Cybersecurity Strategy for the AI-Driven Era

Third Edition

Proven strategies and data-driven tactics to disrupt attacks and strengthen enterprise defenses

Tim Rains

<packt>

Cybersecurity Threats and Strategies Handbook

Third Edition

Portfolio Director: Vijin Boricha
Relationship Lead: Rahul Nair
Project Manager: Gandhali Raut
Content Engineer: Shubhra Mayuri
Technical Editor: Nithik Cheruvakodan
Copy Editor: Safis Editing
Indexer: Tejal Soni
Production Designer: Jyoti Kadam
Growth Lead: Ankita Thakur

First published: May 2020
Second edition: January 2023

Production reference: 1270326

Published by Packt Publishing Ltd.
Grosvenor House
11 St Paul's Square
Birmingham
B3 1RB, UK

ISBN 978-1-80602-857-3
www.packtpub.com

I would like to dedicate this book to my wife, Brenda, and my sons, Tristan and Liam, whose support and patience made this book possible.

– Tim Rains

Foreword

I began my career in cybersecurity in 1987, after graduating with a degree in computer engineering, when the field itself was still trying to define what "computer security" really meant. I joined the Computer Security Office at a federally funded research center, working closely with the National Computer Security Center—now part of the National Security Agency—during a period when the industry was being encouraged, sometimes gently and sometimes not, to build operating systems with security designed in from the start rather than bolted on later as an afterthought.

In the early 1990s, I joined Trusted Information Systems during a formative period for Internet security. Our team released the TIS Firewall Toolkit and one of the earliest commercial Internet firewalls, and I had the opportunity to conduct security consulting engagements, perform risk assessments, and participate in research projects sponsored by ARPA and DARPA. When TIS was later acquired by Network Associates (McAfee), I eventually served as Vice President of Product Management overseeing firewall, intrusion detection, and encryption product lines. That arc reinforced a lesson that has stayed with me: security is never purely technical. It shows up in operations, in organizations, and in people.

In 2002, my former boss, Steve Lipner, convinced me to join Microsoft's Trustworthy Computing initiative. Steve argued—correctly, as it turned out—that there was no better place to drive meaningful security impact than inside a platform used by hundreds of millions of people and organizations worldwide. It was there that I met Tim Rains.

Tim and I worked together for roughly a decade during a period when Microsoft was reshaping how large technology companies approached security and trust. We collaborated on best-practice guidance for securing Windows environments and later on efforts focused on secure and trusted cloud operations. We also worked closely with Trustworthy Computing leadership through some of the most challenging moments the industry has faced, including the fallout from the Edward Snowden disclosures, when questions of trust, transparency, and government access to data stopped being abstract policy debates and became day-to-day customer concerns.

We also spent many years contributing to the Microsoft Security Intelligence Report. My role focused heavily on industry-wide vulnerability analysis, which means I may claim a small amount of responsibility for inspiring Tim's expanded treatment of vulnerability disclosure trends in this new edition. Fortunately for readers, he takes those ideas much further and grounds them in the kind of operational experience you only get from being responsible for outcomes.

Over the past decade, my own career has shifted toward leading crisis communications and issues management, and I would not describe myself today as a modern cybersecurity leader. Tim, however, very much is. He has spent years managing security operations and solving real problems across some of the largest and most complex enterprise environments in the world. That difference shows up in the way he writes, and it shows up in what he emphasizes.

Many cybersecurity books do a good job explaining threats. Others focus on frameworks or technologies. Far fewer capture what it actually feels like to be accountable for defending a living organization—one constrained by budgets, legacy systems, competing business priorities, regulatory pressures, and human behavior. Operational security leadership is constant prioritization, imperfect tradeoffs, and decisions made with incomplete information. Success rarely comes from adopting the newest tool; it comes from understanding which risks matter most and then doing the sustained work to reduce them.

One of Tim's defining strengths, which I observed repeatedly while working with him, is his ability to simplify complex security problems without turning them into slogans. He identifies the small number of factors that truly drive risk and then focuses teams on practical, achievable steps. That mindset runs throughout this book.

This edition builds on the foundation of Tim's earlier work while expanding into areas that now sit at the center of modern security programs. New and updated chapters cover vulnerability disclosure trends, API security, living-off-the-land techniques, and the rapidly evolving intersection of artificial intelligence and cybersecurity—both securing AI systems and using AI to strengthen defense. He doesn't chase buzzwords—he carries the fundamentals forward into environments that keep getting more interconnected and more complex.

A second strength of the book is how it stays anchored in data. Tim does not rely on anecdotes or fear-based narratives. Instead, he connects threat intelligence, vulnerability data, operational experience, and measurable outcomes into guidance you can actually use. You'll find descriptions of threats, but you'll also find help with the harder questions: how to evaluate tradeoffs, how to allocate resources, and how to tell whether your security program is getting better in ways that matter.

Just as important, the book is honest about where security succeeds or fails in the real world: incentives, leadership decisions, cultural resistance, and the grind of execution over time. These are not side topics in operational security; they are often the main event. Tim addresses them with clarity and practicality.

Cybersecurity professionals, executives, and technologists alike will benefit from this perspective. Those new to the field will gain a grounded understanding of how modern organizations are attacked and defended. Experienced practitioners will recognize the constraints and decisions described throughout these chapters and may find language that helps them explain those realities inside their own organizations.

Having worked alongside Tim during some of the industry's most consequential security transformations, I have deep respect for his judgment, pragmatism, and commitment to improving how organizations defend themselves. This book reflects decades of experience, but more than that, it reflects a disciplined way of thinking about risk and responsibility that leaders need if they want to make progress without pretending the job is ever "done."

Cybersecurity is not a problem that gets solved once and finished. It is ongoing stewardship under uncertainty, where progress is measured not by perfection, but by resilience. Books that help leaders think clearly about that responsibility are rare. This is one of them.

Jeff Jones, Sr. Director, Microsoft

Contributors

About the author

Tim Rains is a cybersecurity leader who has spent more than two decades helping organizations and governments understand and defend against modern threats. He has held senior security leadership roles at Microsoft, Amazon Web Services, T-Mobile, and ADT, and has advised enterprises and public-sector institutions around the world on threat intelligence, incident response, cloud security, and risk management. Tim also served on a subcommittee of the National Security Telecommunications Advisory Committee (NSTAC), contributing national-level guidance to the President of the United States on incentivizing and measuring the adoption of cybersecurity best practices. His research on vulnerabilities, malware, and attacker behavior has shaped industry practices, and he brings a practical, data-driven perspective to helping organizations build security strategies that work in the real world.

I'd like to thank my family, my wife Brenda and my sons Tristan and Liam, for their support and patience while I wrote this book. Their encouragement during the writing and editing process for this 600+ page technical book kept me going. I'd like to thank all my current and former colleagues for allowing me to learn from you. Thank you to our Technical Reviewer, Karen Kent, for her help improving my last two books – I'm grateful for having the benefit of your considerable technical acumen. And finally, thank you to Packt Publishing and their fantastic staff for their help and support getting me through the publishing process for the third time.

About the reviewer

Karen Kent of Trusted Cyber Annex has been helping others communicate high-quality cybersecurity information for over 25 years. She was formerly a Senior Computer Scientist at the National Institute of Standards and Technology (NIST) and has co-authored more than 150 technical reports and papers for NIST, including the Cybersecurity Framework (CSF), the Secure Software Development Framework (SSDF), and the Common Vulnerability Scoring System (CVSS). See her full portfolio at `https://kkentwrites.com`.

Table of Contents

Chapter 11: Cybersecurity Strategy Implementation 507

Chapter 15: Artificial Intelligence: Security of AI Systems and Using AI for Better Cybersecurity

Preface

Imagine you are in a submarine hundreds of feet below the surface, surrounded by dark, freezing water. The hull is under immense pressure from all directions, and a single mistake in its design, construction, or operation could spell disaster for the vessel and everyone aboard.

Inside are 150 crew members, several guests, and technologies sourced from 50 different vendors. Three crew members plan to leave the organization after this voyage and are quietly collecting copies of files containing their most important work. One crew member, angry about a promotion he believes he deserved, is plotting how to sabotage the submarine's systems after the voyage in retaliation. Two others have repeatedly exercised poor judgment in their operational roles, putting the entire crew at risk. Unbeknownst to anyone, one of the guests is an agent of a competing organization, searching for sensitive data and intellectual property to steal, and for opportunities to extort the organization for profit.

Meanwhile, back at the crew's headquarters onshore, third-party consultants and industry vendors are meeting with executives and members of the Board of Directors, insisting that the submarine lacks the right technologies and that the captain is not up to the task without their help. Their claims have led some executives to openly question the captain's leadership and competency.

Although the submarine is relatively new, the technologies installed onboard are connected by communications protocols developed in the 1970s. These protocols make integration easy and enable communication with the public Internet, but they also expose the submarine to tens of thousands of software and hardware vulnerabilities and hundreds of millions of pieces of malware. The number of threat actors interested in disrupting the organization's operations has steadily grown for decades, including nation-state groups that now operate openly on the public Internet with impunity.

This is the situation the captain and crew find themselves in—and it is analogous to the challenge that **Chief Information Security Officers (CISOs)** and their teams face today. Their organizations are surrounded on the Internet by adversaries constantly probing for ways to penetrate and compromise their IT infrastructures. Their people receive wave after wave of social engineering attacks designed to trick them into making poor trust decisions that undermine the controls their security teams have implemented. The specters of ransomware and data breaches haunt CISOs, **Chief Information Officers (CIOs)**, **Chief Technology Officers (CTOs)**, and Boards of Directors at even the most sophisticated organizations. Driven by the continuous adoption of new technologies, the attack surfaces of modern enterprises continue to expand faster than proportional investments in cybersecurity programs.

After conducting hundreds of incident response investigations for Microsoft's enterprise customers, publishing thousands of pages of threat intelligence, and assisting some of **Amazon Web Services' (AWS)** largest customers, I have had the opportunity to learn from and advise thousands of businesses and public sector organizations in nearly every country around the world. I have also had the privilege of leading operational cybersecurity teams at some of America's best companies. I wrote this book to share some of the insights and lessons I've learned during my career.

The views and opinions expressed in this book are my own and not those of my current or former employers.

Who this book is for

This book is written for cybersecurity leaders, practitioners, and technologists who are responsible for protecting modern organizations from increasingly complex digital threats. It serves executives, security teams, IT operators, public-sector leaders, students, and anyone seeking a deeper, real-world understanding of today's cybersecurity landscape.

What this book covers

Chapter 1, How Enterprises Get Hacked, explains how enterprises get hacked by detailing real-world attack scenarios, the five main ways organizations are initially compromised, and the importance of focusing on cybersecurity fundamentals to build effective strategies.

Chapter 2, What to Know about Threat Intelligence, provides an overview of **Cyber Threat Intelligence (CTI)**, including its sources, uses, sharing protocols, and guidance for identifying credible CTI versus industry noise.

Chapter 3, Industry Vulnerability Disclosure Trends, provides an in-depth analysis of industry vulnerability disclosure trends, examining how leading vendors manage vulnerabilities, and introduces a framework to help organizations reduce risk and costs through effective vulnerability management strategies.

Chapter 4, Product Vulnerability Disclosure Trends, analyzes vulnerability disclosure trends for popular hardware and software products, evaluates these trends using a vulnerability improvement framework, and provides practical guidance for enterprise vulnerability management programs.

Chapter 5, The Evolution of Malware, provides a comprehensive, data-driven overview of the evolution, prevalence, and impact of malware, especially ransomware, on global IT environments, with practical insights for CISOs and security teams to understand and mitigate modern cyber threats.

Chapter 6, Internet-Based Threats, covers the evolution, tactics, and mitigation strategies for internet-based threats, including phishing, drive-by downloads, and DDoS attacks facing organizations and individuals today.

Chapter 7, Application Programming Interface Security, offers a comprehensive look at API security, covering common vulnerabilities, the evolving threat landscape, secure development practices, privacy considerations, threat modeling, risk management, and practical mitigation strategies tailored for CISOs, developers, and security teams.

Chapter 8, Friend or Foe? The Roles Governments Play in Cybersecurity, examines how governments influence cybersecurity as market participants, standards setters, enforcers, defenders, and even potential threats, and explores the risks and mitigations associated with government access to data in the context of international regulations, surveillance, and cloud computing.

Chapter 9, Ingredients for a Successful Cybersecurity Strategy, explains the essential ingredients of a successful cybersecurity strategy, emphasizing the importance of governance, risk management, compliance, mastering cybersecurity fundamentals, protecting high-value assets, aligning with business objectives, fostering a strong security culture, and overcoming organizational constraints to effectively defend against evolving threats.

Chapter 10, Cybersecurity Strategies, provides an in-depth examination of various cybersecurity strategies used by organizations, evaluates their effectiveness in mitigating common risks through the Cybersecurity Fundamentals Scoring System (CFSS), and offers guidance on selecting and combining approaches to build a resilient and effective cybersecurity posture.

Chapter 11, Cybersecurity Strategy Implementation, provides a practical guide to implementing the Intrusion Kill Chain cybersecurity strategy in real IT environments, including modernizing the framework, mapping controls, identifying gaps and investments, and integrating complementary approaches like the MITRE ATT&CK® framework to strengthen organizational defenses against traditional network intrusions.

Chapter 12, Measuring Performance and Effectiveness, shows how CISOs and cybersecurity teams can use data-driven methods, such as vulnerability management, intrusion reconstructions, and attack-centric frameworks, to assess the performance of their security strategies, demonstrate value, identify gaps, and drive continuous improvement.

Chapter 13, Modern Approaches to Security and Compliance, explores how cloud computing is transforming cybersecurity and compliance practices, emphasizing the power of APIs and automation to modernize security strategies, enhance resilience, and streamline compliance in cloud environments.

Chapter 14, Mitigating "Living Off the Land" Techniques, explores the persistent threat of **Living Off the Land** (LOTL) techniques in cybersecurity, detailing how attackers leverage trusted tools, binaries, and legitimate resources to evade detection, and providing comprehensive strategies for organizations to detect, mitigate, and defend against these sophisticated attacks.

Chapter 15, Artificial Intelligence: Security of AI Systems and Using AI for Better Cybersecurity, examines the safety and security risks of generative and agentic AI systems, explores how attackers leverage AI in cyberattacks, and outlines strategies for securely deploying enterprise AI tools like Microsoft Copilot.

To get the most out of this book

- You should be comfortable with the basic vocabulary of enterprise IT—networks, identity, cloud services, applications, and how systems interact in modern environments.
- A foundational understanding of core cybersecurity concepts—threat actors, common attack techniques, and the purpose of security controls—will make the material easier to follow.
- No special tools or installations are required to read the book. When external frameworks such as NIST, MITRE ATT&CK, or MITRE ATLAS are referenced, the book provides the necessary context and includes links or citations if you want to explore them further.
- If you want to apply the models as you read, having access to your organization's architecture diagrams, security documentation, or incident reports can make the exercises more concrete, but these are optional.
- You'll get the most value by pausing periodically to map each concept to your own environment and by approaching the material with curiosity and a willingness to challenge long-held assumptions—especially as AI reshapes both attack and defense.

Download the color images

We also provide a PDF file that has color images of the screenshots and diagrams used in this book. You can download it here:`https://packt.link/gbp/9781806028573`.

Conventions used

There are a number of text conventions used throughout this book.

`CodeInText`: Indicates code words in text, database table names, folder names, filenames, file extensions, pathnames, dummy URLs, user input, and Twitter handles. For example: " This enables them to crack the weakest passwords in stolen Active Directories (`ntds.dit` files) within minutes "

A block of code is set as follows:

```
{
  "date": "2025-10-31",
  "explanation": "This is the picture you requested...",
  "hdurl": "https://api.packt.com/images/610/picture_610.jpg",
  "media_type": "image",
  "title": "Your Picture",
  "url": "https://api.packt.com/images/610/picture_610.jpg"
}
```

Any command-line input or output is written as follows:

```
aws ec2 run-instances --image-id ami-60a54009 --count 5 --instance-type t2.micro
--key-name my-key-pair
```

Bold: Indicates a new term, an important word, or words that you see on the screen. For instance, words in menus or dialog boxes appear in the text like this. For example: " The OWASP project most relevant to our discussion in this chapter is the **OWASP API Security Project**. OWASP typically publishes updated Top 10 lists every two or three years."

> **Note**
>
> Warnings or important notes appear like this.

> **Tip**
>
> Tips and tricks appear like this.

Get in touch

Feedback from our readers is always welcome.

General feedback: If you have questions about any aspect of this book or have any general feedback, please email us at `customercare@packt.com` and mention the book's title in the subject of your message.

Errata: Although we have taken every care to ensure the accuracy of our content, mistakes do happen. If you have found a mistake in this book, we would be grateful if you reported it to us. Please visit `http://www.packt.com/submit-errata`, click **Submit Errata**, and fill in the form.

Piracy: If you come across any illegal copies of our works in any form on the internet, we would be grateful if you provided us with the location address or website name. Please contact us at `copyright@packt.com` with a link to the material.

If you are interested in becoming an author: If there is a topic that you have expertise in and you are interested in either writing or contributing to a book, please visit `http://authors.packt.com/`.

Free benefits with your book

This book comes with free benefits to support your learning. Activate them now for instant access (see the "*How to Unlock*" section for instructions).

Here's a quick overview of what you can instantly unlock with your purchase:

DRM-Free PDF Version

Download DRM-free PDF and ePub copies of this book.

7-Day Packt Library Access

Get 7-day unlimited access to 8,000+ books and videos. No credit card required.

Available for first-time Packt+ trial users only.

Next-Gen Reader Access

Read this book on Packt Reader with progress sync, dark mode and note-taking.

How to Unlock

Scan the QR code (or go to `packtpub.com/unlock`). Search for this book by name, confirm the edition, and then follow the steps on the page.

UNLOCK NOW

Note: Keep your invoice handy. Purchases made directly from Packt don't require one

Share your thoughts

Once you've read *Cybersecurity Strategy for the AI-Driven Era*, we'd love to hear your thoughts! Scan the QR code below to go straight to the Amazon review page for this book and share your feedback.

https://packt.link/r/1806028573

Your review is important to us and the tech community and will help us make sure we're delivering excellent quality content.

Part 1

Introduction to Cybersecurity Strategies and Threat Intelligence

In this opening section, you'll learn how modern enterprises are actually breached. Through three real-world attack scenarios, you'll see how intrusions unfold and how they can be mitigated. You'll be introduced to the Cybersecurity Usual Suspects, the five primary paths attackers use to gain initial access, why cybersecurity fundamentals matter more than ever, and how to apply threat intelligence effectively, while understanding its limits. You'll also trace the evolution of vulnerabilities, malware, and internet-based threats, giving you the insight needed to make informed decisions and strengthen your organization's defenses. By the end of this section, you'll know how to use credible threat intelligence and insights into attacker tradecraft to build a more effective security program.

This part of the book includes the following chapters:

- *Chapter 1, How Enterprises Get Hacked*
- *Chapter 2, What to Know about Threat Intelligence*

1

How Enterprises Get Hacked

Welcome to *Cybersecurity Strategy for the AI-Driven Era*. This is the third edition of this book that I've written. Why write these books? In my career, I have had the opportunity to work as the most senior cybersecurity advisor at both **Microsoft** and **Amazon Web Services** (**AWS**). I've also had the opportunity to lead operational security teams at some very large, well-known companies. After advising thousands of commercial and public sector organizations all over the world and managing large operational cybersecurity teams myself, I concluded that most organizations do not have a cybersecurity strategy that their security executives or security teams can articulate. In fact, thinking about all the security briefings I provided and meetings I had with executives and their teams over the last couple of decades, I recall meeting fewer than 10 organizations that had a written cybersecurity strategy that the **Chief Information Security Officers** (**CISOs**) could describe and that security team members could repeat. Instead of discussing cybersecurity domains such as risk management and **Identity and Access Management** (**IAM**), I found myself advising CISOs on cybersecurity strategies almost exclusively. That's not surprising, since industry frameworks and certifications offer extensive guidance on individual cybersecurity domains, but rarely provide meaningful direction on strategy itself.

Most of the security teams I advised were approaching cybersecurity as a problem to be solved by procuring the *right* combination of tools. But without a clear strategy guiding them, gaps, areas of over-investment, and areas of under-investment were always the result. Besides, teams with big budgets and lots of cybersecurity tools still get hacked. If cybersecurity could be achieved by procuring some tools, it wouldn't be the massive global problem it is today. It is an inconvenient truth that effective operational cybersecurity is much more challenging than simply procuring cybersecurity tools.

Given this, I decided to write a book about cybersecurity strategies for CISOs, **Chief Information Officers** (**CIOs**), **Chief Technology Officers** (**CTOs**), aspiring cybersecurity executives, cybersecurity teams, and **Information Technology (IT)** professionals who have significant cybersecurity responsibilities. *Cybersecurity Threats, Malware Trends, and Strategies* (Tim Rains) was published by Packt in May 2020. The response to that book in the industry was very positive, and I wrote a second edition that was published in January 2023. Things continue to change very quickly in the IT industry: cyberattacks are non-stop, and cybersecurity strategies continue to garner overwhelming interest. This is why I have written this third edition.

This chapter will cover the following topics:

- The world CISOs live in
- Tales from the frontlines: Real-world attack scenarios
- How organizations get initially compromised
- Focus on the cybersecurity fundamentals
- Understanding the difference between attackers' motivations and their tactics
- Different types of CISOs: The CISO spectrum

> Note
>
> **Your purchase includes a free PDF copy + exclusive extras**
>
> Your purchase includes a DRM-free PDF copy of this book, 7-day trial to the Packt+ library (no credit card required), and additional exclusive extras. See the *Free benefits with your book* section in the *Preface* to unlock them instantly and maximize your learning.

The world CISOs live in

In 2021, the global cybersecurity industry was estimated to be valued at around $140 billion. That number ballooned to an estimated $271 billion in 2025 (Grand View Research, 2025). Combine that with an estimated **Compound Annual Growth Rate (CAGR)** of 11.9% and this results in an estimated industry market size that is expected to reach $633.24 billion by 2033 (Grand View Research, 2025). Most of this revenue growth has put immense pressure on cybersecurity industry vendors' sales and marketing teams. In turn, vendors target roles that are typically cybersecurity spend approvers or key influencers—CISOs, cybersecurity executives, and directors of the boards of companies.

To give you an idea of how both the pressure to ensure effective cybersecurity and the rapid growth of the cybersecurity industry manifest for CISOs, let me share some insights from my own experience. At one point in my career, I would get, on average, nine calls each weekday from cybersecurity vendors trying to sell their products and/or services to me. That's 45 calls per week or 180 calls per month, on average. In six months, my LinkedIn message inbox received 643 unsolicited messages from cybersecurity vendors. That's an average of 4 unsolicited messages every day of the week or 129 messages per month, month after month. In addition to the combined 309 phone calls and LinkedIn messages I received per month on average, I was also contacted by vendors almost daily through other people on my team or executives in other parts of the company. These vendors typically want CISOs to meet with them and explain their priorities and initiatives to determine where their products or services can help. Most CISOs and security team members already spend a lot of time meeting with the vendors they already leverage or plan to leverage. Those vendors are constantly looking for ways to add value and expand their organizations' footprints within their accounts.

Personally, I feel it's impolite if I don't respond to well-meaning industry professionals trying to represent their organizations and share products they believe in. However, professionally, I simply could not keep up with the volume of requests from vendors. If you are a vendor that reached out to me on LinkedIn and didn't get a response, I apologize, but I do hope you understand. Many of the CISOs I have met share the same challenge.

> **Note**
>
> CISOs and security teams can't be successful without the vendors that support them, but they need to spend most of their time on the job practicing cybersecurity.

As the industry grows, more and more cybersecurity vendors use the specter of the "ever-changing threat landscape" to market and sell their wares to anxious and often punch-drunk organizations across every industry. What started out as a relatively simple concept to use computers to make faster and potentially better business decisions has led to a proliferation of technologies, regulations, and standards that require an ever-expanding set of people, processes, and technologies to protect them.

When I started working at Microsoft in the late 90s, they had little to no material revenue from developing and selling cybersecurity products. In 2021, revenue from Microsoft's cybersecurity business exceeded $10 billion (Jakkal, 2021), in 2024 it was over $20 billion, and it was estimated that it will exceed $37 billion in 2025 (Krause, 2024). In 2016, I could walk customers through Microsoft's relatively large and complicated security reference model crammed into a single PowerPoint slide. Since then, this has evolved into what they now call **Microsoft Cybersecurity Reference Architectures** (**MCRA**), which includes numerous different reference models. Microsoft writes the following:

> *"MCRA describes end-to-end security for the 'hybrid of everything' technology estate spanning legacy IT, multicloud, Internet of Things (IoT), Operational Technology (OT), Artificial Intelligence (AI), and more" (Microsoft Corporation, 2025).*

Similarly, when I started working at AWS in 2017, they had around 40 cloud services in their portfolio. When I left AWS almost four and a half years later, they offered over 300 cloud services and had a growing portfolio of security services. Besides the introduction of new services, existing services were constantly improved, and their functionality expanded. Many IT teams that took the time to evaluate AWS' services before they adopted them would have to re-evaluate them annually to ensure they still fully understand them.

Combine the growth from just these two vendors with the growth of other major IT and cloud vendors (Oracle, IBM, Google, etc.) that enterprises typically also leverage, and *thousands* of cybersecurity vendors all vying for their business, and you have *a lot* of options, complexity, noise, and confusion.

Of course, the backdrop to all this technology proliferation, industry growth, and complexity is the constant drumbeat of successful cybersecurity attacks. New technologies have enabled attackers to increase the speed and impact of their attacks. For instance, new ways of performing very large international financial transactions have enabled attackers to build sophisticated business models based on extortion and human-operated ransomware. Similarly, the state of international relations between China, the Democratic People's Republic of Korea, Iran, and Russia with much of the rest of the world has heightened nation-state cyberattacks and enabled ransomware gangs and other criminals perpetuating cybersecurity attacks from these countries to operate in the open with impunity.

As a result, all commercial sector organizations in the Western world have largely been left to fend for themselves, while governments desperately try to protect their critical infrastructures, such as the communications and energy sectors, as well as water systems, from attacks.

> **Note**
>
> If you skipped reading the *Preface* (specifically, the submarine analogy), please read it as it captures the pressurized environment that all enterprises operate in today. I'll refer to this analogy repeatedly in this book.

Subsequently, many of the organizations that I advised would often ask very basic questions:

- *Which cybersecurity capabilities are most important?*
- *What do we do first? How do you prioritize requirements and capabilities?*

- *What are other organizations in our industry doing?*
- *Do you have any threat intelligence from other organizations in our industry? Is there an algorithm that helps us determine the right priorities?*

After having thousands of these discussions and reading between the lines, what they were really asking me about was a **cybersecurity strategy**. The fundamental question they were asking me was: *Which cybersecurity strategy or combination of strategies will be most effective for our organization given the industry we are in, the locations where we do business, our regulatory compliance requirements, and the appetite for risk our business has?*

Before we dive into cybersecurity strategies, it is important to level-set our understanding of the types of threats such strategies are designed to help with. I'll also discuss tactics and mitigations that many security teams leverage to protect, detect, and respond to modern cybersecurity attacks. Let's start by looking at how large organizations typically get hacked.

Tales from the frontlines: Real-world attack scenarios

In my career, I've been involved in literally thousands of **incident response** (**IR**) investigations. I was a technical lead on a team of over 120 IR investigators and engineers at Microsoft that performed IR investigations for their enterprise customers. I developed most of the tools (wrote the code) that these teams used to gather and analyze evidence during their investigations. I also had the opportunity to lead numerous IR investigations at the various companies I have worked at during my career, working with top-tier IR response teams from some of the industry's best vendors. I've also spent a considerable amount of time working with attorneys in the wake of data breaches to comply with various industry breach disclosure obligations and as a subject matter expert in resulting lawsuits. As difficult and pressurized as IR typically is, I learned a lot by unraveling and explaining complex attacks in these roles. Let me share some of the lessons I learned doing IR investigations over the years, to demystify cyberattacks and shed light on how you can develop effective strategies to counter them.

One of the most difficult tasks that CISOs perform as part of their jobs is informing their organizations' senior leadership teams that they have had a data breach. Breaking this kind of bad news to CEOs and potentially many of their direct reports leads to all sorts of questions that CISOs rarely have the answers to at the beginning of an IR investigation. In fact, most of the initial assessments made by incident responders will turn out to be inaccurate by the end of the investigation when more facts have been established.

In a complex IR investigation, the organization's IR team seeks to create a timeline of the attackers' actions to establish how the attack started and whether it has been contained. This essentially involves IR investigators hypothesizing about actions attackers could have taken at each step in their attack and then looking for evidence that their hypotheses are correct. If their hypotheses are proven untrue, they create new hypotheses based on any new information they might have received.

> **Note**
>
> At points in a complex, difficult investigation, when several hypotheses have been unsuccessful, IR teams can start to lose confidence that they truly understand what occurred during the incident. But good IR teams persevere to find more evidence and continue to iteratively make informed hypotheses. As they do this, their disillusionment fades and they make progress.

Figure 1.1 illustrates the contrast between what IR teams think they know versus what they actually know during a typical complex, high-severity incident investigation. In this notional illustration, the horizontal axis represents the first 30 days of an investigation in which new information about the incident was discovered:

Figure 1.1 – A typical IR investigation knowledge trend

> **Note**
>
> Stakeholder demands for information at the beginning of an incident are typically high, when investigators have the least amount of information and their initial hypotheses are not completely tested.

An IR investigation of a complex incident typically takes time, sometimes weeks or months. During the investigation, the stakeholders that the CISO keeps informed tend to ratchet up the pressure for answers to their questions. After all, if they are a publicly traded company, they likely have numerous disclosure timelines that they must comply with, such as the **Securities and Exchange Commission** (**SEC**), potentially US state **Attorneys Generals** (**AGs**), business partners that impose contractual obligations for notifications, and customers that were impacted. As soon as a company makes an "8-K" disclosure to the SEC, the details become public knowledge and negative news cycles about the breach typically commence.

Further, news of data breaches tends to travel fast. Based on this news, business partners and customers naturally want to know whether their data or systems were impacted and proactively contact the disclosing company with questions of their own. In large, high-profile data breaches, the combined volume of such requests can disrupt IR investigations, as cybersecurity teams are forced to shift their focus from the investigation and potentially containing the attack to communicating with the company's stakeholder community. Sometimes, business partners disconnect their networks from victim organizations and even stop accepting emails from them in an attempt to protect themselves from the attack. Industry vendors, such as threat intelligence providers, start briefing their customers on attacks using details from the victim's 8-K filings and the resulting news cycles, potentially further perpetuating inaccuracies.

None of this is helpful for CISOs who are in the midst of a high-severity IR investigation, trying to gather evidence and determine what happened and whether the attacker has been contained. All of this can decelerate IR investigations, giving attackers more time to burrow into the victim's infrastructure, find ways to stay persistent, deploy ransomware, and exfiltrate data.

Further, CISOs and security teams face the challenge of communicating with their stakeholders that not all "data breaches" or "cyberattacks" are the same, even though they are reported in news or threat intelligence briefings the same way, that is, using a set of underlying, often inaccurate, assumptions. In these scenarios, a key part of the CISO's role is to provide clear, accurate context to senior executives and stakeholders.

> **Tip**
>
> Recognizing that different types of attacks represent very different potential cybersecurity outcomes for the victim organization and their stakeholder community is key.

Over-reacting or under-reacting to an incident both have potential consequences; executives typically prefer a straightforward, accurate assessment of the potential impacts of an incident over a minimized or overblown rendering.

In this section, I'll describe the following three types of attacks, how they work, how to mitigate them, and how severe the risk they pose is for enterprise organizations:

- Global malware attack
- Traditional network intrusion
- Data breaches via insecure APIs

I'll refer to these attacks throughout the rest of the book when providing an example of an attack is helpful. The details I provide are fictional unless otherwise stated.

Global malware attack: Worms

Let me paint you a picture of a worst-case scenario based on past successful global worm attacks. I helped lead Microsoft's IR through more than a few global worm attacks, including *SQL Slammer*, *Blaster*, *Sasser*, *MyDoom*, and *Conficker*. Thankfully, large-scale worm attacks aren't as common as they used to be, but this doesn't mean CISOs and security teams can ignore the threat they pose—unfortunately, wormable vulnerabilities are common. Among worms, there were two predominant types propagating around the internet back in 2003–2004, when several big global worm attacks occurred. There were worms that exploited unpatched vulnerabilities and those that exploited design flaws in peer-to-peer and email platforms. In this example, I'll describe the former type, since the exploitation of unpatched vulnerabilities is still leveraged today by threat actors and purveyors of malware alike.

> **Note**
>
> If you aren't exactly sure what a worm is in this context, no problem—please read *Chapter 5, The Evolution of Malware*, dedicated to malware, where I provide quite a bit of background information on different types of malware, including worms. Similarly, if you aren't familiar with the exploitation of unpatched vulnerabilities, please read *Chapters 3, Industry Vulnerability Disclosure Trends* and *4, Product Vulnerability Disclosure Trends*, which provide a deep dive into vulnerabilities.

In the past, several global malware attacks started with an attacker discovering a new zero-day vulnerability in a Microsoft Windows service. This service happens to run by default on the vast majority of Windows systems in the world.

This vulnerable service uses a well-known **Transmission Control Protocol** (**TCP**) port to listen on the network for connection attempts. There is a default rule in Windows Firewall on every system that allows network connections directly to the vulnerable service. The attacker develops a program capable of exploiting this zero-day vulnerability. Technically, this program is called an **exploit**. Exploits are capable of taking advantage of the specific vulnerabilities they are designed for, but have no delivery mechanism built into them. The attacker wants to maximize the number of systems this exploit runs on, so they add the capability for the program to self-propagate.

This means that when the exploit runs successfully on a vulnerable system, one of the things it does is use the compromised system to look for other vulnerable systems to compromise and distribute the exploit program to. This type of malware is called a **worm**. The attacker releases the worm on the internet by running it on internet-connected systems in several different locations.

The worm uses the vulnerability to spread before Microsoft is aware of the vulnerability and before a security update is available to patch it. The default rule in Windows Firewall allows the worm to talk directly to the TCP port that the vulnerable service is listening on, so there is nothing preventing the worm from exploiting the vulnerability on virtually every consumer system running Windows that is directly connected to the internet and that does not have an additional firewall protecting it. *Figure 1.2* illustrates how services running on Windows systems use TCP and **User Datagram Protocol** (**UDP**) ports to process network requests. If those services are not kept up to date with security updates, they become vulnerable to malware attacks, such as worm attacks. It shows a worm checking whether the **Remote Procedure Call** (**RPC**) endpoint mapper service is fully patched, as it accepts network traffic on TCP port 135. If the RPC endpoint mapper service is not patched for the vulnerability that the worm was designed to exploit, it will infect the system and use it to attack other systems.

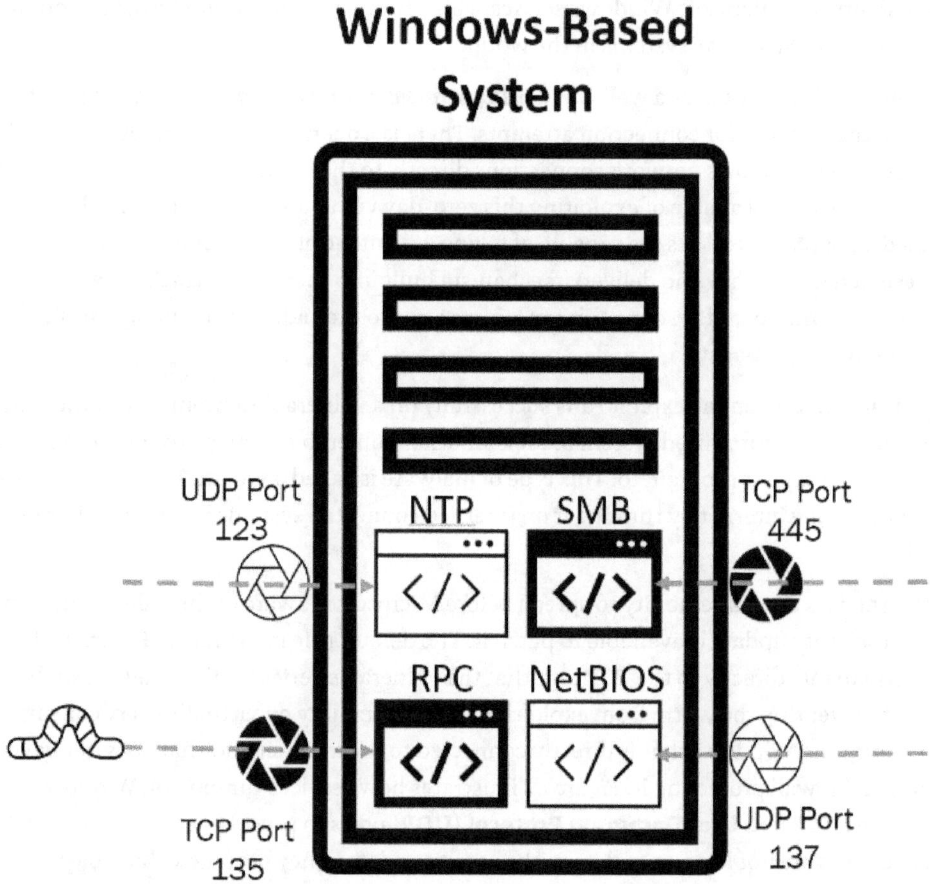

Figure 1.2 – A diagram of a Windows-based computer with the services listening on a network using different TCP and UDP ports. A worm is targeting TCP port 135, where the RPC endpoint mapper service is bound

Anti-malware software doesn't detect the worm because it is brand new, and a sample of it is yet to be provided to a major anti-malware lab for analysis. Vulnerable Windows systems behind professionally managed enterprise firewalls wouldn't be safe either, as infected laptops would introduce the worm into corporate IT environments when they connect via VPN or on their wireless networks (Microsoft Corporation, n.d.). The worm propagates from system to system around the world in a matter of minutes, and the following takes place:

1. The public internet and most private networks are disrupted and rendered unusable, or their performance is severely degraded.

2. The network traffic generated by the worm as it attempts to propagate and re-propagate, from system to system, significantly disrupts legitimate network traffic on the internet, as well as the private networks it has found its way into.
3. After a system gets infected, the worm tries to infect all the systems it has network connectivity with, repeatedly. Hundreds of millions of systems doing this simultaneously disrupt the global internet and private networks.
4. When the worm exploits the unpatched vulnerability, it causes the target system to destabilize, causing a *blue screen of death*, a memory dump, and a system reboot. This exacerbates the problem because it's hard to disinfect and patch systems that are constantly rebooting. Additionally, all the systems rebooting generates even more network traffic.
5. When each system comes back up, they generate **Address Resolution Protocol** (**ARP**) traffic and ask their **Dynamic Host Configuration Protocol** (**DHCP**) servers for IP addresses. When the network segments with DHCP servers get saturated with requests for IP addresses, the DHCP servers are prevented from giving rebooting systems IP addresses.
6. Subsequently, rebooting systems start using automatic private IP addresses that are typically non-routable (`169.254.x.x`). In some cases, these systems can no longer be reached by management software used to patch them, update their anti-malware signatures, or deploy possible mitigations or workarounds to them.

Therefore, the damage such an attack could do shouldn't be underestimated. The US government has identified 16 critical infrastructure sectors deemed critical because if their network or systems are disrupted, it would have dire consequences on the security, economy, and public health and safety of the country. These sectors include the following:

- The chemical sector
- The commercial facilities sector
- The communications sector
- The critical manufacturing sector
- The dams sector
- The defense industrial base sector
- The emergency services sector
- The energy sector
- The financial services sector
- The food and agriculture sector

- The government facilities sector
- The healthcare and public health sector
- The IT sector
- The nuclear reactors, materials, and waste sector
- The transportation systems sector
- The water and wastewater systems sector (US Department of Homeland Security, n.d.)

If a worm exploits a zero-day vulnerability on vulnerable systems in one of these sectors, the economy, energy, water, communications, transportation, hospitals, or other critical functions for society will be disrupted and potentially taken offline. Further, if the attacker includes a malicious payload with the worm, such as encrypting operating system files or data or destroying storage media, recovery would be time-consuming, requiring substantial manual intervention as management software tools and automation systems would be disrupted along with the networks they are connected to. Additionally, if the underlying storage media on infected systems also need to be replaced, the damage from such an attack would linger for years.

Of course, I've painted a picture of a worst-case scenario. But what are the chances that such a worm attack could actually be perpetrated? To answer the question, let's look at confirmed *wormable* vulnerabilities in Windows operating systems disclosed between 2019 and 2025:

Year	CVE ID	CVSS BaseScore	Description	Exploit Availability Status
2019	CVE-2019-0708	9.8	BlueKeep: Unauthenticated RCE in RDP allowing worm-like propagation across exposed systems.	Public exploit exists
2019	CVE-2019-1181	9.8	DejaBlue: Critical RDP flaw enabling unauthenticated remote code execution and potential self-propagation.	
2019	CVE-2019-1182	10.0	DejaBlue variant: Another RDP RCE enabling worm-like spread across vulnerable hosts.	

Year	CVE ID	CVSS BaseScore	Description	Exploit Availability Status
2019	CVE-2019-1222	9.8	Additional RDP RCE enabling remote code execution without authentication.	
2019	CVE-2019-1226	9.8	RDP service flaw allowing unauthenticated RCE with worm potential.	
2020	CVE-2020-0796	10.0	SMBGhost: Unauthenticated RCE in SMBv3 compression enabling rapid worm-like propagation.	Public exploit exists
2020	CVE-2020-16898	8.8	Bad Neighbor: Zero-click RCE triggered by malicious ICMPv6 packets.	Potential exploit exists
2021	CVE-2021-31166	9.8	HTTP.sys RCE allowing unauthenticated network-based exploitation.	Potential exploit exists
2024	CVE-2024-38063	9.8	Zero-click IPv6 RCE in TCP/IP stack with worm-like propagation characteristics.	Public exploit exists
2025	CVE-2025-47981	9.8	Heap overflow in NEGOEX negotiation enabling unauthenticated RCE.	No publicly available exploit code is available, or an exploit is theoretical

Year	CVE ID	CVSS BaseScore	Description	Exploit Availability Status
2025	CVE-2025-21376	8.1	LDAP race-condition RCE enabling propagation between affected servers.	No publicly available exploit code is available, or an exploit is theoretical

Table 1.1 – Wormable vulnerabilities disclosed between 2019 and 2025, including CVE ID, CVSS (v3.x) base score, description, and currently known exploit availability status

Each one was assigned a **Common Vulnerabilities and Exposures** (**CVE**) ID by the MITRE Corporation and a **Common Vulnerability Scoring System** (**CVSS**) base score quantifying its severity. I'll discuss both of these in detail in *Chapter 3*. For now, recognize that the CVSS scores reflect the seriousness of these vulnerabilities in that the closer they are to 10, the more likely remote exploitation with no human interaction is—which is exactly what worms need to execute.

Let's look at some of the vulnerabilities from *Table 1.1* in more detail. On May 14, 2019, Microsoft announced the existence of a critical-rated vulnerability (CVE-2019-0708) in Windows Remote Desktop Services that was wormable (NIST, n.d.). In their announcement, the **Microsoft Security Response Center** (**MSRC**) wrote the following:

> *"This vulnerability is pre-authentication and requires no user interaction. In other words, the vulnerability is 'wormable', meaning that any future malware that exploits this vulnerability could propagate from vulnerable computer to vulnerable computer in a similar way as the WannaCry malware spread across the globe in 2017. While we have observed no exploitation of this vulnerability, it is highly likely that malicious actors will write an exploit for this vulnerability and incorporate it into their malware." —(Microsoft Corporation, n.d.)*

CVE-2019-0708, the so-called *BlueKeep* vulnerability, applied to Windows 7, Windows Server 2008, and Windows Server 2008 R2; a third of all Windows systems were still running Windows 7 in 2019 (Keizer, 2020). This vulnerability was so serious that Microsoft released security updates even for old, unsupported operating systems, such as Windows XP and Windows Server 2003, to protect the large number of systems that had never been upgraded from old, out-of-support operating systems. Protecting these legacy systems, which no longer get regular security updates, from a highly probable worm attack leaves less "fuel" for a worm and results in fewer attacks on supported systems.

Then, on August 13, 2019, Microsoft announced the existence of two more wormable vulnerabilities (CVE-2019-1181 and CVE-2019-1182). More Windows versions contained these vulnerabilities, including Windows 7, Windows Server 2008 R2, Windows Server 2012, Windows Server 2012 R2, Windows 8.1, and all versions of Windows 10 (including Server versions).

In each of these three cases in 2019, Microsoft was able to find and fix these critical, wormable vulnerabilities before would-be attackers discovered them.

Unfortunately, there have been other potentially wormable CVEs since 2019. As *Table 1.1* reveals, there have been at least 11 wormable vulnerabilities in Windows-based systems between January 2019 and June 2025. In most of these cases, the vulnerabilities had a CVSS base score of 9.8 or 10 and could enable code execution for attackers without any user interaction. At least three of these vulnerabilities had public exploit code available at the time of writing. In 2025, at least two wormable vulnerabilities in Windows were disclosed.

> **Tip**
>
> Windows isn't the only operating system that has had wormable vulnerabilities, and Microsoft isn't the only software manufacturer that has had such flaws in its products. Therefore, simply selecting a different operating system or software vendor to leverage isn't a meaningful mitigation of this type of threat.

Mitigating global worm attacks

The probability and potential impact of these types of global malware attacks mean that CISOs and security teams need to have a well-run vulnerability management program. I cover this in detail in *Chapters 3* and *4*, which are devoted to vulnerability management. Mitigating high-severity vulnerabilities as quickly as possible makes it harder for attackers to exploit them. Some IT teams opt to use workarounds instead of security updates to mitigate vulnerabilities. This helps them avoid the dreaded system reboot requirement that many security updates impose, which in turn helps them keep their system uptime **Service-Level Agreements** (**SLAs**). However, I'm not a fan of this approach to mitigate high-severity vulnerabilities when security updates are available because, in many cases, it leaves the system one configuration change away from disaster. The use of workarounds is not typically documented well and leaves knowledge of their use for the tribe to remember.

> **Tip**
>
> Installing security updates provides more certainty and permanence than using workarounds.

Unfortunately, purveyors of malware have evolved their worms over the years to give them a better chance of compromising as many systems as possible. Back in 2008, variants of the Conficker worm demonstrated that worms could use a combination of methods to propagate. It used specific unpatched vulnerabilities (such as MS08-067), it attempted to log in to network file shares using a hardcoded list of easy-to-guess passwords, and it also used social engineering via Windows AutoRun feature abuse.

This means that security teams can't simply keep systems patched to mitigate this type of threat. The following approaches to mitigation can be useful:

- Enforcing a policy requiring long, complex, hard-to-guess passwords and using **Multi-Factor Authentication** (**MFA**) will mitigate the type of dictionary attack that Conficker used and other attacks that seek to leverage weak, leaked, or stolen passwords.
- Blocking USB drive use for most users is a best practice to help manage **Data Loss Prevention** (**DLP**), as well as malware that attempts to use removable storage media.
- Running anti-malware or modern endpoint detection and response software will help detect infection attempts and potentially prevent systems from being infected by such malware.
- IT teams can't always keep up with the pace of attackers, especially in the case of a zero-day attack, as described earlier. In such cases, Zero-Trust design principles can be helpful; for example, **host-based firewalls** such as Windows Firewall, running on all workstations and servers, are key, as well as network micro-segmentation. If the worm can't get to the vulnerable service because firewalls are blocking the associated network ports, it makes it harder for the attack to succeed.

> **Note**
>
> Although running host-based firewalls on workstations is relatively easy, running them on servers can be much more difficult to accomplish since exposing network ports to provide services is a primary function of servers.

The stakes are super high. Attackers have further evolved worms to leverage ransomware as their payloads. Successful worms such as *WannaCry*, *Petya*, and *NotPetya* demonstrated that CISOs and security teams must work to mitigate worms or they could result in an extinction event for their organizations.

Next, let's examine what a traditional network intrusion looks like.

Traditional network intrusion

Instead of relying on the randomness of a global malware attack, attackers carrying out network intrusion attacks tend to target *specific* victim organizations. This is the type of attack that the MITRE ATT&CK enterprise matrix (MITRE Corporation, n.d.) and the classic intrusion kill chain frameworks (Hutchins, E.M., Cloppert, M.J., Amin, R.M., Ph.D., n.d.) seek to help mitigate. The MITRE ATT&CK framework provides lists of known attacker tactics and techniques across the stages attackers can leverage during their attacks. These include **reconnaissance**, **resource development**, **initial access**, **execution**, **persistence**, **privilege escalation**, **defense evasion**, **credential access**, **discovery**, **lateral movement**, **collection**, **command and control**, **exfiltration**, and **impact** (MITRE Corporation, n.d.).

> Note
>
> Attackers do not necessarily have to leverage every one of these stages in every attack, nor do they have to leverage them in the order described by MITRE. Nevertheless, this list gives you a very good idea of what a traditional network intrusion looks like.

This type of attack can progress as follows:

1. Attackers decide which organization(s) they want to victimize and what their objectives are (I will discuss attacker motivations later in this chapter).
2. They build, buy, or partner to develop weapons to use in the attack.
3. They gain initial access to the victim's network, deploy tools, find ways to stay persistent on the network even after they are discovered, and evade defenders' efforts to find them.
4. They use stolen credentials and add their own accounts in order to give themselves permissions to access network resources and perform reconnaissance to discover sensitive systems and data that can be collected and exfiltrated from the network.
5. They typically deploy command and control tools so that they can maintain access to the network and take actions such as exfiltrating data or deploying ransomware, as well as other illicit actions that align with their objectives.

Figure 1.3 illustrates an example of a traditional network intrusion on an enterprise IT environment behind a firewall, where attackers deployed ransomware. Initial compromise is achieved using one or more of the Cybersecurity Usual Suspects, which I'll discuss in detail later in this chapter.

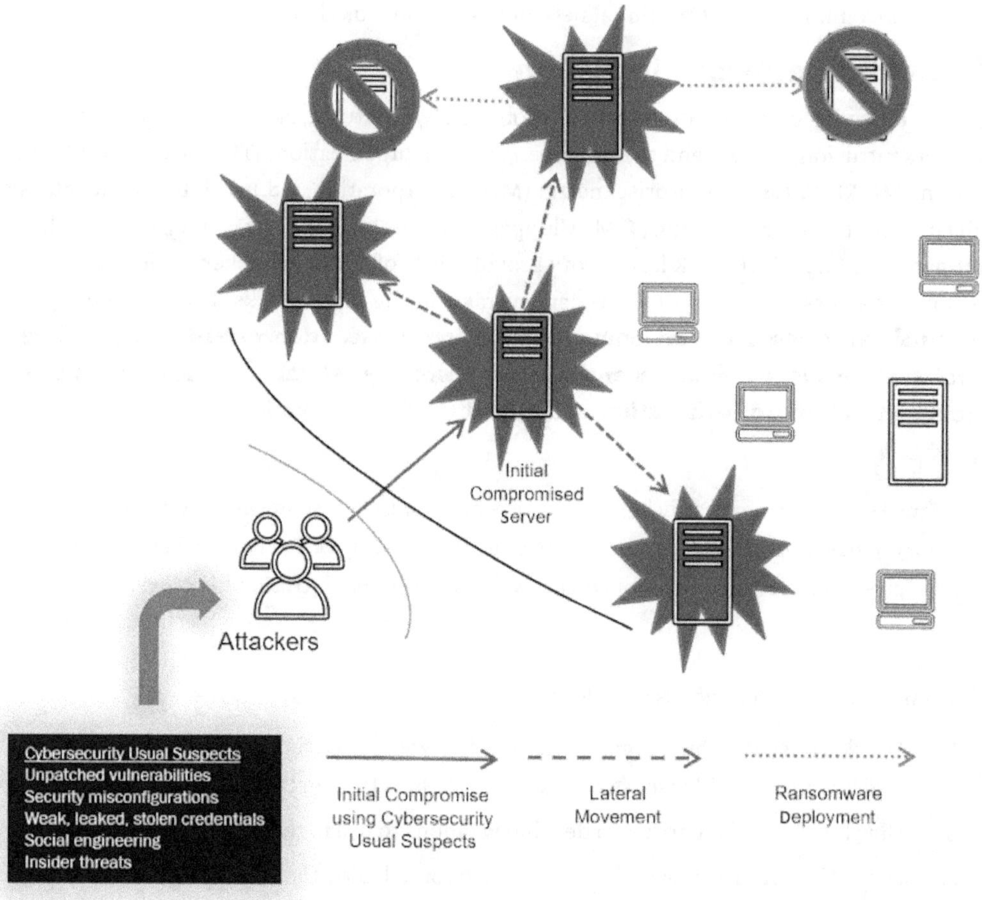

Figure 1.3 – An illustration of a traditional network intrusion where attackers deployed ransomware

The following subsections paint a more detailed picture of what one of these attacks looks like by using a specific fictional example. The attack events have been categorized using some of the tactics defined in the MITRE ATT&CK framework mentioned earlier.

Initial access and execution

Attackers use a targeted phishing email campaign to target specific users at a healthcare organization. They send convincing phishing emails to 10 employees, identified using

LinkedIn, who are likely to have administrator access to the network, and who are also likely to have IAM and service desk roles at the victim organization. Four of the 10 employees who receive the phishing email open it and click on the embedded link. The link takes them to a site that looks just like the Microsoft 365 portal they are accustomed to logging in to. One of the four employees is a little more cautious and suspects that it might be a phishing site prior to entering their credentials into it, while the other three are successfully tricked and enter their valid login credentials into the web page.

The attackers have scripts that automatically use the harvested credentials to immediately log in to the legitimate Microsoft 365 portal. All the employees had MFA enabled on their accounts. Subsequently, when attackers attempt to log in to the employees' Microsoft 365 accounts, their smartphones prompt them to complete the portal login process by granting approval in an authenticator app. The employees think they are logging in to the legitimate Microsoft 365 portal, so the MFA prompt they receive is expected behavior, and they approve the authentication request as they normally do. This gives attackers access to their accounts, and they immediately add their own burner mobile devices as second factors to the accounts to enable future logins without the employees' knowledge or participation. Now the attackers have valid usernames, passwords, and second factors that will enable them to access Microsoft 365 and other access points to the network, such as via a **Virtual Private Network** (**VPN**) and **Virtual Desktop Infrastructure** (**VDI**), anytime.

The attackers can now connect to the victim's network using a VPN connection with one of the stolen credentials. Attackers perform some reconnaissance on the victim's network by running legitimate tools (which are used by attackers regularly), such as Nmap, Advanced IP Scanner, PowerShell, Mimikatz, and PsExec. This helps them identify all the administrator accounts in the Active Directory and discover information that helps them move laterally on the network.

Privilege escalation

Now, the attackers focus on elevating their privileges by compromising some of the administrator accounts they discovered. To do this, they successfully exploit a vulnerability (such as CVE-2024-30088) that gives them system-level access to a domain controller that wasn't patched. This enables them to add new administrator accounts in the Active Directory for their own use.

Exfiltration and credential access

Next, they use a utility that's installed by default on the domain controller called `ntdsutil.exe` to export a copy of the healthcare organization's Active Directory. They upload that file (called `ntds.dit`) to a Google Drive account that they had previously compromised. They begin an offline crack of the passwords that are encrypted in the `ntds.dit` file, which starts yielding results within minutes. The shortest passwords get cracked almost instantly using virtual machines with GPUs in the cloud. Now, the attackers have even more credentials to help them stay persistent, move laterally, get access to sensitive data and exfiltrate it, and deploy ransomware. This includes the KRBTGT user object that is created by default in every Active Directory. Once the attackers are able to impersonate this object, they can impersonate any user object in the Active Directory. At this point, containing the attack and recovering the Active Directory to a known good state are aspirational goals for the victim organization.

Impact

After harvesting accounts and data from the victim's network for weeks or even months, the attackers start to encrypt valuable sensitive data and the organization's most valuable systems, including sensitive patient data, confidential financial data, and valuable intellectual property. Encrypting only a portion of each file, instead of the entire file, with their ransomware allows the attackers to devastate the victim's network and core infrastructure before the latter can understand what is happening. The attackers leave a ransom note behind instructing the organization to transfer $1.5 million in Bitcoin to them, giving the organization 48 hours to comply. They pledge to destroy the key that would decrypt and unlock their systems if this deadline is not met.

The attackers also threaten to publish the terabytes of data they exfiltrated to a victim-shaming site that they manage. If this happens, it will make the attack public knowledge because several media outlets and threat intelligence firms monitor the site for such disclosures.

The healthcare organization's finance department has no idea how to buy and transfer Bitcoin if they were to cede to the attackers' demands. Their senior management is hopeful that the FBI will be able to help them. The likelihood of that happening is low, since the victimshaming site the attackers referenced contains data from over 100 victims collected across three years, showing that law enforcement has not been successful in assisting others.

After consulting with a ransomware negotiation firm, the healthcare organization is more confident that they could pay the ransom and not violate the US Department of Treasury's **Office of Foreign Assets Control** (**OFAC**) regulations or other legal prohibitions, since the attackers aren't likely to be a known terrorist organization. The company makes the ransom payment, and the attackers provide a decryption program and key. However, it quickly becomes evident that it will take more time for the decryption program to decrypt files than restoring them from backups the company took prior to the attack.

The attackers now issue a second ransom demand for $650,000 in exchange for their promise not to sell access to the organization's network to other attackers who might perpetrate their own network intrusions, steal sensitive data, encrypt files, and extort the victim all over again. The CISO of the healthcare organization cannot guarantee that another threat actor wouldn't be able to access their network, given all their credentials were stolen, and the attackers had months of time to burrow into their infrastructure and systems. The CISO knows that, according to industry estimates, it takes 290 days to detect and contain these types of breaches (Okta, n.d.); the reality of the situation is that it will take months of work to contain and eradicate the attackers' presence on their network.

Samples of the healthcare organization's sensitive data are posted to dark web victim-shaming sites offering the full dataset for sale. A few hours later, a negative news cycle about the attack starts with three articles published by different news outlets that saw the posts on dark websites they monitor. Shortly afterward, the organization's customers and partners start calling them to find out what is happening, whether their data was stolen, and whether they need to take steps to protect themselves. The call volume overwhelms their call centers. The organization struggles to meet the data breach disclosure rules that they need to comply with because their systems are still mostly down, and they still don't have all the details needed to explain how the attack happened, what specific datasets were exfiltrated by attackers, and when the attack started. It only takes a few days before attorneys, threatening class action lawsuits on behalf of customers, start contacting the organization, although it's still not clear exactly which customers were impacted.

In the wake of this attack, the CISO and other executives prepare for months of meetings with attorneys, regulators, auditors, customers, and partners in order to meet all legal and regulatory requirements, defend themselves from legal actions, retain their customers and partners, and try to repair the organization's damaged reputation.

Mitigating traditional network intrusions

From the description I provided, it should be clear that a traditional network intrusion is hardly fun or even easy to deal with. This is why most CISOs and security teams focus on protecting assets in ways that make it harder for attackers to succeed and easier for defenders to detect their presence on the network as early in the attack as possible.

> **Tip**
>
> Reducing the "dwell time" during which attackers have access to your environment and restricting the actions they can take while on your network is key because it can reduce the damage and the cost to recover.

Mitigating traditional network intrusions in large enterprise environments is very challenging. If it were easy, cybersecurity would not be a multi-billion-dollar industry growing at double digits annually. In this attack scenario, a holistic cybersecurity strategy is required because the attack surface of a typical enterprise is too large for a narrower approach to be successful. There are several chapters in this book dedicated to helping you understand cybersecurity strategies and developing a strategy or combination of strategies that will give you the best chance of success.

Next, let's look at another common type of attack—data breaches caused by insecure APIs.

Data breaches via insecure APIs

Today, enterprises use APIs for everything from publishing and consuming data to provisioning and remotely controlling huge fleets of virtual systems. APIs are everywhere. Securing APIs can be complicated because it typically requires participation across disciplines to accomplish; developers and testers, IT systems and infrastructure operators, and cybersecurity roles all play parts in securing APIs. Attackers know that APIs are everywhere and that it is challenging to secure them. Subsequently, data breaches due to insecure APIs have become a common attack vector. Let's look at a fictional but realistic example of such an attack.

In this scenario, a municipal government department wants to enable self-service for their customers on their website, for better customer satisfaction while also reducing costs associated with calls to their call center. The department wants to allow their customers to request additional garbage cans, reduce the number of garbage cans they pay for, or cancel their service.

To facilitate this, they publish a web page with instructions for their customers, which includes a field for customers to enter their municipality account numbers. The account number entered is used to validate that they are a legitimate customer. Legitimate customers are redirected to another web page that asks them more questions to prove that they are the customer they say they are, such as their name, address, phone number, zip code, and date of birth. People without a known customer account are directed to a web page where they can open an account if their residence is in the municipality and they qualify for the garbage pickup service.

One morning, the CISO of the department is approached by a news reporter for comment on the data breach that they have apparently suffered. The CISO is confused because they are not aware of any data breach. The CISO gets their **Cyber Threat Intelligence** (**CTI**) program manager to check their CTI vendor's portal for any threat intelligence indicating a data breach. It is found that a dark website claims that the department has suffered a data breach, presenting a small sample of "stolen" customer data as evidence. The CISO asks the CTI program manager to work with the department's database administrator to determine whether the data is legitimate customer data, and it is found that it is.

The CISO immediately mobilizes their IR team to start an investigation. They have many questions:

- How did their network get compromised?
- Are their key systems going to be encrypted next?
- Should they be preparing for a ransom demand? Which user accounts do the attackers have control of?
- What steps should they be taking to contain the attacker?

The department's IR lead traces the data back to a specific database that contains the same fields as the stolen data. Although it is still too early in the investigation to be conclusive, they have found no **Indicators of Compromise** (**IOCs**) for the database or any of the servers. There is no indication of any unauthorized access in the log files. Over the next few days, the IR team performs a painstaking forensic examination of the database and all the servers. At the end of their analysis, they are convinced that there was no network intrusion. The investigation also strongly suggests that the data was not stolen by a malicious insider because there were no abnormal authentication events in the system logs.

The CISO receives an email from one of the network operations engineers who works with the development team. Her email indicates that she has identified some anomalous network traffic on the municipality's website a week before the leaked data was discovered on the dark web. The traffic to the website was normal but showed a sudden spike that lasted a few hours. She determines that the network traffic spike was due to traffic to and from the new customer self-service web page. Her analysis shows that a dozen IP addresses in different countries around the world used that web page. The web page generated queries that were sent to the backend database via an API. This caused the spike in network traffic.

The network operations engineer shares her findings with the IR team, the development team, and the IT operations team. From this data, the development team determines that the API was used to query the database for customer accounts in quick succession, by simply incrementing the account number for each new query. Each time a query was sent, a response came back from the database to the API. There were numerous "account number not valid" responses, but there were also hundreds of responses to queries where valid account numbers were provided.

The CISO is irate. How could this happen? After all, the department has a **Web Application Firewall** (**WAF**) that is supposed to block such attacks. Plus, that API shouldn't be returning customer data to that public web page; if the purpose of the query is just to determine whether the account number is valid, it should just return "account number not valid" or "account number valid." The development manager explains to the CISO that a developer on their team used the wrong API for the query on the web page. Instead of the API returning an "account number valid" response when a valid account number is entered, the API returns several fields in the database record that contain the customer's personal information. This is the information that was leaked to the dark web by attackers. The developer had used an API designed for use on the department's internal network, not for use on a publicly accessible web page on the internet. They didn't think anyone would see the customer information that the API returns because it isn't displayed on the web page. It was a simple mistake, but devastatingly naive.

This issue wasn't caught in testing because the web page wasn't designed to display any of the data that the API returned—it just indicates whether a valid customer account was found. However, if the attacker captured the network packets going between their workstations and the department's website or used free web development tools to debug the department's customer self-service web page, all the data being returned by the API would be visible to them. The department's WAF didn't prevent the attack because the web page and API were not being attacked using **SQL injection**, **Cross-Site Request Forgery**, or any of the typical web application attacks. The web page and API were operating exactly how they had been designed to operate.

> **Note**
>
> There are many cases where security infrastructure cannot compensate for poor developer judgment. This example can be considered one of those cases.

As the IR investigation progresses, customers begin to hear in the news and from some industry vendors that the department's network has been compromised. This frustrates the CISO because the attackers never penetrated their perimeter, never moved laterally on their network, and never found a way to stay persistent in their IT environment. There was no network intrusion. The attacker simply sat on the public internet and sent queries to an insecure API that returned data that it shouldn't have returned.

This type of data breach via an insecure API seems to be a daily occurrence across industries and around the world. The proliferation of APIs exposed to the internet has outpaced the adoption of security and privacy standards by developers that would help minimize the number of vulnerable APIs. Given the rapid and largely ungoverned proliferation of APIs, the number of APIs with vulnerabilities today is incalculable.

Mitigating data breaches via insecure APIs

Mitigating these types of issues with APIs is very challenging. There are at least two categories of applications that need attention:

- Applications that are currently being developed for release in the future that expose APIs
- Applications that are already in production that expose APIs

A **security development life cycle** that includes security and privacy requirements and standards for the development of APIs can help in both categories. However, what triggers a security review for applications already in production? This is the difficult question. Asked another way, when should developers in your organization stop developing new applications and spend time reviewing the old ones that were already released? Unfortunately for most organizations, the answer is when the exploitation of a critical vulnerability in the old application has been demonstrated either by attackers or in a penetration test. In a world with limited resources, most organizations simply can't afford to shift resources from work that will attract more customers, lower costs, and help beat the competition to vulnerabilities they view as theoretical. Regardless, developers need to be educated on **privacy by design** principles that help inform the decisions they make when designing and developing applications.

Threat modeling can also be an immensely powerful tool. Identifying the things that could go wrong before developers start writing code means issues can be addressed in the design rather than after the code is in production. Developers and architects should be trained to perform threat modeling, and it should be required for new application development.

Firewalls, **WAFs**, and **API security platforms** can all play roles in mitigating some issues with APIs. For example, configuring API query rate limits so that attackers can't drain the database in a short period of time will give defenders a better opportunity to detect attacks and respond. In the fictional scenario I described, there was no valid reason for the municipal department to allow network traffic or API queries from outside their own country; after all, they aren't going to pick up garbage for customers in other countries. They could not have saved any money by allowing their customers to adjust the number of garbage cans they have at their home in the US from Russia or China. There is much more risk than reward in such cases. Restricting inbound and outbound internet traffic on firewalls to the bare minimum will make it harder for attackers. By themselves, none of these are silver bullet solutions, but together, they make it harder for attackers to be successful. Every enterprise and CISO shares the challenge of API security. So, I have dedicated *Chapter 7, Application Programming Interface Security*, to API security.

The next section discusses the conclusions we can draw from comparing and contrasting the three types of attacks described in this section.

Lessons learned: Real-world attack scenarios – conclusions

The reason I wanted to show you three different types of attacks was to illustrate that not all data breaches are the same. When you hear about a data breach in the news or your organization experiences one, don't assume the worst-case scenario. The difference between a traditional network intrusion and the other two real-world attack scenarios can be pronounced for victims.

A **traditional network intrusion** can be an extinction event for victims, depending on the attacker's motivations and whether the attack goes undetected. While a **data breach via an API** can expose sensitive information, victims' infrastructures aren't typically impacted in this case, and the business can typically continue unabated. Both types of attacks can potentially have bad legal, regulatory, and reputational outcomes, but extinction for the organization is unlikely when an attacker simply repeatedly queries an insecure API from the internet.

The potential impact of worms is typically more random. Once a worm is released into the wild, where it ends up is largely uncontrolled. Even when a worm's developer has a specific target in mind, they can rarely control the unintended consequences once the worm is released.

Take the *Stuxnet worm* as an example, which was developed to target **Programmable Logic Controllers** (**PLCs**) leveraging four vulnerabilities. The purported and specific goal of the attack was to disrupt centrifuges used to enrich uranium at a nuclear facility in Iran. However, since three of the vulnerabilities that the worm leveraged were in Microsoft Windows, once the worm was released at the nuclear facility, it found ways to escape onto the public internet, where it continued to infect systems for years after the initial attack. Other purveyors of malware began using the same vulnerabilities Stuxnet used in their own malware and continued to compromise unpatched systems for years (Kaspersky, 2014).

Organizations might or might not be impacted by worms released to the internet. The impacts on affected organizations might be terrible or limited. There are a number of factors that influence such outcomes.

You might still be wondering, how do attackers continue to be successful despite organizations' substantial investments in cybersecurity? Is there a secret to their success? To answer this question, let's examine how enterprise IT environments get compromised in the first place, that is, so-called initial access. This is key to understanding, developing, and evaluating the effectiveness of cybersecurity strategies for enterprise IT environments.

How organizations get initially compromised

The foundation of an effective cybersecurity strategy is what I call the **cybersecurity fundamentals**. The cybersecurity fundamentals are based on decades of threat intelligence that I discuss in detail later in this book. After performing hundreds of IR investigations and studying Microsoft's and other vendors' threat intelligence for over a decade, I can tell you with confidence that there are only five ways that organizations initially get compromised. I call them the "Cybersecurity Usual Suspects":

- Unpatched vulnerabilities
- Security misconfigurations
- Weak, leaked, and stolen credentials
- Social engineering
- Insider threats

After the initial compromise, there are many, many **Tactics, Techniques, and Procedures (TTPs)** that attackers can use to move laterally, steal credentials, compromise infrastructure, remain persistent, gain illicit access to information, destroy data and infrastructure, and so on. Some of these have been around for decades, and some are newer and novel.

Let's look at each one of these usual suspects in more detail, starting with the exploitation of unpatched vulnerabilities.

Unpatched vulnerabilities

A vulnerability is a flaw in software or hardware design and/or the underlying programming code that allows an attacker to make the affected system do something unintended. The most severe vulnerabilities allow attackers to take complete control of the affected system, running arbitrary code of their choice. Less severe vulnerabilities lead to systems disclosing data in unintended ways or denying service to legitimate users.

> Note
>
> In *Chapter 3*, I provide a deep dive into vulnerability management and some of the key vulnerability disclosure trends over the past 20+ years. I'll save that in-depth discussion for that chapter, but I will provide some more context here.

Attackers have been using vulnerabilities to compromise systems at scale since at least the days of Code Red and Nimda in 2001. In 2003, SQL Slammer and Blaster successfully disrupted the internet and compromised hundreds of thousands of systems worldwide by exploiting unpatched vulnerabilities in Microsoft SQL Server and Microsoft Windows operating systems. In the years following these attacks, a cottage industry developed an ongoing effort to help enterprise organizations—those with the most complex environments—inventory their IT systems, identify vulnerabilities in them, deploy mitigations for vulnerabilities, and patch them. At the end of January 2026, over 241,000 vulnerabilities had been disclosed in software and hardware products from across the industry in the National Vulnerability Database (National Vulnerability Database, n.d.). As you'll read in *Chapter 3*, the number of vulnerabilities disclosed across the industry surged by 128% between 2016 and 2017, reaching levels never seen before. The number of vulnerability disclosures has increased year over year every year since, exceeding 48,400 disclosures in 2025.

An economy has evolved around the supply and demand for vulnerabilities and exploits, with a varied list of participants, including vendors, attackers, defenders, various commercial entities, and governments. The number of participants in this economy and their relative sophistication make it harder for organizations to protect themselves from the exploitation of vulnerabilities in their IT environments. Therefore, using unpatched vulnerabilities becomes a mainstay of attackers' toolkits.

Organizations that are highly competent at vulnerability management make it much harder for attackers to successfully attack them. A well-run vulnerability management program is a fundamental component and a critical requirement of an effective cybersecurity strategy. Without it, organizations' cybersecurity efforts will fail regardless of their other investments. Unpatched vulnerabilities in operating systems and the underlying platform components that even advanced cybersecurity capabilities rely on enable attackers to completely undermine the effectiveness of these investments. Failing to efficiently address ongoing vulnerability disclosures in the "trusted computing base" that your hardware and software rely on renders your hardware and software untrustworthy.

The importance of asset inventories

An accurate inventory of all IT assets is critical for a vulnerability management program. Organizations that can't perform accurate and timely inventories of all their IT assets, scan all IT assets for vulnerabilities, and efficiently mitigate and/or patch those vulnerabilities end up accepting a lot of risk. The following is some advice about asset management inventories.

The risk of incomplete asset inventories

Assets that don't show up in inventories won't get scanned or patched and will become the weak link in your security chain. Therefore, if the CISO and vulnerability management program managers rely on their organization's IT group or other internal partners to provide IT asset inventories, those inventories need to be complete and not just include systems that they are willing to patch. I've seen asset owners and operators willfully conceal IT assets from their vulnerability management teams because they didn't want those assets to be enrolled in the regular vulnerability scanning process and subject to the SLAs specified in their organization's vulnerability management policy. I've seen a range of reasons stated for this behavior, including the belief that security updates would destabilize critical systems, or that the systems were just test systems on the production network that the policy didn't apply to.

However, more commonly, the asset owners simply can't keep up with the pace of new vulnerability disclosures because they haven't increased resource levels over the years to do so.

The tension with uptime goals

Another reason asset owners and operators choose to conceal assets or consistently ask for vulnerability management policy exceptions to delay patching assets is the *reboots associated with patching*. Rebooting systems after they have been patched is at odds with the uptime objectives that IT organizations are measured against, because patching vulnerabilities increases the number of system reboots and, subsequently, decreases uptime even if everything goes smoothly.

Rebooting a healthy but very busy database server, for example, can take more time than the annual downtime budget permits for a server. Organizations that view the time it takes to install security updates as a blight on their uptime objectives need to reconsider their objectives. Organizations require systems to be online to serve their stakeholders' interests. However, if those servers are taken offline, temporarily or indefinitely, by an avoidable cybersecurity attack, those objectives clearly aren't met. Only by realizing that IT asset owners, operators, and their cybersecurity teams all have a shared destiny can they be successful. They need to adopt SLAs that help them keep fully patched systems continuously meeting stakeholder requirements, not just running in production. Renegotiating SLA uptime goals with provisions for regular and emergency security updates is one potential way to accomplish this.

The importance of independent verification

My advice in scenarios where asset inventories are provided by parties other than the vulnerability management program itself is to *trust but verify*. Spend the extra effort and budget to continually check asset inventories against reality. This includes those official and unofficial development and test environments that have been responsible for so many breaches in the industry over the years. Shadow IT and unofficial cloud accounts also fall into this category. Customers, partners, and employees won't care any less if their data was stolen from a test account instead of a production account.

> **Tip**
>
> If it is worth operating, it is worth maintaining and securing.

If the sources of asset inventories resist this requirement or fail to provide accurate, timely inventories, this represents a risk that the organization's senior leadership and the board of directors should be aware of. Providing senior leadership with a view of the estimated percentage of the total asset inventory currently not managed by your vulnerability management program should result in the sources of asset inventories reprioritizing their work—a disruption of a dangerous status quo.

> **Tip**
>
> **Cloud Access Security Brokers (CASBs)**, attack surface management products, **Software-as-a-Service (SaaS)** posture management products, **Identity Provider (IdP)** products, and asset management products can all help identify unknown and rogue assets.

Some of the CISOs I have talked to have taken ownership of the IT asset management programs for their organizations. This can be a significant amount of work in large IT environments. However, they do this because asset management is critical to operating a successful vulnerability management program.

I'll discuss traditional vulnerability management in greater detail in *Chapter 3*, and *Chapter 4*. I'll also discuss modern approaches to vulnerability management in *Chapter 13, Modern Approaches to Security and Compliance*. The cloud can render the old-fashioned methods of inventorying, scanning, and patching security vulnerabilities obsolete.

Bring your own device

Of course, one challenge with the approach I just described is environments that have embraced **Bring-Your-Own-Device (BYOD)** policies that allow employees to use their personal mobile devices to access and process enterprise data. The underlying question is whether enterprise vulnerability management teams should inventory and manage personal devices. This debate is one reason why many security professionals originally dubbed BYOD as "bring your own disaster."

Different organizations take different approaches when answering this question. Here are some of the approaches I've seen:

- **Corporate-owned devices**: Some organizations decide to solve their mobile computing requirements by procuring mobile devices for their workers and fully managing them. This gives them full control of these devices, but it is typically an expensive option considering the costs of buying the hardware and actively managing it over time.
- **Personal devices**: Many cost-conscious organizations simply allow their workers to use their own devices for business purposes. This is typically the least expensive option but provides the least amount of control and visibility. These organizations rely on their workers to patch their mobile devices and report any misplacements. Hope plays a big part in the security strategy for organizations that employ this approach. They

hope nothing bad will happen to these devices because some of their data is accessible from these devices or might even be stored on these devices. However, they likely won't know if something bad does happen as these devices are completely unmanaged.

- **Hybrid or passive management approach**: A popular approach is a passive management model, where users are required to have an access PIN on their personal devices. This provides at least one layer of protection for the device contents if the device is lost or stolen.

  Additionally, these devices aren't allowed to connect to their employers' networks if the latest mobile operating system version isn't installed. Some organizations take device health verification one step further by employing **Network Access Control** (**NAC**) or **Network Access Protection** (**NAP**) technologies to help enforce policies related to the health of systems connecting to their network. Microsoft Intune and Jamf are popular choices for mobile device management, among many others.

  > Note
  >
  > Some vendors have made this model a cornerstone of the Zero-Trust architectures that they offer to their customers. They won't trust endpoints unless their health has been verified to meet the organization's mobile device security policies. This typically includes running the latest operating system version and being patched for all known vulnerabilities.

  These characteristics make endpoints more trustworthy because they meet minimum security standards, thus reducing the likelihood that they are compromised and could provide attackers with entry into the corporate network. If an endpoint doesn't meet these minimum standards, remote connection requests from it are refused until it complies with the policy and has a "clean bill of health."

Regardless of the approach adopted, minimizing the number of unpatched systems allowed to connect to enterprise networks is a best practice.

Next, we'll consider security misconfigurations. Like unpatched vulnerabilities, security misconfigurations can potentially enable attackers to take a range of actions on a system, including disrupting its operation, stealing information, lowering security settings, disabling security features, seizing control of it, and using it to attack other systems.

Security misconfigurations

Security misconfigurations can be present in a system as a default setting, such as a preset key or password that is the same on every system manufactured by a vendor. Security misconfigurations can also be introduced gradually as a system's configuration changes incrementally as it gets managed over time.

> Tip
>
> After performing hundreds of IR investigations while I was on the customer-facing IR team at Microsoft, I can tell you that a significant percentage of systems initially get compromised through security misconfigurations.

This is especially true of internet-facing systems such as **web servers**, **firewalls**, and other systems found in enterprise **Demilitarized Zones** (**DMZs**). If a misconfiguration lets an attacker take control of a system in the DMZ—or use it to issue authenticated requests on their behalf, such as through a server-side request forgery—they will try to use that foothold to access other systems in the DMZ and eventually pivot into the organization's internal network. This has been a common pattern in attackers' playbooks for more than 20 years.

Security misconfigurations have also plagued endpoint devices, such as PCs, smartphones, and **Internet of Things** (**IoT**) devices. The infrastructure that these endpoints connect to, such as wireless access points, is also frequently probed by attackers for common misconfigurations. Security misconfigurations have also been an issue in **Industrial Control Systems** (**ICSs**) for many years. For example, one scenario involving ICSs that has burned security teams in the past is "fall back to last known status," which can override more recent security configuration changes in favor of former, less secure settings. Hardcoded credentials, which are the same on every device that a manufacturer sells, and vulnerable default configurations have long-haunted manufacturers of all sorts of software and hardware across the industry. Once attackers learn that specific devices from specific manufacturers all have the same default password or unchangeable backdoor for their developers, they quickly become perennial targets.

A well-run vulnerability management program typically includes identifying security misconfigurations as part of its scope. Many of the same vulnerability scanners and tools that are used to identify and patch security vulnerabilities are also capable of identifying security misconfigurations and providing guidance on how to address them. Some vulnerability scanners can assess whether system configurations align with widely adopted security baselines, such as the **Center for Internet Security (CIS)** Benchmarks (Center for Internet Security, n.d.) or an organization's own internal configuration standards.

Again, organizations should forego big investments in advanced cybersecurity capabilities if they aren't already very proficient at identifying and mitigating security misconfigurations in their environment. For instance, there's no point in spending a lot of money and effort looking for **Advanced Persistent Threats** (**APTs**) in an environment if attackers can use decades-old lists of hardcoded passwords available on the internet to successfully compromise and move around the environment. Even if CISOs found such attackers in their IT environment, they would be powerless to exorcise them with common security misconfigurations present.

Some of the biggest breaches in history were a result of an initial compromise through a combination of unpatched vulnerabilities and security misconfigurations. Both can be managed through a well-run vulnerability management program. Some CISOs rely on their offensive security teams to ferret out misconfigurations during **red team operations**, **attack simulations**, or **cybersecurity control testing**. In some cases, these will be more effective approaches than leveraging vulnerability management tools.

> Tip
>
> **Remember**
>
> It is easier to manage things you can measure; complete, accurate, and timely IT asset inventories are critical for successful vulnerability management programs, as well as finding and remediating security misconfigurations. Trust but verify asset inventories, always. It's worth keeping in mind that the cloud provides several advantages over the old on-premises IT world. I'll discuss this in detail in *Chapter 13*.

Security misconfigurations can be present by default in new hardware and software or may creep in over time. Another ongoing threat that requires constant attention is that of compromised credentials, discussed next.

Weak, leaked, and stolen credentials

There's an old saying in the cybersecurity industry: "attackers don't break in, they log in." You might have also heard, "identity is the new firewall." These reflect the fact that compromised IT environments due to weak, leaked, or stolen credentials are common. In 2024, Microsoft reported, "Microsoft Entra data shows that of more than 600 million identity attacks per day, more than 99% are password-based" (Microsoft, 2024). That's 7,000 password attacks blocked per second, on average, for the entire year!

There are several ways that credentials get leaked and stolen: **social engineering**, such as **phishing**, malware that does **keystroke logging** or steals credentials from operating systems and browsers, and **compromised systems** that cache, store, and/or process credentials. Sometimes, developers accidentally expose secrets by uploading projects to code-sharing sites and forgetting to remove any keys or passwords that were embedded in their code. When those code-sharing sites get compromised, all those secrets are exposed. Similarly, old development and test environments that are abandoned but left running ultimately yield credentials to attackers after not being patched over time. Further, some attackers pay insiders to provide stolen credentials to them. And, of course, as you read in the traditional network intrusion scenario earlier in the chapter, if attackers successfully exfiltrate an organization's `ntds.dit` (a copy of their Active Directory), all their credentials are now potentially exposed and can be sold by access brokers or might simply start to show up in lists of compromised credentials on the dark web. In fact, many organizations struggle to rotate all their passwords after such an intrusion because non-human accounts, such as service accounts, likely have never been rotated before. It can take months to rotate all passwords, while in the meantime, attackers can continue to use credentials that haven't been rotated.

Massive lists of stolen and leaked credentials have been discovered on the internet over the years. In addition to these lists, the availability of **High-Performance Computing Clusters** (**HPCs**) and GPU-based password-cracking tools has rendered passwords, by themselves, ineffective in protecting resources and accounts.

The following describes in detail how attackers might use stolen credentials:

1. When an on-premises enterprise environment is initially compromised, attackers use leaked or stolen credentials for reconnaissance and look for other credentials that are cached or stored in the environment. They especially look for administrator credentials that could give them unlimited access to resources in the compromised environment.
2. Typically, within seconds of the initial compromise, attackers try to access the victim organization's user account directory service, such as Microsoft Active Directory, to dump all the credentials in the directory (the aforementioned `ntds.dit` file). The more credentials they have at their disposal to move and stay persistent, the harder it is to expel them from the environment—they can persist indefinitely.
3. Attackers will also try to steal user account databases. If attackers successfully get all the credentials from their victim's directory service, then recovery really is aspirational.
4. Once attackers have stolen hashed credentials, traditionally the weakest of these credentials can be cracked in offline attacks in under an hour (Kaspersky, 2024).

Longer, uncommon, and truly complex passwords will get cracked last. There have been raging debates for decades about the efficacy of passwords versus passphrases, as well as appropriate character lengths, character sets, password lockout policies, password expiration policies, and the like. Guidance for passwords has changed over the years as threats and risks have changed and new data has become available. Microsoft has published guidance for Microsoft 365 password policies that is definitely worth a read (Microsoft 2025).

When credentials are leaked or stolen from an organization, it doesn't take attackers long to run them through scripts that try to log in to financial institutions, e-commerce sites, social networking sites, and other sites in the hopes that the credentials were reused somewhere. Reusing passwords across accounts is a terrible practice. Simply put, credentials that provide access to more than one account have a higher ROI for attackers than those that don't. Sets of compromised credentials that can provide access to corporate resources and information, as well as social networks, which can also serve as a rich source of information and potential victims, are valuable.

The usefulness of passwords by themselves to protect enterprise resources has long passed. Consequently, using MFA is a requirement for enterprises and consumers alike. MFA can mitigate stolen and leaked credentials in many, but not all, scenarios. When MFA is used, even if attackers possess a valid username and password for an account, they won't get access to the account unless they also possess the other authentication factor required. These other factors include digital certificates, one-time passwords, and PINs generated on dedicated hardware or smartphone apps; a call to a preregistered landline or mobile phone; fingerprints; and facial recognition.

However, there have been some successful attacks on some MFA methods as well, for example, **SIM-swapping attacks** to intercept PIN codes sent to preregistered mobile phones via SMS. Another limitation of MFA is that it isn't ubiquitous in enterprise IT environments. Organizations with decades-old legacy applications using old-fashioned authentication and authorization methods are less likely to fully mitigate the risk with MFA. Even if the latest systems and cloud-based services require MFA, chances are there are more legacy applications that cannot utilize it easily.

Several CISOs that I've talked to have experienced this limitation firsthand during penetration tests that exposed the limitations of MFA in their environments. Some vendors specialize in mitigating such MFA-related risks; one such vendor is called Silverfort (Silverfort, n.d.).

The following are some best practices to follow to protect your organization against credential leaks or theft:

- Using unique passwords for every account can help mitigate this risk. If a password is unique and it is leaked or stolen, its potential usefulness to attackers will be limited. If you have too many accounts to assign and track unique passwords for, then use a password vault to make life easier. There are numerous commercially available products for consumers and enterprises.
- MFA can be very effective; use it everywhere that usernames and passwords are in use. Microsoft has published a great blog post about the effectiveness of MFA called *Your Pa$$word Doesn't Matter* (Weinert, 2019), which is recommended reading.
- Leveraging passkeys can also be very helpful. Passkeys are a passwordless authentication method that uses cryptographic key pairs stored on a user's device to verify identity without ever transmitting a secret that can be phished or stolen. They replace passwords by relying on biometrics or device-level unlock mechanisms. This

makes them resistant to credential theft and replay attacks. More information is available on the FIDO Alliance website at `https://fidoalliance.org/passkeys/`.

- Plan for failure; that is, plan for when your organization's `ntds.dit` file gets stolen. Relatively long passwords or passphrases will make offline cracking of stolen passwords harder and slower for attackers, which in turn will give your organization more time to rotate all their passwords before attackers can harvest and use them. Passwords or passphrases that are 15 characters or longer pose a significant hurdle for offline cracking tools. Where possible, prevent users from using variations of their old passwords. Attackers have developed novel methods of using old leaked and stolen passwords to derive uncreative users' likely new passwords. Use a password manager solution if these requirements are too hard for users to manage.
- You should know whether your organization is leaking credentials and how old those leaked credentials are. Using a service that collects leaked and stolen credentials and looks for your organization's credentials being sold and traded online can give you a little peace of mind that you aren't missing something obvious. Getting some idea of the age of these credentials can help you decide whether password resets are necessary and the number of people potentially impacted.
- Privileged access management solutions can detect credential theft and credential misuse attacks (such as pass-the-hash, pass-the-ticket, and golden ticket attacks), as well as attackers' lateral movement and reconnaissance in your infrastructure:
    - Many of these solutions also offer password vaulting, credential brokering, and specialized analytics. Some of these solutions can be noisy and prone to false positives, but still, they can help you to manage and detect weak, leaked, and stolen credentials.

  In cloud-based environments, IAM controls are the most powerful controls you have. Taking advantage of all the power that IAM controls offer can help you to protect and detect threats to resources in the cloud. But this is one control set area that can proliferate into an unmanageable mess quickly. Extra thoughtful planning around your organization's IAM strategy will pay huge security dividends.

I will discuss identity a little more in *Chapter 10, Cybersecurity Strategies*.

An important aspect of protecting credentials involves educating information workers to be aware of social engineering attacks in which attackers may attempt to steal credentials through methods such as phishing. This is not the only way in which social engineering is used to compromise systems, however. I'll cover social engineering in a little more detail next.

Social engineering

Of the Cybersecurity Usual Suspects, social engineering is the most widely used method. Simply put, social engineering involves tricking users into making poor trust decisions. Examples of poor trust decisions include lowering the security posture of a system by changing its settings without understanding the possible outcomes of doing so or unknowingly installing malware on a system. Attackers rely on the naivety of their victims in social engineering attacks.

The volume of social engineering attacks is orders of magnitude larger than other types of attacks. For example, the volume of email phishing attacks Microsoft reported for July 2019 was 0.85% of the more than 470 billion email messages that flowed through Office 365 that month (Microsoft Corporation, n.d.). That's 4 billion phishing emails that all relied on social engineering detected in a single month. Microsoft reported that the domains used in phishing attacks grew consistently between July 2022 and June 2023, with the period ending with four times more domains used for phishing (Microsoft, 2023). Attackers continue to use phishing because it continues to be successful for them. Microsoft reported that between April and June 2023, they alerted users about roughly 10,000 instances per month in which passwords were entered into malicious websites (Microsoft, 2023). Although it doesn't appear that Microsoft has published updated phishing volume data for more recent time periods, they have shared how they have observed attackers leveraging AI to improve phishing attacks:

> *"AI-automated phishing emails achieved 54% click-through rates compared to 12% for standard attempts—a 4.5x increase. AI enables more targeted phishing and better phishing lures. More concerning, AI automation has the potential to increase phishing profitability by up to 50 times by scaling highly targeted attacks to thousands of targets at minimal cost." (Microsoft, 2025)*

I discuss phishing in greater detail in *Chapter 6, Internet-Based Threats.*

Trojan, a category of malware that relies on social engineering to be successful, has been the most prevalent category of malware for many years. In a recent Microsoft Digital Defense Report, data from Microsoft Defender for Office 365 indicates that 775 million email messages contained malware between July 2023 and June 2024 (Microsoft Corporation, 2024). I'll discuss this category of malware and many others in detail in *Chapter 5.*

Given the massive volume of social engineering attacks and their historical record of success, mitigating these attacks really isn't optional for enterprises. A fundamental component of an enterprise cybersecurity strategy is a mitigation strategy for social engineering attacks. Put another way, not including social engineering attacks in your cybersecurity strategy would mean ignoring the most common way that organizations initially get compromised.

Social engineering attacks are typically perpetrated by attackers external to organizations, so users must be prepared through appropriate education and training.

Another challenging threat to defend against is one from within. The final potential route of initial compromise, which we'll discuss next, is that of the insider threat.

Insider threats

When discussing insider threats with CISOs and security teams, I find it useful to break them down into two different categories, listed here from most likely to least likely:

1. **Non-malicious intent**: This includes mistakes or poor trust decisions that lead to bad security outcomes. Unfortunately, I've seen too many incidents start with this subcategory of insider threats. Some of the worst outcomes include administrators making high-risk configuration changes without going through their organization's governance or change control approval processes because they were in a hurry or were troubleshooting something. Further, poorly thought-through changes to internet-facing firewalls and WAFs that have very bad outcomes seem to be two perennial examples of such mistakes.
2. **Malicious intent**: This includes insiders, such as employees or contractors who use their privileged access to steal information or otherwise negatively impact the confidentiality, integrity, or availability of the organization's IT and/or data. Malicious insiders can be motivated by many different things, including their compensation or title not progressing relative to their expectations, or if they get enticed by financial incentives offered by attackers. I discuss a broader range of motivations later in this chapter. Most CISOs I've talked to have three subcategories of malicious insiders in mind:
   The **lone wolf insider** who works by themselves, abusing the privileged access they have to their organization's infrastructure and data for their own benefit.

   A **small group** of individuals who work together to accomplish unauthorized activities that none of the group members could achieve alone.

   A **mass conspiracy**, where multiple insiders work together to overcome the separation of duties that distributes the span of security control. I've found that CISOs typically bring this subcategory up in discussions about risks in managed service provider environments and the cloud, asserting that the entirety of US cloud service providers are corrupt. I discuss this in more detail in *Chapter 8, Friend or Foe? The Roles Governments Play in Cybersecurity*.

Mitigating insider threats should be fundamental to enterprise-wide cybersecurity strategies. Enforcing *meaningful separation of duties* and embracing *the principle of least privilege* are helpful, as are *automation*, *monitoring*, and *auditing*.

> Tip
>
> The revelation of a clandestine insider threat program is one of the easiest ways to create lasting distrust within an organization. Revealing the program's existence only when the security team needs other people's help can lead to trust issues. Setting up an **insider threat program steering committee** composed of senior representatives from the office of the CISO and legal, HR, fraud, privacy, and IT departments will help CISOs avoid or minimize issues later if the program identifies malicious insiders and action is warranted. A steering committee that sets the program's charter and scope and approves its playbooks can help CISOs avoid alienating their partners and allow them to manage the program more effectively. However, the decision to keep the program confidential or make its existence broadly known within an organization (to leverage its potential deterrent value) is largely a function of culture (both corporate and regional).

From a tools perspective, it has been interesting to watch different approaches emerge in this space. Some vendors offer products that are grounded in **endpoint forensics** that enable investigators to get visibility into every keystroke and mouse click users make. Other vendors have developed products where DLP is central, tracking how users access data and how and where data moves. Some others offer **deception technology** that helps identify insiders who poke around network resources without any business cause to do so.

I became a big fan of deception technology after seeing how it can be used to detect insider threats. There are a few different approaches to deception technology, but the basic concept is to present attackers with a system, potentially with publicly known vulnerabilities or common security misconfigurations, that alerts defenders to the presence of attackers when attackers interact with the system. I've heard some security professionals refer to this as a "canary in the coal mine" for IT environments.

Something to consider as part of the insider threat tool selection process is to develop some **insider threat risk indicators**. These indicators can help predict whether an insider might turn malicious. Some common indicators include declining performance, declining interest in the goals of the organization, spending less time at work, suddenly printing lots of documents, or exfiltrating files from work to their personal cloud storage service. Other effective indicators might be associated with the type of organization, the organization's culture, the country where they work, and their customs and culture. Some insiders turn malicious after they have tendered their resignations. This is a key time to watch for and detect malicious activities such as data exfiltration. Developing a list of the indicators that you think will be effective can help with choosing the right insider threat tool for your program and give you a better chance at detecting insider threats.

You are now well versed in the Cybersecurity Usual Suspects, that is, the five ways organizations are initially compromised. Defending against these five vectors of attack is fundamental to effective cybersecurity.

Focusing on the cybersecurity fundamentals

In order to achieve a successful cybersecurity program, organizations need to get very good at continuously mitigating all five of the Cybersecurity Usual Suspects. This competency forms the foundation of a sound cybersecurity strategy. Other cybersecurity-related investments will potentially have diminishing returns if the foundation of the strategy is not solid.

After an attacker uses one or more of these five ways to initially compromise an organization, they might employ a plethora of novel and advanced TTPs. Organizations that focus on the cybersecurity fundamentals make it much harder for attackers to be successful; that is, by focusing on the inside 85% of the bell curve shown in *Figure 1.4*, in which the cybersecurity fundamentals sit, instead of the activities in the outlying 7.5% on either end of the curve, security teams will have a better chance at success.

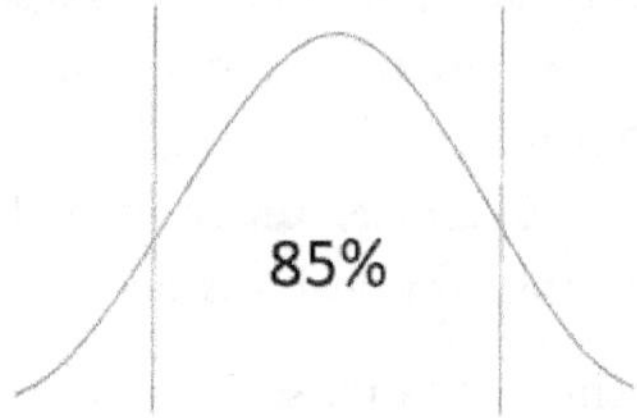

Figure 1.4 – A bell curve illustrating that most security teams should spend their time on the cybersecurity fundamentals

Unfortunately, the allure of hunting APTs can take resources away from the less sexy but critical work in the middle of the curve.

If there really are only five ways that organizations get initially compromised, why does there seem to be so much confusion in the industry on proper priorities for cybersecurity programs? I think there are a bunch of factors contributing to this confusion. One reason is that the way attacks, security incidents, and data breaches are reported in popular media outlets sometimes confuses attackers' tactics with their motivations.

This lack of clarity can lead organizations to make wrong security prioritization decisions. The next section explains the differences between attackers' motivations and tactics.

Understanding the differences between attackers' motivations and tactics

One of the reasons I've found that so many organizations lack focus and competency around the cybersecurity fundamentals is confusion surrounding how attacks are perpetrated. There are a lot of different ways organizations get attacked, as I illustrated with the three real-world attack examples earlier in this chapter. However, when you take a closer look at these attacks, the victim organization was *always initially* compromised by attackers using one or more of the Cybersecurity Usual Suspects.

Why the volume of attacks has increased

There are more attackers operating out in the open than ever before, because they don't believe there are consequences for their illicit activities, based on their location, legal jurisdiction, or who sponsors their work. It used to be the exception to the rule that they wouldn't obfuscate their true affiliations and identities. However, there has been a proliferation of nation-state threat groups, and some threat intelligence providers are now tracking many such groups that they identify as *bona fide nation states*. For example, a recent Microsoft Digital Defense Report shares that "Microsoft Threat Intelligence now tracks more than 1,500 unique threat groups—including more than 600 nation-state threat actor groups, 300 cybercrime groups, 200 influence operations groups, and hundreds of others" (Microsoft Corporation, 2024).

The world has changed over the past several years in ways that enable more cyberattacks than in the past. The poor international relations between Western nations and Russia, China, Iran, and North Korea enable criminal groups in those countries to attack non-military targets in the US, Canada, the UK, and other Western nations without consequences. Law enforcement in those countries has demonstrated their unwillingness to stop attacks against industries in the Western world. This has emboldened attackers in these locations with literally no downside to attacking commercial sector organizations. When these attackers' TTPs are discovered and publicized, it lowers the barrier for entry to lower-skilled criminals in other parts of the world.

The evolving challenge of attribution

Attributing an attack to an individual or group used to be very aspirational because the internet is based on a suite of protocols that were developed over 40 years ago. The engineers who developed these immensely scalable and sophisticated protocols never envisioned a future world where an entire $271 billion+-dollar-a-year industry (Grand View Research, 2025) would be based on the discoveries of new security vulnerabilities, malware research, social engineering protection, and the proliferation of sophisticated criminal organizations and nation-state actors. The **TCP/IP (version 4) protocol** suite, the basis of the internet, was never designed to help investigators perform attribution for cyberattacks that leverage vast networks of compromised distributed systems around the world. Finding "patient zero," where the compromise started, in large environments that have been compromised for months or years, using evidence collected from compromised systems, can rarely be done with complete confidence.

However, attackers that have embraced the modern ransomware business model have made it easier to do attribution with much more confidence. They essentially identify themselves, or at least their ransomware gang affiliation, when they demand a ransom from their victims. Having a known ransomware gang designation can help strike fear in the minds of victims, especially when the gang has a history of successful attacks. Victims take them seriously when they have a record of keeping their promises—both good and bad.

Attribution is relatively easy when a known ransomware gang posts a dark web blog post in the same way they have in the past, publishing some of their latest victim's data. It proves they have possession of stolen data and are demanding one or more ransoms from the victim. I examine some of the ways that ransomware has evolved in *Chapter 5*.

When security teams find IOCs that precisely match the "rat droppings" of a known threat actor, it's hard *not to* conclude that the associated threat actor is involved in an attack.

> Note
>
> I discuss IOCs in more detail in *Chapter 2, What to Know about Threat Intelligence*. But I still think it's important to keep in mind that even if you were able to identify an attacker and capture them, they likely would never tell you their true motivations—criminals rarely do. This is especially true of organized crime and nation states—you will be left with a lot of assumptions about their motivations. I discuss governments and the myriad motivations they have in *Chapter 8*.

Attackers' motivations

In the case of ransomware, it would seem like the motivation is quite straightforward—profit. However, some Microsoft threat research suggested that attackers used "fake" ransomware against Ukrainian government targets during the Russian invasion in 2022. The motivation of these "fake" ransomware attacks wasn't profit; it was really the destruction of Ukrainian assets. At the time, Microsoft reported, "MSTIC assesses that the malware, which is designed to look like ransomware but lacking a ransom recovery mechanism, is intended to be destructive and designed to render targeted devices inoperable rather than to obtain a ransom" (Microsoft Corporation, January 15, 2022). Apparently, wiper malware was disguised as ransomware. The difference is that this wiper malware wasn't designed to encrypt data in a way that is reversible using a decryption key; the data was instead destroyed ("crypto deleted"). This wasn't the first time, nor will it be the last, that attackers try to make their motivations opaque.

Still, many cybersecurity professionals use this type of evidence to surmise the attackers' motivations, affiliations, and identities. Attacker motivations can include the following:

- **Notoriety**: The attacker wants to prove that they are smarter than the big high-tech companies and their victims.
- **Profit**: As I discuss in *Chapter 4*, after the successful global worm attacks in 2003, malware began to evolve to support a profit motive that continues to the present day.
- **Economic espionage**: For example, alleged activities by groups in China to steal valuable intellectual property from Western nations to give their own industries a competitive and economic advantage.
- **Military espionage**: A motivation as old as governments themselves, where governments want to understand the military capabilities of their adversaries and allies.
- **Hacktivism**: Attacks against organizations and institutions based on disagreements on political or philosophical issues.
- **Foreign policy objectives**: Governments run sophisticated cyber-influence operations using cultural manipulation and information warfare tactics, amplifying false narratives to influence and manipulate target populations. Examples include influencing elections and lowering the morale of enemy civilian populations during wartime.
- **Many others**: Watch any James Bond movie where the **Special Executive for Counterintelligence, Terrorism, Revenge, and Extortion** (**SPECTRE**) is part of the plot, and you'll see some creative motivations.

Here are some examples of things I see get confused with motivations all the time:

- **Cryptocurrency theft**: This isn't a motivation; it's an *action* attackers take based on their motivation. Based on the preceding list, obvious motivations for cryptocurrency theft could be notoriety, revenge, and/or profit. *Theft itself is not a motivation.*
- **Data destruction**: Again, this is an action attackers take in pursuit of their objectives, which follows one of the motivations on the previously discussed list.
- **Ransomware**: This is a family of malware and a *type of attack*, but not a motivation. As mentioned earlier, profit, revenge, and pursuing foreign policy objectives are three examples of possible motivations for leveraging ransomware.

This is a subtle but important nuance that CISOs should keep in mind when developing their cybersecurity strategies, communicating with their stakeholders, and talking with cybersecurity vendors, especially during IR investigations when it's easy to get distracted. Focusing on *how* organizations get attacked instead of *why* they get attacked will help you develop a more holistic cybersecurity strategy with measurable efficacy.

Attribution is not a prerequisite to success

You might wonder, if attackers' motivations are unclear, how are CISOs supposed to know what a proportional response is? Who should help the victim organization with the response to the attack—local authorities, national law enforcement such as the FBI, the military, or an international coalition?

Security teams armed with the knowledge of attackers' TTPs, catalogs of IOCs, and improved detection and response automation can definitely defend against known threat actors much more effectively and efficiently than ever before. However, as successful and promising as new threat intelligence capabilities are, and even when attackers identify their affiliations with ransom demands and data leak blog posts, attacks continue unabated, and arguably, attackers have never been more successful than they are today.

Fortunately, understanding who the attackers are is not a prerequisite for a successful cybersecurity strategy. Regardless of who sponsors their work or how sophisticated attackers are, they all use the Cybersecurity Usual Suspects to achieve initial compromise: "the tools used by nation states to compromise victim networks are most frequently the same tools used by other malicious actors" (Microsoft Corporation, October 2021). I believe we can, with 99.9% certainty, predict the tactics that attackers will use when they try to initially compromise an enterprise IT environment. This is what organizations should invest in first—the cybersecurity fundamentals to mitigate the Cybersecurity Usual Suspects.

> **Note**
>
> A large and thriving threat intelligence industry has grown out of the insatiable desire for attribution, TTPs, and IOCs. In the next chapter, we'll dive deep into CTI. You'll learn what threat intelligence is, how to distinguish good intelligence from bad, and how enterprise cybersecurity teams use it. This will help prepare you to evaluate the cybersecurity strategies that are designed to mitigate intrusion attempts that are discussed in later chapters of this book.

Given everything I've discussed in this chapter, you might be wondering who would be crazy enough to take a CISO job! In my experience, CISOs can have different motivations, which are typically based on their experience and backgrounds. I mentioned that I wrote this book for

CISOs, aspiring CISOs, and other professionals who work with CISOs. Did you know that there are different types of CISOs? Whether you are a CISO yourself, a security team member of a vendor account team supporting a CISO, a salesperson trying to sell to a CISO, or a member of a board of directors that a CISO reports to, understanding the type of CISO you are working with can help make communicating with them a lot more predictable, efficient, and perhaps even enjoyable.

Different types of CISOs: "The CISO spectrum"

Different types of CISOs can have different approaches to cybersecurity that dictate, or at least strongly influence, the focus of their security programs. I call this list of types of CISOs the *CISO spectrum*. This list isn't exhaustive; it simply contains the types of CISOs I encountered over the past couple of decades of my career:

- **Type 1 – the IT director with cybersecurity responsibility**: They were perhaps the most technical of all the types of CISOs I encountered, typically having had more IT expertise than cybersecurity expertise. They knew all about the IT infrastructure that they supported and were trusted members of the IT leadership team. They were assigned cybersecurity as part of their job function. They had the aptitude and the desire to learn about security and compliance, sometimes purely out of a sense of self-preservation. Their comfort zone was IT systems, and when they met with me, they were typically keen for insights and help with cybersecurity.
- **Type 2 – the incident responder**: Some of the CISOs I met became CISOs because they were the go-to person for responding to incidents for their organization. They were IR and remediation experts. Their organizations trusted them during crises and looked to them to help the organization avoid crisis situations in the future. They tended to be threat intelligence geeks and focused on making it harder for attackers to succeed, using their technical knowledge. They had deep knowledge of IT systems as they were typically involved in building and administrating these systems earlier in their career.
- **Type 3 – the compliance or audit expert**: These folks tended to focus on control sets that helped meet regulations and industry standards. Their experience in managing compliance or audit programs gave them deep expertise in managing large control sets in large complex IT environments that were required to comply with multiple standards, such as PCI DSS, CMMC, the NIST **Risk Management Framework** (**RMF**) that uses NIST SP 800-53, ISO 27000, and so on. They'd typically rather discuss control sets and compliance challenges than threats or threat actors. For this type of CISO, "good" cybersecurity is strict compliance with standards.

- **Type 4 – the policy wonk**: I met two different types of CISOs who rely on their strong policy backgrounds:
    - **Governance, Risk, and Compliance (GRC) policy experts**: These CISOs typically had lots of experience writing and enforcing GRC-related policies. To get things done, they relied on policies the same way police rely on laws.
    - **Cybersecurity public policy experts**: These CISOs typically weren't IT experts or enterprise cybersecurity experts. Rather, they tended to be attorneys with deep public policy and privacy expertise. They had experience with national cybersecurity policies, that is, cybersecurity policies that national or federal governments implement to protect citizens, as well as private sector and public sector organizations within their borders.
- **Type 5 – the strategist**: These CISOs tended to focus on aligning resources around frameworks. To do this, they required some cybersecurity expertise along with some business acumen. Many of these folks had experience in at least a couple of different cybersecurity domains, such as IR and risk management. They were always on the lookout for technologies or processes that would help them address known gaps in their capabilities and improve the effectiveness of their strategies.
- **Type 6 – the risk expert**: In my experience, this type of CISO was rarer than the rest. Their area of expertise was risk management. They approached cybersecurity like an actuary, using quantitative risk calculations to determine the potential cost range of different types of exposures, which helped inform areas of investment for their cybersecurity program. I met this type of CISO typically when I was advising insurance companies. They tended to report to the **Chief Risk Officer** (**CRO**).
- **Type 7 – the cybersecurity advisor**: These CISOs saw themselves as advisors to the businesses they supported. Typically, their position was that they didn't actually "own" anything—the business did. They advised the business to make cybersecurity investments but didn't necessarily design and operate cybersecurity capabilities themselves—the IT team would instead. This type of CISO was typically able to avoid the conflict that naturally occurs when there is tension between the autonomy the business wants and the control necessary to defend the business' assets. Many CISOs of this ilk didn't believe their role was to provide oversight, just advice.
- **Type 8 – the trusted business executive**: These CISOs weren't cybersecurity experts and sometimes weren't IT experts either. They were executives who had proven themselves to senior leadership by managing different parts of the business or particularly difficult or important projects or initiatives. The leadership trusted them because of their track record of success at the company. Since they had proven that they

could manage challenging assignments, they were given cybersecurity to manage. These organizations believed that these CISOs would succeed given their ability to lead and manage, and that cybersecurity expertise was not a prerequisite for success. Many of the CISOs that I met in this category were attorneys.

That is the CISO spectrum. The types of CISOs discussed probably describe 90% of the thousands of CISOs I have met. I don't view any of them as better than the others; they simply have different backgrounds and approaches to cybersecurity. However, frequently, factors within the organizations dictate the approach to cybersecurity that their CISOs take, regardless of their backgrounds or personal preferences.

> **Tip**
>
> Many CISOs I met were frustrated because they wanted to be a specific type of CISO while their organizations demanded a different type, proving once again that even at the top of a business discipline, you can't always get what you want.

I learned to identify the type of CISO I was advising as quickly as possible in order to make the conversation more meaningful for us both. For example, if a CISO was really interested in discussing how a new exploit worked, it would be a short and annoying conversation trying to discuss risk management with them. For this reason, many of the sales teams that I supported at Microsoft and AWS were intimidated by the CISOs of their accounts. Once they learned about the CISO spectrum, it made it easier for them to understand the CISOs they supported and connect them with the people and resources that could really address the things they were most interested in.

In most cases, this would earn some trust with CISOs because the salespeople were perceived as helpful and not just interested in sales transactions.

> **Tip**
>
> Recognizing the type of CISO you support can help you become a trusted advisor to them.

On occasion, I've been asked about the type of CISO I am. After working in IT roles for many years, I started my cybersecurity career in IR. I worked as a cybersecurity advisor for many years and spent a lot of time working on threat intelligence. However, believe it or not, as hard as IR jobs tend to be, my "happy place" is IR. For me, understanding how threat actors *really* operate gives me the confidence to develop and execute on cybersecurity strategies as a CISO. But, as I'll discuss in *Chapter 9, Ingredients for a Successful Strategy*, the challenge CISOs and security teams face can't be met with confidence alone; managing cybersecurity for large enterprises is a much harder job than that.

Summary

In this chapter, I shared examples of different types of cyberattacks and introduced some key concepts that I will refer to throughout the rest of this book.

First, I introduced the *IR investigation knowledge trend* to illustrate how IR investigators develop hypotheses during an investigation and collect evidence to test their hypotheses. Tenacity fuels good IR teams to make progress and uncover as much about an incident as possible.

I also described three different types of cyberattacks to provide insight into how such attacks are perpetrated and to illustrate that not all "data breaches" are the same in terms of damage, remediation efforts, and costs. The three types of attacks I described were as follows:

- Global malware attack
- Traditional network intrusion
- Data breaches via insecure APIs

It can be very difficult to contain and eradicate attackers that successfully perpetrate traditional network intrusions; for example, data published by Okta suggests that the average time to detect and contain a breach is 290 days (Okta, n.d.). Although a data breach via insecure APIs can also negatively impact an organization's employees, customers, and reputation and have costly legal and regulatory outcomes, attackers aren't typically inside the victims' networks. Subsequently, the effort and costs to contain attackers in this scenario are typically a small fraction of what it takes to do so in a traditional network intrusion.

Next, I introduced the Cybersecurity Usual Suspects, which covers the five ways enterprises initially get compromised by attackers and the cybersecurity fundamentals. They include the following:

- Unpatched vulnerabilities
- Security misconfigurations
- Weak, leaked, and stolen credentials
- Social engineering
- Insider threats

Organizations that are very proficient at managing the cybersecurity fundamentals and seek to mitigate the Cybersecurity Usual Suspects make it much harder for attackers to be successful. A solid foundation, focused on the fundamentals, is required for a successful strategy.

I hope the combination of the real-world attack types I described, the Cybersecurity Usual Suspects, and the difference between attackers' tactics and motivations helps you understand how enterprises get hacked. Ensuring your organization's cybersecurity team has enough consistent investment in the cybersecurity fundamentals can make initial compromise much harder for threat actors. I'll discuss post-compromise tactics that attackers use in detail in other chapters of this book—they need attention and investment as well.

Finally, I introduced the *CISO spectrum*, which covers the eight types of CISOs I've encountered in my career. Understanding the type of CISO you are working with or selling to can make things easier for everyone.

The next chapter dives into one of my favorite topics—threat intelligence. Threat intelligence can inform your cybersecurity strategy in some key ways that will be discussed in detail.

References

- Rains, T. (2020). *Cybersecurity Threats, Malware Trends, and Strategies.* Packt Publishing. Retrieved from `https://www.packtpub.com/product/cybersecurity-threats-malwaretrends-and-strategies/9781800206014`.
- Jakkal, V. (2021). *Microsoft surpasses $10 billion in security business revenue, more than 40 percent year-over-year growth.* Microsoft.com. Retrieved from `https://www.microsoft.com/en-us/security/blog/2021/01/27/microsoft-surpasses-10-billion-in-security-business-revenue-more-than-40-percent-year-over-year-growth/`Krause, R. (January 30, 2024). *Microsoft's Cybersecurity Business Is Booming. Critics Say It's The Problem.* Investor's Business Daily. Retrieved from `https://www.investors.com/news/technology/microsoft-stock-cybersecurity-business-booms-critics-say-its-the-problem/`.
- Microsoft. (2025). *Microsoft Cybersecurity Reference Architectures.* Microsoft Corporation. Retrieved from `https://learn.microsoft.com/en-us/security/adoption/mcra`.
- Mitre Corporation. (n.d.). *ATT&CK Enterprise Matrix.* Mitre Corporation. Retrieved from `https://attack.mitre.org/matrices/enterprise`.
- Hutchins, E.M., Cloppert, M.J., Amin, R.M. Ph.D. (n.d.). *Intelligence-Driven Computer Network Defense Informed by Analysis of Adversary Campaigns and Intrusion Kill Chains.* Retrieved from Lockheed Martin: `https://lockheedmartin.com/content/dam/lockheed-martin/rms/documents/cyber/LM-White-Paper-Intel-Driven-Defense.pdf`.

- Okta. (n.d.). *Visibility is power*. Retrieved from https://www.okta.com/sites/default/files/2025-04/Threat-Visibility-Infographic.pdf.
- Kaspersky (2014). *Stuxnet's 'hole': the vulnerability is still around*. Kaspersky. Retrieved from https://www.kaspersky.com/blog/stuxnets-hole-the-vulnerability-is-still-around/14993/.
- Microsoft. (2025). *Microsoft Digital Defense Report 2025*. Microsoft Corporation. Retrieved from https://cdn-dynmedia-1.microsoft.com/is/content/microsoftcorp/microsoft/msc/documents/presentations/CSR/Microsoft-Digital-Defense-Report-2025.pdf.
- Microsoft (2024). *Microsoft Digital Defense Report 2024*. Microsoft Corporation. Retrieved from https://cdn-dynmedia-1.microsoft.com/is/content/microsoftcorp/microsoft/final/en-us/microsoft-brand/documents/Microsoft%20Digital%20Defense%20Report%202024%20%281%29.pdf.
- Silverfort (n.d.). Retrieved from https://www.silverfort.com/.
- Kaspersky (2024). *How hackers can crack your password in an hour*. Kaspersky. Retrieved from https://www.kaspersky.co.in/blog/password-can-be-hacked-in-one-hour/27588/.
- Microsoft (2025). *Password policy recommendations for Microsoft 365 passwords*. Microsoft Corporation. Retrieved from https://learn.microsoft.com/en-us/microsoft-365/admin/misc/password-policy-recommendations?view=o365-worldwide.
- Microsoft. (2023). *Microsoft Digital Defense Report 2023*. Microsoft Corporation. Retrieved from https://www.microsoft.com/en-us/security/security-insider/microsoft-digital-defense-report-2023.
- Kark K., Aguas, T. (March 12, 2017). *The New CISO: Leading the Strategic Security Organization*. The Wall Street Journal. Retrieved from https://deloitte.wsj.com/riskandcompliance/the-new-ciso-leading-the-strategic-security-organization-1489381336?gaa_at=eafs&gaa_n=ASWzDAjzyCqhhrpeiSLgJ6Fnthr9s0nnua2D-kcVn1NATuMBHBMH4K2FQtDB&gaa_ts=68ec5b14&gaa_sig=n-nq9KV6tN3Qj4yaJ4wwTBiKU41DyE2e8CMNP_LXKyKBT4FHq_gt09mDKyb9JNw4YPuSIQ8BwvZmsGGUbnZHTA%3D%3D.
- National Vulnerability Database (n.d.). Retrieved from https://nvd.nist.gov/vuln.

- Center for Internet Security (n.d.). Retrieved from `https://www.cisecurity.org/cis-benchmarks`.
- Weinert, A. (July 9, 2019). *Your Pa$$word doesn't matter*. Microsoft Corporation. Retrieved from `https://techcommunity.microsoft.com/blog/microsoft-entra-blog/your-paword-doesnt-matter/731984`.
- Microsoft Corporation (n.d.). *2023 Microsoft Digital Defense Report*. Microsoft Corporation. Retrieved from `https://www.microsoft.com/securityinsights/Phishing`.
- Microsoft Corporation (January 15, 2022). *Destructive malware targeting Ukrainian organizations*. Microsoft Corporation. Retrieved from `https://www.microsoft.com/en-us/security/blog/2022/01/15/destructive-malware-targeting-ukrainian-organizations/`.
- Microsoft Corporation (October 2021). *Microsoft Digital Defense Report 2021*. Microsoft Corporation. Retrieved from `https://www.microsoft.com/en-us/security/security-insider/threat-landscape/microsoft-digital-defense-report-2021`.
- Grand View Research. (2025). *Cyber Security Market*. Retrieved from `https://www.grandviewresearch.com/industry-analysis/cyber-security-market`.

Get this book's PDF version and more

Scan the QR code (or go to `packtpub.com/unlock`). Search for this book by name, confirm the edition, and then follow the steps on the page.

UNLOCK NOW

Note: Keep your invoice handy. Purchases made directly from Packt don't require an invoice.

2

What to Know About Threat Intelligence

I admit it, I'm a threat intelligence data geek. I really enjoy studying threat intelligence. It helps me understand the tactics and techniques that are in vogue with attackers and how the threat landscape is evolving. One of the best jobs I had at Microsoft was working as a Director of Trustworthy Computing. In this role, I was the executive editor and a contributor to the **Microsoft Security Intelligence Report**, which we called "**the SIR**." During the 8 or 9 years I helped produce the SIR, we published more than 20 volumes and special editions of this report, spanning thousands of pages. I gave literally thousands of threat intelligence briefings for customers around the world, as well as press and analyst interviews. I can tell you from experience, interviews on live television in front of millions of people, discussing threat intelligence, are nerve-racking! (BBC News, 2013).

Building and publishing the SIR was a *lot* of work, but very rewarding. In this role, I had the opportunity to work with so many smart people in the **Microsoft Security Response Center** (**MSRC**), the **Microsoft Malware Protection Center** (**MMPC**), the Microsoft **Digital Crimes Unit** (**DCU**), the **Security Development Lifecycle** (**SDL**) team, Microsoft IT, and many others. Doing this work gave me a deep appreciation for the value of good threat intelligence and some of the ways it is produced. Microsoft has continued to invest in threat intelligence, and they have a center dedicated to it called the **Microsoft Threat Intelligence Center** (**MSTIC**), in which a few of my former colleagues still work. I provide some data and insights from the SIR in *Chapter 5, The Evolution of Malware*. I also provide a deep dive into security vulnerabilities in *Chapter 3, Vulnerability Disclosure Trends*.

Since those days, I have been a consumer of threat intelligence in all the jobs I've had, both in vendor roles and as an operational cybersecurity team leader. Perhaps, because I spent so much time in my career developing threat intelligence, I have high expectations about the intelligence I spend my time studying. Spending time consuming vendors' marketing content —instead of real threat intelligence that can help operational cybersecurity teams—is something I avoid like the plague. I'll describe the difference between helpful threat intelligence and the noise that echoes across the industry as vendors and industry professionals try to draw attention to themselves, later in this chapter.

In this chapter, I'll provide you with some context that will help you understand the analysis of various threats that I'll discuss in the rest of this book. By the end of this chapter, you'll be able to recognize the difference between credible threat intelligence and questionable threat intelligence.

In this chapter, we'll cover the following topics:

- What is threat intelligence
- Using CTI
- Sharing CTI
- How to identify credible CTI

Let's get started!

What is threat intelligence?

Threat intelligence (**TI**) is sometimes referred to as **cyber threat intelligence** (**CTI**) to clarify that the intelligence focuses on cybersecurity threats as opposed to other types of threats. The concept is ancient: the more you know about your enemies and how they plan and execute their attacks, the more prepared you can be for those attacks.

Simply put, CTI provides organizations with data and information on how attackers have been leveraging the *Cybersecurity Usual Suspects* we discussed in *Chapter 1, How Enterprises Get Hacked* to gain initial access to their victims' environments, what they have been doing in their victims' environments post initial compromise, and sometimes attribution for attacks to specific threat actors. Threats can also include various categories of malware, tools, exploitation of vulnerabilities, web-based attacks, **distributed denial of service** (**DDoS**) attacks, social engineering attacks, and others. Of course, as I wrote in *Chapter 1* there is also high interest in information about the attackers themselves—who they are, where they are located, whether they are state-sponsored or an independent criminal organization, and details on their modus operandi from their past attacks. An entire industry has grown around the demand for attribution and information on threat actors. Over time, as the world changed in ways that allowed many attackers to work in the open without concealing their existence, performing attribution for their attacks became easier.

Where does CTI come from?

Purveyors of CTI collect and analyze data from data sources. Understanding where your CTI comes from is very important. How CTI is collected, and the way it should be interpreted, are typically defined by its source. Without knowledge of the source, there's a good chance that CTI will be misinterpreted.

There are many potential sources of data that CTI providers can use. Here are some examples:

- Data on malware threats can come from anti-malware products and services running on endpoints, networks, email servers, web browsers, cloud services, honeypots, and so on.
- Data on weak, leaked, and stolen credentials can come not only from identity providers such as Microsoft Entra ID (formerly called Azure Active Directory), Google's identity offerings, and Okta, but also from monitoring illicit forums where such credentials are bought, sold, and leaked.
- Data on social engineering attacks can come from phishing and spam filtering services, as well as social networking services.

There is also **open source intelligence** (**OSINT**), which leverages publicly available data sources such as social media, news feeds, court filings, public records such as arrest records, information attackers disclose about their victims, activity in illicit forums, and many others. OSINT can help defenders in at least a couple of ways. First, it can help notify you that your IT environment has been compromised. Observing attackers offering your data for sale or chattering about illicit access to your network can be leading indicators of a breach that has gone undetected. Another way many organizations use OSINT is for researching attackers and the tactics they use.

Of course, attackers can use OSINT to research and perform reconnaissance on their potential targets as well. We'll discuss some of the ways attackers perform reconnaissance in *Chapter 10, Cybersecurity Strategies* and *11, Cybersecurity Strategy Implementation*. There is a plethora of tools to help find OSINT, including **Maltego**, **Shodan**, **theHarvester**, and many others. A more comprehensive list of OSINT tools can be found at the OSINT Framework website (OSINT Framework, n.d.). There are also hundreds of public repositories on GitHub offering OSINT tools (GitHub, n.d.).

Purveyors of CTI can use data sources that they own and operate, CTI data procured from third parties, and OSINT data sources. For example, anti-malware vendors that operate their own research and response labs collect malware for analysis and operate various anti-malware offerings. They can get malware samples from their customers, partners, and competitors. The more customers they have running their anti-malware offerings, the more samples they can collect and the more telemetry they can receive on malware and the systems attacked.

Anti-malware vendors have their customers agree to submit malware samples that they encounter, and the vendors' products and services generate data from detections, installation blocking, and disinfections in the course of operating. All this data can be collected, aggregated, and analyzed to provide the vendor with insight into how their products and services are operating and steer future research, response activities, and investments.

Many vendors also publish TI reports and provide CTI to their customers via web portals and emails, but also integrate it into APIs, products, and services. Examples of vendors that do this include CrowdStrike, Google, Kaspersky Lab, Mandiant, McAfee, Microsoft, Palo Alto Networks, Recorded Future, Sophos, Symantec, and many others. They primarily do this to share their CTI and help organizations understand what is happening in the threat landscape. However, they also integrate reports to generate new business by demonstrating the breadth and depth of their CTI. Many vendors like to claim they provide better visibility than their competitors, and thus better protection from threats. This is where scale can be a differentiator.

> **Note**
>
> When I worked at Microsoft, some anti-malware vendors would make claims like this. However, *hundreds of millions* of Windows users around the world agreed to share threat data with Microsoft. Layer in data from web browsers, the Bing internet search engine, Microsoft 365, the world's most popular productivity suite, and very large-scale enterprise identity products and services, and the CTI generated is impressive. This massive reach enabled Microsoft to develop an excellent understanding of the global threat landscape and share it with its customers via the SIR, blogs, whitepapers, products, services, and APIs. I demonstrate the reach of such data sources in detail in *Chapter 5*. This is one of the reasons why it was such a great experience for me working so closely with the MMPC at Microsoft – no one receives more malware telemetry than Microsoft.

Some CTI vendors differentiate themselves not necessarily by scale, but by the quality of their data and analysis. They can correlate data they have to specific industries and to specific customers within those industries and provide more actionable insights than high-level, anonymized, global trends will typically enable.

For example, if I'm the CISO of an organization in the healthcare industry, I am likely interested in CTI from a vendor that really understands my industry and its unique challenges and has data on attackers that target this industry, and in the geographic locations my organization does business. This combination will help me understand the threats specifically impacting my industry and better prepare for them in a healthcare context that potentially includes heavy regulation, a big focus on patient privacy, expensive equipment certification requirements, and risk to human life. Further, I'm always looking for insights into what other organizations similar to mine are doing to protect, detect, and respond to these threats. This information will inform some of my efforts and make it easier to convince the business I support to provide the budget and resources I need.

Some CTI vendors tout their abilities to perform attribution and their knowledge of nation-state attackers. They have coined sometimes fun, but always intriguing names for such attack groups. Examples include **Lazarus Group**, **Sandworm Team**, **PHOSPHORUS**, and many others. Each CTI vendor gave their own name to each threat actor group, just as each anti-malware lab gave their own names to malware they discovered. Different vendors using different names for the same threat actor group made it confusing for their customers and the industry. In June 2025, CrowdStrike and Microsoft announced plans to harmonize cybersecurity threat attribution:

> *"AUSTIN, TX — June 2, 2025 —CrowdStrike[https://www.crowdstrike.com/en-us/](NASDAQ: CRWD) and Microsoft today announced a collaboration to bring clarity and coordination to how cyber threat actors are identified and tracked across security vendors. By mapping threat actor aliases and aligning adversary attribution across platforms, the collaboration minimizes confusion caused by different naming systems and accelerates cyber defenders' response against today's and tomorrow's most sophisticated adversaries."*
>
> *(CrowdStrike, June 2025)*

It can be very interesting to get some insight into how well-funded attackers operate. It doesn't take long for other attackers to try to mimic the tactics and techniques that the professionals use once they are revealed via CTI. In this way, nation-state threat actors have been lowering the barrier to entry for criminals for decades.

However, no matter how well-funded attackers are, they will use one or more of the Cybersecurity Usual Suspects to initially compromise their targets' IT environment, just like common criminals will.

> **Tip**
>
> In my experience advising many organizations over the years, the threat of nation-state actors can skew the security approach in a way that isn't helpful. Focusing on threat actors that potentially have unlimited resources (governments can print money) can distract CISOs and security teams from focusing on the cybersecurity fundamentals. CISOs need to ask themselves, "Do we really need to be concerned with these nation-state threat actors now, or do we have more fundamental challenges to address first?"

> After all, becoming excellent at the cybersecurity fundamentals will drive down the ROI for all potential threat actors that target your organization.
>
> I have talked with plenty of security teams at public sector and private sector organizations where paying attention to nation-state threat actors is not optional due to their organizations' own charters or the intellectual property they possess. But even in these cases, focusing on the cybersecurity fundamentals can pay big dividends.

Using CTI

Cybersecurity programs can make use of CTI in several ways. Here are some examples (this list is not exhaustive):

- CTI is essential to the effective operation of **security operations centers** (**SOCs**); they are only as good as the CTI they have
- CTI can help inform **cybersecurity incident response teams**' (**CIRT**) investigations
- CTI can inform threat hunting, red, blue, and purple teams' efforts, and cybersecurity control testing
- CTI can help defenders profile attackers in order to be better prepared for them
- CTI can inform executive protection programs designed to protect executives and their families
- CTI is an important input for risk management programs

Let's dig into that last example a bit more: inform risk management. CTI can highlight the risks that organizations pay attention to. Recall that risk is composed of probability and impact. CTI can help quantify both the probability and the impact of risk calculations. For example, let's say you are a CISO and the business leaders you support are very concerned about ransomware because they keep seeing news stories about attacks. CTI can provide some idea of the probability of encountering ransomware.

I'll discuss ransomware in detail in *Chapter 5* but for now, note that ransomware (the category of malware) is typically one of the least prevalent categories of malware. There are some logical reasons why this is the case that I'll cover in *Chapter 5*. Generally, if you were to stack-rank risks by priority based on probability alone, ransomware would likely show up near the bottom of the list. However, once we quantify the potential impact of ransomware to reflect that encountering it could be an extinction event for your business, it likely bumps it way up in the ranking in the list of risks.

Using TTPs

Another use for CTI is to help security teams mitigate risks by providing details about specific threats and how they operate. Understanding the **tactics, techniques, and procedures (TTPs)** that attackers employ can provide some concrete ideas on how they can be mitigated. NIST defines TTPs as, "*The behavior of an actor. A tactic is the highest-level description of this behavior, while techniques give a more detailed description of behavior in the context of a tactic, and procedures an even lower-level, highly detailed description in the context of a technique.*" (Badger et al, 2016).

A tactic is the reason the attacker performs a particular action. Why do they decide to take specific action? It is because it was a tactical goal. For example, once an attacker is inside their victim's network, they typically need to move laterally to explore the network and find sensitive data. The tactic in this example is lateral movement. Other examples of tactics include reconnaissance, persistence, and exfiltration.

Techniques are how the attacker tries to accomplish the tactic—the specific actions they take. For example, suppose an attacker needed to move laterally (the tactic) on the victim's network, so they used *pass the hash* and stolen web authentication cookies (the techniques) to do this.

Using this combination of tactics and techniques enables security teams to take a structured approach to planning attacks. Knowing the tactics and techniques that attackers use allows defenders to put people, processes, and technologies in place that will detect or mitigate the techniques when they are employed. In our example, where *pass the hash* was employed, we could plan to mitigate this technique using some guidance from Microsoft or by procuring a security product designed to detect it.

Using TTPs this way might seem like a daunting task because there can be many combinations and permutations of attacker tactics and techniques. A great resource to help security teams is the MITRE ATT&CK® knowledge base (found at `https://attack.mitre.org/`). This knowledge base contains tactics and techniques that have been seen in use during attacks. It maps techniques to tactics and provides ways that each technique can potentially be mitigated and detected. Many cybersecurity teams have standardized their approach to cybersecurity based on this model. Further, many cybersecurity products have this same model baked into them to make it easy for cybersecurity teams to use them.

Using IOCs

Many security teams also use **indicators of compromise (IOCs)** to help determine whether their enterprise IT environments have been compromised. IOCs can help in post-compromise situations when response teams are trying to determine when and how the initial compromise happened, and what the attackers did with their illicit access afterward. IOCs are described in *NIST Special Publication 800-53 Revision 5*:

> *"Indicators of compromise (IOC) are forensic artifacts from intrusions that are identified on organizational systems at the host or network level. IOCs provide valuable information on systems that have been compromised. IOCs can include the creation of registry key values. IOCs for network traffic include Universal Resource Locator or protocol elements that indicate malicious code command and control servers. The rapid distribution and adoption of IOCs can improve information security by reducing the time that systems and organizations are vulnerable to the same exploit or attack. Threat indicators, signatures, tactics, techniques, procedures, and other indicators of compromise may be available via government and non-government cooperatives, including the Forum of Incident Response and Security Teams, the United States Computer Emergency Readiness Team, the Defense Industrial Base Cybersecurity Information Sharing Program, and the CERT Coordination Center."*
>
> *(NIST Special Publication 800-53 Revision 5, September 2020)*

Examples of IOCs include unusual network traffic (destination, origin, or volume), network traffic to or from known malicious domain names or IP addresses, unusual volumes of authentication failures, the presence of specific tools, files, or registry entries, recently added unrecognized accounts, and many others. Incident response and forensics teams can use IOCs to help them identify compromised systems. To do this, they typically need **SHA-256** hashes for files, scripts, and tools that attackers leave behind. File hashes can help identify the presence of files that were potentially used during attacks among the mountains of legitimate files on systems.

IP addresses for command-and-control servers, data exfiltration locations, and other attacker-controlled resources can also be helpful to investigators as they comb through network flow data logs on firewalls, proxy servers, and other devices on a network.

Figure 2.1 provides some fictional examples of IOCs, including example file hashes for different types of scripts as well as IP addresses for command-and-control servers. IOCs can be shared in a few different formats, such as CSV, JSON, or STIX format. I'll discuss sharing CTI in more detail later in this chapter.

PowerShell Scripts	
Filename	SHA-256 Hash
bad-file1.ps1	a4f9c2b1e7d84f0a3c1d9b6f52e0a7c4d8f1b2e9c7a3d0f4b1e6c2d9f0a7b3c5
bad-file2.ps1	f1c3a9e0d7b4c6a2e8f0b1d3c4a7e9f2d0c6b3a1e4f8d2c7b9a0e1f3c5d7a2b4

Additional PowerShell Filenames	
psexec.ps1	cmd.ps1
rundll32.ps1	

Batch Scripts	
Filename	SHA-256 Hash
os-checker.bat	9c7e1a4d3b0f2e8c6d1a5b3f7e0c4a9d2b6f1e3c8a0d7b5f9c2e4a1b8d3f0c6
download-libs.bat	d2f7b1c4e9a0d3c6f8b2e1a4c7d0f5a9e3b6c1f4d8a2e7c0b5f9d1a3c6e4b8
disable-av.bat	b8e1c3f4a7d0b2e9c6f1a4d3c8b0e2f7d1a5c9e0b3f6a8d4c1e7b9f2a0c5d3

Executables and DLLs	
Filename	SHA-256 Hash
rpcdump.exe	c5a0e7d2b9f4c1a8e3d6b0f2a5c8e1d3b7f9a4c0e6d1b3f8a2c7e0d5b1f3a9
gmode.exe	f9b3e1c6a4d0f2b8e5c7a1d3f6b0e4c9a2d7f1b5e0c3a8d4f7b1e9c2a6d0f5
gmode.dll	e0d4c1b7f9a3d6c2e8b1f4a7c0d5e9b3a6f1c4d8b0e2f7a5c9d1e3b6f0a4c7

Filename	SHA-256 Hash
my-encoder.exe	a1c8e3b5f0d2a7c4e9b1f6d3a0c5e8b2f7d4a9c1e6b0f3d8a2c7e1b4f9d0a5
my-mimikatz.exe	d7e2c0b5f9a1d4c8e3b6f0a2c9e1d3b7f5a0c4e8b1f6d9a3c5e0b2f4d1a7c6

Command & Control IP Addresses	
169.254.66.22	169.254.66.25
169.254.66.23	169.254.66.26
169.254.66.24	169.254.66.27

Figure 2.1 – An example of IOCs with fictional filenames, hashes, and IP addresses

I learned so much about the tricks that attackers like to use when I worked on Microsoft's customer-facing incident response team. We built tools to collect system data on live-running Windows systems that were suspected of being compromised. We'd compare the data on system configurations and running states with known good and known bad datasets—essentially looking for IOCs. This was as much art as it was science because attackers were using all sorts of creative tricks to try to avoid detection, stay persistent, and perform data exfiltration.

Some memorable tricks include attackers using IP addresses in Base-8 instead of Base-10 format to bypass proxy server rules, taking advantage of bugs in browsers and proxy servers when domain names in Cyrillic were used, running processes using the same name as well-known legitimate Windows system processes, but from slightly different directories to avoid detection, and so many more. Interesting stuff!

Since then, intrusions have become more science than art, in that many attackers are much more organized, and their attacks are methodical and leverage automation. After they use one or more of the Cybersecurity Usual Suspects to gain initial access to a victim's environment, they can execute their attack and accomplish their objectives before the victim's cybersecurity detection capabilities even flag their potential presence. This sophisticated approach to attacks has decreased the dwell time that many attackers require after they gain initial access, thus putting more pressure on security teams to detect attackers as quickly and efficiently as possible. Recall the traditional network intrusion I described in *Chapter 1*. In my experience responding to and investigating these types of attacks, after gaining initial access, most attackers go straight for their victims' Active Directory so that they can harvest credentials that will enable them to stay persistent longer, move laterally, access more systems and data, exfiltrate data, deploy command-and-control tools and other malware, and so on. They automate the steps needed to do this using batch files, PowerShell scripts, **Windows Management Instrumentation** (**WMI**), the victims' own development tools, and so on. Attackers leverage this type of automation frequently because it reduces their level of effort and costs associated with their attacks. It can also be very challenging to defend against these attacks because attackers are using many of the same system commands and legitimate tools that their victims' IT departments use. Because this is so common, I have dedicated *Chapter 14* to mitigating *living off the land* tactics in this book.

This is one reason threat hunting has become such a powerful cybersecurity discipline; instead of waiting for the bad guys to make a mistake or announce they are in your environment at the end of their attack, find them and disrupt their attack before they can finish what they plan to do.

Security teams can leverage TTPs and IOCs with a variety of security tools, products, and services. Examples include **security information and event management** (**SIEM**) systems, behavioral analytics tools, data visualization tools, email filtering services, web browsing filtering services, endpoint protection products, **extended detection and response** (**XDR**) products, **security orchestration, automation, and response** (**SOAR**) products, and many others. There are a vast number of ways to leverage CTI to protect, detect, and respond to modern threats.

Different roles in security teams can leverage CTI in slightly different ways. For example, as I mentioned earlier, CIRTs use IOCs when performing intrusion investigations. Meanwhile, IT analysts use CTI to ensure that protection and detection capabilities are optimized. Analysts in SOCs monitor and triage alerts based on data enriched with CTI. Threat hunters use CTI to inform their hunts. CISOs use CTI to understand whether their cybersecurity strategy is effective and identify areas that require change or further investment. CTI has the potential to inform the efforts of many different roles and stakeholders.

The key to using threat intelligence

It's important to recognize that although CTI is a product offered by many vendors and organizations, it's also a process – a process used to collect data, process that data, analyze the processed data, and then share the results with stakeholders who need them. This typically takes time, budget, and resources to accomplish. I haven't met a security team yet that has unlimited resources and does not need to make trade-offs.

The combination of so many potential sources and uses of CTI and limited resources can lead to security teams drowning in CTI that might not be helpful to them. This is why it is very important for teams to take the time to develop a set of requirements for their CTI program. In this context, "requirements" are statements about the specific problems the CTI program is trying to solve. These requirements tie the specific CTI collected and analyzed to the specific needs of the program's stakeholders, thus rationalizing its use. If some CTI source has interesting data, but the data it provides doesn't help fulfill a requirement defined by a program stakeholder, then that source likely should not be leveraged.

This approach helps the CTI program optimize its resources and prevents it from drowning in CTI. I've seen a few different approaches to documenting requirements. *Figure 2.2* provides an example.

Outcome	Requirement Statement	Priority	Data Sources	Stakeholders	Reporting Speed	CTI Shared
Detection	CTI program will collect and analyze data that enables early detection of attacks on our firm's internet-facing systems.	High	OSINT; Palo Alto Networks; X-Force Exchange	CISO; CIRT; Digital Marketing Team; Server Operations	Immediate	Stakeholder alert email; CIRT incident tool
Respond	CTI program will support CIRT team before, during, and after security incidents to enable fast and effective response to failed, partially successful, and fully successful attacks.	Medium	Internal sources; OSINT; Law Enforcement	CIRT; CISO; SLT; BoD; Compliance team; Legal; Fraud team	As scenario warrants	CIRT incident tool; SLT alert email; BoD incident review deck
...						

Figure 2.2 – An example of CTI requirements

> **Tip**
>
> If your CTI program doesn't have a set of documented requirements, I recommend working with the program's stakeholders to develop them, as they are the key to an optimized approach.

There is no single right way for a CTI team to operate. CTI teams have operated in very different ways over the years based on the requirements of the organizations they support and the people managing the teams. For example, some CTI teams support fraud investigations, and some don't, because some cybersecurity teams have fraud included in their charters, while others do not.

As a CISO, I always had three functions in mind for my CTI teams:

1. **Maximize the value of IOCs and TTPs**: In addition to all the sources of OSINT I mentioned earlier, more and more cybersecurity vendors are now including CTI with their product and service offerings. A large enterprise that leverages many vendors typically has some CTI sources it is unaware of or does not leverage. Maintaining an accurate inventory of CTI sources can be very helpful for CTI teams and their stakeholders. Many cybersecurity products and tools are capable of consuming CTI by integrating feeds from CTI sources. In order to maximize the CTI benefits that enterprises have, I recommend that CTI teams track the following information:
    - All the CTI sources and feeds that their organization is entitled to
    - The type of CTI each source and feed provides
    - Information that is available on automated CTI feeds/APIs
    - Each source's funding renewal date (typically part of the product or service licensing annual renewal)
2. **Validate your cybersecurity strategy**: For CISOs, it is important for them to understand what threats made their way onto their networks each day or week. Some CISOs do this by attending daily SOC stand-up meetings where the staff in the SOC brief each other on the alerts they have been triaging and any other noteworthy work items. However, I always found this to be a little disruptive to the SOC meetings, and it didn't help me understand what trends might be emerging in our environment. As a workaround, I typically ask my CTI team to pull together a snapshot of what happened each week, from a cybersecurity perspective. Try to provide a 360-degree view by aggregating threat detection data from the various tools and products that generate it. This includes detections such as the following:
    - ***Email threats identified by Microsoft 365, and other filters***: I like to understand the volume of attacks and what kinds of attacks are trying to make their way into our users' inboxes. Also, I like to get an idea of whether the filters are being effective by understanding how many threats made it through the filters into users' inboxes and how many were reported by users. This tells me whether my team's approach to mitigating email-based threats is being effective or if changes should be considered. Potential changes could include changes to configurations of the email protections used and changes to the vendors and products used for email protection.

- ***External attack surface detections***: These include meaningful alerts from attack surface management tools and firewalls, brute-force attacks on VPN servers, and issues identified by third-party risk management platforms such as BitSight, Security ScoreCard, UpGuard, and so on. This also includes data from **web application firewalls (WAFs)** that protect applications. Were there any application attacks, such as password spray or SQL injection attacks, and did the WAF blunt them successfully?
- ***Detections from endpoint products***: These include anti-malware and XDR/EDR. I am always interested in understanding what families of malware made their way into our environment, how, the method of propagation, and what the intended payload was. Further, understanding which of the Cybersecurity Usual Suspects the malware used to gain initial access is also significant. This information points to the weakness in our approach that needs to be addressed.
- ***Network detections*** from IDS/IPS, firewalls, network traffic analysis, and **cloud access security broker (CASB)** data on websites that users are accessing. This helps security teams understand whether network detection tools identified potential threats that endpoint detection products didn't identify. For example, attackers were able to execute a file transfer tool from a compromised endpoint. The endpoint protection suite (EDR/XDR or anti-malware software) didn't detect that the endpoint was compromised. However, network detection tools identified suspicious outbound network connection attempts to a known bad destination on the internet.
- ***Application programming interfaces* (*APIs*)**: These are alerts from any APIs abused over the past week, whether there were alerts that API rate limits were hit, or whether the request volume for APIs looks normal. Remember the data breach via insecure APIs attack that I described in *Chapter 1* – this data can help us understand what is happening on the "API front of the cyber-war."
- ***Data and database-related detections***: These include details such as whether there were anomalous database access requests and whether query volume had unexpected spikes. **Data loss prevention (DLP)** detections also fall into this category, such as whether someone tried to use mass storage devices or move a large amount of data unexpectedly.

- ***Identity and access management detections***: These include repeated login failures, especially for highly privileged accounts, MFA failures, failed VPN login attempts, and so on.
- ***Meaningful alerts from assets in the cloud and cloud services***: These include alerts from any of the built-in security features/functionality in the cloud services used. Examples include any alerts from Amazon GuardDuty in AWS or Microsoft Defender for Cloud in Azure.

  If security teams can get this type of aggregate visibility once every week or two, it gives them the opportunity to identify areas that need improvement in the short term rather than waiting until attackers point those out through a successful attack. Automating as much of the data collection and aggregation as possible ensures that gaining this visibility doesn't become a burdensome, time-consuming chore. This is one area where AI tools such as Microsoft Security Copilot, Google Gemini, Bricklayer AI, and many others can help by summarizing such data in seconds.

3. **Synthesize industry CTI reports and news**: The third function I typically ask my CTI teams to fulfill is to monitor and analyze cybersecurity industry news to help us understand how it might apply to our organization – for example, news about zero-day vulnerabilities or vulnerabilities added to CISA's **Known Exploited Vulnerabilities** (**KEV**) catalog. These are topics I will discuss in *Chapter 3*. This is an area where CTI teams and vulnerability management teams can collaborate. CTI teams can inform vulnerability management teams of breaking news that potentially represents high risk to the organization. As a CISO, it helps me sleep better at night knowing that my CTI team is paying attention to the daily deluge of cybersecurity industry news and trends, and flagging potentially important news for other parts of the organization as needed. This also includes the annual and semi-annual threat reports that major vendors publish, such as the Verizon **Data Breach Investigations Report** (**DBIR**), the Microsoft Digital Defense Report, CrowdStrike's Global Threat Report, the Palo Alto Networks Unit 42 Global Incident Response Report, and Mandiant's various reports as examples.

It's also worth mentioning that **artificial intelligence** (**AI**) and machine learning capabilities have matured dramatically in the last few years. Services that leverage these capabilities can churn through massive amounts of CTI very quickly compared to human analysts. This can help your organization manage large volumes of CTI on an ongoing basis. Of course, like many aspects of computer science and cybersecurity, the value derived here is a function of the effort that is put into it. Using AI to get more value out of CTI seems like a great use case, and I know every purveyor of CTI is looking at how they can leverage AI.

Sometimes organizations want to share the CTI they possess with other organizations, such as partners, vendors, or their industry at large. This turns out to be more complicated than it sounds. Let's explore this aspect of TI next.

Threat intelligence sharing

Security teams can find themselves in situations where they want to share the CTI they possess with security teams at other organizations. There are lots of different scenarios where this happens. For example, a parent company might want all the security teams at its subsidiaries to share CTI with each other. Another example is an industry-specific **information sharing and analysis center** (**ISAC**) that facilitates CTI sharing among its member organizations. When the **Financial Services ISAC** (**FS-ISAC**) shares CTI on a specific threat actor that has been actively attacking financial services firms, it helps all the firms in the industry better protect themselves from the threat actor. Sharing CTI across organizations in the same industry potentially makes it more challenging for attackers to victimize individual members because they all have the TTPs that threat actors use when targeting the industry. For this reason, the financial services industry, the retail industry, and the healthcare industry all have ISACs, as examples.

> Note
>
> NIST published *Special Publication 800-150, Guide to Cyber Threat Information Sharing*, which provides some guidelines for sharing CTI, as well as a good list of scenarios where sharing CTI can be helpful. The benefits of sharing CTI that the authors cite are numerous, including shared situational awareness, improved security posture, knowledge maturation, and greater defensive agility. (NIST Special Publication 800-150 Badger et al., October 2016).

However, sharing CTI can be more complicated than it sounds. It is not without risk. Sensitive information, such as **personally identifiable information** (**PII**), can be swept up as part of an investigation into an intrusion. If its context and sensitivity are lost and the CTI is shared without the proper safeguards, it could be used as an example of how the organization failed to keep its regulatory compliance obligations to standards such as PCI DSS, SOX, GDPR, and a host of others. This could lead to large fines, unwanted scrutiny from regulators, and reputational damage.

For public sector organizations with classified information that requires security clearance, information-sharing programs can be fraught with challenges. In many cases, CTI would need to be declassified before it could be shared, and the inappropriate sharing of that CTI could have drastic consequences, such as criminal prosecution. Because of all the sensitivities and potential land mines, many organizations share CTI anonymously. However, CTI that isn't attributed to a credible source might not inspire the requisite confidence in its quality among the security teams that receive it and go unused.

> Tip
>
> If your security team is considering sharing CTI with other organizations, I suggest they leverage NIST Special Publication 800-150 to inform their deliberations.

CTI-sharing protocols

I can't discuss sharing CTI without at least mentioning some of the protocols for doing so. Recall that protocols are used to set rules for effective communication. Some protocols are optimized for human-to-human communication, while others are optimized for machine-to-machine (automated) communication, machine-to-human communication, and so on. The three protocols I'll discuss in this section include **Traffic Light Protocol** (**TLP**), **Structured Threat Information eXpression** (**STIX**), and **Trusted Automated eXchange of Indicator Information** (**TAXII**).

Traffic Light Protocol

TLP has become a popular protocol for sharing CTI and other types of information. TLP can help communicate the expected treatment of CTI shared between people. I don't think it is especially optimized for automated CTI sharing between systems – it's really a protocol for humans to use when sharing potentially sensitive information with each other. For example, if a CTI team decides to share some CTI with another CTI team or a CIRT via email or in a document, they could use TLP.

As its name suggests, TLP uses a traffic light analogy to make it easy for people to understand information senders' expectations and their intended information sharing boundaries. The "traffic light" analogy in this case has four colors: red, amber, green, and clear (*FIRST*, n.d.). The colors are used to communicate different information-sharing boundaries, as specified by the sender.

The rule the protocol sets is that the color be specified as follows, when the CTI is being communicated in writing (in an email or document): *TLP:COLOR*. "*TLP:*" is followed by one of the color names in caps – for example, *TLP:AMBER*.

TLP:RED specifies that the shared information is "*not for disclosure, restricted to participants only*" (*FIRST*, n.d.). Therefore, the information is limited to only the people the sender shared it with directly and is typically communicated verbally as a further step to limit how the information can be shared, and to make it harder to attribute the information to a particular sender, thus protecting their privacy. Senders use this color when they want to limit the potential impact on their reputation or privacy, and when other parties cannot effectively act on the information shared.

TLP:AMBER specifies "*limited disclosure, restricted to participants' organizations*" (*FIRST*, n.d.). Receivers are only permitted to share *TLP:AMBER* information within their own organization and with customers with a need to know. The sender can also specify more restrictions and limitations that it expects the receivers to honor.

TLP:GREEN permits "*limited disclosure, restricted to the community*" (*FIRST*, n.d.). Senders that specify *TLP:GREEN* are allowing receivers to share the information with organizations within their community or industry, but not by using channels that are open to the general public. Senders do not want the information shared outside of the receiver's industry or community. This is used when information can be used to protect the broader community or industry.

Lastly, using **TLP:CLEAR** means the "*disclosure is not limited*" (*FIRST*, n.d.). In other words, there are no sharing restrictions on information that is disclosed using *TLP:CLEAR*. Receivers are free to share this information as broadly as they like. This is meant to be used when sharing information has minimal risk.

The TLP convention dictates that emails should have the TLP designation in the subject line and at the top of the email, while the designation should appear in the page headers and footers in documents (CISA, n.d.). This makes it clear to the receiver what the sender's expectations are before they read the CTI. Again, the sender trusts the receiver to honor the TLP designation and any sharing boundaries they have specified.

> **Note**
>
> TLP helps set expectations between the sender of the information and the receiver of the information on how the information should be handled. The sender is responsible for communicating these expectations to the receiver. However, the receiver could choose to ignore the sender's instructions. Therefore, trust between the sharing parties is very important. The receiver is trusted by the sender to honor the sender's specified information-sharing boundaries. If the sender doesn't trust the receiver to honor their expectations, they shouldn't share the CTI with the receiver.

If you are doing research on the internet on threats, you'll likely come across documents marked with *TLP:CLEAR*. For example, both the **Federal Bureau of Investigation** (**FBI**) and **Cybersecurity and Infrastructure Security Agency** (**CISA**) publish threat reports for public consumption labeled *TLP:CLEAR*. If you weren't aware of TLP before, these markings will make more sense to you now.

STIX and TAXII

Now that we've covered a protocol for use among humans, let's look at two complementary protocols that enable automated CTI sharing: STIX and TAXII. Employing protocols that are optimized to be processed by machines can dramatically accelerate the dissemination of CTI to organizations that can benefit from it and operationalize it, as well as across different types of technologies that know how to consume it.

STIX is a structured language or schema that describes threats in a standard way. The STIX schema includes core objects and meta-objects used to describe threats. The specification for STIX version 2.1 is 313 pages (STIX Version 2.1, June 2021). Needless to say, it's very comprehensive and can be used to describe a broad range of threats.

> **Note**
>
> "OASIS," "STIX," "Structured Threat Information eXpression," "TAXII," and "Trusted Automated eXchange of Indicator Information" are trademarks of OASIS, the open standards consortium where the "STIX," "Structured Threat Information eXpression," "TAXII," and "Trusted Automated eXchange of Indicator Information" specifications are owned and developed. "STIX," "Structured Threat Information eXpression," "TAXII," and "Trusted Automated eXchange of Indicator Information" are copyrighted © works of OASIS Open. All rights reserved.

To give you an idea of what STIX looks like, next, you'll find an example of a campaign described using STIX. All the data in this example is random and fictional – it's provided so you can see an example of the format:

```
{
"type": "campaign",
"spec_version": "2.1",
"id": "campaign—3a3b4a4b-16a3-0fea-543e-10fa55c3cc2c",
"created_by_ref": "identity—e552e362-722c-33f1-bb4a-7c4455ace3ef",
"created": "2022-07-09T15:02:00.000Z",
"modified": "2022-07-09T15:02:00.000Z",
"name": "Attacker1 Attacks on Retail Industry",
"description": "Campaign by Attacker1 on the retail industry."
}
```

While STIX is used to describe threats in a standard way, TAXII is an application-layer protocol used to communicate that information between systems that can consume it. TAXII standardizes how computers share CTI with each other. Stated another way, TAXII is a protocol designed to exchange CTI between the sender and receiver(s) and enables automated machine-to-machine sharing of CTI over HTTPS. TAXII supports various sharing models, including hub and spoke, source and subscriber, and peer-to-peer. To do this, TAXII specifies two mechanisms: ***collections*** and ***channels***.

These enable CTI producers to support both push and pull communications models. Collections are sets of CTI data that CTI producers can provide to their customers when requested to do so. Channels enable CTI producers to push data to their customers – whether it's a single customer or many customers. This same mechanism also enables customers to receive data from many producers (STIX Version 2.1, June 2021). The TAXII version 2.1 specification is 79 pages and contains all the details needed to implement client and server participants in the CTI-sharing models I mentioned earlier.

> **Note**
>
> Threats described using STIX are not required to be shared via TAXII – any protocol can be used to do this as long as the sender and receiver both understand and support it.

A key benefit of using STIX and TAXII is standardization. When CTI producers publish CTI using a standardized schema such as STIX, it makes it easier for organizations to consume it, even when they are using technologies from different vendors. If everyone uses the same standard way to describe threats versus proprietary protocols, CTI consumers get the benefit regardless of the vendors they procure their cybersecurity capabilities from. In other words, cybersecurity vendors and teams can focus on innovation using CTI, instead of spending time devising ways to model and share it. In this manner, these protocols help scale CTI sharing to organizations and technologies around the world.

Reasons not to share CTI

Many of the security teams I have talked to opt not to share CTI with other organizations, even when they have good relationships with them. This might seem counterintuitive. Why wouldn't a security team want to help other organizations detect threats they have already discovered in their own IT environment?

There are at least a couple of good reasons for this behavior. First, depending on the exposure, disclosing CTI could be interpreted as an admission or even an announcement that the organization has suffered a data breach. If the organization has suffered a breach, they'll want to manage it on their own terms and on their own timeline if possible. Keeping such matters close to the chest minimizes potential legal risks and PR risks, or at least gives the organization some time to complete its investigation if one is ongoing. Further, many organizations simply won't share CTI because it could end up disrupting their incident response processes and crisis communication plans, potentially leading to litigation and class action lawsuits.

A second reason some security teams opt not to share CTI is that they don't want to signal to the attackers that they know that their IT environment is compromised. For example, when they'd find a file suspected of being malware on one of their systems, instead of uploading a copy of it to VirusTotal or their anti-malware vendor for analysis, they'd prefer to do their own analysis behind closed doors so as not to tip off the attackers.

A *best practice* that many malware purveyors use is to scan the malware they develop offline with multiple anti-malware products to ensure that their new malware is not detected by any of them. This gives them a measure of confidence that they are still undetected in their victims' IT environments. So, once a security team uploads the malware sample to an anti-malware vendor, that vendor will develop signatures to detect, block, and clean that malware. They will also distribute those signatures to their customers and samples of the malware to other anti-malware vendors and add the malware to their online threat encyclopedias.

This will let the attacker know that one or more of their victims has found their malware, submitted it to an anti-malware vendor, and is likely investigating further to determine the extent of the intrusion. This could accelerate the attackers' timeline with a severe impact on their victims. For example, knowing that their presence has been detected, attackers might deploy ransomware and demand a ransom before their victims' incident response teams can take action.

Subsequently, many security teams do their own in-house malware reverse engineering and do not share CTI with other organizations or even their security vendors, until they believe there is no opportunity cost in doing so. They do not want to give attackers any advantage and do not want to deal with potential negative legal, regulatory, or reputational outcomes that could arise. This approach gives them the best chance to find and exorcize the attackers before they decide to perform actions on objectives, such as deploying ransomware or destructive wiper malware.

Now that we've discussed what CTI is and how it is shared between organizations, let's explore the characteristics of *credible CTI*. Knowing how to tell the difference between credible CTI and not-so-credible CTI can help CISOs and security teams consume and operationalize CTI more efficiently.

How to identify credible CTI

In this section, I'm going to give you some guidance on how to identify good CTI versus the questionable TI I see so often in the industry today. After publishing one of the industry's best

TI reports for the better part of a decade (OK, I admit I'm biased), I learned a few things along the way that I'll share with you here.

The only way you'll be able to truly understand whether or how specific threat intelligence can help your organization is to understand its data sources, as well as the methodology that the vendor used to collect and report the data; without this context, TI can be distracting and the opposite of helpful.

There are two challenges security teams must overcome with respect to CTI:

- First, they only have so much time to consume and potentially operationalize CTI. Every minute they spend consuming CTI that won't help them is a minute lost during the constant deluge of attacks on their organization. Frankly, most security teams are not resourced well enough that they can spend time consuming CTI that isn't helpful to them.
- The second related challenge they need to overcome is operationalizing the wrong CTI. In other words, they spend the time, effort, and budget to develop capabilities that defend against low probability or low impact threats instead of the threats with the highest probability and potential impact on them. There are a lot of threats that security teams can spend their time and resources on, but most teams need to be very good at choosing the most important areas to invest in.

Keep in mind that many cybersecurity vendors, including those that publish CTI, leverage modern marketing techniques to drive demand for their products and services and build their brands. Focusing your precious attention on CTI that is designed to help operational cybersecurity teams instead of marketing vehicles that leverage CTI will help your security teams stay sane in this noisy industry.

As I previously mentioned, understanding the source of the CTI you consume is very important. Let's explore this aspect next.

Data sources

First and perhaps most importantly, always review the sources of CTI data that you are using and how the vendors involved are interpreting the data. If the data source is unknown or the vendors won't share the source of the data, then you simply cannot trust it and the interpretations based on it.

> Tip
>
> If the vendors don't tell you what their methodology is, then you can't trust their data, period.

For example, suppose a vendor claims that 85% of all systems have been successfully infected by a particular family of malware. But when you dig into the data source used to make this claim, you find that *85% of systems that used the vendor's online malware cleaner website* were infected with the malware referenced. Note that "85% of all systems" is a dramatic extrapolation from "85% of all systems that used their online tool."

Additionally, you also find that the online tool is only offered in US English, meaning it's less likely that consumers who don't speak English will use it even if they know it exists, which further skews the data. For example, if you work at a public sector organization in Japan, how valuable is CTI to you that focuses on a specific industry vertical in the private sector in the US? The answer is you don't know until you understand the sources of data and what they might mean to your organization.

Finally, you discover that the vendor's desktop antivirus detection tool refers users to the online tool to get disinfected when it finds systems to be infected with the threat. The vendor does this to drive awareness that their super-great online tool is available to their customers. This skews the data, as 100% of users referred to the online tool from the desktop antivirus tool were already known to be infected with that threat. I can't count how many times I've seen stunts like this over the years.

Examples such as these illustrate why it's always important to dive deep into the data sources to understand what the data actually means to you.

> Note
>
> In *Chapter 5*, I will spend a lot of time describing the intricacies of the sources of data used in that chapter. This is the only way to understand the picture the data is providing, relative to your organization and the risks it cares about.

Specificity is your friend in this context. Understanding where the data was collected from and how, the limitations of the data sources, and the underlying assumptions and biases present while processing the data are all key to understanding how the resulting CTI might help your organization. Purveyors of credible CTI are happy to provide this context to you. However, they might not volunteer this information, and you might need to request it. Providing such information tends to highlight the limitations of the CTI and the CTI provider's capabilities. Also, I've found that not everyone is a connoisseur of the finer points of CTI; being prepared to ask your own questions is typically the best way to get the context you need to truly understand CTI.

Regarding marketing communications from vendors that leverage CTI, marketing professionals do this for at least a couple of good reasons. First, if they lead their communications with new CTI data, they can potentially drive a news cycle that amplifies their message and helps drive demand for whatever they are selling. Secondly, including real CTI in their marketing message gives the message some semblance of credibility. Your job as a CTI consumer is to recognize the difference between marketing messages that leverage CTI and CTI that will help your operational security team. Although these aren't mutually exclusive, recognizing the difference will help avoid randomizing your operational security team with CTI that is relatively low value for them.

Time periods

When consuming TI, understanding the time scale and time periods of the data is super important. Are the data and insights provided from a period of days, weeks, months, quarters, or years? The answer to this question will help provide the context required to understand the intelligence.

The events of a few days will potentially have a much different meaning to your organization than a long-term trend over a period of months or years. Anomalies will typically warrant a different risk treatment than established patterns. Additionally, the conclusions that can be made from CTI data can be dramatically altered based on the time periods the vendor uses in their report.

Let me provide you with an example scenario. Let's say a vendor is reporting on how many vulnerabilities were exploited in their products for a given period. If the data is reported in regular sequential periods of time, such as quarterly, the trend looks really bad, as large increases are evident. But instead of reporting the trend using sequential quarterly periods, the trend looks much better when comparing the current quarter to the same quarter last year; there could actually be a decrease in the exploitation of vulnerabilities in the current quarter versus the same quarter last year. This puts a positive light on the vendor and obscures the increase in the exploitation of vulnerabilities in their products quarter over quarter.

Another potential red flag is when you see a vendor report data that isn't for a normal period of time, such as monthly, quarterly, or annually. Instead, they use a period of months that seems a little random. If the time period is irregular and the reason it's used isn't obvious, the rationale should be documented with the CTI. If it's not, ask the vendor why they selected the time periods they used. In some cases, the timeframe changes for valid reasons, such as updates to a product or methodology, or the adoption of a new reporting cadence. However, sometimes, you'll find some vendors use a specific time period because it makes their story more dramatic, garnering more attention, if that's their agenda. Alternatively, the period selected might help downplay bad news by minimizing changes in the data.

Understanding why the data is being reported in specific time scales and periods will give you some idea about the credibility of the data, as well as the agenda of the vendor providing it to you.

Recognizing hype

One of the biggest mistakes I've seen organizations make when consuming CTI is accepting their vendor's claims about the scope, applicability, and relevance of their data. For example, suppose a CTI vendor publishes data that claims 100% of attacks in a specific time period involved social engineering or exploited a specific vulnerability. The problem with such claims is that no one in the world can see 100% of all attacks, period.

They'd have to be omniscient to see all attacks occurring everywhere in the world simultaneously, on all operating systems and cloud platforms, in all browsers and applications. Similarly, claims such as 60% of all attacks were perpetrated by a specific **Advanced Persistent Threat** (APT) group are not helpful. Unless the vendor making this claim has knowledge of 100% of attacks, they can't credibly make claims about the characteristics of 60% of them. A claim about the characteristics of all attacks or a subset that requires knowledge of all attacks, even when referencing specific time periods, specific locations, and specific attack vectors, simply isn't possible or credible. I call these types of claims *claims of omniscience*.

A good litmus test for CTI is to ask yourself, does the vendor have to be omniscient to make this claim? This is where understanding the data sources and the time periods will help you cut through the hype and derive any value the intelligence might have. Purveyors of CTI that openly state the limitations of their data and properly qualify the conclusions they make earn trust with me because they are more credible. Outlandish conclusions-based questionable CTI claims don't impress me, even if they are highly entertaining.

Many times, the vendor publishing the data doesn't make such claims directly in their TI reports, but the way new intelligence is reported in the headlines is generalized or made more dramatic in order to draw attention to it. Don't blame CTI vendors for the way the news is reported, as this is typically beyond their control. But if they make such claims directly, recognize them and adjust the context in your mind appropriately. For many years, I made headlines around the world regularly speaking and writing about threats using threat detection data from a billion Windows systems, but we were always very careful not to overstep the mark from conclusions supported by the data. Making bolder claims would have required omniscience and omnipotence.

Predictions about the future

I'm sure you've seen some vendors make predictions about what's going to happen in the threat landscape in the future, and they might even provide data that leads you to believe that their predictions are accurate.

For this purpose, some CTI vendors use a trick that is again related to time periods. Let's say I'm publishing a TI report about the last 6-month period covering January through June. By the time the data for this period is collected and the report is written and published, a month or two might have gone by. Now it is September. If I make a prediction about the future in this report, I have two months of data from July and August that tell me what's been happening since the end of the reporting period.

If my prediction is based on what the data tells us already happened in July and August, readers of the report will be led to believe that I actually predicted the future accurately, thus reinforcing the idea that my firm knows more about the threat landscape than anyone else. Understanding when the prediction was made relative to the time period it was focused on will help you decide how credible the prediction and results are, and how trustworthy the vendor making the prediction is. Remember, predictions about the future are guesses —what happened in the past does not define what can happen in the future.

Vendors' motives

Trust is earned with people by behaving with a combination of credibility and character that they appreciate. You can use both to decide how trustworthy your vendors are. Transparency around CTI data sources, time scales, time periods, and predictions about the future can help vendors prove they are credible. Their motives communicate something about their character. Do they want to build a relationship with your organization as a trusted advisor, or is their interest limited to a financial transaction? There's a place for both types of vendors when building a cybersecurity program, but knowing which vendors fall into each category can be helpful, especially during incident response-related activities, when the pressure is on.

> **Tip**
>
> Knowing who you can rely on for real help when you need it is important.

Those are some of the insights I can offer you from a decade of experience publishing TI reports. Again, the big takeaway here is understanding the methodology and data sources of the CTI you consume—*this context is not optional.* One final word of advice: do not consume TI that doesn't meet this criterion. There is too much fear, uncertainty, doubt, and complexity in the IT industry. You need to be selective about who you take advice from.

Summary

I hope you enjoyed this chapter. Over the last 10 years, the CTI industry has exploded. Finding credible sources of CTI shouldn't be a challenge for well-funded cybersecurity programs. CTI is being integrated into cybersecurity products and services more and more, which means protecting, detecting, and responding to threats should be easier and faster than ever. However, I have to wonder, if this is true, how are attackers being more successful now than ever before? There are many historical examples that teach us that TI isn't sufficient by itself to mitigate attacks; defenders need to be willing to act on the intelligence they have and need the capabilities to do so effectively. Despite the proliferation of CTI, organizations need effective cybersecurity strategies to be successful. In order to develop an effective strategy for your organization, it is helpful to first understand the types of threats you face and how they operate. This is the theme of the next six chapters of this book.

In this chapter, you learned about different aspects of CTI. CTI provides organizations with data and information on potential cyber threats. Those threats can include various categories of malware, exploitation of vulnerabilities, web-based attacks, DDoS attacks, social engineering attacks, and others. OSINT leverages publicly available data sources such as social media, news feeds, court filings, and arrest records, as well as information attackers disclosed on their victims, activity in illicit forums, and many others.

I also described how cybersecurity programs can make use of CTI, including in SOCs, to inform CIRT investigations, to inform threat hunting, red, blue, and purple teams' efforts, and many others. I discussed how cybersecurity teams use TTPs and IOCs.

I introduced the TLP, which has become a popular protocol for sharing CTI and other types of information. Finally, we explored how to recognize credible CTI versus noise. To do this, you need to dive deep into data sources, understand how time periods are being used, learn to recognize hype, and seek to understand your vendors' motives.

This chapter provided some context to help you understand the analysis of various threats in the next six chapters: *Chapter 3, Industry Vulnerability Disclosure Trends*; *Chapter 4, Product Vulnerability Disclosure Trends*; *Chapter 5, The Evolution of Malware*; *Chapter 6, Internet-Based Threats*; *Chapter 7, Application Programming Interface (API) Security*; and *Chapter 8, Friend or Foe? The Roles Governments Play in Cybersecurity*.

In *Chapter 3, Industry Vulnerability Disclosure Trends*, we'll dive deep into the world of security vulnerabilities.

References

- BBC News. (2013). *Microsoft sees rise in net attacks*. BBC News. Retrieved from `https://www.bbc.com/news/av/business-22348290`.
- OSINT Framework. (n.d.). *OSINT Framework*. Retrieved from `https://osintframework.com/`.
- GitHub (n.d.). *#osint-tools*. Retrieved from `https://github.com/topics/osint-tools`.

- CrowdStrike. (June 2025). *CrowdStrike and Microsoft Collaborate to Harmonize Cyber Threat Attribution*. CrowdStrike. Retrieved from `https://www.crowdstrike.com/en-us/press-releases/crowdstrike-microsoft-collaborate-deconflict-cyber-threat-attribution/`.
- Badger, L.; Johnson, C.; Skorupka, C.; Snyder, J.; Watermire, D. (October 2016). *NIST Special Publication 800-150*. NIST. Retrieved from `https://nvlpubs.nist.gov/nistpubs/SpecialPublications/NIST.SP.800-150.pdf`.
- MITRE ATT&CK® (n.d.). Retrieved from `https://attack.mitre.org/`.
- *NIST Special Publication 800-53 Revision 5*. (September 2020). NIST. Retrieved from `https://nvlpubs.nist.gov/nistpubs/SpecialPublications/NIST.SP.800-53r5.pdf`.
- FIRST. (n.d.). Retrieved from `https://www.first.org/tlp/`.
- CISA. (n.d.). Retrieved from `https://www.cisa.gov/tlp`.
- *STIX Version 2.1*. (10 June 2021). OASIS Standard. Retrieved from `https://docs.oasis-open.org/cti/stix/v2.1/os/stix-v2.1-os.pdf`.
- *TAXII™ Version 2.1*. (10 June 2021). OASIS Standard. Retrieved from `https://www.oasis-open.org/standard/taxii-version-2-1/`.

Get this book's PDF version and more

Scan the QR code (or go to `packtpub.com/unlock`). Search for this book by name, confirm the edition, and then follow the steps on the page.

UNLOCK NOW

Note: Keep your invoice handy. Purchases made directly from Packt don't require an invoice.

Part 2

Evolution of the threat landscape

In this section, you'll gain a deeper understanding of how the modern threat landscape has evolved and what that evolution means for your security strategy. You'll learn from long-term trends in both industry-wide and product-specific vulnerability disclosures, including a detailed look at the Cybersecurity and Infrastructure Security Agency's Known Exploited Vulnerabilities catalog and what it reveals about real-world attacker behavior. You'll explore how malware, especially ransomware, has transformed into one of the most disruptive and financially damaging tools in an attacker's arsenal.

You'll examine the shifting nature of internet-based threats, from phishing and drive-by downloads to large-scale distributed denial-of-service attacks, and understand how these techniques continue to adapt to modern environments. You'll also see why **Application Programming Interfaces (APIs)** have become one of the most consequential enterprise attack surfaces and learn how to evaluate and secure them effectively.

Finally, you'll unpack the complex and sometimes contradictory roles governments play in cybersecurity as market participants, standards bodies, regulators, defenders, and at times adversaries, so you can navigate policy, compliance, and geopolitical risk with clarity and confidence.

This part of the book includes the following chapters:

- *Chapter 3, Industry Vulnerability Disclosure Trends*

- *Chapter 4, Product Vulnerability Disclosure Trends*
- *Chapter 5, The Evolution of Malware*
- *Chapter 6, Internet-Based Threats*
- *Chapter 7, Application Programming Interface Security*
- *Chapter 8, Friend or Foe? The Roles Governments Play in Cybersecurity*

3

Industry Vulnerability Disclosure Trends

Vulnerabilities represent risk and expense to all organizations that use technology. Technology vendors who are serious about reducing both risk and costs for their customers focus on reducing the number of vulnerabilities in their products and work on ways to make it hard and expensive for attackers to exploit their customers, thereby driving down attackers' return on investment. Identifying the vendors and the products that have been successful in doing this can be time-consuming and difficult.

Organizations that develop and operate their own software and hardware share this challenge. It is their responsibility to take commercially reasonable steps to protect their customers' and employees' data, their intellectual property, and other confidential business data. Failure to take this responsibility seriously can lead to expensive incident response events, expensive product rework or canceled products, a diminished brand, expensive lawsuits, fines, and poor regulatory outcomes. Vulnerability management is a cornerstone of most successful cybersecurity programs because it is fundamental to cybersecurity.

In this chapter, I will provide you with valuable background information and an in-depth analysis of how some of the industry's leaders have managed vulnerabilities in their products over the last several years. I will introduce a vulnerability improvement framework that can help you identify vendors and products that have been reducing risks and costs for their customers. This data and analysis can inform your organization's vulnerability management strategy.

In this chapter, we'll cover the following topics:

- From worms to resilience: the evolution of vulnerability management
- Vulnerability management primer

- Industry vulnerability disclosure trends
- Vendor vulnerability trends

Let's begin by looking at what vulnerability management is.

From worms to resilience: the evolution of vulnerability management

Over the past 25 years, organizations have been challenged to manage a continual volume of new vulnerabilities in software and hardware. Attackers and malware constantly attempt to exploit unpatched vulnerabilities on systems in every industry and every part of the world. Vulnerabilities are a currency for many interested groups, including security researchers, the vulnerability management industry, governments, various commercial organizations, and, of course, attackers and purveyors of malware. These groups have different motivations and goals, but they all value new vulnerabilities, with some willing to pay handsomely for them.

I had a front-row seat at ground zero for the tumultuous period where worms and other malware first started exploiting vulnerabilities in Microsoft software at scale. After working on the Enterprise Network Support team at Microsoft for a few years, I was asked to help build a new customer-facing security incident response team. I accepted that job on Thursday, January 23, 2003. Two days later, on Saturday, January 25th, *SQL Slammer* hit the internet, disrupting networks worldwide. That Saturday morning, I got into my car to drive to the office but had to stop for gas. Both the cash machine and the pumps at the gas station were offline due to "network issues." At that point, I realized just how widespread and serious that attack was. Then, one day in August 2003, *Blaster* disrupted the internet to an even greater extent than SQL Slammer had. Over the course of the following year, Blaster variants followed, as well as *MyDoom*, *Sasser*, and other widespread malware attacks. It turns out that millions of people were willing to double-click on an email attachment labeled *MyDoom*. Most of these attacks used unpatched vulnerabilities in Microsoft products to infect systems and propagate. This all happened before Windows Update or any of the tools that are available today for servicing software existed. Because Microsoft had to release multiple security updates to address the underlying vulnerabilities in the components that Blaster used, many IT departments began a long-term pattern of behavior, delaying patching systems to avoid patching the same components repeatedly and rebooting systems repeatedly. Most internet-connected Windows-based systems were not running antivirus software in those days either, and many of those that were didn't have the latest signatures installed. Working on a customer-facing security incident response team, supporting security updates, and helping enterprise customers with malware infections and hackers was a very tough job in those days—you needed thick skin. Subsequently, I had the opportunity to learn a lot about malware, vulnerabilities, and exploits in this role.

Later in my career at Microsoft, I managed marketing communications for the **Microsoft Security Response Center** (**MSRC**), the Microsoft **Security Development Lifecycle** (**SDL**), and the **Microsoft Malware Protection Center** (**MMPC**). The MSRC is the group at Microsoft that manages the incoming vulnerability and attack reports. The MMPC was Microsoft's antivirus research and response lab back then. The SDL is a software development methodology that was instituted at Microsoft in the years that followed these devastating worm attacks. I learned a lot about vulnerabilities, exploits, malware, and attackers in the 8 or 9 years I worked in this organization, called *Trustworthy Computing*. I often get asked whether things are better today than they were 10 or 15 years ago. *Chapters 3* and *4* in this book are dedicated to answering this question and providing some insights into how things have changed from a vulnerability management perspective. These chapters also provide you with a way to identify vendors and products that have been reducing risk and costs for their customers.

Vulnerability management primer

Before we dive into the vulnerability disclosure trends for the past 25 years, let me provide you with a quick primer on vulnerability management so that it's easier to understand the data and analysis I provide in this chapter, and how some vulnerability management teams use such data.

There are many different definitions of what a vulnerability is. Let's use the definition provided by the **National Institute of Standards and Technology** (**NIST**):

> *"A weakness in the computational logic (e.g., code) found in software and hardware components that, when exploited, results in a negative impact to confidentiality, integrity, or availability. Mitigation of the vulnerabilities in this context typically involves coding changes, but could also include specification changes or even specification deprecations (e.g., removal of affected protocols or functionality in their entirety)."*
>
> *NIST, August 2023*

If you are wondering what a vulnerability actually looks like, this little C code snippet is a good example, as its author explains in the following quote:

```
void func(int index, int value)
{
    char buf[4];
    buf[index] = value;
}
```

> *"Let's assume the arguments index and value come from a call to recv() which reads a packet from the Internet. Is this a security bug? Heck yeah. The attacker controls everything about that poor old buffer. Even with /GS and ASLR in place, this would be a serious bug and would be fixed at the earliest."*
>
> *Howard, May 9, 2021*

> **Note**
>
> Vulnerabilities, such as this example, can be obvious bugs that are identified by developers reviewing code, the development tools they use, or **Static Application Security Testing** (**SAST**) and **Dynamic Application Security Testing** (**DAST**). Other vulnerabilities can be very subtle and hard to find.

In this example, the author is alluding to the developer's failure to validate the input before processing it. The developer appears to be making the assumption that `index` and `value` passed into the function will always be valid numbers that can be used to set the value of each character in the character array buffer allocated (called `buf`). Since the values of `index` and `value` are set by the contents of a network packet from the internet, what if attackers set those values to something the developer didn't expect? Could an attacker corrupt some memory by passing an `index` value to the function that is beyond the end of the defined buffer? Without including input validation and error handling in this function, this developer has developed a potentially exploitable bug. As the author of the code mentions, even enabling compiler options such as /GS and ASLR, which are designed to make exploitation of vulnerabilities harder, can't always compensate when developers make mistakes.

Remember the real-world example of the incident I described in *Chapter 1, How Enterprises Get Hacked,* called *Data breaches via insecure APIs*? The root cause in both these cases is the same; developers make mistakes that tools and automation can't always discover. To be fair to developers, many security class bugs that are exploitable are far more nuanced and harder to identify than this simple example; modern compilers would likely flag this bug for the developer. Still, **memory corruption** vulnerabilities constitute the second largest category of vulnerability type behind **cross-site scripting**, causing 20,789 vulnerabilities between 2016 and the end of 2025 (CVE Details, n.d.). These *weaknesses* in hardware and software that could lead to bad security outcomes are tracked and shared.

This vulnerability management primer provides some background and context that will help you digest all the vulnerability data I share in this chapter as well as the next chapter.

Understanding how vulnerabilities are tracked, scored, and their impact on front-line enterprise vulnerability management teams will help you interpret the data. Let's start with Common Weakness Enumeration.

Common Weakness Enumeration

The MITRE Corporation is a not-for-profit organization that manages federally funded research centers for, among other things, cybersecurity. MITRE supports the NIST in a mission to build trustworthy information systems for US government agencies. These two organizations are central to how vulnerability management operates across industries around the world. When a vulnerability in a commercial software or hardware product is discovered, MITRE and NIST record and track the vulnerability so that anyone using the product can understand the risk of doing so and what mitigations for the vulnerability exist. As part of this, MITRE manages a list of common software and hardware weakness types to which vulnerabilities discovered are mapped. This list is called **Common Weakness Enumeration** (**CWE™**). MITRE offers the CWE for free for public sector and commercial sector organizations, as well as individuals, at `https://cwe.mitre.org/index.html`. MITRE describes why they offer the CWE this way:

> *"Knowing the weaknesses that result in vulnerabilities means software developers, hardware designers, and security architects can eliminate them before deployment, when it is much easier and cheaper to do so."*
>
> *MITRE, n.d.*

At the time of writing, version 4.19.1 of the CWE list had 944 weaknesses listed in it. The list can be navigated based on the area of research you are interested in, such as software, hardware, or more specific areas, such as **OWASP Top 10**, software written in C++, software written in Java, and so on. Regardless of the programming language used or the type of product developed, common weaknesses can be introduced in the development process that can be identified and fixed before they become vulnerabilities that technology operators must manage downstream. I mentioned two types of weaknesses earlier, memory corruption and cross-site scripting. Other examples include exposure of sensitive information to an unauthorized actor, deserialization of untrusted data, and use of hardcoded credentials.

The CVE Program and NIST

When a vulnerability is discovered in a released software or hardware product and reported to the vendor that owns the vulnerable product or service, the vulnerability will ultimately be assigned a **Common Vulnerabilities and Exposures** (**CVE**) identifier, referred to as a **CVE ID**, at some point. CVE IDs are alphanumeric strings used to identify publicly disclosed vulnerabilities. The format of CVE IDs is **CVE-YYYY-NNNN**, where *YYYY* is the year the CVE ID was assigned, and *NNNN* is a unique identifier. *CVE-2018-8653* is an example of a CVE ID that was assigned in 2018.

MITRE Corporation started a catalog of all CVEs, called the CVE list, in 1999. There were 321 CVE records in the list at that time. Twenty-five years later, at the time I wrote this, there were over 332,000 records, representing an increase of about 103,327%. The CVE list can be accessed at `https://www.cve.org/`, and the history of the CVE list can be found at `https://www.cve.org/About/History`.

The exact date when a CVE ID is assigned to a vulnerability is a function of many different factors, to which an entire chapter in this book could be dedicated. In fact, I co-wrote a Microsoft white paper on this topic called *Software Vulnerability Management at Microsoft*, which described why it could take a relatively long time to release security updates for Microsoft products. It appears that this paper has disappeared from the Microsoft Download Center with the sands of time. However, the following are some of the factors explaining why it can be a long time between a vendor receiving a report of a vulnerability and releasing a security update for it:

- **Identifying the bug**: Some bugs only show up under special conditions or in the largest IT environments. It can take time for the vendor to reproduce the bug and triage it. Additionally, the reported vulnerability might exist in other products and services that use the same or similar components. All of these products and services need to be fixed simultaneously so that the vendor doesn't inadvertently produce a zero-day vulnerability in its own product line. I'll discuss zero-day vulnerabilities later in this chapter.
- **Identifying all variants**: Fixing the reported bug might be straightforward. However, finding all the variations of the issue and fixing them too is important, as it will prevent the need to re-release security updates or release multiple updates to address vulnerabilities in the same component. This can be the activity that takes the most time when fixing vulnerabilities.
- **Code reviews and testing**: Ensuring that the updated code actually fixes the vulnerability and doesn't introduce more bugs and vulnerabilities is important and sometimes time-consuming.
- **Functional testing**: This ensures that the fix doesn't impact the functionality of the product—customers don't appreciate it when this happens.
- **Application compatibility testing**: In the case of an operating system or web browser, vendors might need to test thousands of applications, drivers, and other components to ensure that they don't break their ecosystem when they release the security update.

For example, the integration testing matrix for Windows is huge, including thousands of the most common applications that run on the platform.

- **Release testing**: Ensuring that the distribution and installation of the security update works as expected and doesn't make systems unbootable or unstable is vital. The last thing software vendors want to do is push an update to all of their customers that makes operating systems unbootable. The latest high-impact example of this is "*KB5042421: CrowdStrike issue impacting Windows endpoints causing an 0x50 or 0x7E error message on a blue screen*" (Microsoft, n.d.).

> Note
>
> Note that the date that a CVE identifier is assigned to a vulnerability isn't necessarily related to the date that the vendor releases a security update addressing the underlying vulnerability; that is, these dates can be different.

The allure of notoriety that comes with announcing the discovery of a new major vulnerability leads some security researchers to release details publicly before vendors can fix the flaws. The typical best-case scenario is when the public disclosure of a vulnerability occurs on the same date that the vendor releases a security update for the vulnerability. This reduces the window of opportunity for attackers to exploit the vulnerability to the time it takes for each organization to test and deploy the update in their IT environments.

Let's take a closer look at the details for that example CVE ID I introduced earlier, *CVE-2018-8653*. This will help you understand some of the aspects of vulnerabilities that are tracked and how that information is used by vulnerability management teams. As you can tell from the CVE ID, the number *8653* was assigned to the vulnerability it was associated with in 2018. When we look up this CVE identifier in the CVE list, we can get access to some basic information including a short description, the vendor whose code has the vulnerability in it along with the known affected products and their versions, the CVE Numbering Authority that assigned the vulnerability, its CVE ID, references to more information, the date the CVE ID was added to the list, and other information. Here is the description of that CVE ID:

> *"A remote code execution vulnerability exists in the way that the scripting engine handles objects in memory in Internet Explorer, aka "Scripting Engine Memory Corruption Vulnerability." This affects Internet Explorer 9, Internet Explorer 11, Internet Explorer 10. This CVE ID is unique from CVE-2018-8643."*
>
> *CVE, 2018*

National Vulnerability Database and CVSS

The **Internet Category of Attack Toolkit** (**ICAT**) was started in 1999. It was rebranded as the **National Vulnerability Database** (**NVD**) in 2005 by NIST. The NVD imports data from the CVE list and adds metadata to it, including metrics and scoring information, in a process referred to as "*enrichment*" (CVE, n.d.). The NVD can be used to track publicly disclosed vulnerabilities in all sorts of software and hardware products across the entire industry. The NVD is a publicly available database that can be accessed at `https://nvd.nist.gov`.

When we look up the CVE ID mentioned earlier, *CVE-2018-8653*, in the NVD, we can get even more details about it that weren't available in the CVE ID's record in the CVE list. Examples of these extra details include the severity scores for the vulnerability, potentially from multiple different sources, whether the vulnerability can be accessed remotely, whether user interaction is required to exploit the vulnerability, its potential impact on confidentiality, integrity, and availability, and its exploitability score. Enriching the CVE can also include assigning a CWE ID and adding **Common Platform Enumeration** (**CPE**) applicability statements (NIST, 2022).

The CPE provides a standard naming convention for software and hardware affected by vulnerabilities. This is helpful, as in the past, different names for the same product appeared in the NVD. For example, "Internet Explorer" and "IE" would both appear as affected products in different CVE ID records referring to the same product. This made it hard to get an accurate inventory of CVE IDs for a specific product that suffered from this problem. The CPE addresses this problem and provides a format that makes CPE applicability statements more machine-readable so that vulnerability management tools and products can consume them more easily. Here is an example of a CPE applicability statement: `"cpe:2.3:a:microsoft:internet_explorer:8.0.6001:beta:*:*:*:*:*:*"`. If you are interested in learning more about the CPE and its format, check out the CPE specifications on NIST's website at `https://nvd.nist.gov/products/cpe`.

You might wonder what all the other additional information the NVD provides is used for. A score is assigned to each CVE ID in the NVD that represents a risk calculation for each vulnerability. Risk is the combination of probability and impact. In the context of vulnerabilities, risk is the combination of the probability that a vulnerability can be successfully exploited and the impact on the system if it is exploited. The **Common Vulnerability Scoring System** (**CVSS**) is used to estimate the risk for each vulnerability in the NVD. The **Forum of Incident Response and Security Teams** (**FIRST**) CVSS **Special Interest Group** (**SIG**) is the custodian of the CVSS with the goal of improving it over time. You can find more information on this SIG at `https://www.first.org/cvss/`.

Before getting into the details on the latest version of the CVSS, it is important to know that the CVSS has evolved over time. Subsequently, there have been different versions released over time, such as v1, v2, v3, v3.1, and v4.0. Each newer version incorporated feedback from the CVSS stakeholder community and improved the industry's ability to manage vulnerabilities in technologies, and enabled security measurement and compliance objectives.

As the CVSS evolved and different versions were published, a natural question arose. Assuming organizations will strive to use the latest CVSS version to get its advantages, will all the CVE IDs that were published in the past get updated with scores using the newest CVSS version? For example, when we look up the example CVE ID we've been discussing, *CVE-2018-8653*, in the NVD, it currently has CVSS scores using CVSS versions 2.0 and 3.x, but not 4.0 (the latest version). If we look up a newer CVE ID, *CVE-2024-24747*, for example, it has a CVSS v3.x score, but not a CVSS 2.0 or CVSS 4.0 score assigned to it. This is the case despite more than 18 months having passed since *CVE-2024-24747* was published and CVSS version 4.0 became available months before the CVE ID was published. The answer to this question can be found in the NVD's FAQ on CVEs:

> *"Q. Have all older CVEs been updated to CVSSv3?*
>
> *A. The NVD is [sic] prioritizes the enrichment of new vulnerabilities or vulnerabilities that have changed since their last enrichment. At this time, there are no plans to retroactively assess vulnerabilities published before Dec 20, 2015 with CVSS v3.0 scores.*
>
> *A similar approach is planned for after the release of CVSSv4."*
>
> *NIST, 2022*

While the lack of CVSS version continuity amid the ever-growing population of CVE IDs introduces a few challenges, the fact that newer versions of the CVSS continue to improve the industry's ability to manage risks associated with vulnerabilities is very positive. However, in 2024, a variety of factors impacted NIST's ability to keep pace with the volume of CVE IDs being published by CVE Numbering Authorities. This led to a large backlog of CVE IDs that were published but had not gone through NIST's NVD enrichment process. NIST published the following statement about the situation on their website in February 2024 and later updated it in April of the same year:

> *"NVD Program Announcement UPDATED - April, 25th 2024*
>
> *NIST maintains the National Vulnerability Database (NVD), a repository of information on software and hardware flaws that can compromise computer security. This is a key piece of the nation's cybersecurity infrastructure.*

> *There is a growing backlog of vulnerabilities submitted to the NVD and requiring analysis. This is based on a variety of factors, including an increase in software and, therefore, vulnerabilities, as well as a change in interagency support.*
>
> *Currently, we are prioritizing analysis of the most significant vulnerabilities. In addition, we are working with our agency partners to bring on more support for analyzing vulnerabilities and have reassigned additional NIST staff to this task as well.*
>
> *We are also looking into longer-term solutions to this challenge, including the establishment of a consortium of industry, government, and other stakeholder organizations that can collaborate on research to improve the NVD.*
>
> *NIST is committed to its continued support and management of the NVD. Currently, we are focused on our immediate plans to address the CVE backlog, but plan to keep the community posted on potential plans for the consortium as they develop."*
>
> *NIST, 2024*

Some industry estimates put the backlog of new CVE IDs that needed enrichment at over 16,000 by July of 2024 (Phoenix Security, 2024). At the time of writing (February 2026), CVE IDs in the NVD that have not gone through the enrichment process can still be found. A note in the details of such CVE IDs in the NVD states: "*AWAITING ANALYSIS. This CVE record has been marked for NVD enrichment efforts.*" Apparently, the backlog for enriching CVE IDs has not been cleared yet. The NVD plays a critical role for governments and industry worldwide, and such a backlog hinders its reliable operation. To reduce reliance on the US NVD, the European Union created its own equivalent—the **European Union Vulnerability Database** (**EUVD**)—which released its first public vulnerability data in April 2025. The EUVD can be accessed at `https://euvd.enisa.europa.eu/`.

Now that you've gained some insight into the importance and drama surrounding CVE IDs, let's look at the latest version of the CVSS more closely. CVSS version 4 was published on November 1st, 2023 (FIRST, 2023). To calculate a CVSS score, this version of the CVSS uses four metric groups, including **Base**, **Threat**, **Environmental**, and **Supplemental**.

The *Base* metric group leverages two sets of metrics: **exploitability metrics** and **impact metrics**. Notice how these sets of metrics map to probability and impact, respectively. Exploitability metrics include metrics such as the following:

- **Attack vector**: How exploitation is made possible
- **Attack complexity**: How hard it is to exploit the vulnerability
- **Attack requirements**: Conditions that must be true for an attack to succeed
- **Privileges required**: The level of privileges the attacker must have
- **User interaction**: Whether a user needs to take action to exploit the vulnerability (FIRST, 2023)

To calculate an estimate of the impact on a system if a vulnerability is successfully exploited, the CVSS uses impact metrics, such as the expected impact on confidentiality, integrity, and availability (FIRST, 2023).

The exploitability metrics and impact metrics are provided in the NVD's details on each CVE ID. The CVSS uses these details in some mathematical calculations to produce a base score for each vulnerability (NIST, n.d.). The NVD provides CVSS calculators to help organizations calculate vulnerability scores. NVD calculators are available on NIST's website for CVSS v2.0, v3.0, v3.1, and v4.0. CVSS scores can range from 0.0 to 10.0. The scores can be mapped into qualitative ratings such as *low*, *medium*, *high*, and *critical* to make it easier to manage than using granular numeric scores (FIRST, 2023). *Table 3.1* summarizes the CVSS scoring ranges for each rating:

Rating	CVSS Score
None	0.0
Low	0.1–3.9
Medium	4.0–6.9
High	7.0–8.9
Critical	9.0–10.0

Table 3.1 – Rating descriptions for ranges of CVSS version 4.0 scores

Vulnerabilities with higher scores have higher probabilities of exploitation and/or greater impacts on systems when exploited. Put another way, the higher the score, the higher the risk. This is why many vulnerability management teams use these scores and ratings to determine how quickly to test and deploy security updates and/or mitigations for vulnerabilities in their environments, once the vulnerabilities have been publicly disclosed.

Vulnerability management professionals can further refine the base scores for vulnerabilities by using the other aforementioned metric groups, including *Threat*, *Environmental*, and *Supplemental*.

Threat metrics are meant to provide insight into the current state of exploit techniques or the availability of exploit code for each CVE ID scored. The intent of the *exploit maturity* metric is to provide some insight into the likelihood that a particular vulnerability will be exploited. The source for such a metric is **Cybersecurity Threat Intelligence** (**CTI**), as we discussed in *Chapter 2, What to Know About Threat Intelligence*. The possible values for this metric are as follows:

- **Not Defined**: No reliable CTI is available
- **Attacked**: The vulnerability has been used in attacks, or attacks seem imminent
- **Proof-of-Concept**: Proof-of-concept code publicly available, no knowledge of actual attacks
- **Unreported**: Based on CTI, no knowledge of proof-of-concept code or attacks

This can be very helpful information if your vulnerability management team is trying to prioritize which vulnerabilities to address; for instance, vulnerabilities that are categorized as "attacked" are no longer only theoretically exploitable. Because of this, many CISOs and vulnerability management policy **service level agreements** (**SLAs**) expedite patching for vulnerabilities with known exploitation.

> Tip
>
> Remember one of the key lessons from *Chapter 2*: a metric that is based on CTI is only as good as the CTI.

The *Environmental* metric group provides another way to tailor CVSS scores. Rather than measuring the likelihood of exploitation, these metrics reflect how critical the affected systems are to a specific organization, based on their potential impact on **confidentiality, integrity, and availability**—the classic **CIA** triad. Vulnerability management analysts can assign greater importance or less importance to each member of the CIA triad. For example, a system that absolutely must be online always could have a high impact on an organization if availability is impacted by the exploitation of the vulnerability. At the same time, the confidentiality of the same system may not represent as big an impact if it is compromised, because that system is only processing non-confidential, publicly available information.

The *Environmental* metric group also contains modified *Base* metrics, which can be used to customize CVSS scores based on specific circumstances of an organization's environment, such as the existence of mitigating factors or controls in a specific IT environment. For example, the impact of a particular vulnerability might be blunted because a mitigation for the vulnerability had already been deployed by an organization in their previous efforts to harden their IT environment. While the CVSS base score for the vulnerability might be deemed high severity (a CVSS score between 7.0 and 8.9), in this organization's environment, the threat of exploitation has been blunted by system hardening and represents a medium severity vulnerability (a CVSS score between 4.0 and 6.9) to the organization.

Finally, the *Supplemental* metric group can also be leveraged to customize the CVSS score for CVE IDs. Metrics in this group include the following:

- **Safety**: Is the safety of humans at risk?
- **Automatable**: Can exploitation be automated across targets?
- **Value Density**: Can the attacker gain control over diffuse or concentrated systems using the vulnerability?
- **Vulnerability Response Effort**: How difficult or easy is it to mitigate the vulnerability/

All the gory details on the metric groups I discussed are available in the *CVSS version 4.0: Specification Document*, available on `www.first.org`.

Now, let's examine how actively exploited vulnerabilities are tracked, since this information is crucial for prioritizing remediation.

CISA Known Exploited Vulnerabilities catalog

Once a vulnerability has been successfully exploited in the wild, that is someone has developed exploit code or tooling and used it against real systems, the risk profile changes dramatically. As a result, many vulnerability management and remediation teams prioritize patching known exploited vulnerabilities before all others. This approach provides remediation teams more time to address vulnerabilities when there is no CTI indicating active exploitation.

The **Cybersecurity and Infrastructure Security Agency** (**CISA**) maintains a list of vulnerabilities that are known to have been exploited, called the **Known Exploited Vulnerabilities** (**KEV**) catalog. All US federal civilian executive branch agencies are required by a *Binding Operational Directive* to remediate the vulnerabilities added to the KEV catalog. Given this, along with the aggressively growing number of vulnerability disclosures across the industry, some vulnerability management teams I've talked to have decided to prioritize remediation of only the vulnerabilities found in the KEV catalog. Other vulnerabilities, such as critical and high-severity vulnerabilities, get addressed with much less urgency, as they are viewed by these teams as merely *theoretically exploitable*. Until proof that they have been exploited surfaces, they view CVE IDs, even critical-severity CVE IDs, as lower risk and address them with a slower cadence. I examine the efficacy of this approach later in this chapter in the section called *Analysis of CISA's KEV catalog*.

The risk trade-offs of CTI-driven prioritization

Arguably, organizations that use this approach accept more risk, at least until all critical and high-severity vulnerabilities in their IT estates have been addressed. Essentially, they are gambling on the quality and timeliness of the CTI they use to inform their vulnerability remediation priorities. However, for organizations that struggle with vulnerability management and remediation, this approach helps them maintain a manageable scope for their remediation efforts while genuinely reducing risk. The key, though, is to address the other critical and high-severity vulnerabilities that weren't being actively exploited when they were initially evaluated, in a reasonable period of time. Allowing these vulnerabilities to sit in inventory and accumulate over time is foolhardy. Remember what I wrote in *Chapter 2*—no one is omniscient, and subsequently, no one can see 100% of all attacks. Understanding the sources of data and the limitations of the CTI used to inform vulnerability management is critical when using this approach.

Leveraging CTI to prioritize vulnerability remediation has become so popular that major vulnerability scanner vendors offer CTI integrations into their vulnerability scanner products, and the NVD integrates exploitation information into the details of each CVE ID.

> *"The NVD has added information to its CVE detail pages to identify vulnerabilities appearing in CISA's Known Exploited Vulnerabilities (KEV) Catalog. CVE [sic] appearing in the catalog will now contain a text reference and a hyperlink to the catalog. CVE not appearing in the catalog will not see any change. Information on exploited vulnerabilities and the affected products will also become available to developers when the NVD releases new APIs in late 2022."*
>
> *NIST, n.d.*

To the uninitiated, these approaches and the trade-offs might not make much sense.

The primary pain point that deploying security updates for vulnerabilities creates, besides the expense, is disruption to the business. For example, historically, most updates for Windows operating systems required reboots. When systems get rebooted, the downtime incurred is counted against the uptime goals that most IT organizations are committed to. Rebooting a single server might not seem material, but the time it takes to reboot hundreds or thousands of servers starts to add up. Keep in mind that organizations trying to maintain 99.999% (5 "9s") uptime can only afford to have 5 minutes and 15 seconds of downtime per year. That's 26.3 seconds of downtime per month. Servers in enterprise data centers, especially database and storage servers, can easily take more than 5 minutes to reboot when they are healthy. Additionally, when a server is rebooted, this is a prime time for issues to surface that require troubleshooting, thereby exacerbating downtime. The worst-case scenario is when a security update itself causes a problem. The time it takes to uninstall the update, to remediate the problem it's causing, and reboot yet again, on hundreds or thousands of systems, leaving them in a vulnerable state, also negatively impacts uptime.

Additionally, patching and rebooting systems can be expensive, especially for organizations that perform supervised patching in off-hours, which can require overtime and weekend wages. The concept of the conventional maintenance window is no longer valid, as many businesses are global and operate across borders, 24 hours per day, 7 days per week. A thoughtful approach to scheduled and layered patching, keeping the majority of infrastructure available while patching and rebooting a minority, has become common.

Reboots are the top reason that many organizations decide to accept some risk by patching quarterly or semi-annually, so much so that the MSRC that I worked closely with for over a decade used to try to minimize the number of security updates that required system reboots to every second month. To do this, when possible, they would try to release all the updates that required a reboot in one month, and then release updates that didn't require reboots the next month. When this plan worked, organizations that were patching systems every month could at least avoid rebooting systems every second month. But the "out of band" updates, which were unplanned updates necessitated by rapidly changing assumptions about the exploitability of vulnerabilities, seemed to spoil these plans frequently.

Rebooting servers has traditionally created tension between IT operations teams focused on uptime as an indicator of success and cybersecurity teams focused on preventing long-running unpatched systems from being the Achilles heel in their security postures. So much so that in 2025, Microsoft announced "*hotpatching*" [sic] for security updates for select versions of Windows Server and Windows 11 Enterprise (Microsoft, April 24, 2025). Windows "*hotpatch*" [sic] packages install without the need to schedule a reboot. Other update packages for Windows that install features are released quarterly and likely will require a reboot after installation. The net is that using hotpatching enables rapid installation of security updates while reducing the requirement to reboot to quarterly for select Windows Server and client versions. For organizations that run the latest versions of Windows, this new capability is sure to reduce the tension between IT operations teams and cybersecurity teams by allowing security updates to be deployed faster.

When you see how vulnerability disclosures have trended over time, the trade-offs that organizations make between the risk of exploitation and uptime might make more sense. Running servers in the cloud can dramatically change this equation—I'll cover this in more detail in *Chapter 13, Modern Approaches to Security and Compliance*. There are many other aspects and details of the NVD, CVE, and CVSS that I didn't cover here, but I've provided enough of a primer that you'll be able to appreciate the vulnerability disclosure trends that we dive into next. I'll introduce a few more CVE ID-related concepts as we make our way through the data.

Zero-day vulnerabilities

Another important term to understand is **zero-day vulnerability**. A zero-day vulnerability is a vulnerability that has been publicly disclosed before the vendor responsible for it has released a security update to address it. These vulnerabilities are the most valuable of all vulnerabilities, with attackers and governments willing to pay relatively large sums for them.

A scenario that vulnerability management teams dread is when a critical-rated zero-day vulnerability in their software or hardware has been publicly disclosed. This means the risk of exploitation could be significantly high, and that a security update to prevent exploitation of the vulnerability is not publicly available. Sometimes in these scenarios, there are *workarounds* that can be implemented to help make exploitation of the vulnerability harder or impossible. Workarounds, such as specific system configurations that prevent exploitation, are typically meant to be temporary. After all, if the only thing preventing exploitation is a configuration setting, what happens if that setting gets changed inadvertently or by an attacker who already has initial access? Often, changing a configuration setting as a workaround also disables functionality that was previously available. The one way to address vulnerabilities with the highest confidence and least impact is to install an update that fixes them.

An even worse scenario is when a vendor releases a security update for an exploitable, critical-rated vulnerability, but the update doesn't fix the vulnerability completely. In this scenario, the existence of the vulnerability is public knowledge, and the publicly available security update that isn't 100% effective essentially draws a map to the vulnerability for attackers to use. Typically, in such scenarios, the exploit code for such a vulnerability becomes publicly available and widely circulated on the internet very quickly.

This scenario might sound theoretical, but unfortunately, it has occurred numerous times over the past two decades. Perhaps the best examples are the dreaded *Log4j* vulnerabilities (*CVE-2021-44228* and *CVE-2021-45046*). These vulnerabilities were in the ubiquitous Java logging library Apache Log4j2. *CVE-2021-44228* has a "perfect" 10 CVSS v3.x score (9.3 CVSS 2.0 score, no CVSS 4.0 score published), meaning it is easy to exploit and can result in attackers taking complete control of impacted systems. It is so easy to exploit that some cybersecurity professionals nicknamed it *Log4Shell*—a tongue-in-cheek reference to the ability to remotely run any command on systems compromised using this vulnerability. The Software Engineering Institute CERT Coordination Center at Carnegie Mellon University described it this way:

> *"Apache Log4j allows insecure JNDI lookups that could allow an unauthenticated, remote attacker to execute arbitrary code with the privileges of the vulnerable Java application using Log4j."*
>
> *Software Engineering Institute CERT Coordination Center, Carnegie Mellon University 2021-12-15*

Because this vulnerability was in a very popular software library, it impacted literally thousands of products that leveraged that library across operating systems such as Windows, Linux, and macOS. Recall that I mentioned that NIST adds CPE applicability statements to CVE IDs as part of its enrichment process. The "*known affected software configurations*" section of *CVE-2021-44228* has pages of CPE applicability statements listing impacted products, including everything from firmware to Linux operating systems, to email platforms, to identity services, and so on.

For many security teams, the ubiquity of Log4j and the wide variety of places it could be present in enterprise IT environments made it challenging to find and remediate. Organizations that had immature asset management practices or imperfect asset inventories (almost everyone) were left with a ticking time bomb on their hands. Subsequently, many of the customers I advised managed the remediation of this vulnerability the same way they would manage an active cybersecurity incident. Using incident response processes instead of their vulnerability management processes enabled these teams to deem remediation as a top priority for their organizations and get access to resources commensurate with this declaration.

However, to make matters worse, more than one security update had to be released to fully address this critical-rated vulnerability, which was already in active use by attackers at the time. *CVE-2021-45046* stated, "*It was found that the fix to address CVE-2021-44228 in Apache Log4j 2.15.0 was incomplete in certain non-default configurations*" (CVE, December 14, 2021).

These factors resulted in much more work for cybersecurity and IT teams than remediating a typical critical-rated vulnerability. This scenario occurred at Christmas time in 2021 and spilled over into the new year, forcing many security teams to work through the holiday season on remediation. All these factors conspired to exhaust many cybersecurity and IT professionals. Months later, vulnerable versions of Log4j continued to endear themselves to cybersecurity and IT teams around the world, by continuing to "pop up" unexpectedly in many enterprise IT environments, seeping back in from a variety of sources such as vulnerable systems restored from backups, spinning up virtual machines from unpatched images, vendors continuing to deploy unpatched applications and appliances, continuing to operate systems past the end of their supportability dates, and many others. This fun and the associated risks will be around for years to come.

If you are interested in reading all the details about how the Log4j vulnerabilities were reported and the crisis unfolded, the US Cyber Safety Review Board investigated and published a report on their findings. I saw the board's chair from the Department of Homeland Security and the deputy chair from Google discuss the report and their findings at the Black Hat 2022 conference. It was interesting to hear about the **People's Republic of China** (**PRC**) government's reaction to the security researcher from Alibaba who found the vulnerability and initially reported it to the Apache Software Foundation, instead of to the PRC's **Ministry of Industry and Information Technology** (**MIIT**).

> *"Independent of a possible sanction against Alibaba, the Board noted troubling elements of MIIT's regulations governing disclosure of security vulnerabilities. The requirement for network product providers to report vulnerabilities in their products to MIIT within two days of discovery could give the PRC government early knowledge of vulnerabilities before vendor fixes are made available to the community. The Board is concerned this will afford the PRC government a window in which to exploit vulnerabilities before network defenders can patch them. This is a disturbing prospect given the PRC government's known track record of intellectual property theft, intelligence collection, surveillance of human rights activists and dissidents, and military cyber operations."*
>
> *Cyber Safety Review Board. July 11, 2022*

This quote lays bare how globally important and politically charged vulnerability disclosures can get! I'll discuss this tension in *Chapter 8, Friend or Foe? The Roles Governments Play in Cybersecurity*. If you are interested in reading the report, it can be downloaded from `https://www.cisa.gov/sites/default/files/publications/CSRB-Report-on-Log4-July-11-2022_508.pdf`.

Zero-day vulnerabilities aren't as rare as you might think. Data published by Microsoft indicates that, of the CVEs that were known to be exploited in Microsoft products in 2017, the first time they were exploited, 100% were zero-day vulnerabilities, and, in 2018, 83% were zero-day vulnerabilities (Miller, Matt, 2019).

Since then, data published by Google indicates there were a total of 490 zero-day vulnerabilities exploited in the wild between 2019 and 2025. That's an average of 70 zero-day vulnerabilities disclosed across the industry per year (an average of 6 per month) over a seven-year period. *Figure 3.1* illustrates the number of zero-day vulnerabilities that were confirmed to have been exploited in the wild between 2019 and 2025, published by Google.

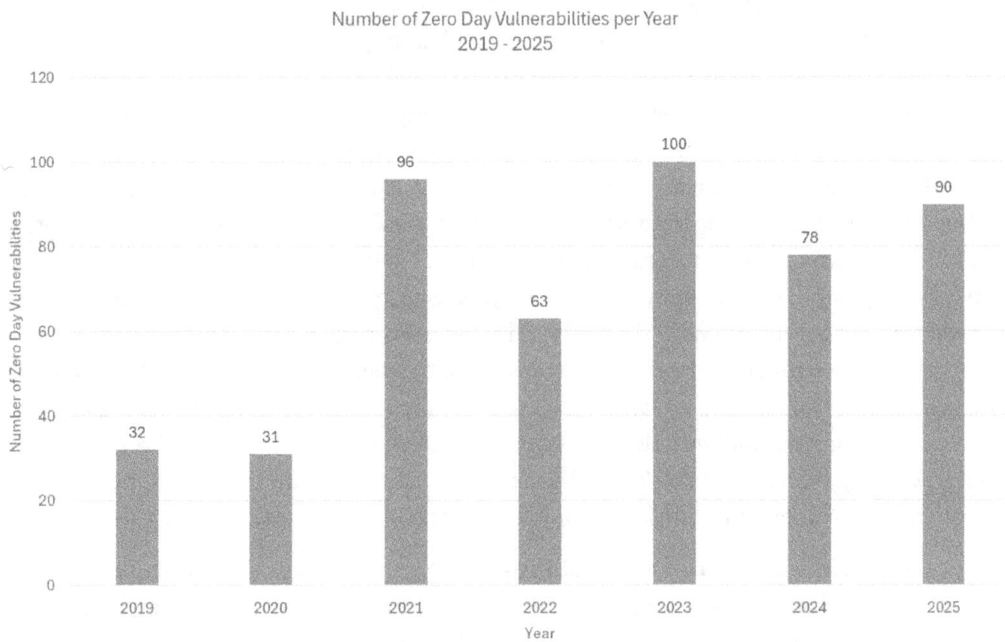

Figure 3.1 – Number of zero-day vulnerabilities disclosed across the industry per year between 2019 and 2025

> **Note**
>
> Here is a fun fact for you. I created a large, sensational news cycle in 2013 when I coined the term "*zero day forever*" in a blog post I wrote on Microsoft's official security blog. I was referring to any vulnerability found in Windows XP after official support for it ended. In this scenario, any vulnerability found in Windows XP after the end of support would be a *zero day forever*, as Microsoft would not provide ongoing security updates for it.
>
> Let me explain this in a little more detail. Attackers can wait for new security updates to be released for currently supported versions of Windows, such as Windows 11. Then, they reverse-engineer these updates to find the vulnerability that each update addresses. Then, they check whether those vulnerabilities are also present in Windows XP. If they are, and Microsoft won't release security updates for that operating system, then attackers will have zero-day vulnerabilities for Windows XP forever. To this day, you can search for the term "*zero day forever*" and find many news articles quoting me. I became the poster boy for the end-of-life of Windows XP because of that news cycle.

Over the years, I have talked to thousands of CISOs and vulnerability program managers about the practices they use to manage vulnerabilities for their organizations. These teams' time is typically consumed with ensuring that their asset management inventories are as accurate as possible, triaging incoming volumes of CVE IDs, ensuring that the design and operation of their vulnerability scanning infrastructure is sufficient, scanning for vulnerabilities and misconfigurations, communicating scan results and SLA compliance status, patching systems, and/or working with asset operators to patch systems, ideally within SLAs. Ideally, this work is like a well-oiled machine, but all too often, it is stressful and frustrating because of the tension between the goals of asset operators and their cybersecurity teams' desire to constantly reduce the risk for their organizations. If the goals and resources are not aligned between these two teams, they both struggle to meet expectations while the risks increase. This can lead CISOs and vulnerability management team managers to adopt different processes to manage vulnerabilities and misconfigurations based on the different philosophies and risk appetites their leadership expresses. Historically, the four most common groups of thought on the best way to manage vulnerabilities in large, complex enterprise environments are as follows:

- **Prioritize critical-rated vulnerabilities**: When updates or mitigations for critical-rated vulnerabilities become available, they are tested and deployed immediately. Lower-rated vulnerabilities are tested and deployed during regularly scheduled IT maintenance in order to minimize system reboots and disruption to business. These organizations are mitigating the highest-risk vulnerabilities as quickly as possible and are willing to accept significant risk in order to avoid constantly disrupting their environments with security update deployments.

  > **Tip**
  >
  > Remember, the difference between a critical-rated vulnerability and a high-severity vulnerability might be that the user needs to take some action, or a race condition exists on systems for successful exploitation.

  These organizations are gambling that high-severity vulnerabilities won't be exploited as quickly as critical-severity vulnerabilities. This reduces the number of CVE IDs they need to patch quickly, as the number of critical-rated vulnerabilities is typically a fraction of high-severity vulnerabilities. For example, in 2024, the number of high-severity vulnerabilities was 2.6 times that of critical-severity vulnerabilities (CVE Details, n.d.).

- **30/60/90-day policy approach**: This approach addresses critical and high-risk vulnerabilities within 30 days, medium-risk vulnerabilities within 60 days, and low-risk vulnerabilities within 90 days. Alternatively, I've seen 30-day SLAs assigned to critical-severity CVE IDs, 60 days to high-severity CVE IDs, and 90 days for medium- and low-severity CVE IDs. When high- and critical-rated vulnerabilities are publicly disclosed and are being actively exploited on the internet, these organizations' vulnerability management policies dictate that they will patch critical vulnerabilities or deploy available mitigations within 24 hours and high-rated vulnerabilities within a month. This approach aims to strike a balance between the number of CVE IDs that need to be addressed immediately, those that can wait a month, and those that can wait much longer. It is noteworthy that the number of medium-severity CVE IDs is typically comparable or even higher than the number of high-severity vulnerabilities in any given year.

- **No prioritization—just patch everything**: Some organizations have concluded that, given the continuous and growing volume of vulnerability disclosures that they are forced to manage, the effort they put into analyzing CVSS scores and prioritizing updates isn't worthwhile. Instead, they simply test and deploy all updates on essentially the same schedule. This schedule might be monthly, quarterly, or, for organizations with inflated risk appetites, semi-annually. These organizations focus on being really efficient at deploying security updates regardless of their severity ratings. Believe it or not, these vulnerability management teams tend to be the happiest of those I've met over the years. Expectations are set across the entire organization that this is simply the way IT is done, which dramatically reduces all the analysis paralysis, arguing, and negotiating timelines and scope that typically accompany processes that rely on CVSS scores for prioritization.
- **Delay deployment**: For organizations that are acutely sensitive to IT disruptions and have been disrupted by poor-quality security updates in the past, delaying the deployment of security updates has become an unfortunate practice. In other words, these organizations accept the risk related to all publicly known, unpatched vulnerabilities in the products they use for a period of months to ensure that security updates from their vendors aren't re-released due to quality issues. These organizations have decided that the cure is potentially worse than the disease; that is, disruption from poor-quality security updates poses the same or higher risk to them than all potential attackers in the world. The organizations that subscribe to this school of thought tend to bundle and deploy months' worth of updates. The appetite for risk among these organizations is high, to say the least.

A newer approach to managing vulnerabilities in large enterprise IT environments focuses even further on prioritizing specific vulnerabilities for remediation. It has become very popular among security teams. As I wrote in *Chapter 2*, **CTI** has many uses. One of those uses is to inform the priority of vulnerability remediation. Most of the organizations I have advised now use CTI to identify the vulnerabilities that are being used in active attacks on the internet. They view these vulnerabilities as the highest risk because their exploitation isn't just theoretical, which is what a CVSS score represents to many people. CVSS v4.0 does have an *exploit maturity* metric that can influence the CVSS scores for vulnerabilities with active exploits. Also, in an effort to help organizations prioritize remediation of CVE IDs, FIRST offers the **Exploit Prediction Scoring System** (**EPSS**). It provides the probability of exploitation in the wild for each CVE ID during the 30 days following its publication. FIRST describes the EPSS this way:

> *"The Exploit Prediction Scoring System (EPSS) is a data-driven effort for estimating the likelihood (probability) that a software vulnerability will be exploited in the wild. Our goal is to assist network defenders to better prioritize vulnerability remediation efforts. While other industry standards have been useful for capturing innate characteristics of a vulnerability and provide measures of severity, they are limited in their ability to assess threat. EPSS fills that gap because it uses current threat information from CVE and real-world exploit data. The EPSS model produces a probability score between 0 and 1 (0 and 100%). The higher the score, the greater the probability that a vulnerability will be exploited."*
>
> *FIRST, n.d.*

You can get all the details on this model at `https://www.first.org/epss/model`.

The bulk of the rest of this chapter is devoted to data and analysis with many graphs and tables. If you aren't interested in seeing the data and analysis, you can skip it and go right to the summary called *Vulnerability improvement framework summary*.

Industry vulnerability disclosure trends

Before we dig into the vulnerability disclosure data, let me tell you where the data comes from and provide some caveats regarding the validity and reliability of the data. There are three primary sources of data that I used for *Chapters 3* and *4*:

- The CVE list: `https://www.cve.org/`
- The NVD: `https://nvd.nist.gov/vuln/search`
- CVE Details: `https://www.cvedetails.com/`

The CVE list is the *de facto* authoritative source of vulnerability disclosures for the industry. The NVD imports data from the CVE list and adds metadata to it (including metrics and scoring information) (CVE, 2020). Finally, the CVSS is used to calculate severity scores for each CVE ID imported into the NVD.

However, this doesn't mean the data in the CVE list or the NVD is perfect, nor is the CVSS. I attended a session at the Black Hat USA conference in 2013 called *Buying into the Bias: Why Vulnerability Statistics Suck* (Martin, Brian, 2013). This session covered numerous biases in CVE data. You might be able to find this talk or the associated paper online, and I recommend watching the video or reading the paper so that you understand some of the limitations of the CVE data that I discuss in this chapter.

CVE Details is a great website that saved me a lot of time collecting and analyzing CVE data. CVE Details inherits the limitations of the NVD because it uses data from the NVD. It's worth reading how CVE Details works and its limitations (CVE Details, n.d.). Since the data and analysis that I provide in this chapter are based on the NVD and CVE Details, they inherit these limitations and biases. As I discussed earlier in this chapter, the CVSS versions were updated over time, and older CVE IDs were not going to be re-scored using the latest CVSS version. Subsequently, my analysis of CVSS scores mostly uses CVSS v3 as it was consistently the newest version of the CVSS that was used to score most of the CVE IDs I examined. For really long timelines, I was forced to use a mix of CVSS v3 and v2. The lack of CVSS version continuity across CVE IDs is not ideal for such an analysis.

Given that the two primary sources of data that I used for the analysis in this chapter have stated limitations and the CVSS has changed dramatically over the years, I can state with confidence that my analysis is not entirely accurate or complete. Also, vulnerability data changes over time as the NVD is updated constantly. My analysis is based on a snapshot of the CVE data taken months ago that is no longer up to date or accurate. I'm providing this analysis to illustrate how vulnerability disclosures were trending over time, but I make no warranty about this data—use it at your own risk.

Vulnerability disclosures 1999 to now

First, let's look at the vulnerability disclosures each year since the CVE list was started in 1999. It is interesting to note that I can find vulnerabilities with publication dates going back to January 1989 (*CVE-1999-1471*) in the NVD. Vulnerabilities published prior to 1999 appear to have been assigned CVE IDs starting with "1999" because that's when the first CVE list was collected and published by MITRE. An archived bulletin published by the **Computer Security Division Information Technology Laboratory** (**ITL**) at NIST in July 2000 provides some historical insight into the early days of the NVD. NIST's original CVE search service was called ICAT, as described here:

> *"The Computer Security Division at NIST's Information Technology Laboratory has created a searchable index containing 700 of the most important publicly known computer security vulnerabilities. This index, called ICAT (pronounced eye-cat), helps the user to search for specific vulnerabilities and identify those vulnerabilities that are applicable to their organizations... The vulnerability information indexed*

> *by ICAT pertains to those vulnerabilities included in a standard vulnerability naming scheme called CVE (Common Vulnerabilities and Exposures)... Since the current list of 700 vulnerabilities is too large for system administrators to manually review, we created ICAT to allow one to search for vulnerabilities applicable to a particular organization's hosts."*
>
> *Mell, Peter. NIST. 2000*

The reviewer for the second and third editions of this book, Karen Kent, worked closely with Peter Mell and others at NIST to develop the NVD as the successor to ICAT. The NVD was launched in mid-2005. Analysts at NIST performed CVSS v1 scoring for all the existing ICAT vulnerabilities. They then used that body of scoring data to inform improvements for CVSS v2 (Kent, Karen, personal communication, September 4, 2022).

The total number of vulnerabilities assigned a CVE ID between 1999 and the end of 2025 was over 309,000 (CVE Details, n.d.). As *Figure 3.2* illustrates, there was a large increase in disclosures in 2017 that has not receded to historically typical volumes since; a new era in vulnerability disclosures started in 2017.

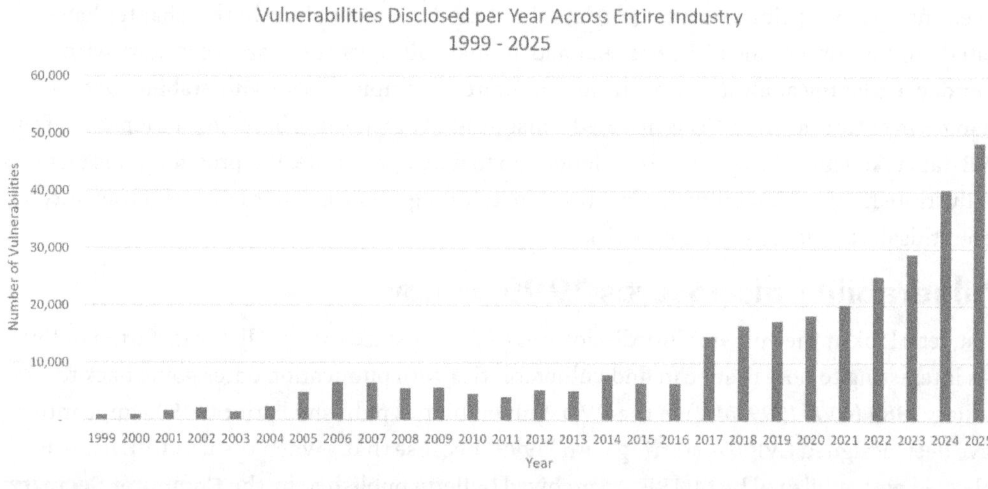

Figure 3.2 – Vulnerabilities disclosed across the industry per year (1999–2025)

There was a 128% increase in disclosures between 2016 and 2017, and a 157% increase between 2016 and 2018. Put another way, in 2016, vulnerability management teams were managing 18 new vulnerabilities per day on average. That number increased to 40 vulnerabilities per day in 2017 and 45 per day in 2018, on average. As *Figure 3.3* illustrates, vulnerability management teams were managing 55 new vulnerabilities per day on average in 2021, a 206% increase from 2016 levels:

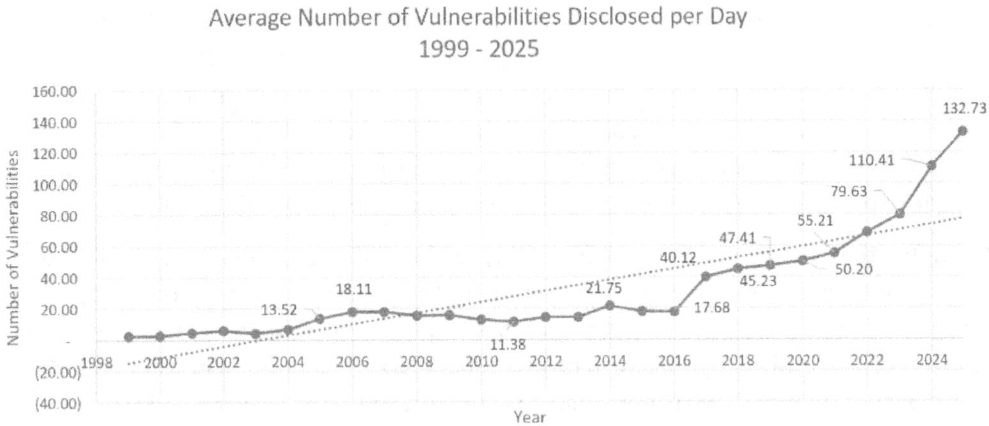

Figure 3.3 – Average number of vulnerabilities disclosed per day between 1999 and 2025

If things couldn't be more challenging for vulnerability management teams, the number of disclosures continued to increase rapidly during the next three years. Average daily vulnerability disclosures increased 25% in 2022, another 16% in 2023, another 39% in 2024, and 20% in 2025. That's a 651% increase in the average number of daily disclosures between 2016 and 2025, with vulnerability management teams facing 110 disclosures per day on average in 2024 and 133 disclosures per day in 2025.

> **Note**
>
> Many of the organizations I advised during these years did not increase the staffing levels or budget for their vulnerability management and remediation teams commensurate with these increases. This is one factor that helps explain why so many enterprises carry large inventories of unpatched vulnerabilities, dramatically increasing the risk to them. If their remediation teams are not keeping up with 133 or more new vulnerability disclosures every day (including weekends and holidays), that's potentially 931 vulnerabilities per week, 3,990 per month, and over 48,500 new vulnerabilities in a year to triage.

Vulnerability management teams review new disclosures to determine which ones affect the software and hardware in their asset inventories. No organization—unless it's a technology museum—runs every affected product, but most will have a subset of disclosures that apply to them each week or month. Larger and older organizations typically face a broader impact because they carry decades of legacy technology alongside modern systems.

Once affected technologies are identified, vulnerability teams work with asset owners to remediate them. The workload scales with both the number of new vulnerabilities and the number of systems, devices, or instances they impact. Organizations that can't keep pace quickly accumulate a backlog while still facing a constant stream of new CVE disclosures, dramatically increasing their risk exposure. In large enterprises without mature vulnerability management capabilities, this can balloon into hundreds of thousands or even millions of unpatched vulnerabilities. At that scale, the problem becomes overwhelming, and teams struggle to see a viable path to reducing the inventory of unpatched vulnerabilities.

Remember that a single unpatched vulnerability can be all the opportunity attackers need to initially compromise an enterprise IT environment. There are many examples of a single unpatched vulnerability leading to data breaches of major corporations that made headlines. Attackers can take advantage of unpatched vulnerabilities in many different ways, including using purpose-built tools, malware, email attachments, and drive-by download attacks, among other methods. Unpatched vulnerabilities are also used by attackers to move laterally, persist, and get access to systems post-compromise. Unpatched vulnerabilities are also used in dreaded mass ransomware attacks—remember the WannaCry "crypto-worm" ransomware attack that impacted hundreds of thousands of systems around the world?

Subsequently, carrying massive inventories of unpatched vulnerabilities is like setting sail in a submarine that you know has holes in the hull. I'd often ask executives that I advised, who were a little cavalier about the state of vulnerability management in their IT environments, whether they would put their families and retirement savings in such a submarine and set sail, knowing the state of the condition of the hull. To date, I haven't found one executive who said they would do such a thing.

A risk-based approach, informed by the **CTI** that I discussed in *Chapter 2*, that makes heavy use of automation can help manage this new normal. Alternatively, as I have pleaded with so many enterprises to do, moving to modern compute environments such as the cloud can dramatically change this calculus. I'll share more on this approach in *Chapter 13*.

CVE Numbering Authorities

You might be wondering what factors contributed to such a large increase in vulnerability disclosures since 2016. The primary initial factor was likely a change made to how CVE identifiers are assigned to vulnerabilities in the CVE list. During this time, the CVE anointed and authorized what they call **CVE Numbering Authorities** (**CNAs**) to assign CVE identifiers to new vulnerabilities (CVE, n.d.). According to MITRE, the organization that manages the CVE process that populates the NVD with data,

> *CNAs are vendor, researcher, open source, CERT, hosted service, bug bounty provider, and consortium organizations authorized by the CVE Program to assign CVE IDs to vulnerabilities and publish CVE Records within their own specific scopes of coverage.*
>
> *CVE (n.d.)*

> Note
>
> CVE usage
>
> MITRE hereby grants you a perpetual, worldwide, non-exclusive, no-charge, royalty-free, irrevocable copyright license to reproduce, prepare derivative works of, publicly display, publicly perform, sublicense, and distribute Common Vulnerabilities and Exposures (CVE™). Any copy you make for such purposes is authorized, provided that you reproduce MITRE's copyright designation and this license in any such copy.

The advent of CNAs means that there are now many more organizations assigning CVE identifiers since 2016. On January 1, 2020, there were 110 organizations in 21 countries participating as CNAs. By July 2022, the number of CNAs had grown to 232 organizations in 35 countries, and by July 2025, there were 458 CNAs in 39 countries (CVE, n.d.). That's a 316% increase in the number of organizations entering CVEs into the NVD, in less than 6 years! The names, locations, and program roles of the CNAs are available at `https://www.cve.org/PartnerInformation/ListofPartners`.

CNAs using automation to rapidly find and document more CVEs have also been credited, or blamed (depending on your point of view), for the exponential increases in CVE IDs over the past few years. The quality and efficacy of such CVE IDs have been questioned. Clearly, allowing CNAs to assign CVE IDs has made the process of assigning CVE identifiers more efficient, thus leading to a large increase in vulnerability disclosures in 2017 and every year since.

There are several other factors that have contributed to the higher volumes of vulnerability disclosures since 2017. First, the software industry has expanded dramatically with more people and machines churning out code than ever before. AI coding assistant tools have enabled developers to churn out more code than ever before. There have been studies that detract from such tools, claiming they actually make developers slower. However, the developers I work with indicate that these tools that write, fix, and improve code have definitely helped them write code faster. More code means more vulnerabilities in the code.

There are more people and organizations doing vulnerability research than ever before, and they have better tools than in the past. Finding new vulnerabilities is big business, and a lot of people are eager to get a piece of that pie. However, most of the focus has been on critical and high-severity vulnerabilities. This is where the money is, and many security researchers are only interested in finding the most valuable vulnerabilities to maximize the return on their investments in time, expertise, and expenses. This leaves reporting of lower severity vulnerabilities largely to the vendors themselves. Stated another way, vendors largely engage in the honor system to self-report low-rated vulnerabilities. This has likely led to the under-reporting of low-rated vulnerabilities. After all, it is easier to simply fix low-risk bugs that aren't exploitable, for the next product update, than go through the vulnerability-reporting process and patch them individually.

The distribution of the severity of the CVE IDs assigned between 1999 and 2025 is illustrated in *Figure 3.4* (CVE Details, n.d.):

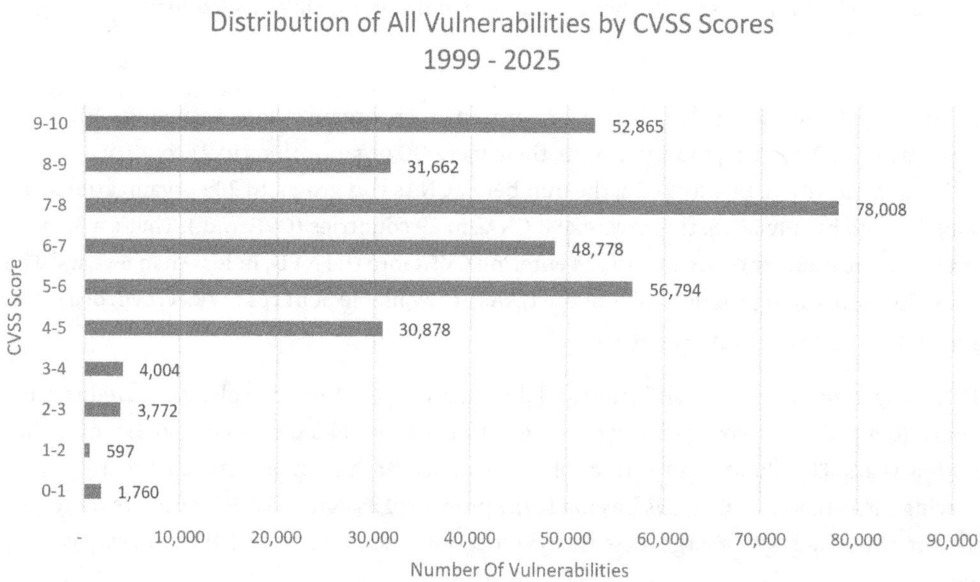

Figure 3.4 – CVSS scores by severity (1999–2025)

There are almost three times more CVEs rated medium severity (136,450 CVEs with CVSS scores between 4 and 6.9) than critical severity (52,865 CVEs with CVSS scores between 9.0 and 10.0). The number of critical and high-severity vulnerabilities combined constitutes a little more than half (53%) of all the vulnerabilities disclosed in this 26-year period. The weighted average CVSS score over this period is 7.6.

> **Tip**
>
> Keep in mind that since low-severity vulnerabilities are likely under-reported, the weighted average of all vulnerabilities, including those not reported, is almost certainly lower than that of reported vulnerabilities.

For organizations that have vulnerability management policies dictating the emergency deployment of all critical-rated vulnerabilities, that's potentially almost 53,000 emergency deployments over this 26-year period. For most organizations, it will be a fraction of this number, but this is still likely to represent hundreds or thousands of emergency deployments over the years. This is one reason why some organizations decide not to prioritize security updates based on severity—there are too many high- and critical-severity vulnerabilities to make managing them differently from lower-rated vulnerabilities an effective use of time.

Many of the best vulnerability management teams I've advised over the years focused on becoming really efficient at testing and deploying security updates in their environment so that they could deploy all updates as quickly as possible without disrupting the business, regardless of their severity. This represents real risk reduction for their organizations and, frankly, they were among the most satisfied vulnerability management teams I met.

It is easy for vulnerability management teams to feel overwhelmed and underappreciated. Many of them focus on crunching numbers and over-analyzing data to justify testing and patching fewer security updates, reducing their workloads, and asking the organization to accept more risk. These teams tend to spend more time analyzing and arguing about asset inventories, asset ownership, the efficacy of workarounds, and modified CVSS base scores than turning the crank and just patching. I have a high level of empathy and a lot of respect for all vulnerability management teams, regardless of the approach they adopt—these are among the hardest jobs in cybersecurity and tend to be under-resourced.

Let's dive a little deeper into the long-term trends of critical and high-severity vulnerabilities that have CVSS scores of 7 and higher. As I mentioned previously, most security teams focus on remediating these vulnerabilities first because they are the highest risk. As *Figure 3.5* illustrates, the number of critical and high-severity vulnerabilities jumped dramatically between 2016 and 2017, moving from 3,879 in 2016 to 8,994 CVE IDs disclosed in 2017.

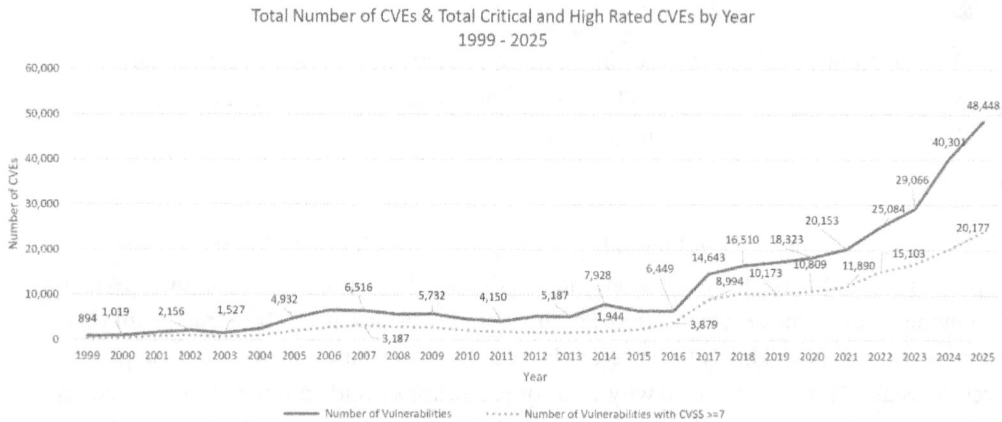

Figure 3.5 – Total number of CVEs by year and the total number of critical- and high-severity CVEs by year (1999–2025)

This represents a 132% increase in disclosures of the most severe vulnerabilities in a single year. The figure also shows us that although the number of critical and high-severity vulnerabilities was relatively flat between 2018 and 2020, as the total number of vulnerabilities continued to increase, there has been a dramatic upward trend since (CVE Details, n.d.). The advent of the CNAs assigning CVE IDs and publishing CVE records has essentially supercharged vulnerability disclosures compared to the prior 17 years of the NVD. Clearly, the CNAs are not just filing low- and medium-severity vulnerabilities, when more critical and high-severity vulnerabilities were filed in 2017 than vulnerabilities of all severities in 2016.

Figure 3.6 reveals that 2018 was the year that the industry hit an all-time high of 62.8% of total vulnerability disclosures rated critical and high severity:

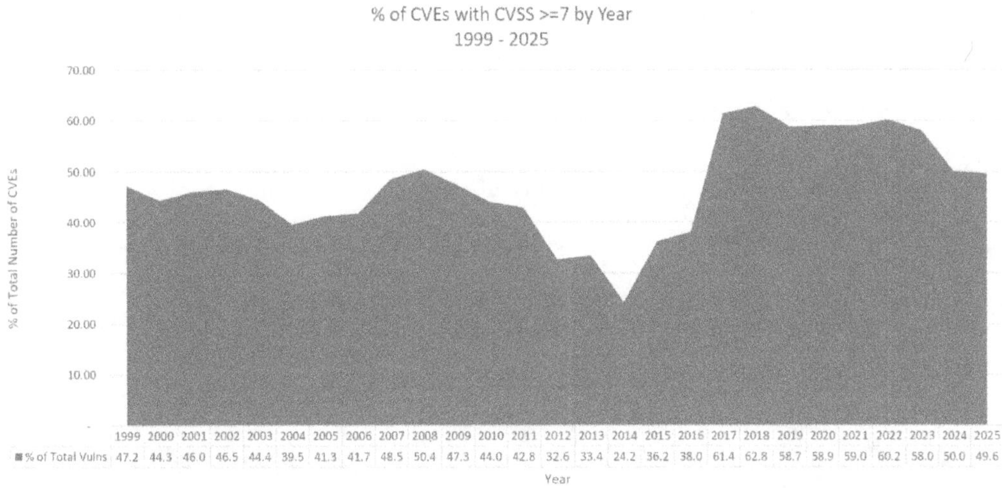

Figure 3.6 – CVEs rated critical or high severity as a percentage of the total of all CVEs, by year (1999–2025)

The figure also shows us that in 2021, critical and high vulnerabilities represented 59% of all vulnerability disclosures that year, and 60% in 2022. These recent highs receded to 58%, 50%, and 49.6% in 2023, 2024, and 2025, respectively.

However, don't open the champagne just yet. The aforementioned 132% increase between 2016 and 2017 is plain as day in *Figure 3.7*. When translated into potential work for vulnerability management teams and remediation teams, *Figure 3.7* reveals that the average number of vulnerability disclosures per day that have CVSS scores of 7 or higher has never been higher:

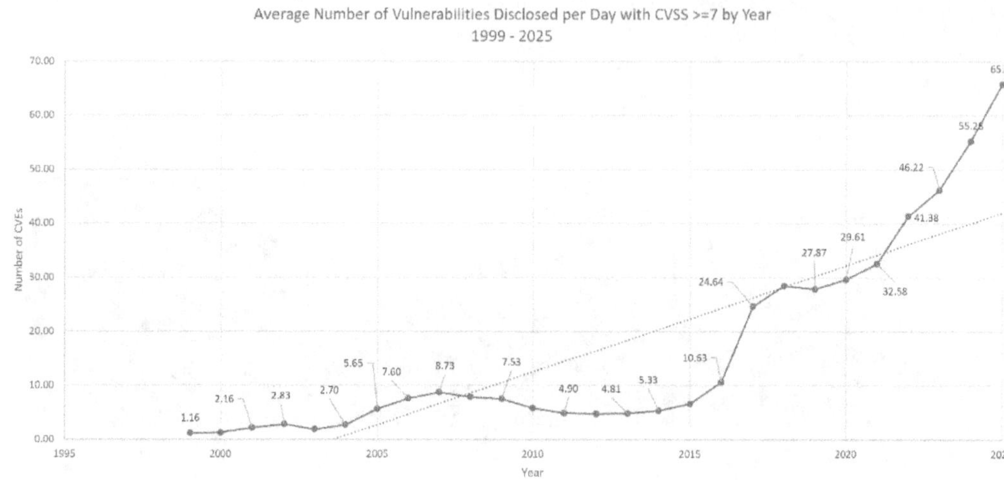

Figure 3.7 – Average number of vulnerabilities disclosed per day that are rated critical or high severity, by year (1999–2025)

With an average of 66 new critical or high-rated CVEs disclosed every day in 2025, vulnerability management teams and remediation teams need highly efficient people, processes, and technologies to keep up with the volume. Left untended, that volume is potentially 461 CVEs per week, 1,975 CVEs per month, and over 24,000 CVEs per year, all of which have the highest probability of exploitation. The number of vulnerabilities multiplied by the number of instances, systems, and IoT devices that these vulnerabilities impact means the inventory of unpatched vulnerabilities can get very large, very fast.

Remember my story about all the successful worm attacks in 2003? The daily average volume of critical- and high-severity vulnerability disclosures back then was 30 times less than it was in 2024. How times have changed. Fortunately, the volume of vulnerability disclosures isn't the only thing that has changed; capabilities to detect, block, contain, and respond to exploitation have as well.

For example, security teams would have been able to reduce the potential maximum average number of new vulnerabilities to investigate every day from 110 to 55 in 2024 by using vulnerability severity to prioritize near-term remediation. Focusing on the most severe vulnerabilities helps reduce the number of vulnerabilities to triage every day and reduces risk.

After 8 years of significantly increased volumes of vulnerability disclosures, which continue to grow every year, this appears to be the new normal for the industry, leading to much more risk and more work to manage. And with the specter of ransomware, which could be an extinction event for a business, the pressure on security teams has never been higher. I attended multiple briefings at the Black Hat conference in 2025, where the topics discussed included how to use

AI (large language models specifically) to find, exploit, and fix vulnerabilities. This area of security research is nascent and promises to help identify vulnerabilities faster and more efficiently than ever. Given this, CVE ID volumes are likely to continue increasing.

Analysis of CISA's KEV catalog

Security teams that use CTI on active exploitation can potentially reduce the number of CVE IDs to triage every day, even further. As I mentioned earlier in this chapter, CISA provides an authoritative list of CVE IDs that are known to have been exploited in the wild, called the KEV catalog. Although I use the KEV catalog frequently in my job as a CISO, since I'm not intimately familiar with this source of CTI, my observations here are more speculative and limited to comments about the data itself. At the time of writing, I counted 1,483 CVE IDs in the KEV catalog entered in the 5 years between 2021 and 2025. I counted 185 CVE IDs that were added to the KEV catalog in 2024 and 245 added in 2025 (a 32% increase from 2024). This means CISA identified 185 CVE IDs that were being actively exploited in the wild in 2024 and 245 in 2025, which were previously not known to be exploited by CISA. *Figure 3.8* shows the volume of CVE IDs published in the KEV catalog each year since 2021.

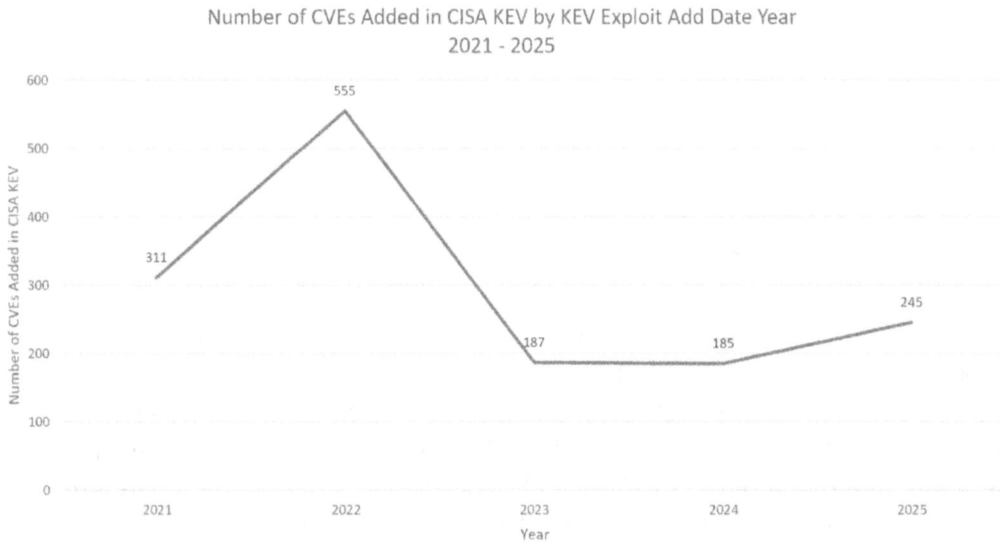

Figure 3.8 – Number of CVE IDs added to the KEV catalog each year between 2021 and 2025

CISA started publishing the KEV catalog in November 2021. This means they only had 2 months of operating time in 2021, in which they managed to add 311 vulnerabilities that they had confirmed were exploited in the wild. 2022 was the first full year of the KEV catalog's operation, in which CISA added 555 CVE IDs to the catalog of known exploited CVE IDs. They had public exploitation of CVE IDs from the prior 20 years to potentially enter into the KEV catalog, which might explain why so many were entered in 2022 compared to other years. In 2023 and 2024, the volume of CVE IDs added to the KEV catalog was 187 and 187 CVE IDs, respectively, as *Figure 3.8* illustrates. My uninformed interpretation of these five years of data is that 2022 was an outlier, as they likely had a large backlog of known exploited vulnerabilities that they processed that year. I surmise that after the backlog was processed, 2023 and 2024 represented more typical years in terms of the volume of new CVE IDs added to the KEV catalog. To test this hypothesis, I analyzed which year each CVE ID was published in and the year it was added to the KEV catalog. I wanted to see which year each CVE ID was added to the catalog to get a view into how old each CVE ID was when it was added to the catalog. *Figure 3.9* provides the results of this analysis:

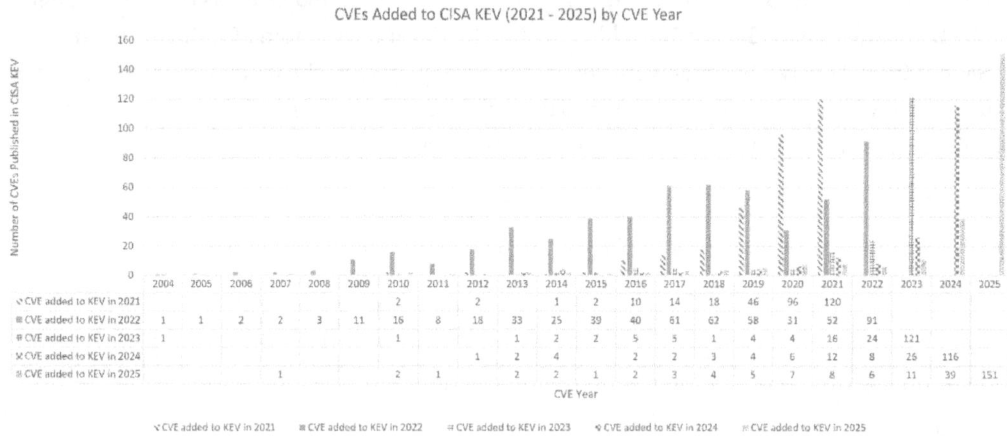

Figure 3.9 – Number of CVE IDs added to the KEV catalog each year between 2021 and 2025 by the date when the CVE ID was first published

Looking at the CVE IDs added to the KEV catalog in 2022, we can see that CVE IDs that were published in 19 different years were added to the catalog that year, going as far back as 2004. There's no other year where CISA added so many CVE IDs published from so many different years. The data suggests that CISA added 91 CVEs that were published in 2022 to the KEV catalog that same year. However, the other 464 CVE IDs (84%) were from other years. The average age of CVE IDs added to the KEV catalog in 2022 was 5 years, because of the age of the CVE IDs in the backlog that were added that year. The average age of CVE IDs added to the KEV catalog in 2023, 2024, and 2025 was 1.2 years, 1.3 years, and 1.5 years, respectively. However, note that very old CVE IDs were added to the KEV in all these years, the oldest being 19 years old in 2023, 12 years old in 2024, and 18 years old in 2025.

Now, let's look at the severity of the CVE IDs added to the KEV during those five years. To do this, we need to use data from CVE Details because CISA doesn't publish CVSS scores in the downloadable version of the KEV catalog. At the time of writing, CVE Details provides a subset (1,348 CVE IDs) of the 1,483 CVE IDs in the KEV. The average, median, and lowest CVSS scores of the CVE IDs added to the KEV catalog during this time period are 8.6, 8.8, and 3.3, respectively. *Figure 3.10* illustrates the CVSS max base score distribution of the 1,348 CVE IDs added to the KEV catalog between 2021 and 2025:

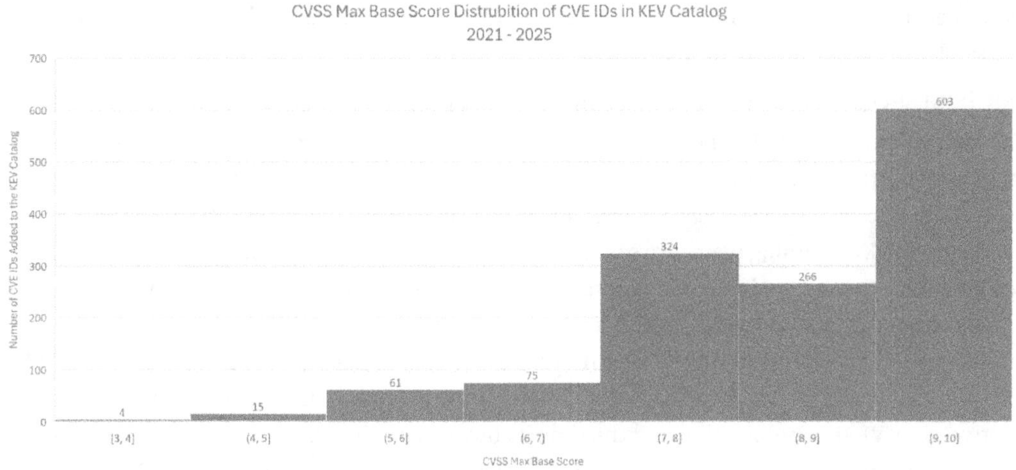

Figure 3.10 – CVSS max base score distribution of the CVE IDs added to the KEV between 2021 and 2025 (CVE Details, n.d.)

This shows us that 4 CVE IDs (0.15% of the total) were low severity, 151 (11.2% of the total) were medium severity, 590 (43.8%) were high severity, and 603 (44.7%) were critical severity. Looking at only the CVE IDs added to the KEV catalog in 2025 (the last full year we have data for), the average CVSS score of CVE IDs added was 8.3, the median score was 8.8, and the lowest CVSS score added was 4.

The rate at which CVE IDs were added to the KEV catalog was 0.5 CVE IDs per day, on average, in both 2023 and 2024. In 2025, this increased to 0.67 CVE IDs added to the KEV catalog per day. This represents a substantial increase in the number of CVE IDs that CISA saw exploited in the wild in 2025 compared to the previous two years. One could argue that CISA has just gotten more efficient at finding evidence of vulnerability exploitation, but this data suggests that vulnerability management teams will continue to have their hands full managing vulnerabilities with the highest possible risk.

What other conclusions do I draw from this analysis? First, it is very helpful to have an authoritative source of exploited vulnerabilities to help drive remediation of vulnerabilities with the highest probability of exploitation. Every time old, known exploited CVE IDs seep back into your environment or new ones are added to the KEV catalog, having a list of them at your fingertips makes it easier to identify them in your asset inventory and track their remediation. Sometimes, this type of data is necessary to get stubborn stakeholders to approve near-term action.

My second observation is that 5 years of KEV catalog data is likely not enough data to draw solid conclusions from, given that the first 2 years of data reported were during the years the KEV catalog program was bootstrapping and addressing a 20-year backlog. The question is whether the volume of CVE IDs added to the KEV catalog in 2025 is the beginning of a new normal or an outlier? Only time will tell.

My third observation is that, assuming that the data from 2023 and 2024 describe more normal volumes of CVE IDs being added to the KEV catalog, vulnerability management teams will have to triage fewer than 200 CVE IDs per year if all they focused on was CVE IDs that were added to the KEV catalog. However, in each of those years, about one-third of all CVE IDs added to the KEV catalog were years old, and in several cases, over a decade old. The requirement to have evidence of exploitation means that by the time vulnerability management teams understand the need to triage a given vulnerability, it has already been used for attacks on the internet. It's hard to believe that CVE IDs that are 5, 10, or 20 years old haven't been used in attacks until they suddenly show up in the KEV catalog. The time between a CVE ID's publication and the time it shows up in the KEV catalog represents risk to those vulnerability management teams that choose to only take action once CVE IDs show up in the KEV.

There is time between when attackers can start exploiting a vulnerability, when they are observed doing so, and when up-to-date CTI that reflects this is distributed. Some exploitations might never be observed. Most vulnerability management teams would be uncomfortable leaving a 10-year-old critical-rated vulnerability unpatched on internet-facing assets because it hasn't appeared in the KEV catalog. CISA doesn't advocate such an approach, but I still run into CISOs that gravitate heavily towards it because it reduces the amount of work their over-worked vulnerability management and remediation teams must do. Using the KEV catalog to inform a broader vulnerability prioritization framework seems to be a less risky approach to vulnerability management than mitigating only those CVE IDs that appear in the KEV catalog.

> **Note**
>
> The KEV catalog is available for download from `https://www.cisa.gov/known-exploited-vulnerabilities-catalog`.

Finally, it is likely surprising to some that there are low- and medium-severity CVE IDs in the KEV catalog. About 11% of CVE IDs added to the KEV catalog between 2021 and 2025 weren't high- or critical-severity CVE IDs. Lower severity CVE IDs generally get forgotten among the huge volumes of higher severity vulnerabilities. This raises the question as to whether deprioritizing medium-severity vulnerabilities is the right approach for more risk-averse organizations.

In June of 2025, it was reported that CISA faced dramatic budget and staffing cuts of approximately $495 million and 1,000 staff (Scroxton, June 2, 2025). However, it doesn't appear that those reductions impacted the operation of the KEV catalog, given there was a 32% increase in CVEs entered into the KEV catalog in 2025. The future volumes of CVE ID additions to the KEV catalog can be compared to *Figure 3.8* to gain insight into volume changes.

Now that we have visibility into the growing volume of vulnerability disclosures across the industry, it is likely obvious that huge backlogs of unpatched vulnerabilities mount quickly if teams don't work with enough urgency to address them. Let's discuss how quickly vulnerability management and remediation teams should work to address vulnerabilities.

Vulnerability remediation SLAs

Today, many security teams use CTI to identify and remediate the CVE IDs that are actively being exploited as quickly as possible. Then, they work to meet the SLAs that their organization has put in place for critical and high-severity vulnerabilities. Many CISOs and vulnerability management teams I've met use the 30/60/90-day policy approach; they address critical and high-risk vulnerabilities within 30 days, medium-risk vulnerabilities within 60 days, and low-risk vulnerabilities within 90 days. Alternatively, I've seen 30-day SLAs assigned to critical severity CVE IDs, 60 days to high severity CVE IDs, and 90 days for medium and low severity CVE IDs. I have also seen much more aggressive SLAs and much less aggressive SLAs—theoretically, these SLAs are a function of the risk appetite of each organization. However, I have met very few executives who really understand just how much risk their vulnerability remediation SLAs represent to their organizations; these SLAs and compliance with them are typically a function of how fast their remediation teams can work based on target resourcing levels.

As a CISO who has managed several vulnerability management teams in my career, I typically advocate for aggressive vulnerability remediation SLAs, especially if there is a large backlog of vulnerabilities. To do this, I have found it helpful to define different SLAs based on asset value or the probability of unpatched vulnerability exploitation. Using this approach, there are typically three different categories of assets I employ: internet-facing, crown jewels, and everything else.

Internet-facing

Internet-facing IT assets are systems that are not only accessible from inside the organization's network perimeter, but also from the internet. This includes systems behind firewalls and inside **demilitarized zones (DMZs)**. For example, an application server that hosts applications to users on the internet is internet-facing even if it is behind a firewall or inside a DMZ. Another example is an email server; they typically process inbound and outbound email using network connections to other email servers on the internet. It doesn't matter that the email server is behind firewalls because it is receiving packets from the internet regardless of whether those packets get proxied by firewalls or proxy servers. The increased risk for these systems is that attackers can interact with them, by design, regardless of how many firewalls they are behind. Application servers, email servers, and other internet-facing systems expose network ports and potentially receive input from actors on the internet. These systems are more accessible to attackers than other systems (insider threat scenarios aside). The internet-facing category of assets is important to get right because assets in this category have the highest probability of getting attacked, given their proximity to attackers and their functions. If a system accepts unsolicited TCP/IP packets from the internet, even if they go through multiple firewalls or other routing and switching equipment, it's an internet-facing asset for vulnerability management purposes.

Some vulnerability remediation teams love to get lawyerly in conversations about this asset category, coming up with imaginative arguments about why assets that receive network traffic from the internet shouldn't be considered internet-facing. Successfully claiming that an asset isn't really internet-facing means they'd have to comply with a much less aggressive remediation SLA. An example is arguing that since an asset has two network interfaces and one is used for management and only connected to a management network, then the asset isn't internet-facing, although the other network interface sends and receives network traffic to and from the internet. They are essentially arguing that the system can only be attacked using the vulnerability in question via the management interface on an internal network. Sometimes, the vendor that owns the technology in which the vulnerability is, makes these statements when they release the update to address it. But I can tell you from my experience working in the MSRC, attackers live to prove such vendors wrong.

> **Tip**
>
> My advice to vulnerability remediation teams is to avoid the temptation to spend time debating the conditions under which a critical or high-severity vulnerability, especially one in the KEV catalog, can be exploited. Instead, focus your time on developing the people, processes, technologies, and automation that enable you to patch vulnerabilities of any severity as efficiently as possible. Your stakeholders will be happier; you'll be happier and more effective at reducing real risk for your organization.

Internet-facing assets need to be patched aggressively, especially critical and high-severity vulnerabilities, and those CVE IDs in the KEV catalog. If a vulnerability on an internet-facing asset is in the KEV catalog, an aggressive SLA is appropriate. I've seen organizations use SLAs between immediately and 15 days for these types of vulnerabilities. Although I'm sure there are organizations that don't prioritize this category of vulnerability and patch them with other CVE IDs 30 days or 60 days after the updates have been published. In my opinion, giving attackers more than 24 hours to attack unpatched and proven exploitable vulnerabilities on internet-facing assets is a recipe for failure. It's not the kind of failure you learn from, because this failure is predictable and not something you have to experience to learn from. It is also the very type of risk that cybersecurity teams get paid to mitigate.

Critical and high-severity CVE IDs without known exploitation on internet-facing assets get a bit more lead time, such as 48 or 72 hours. These can be super aggressive and hard to achieve, depending on the size and complexity of the environment. Often, remediating operating systems and applications is managed by two different teams. Application owners and operators tend to have the most challenging job patching because they need to test that their applications will still work as designed after security updates are deployed. Compressed timeframes in which to accomplish this add pressure on these teams. This is why so many organizations opt to patch every quarter or every 6 months.

> **Note**
>
> As I'll discuss in *Chapter 9, Ingredients for a Successful Cybersecurity Strategy*, your application owners' constraints are not shared by attackers who don't wait until application owners are ready before attacking. Developing the people, processes, technologies, and automation to patch vulnerabilities quickly on internet-facing assets, which attackers already know how to exploit, is not optional today. Failure to do so means your cybersecurity strategy is based on hope. These leaders hope that attackers do not find unpatched vulnerabilities in the assets they can discover and access from the internet, and they hope attackers do not decide to exploit those vulnerabilities using exploits that are already available or might become publicly available, while they are unpatched for days or months. They are true gamblers at heart.

Finally, it seems like medium- and low-severity vulnerabilities are an afterthought for most organizations. Most organizations rightfully focus their attention and efforts on the constant drumbeat of new critical and high-severity CVE IDs. But they rarely get the time to drain the swamp of the growing number of lower-severity vulnerabilities. Simply failing to patch medium- and low-severity vulnerabilities is riskier than it seems. Since many security teams focus on mitigating critical and high-severity vulnerabilities first, attackers have been using combinations or *chains* of lower-severity vulnerabilities to compromise systems for many years. Failing to address such vulnerabilities in a timely fashion and allowing large inventories to accumulate is not a best practice of a well-run vulnerability management program. Remember, critical and high-severity vulnerabilities combined only comprise roughly 50–60% of all CVE IDs in any given year.

Crown jewels

The second category of assets that I typically assign a vulnerability remediation SLA to is the **crown jewels**. Crown jewels are the *highest-value assets* an organization has. These assets can be **systems**, **infrastructure**, **processes**, and **data**. Examples of crown jewels include systems that process, store, or transmit customer data, employee data, intellectual property, and unreleased financial data. I will discuss the crown jewels in more detail in *Chapter 9, Ingredients for a Successful Cybersecurity Strategy*. Given their value to the organization, if a crown jewel were compromised, it would be very impactful to the organization, perhaps devastating. Subsequently, the crown jewels should have aggressive vulnerability remediation SLAs assigned to them. If a crown jewel is internet-facing, it already should have a super-aggressive SLA assigned to it, as I previously discussed. Crown jewels that are not internet-facing typically do not need such an aggressive SLA, but vulnerabilities in them should be remediated faster than the average IT asset. After all, crown jewels are the highest value assets. If the SLA to address a critical-rated vulnerability is 30 days for ordinary assets, for example, the SLA for a crown jewel should be half that: 15 days. Unlike an internet-facing asset's super-aggressive SLA for critical vulnerabilities in the KEV catalog, crown jewels get more lead time for testing and deployment, such as 5 days instead of 24 hours. This approach acknowledges the outsized importance of crown jewels but gives their owners and operators time to test updates before deploying them, so they don't disrupt regular operations. Again, I've seen a range of SLAs used for crown jewels among the vulnerability management teams I've advised over the years. Some teams adopt aggressive SLAs to reduce the risk of a potential extinction event, while others assign the same SLAs they have on all other assets to their highest value assets. We'll revisit this topic in *Chapter 9*.

Everything else

These assets aren't internet-facing and aren't crown jewels, so they generally carry lower inherent risk. They're less likely to be compromised because they sit behind multiple layers of protection, and a breach typically has a smaller organizational impact. As a result, they often have longer vulnerability-remediation SLAs.

However, once attackers gain initial access, they readily exploit unpatched vulnerabilities and misconfigurations on these lower-value systems to move laterally, maintain persistence, exfiltrate data, or deploy ransomware. An organization may view these assets as low risk, but attackers do not.

Establishing remediation SLAs that accurately reflect your organization's risk appetite and regularly reporting SLA performance to senior leadership is strongly recommended.

So far, we've looked at the growing volume of vulnerability disclosures and discussed how quickly they need to be remediated based on the relative value of assets and the likelihood of exploitation. Now, let's dive deeper into the vulnerability disclosure trends for specific popular vendors. This will give you some idea of the volume of vulnerability disclosures that your organization faces if it is leveraging these vendors.

Vendor vulnerability trends

At this point, you might be wondering what type of products these vulnerabilities are in. Both **Information Technology** (**IT**) and **Operational Technology** (**OT**) have vulnerabilities. In this section, we'll look at the aggregate vulnerabilities of three top vendors that millions of enterprises and consumers use around the world.

Table 3.2 categorizes the top 25 products with the highest number of CVE IDs assigned to them into operating systems, web browsers, and applications. It shows us that there are no applications in the top 25 products with the most CVE IDs (CVE Details, retrieved February 2026); the entire list is comprised of operating systems and web browsers:

Rank	Product Name	Vendor Name	Product Type	Number of CVE IDs
1	Linux Kernel	Linux	OS	13,888
2	Debian Linux	Debian	OS	9,908
3	Android	Google	OS	7,926
4	Fedora	Fedoraproject	OS	5,352
5	Windows Server 2016	Microsoft	OS	4,438
6	Windows Server 2019	Microsoft	OS	4,135
7	Ubuntu Linux	Canonical	OS	4,107
8	Iphone Os	Apple	OS	3,852
9	Chrome	Google	Browser	3,777
10	Windows Server 2012	Microsoft	OS	3,692
11	Windows Server 2008	Microsoft	OS	3,556

Rank	Product Name	Vendor Name	Product Type	Number of CVE IDs
12	Mac Os X	Apple	OS	3,207
13	Windows 10	Microsoft	OS	3,006
14	Firefox	Mozilla	Browser	2,938
15	Windows Server 2022	Microsoft	OS	2,474
16	Macos	Apple	OS	2,460
17	Windows 7	Microsoft	OS	2,368
18	Windows 8.1	Microsoft	OS	2,216
19	Windows Rt 8.1	Microsoft	OS	2,021
20	Tvos	Apple	OS	1,931
21	Enterprise Linux Desktop	Redhat	OS	1,928
22	Enterprise Linux	Redhat	OS	1,917
23	Leap	Opensuse	OS	1,901
24	Enterprise Linux Server	Redhat	OS	1,891
25	Enterprise Linux Workstation	Redhat	OS	1,845

Table 3.2 – The top 25 products with the most CVE IDs, 1999–2025 (CVE Details. 2026)

This isn't surprising given that vulnerabilities in operating systems and browsers typically have a higher value to attackers, security researchers, and vendors. This is due to the relatively large installation bases these products have. The first application, Acrobat Reader DC, is ranked 26th and subsequently does not make it onto the list of the top 25. Operating systems dominate this list, making up 92% of the total, meaning there are more CVE IDs impacting operating systems than browsers and applications combined in the list of top 25 products. This means that 8% of the top 25 products with the most vulnerabilities are web browsers—there are only

2 on the list. The concentration is striking: the 25 products with the highest CVE ID counts account for 29% of all entries in the NVD, and the top 50 products make up 40%.

Predictably, as the number of products on this list is expanded from 25 to 50, this distribution starts to shift quickly. There are 9 applications (18%) in the top 50 products with the most CVE IDs. As the number of products included in this analysis increases, applications would eventually have more CVE IDs than the other categories, for no other reason than the fact that there are many, many more applications than operating systems and browsers. Also, keep in mind that the impact of a vulnerability in a popular development library or framework, such as Django, Log4j, or Microsoft .NET, can be magnified because of the millions of applications that leverage them.

This list shouldn't be all that surprising, as some vendors in this list are also the top vendors based on the number of products they have had in the market over the last 20+ years. The more code you write, the more potential for vulnerabilities there is, especially in the years prior to 2003 when the big worm attacks (SQL Slammer, Blaster, and Sasser) were perpetrated. After 2004, industry leaders such as the ones on this list started paying more attention to security vulnerabilities in the wake of those attacks. I'll discuss malware more in *Chapter 5, The Evolution of Malware*. Additionally, operating systems and web browser vendors have had a disproportionate amount of attention and focus on their products because of their ubiquity. A new critical or high-rated vulnerability in an operating system or browser is worth considerably more than a vulnerability in an obscure application. *Table 3.3* presents the leading software and hardware vendors by total CVE ID count, along with the number of products they publish and the average number of CVE IDs per product (retrieved from CVE Details in February 2026).

Rank	**Vendor**	**Number of Products**	**Number of CVE IDs**	**Number of CVE IDs/ Number of Products**
1	Linux	23	13,960	607
2	Microsoft	1,218	13,649	11
3	Google	271	12,456	46
4	Oracle	1,147	10,111	9
5	Debian	123	10,053	82

Rank	Vendor	Number of Products	Number of CVE IDs	Number of CVE IDs/ Number of Products
6	Apple	265	8,367	32
7	IBM	1,732	7,999	5
8	Adobe	355	6,916	19
9	Cisco	6,847	6,626	1
10	Redhat	644	5,871	9

Table 3.3 – Top 10 vendors/distributions with the most CVE ID counts, 1999–2025 (CVE Details. Retrieved February 2026)

Back in 2003, when the big worm attacks on Microsoft Windows occurred, many of the organizations I talked to at the time believed that only Microsoft software had vulnerabilities, and other vendors' software was free from them. This is despite the fact that thousands of CVE IDs were being assigned each year before and after 2003 to software from many vendors.

More than two decades later, I haven't talked to any security teams recently that still believe this myth, as they are dealing with vulnerabilities in all software and hardware. This data is not perfect, and counting the total number of CVE IDs in this manner does not necessarily tell us which of these vendors and products have improved over the years or whether the industry has improved its security development practices as a whole. Let's explore these aspects more next.

In the next sections of this chapter, I provide a deep dive analysis of select vendors that have had the most vulnerability disclosures over the years. All these numbers and graphs will provide you with insight into how these popular vendors have been trending with regard to the volume of CVE IDs assigned to them.

Interpreting vendor and product vulnerability data

Before we dive into more data, I wanted to offer a few thoughts on the reliability of this data and how to use it.

First, this data is not perfect. As I mentioned previously, at the time of writing, there is a backlog of data that has not been through the NVD enrichment process. Since I am counting and analyzing CVE IDs with specific characteristics, this will undoubtedly have an impact on the accuracy of the data, especially for more recent years, such as 2023, 2024, and 2025.

Second, this data is only a snapshot of the available data. The data at their sources continued to change the moment I took each snapshot. The NVD constantly receives new information and improves the accuracy of the data it has. The world keeps rotating, meaning researchers and attackers are constantly looking for new discoveries in new and existing CVE IDs. Things are constantly changing, but the data I provide next is only a snapshot at one point in time. In the analysis in this section, I used CVSS v3 in most cases because CVSS v3 scores were available for almost all the CVE IDs I examined in the years between 2017 and 2025. In some cases, when I examined data from earlier time periods, I used CVSS v1 or v2 scores because CVSS v3 scores were not available. This isn't ideal, but it helped ensure consistent CVSS scoring for the CVE IDs in the most recent years. Also note that I used the publication dates of CVE IDs, not the year when the CVE ID was first assigned. This helps ensure the CVE ID is counted in the year it was added to the NVD.

One way to interpret this data is through the lens of an SDL. In the wake of the big worm attacks in 2003, Microsoft started developing the Microsoft SDL (Microsoft, n.d.). Microsoft continues to use the SDL to this day. I managed marketing communications for the SDL for several years, so I had the opportunity to learn a lot about this approach to development. The stated goals of the SDL are to decrease the number and severity of vulnerabilities in Microsoft software. The SDL also seeks to make vulnerabilities found in software after development harder or impossible to exploit.

It became clear that even if Microsoft were somehow able to produce vulnerability-free products, the applications, drivers, and third-party components running on Windows or in web browsers would still render systems vulnerable. Subsequently, Microsoft shared some versions of the SDL and some SDL tools with the broader industry for free. It also baked some aspects of the SDL into some of their publicly available development tools. You can get access to these resources at `https://www.microsoft.com/en-us/securityengineering/sdl`.

We can use the goals of the SDL as an informal **vulnerability improvement framework** to get an idea of whether the risk (probability and impact) of using a vendor or a specific product has increased or decreased over time. This framework has four criteria:

- Is the total number of vulnerabilities trending up or down?
- Is the severity of those vulnerabilities trending up or down?
- Are the EPSS scores trending lower or higher?
- Is the number of CVE IDs added to the KEV catalog trending up or down?

Why does this seemingly simple framework make sense? Let's walk through it.

Is the total number of vulnerabilities trending up or down? Vendors should be working to reduce the number of vulnerabilities in their products over time. An aspirational goal for all vendors should be to have zero vulnerabilities in their products. But this isn't realistic, as humans write code, and they make mistakes that can lead to vulnerabilities. However, over time, vendors should be able to show their customers that they have found ways to reduce vulnerabilities in their products to reduce risk and costs for their customers.

Is the severity of those vulnerabilities trending up or down? Given that there will be some security vulnerabilities in products, vendors should work to reduce the severity of those vulnerabilities. Reducing the severity of vulnerabilities reduces the number of emergency security update deployments I mentioned earlier in the chapter. It also gives vulnerability management teams more time to test and deploy vulnerabilities, which reduces disruptions to the organizations they support. More specifically, the number of critical and high-severity CVEs should be minimized as these pose the greatest risk to systems.

Are the EPSS scores of those vulnerabilities trending up or down? Again, if there are vulnerabilities in products, making those vulnerabilities as hard as possible to exploit should be something vendors focus on. EPSS is an estimate of the probability of exploitation of a vulnerability for the first 30 days after it is published.

Is the number of CVE IDs added to the KEV catalog trending up or down? The number of vulnerabilities that are added to the CISA KEV catalog is also a good indicator of whether exploitation is getting harder over time. As we discussed, CISA's KEV catalog is an authoritative list of CVE IDs that have been exploited in the wild. Vendors that pay attention to this measure and demonstrate they can effectively reduce the number of their vulnerabilities that get exploited are vendors who are reducing risk for their customers.

Using these measures, we want to see vendors making the vulnerabilities in their products consistently hard to exploit. We also want to see fewer vulnerabilities that attackers actually end up exploiting and that get added to the KEV catalog.

When you interpret CVE ID data for vendors or their products, I suggest you keep these questions in mind:

- Is the CVE ID count increasing or decreasing each year?
- Are the numbers of critical-rated and high-rated CVE IDs increasing or decreasing each year?
- Are the EPSS scores advantageous for you or attackers?
- Is the number of CVE IDs added to the KEV catalog increasing or decreasing each year?

One limitation of this approach is that it won't be helpful in cases where vendors and/or their products are new, and there isn't enough data to evaluate. Another limitation is the *mergers and acquisitions* scenario, where vendors acquire new companies and their products. For example, Oracle acquired numerous technology companies and new technologies along with their vulnerabilities, including MySQL and Sun Microsystems. Acquisition of new technologies can lead to significant changes in CVE ID numbers for vendors. It can take time for vendors to shape the products they obtain to meet or exceed their standards, during which their customers manage increased volumes of CVE IDs in their products.

Let's start our deep dive by examining some vulnerability disclosure trends for some big software and cloud vendors, those with the most CVE IDs. Let me make one more important point before we dive into the data. As I mentioned earlier, I've done thousands of threat intelligence briefings around the world. I've given enough briefings to enough people to recognize behavioral curiosities among the audiences I've briefed. There were typically one or two people in every audience who, upon seeing vulnerability disclosure trends, even for vendors they said they weren't fans of, suddenly became *vendor apologists*. The typical refrain was that we can't really see how vendors are performing by counting CVE IDs unless we examine specific products, or even a subset of distributions of products. After all, they could be developed by different development teams, and we really want to measure how those specific development teams improve over time.

However, after working at two of the world's pre-eminent technology companies for more than two decades in my career, I have a different view. Every product and every distribution is the output of the people, processes, and technologies that each vendor uses to develop them. The vendors we will examine in this chapter are some of the biggest software vendors in the world. They all have **Software Development Lifecycles** (**SDLCs**) and **Security Development Lifecycles** (**SDLs**) of some sort to meet their own requirements for minimum viable products, while improving security and controlling development costs. Some smaller vendors might suffer from inconsistent quality across the products they develop because they lack these things, but these big vendors have people, processes, and technologies that help them meet their minimum requirements to ship their products. If they don't have effective processes and tools, that's worth knowing. This is what we are measuring in this chapter—the effectiveness of their people, processes, and technologies, to continuously develop better quality products, measured by the number of serious vulnerability disclosures they have had. Once a product or distribution is released to its customers, the customers bear the brunt of the volume of security updates that follow, in the form of dramatically increased risk, disruptions to their operations, and associated expenses. Remember, *all* vulnerability management teams dealt with 133 new CVE IDs per day on average in 2025, with an average of 55 new critical or high-rated CVEs disclosed every day. Don't make excuses for the vendors that have the most vulnerabilities—demand better products instead. All these vendors have the best access to security tools, cloud services, and AI in the world. If they can't reduce the number and severity of vulnerabilities in their own products over a period of years, then what chance do smaller, less sophisticated organizations have?

In this section, I'll focus on three years of data. At the time of writing, CVE data for 2025 is still being updated frequently, so I'll use data from 2022 to 2024, which is likely more stable at this point. Three years is sufficient time to make performance course corrections to individual products, especially in an industry where Agile, continuous integration, continuous deployment, and AI code assist tools are the mantra. They all take security seriously, so let's take an objective, quantitative approach to examining their performance. Now let's dive into the data!

Microsoft vulnerability trends

Let's look at how Microsoft has been managing vulnerabilities in its products over the past 26 years. They typically top the list of vendors with the most CVE IDs, with approximately 13,008 between 1999 and the end of 2025 (CVE Details, n.d.). However, in 2025, Linux ascended to the top of the list of vendors with the most CVE IDs. I will discuss this in more detail in the next chapter, which focuses on CVE IDs in products. Remember, these numbers are constantly being updated. Of the aforementioned 13,008 CVE IDs assigned to Microsoft products, 8,450 were rated critical or high. That's 65% of all CVE IDs assigned to Microsoft during this time that had CVSS scores of 7 or higher. However, note that these CVSS scores were calculated using a mix of CVSS v1, v2, and v3 base scores because of CVSS version changes during those 26 years. *Figure 3.11* provides a very long-term view of the volume of vulnerability disclosures, as well as those CVE IDs with critical or high-severity ratings:

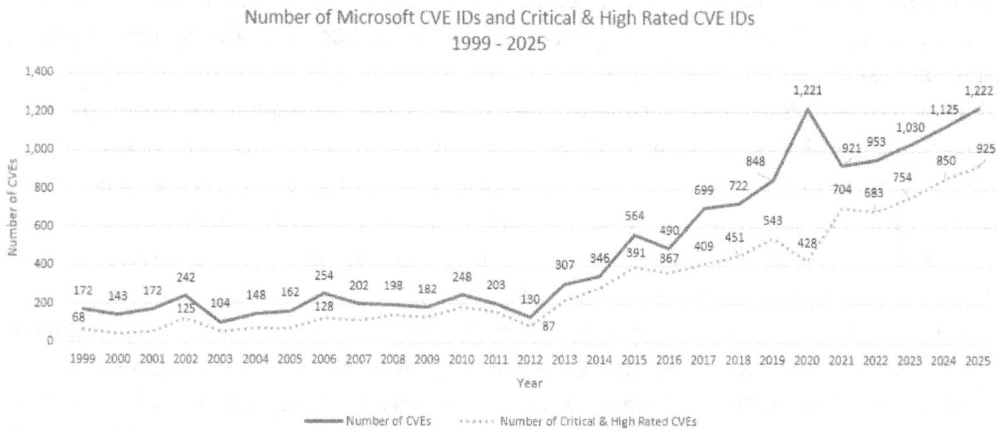

Figure 3.11 – The number of CVEs and the number of CVEs rated critical or high in Microsoft products per year (1999–2025) (CVE Details, n.d.)

The products that contributed the most to Microsoft's overall CVE ID count include Windows Server 2016, Windows Server 2019, Windows Server 2012, Windows Server 2008, and Windows 10 (CVE Details, n.d.).

Let's focus on the last three years for which we have full-year data: 2022, 2023, and 2024. *Figure 3.12* illustrates the key statistics regarding the questions I previously posed.

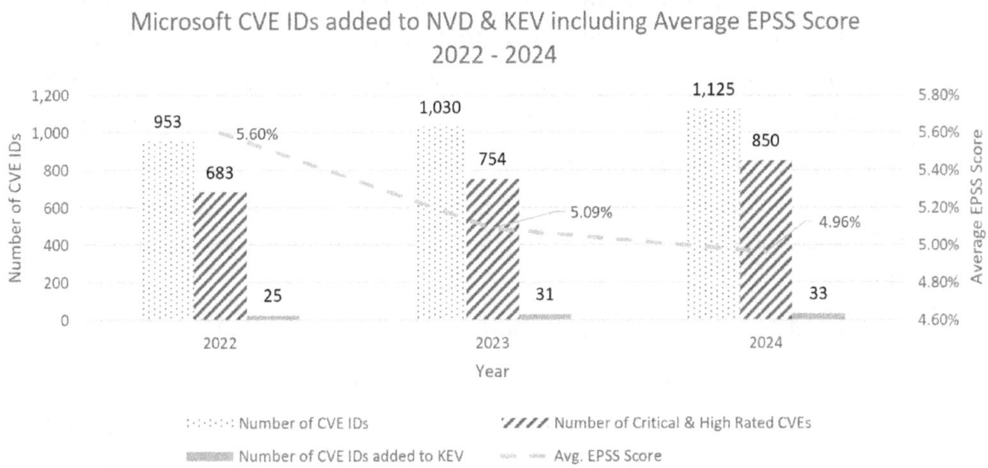

Figure 3.12 – Volumes of CVE IDs and CVE IDs with CVSS scores 7 or higher added to NVD assigned to Microsoft products; the percentage of total CVE IDs added to CISA's KEV catalog, including average EPSS scores (2022–2024) (CVE Details, 2025)

The following is clear from the preceding figure:

- First, it shows us that the number of CVE IDs for Microsoft products increased each year, from 953 in 2022 to 1,030 in 2023, and to 1,125 in 2024. That's a total of 3,108 CVE IDs assigned to Microsoft products in 3 years, equivalent to 2.8 new CVE IDs per day on average.
- Second, it shows us that the number of critical and high-severity CVE IDs also grew each year, starting with 683 in 2022, to 754 in 2023, to 850 in 2024, for a total of 2,287 in 3 years. That's an average of two critical or high-severity CVE IDs disclosed per day. Neither of these measures is moving in the direction we want them to go. Ideally, we want fewer vulnerabilities for our vulnerability management and remediation teams to triage, test, and deploy, and especially fewer of the most severe vulnerabilities. There was a 17% increase in the number of CVE IDs assigned to Microsoft during these years and a 22% increase in critical and high severity vulnerabilities.
- *Figure 3.12* also shows us that the probability that these CVE IDs would be exploited during the first 30 days after they were published was, on average, 5.6% in 2022, 5.09% in 2023, and 4.96% in 2024. This measure did reduce each year, which is positive news for Microsoft customers.
- Finally, *Figure 3.12* also shows us that the number of CVE IDs assigned to Microsoft products that CISA put into the KEV catalog was 25 in 2022, 31 in 2023, and 33 in 2024. A total of 89 CVE IDs assigned to Microsoft products entered the KEV catalog, meaning

they were being exploited in the wild. This is equivalent to 2.5 CVE IDs for Microsoft products added each month, on average, to the CISA KEV catalog during these years.

The most frequently identified common weaknesses enumerated in Microsoft's vulnerabilities during these three years included cross-site scripting (37 CVE IDs), memory corruption (23 CVE IDs), and classic buffer overflows (12 CVE IDs).

Now, let's apply the vulnerability improvement framework that I introduced earlier in this chapter to the Microsoft CVE ID data from 2022 to 2024. The four measures of the framework are the following:

- Did they reduce the number of CVEs during this three-year period? *No.*
- Did they reduce the number of critical and high-severity CVEs? *No.*
- Did they reduce the average EPSS scores, thus reducing the probability of exploitation after CVE IDs are published? *Yes.*
- Did they reduce the number of CVE IDs added to CISA's KEV catalog? *No.*

As you can see, Microsoft only accomplished one of the goals defined by the framework. Let's see how some other vendors performed across these same four measures.

Google vulnerability trends

Since Google is #3 in the top 10 list of vendors with the most CVE IDs since the NVD's inception, let's examine their CVE trends next (CVE Details, n.d.). *Figure 3.13* shows us that between 2017 and 2025, there were 10,110 CVE IDs assigned to Google. Of those CVE IDs in Google products, 5,529 or 55% were rated critical or high severity:

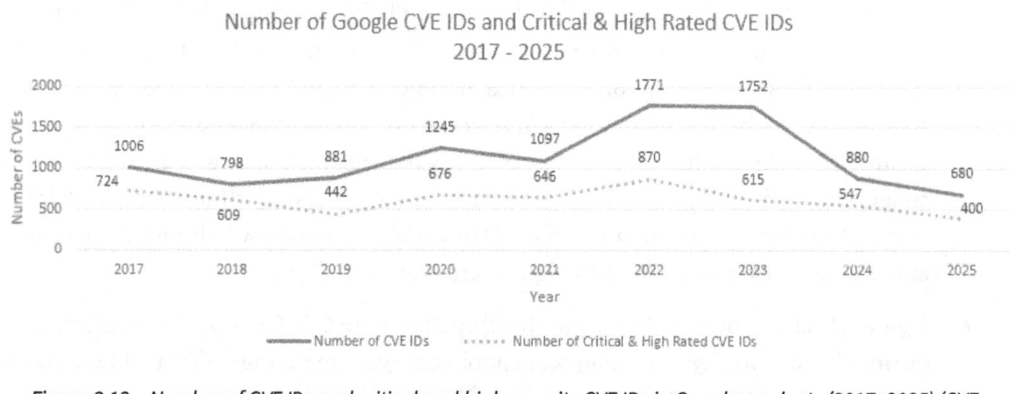

Figure 3.13 – Number of CVE IDs and critical and high-severity CVE IDs in Google products (2017–2025) (CVE Details, n.d.)

According to CVE Details, the products contributing the most CVE IDs to Google's totals included Android, Chrome, and TensorFlow.

Looking at the 3 years between 2022 and the end of 2024, there was a 67% decrease in CVE IDs assigned to Google products. This dramatic decrease in CVE IDs is further illustrated by *Figure 3.14*.

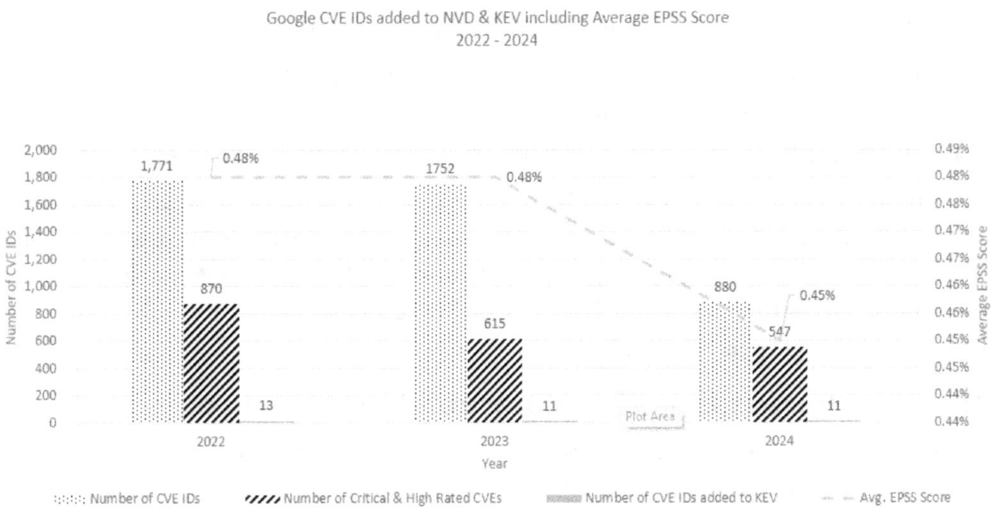

Figure 3.14 – Volumes of CVE IDs and CVE IDs with CVSS scores 7 or higher added to NVD assigned to Google products; the percentage of total CVE IDs added to CISA's KEV catalog, including average EPSS scores (2022–2024) (CVE Details, 2025)

The total number of CVE IDs assigned to their products during these three years was 4,403, of which 2,032 or 46% were rated critical or high severity. This is equivalent to 4 new CVE IDs disclosed per day on average and 1.9 critical or high-severity CVE IDs per day on average. As *Figure 3.14* illustrates, 2024 was a curious year for Google CVE IDs, as the total number was dramatically reduced, while the proportion of critical and high-severity CVE IDs increased to 62%, but the number of CVE IDs that were added to the KEV catalog remained the same from the previous year. The raw number of CVE IDs added to the KEV catalog in 2024 was the same as in 2023 (11 CVE IDs added), but the reduction in total CVE IDs in 2024 meant the proportion of that year's total CVE IDs added to the KEV catalog increased. However, Google did reduce the total raw number of CVE IDs from 13 in 2022 to 11 in 2024. The same thing happened with critical and high-severity CVE IDs—the raw total number decreased while the proportion of the total increased. The average EPSS score was also reduced in 2024 to 0.45%.

The most frequently identified common weaknesses enumerated in Google's vulnerabilities during these three years included memory corruption (919 CVE IDs), overflow (330 CVE IDs), and input validation (146 CVE IDs).

Let's apply the vulnerability improvement framework that I introduced earlier in this chapter to Google's CVE ID data from 2022 to 2024. The four measures of the framework are as follows:

- Did they reduce the number of CVEs during this three-year period? *Yes.*
- Did they reduce the number of critical and high-severity CVEs? *Yes.*
- Did they reduce the average EPSS scores, thus reducing the probability of exploitation after CVE IDs are published? *Yes.*
- Did they reduce the number of CVE IDs added to CISA's KEV catalog? *Yes.*

Google met the four goals of our vulnerability improvement framework between 2022 and 2024. Congratulations Google! The dramatic reduction in total CVE IDs in 2024, as well as the reduction in 2024's average EPSS score, fewer critical and high-severity vulnerabilities each year, and ending the three-year period with fewer CVE IDs added to the KEV are all risk reductions for Google's enterprise customers.

Microsoft versus Google vulnerability disclosures

Google and Microsoft are fierce competitors, both offering consumers and enterprises operating systems, web browsers, and cloud services, among other products. They are under similar competitive, legal, and regulatory pressures. They are both based on the West Coast of the US and have global operations, and they compete for the same pool of technical talent for their workforces. So, you might wonder how they compare when it comes to vulnerability disclosures? *Figure 3.15*, *Table 3.4*, and *Table 3.5* reveal the answer to this question. There are some differences, but it is interesting how similar these tech titans' CVE data points are at the end of the six-year period.

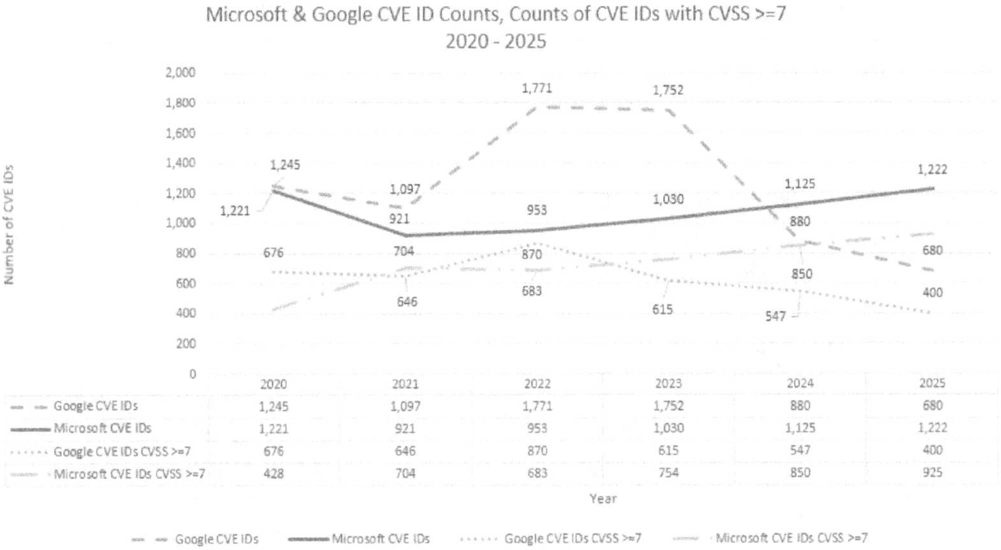

Figure 3.15 – Number of CVE IDs and CVE IDs with critical and high severity in Google and Microsoft products (2020–2025) (CVE Details, n.d.)

Even though Google ended the 6-year period with a lower CVE ID count for 2025, Google had 953 more CVE IDs during this 6-year period than Microsoft. Over the 6-year period, this translated into an average of 3.4 new CVE IDs per day for Google products versus 3.0 new CVE IDs per day on average for Microsoft. However, despite having more CVE IDs, Google had fewer CVE IDs with CVSS scores equivalent to critical and high severity than Microsoft during this period. Additionally, *Table 3.4* shows us that Google's CVE IDs also had significantly lower average EPSS scores in every one of the six years during this period.

Year	**Google Avg. EPSS Score**	**Microsoft Avg. EPSS Score**
2020	0.90%	6.37%
2021	1.22%	6.25%
2022	0.48%	5.60%
2023	0.48%	5.09%
2024	0.45%	4.96%

Year	Google Avg. EPSS Score	Microsoft Avg. EPSS Score
2025	0.19%	1.79%

Table 3.4 – Average EPSS scores, as a percentage, for Google and Microsoft CVE IDs (2020–2025)

Table 3.5 compares the number of CVE IDs from both vendors that were added to CISA's KEV catalog between 2022 and 2025. Recall that the KEV catalog was founded in November of 2021 and only had two months of operations that year. Subsequently, I decided to compare four full years of KEV catalog operations. Each year, significantly more Microsoft CVE IDs were added to the KEV catalog than Google CVE IDs.

Year	Number of Microsoft CVE IDs added to KEV	Number of Google CVE IDs added to KEV
2022	25	13
2023	31	11
2024	33	11
2025	39	10

Table 3.5 – The number of Microsoft and Google CVE IDs added to CISA's KEV catalog (2022-2025)

Although Google had more vulnerabilities than Microsoft, it had fewer CVE IDs that were rated critical and high severity, its average EPSS scores were significantly lower, and fewer CVE IDs were added to the KEV catalog. Its CVE IDs tended to be less exploitable according to the data compared here. As I discussed earlier in the chapter, CVE IDs with lower exploitability tend to relieve pressure on front-line vulnerability management and remediation teams. It appears as though Google had a superior track record of doing this in the years I examined here.

Next, let's examine the CVE ID trends of another immensely successful company, Oracle.

Oracle vulnerability trends

Since Oracle is #4 in the top 10 list of vendors with the most CVEs since 1999, let's examine their CVE trends next (CVE Details, n.d.). There are CVEs in the NVD for Oracle products dating back to 1999. *Figure 3.16* illustrates the number of CVE IDs published each year for Oracle products between 2017 and 2025, as well as the number of CVE IDs with critical and high-severity ratings.

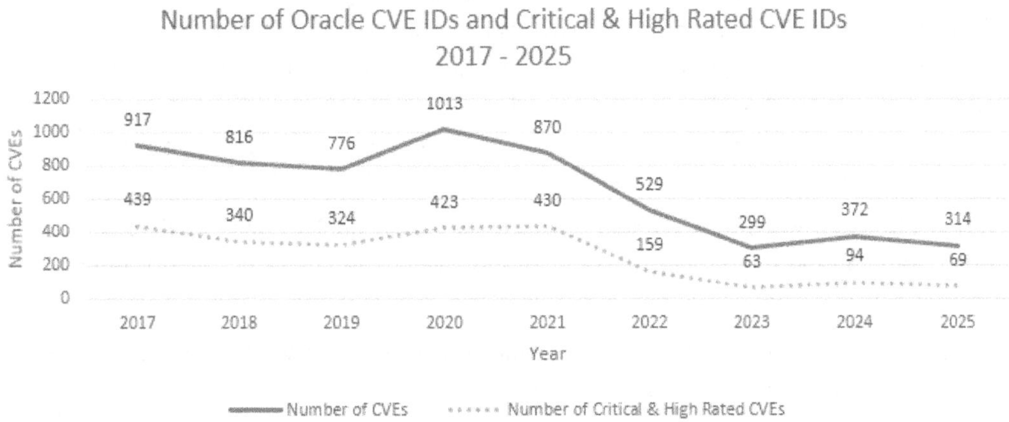

Figure 3.16 – Number of CVE IDs, critical and high CVE IDs in Oracle products (2017–2025) (CVE Details, n.d.)

During this period, 5,906 CVE IDs were assigned to Oracle products. Of these CVE IDs, 2,341 or 40% were rated critical or high severity. During this period, the number of vulnerability disclosures in Oracle products appears to have peaked in 2020 before trending downward.

According to CVE Details, the products contributing the most CVE IDs to Oracle's CVE ID totals included MySQL, JRE, JDK, Solaris, and Database Server (CVE Details, n.d.).

Looking at the 3 years between 2021 and the end of 2024, there was a 30% decrease in CVE IDs assigned to Oracle products. This big decrease in CVE IDs is illustrated by *Figure 3.17*.

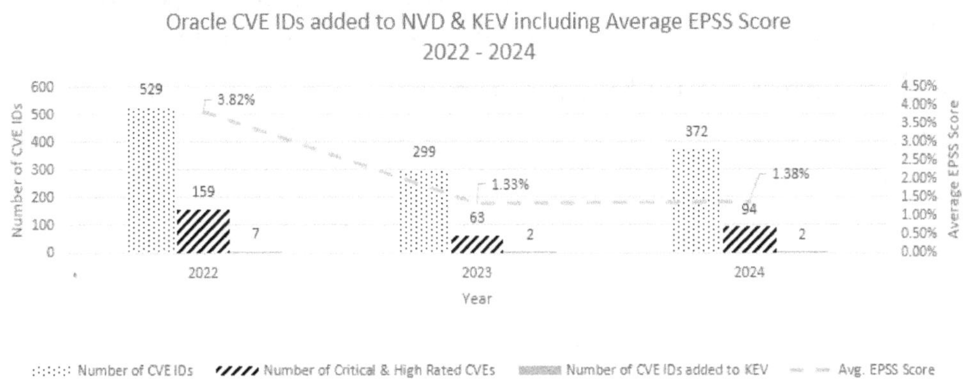

Figure 3.17 – Volumes of CVE IDs and CVE IDs with CVSS scores 7 or higher added to NVD assigned to Oracle products; the percentage of total CVE IDs added to CISA's KEV catalog, including average EPSS scores (2022–2024) (CVE Details, n.d.)

The total number of CVE IDs assigned to their products during these 3 years was 1,200, of which 316 or 26% were rated critical or high severity. This is equivalent to 1.1 new CVE IDs disclosed per day on average and 0.29 critical or high-severity CVE IDs per day on average. As *Figure 3.17* illustrates, the number of CVE IDs that were added to the KEV catalog was also relatively low, totaling 11 CVE IDs across all 3 years. The average EPSS score was also reduced between 2022 and 2024, ending the period at 1.38% (CVE Details, n.d.).

The most frequently identified common weaknesses enumerated in Oracle's vulnerabilities during these three years included cross-site scripting, overflow, and memory corruption (CVE Details, n.d.).

Let's apply the vulnerability improvement framework to Oracle's CVE ID data from 2022 to 2024. The four measures of the framework are as follows:

- Did they reduce the number of CVEs during this three-year period? *Yes*. The number of CVEs was lower in the third year than the first year.
- Did they reduce the number of critical and high-severity CVEs? *Yes*. The number of CVEs was lower in the last year of the period than the first year.
- Did they reduce the average EPSS scores, thus reducing the probability of exploitation after CVE IDs are published? *Yes*. The score was lower in the last year than the first year.
- Did they reduce the number of CVE IDs added to CISA's KEV catalog? *Yes*.

As *Figure 3.16* reveals, Oracle has done a great job of reducing the number and severity of the vulnerabilities in its products since 2020. The relatively low number of critical and high-severity CVE IDs in the three years examined, compared to their peers, is impressive, as is the very low number of Oracle CVE IDs added to CISA's KEV catalog. Great job, Oracle!

Vendor vulnerability trend summary

Figure 3.18 summarizes some of the key measures discussed in this section.

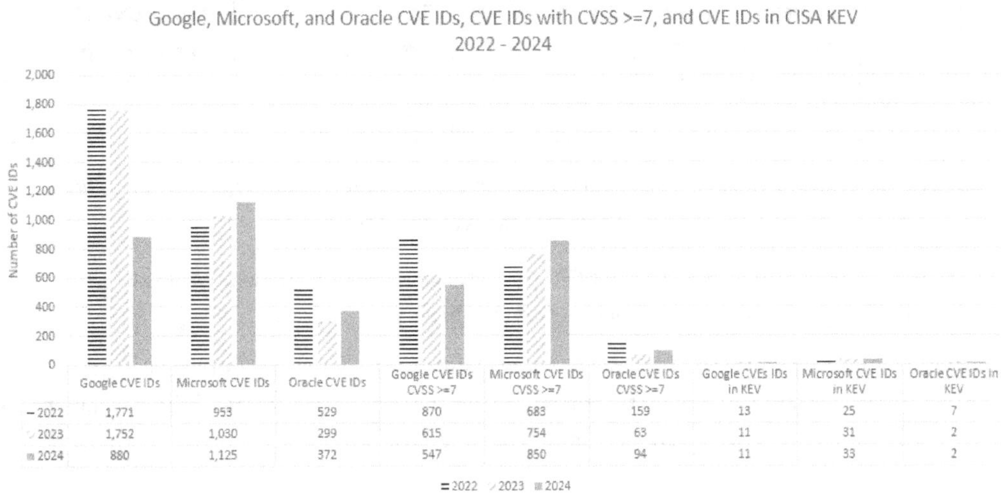

Figure 3.18 – CVE ID count, count of CVE IDs with CVSS >=7, and count of CVE IDs in CISA's KEV catalog for Google, Microsoft, and Oracle (2022–2024) (CVE Details, n.d.)

Google had the most CVE IDs of these three vendors during the three years studied. Microsoft had the most critical and high-severity CVE IDs, the highest average EPSS scores, and the most CVE IDs added to the KEV during the period studied. Oracle had the fewest CVE IDs, the fewest CVE IDs with CVSS scores 7 and higher, and the fewest CVE IDs added to CISA's KEV catalog during this period, by far. However, Oracle did have a consistently higher average EPSS score than Google. Google and Oracle both met the four vulnerability improvement framework measures in the

three years examined.

Let's finish this section on vendor vulnerability trends with a summary of how the vendors we examined fared with regard to our vulnerability improvement framework.

Table 3.6 summarizes how each vendor that we examined performed across the four measures of the vulnerability improvement framework.

Vendor	**Fewer CVE IDs?**	**Fewer CVE IDs with CVSS Score <=7?**	**Lower Average EPSS Score?**	**Fewer CVE IDs in KEV Catalog?**
Google	Yes	Yes	Yes	Yes
Microsoft	No	No	Yes	No

Vendor	Fewer CVE IDs?	Fewer CVE IDs with CVSS Score <=7?	Lower Average EPSS Score?	Fewer CVE IDs in KEV Catalog?
Oracle	No	No	No	Yes

Table 3.6 – Summary of whether the vendors examined in this chapter met the criteria of the vulnerability improvement framework during 2022-2024

Google and Oracle both improved their CVE ID data across all four measures of the vulnerability improvement framework during the three-year period..

I hope this lengthy analysis has given you some insights into which vendors have been improving recently across some of the key measures that enterprise vulnerability management and remediation teams can leverage to manage vulnerabilities.

Summary

Vulnerability management is a cornerstone of cybersecurity programs. I started this chapter by mentioning that I get asked frequently whether cybersecurity is better now than 10 or 15 years ago. The data we examined in this chapter suggests that things have become much worse, as evidenced by much higher volumes of severe security vulnerabilities. It is not all bad news, though, as the data also suggests that some of the vendors we examined have improved in important ways.

Risk is the combination of probability and impact. The CVSS is used to estimate the risk for each vulnerability (CVE) in the NVD. This freely available data should be used to inform your vulnerability management program. Using vendors who have been successful at reducing the number of vulnerabilities in their products can potentially reduce the time, effort, and costs related to your vulnerability management program. If you choose vendors who have also invested in reducing attackers' return on investment by making the exploitation of vulnerabilities in their products hard or impossible, you'll also be reducing your risk and costs.

Of the three vendors examined in this chapter, Google and Oracle met the criteria of our vulnerability improvement framework by reducing the number of vulnerabilities in their products, reducing the severity of vulnerabilities in their products, and reducing the number of exploited vulnerabilities during the years studied.

Please keep in mind that the data used for these comparisons has many biases and is not complete or completely accurate. But you can do your own CVE ID research and use the informal vulnerability improvement framework I've provided in this chapter.

In the next chapter, we are going to dive into the vulnerability disclosure trends for workstation, server, and mobile operating systems, as well as some popular web browsers. I'll also provide some guidance on vulnerability management programs based on the lessons I've learned in the trenches over the years.

References

- NIST. (August 3, 2023). Retrieved from National Vulnerability Database: `https://nvd.nist.gov/vuln#`
- CVE. (March 5, 2020). *CVE Numbering Authority (CNA) Rules*. Retrieved from `https://www.cve.org/ResourcesSupport/AllResources/CNARules`
- Howard, M. (May 9, 2021). *The Best Security Advice I Can Give....* Retrieved from `https://michaelhowardsecure.blog/2021/05/09/the-best-security-advice-i-can-give/`
- MITRE. (n.d.). Common Weakness Enumeration. Retrieved from `https://cwe.mitre.org/index.html`
- CVE Details. (n.d.). Vulnerabilities by Types/Categories. Retrieved from CVE Details: `https://www.cvedetails.com/vulnerabilities-by-types.php`
- Microsoft. (n.d.). Support. Retrieved from Microsoft: `https://support.microsoft.com/en-us/topic/kb5042421-crowdstrike-issue-impacting-windows-endpoints-causing-an-0x50-or-0x7e-error-message-on-a-blue-screen-b1c700e0-7317-4e95-aeee-5d67dd35b92f`
- CVE. (n.d.). CVE-2018-8653 Detail. Retrieved from `https://www.cve.org/CVERecord?id=CVE-2018-8653`
- NIST. (September 20, 2022). CVEs and the NVD Process. Retrieved from `https://nvd.nist.gov/general/cve-process`
- NIST. (September 20, 2022). CVE FAQs. Retrieved from `https://nvd.nist.gov/general/FAQ-Sections/CVE-FAQs#faqLink10`
- NIST. (February 13, 2024). NVD Program Announcement. Retrieved from `https://nvd.nist.gov/general/news/nvd-program-transition-announcement`
- Phoenix Security. (July 14, 2024). *NVD Backlog, are we there yet? has [sic] CISA, and the Vulnrichment Program created a dent?* Retrieved from `https://phoenix.security/nvd-backlog-burndown-update/`
- FIRST. (November 3, 2023). CVSS v4.0 is now available. Retrieved from `https://www.first.org/newsroom/releases/202310-3`

- FIRST. (November 1, 2023). Common Vulnerability Scoring System version 4.0: Specification Document. Retrieved from `https://www.first.org/cvss/specification-document`
- NIST. (n.d.). Common Vulnerability Scoring System Calculator. Retrieved from `https://nvd.nist.gov/vuln-metrics/cvss/v3-calculator`
- CVE. (n.d.). CVE and NVD Relationship. Retrieved from `https://cve.mitre.org/about/cve_and_nvd_relationship.html`
- CVE. (December 14, 2021). "CVE-2021-45046 Detail". Retrieved from `https://cve.mitre.org/cgi-bin/cvename.cgi?name=CVE-2021-45046`
- Software Engineering Institute CERT Coordination Center, Carnegie Mellon University (December 15, 2021). *Apache Log4j allows insecure JNDI lookups, Vulnerability Note VU#930724*. Retrieved from `https://www.kb.cert.org/vuls/id/930724`
- Cyber Safety Review Board. July 11, 2022. Review of the December 2021 Log4j Event. Retrieved from `https://www.cisa.gov/sites/default/files/publications/CSRB-Report-on-Log4-July-11-2022_508.pdf`
- Miller, Matt M. (February 14, 2019). BlueHat IL 2019 – Matt Miller. Retrieved from YouTube: `https://www.youtube.com/ watch?v=PjbGojjnBZQ`
- Google Threat Intelligence Group. (April 29, 2025). *Hello 0-Days, My Old Friend: A 2024 Zero-Day Exploitation Analysis*. Retrieved from `https://cloud.google.com/blog/topics/threat-intelligence/2024-zero-day-trends`
- NIST. (n.d.). *Known Exploited Vulnerabilities*. Retrieved from `https://nvd.nist.gov/General/News/cisa-exploit-catalog`
- Microsoft. (April 24, 2025). *Tired of all the restarts? Get hotpatching for Windows Server*. Retrieved from `https://www.microsoft.com/en-us/windows-server/blog/2025/04/24/tired-of-all-the-restarts-get-hotpatching-for-windows-server/?msockid=31172e3ff77a656817c33ec5f6c964c4`
- Martin, Brian S. C. (December 3, 2013). *Black Hat USA 2013 - Buying into the Bias: Why Vulnerability Statistics Suck*. Retrieved from YouTube: `https://www.youtube.com/watch?time_continue=20&v=3Sx0uJGRQ4s`
- CVE Details. (n.d.). *How does it work?* Retrieved from CVE Details: `https://www.cvedetails.com/how-does-it-work.php`
- Mell, Peter. (July, 2000). Computer Security Division Information Technology Laboratory, National Institute of Standards and Technology, ITL Bulletin. Retrieved

fromhttps://csrc.nist.gov/csrc/media/Publications/Shared/documents/itl-bulletin/itlbul2000-07.pdf

- Common Vulnerabilities and Exposures. (n.d.). *CVE Numbering Authorities (CNAs)*. Retrieved from Common Vulnerabilities and Exposures: https://www.cve.org/ProgramOrganization/CNAs
- FIRST. (n.d.). *Exploit Prediction Scoring System*. Retrieved from https://www.first.org/epss/
- CISA. (n.d.). *Known Exploited Vulnerabilities Catalog*. Retrieved from https://www.cisa.gov/known-exploited-vulnerabilities-catalog
- Scroxton, Alex. (June 2, 2025). ComputerWeekly.com. *US cyber agency CISA faces stiff budget cuts*. Retrieved from https://www.computerweekly.com/news/366625236/US-cyber-agency-CISA-faces-stiff-budget-cuts
- CVE Details. (Retrieved February, 2026). *Top 50 List of Products with the most CVEs*. Retrieved from CVE Details: https://www.cvedetails.com/top-50-products.php
- CVE Details. (Retrieved February, 2026). *Top 50 List of Vendors with the most CVEs*. Retrieved from CVE Details: https://www.cvedetails.com/top-50-vendors.php
- CVE Details. (n.d.). Current CVSS Score Distribution For All Vulnerabilities. Retrieved from CVE Details: https://www.cvedetails.com/index.php
- Microsoft. (n.d.). *Security Engineering*. Retrieved from Microsoft: https://www.microsoft.com/en-us/securityengineering/sdl
- CVE Details. (n.d.). Microsoft Vulnerability Statistics. Retrieved from CVE Details: https://www.cvedetails.com/vendor/26/Microsoft.html
- CVE Details. (n.d.). Google Vulnerability Statistics. Retrieved from CVE Details: https://www.cvedetails.com/vendor/1224/Google.html
- CVE Details. (n.d.). Oracle Vulnerability Statistics. Retrieved from CVE Details: https://www.cvedetails.com/vendor/93/Oracle.html

Get this book's PDF version and more

Scan the QR code (or go to `packtpub.com/unlock`). Search for this book by name, confirm the edition, and then follow the steps on the page.

UNLOCK NOW

Note: Keep your invoice handy. Purchases made directly from Packt don't require an invoice.

4

Product Vulnerability Disclosure Trends

In *Chapter 3, Vendor Vulnerability Disclosure Trends*, we took a close look at the three vendors with the most CVE IDs assigned to them. Now, let's examine vulnerability trends for some specific popular products. Most enterprises leverage a mix of different hardware and software products from different vendors. Most of the enterprises I've worked at employ multiple operating systems and web browsers from different vendors. This adds complexity for the vulnerability management teams that track vulnerabilities in their technology estates. Leveraging hardware and software products with consistently elevated levels of vulnerabilities makes it more expensive and riskier for enterprises. Using vulnerability disclosure trends as an input to your product selection process can help you understand the relative risks and costs associated with the products you consider adding to your technology estate. Let's explore some of the data.

This chapter will cover the following topics:

- Product vulnerability trends
- Vulnerability management guidance

Product vulnerability trends

The aggregate vulnerability trend of an individual vendor helps us understand whether and how that vendor is trying to improve their overall security development processes and drive costs down for their enterprise customers. However, enterprise customers use products such as operating systems, web browsers, applications, routing and switching equipment, firewalls, and so on. Does your organization use vulnerability statistics to inform its IT product procurement process? Using products that have fewer vulnerabilities, fewer severe vulnerabilities, and fewer exploitable vulnerabilities can help reduce the total cost of ownership and the unwanted drama that comes with emergency security patching. Let's start by examining the vulnerability trends for some popular operating systems.

Operating system vulnerability trends

Operating systems have garnered a lot of attention from security researchers over the past 25+ years. A working exploit for a zero-day vulnerability in a popular desktop or mobile operating system can be potentially worth a lot of money. Let's look at the vulnerability disclosure trends for operating systems and look closely at a few of the products that have the highest vulnerability counts. *Figure 4.1* illustrates the operating systems that had the most unique vulnerabilities between 1999 and February 2026, according to CVE Details (CVE Details, n.d.):

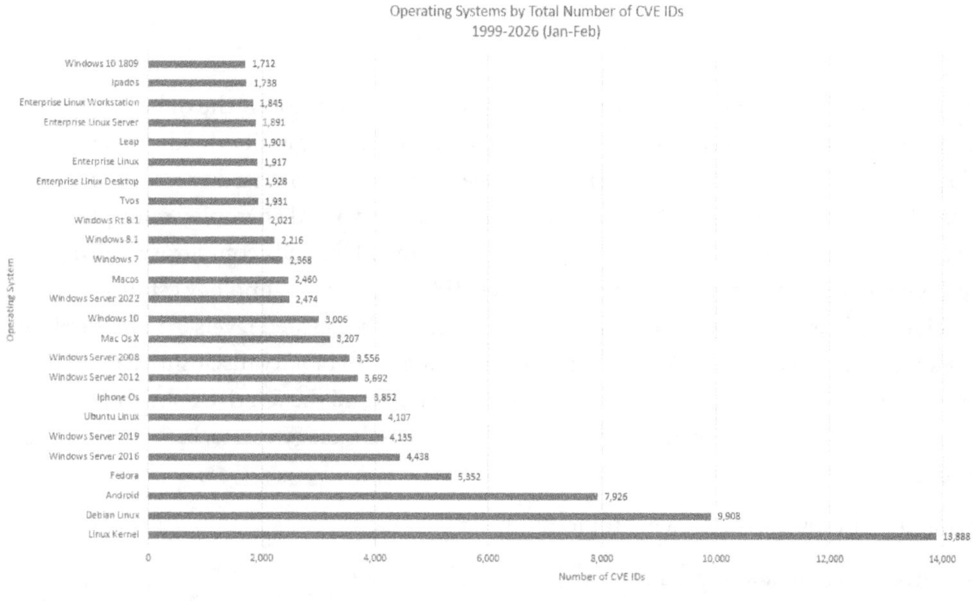

Figure 4.1 – Operating systems with the most unique vulnerabilities by total number of CVE counts (1999 to 2026 (Jan–Feb) (CVE Details, n.d.))

The list contains desktop, server, and mobile operating systems from an array of vendors, including Apple, Google, Linux vendors, Microsoft, and others. Note that *Figure 4.1* does not include firmware products, which also have vulnerabilities in them.

In this section, I'll select a few **operating systems** (**OSes**) and examine three full years of vulnerability disclosure measures, as I did with vendors in the last chapter. I'll examine CVE ID data from 2022, 2023, and 2024, as at the time of writing (January 2026), CVE ID data from 2025 is still being updated frequently. The OSes I select will be based on their popularity with the enterprise customers I've advised in the past. Since Debian Linux has one of the highest CVE ID counts, let's start with it.

As we did in *Chapter 3*, we will use the goals of the **Security Development Lifecycle** (**SDL**) as an informal **vulnerability improvement framework** to get an idea of whether the risk (probability and impact) of using a specific product has increased or decreased over time. This framework has four criteria:

1. Is the total number of vulnerabilities trending up or down?
2. Is the severity of those vulnerabilities trending up or down?
3. Are the **Exploit Prediction Scoring System (EPSS)** scores trending lower or higher?
4. Is the number of CVE IDs added to the KEV catalog trending up or down?

Let's start with a popular Linux distribution – Debian Linux.

Debian Linux vulnerability trends

According to CVE Details, Debian Linux accumulated 9,908 CVE IDs in the NVD between its inception and February 2026. There are numerous versions of Debian Linux that have CVE IDs assigned to them, including version 9, version 10, version 11, and others. As *Figure 4.2* illustrates, between 2017 and 2024, there were 7,341 CVE IDs assigned to Debian Linux, of which 4,223 or 58% were rated critical or high severity:

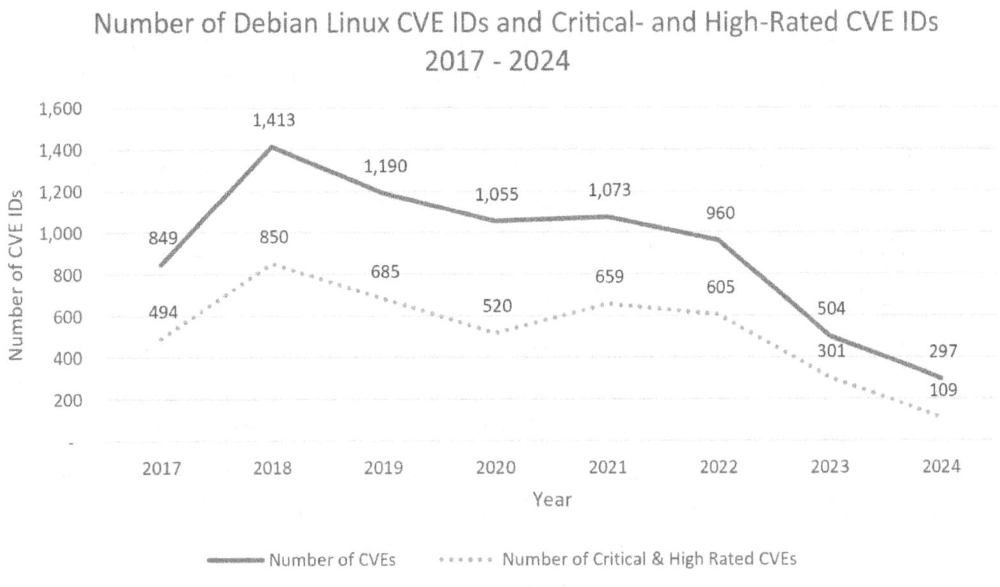

Figure 4.2 – Number of CVE IDs and critical- and high-rated CVE IDs in Debian Linux (2017–2024) (CVE Details, n.d.)

Focusing on the three years between the beginning of 2022 and the end of 2024, *Figure 4.3* reveals that Debian was able to reduce the number of CVE IDs, the severity of CVE IDs, and make them harder to exploit in Debian Linux. There was a 69% decrease in the number of CVE IDs in Debian Linux by the end of this three-year period, with an 82% decrease in the most severe CVE IDs. On average, there were 1.61 new vulnerability disclosures per day in Debian Linux during these three years and 0.93 new critical or high-severity vulnerabilities per day. With just three Debian Linux CVE IDs added to the KEV catalog in 2024 and 0.3 critical or high-severity vulnerability disclosures per day on average, vulnerability management teams had minimal drama that year.

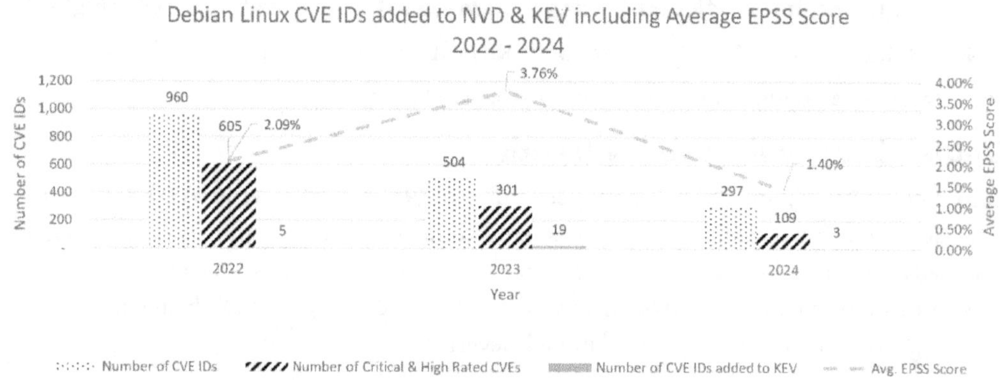

Figure 4.3 – Volumes of CVE IDs and CVE IDs with CVSS scores of 7 or higher added to NVD assigned to Debian Linux; the percentage of total CVE IDs added to CISA's KEV catalog, including average EPSS scores 2022-2024 (CVE Details, n.d.)

Now, let's apply the vulnerability improvement framework to the Debian Linux CVE ID data from 2022 to 2024. The four measures of the framework are as follows:

1. Did they reduce the number of CVE IDs during this three-year period? *Yes.*
2. Did they reduce the number of critical- and high-severity CVE IDs? *Yes.*
3. Did they reduce the average EPSS scores, thus reducing the probability of exploitation after CVE IDs are published? *Yes.*
4. Did they reduce the number of CVE IDs added to CISA's KEV catalog? *Yes.*

Debian Linux met the criteria of our vulnerability improvement framework because all four measures were lower at the end of the period than where they started. Well done, Debian! The data suggests that they did a great job of reducing CVE IDs in Debian Linux in the three years we examined. This means the people, processes, and technologies they leveraged had a meaningful security impact and cost reduction for their customers.

Let's examine the vulnerability trends for the Linux kernel next, as it is #1 on the list of operating systems with the most CVE IDs.

Linux kernel vulnerability trends

The Linux kernel isn't a full operating system per se, but it is the kernel that some of the most popular Linux operating systems are based on. The Linux kernel has a long history of relatively low volumes of CVE IDs. The first thing you'll likely notice about *Figure 4.4* is the big spike in CVE IDs in the Linux kernel in 2024:

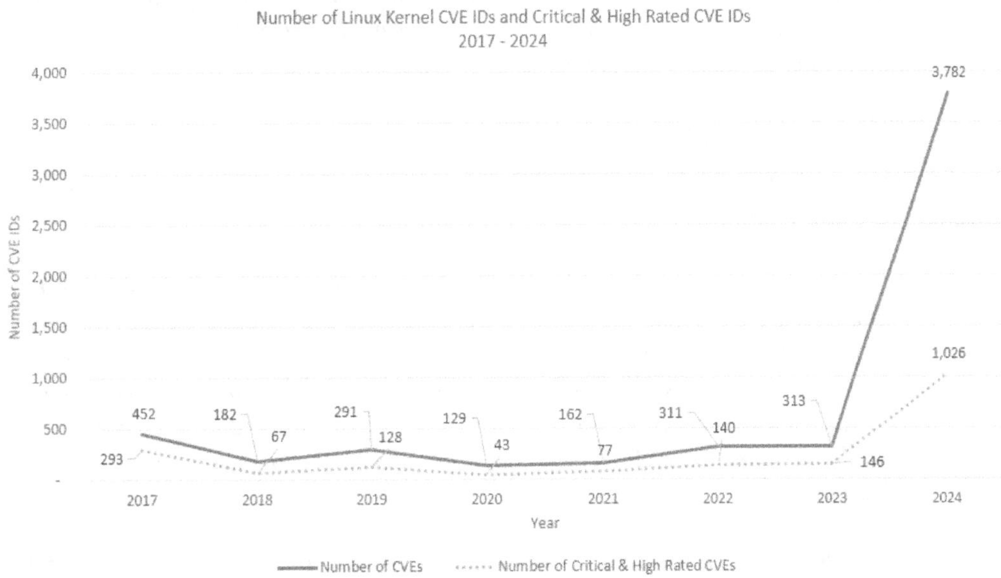

Figure 4.4 – Number of CVE IDs and critical- and high-rated CVE IDs in the Linux kernel (2017–2024) (CVE Details, n.d.)

For vulnerability data geeks like me, there is an interesting backstory behind this big increase. It appears that in the community that develops and maintains the Linux kernel, there were different opinions about whether assigning CVE IDs to vulnerabilities that weren't clearly exploitable in the Linux kernel was necessary. In February of 2024, MITRE announced that kernel.org was becoming a **CVE Numbering Authority** (**CNA**) (MITRE, 2024). This enabled kernel.org to assign CVE IDs to Linux kernel vulnerabilities, which then led to a large number of new CVE IDs being disclosed for the Linux kernel.

Of the 3,782 CVE IDs published in the NVD in 2024 for the Linux kernel, 1,435 (38%) appear to be CVE IDs from the prior few years, from 2019 to 2023. 1,026 of the 3,782 (27%) CVE IDs were rated critical or high severity. That's equivalent to 10.4 new CVE IDs per day and 2.8 critical or high-severity CVE IDs per day.

The following explanation was provided in the official kernel documentation:

> *"Common Vulnerabilities and Exposure (CVE®) numbers were developed as an unambiguous way to identify, define, and catalog publicly disclosed security vulnerabilities. Over time, their usefulness has declined with regards to the kernel project, and CVE numbers were very often assigned in inappropriate ways and for inappropriate reasons. Because of this, the kernel development community has tended to avoid them. However, the combination of continuing pressure to assign CVEs and other forms of security identifiers, and ongoing abuses by individuals and companies outside of the kernel community has made it clear that the kernel community should have control over those assignments."*
>
> *(The kernel development community. n.d.)*

Another explanation was published on LWN.net, the primary news and information source for the Linux software community:

> *"The kernel project has, for the most part, declined to participate in the CVE game. Famously, the project (or, at least, some of the most influential developers within it) has long taken the position that all bugs are potentially security issues, so there is no point in making a fuss over the fixes that have been identified by somebody as having security implications. Still, the kernel has proved fertile ground for those who would pad their resumes with CVE credits, and that grates on both developers and distributors.*
>
> *The situation has now changed, and the kernel will be assigning CVE numbers for itself. If that idea brings to mind a group of grumpy, beer-drinking kernel developers reviewing and rejecting CVE-number requests, though, then a closer look is warranted. The key to how this is going to work can be found in this patch to the kernel's documentation:*
>
> *As part of the normal stable release process, kernel changes that are potentially security issues are identified by the developers responsible for CVE number assignments and have CVE numbers automatically assigned to them. These assignments are published on the linux-cve-announce mailing list as announcements on a frequent basis.*
>
> *Note, due to the layer at which the Linux kernel is in a system, almost any bug might be exploitable to compromise the security of the kernel, but the possibility of exploitation is often not evident when the bug is fixed. Because of this, the CVE assignment team is overly cautious and assigns CVE numbers to any bugfix that*

> *they identify. This explains the seemingly large number of CVEs that are issued by the Linux kernel team."*
>
> *(Corbet, Jonathan. February 14, 2024)*

It turns out that Red Hat products also saw a marked increase in CVE IDs in 2024. Red Hat Linux is based on the Linux kernel. Subsequently, the increase in CVE IDs in the Linux kernel also led to increases in Red Hat Linux in 2024, as described in a Red Hat blog post:

> *"The common vulnerabilities and exposures (CVE) count skyrocketed to 4272, a significant increase from previous years, which were relatively stable. What caused this? The report highlights the Linux Kernel Organization becoming a CVE Numbering Authority (CNA) in February 2024. They began assigning CVEs to numerous kernel issues, many of which wouldn't have received assignments previously. If you filter out those new kernel.org CVEs, the trend line appears more familiar, with a slight increase, likely reflecting Red Hat's growing portfolio but nothing alarming." (Hughes, Maria H. June 6, 2025)*

Figure 4.5 dives a little deeper into the Linux kernel's CVE ID data between 2022 and 2024. As the figure illustrates, despite the high number of CVE IDs in 2024, the average EPSS score was a tiny 0.08%, and only 7 CVE IDs (0.19% of the total) from that year were added to CISA's KEV catalog:

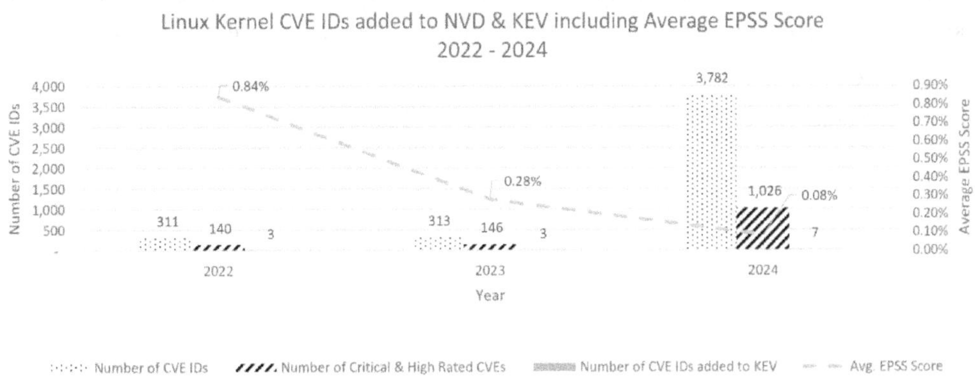

Figure 4.5 – Volumes of CVE IDs and CVE IDs with CVSS scores of 7 or higher added to NVD assigned to Linux Kernel; the percentage of total CVE IDs added to CISA's KEV catalog, including average EPSS scores 2022-2024 (CVE Details, n.d.)

Interestingly, there were many CVE IDs published in 2024 that did not have CVSS v3 scores; however, they all had CVSS v2 scores. The average CVSS v2 score for the 3,782 CVE IDs in 2024 was 5.6, and the median score was 5.5. The lowest CVSS v2 score was zero, and the highest was 9.8.

Let's apply the vulnerability improvement framework to the Linux kernel CVE ID data from 2022 to 2024. The four measures of the framework are as follows:

1. Did they reduce the number of CVE IDs during this three-year period? *No.*
2. Did they reduce the number of critical- and high-severity CVE IDs? *No.*
3. Did they reduce the average EPSS scores, thus reducing the probability of exploitation after CVE IDs are published? *Yes.*
4. Did they reduce the number of CVE IDs added to CISA's KEV catalog? *No.*

Although the Linux kernel does not meet the requirements for our vulnerability improvement framework because of the CVE ID count spike in 2024, it is sure to earn the respect of many CISOs, security teams, and other industry stakeholders for trying to be more transparent and precise about vulnerabilities in the Linux kernel. Typically, it is easier to manage something that you measure. Although in the short term this has generated more work for the developers who work on the Linux kernel and more work for enterprise vulnerability and remediation teams, in the long term, it will be a measurably higher-quality product with higher levels of security assurance. Besides, would CISOs and other industry stakeholders be satisfied if Apple, Google, or Microsoft stopped disclosing kernel vulnerabilities because every bug could be a vulnerability?

Next, let's examine one more flavor of Linux, Ubuntu Linux.

Ubuntu Linux vulnerability trends

Canonical Ubuntu Linux also appears on the list of operating systems with the most CVE IDs (CVE Details, n.d.), with 4,107 CVE IDs in total in February of 2026. As you can see from *Figure 4.6*, there was a dramatic (96%) reduction in CVE IDs in Ubuntu Linux in 2021, which has been sustained since:

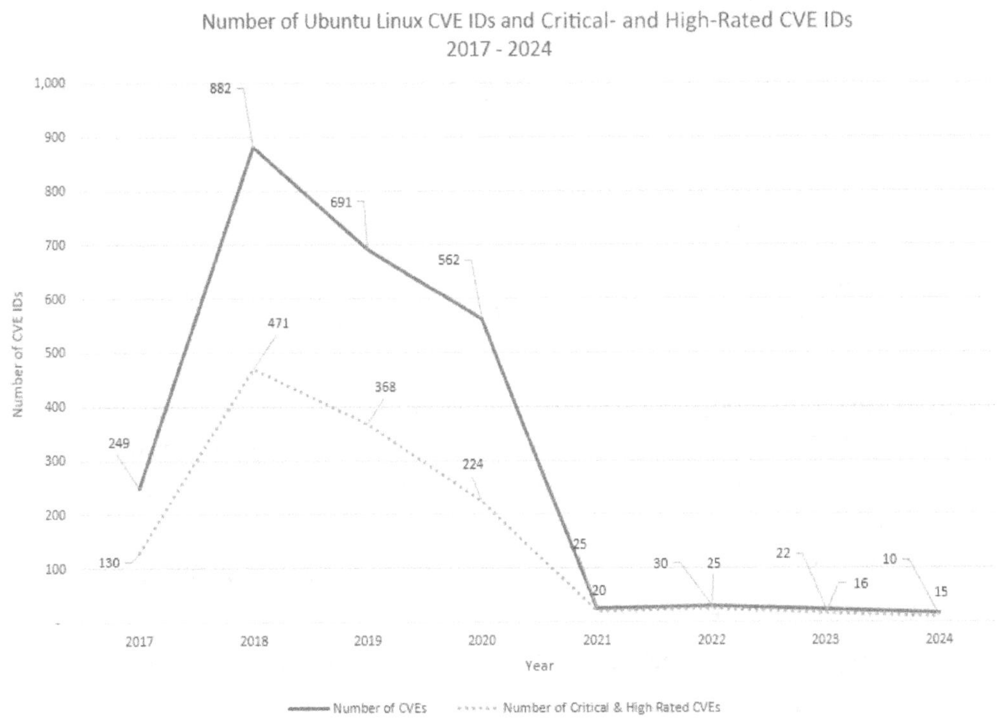

Figure 4.6 – The number of CVEs, critical- and high-rated severity CVEs, and low-complexity CVEs in Ubuntu Linux per year (2017–2024) (CVE Details, n.d.)

In my dataset of Ubuntu-related CVE IDs, there were approximately 1.5 CVE IDs per day on average in 2020. This dropped to 0.069 per day in 2021. However, the proportion of *high* and *critical* severity vulnerabilities increased from 40% in 2020 to 80% in 2021. The proportion peaked at 83% in 2022 before trending down to 73% in 2023 and 67% in 2024. A sharp reduction in CVE volume within a single year often occurs when an older Ubuntu LTS release reaches its end-of-life and is no longer receiving standard security updates. This may be the case here, as Ubuntu 16.04 LTS (Xenial Xerus) reached its end-of-life in April 2021 and transitioned into **Expanded Security Maintenance** (**ESM**) (Ubuntu, n.d.). Regardless of why the big reduction in CVE IDs occurred, Canonical was able to sustain the much lower CVE ID counts for at least four straight years, which is a super achievement.

Figure 4.7 reveals fewer CVE IDs each year for Ubuntu Linux between 2022 and 2024, as well as fewer CVE IDs in CISA's KEV catalog than at the beginning of the period:

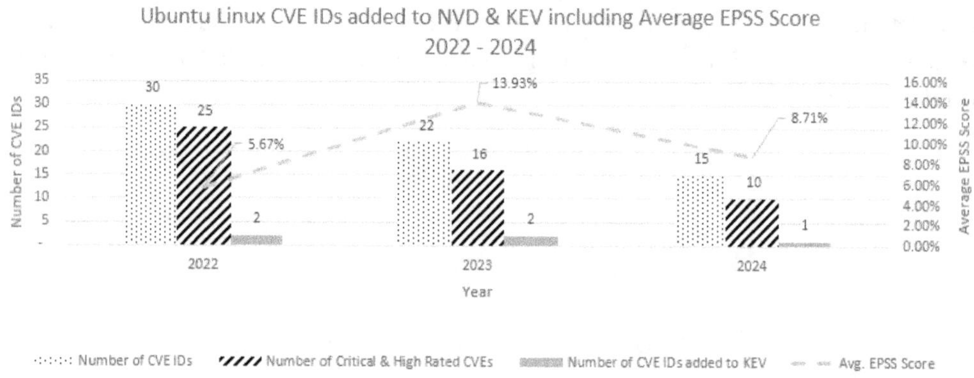

Figure 4.7 – Volumes of CVE IDs and CVE IDs with CVSS scores of 7 or higher added to NVD assigned to Ubuntu Linux; the percentage of total CVE IDs added to CISA's KEV catalog, including average EPSS scores 2022-2024 (CVE Details, n.d.)

The average EPSS score is higher for Ubuntu Linux during these years than for the other vendors we've looked at so far. But frankly, once the number of CVE IDs is driven down to very low levels, as seen here, one or two CVEs with relatively high EPSS scores can impact the average dramatically.

Let's apply the vulnerability improvement framework to the Ubuntu Linux CVE ID data from 2022 to 2024. The four measures of the framework are as follows:

1. Did they reduce the number of CVE IDs during this three-year period? *Yes.*
2. Did they reduce the number of critical- and high-severity CVE IDs? *Yes.*
3. Did they reduce the average EPSS scores, thus reducing the probability of exploitation after CVE IDs are published? *No.*
4. Did they reduce the number of CVE IDs added to CISA's KEV catalog? *Yes.*

Canonical has clearly done an outstanding job managing vulnerabilities in Ubuntu Linux over a period of years. This benefits its enterprise customers' vulnerability management and remediation teams by keeping associated costs low. Unfortunately, because the average EPSS score is higher at the end of the period than at the beginning of the period, Ubuntu Linux does not meet the criteria of our vulnerability improvement framework. It missed by the slimmest of measures.

Next, let's look at one final server operating system on the list of operating systems with the most CVE IDs, Windows Server 2022.

Windows Server 2022 vulnerability trends

Microsoft Windows Server 2012 and Microsoft Windows Server 2016 are both very popular server operating systems. Support for Microsoft Windows Server 2012 ended in October 2023. Windows Server 2016's end-of-support date is January 12, 2027, after which it will no longer get security updates from Microsoft. Windows Server 2022 was released in August 2021. This provides us with three full years of data to study between 2022 and 2024. *Figure 4.8* illustrates the CVE ID counts for Windows Server 2022, along with the average EPSS and the number of CVE IDs added to CISA's KEV catalog each year:

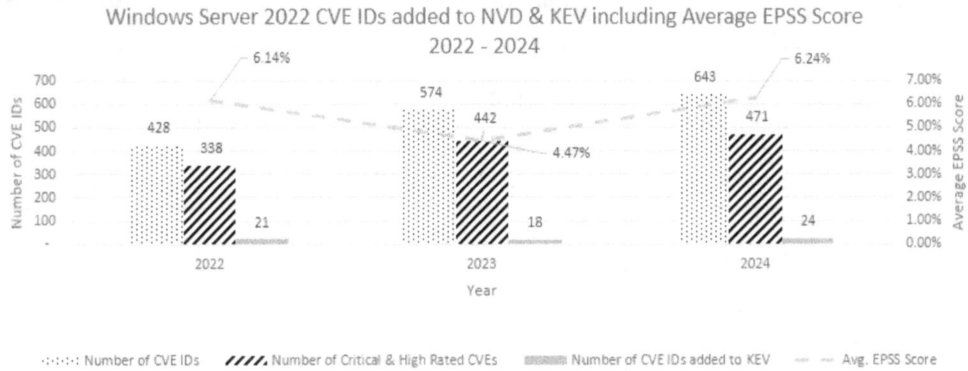

Figure 4.8 – Volumes of CVE IDs and CVE IDs with CVSS scores of 7 or higher added to NVD assigned to Windows Server 2022; the percentage of total CVE IDs added to CISA's KEV catalog, including average EPSS scores 2022-2024 (CVE Details, n.d.)

Let's apply the vulnerability improvement framework to the Windows Server 2022 CVE ID data from 2022 to 2024. The four measures of the framework are as follows:

1. Did they reduce the number of CVE IDs during this three-year period? *No.*
2. Did they reduce the number of critical- and high-severity CVE IDs? *No.*
3. Did they reduce the average EPSS scores, thus reducing the probability of exploitation after CVE IDs are published? *No.*
4. Did they reduce the number of CVE IDs added to CISA's KEV catalog? *No.*

The number of CVE IDs assigned to Windows Server 2022 increased each year during this period, as did the number of critical and high-severity vulnerabilities. 1,251 (76%) of the 1,645 CVE IDs that were published for Windows Server 2022 during these three years were critical or high severity. On average, Windows Server 2022 had 1.5 vulnerability disclosures per day during these years, with 1.14 critical or high-severity CVE IDs per day. This three-year period ended with more CVE IDs in CISA KEV for Windows Server 2022 than when it started and a slightly higher average EPSS score. Because of these factors, Windows Server 2022 does not meet the requirements for our vulnerability improvement framework.

Server operating system vulnerability summary

Table 4.1 provides a summary of the various server operating systems we examined in this section:

Operating System	Total Number of CVE IDs	Number of Critical & High Rated CVEs	Critical & High % of Total	Number of CVE IDs in CISA KEV
Debian Linux	1,761	1,015	57.6%	27
Linux Kernel	4,406	1,312	29.8%	13
Ubuntu Linux	67	51	76.1%	5
Windows Server 2022	1,645	1,251	76.0%	63

Table 4.1 – Summary of server operating systems analysis for 2022 – 2024, including the total number of CVE IDs, the total number of critical and high-severity CVE IDs, the percentage of the total number of CVE IDs represented by critical and high-severity CVE IDs, and the number of CVE IDs added to CISA's KEV catalog

The only server operating system that met the requirements of our vulnerability improvement framework is *Debian Linux*, with an honorable mention for *Ubuntu Linux*.

Now that we've looked at some popular server operating systems, let's shift our focus to a couple of popular client operating systems.

Windows 11

Microsoft Windows 11 was released in October 2021, giving us three full years of data to analyze. Evaluating CVE assignments for Windows 11 is more complex than for other operating systems because Microsoft's annual feature update cadence bundles security fixes into cumulative releases. These feature updates are labeled 21H2, 22H2, 23H2, and 24H2 to indicate the year of release (Microsoft, June 2025).

Both the base Windows 11 product and each feature update receive their own CVE assignments in the NVD. Because Windows 11 devices do not all install feature updates immediately, Microsoft continues assigning CVEs to older feature updates for as long as those versions remain within their official support lifecycle. For example, Windows 11 23H2 was released on October 31, 2023. Although Windows 11 24H2 shipped in October 2024, Microsoft will continue issuing CVEs for 23H2 through November 2026 to support systems that have not yet upgraded (Microsoft, n.d.). I did my best to sort through the CVE IDs published for each feature update to get a view of unique CVE IDs for Windows 11 using CVE Details as my data source. *Figure 4.9* is the result of this analysis:

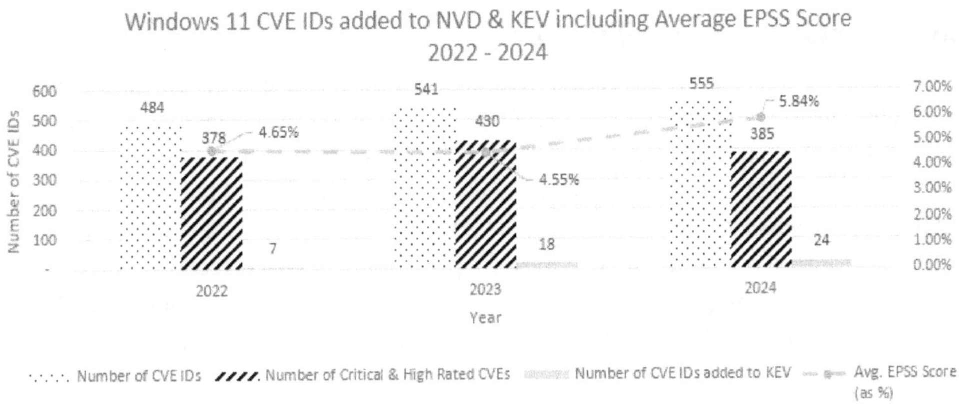

Figure 4.9 – Volumes of CVE IDs and CVE IDs with CVSS scores of 7 or higher added to NVD assigned to Windows 11; the percentage of total CVE IDs added to CISA's KEV catalog, including average EPSS scores 2022-2024 (CVE Details, n.d.)

> **Note**
>
> I did try to cross-reference my CVE ID counts using a few third-party information sources and AI chatbots, but digging through this data is harder than it sounds. Remember, these figures represent a snapshot at a point in time that started changing almost immediately after I took it.

Let's apply the vulnerability improvement framework to the Windows 11 CVE ID data from 2022 to 2024. The four measures of the framework are as follows:

1. Did they reduce the number of CVE IDs during this three-year period? *No.*
2. Did they reduce the number of critical- and high-severity CVE IDs? *No.*
3. Did they reduce the average EPSS scores, thus reducing the probability of exploitation after CVE IDs are published? *No.*
4. Did they reduce the number of CVE IDs added to CISA's KEV catalog? *No.*

The total number of CVE IDs across the three years examined is 1,580, of which 1,193 (76%) were rated critical or high severity. This is equivalent to 1.44 new CVE IDs per day on average over those three years, and 1.09 CVE IDs rated critical or high severity per day on average. The average EPSS score at the start of the three-year period was 4.65% in 2022 and ended the period with 5.84% in 2024. The number of CVE IDs added to CISA's KEV catalog grew every year, totaling 49 over the three years. Because of these factors, Windows 11 does not meet the requirements for our vulnerability improvement framework for the three years examined.

Next let's look at a popular Apple client operating system.

Apple macOS vulnerability trends

Now I'll examine Apple's macOS. Apple started calling this operating system macOS instead of Mac OS X in 2016, with the announcement of macOS 10.12 Sierra. There have been numerous versions of macOS since then. Looking at the period between 2022 and 2024, according to CVE Details there were 1,314 CVE IDs assigned to macOS, of which 660 (50%) had a CVSS score equal to or greater than 7. This is equivalent to 1.20 new CVE IDs per day on average and 0.6 CVE IDs rated critical or high severity on average, per day. *Figure 4.10* reveals that CVE IDs increased each year during the period, although the average EPSS scores declined in each of the three years. The period ended with fewer CVE IDs in CISA's KEV catalog, totaling 34 for the three years.

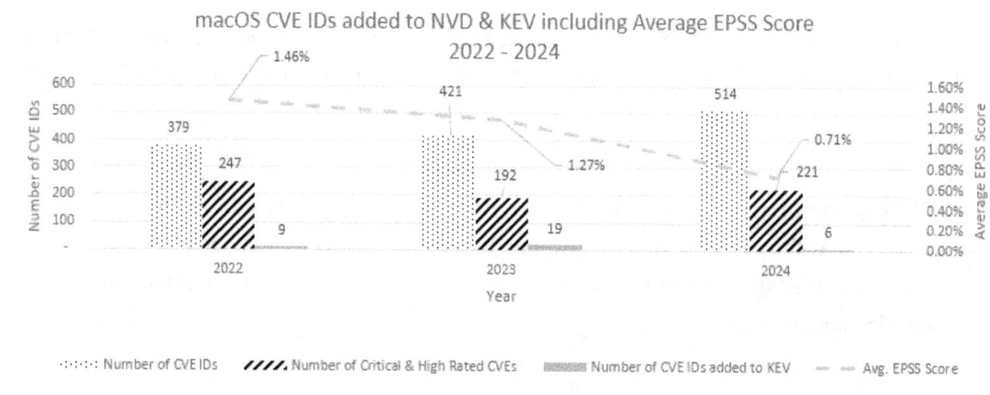

Figure 4.10 – Volumes of CVE IDs and CVE IDs with CVSS scores of 7 or higher added to NVD assigned to Apple macOS; the percentage of total CVE IDs added to CISA's KEV catalog, including average EPSS scores 2022-2024 (CVE Details, n.d.)

How did macOS perform when our vulnerability improvement framework was applied? Because of the growth in CVE IDs during the period, Apple's macOS does not meet the criteria for our vulnerability improvement framework.

Let me summarize the results of the client operating systems we looked at in this section.

Client operating system vulnerability summary

Table 4.2 provides a summary of the two client operating systems we examined in this section:

Operating System	Total Number of CVE IDs	Number of Critical & High-Rated CVEs	Critical & High % of Total	Number of CVE IDs in CISA KEV
Windows 11	1,580	1,193	75.5%	49
macOS	1,314	660	50.2%	34

Table 4.2 – Summary of client operating systems analysis for 2022 – 2024, including the total number of CVE IDs, the total number of critical and high-severity CVE IDs, the percentage of the total number of CVE IDs represented by critical and high-severity CVE IDs, and the number of CVE IDs added to CISA's KEV catalog

Microsoft Windows 11 had 266 CVE IDs more than Apple macOS during the three-year period examined. Apple macOS had 533 fewer critical and high-severity CVE IDs than Windows 11 and 15 fewer CVE IDs in CISA's KEV catalog during the same period.

Now that we've looked at vendors as well as client and server operating systems, let's examine a couple of popular mobile operating systems next.

Google Android vulnerability trends

Let's look at Android, a mobile operating system manufactured by Google. Android's initial release date was in September 2008, and CVE IDs for Android started showing up in 2009. During the three years between 2022 and 2024, 3,554 CVE IDs were filed for Android, equivalent to 3.25 new CVE IDs per day on average. There was a 53% reduction in CVE IDs in 2024 compared to 2023. There was a total of 1,365 CVE IDs rated critical or high severity in these three years. This is equivalent to 38% of all CVE IDs assigned to Android, representing 1.25 new CVE IDs per day on average. The number of these severe CVE IDs decreased each year during this period. The number of CVE IDs added to CISA's KEV catalog during this time was relatively low, given the relatively large number of CVE IDs assigned to Android, totaling just 10 CVE IDs. The average EPSS scores were also relatively low and ended the three-year period lower than where they started. *Figure 4.11* illustrates these measures across the three-year period.

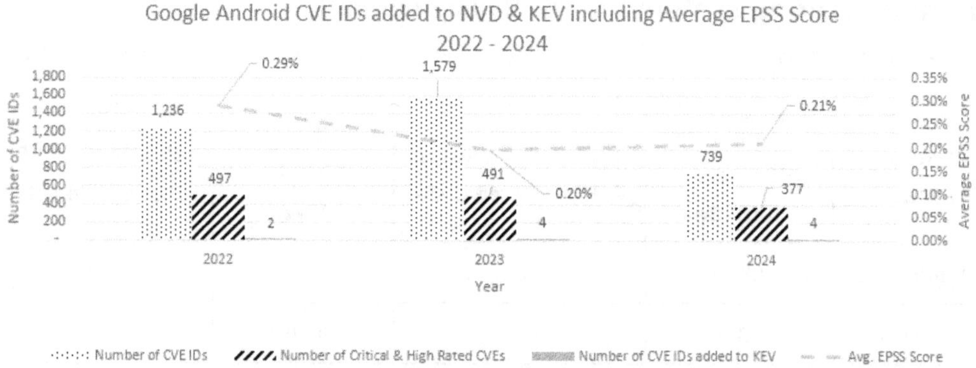

Figure 4.11 – Volumes of CVE IDs and CVE IDs with CVSS scores of 7 or higher added to NVD assigned to Google Android; the percentage of total CVE IDs added to CISA's KEV catalog, including average EPSS scores 2022-2024 (CVE Details, n.d.)

Let's apply the vulnerability improvement framework to the Google Android CVE ID data from 2022 to 2024.

1. Did they reduce the number of CVE IDs during this three-year period? *Yes.*
2. Did they reduce the number of critical- and high-severity CVE IDs? *Yes.*
3. Did they reduce the average EPSS scores, thus reducing the probability of exploitation after CVE IDs are published? *Yes.*
4. Did they reduce the number of CVE IDs added to CISA's KEV catalog? *No.*

Despite the relatively large number of CVE IDs, Android improved in three of the four areas required to meet our vulnerability improvement framework for this time period. The number of CVE IDs added to the KEV catalog was higher at the end of the period than at the start. It's also important to note that despite the relatively high number of CVE IDs, their overall exploitability appears to be low. If an operating system is going to accumulate a large volume of CVE IDs, it is far better for those vulnerabilities to be unlikely to be exploited, as this reduces the number of urgent, out-of-cycle patching events that vulnerability management and remediation teams must handle. Although Android didn't meet all the requirements of our vulnerability improvement framework, they get an honorable mention for improving so much during this three-year time period.

Next, let's look at Apple iOS.

Apple iOS vulnerability trends

Apple started releasing iPhone OS in June 2007, and later it was renamed iOS. iOS had 830 CVE IDs between 2022 and 2024. That's an average of 277 CVE IDs per year and an average of 0.76 new CVE IDs per day. iOS had 405 critical and high-rated CVE IDs, equivalent to 49% of the total and 0.37 new CVE IDs per day on average. *Figure 4.12* illustrates how the CVE IDs, critical and high-severity CVE IDs, average EPSS scores, and CVE IDs added to CISA's KEV catalog trended between 2022 and 2024.

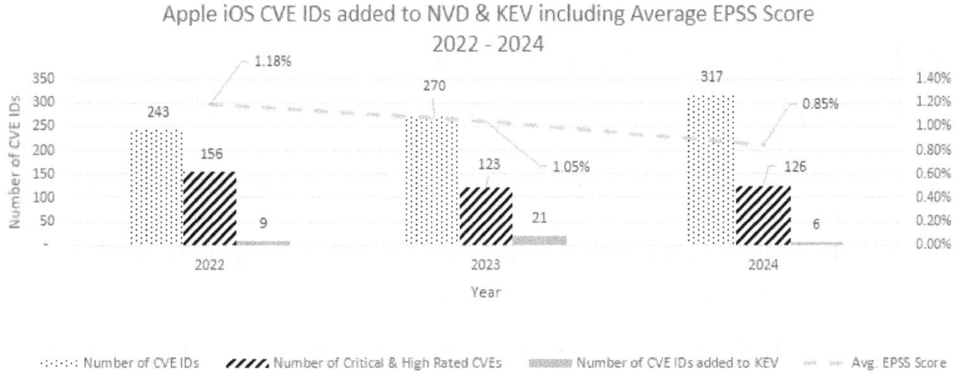

Figure 4.12 – Volumes of CVE IDs and CVE IDs with CVSS scores of 7 or higher added to NVD assigned to Apple iOS; the percentage of total CVE IDs added to CISA's KEV catalog, including average EPSS scores 2022-2024 (CVE Details, n.d.)

Figure 4.12 shows us that Apple iOS almost met the criteria for our vulnerability improvement framework. So close! The slightly elevated number of CVE IDs was the only negative factor in an otherwise great drive to reduce risk for Apple's customers.

Mobile operating system summary

So how did Apple iOS compare to Android? *Table 4.3* provides a summary.

Operating System	Total Number of CVE IDs	Number of Critical & High Rated CVEs	Critical & High % of Total	Number of CVE IDs in CISA KEV
Google Android	3,554	1,365	38.4%	10
Apple iOS	830	405	48.8%	36

Table 4.3 – Apple iOS and Google Android CVE ID comparison 2022–2024

Fewer vulnerabilities, fewer severe vulnerabilities, and fewer exploitable vulnerabilities means less risk and less expense. Apple iOS had significantly fewer CVE IDs during the period but still ended up with more exploited vulnerabilities in CISA's KEV catalog than Google Android.

Next, let's look at one final category of popular software, web browsers.

Web browser vulnerability trends

Web browsers attract a lot of attention from security researchers and attackers alike. This is because they are hard to live without. Everyone uses at least one browser on desktops, mobile devices, and on some types of servers. Operating systems' development teams can bake layers of security features into their products, but web browsers tend to bring threats right through all those host-based firewalls and other security layers. Web browsers have been notoriously difficult to secure, but have improved over the years.

I'll examine two popular web browsers in this section: **Apple Safari** and **Google Chrome**. Everyone tends to have a favorite browser, and some people I've briefed in the past became emotional when their favorite browser had more vulnerabilities than they thought possible.

> Note
>
> Please keep in mind that all of this CVE data is imperfect and is a snapshot in time that can change rapidly. Please don't let this data put you in a bad mood.

Apple Safari vulnerability trends

Apple Safari was introduced in 2003 and runs on a range of devices, including those powered by Apple operating systems, such as macOS and iOS. There were 138 CVE IDs assigned to Safari between 2022 and the end of 2024. This is equivalent to, on average, 46 CVE IDs per year and 0.13 CVE IDs per day. During this three-year period, there were 82 CVE IDs that were rated critical or high severity, the equivalent of 0.07 CVE IDs per day on average. *Figure 4.13* illustrates the three-year trend for the measures in our vulnerability improvement framework:

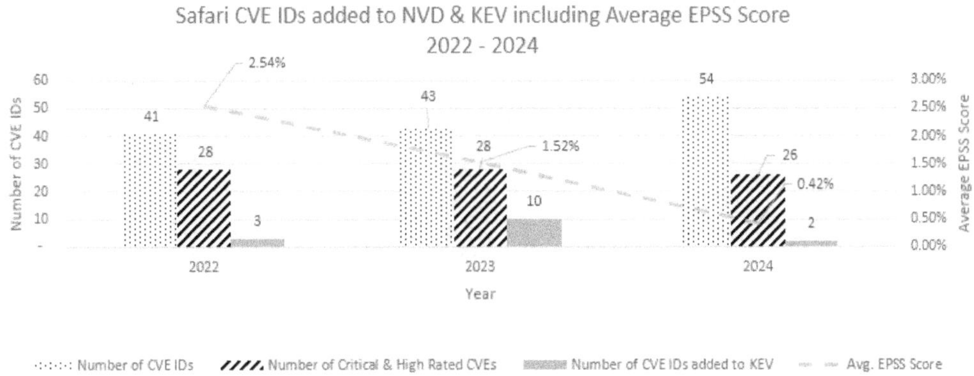

Figure 4.13 – Volumes of CVE IDs and CVE IDs with CVSS scores of 7 or higher added to NVD assigned to Apple Safari; the percentage of total CVE IDs added to CISA's KEV catalog, including average EPSS scores 2022-2024 (CVE Details, n.d.)

Let's apply the vulnerability improvement framework to the Apple Safari CVE ID data from 2022 to 2024:

1. Did they reduce the number of CVE IDs during this three-year period? *No.*
2. Did they reduce the number of critical- and high-severity CVE IDs? *Yes.*
3. Did they reduce the average EPSS scores, thus reducing the probability of exploitation after CVE IDs are published? *Yes.*
4. Did they reduce the number of CVE IDs added to CISA's KEV catalog? *Yes.*

Unfortunately, the slight increase in CVE IDs in 2024 means that Safari did not meet the criteria for our vulnerability improvement framework during this three-year period. But it was very close!

Next, let's dive into the vulnerability trends for another extremely popular web browser, Google Chrome.

Google Chrome vulnerability trends

The Google Chrome browser was released in 2008, first on Windows and then later on other operating systems. Looking at the three-year period between 2022 and 2024, there were 913 CVE IDs assigned to Chrome. This is an average of 304 vulnerabilities per year (CVE Details, n.d.), and 0.83 CVE IDs per day. Of these 913 CVE IDs, 644 of them, or 71%, were rated critical or high severity. This is the equivalent of 0.59 new critical or high-severity CVE IDs per day on average. As illustrated in *Figure 4.14*, the number of critical and high-severity vulnerabilities increased in 2024 but was still lower than at the beginning of the period; thus, Chrome met the criteria of our vulnerability improvement framework. Congratulations, Google!

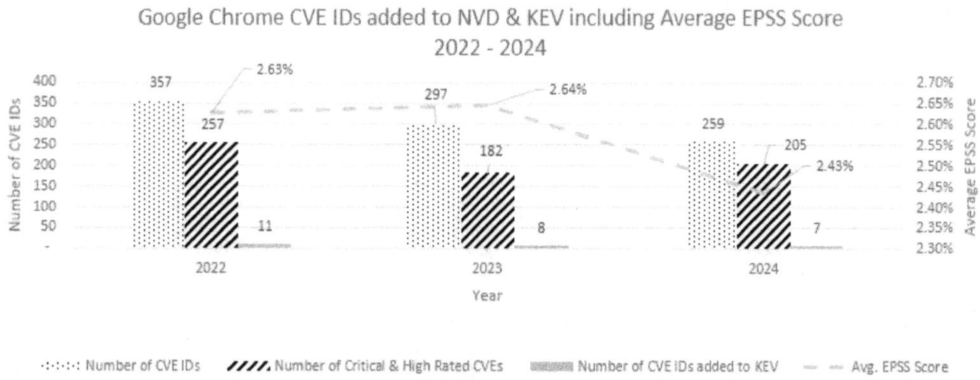

Figure 4.14 – Volumes of CVE IDs and CVE IDs with CVSS scores of 7 or higher added to NVD assigned to Google Chrome; the percentage of total CVE IDs added to CISA's KEV catalog, including average EPSS scores 2022-2024 (CVE Details, n.d.)

Here are the vulnerability improvement framework criteria applied to the Google Chrome CVE ID data from 2022 to 2024:

1. Did they reduce the number of CVE IDs during this three-year period? *Yes.*
2. Did they reduce the number of critical- and high-severity CVE IDs? *Yes.*
3. Did they reduce the average EPSS scores, thus reducing the probability of exploitation after CVE IDs are published? *Yes.*
4. Did they reduce the number of CVE IDs added to CISA's KEV catalog? *Yes.*

You might be thinking, how can I analyze popular web browsers and not include Mozilla Firefox? After all, it's a very popular browser. Okay, let's do it!

Mozilla Firefox vulnerability trends

The good folks at Firefox.com describe themselves this way:

> *"Firefox was created in 2004 by Mozilla as a faster, more private, and customizable alternative to browsers like Internet Explorer. Today, we are still not-for-profit, still not owned by any billionaires and still working to make the internet — and the time you spend on it — better."* (Firefox, n.d.)

During the three years I examined, 527 CVE IDs were assigned to Firefox. That's an average of 176 CVE IDs per year or 0.48 CVE IDs per day. Of these 527 CVE IDs, 282 were critical or high severity, the equivalent of 54% of the total, with 0.26 new CVE IDs per day on average. Firefox had a total of 5 CVE IDs added to CISA's KEV catalog during these three years and kept its average annual EPSS scores below 1%. *Figure 4.15* paints this picture for us:

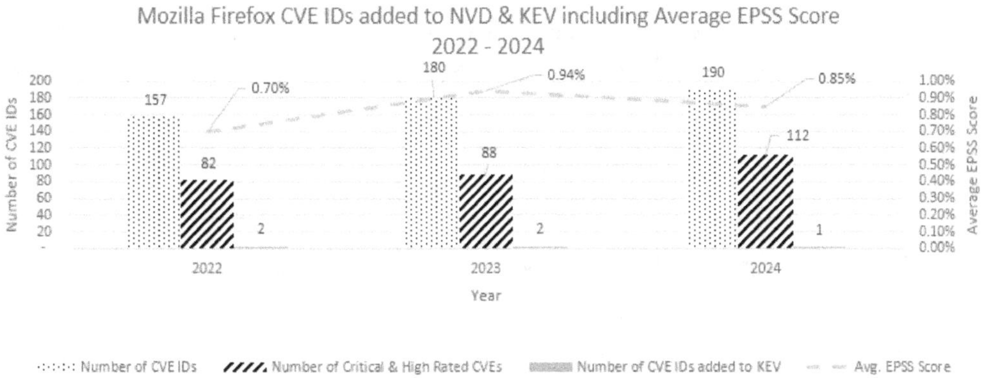

Figure 4.15 – Volumes of CVE IDs and CVE IDs with CVSS scores of 7 or higher added to NVD assigned to Firefox; the percentage of total CVE IDs added to CISA's KEV catalog, including average EPSS scores 2022-2024 (CVE Details, n.d.)

Let's apply the vulnerability improvement framework to the Firefox CVE ID data from 2022 to 2024:

1. Did they reduce the number of CVE IDs during this three-year period? *No.*
2. Did they reduce the number of critical- and high-severity CVE IDs? *No.*
3. Did they reduce the average EPSS scores, thus reducing the probability of exploitation after CVE IDs are published? *No.*
4. Did they reduce the number of CVE IDs added to CISA's KEV catalog? *Yes.*

Firefox had a lower CVE ID count than Google Chrome, and its relatively low CISA KEV catalog CVE ID count is very positive for Firefox users. However, CVE IDs increased each year during the three-year period, as did the CVE IDs rated critical and high severity. For this reason, Firefox did not meet the criteria of our vulnerability improvement framework.

Web browser summary

The data we examined suggests that all three of these vendors are doing an excellent job of managing vulnerabilities in some of the world's most popular web browsers. This is very encouraging. *Table 4.4* summarizes some of the findings from our analysis:

Web Browser	Total Number of CVE IDs	Number of Critical & High Rated CVEs	Critical & High % of Total	Number of CVE IDs in CISA KEV
Apple Safari	138	82	59.4%	15

Web Browser	Total Number of CVE IDs	Number of Critical & High Rated CVEs	Critical & High % of Total	Number of CVE IDs in CISA KEV
Google Chrome	913	644	70.5%	26
Mozilla Firefox	527	282	53.5%	5

Table 4.4 – Apple Safari, Google Chrome, and Mozilla Firefox CVE ID Comparison 2022–2024

While Safari had the fewest CVE IDs by a large margin, Firefox had the lowest proportion of critical and high-severity vulnerabilities and the fewest CVE IDs in CISA's KEV catalog. Perhaps ironically, because it had a relatively high CVE ID count in 2022, Google Chrome met the criteria of our vulnerability improvement framework because it improved so much during the three years examined. But it also illustrates the point of our vulnerability improvement framework – constant improvement.

Vulnerability improvement framework summary

Let's finish this section on vendor and product vulnerability trends with a summary of how the vendors, operating systems, and web browsers we examined fared with regard to our vulnerability improvement framework.

Table 4.5 summarizes how each vendor, operating system, and web browser that we examined did across the three measures of the vulnerability improvement framework:

Vendor / Product	Fewer CVE IDs?	Fewer CVE IDs with CVSS Score <=7?	Lower Average EPSS Score?	Fewer CVE IDs in KEV Catalog?
Google	Yes	Yes	Yes	Yes
Microsoft	No	No	Yes	No
Oracle	No	No	No	Yes
Server OSes	**Fewer CVE IDs?**	**Fewer CVE IDs with CVSS Score <=7?**	**Lower Average EPSS Score?**	**Fewer CVE IDs in KEV Catalog?**

Debian Linux	Yes	Yes	Yes	Yes
Linux Kernel	No	No	Yes	No
Ubuntu Linux	Yes	Yes	No	Yes
Windows Server 2022	No	No	No	No
Client OSes	**Fewer CVE IDs?**	**Fewer CVE IDs with CVSS Score <=7?**	**Lower Average EPSS Score?**	**Fewer CVE IDs in KEV Catalog?**
Windows 11	No	No	No	No
macOS	No	No	Yes	Yes
Mobile OSes	**Fewer CVE IDs?**	**Fewer CVE IDs with CVSS Score <=7?**	**Lower Average EPSS Score?**	**Fewer CVE IDs in KEV Catalog?**
Google Android	Yes	Yes	Yes	No
Apple iOS	No	Yes	Yes	Yes
Web Browsers	**Fewer CVE IDs?**	**Fewer CVE IDs with CVSS Score <=7?**	**Lower Average EPSS Score?**	**Fewer CVE IDs in KEV Catalog?**
Apple Safari	No	Yes	Yes	Yes
Google Chrome	Yes	Yes	Yes	Yes

Mozilla Firefox	No	No	No	Yes

Table 4.5 – Summary of whether the vendors, operating systems, and web browsers examined in this chapter met the criteria of the vulnerability improvement framework during 2022-2024

Debian Linux was the only server operating system to improve its CVE ID data across all four measures of the vulnerability improvement framework during the three-year period. However, Ubuntu Linux missed it by the closest of margins, and clearly has done a fantastic job keeping CVE ID counts very low. Neither of the two client operating systems we examined was able to meet the requirements. Finally, Google Chrome was the only web browser examined that met all the criteria after improving markedly during the three years I studied. However, Safari had ultra-low CVE ID counts for a web browser and missed meeting our criteria by just 14 CVE IDs in 2024.

I hope this lengthy analysis in *Chapters 3* and *4* has given you some insights into which vendors and products have been improving recently across some of the key measures that enterprise vulnerability management and remediation teams can leverage to manage vulnerabilities. Let me finish this chapter by providing some general guidance on vulnerability management.

Vulnerability management guidance

A well-run vulnerability management program is critical for all organizations. As you've seen from the data and analysis in this chapter, there have been lots of vulnerabilities disclosed across the industry, and the volumes have been increasing, not decreasing. By the end of 2025, there were over 309,000 CVE IDs in the NVD. Attackers know this and understand how challenging it is for organizations to keep up with the volume and complexity of patching the various hardware and software products they have in their environments. Defenders must be perfect, while attackers just have to be good or lucky once. Let me provide you with some guidance regarding vulnerability management programs based on my experience managing some large programs.

Asset inventories

First, I cannot overstate the importance of asset management and its role in enabling effective vulnerability management, incident response, and other key aspects of cybersecurity and IT management. If an organization doesn't maintain an accurate inventory of IT assets, it is very difficult, indeed nearly impossible, to effectively manage vulnerabilities and security misconfigurations. For example, let's say a vulnerability management team scans a system for unpatched vulnerabilities. They discover numerous unpatched critical and high-severity vulnerabilities present on the system that exceed remediation time service-level agreements.

The next step would be to quickly remediate these findings. Who should the vulnerability management team or remediation team contact to perform application compatibility testing for the security updates and install the updates on the system? Without an accurate asset inventory, finding the owner of that system might be a daunting task in a large enterprise environment. The same problem is pressurized during an active cybersecurity incident when a system has been compromised, but there isn't an accurate asset inventory to use to find the owner and get other vital details on the system being investigated or other systems that might also need to be investigated. One fundamental question in these scenarios is, who has the administrator credentials?

Organizations that are really good at managing their assets' life cycles and maintaining accurate, detailed inventories have a much easier time in such scenarios. For example, imagine if a vulnerability management team didn't have to scan hundreds of thousands of systems looking for the dreaded Log4j vulnerability during the Christmas holiday period. What if, instead, they could simply query their asset management database and find a list of assets with the vulnerable component? What if the asset management database could provide the name and contact information of the owner of every system where the vulnerable component exists? Remediation could be a lot faster and with less drama than scanning hundreds of thousands of systems looking for the vulnerable component, while active attacks are underway on the internet, and scrambling to try to find system owners to start testing and remediation efforts. There are some powerful integrations between enterprise asset management products and many enterprise vulnerability scanners that make vulnerability management and incident response easier.

Additionally, there are several vendors that make products that help automate asset discovery on large networks. Some examples include **Axonius**, **Lansweeper**, **runZero**, and **Qualys**, among others. These products can help continuously discover assets on-premises and in the cloud and feed their details into asset management solutions such as **ServiceNow**.

The key to efficient vulnerability management, including vulnerability reporting, is good asset management. Investing in asset management will pay dividends in many ways in large enterprise environments. That said, asset management is neither easy nor inexpensive for large enterprises that have complex, diverse computing environments. I have talked to some CISOs who have taken ownership of asset management for their enterprises because it is too critical for the success of their cybersecurity programs to leave it to other teams to half-heartedly manage. In my experience, this is the exception, not the rule. However, I can see some wisdom in this approach. Asset management can be an immense amount of work, especially for organizations that are just starting or resuming that journey after many years without focusing on it. But since it's on the critical path for some key cybersecurity functions, I can understand why some CISOs would want to manage it themselves.

> **Tip**
>
> Asset management can be resource-intensive and could consume resources on a cybersecurity team that should be used for other under-resourced cybersecurity functions instead. In such scenarios, a carefully weighted balance between the two needs to be maintained.

Governance, risk, and compliance

Governance, risk, and compliance (**GRC**) are super important for cybersecurity programs, but are often overlooked or undervalued by CISOs and CIOs of organizations that don't have mature IT operations or cybersecurity programs. If you don't try to govern things rationally upfront, you'll have to deal with them later when they are an unwieldy mess, more resource-intensive, and more costly.

In a vulnerability management context, understanding the risk that unpatched vulnerabilities pose to your organization is a great starting point. The better you are at translating that risk into a dollar figure range representing the potential cost of an exposure, the easier it will be to compare it with other cybersecurity and business risks that the organization pays attention to. For example, if you have credible quantitative risk calculations that show that an unpatched vulnerability on an internet-facing system would likely cost the organization between $250,000 and $2,000,000, it makes it easier for business executives to understand the difference between that risk and other risks they manage, such as legal, human resources, and financial risks. It also makes it easier for everyone to understand why it would be advantageous to spend $150,000 to treat that risk, given that it would be potentially much more expensive to accept the risk.

Once you can articulate the risk, developing a policy that supports managing and minimizing the risk can be very helpful. Most technical CISOs I've advised don't see the value in writing corporate policies because no one reads them, and anyone who does complains about them. It took me a long time in my career to truly appreciate the roles that governance and policies play in supporting a successful cybersecurity program. I discussed vulnerability management SLAs in *Chapter 3*, so I won't duplicate that discussion here. Developing a vulnerability management policy that clearly articulates vulnerability remediation SLAs, as well as other requirements, is important for a few reasons:

- First, it sets expectations among asset owners and operators about how quickly they need to remediate vulnerabilities in the assets they own. Since policies aren't discretionary, asset owners and operators are bound to comply with the policy's requirements or potentially suffer consequences. This tension is helpful to teams as they perform resource and budget planning, to ensure they ask for what they need to meet the requirements of the policy. They aren't "empire building" when asking for more people for vulnerability remediation; they can use vulnerability program data to prove they are under-resourced.

- Second, a good vulnerability management policy reflects the risk appetite of the organization. This is helpful to CISOs and other executives as they navigate the risk-based decisions that unfold in front of them. If a CISO knows that the organization has an enormous risk appetite because it is in a hyper-competitive industry, for example, it makes it easier for them to accept that they need to manage large inventories of vulnerabilities, because this is supported by the policy that the organization approved.
- A third thing that a clearly articulated vulnerability management policy helps with is vulnerability management program reporting. Instead of providing elaborate reports with all sorts of interesting cuts of vulnerability data, simply reporting on whether each part of the organization is complying with the approved policy and what the variances are is typically all that is necessary for most executives.

My advice for organizations that are just developing vulnerability management policies for the first time or trying to mature and operationalize their existing policies is to consider including the following in their policies:

- **Service-level agreements**: Include SLAs based on risk appetite, credible quantified costs of exposures, and asset values to the organization. As I discussed earlier, I typically advocate for different SLAs for internet-facing assets, crown jewels, and a third category for everything else.
- **Technology**: The vulnerability management policy should include requirements for asset owners and operators to install and maintain the specific technologies that the asset management and vulnerability management programs require to function effectively. This could include agents that enable the vulnerability management team to perform authenticated scans of all assets, such as agents from Qualys, Tenable, Rapid7, or others. If every system doesn't have these installed, then every system can't be scanned for vulnerabilities effectively. Your asset inventory and overall security posture depend on ensuring that required technologies are installed on every system in the environment. Embedding these technology requirements directly into policy reinforces that unmanaged or isolated "shadow" networks, often maintained to avoid compliance obligations, are no longer acceptable. All newly provisioned and existing systems must run the tools that allow the organization to track them, assess the risk they introduce, and keep them properly updated.

- **Scope**: Make the scope of the policy clear so that everyone knows it applies to all software and hardware, in on-premises environments, containers, virtual machines, in the cloud, and hosted by third parties. It applies to all software and hardware procured from third parties and developed by your own development teams (whether they are FTEs, contractors, or third-party development organizations). This includes operating systems, web browsers, all applications, appliances such as firewalls and storage arrays, as well as routing and switching equipment.
- **End of Life (EOL)**: EOL software and hardware can pose a grave risk to enterprise environments. Many non-security managers view decommissioning assets, whose vendors will no longer release security updates for them, as an expense. They typically reason, why spend time and effort decommissioning old technology when they could expend that effort getting new capabilities into the hands of customers and partners? Just let it decay in place. But letting EOL software and hardware decay on an enterprise network quickly provides oxygen for attackers. As the inventory of unpatched vulnerabilities and security misconfigurations mounts, it makes it easier and easier for attackers to initially compromise an environment, move laterally, stage their attacks, stay persistent, exfiltrate data, and perform actions on objectives. The inventory of vulnerabilities on EOL software and hardware represents zero-day vulnerabilities to organizations foolish enough to let them persist, because the manufacturers of those technologies will never release security updates for them. Attackers will happily use that to their advantage over and over. In the meantime, most organizations' vulnerability management policies have the most aggressive SLAs for active zero-day exploits. So, then the question becomes *Why perform emergency patch cycles for new zero-day vulnerabilities if you are willing to let them accumulate by running EOL software and hardware on your network perpetually?* Decommissioning EOL software and hardware is the same as patching zero-day vulnerabilities. Including language in your vulnerability management policy that prohibits EOL software and hardware without approved exception requests is strongly recommended. Exceptions of this nature need to be recorded in the organization's cybersecurity risk register and periodically reviewed with senior leadership to ensure the appetite to carry such risk endures.
- **Consequences of lack of compliance**: Some of the IT workers I worked with in the past didn't think the rules applied to them. Some of them spent more time and effort trying to skirt the rules than it would take to comply with them. Since corporate policies are non-discretionary, including language that outlines the consequences for non-compliance gives them gravity they otherwise wouldn't have. It sends the message that it's not acceptable to ignore the policy. The first person who gets terminated for non-compliance is typically the last person to get terminated for non-

compliance because everyone else gets the message. If there truly is no consequence for non-compliance with security policies, then the best effort of some subset of team members is what you can reasonably expect.

- **Policy approvals**: Vulnerability management policies should be signed off by the largest group of most senior executives that is practical. This is to ensure that asset owners and operators can't interpret the lack of their leadership's signatures as a sign that they do not need to comply with the policy. I've literally had senior directors tell me that the company's vulnerability management policy wasn't signed off by their Vice President, so it doesn't apply to them. Having a policy that is approved by the largest group of the most senior leaders sends a message to everyone that security is a priority at the company, and no one is an exception, based on who they report to. The size of the organization, how it is organized, and its culture are all factors in how high and broad security policy approvals need to be. Compliance with vulnerability management policies is not limited to IT groups, and the policy signatories should reflect this. Legal, HR, Finance, Marketing, Sales – anywhere IT and OT asset owners and operators exist – should be covered by the umbrella of the signatories.
- **Education and awareness**: Once you have your vulnerability management policy approved, it's time to drive awareness of the existence of the policy and educate asset owners, operators, and the stakeholder communities they serve about the details. Ultimately, you want all the stakeholders to understand that it is their responsibility to understand and comply with the policy. It's not their vulnerability management team's responsibility to catch them in the act of non-compliance in order to get them to comply with the policy. This is why awareness and education are key to the success of vulnerability management policies. This isn't a one-time activity because every organization has staff turnover and people who change roles over time. Periodic refresher awareness and training sessions on vulnerability management policies are very important to the long-term success of the program. Related to education and awareness is the topic of reporting, which I'll discuss in depth later in this chapter.

That's my advice for developing vulnerability management policies. Next, let's talk about another critical factor for a successful vulnerability management program: how often to scan assets for vulnerabilities.

Scanning for vulnerabilities

One objective of a vulnerability management program is to understand the risk that vulnerabilities present in your IT environment. This understanding is not static or slow-moving. As you saw from the vendor and product CVE ID analysis I provided earlier in this chapter, vulnerabilities are constantly being disclosed in all hardware and software. Because of this, data on the vulnerabilities in your environment can get stale quickly. The organizations that I have met that decided they would deploy security updates once per quarter, or once every six months, have an unusually high appetite for risk. Although, paradoxically, some of these same organizations told me they have no appetite for risk. It is always interesting to meet people who believe their highest priority risks are their vendors, instead of the cadre of attackers who are actively looking for ways to take advantage of them – attackers who, given the chance, will gladly encrypt all their data and demand a ransom for the decryption keys.

When I meet an organization with this type of policy, I wonder whether they really do have a data-driven view of the risk and whether the most senior layer of management really understands the risk that they are accepting on behalf of the entire organization, the Board of Directors, and all of their shareholders. Do they know that 110 new CVE IDs per day on average were published in 2024, with an average of 55 new critical or high-rated CVE IDs disclosed every day? If they are patching quarterly, that is equivalent to 9,900 vulnerabilities they'll need to triage to determine whether they impact their organization.

As an example, let's say a large enterprise runs Windows 11 on 10,000 clients and Windows Server 2022 on 5,000 servers in its data centers. Windows 11 had 1.44 new CVE IDs per day on average between 2022 and 2024, and 1.09 CVE IDs rated critical or high severity per day on average during the same period. That means at the end of the quarter, they'd have almost 1.3 million security updates to deploy on their Windows 11 systems, of which 981,000 would be critical or high severity. Windows Server 2022 had 1.5 vulnerability disclosures per day during these years, with 1.14 critical or high-severity CVE IDs per day. This would add another 675,000 security updates to deploy, of which 513,000 would be critical or high severity. Then add security updates for applications running on those systems, along with firewalls and routing and switching equipment. Double these figures for organizations that patch semi-annually. It is very easy for organizations to become overwhelmed with the number of updates they need to deploy when they have risk appetites this large. One compatibility issue, deployment issue, recalled security update, or high-severity incident, and they could delay deploying some security updates until the next patching cycle, 90 or 180 days in the future, further compounding the numbers.

They also accept the risk associated with large and quickly growing inventories of all those critical and high-severity vulnerabilities every day for 90 or 180 days. All the while, attackers only require one exploitable vulnerability in the right system to successfully initially compromise their environment. Remember the *Cybersecurity Usual Suspects*? Attackers can use any one of them or a combination of them to gain initial access, then use the huge inventory of unpatched vulnerabilities to move laterally, stay persistent, deploy ransomware, and gain access to systems that can be used for data exfiltration.

Instead of avoiding patching and rebooting systems to minimize disruption to their business, most of these organizations need to focus on building very efficient vulnerability management programs, with the goal of reducing risk in a more reasonable amount of time. Attackers have a huge advantage in environments that are both brittle and unpatched for long periods.

For most organizations, my recommendation is that vulnerability management teams *scan everything, every day*. Read that line again if you have to. Remember the submarine analogy I used in the *Preface* section of this book. Your vulnerability management program is one of the ways in which you look for defects in the hull of your submarine. Scanning every asset you have in your environment for vulnerabilities every day will help identify cracks and imperfections in the hull that, if exploited, would sink the submarine. Scanning everything every day for vulnerabilities and misconfigurations provides the organization with important data that will inform its risk decisions.

> **Tip**
>
> Remember the Cybersecurity Usual Suspects—finding and addressing security misconfigurations is just as important as vulnerabilities. Without up-to-date data, they are managing risk in an uninformed way.

For example, scanning everything every day will help identify when the most severe vulnerabilities, such as Log4j, show up in an environment months or years after it was thought to be remediated. Scanning every day provides the organization with the visibility required to identify and mitigate high- and critical-risk vulnerabilities before they can become problematic.

Note that I'm not recommending patching every day, just scanning to get a daily snapshot of the risk. As I discussed earlier in this chapter, remediation-time SLAs should be based on the risk appetite of the organization. Remember what I recommended earlier: use CTI to inform remediation priorities. This will help your organization reduce the highest-risk vulnerabilities first and provide the prescriptive priorities that remediation teams so often want. The combination of CTI and effective asset management can simplify and reduce costs related to your vulnerability management and remediation efforts.

For organizations that can accomplish it, using MITRE ATT&CK® to also inform vulnerability remediation priorities can reduce the number of high-priority vulnerabilities while reducing the risk of exploitation. I discuss this framework in detail in *Chapter 10, Cybersecurity Strategies*. Prioritizing patching the vulnerabilities that can support the techniques and procedures that attackers are known to use makes it harder for them to be successful.

It's important to note that mobile devices, especially of the BYOD variety, pose a significant challenge to vulnerability management teams. The data on mobile OS vulnerabilities provided earlier in this chapter indicates that there are hundreds or thousands of CVEs in popular mobile OSes every year. Most organizations simply can't scan these devices for vulnerabilities the same way they scan other assets. Instead, limiting mobile devices' access to sensitive information and high-value assets is more common. Requiring newer operating system versions and minimum patch levels in order to connect to corporate networks or services is also common. To this end, most of the enterprises I've met with over the years leverage **Mobile Device Management** (**MDM**) or **Mobile Application Management** (**MAM**) solutions.

For some organizations, scanning everything every day will require more resources than they currently have. For example, they might require more vulnerability scanning engines than they currently have in order to scan 100% of their IT assets every day. They might also want to do this scanning during off hours to reduce network traffic generated by scanning during regular work hours. This might mean that they must scan everything, every night, for a defined number of hours. To accomplish this, they'll need a sufficient number of scanning engines and staff to manage them. Another issue that plagues organizations that try to scan everything every day is that their networks were not designed with this requirement in mind. The volume of traffic generated by all that scanning can impair routing and switching equipment, internal firewalls, and proxy servers whose capacities have not been scoped to support such a task. Unfortunately for them, this limitation won't stop attackers. This type of limitation can lead to a rapid proliferation of scanning engines on network segments if the network capacity issues cannot be addressed.

Once vulnerability management teams have up-to-date data on the state of the environment, that data can be used to make risk-based decisions – for example, how quickly newly discovered vulnerabilities and misconfigurations should be addressed. Without up-to-date data on the state of the environment, hope will play a continual and central role in their vulnerability management strategy.

Next, let's discuss one final aspect of vulnerability management that I'd like to provide you with guidance on – reporting.

Reporting

The data generated by all this vulnerability scanning is gold dust for CISOs, especially for security programs that are relatively immature. Providing the C-suite and board of directors with data from this program can help CISOs get the resources they need and communicate the progress they are making with their security program. Effective reporting also helps asset owners and operators understand what their inventory of unpatched security vulnerabilities looks like and how they are performing in complying with remediation SLAs.

This list contains some useful example data points:

- A breakdown of the number of assets in inventory.
- A breakdown of the number of assets in inventory versus the total number of known assets. This provides visibility into the number of systems that are not in inventory and therefore not being scanned for vulnerabilities.
- The number of assets that are authenticated as scanned for vulnerabilities (the vulnerability scanner agent is installed and running on the system being scanned). Authenticated scans provide the maximum visibility to vulnerabilities on a system. Unauthenticated scans are more like network port scans that provide limited visibility of the vulnerabilities that might be present on a system. Note that not all systems support vulnerability scanning agents, so in some cases, unauthenticated scans are as good as it gets.
- The number of critical and high-severity vulnerabilities present.
- The average remediation time for vulnerabilities.

This type of data can inform an estimate of how long it will take to address all these vulnerabilities and can help build an effective business case for more investment in the vulnerability management program and remediation teams. Providing senior management with quantitative data like this helps them understand reality versus opinion.

Asset owners and operators tend to request one of two views of their vulnerability inventories, depending on how efficient they are at remediating them:

- Teams that have effective remediation processes typically request the number of vulnerabilities in inventory, the breakdown by severity, a list of the systems that need to be patched, and guidance on the most effective way to deploy the updates.
- Teams that struggle patching vulnerabilities and meeting SLAs tend not to appreciate this type of reporting because it lays bare how many unpatched vulnerabilities they have in inventory, how far behind remediation SLAs they are, and how much risk they are exposing the organization to. Instead, they typically want reporting to focus on the number of systems that need to be updated as opposed to the number of security updates that need to be deployed. This is typically a much smaller number that they don't feel so embarrassed about. However, the challenge they soon face with this type of reporting is that the numbers don't improve very quickly because all the vulnerabilities on each system need to be patched before their status changes in the reports. Because of this, their progress appears to be super slow, even if they are deploying a lot of security updates.

Another approach is to simply report average days to remediate for each asset type (internet-facing, crown jewels, etc.). That average is easily compared to the SLA for each asset type to reveal how well or poorly they are complying with the policy.

I typically provide my stakeholders with both a dashboard that provides near real-time inventories and weekly roll-up reports. I like the "9-Box" format because it maps to the policy SLAs I discussed earlier and makes it easy for stakeholders to understand. *Figure 4.16* is an example of what it looks like:

	Highest Probability of Exploitation	Biggest Impact if Exploited	
	Internet-Facing **Critical + High + KEV** **8 vulnerabilities** **2 assets**	**Crown Jewels** **Critical + High + KEV** **0 vulnerabilities** **0 assets**	Everything Else Critical + High + KEV 404 vulnerabilities 370 assets
5-week trend			
	Internet-Facing **Critical + High** **100 vulnerabilities** **40 assets**	**Crown Jewels** **Critical + High** **150 vulnerabilities** **40 assets**	Everything Else Critical + High 2,205 vulnerabilities 303 assets
5-week trend			
	Internet-Facing All Severities 1,005 vulnerabilities 350 assets	Crown Jewels All Severities 1,200 vulnerabilities 75 assets	All Vulnerabilities 10,500 vulnerabilities 2,550 assets
5-week trend			
			Least Risk

Figure 4.16 – An example of a "9-Box" vulnerability reporting format designed for executives to understand what their vulnerability inventory looks like

It is evident that the two left boxes on the top row need to be zero all the time. Non-zero values in these boxes mean there's work to do immediately in order to comply with the SLAs in the vulnerability management policy. The 5-week trend sparklines help communicate whether vulnerabilities have been getting remediated regularly or if they just keep accumulating. It's normal for these lines to reveal large increases because many vendors, such as Microsoft, for example, release their security updates once per month. On that day, the number of unpatched vulnerabilities in inventory typically increases, sometimes dramatically.

This is just a basic example of a dashboard. The data in this dashboard can be supplemented by other interesting statistics, such as the average number of vulnerabilities per asset in each box, the average number of days to remediate vulnerabilities in each box, and the variance between that number and the policy SLAs. Asset operators, those typically responsible for patching, need much more granular information in order to identify the systems that need to be patched and the optimal order in which to install the updates. Subsequently, clicking on the boxes in the dashboard allows them to dive into the data to show them the assets and CVE IDs that need to be remediated for each asset. These details can be exported from the dashboard so they can be shared with remediation teams. Of course, the companies that offer vulnerability management software, such as Rapid7, Qualys, and Tenable, offer their own dashboards that can be customized.

The vendor and product CVE ID data we looked at earlier revealed that the volume of vulnerabilities has largely grown unrestrained since 2016. Many cybersecurity and IT professionals have come to the conclusion that the volumes are now too large for reasonably sized vulnerability management teams to be successful and have adopted other approaches. I'll discuss this now to conclude this chapter.

More modern approaches

Of course, there are more modern approaches to vulnerability management that can reduce the number of assets that vulnerability management teams need to scan every day or even deprioritize the type of scanning we've been discussing altogether. This topic could be a lengthy chapter in itself, but let's discuss a few of these approaches.

Using more modern "Zero Trust" approaches that verify systems are fully patched before they are allowed to connect to corporate networks is a popular approach. Requiring systems that are missing security updates to self-remediate prior to being trusted enough to connect to a corporate network can dramatically reduce the amount of vulnerability scanning and patching that vulnerability management and remediation teams must do. Microsoft Defender for Endpoint is an example of a product that supports this approach. However, most large organizations have complex IT estates that were built over a period of decades and that typically rely on significant amounts of legacy technologies. Unfortunately, there's no shortcut to transforming massive legacy IT environments into modern Zero Trust architectures. Most organizations modernize parts of their IT estates over a number of years, never able to modernize everything at once. These environments very often require legacy approaches, such as scanning everything every day, to truly manage them effectively.

Virtual machines (VMs), containers, and the cloud have enabled an approach to patching that some IT professionals call "repaving." Instead of scanning every system for vulnerabilities and security misconfigurations, they scan the images that these transient compute resources are based on and patch them. Then, when they launch new VMs, they are based on a fully patched image with a known good configuration state. This approach can reduce costs and effort related to vulnerability management dramatically. I'll discuss this in *Chapter 13, Modern Approaches to Security and Compliance.*

Finally, there's another approach gaining popularity in the industry that distills much of what we discussed in *Chapters 3* and *4* and marries it with the ability to discover viable attack paths. Since scanning and remediating every critical and high-severity vulnerability has become too difficult to achieve in a reasonable amount of time, prioritizing remediation of the specific vulnerabilities that can be exploited in a non-theoretical attack path helps reduce the risk of exploitation. Tackling the truly exploitable vulnerabilities first provides remediation teams with more time to manage the other vulnerabilities in inventory, regardless of their CVSS scores. If they can't be exploited, they aren't a priority. **Continuous Threat Exposure Management (CTEM)** and Continuous Red Teaming are two such approaches. They both seek to identify the ways and vulnerabilities that attackers could actually use in a successful attack versus prioritizing vulnerability remediations based on the type of CVE ID data we reviewed in this chapter. A Gartner analyst describes CTEM this way:

> *"Continuous threat exposure management is a pragmatic and effective systemic approach to continuously refine priorities and walk the tightrope between two modern security realities. Organizations can't fix everything, nor can they be completely sure what vulnerability remediation they can safely postpone." (Gartner, August, 2023).*

The success of these approaches is highly dependent on their ability to discover all the viable attack paths. If they fail to discover viable attack paths and the infrastructure remains unpatched, it could provide attackers with an advantage. Still, if vulnerability management and remediation teams are faced with ever-growing volumes of severe vulnerabilities, newer, more efficient approaches will prevail.

This is an area ripe with opportunity for AI. Both defenders and attackers are already leveraging AI to find exploitable vulnerabilities faster, both in code and in infrastructure. We'll dive deeper into this in *Chapter 15, Artificial Intelligence: Security of AI Systems and Using AI for Better Cybersecurity.*

Summary

The only operating system of the six that I examined to see whether they achieve the objectives of our vulnerability improvement framework over a 3-year period was Debian Linux. However, Ubuntu Linux was very close to satisfying the criteria. Of the three web browsers I examined, Google Chrome had the best vulnerability management track record between 2022 and 2024, but also had the highest number of CVE IDs assigned to it. Apple Safari was very close to satisfying the criteria as well, and it had the lowest number of CVE IDs assigned to it of any of the browsers I studied. The way vulnerabilities were managed in these browsers during these 3 years reduced the risk to the enterprises that leveraged them.

Please keep in mind that the data used for these comparisons has many biases and is not complete or completely accurate. But you can do your own CVE ID research and use the informal vulnerability improvement framework I've provided in this chapter.

Accurate asset inventories are rare, but crucial for vulnerability management, incident response, and other aspects of operational cybersecurity programs. Don't underestimate the value of governance, risk, and compliance to your vulnerability management program. Quantitative risk estimates help stakeholders understand cybersecurity risks in familiar financial terms, while associated policies should be written to treat these risks with the stakeholders' risk appetite in mind.

Vulnerability management teams that scan everything, every day, provide the best visibility for their organizations to manage risk. Data from vulnerability management programs provides CISOs with some of the data they need to manage the performance of their security programs and steer future investments into the programs. Reporting scan results to asset owners and operators helps drive compliance with the vulnerability management policy.

In the next chapter, we are going to dive into the world of malware and examine how the threat landscape has evolved over the years. Did you know that socioeconomic factors, such as GDP, are related to regional malware infection rates? We are going to look at this as well.

References

- CVE Details. (n.d.). Microsoft Vulnerability Statistics. Retrieved from CVE Details: `https://www.cvedetails.com/vendor/26/Microsoft.html`
- CVE Details. (n.d.). Google Vulnerability Statistics. Retrieved from CVE Details:`https://www.cvedetails.com/vendor/1224/Google.html`
- CVE Details. (n.d.). Oracle Vulnerability Statistics. Retrieved from CVE Details: `https://www.cvedetails.com/vendor/93/Oracle.html`

- CVE Details. (n.d.). Debian Linux Vulnerability Statistics. Retrieved from CVE Details: `https://www.cvedetails.com/vulnerability-list/vendor_id-23/product_id-36/Debian-Debian-Linux.html`
- CVE Details. (n.d.). Linux Kernel Vulnerability Statistics. Retrieved from CVE Details: `https://www.cvedetails.com/vulnerability-list/vendor_id-33/product_id-47/Linux-Linux-Kernel.html`
- CVE Details. (n.d.). Ubuntu Linux Vulnerability Statistics. Retrieved from CVE Details: `https://www.cvedetails.com/vulnerability-list/vendor_id-4781/product_id-20550/Canonical-Ubuntu-Linux.html`
- CVE Details. (n.d.). Windows Server 2022 Vulnerability Statistics. Retrieved from CVE Details: `https://www.cvedetails.com/vulnerability-list/vendor_id-26/product_id-100693/Microsoft-Windows-Server-2022.html`
- CVE Details. (n.d.). Windows 11 Vulnerability Statistics. Retrieved from CVE Details: `https://www.cvedetails.com/product-search.php?vendor_id=0&search=Windows+11`
- Microsoft. (n.d.). Windows 11 Home and Pro follows the Modern Lifecycle Policy. Retrieved from Microsoft: `https://learn.microsoft.com/en-us/lifecycle/products/windows-11-home-and-pro`
- CVE Details. (n.d.). Apple macOS Vulnerability Statistics. Retrieved from CVE Details: `https://www.cvedetails.com/vulnerability-list/vendor_id-49/product_id-70318/Apple-Macos.html`
- CVE Details. (n.d.). Google Android Vulnerability Statistics. Retrieved from CVE Details: `https://www.cvedetails.com/vulnerability-list/vendor_id-1224/product_id-19997/Google-Android.html`
- CVE Details. (n.d.). Apple iOS Vulnerability Statistics. Retrieved from CVE Details: `https://www.cvedetails.com/vulnerability-list/vendor_id-49/product_id-15556/Apple-Iphone-Os.html`
- CVE Details. (n.d.). Apple Safari Vulnerability Statistics. Retrieved from CVE Details: `https://www.cvedetails.com/vulnerability-list/vendor_id-49/product_id-2935/Apple-Safari.html`
- CVE Details. (n.d.). Google Chrome Vulnerability Statistics. Retrieved from CVE Details: `https://www.cvedetails.com/vulnerability-list/vendor_id-1224/product_id-15031/Google-Chrome.html`

- CVE Details. (n.d.). Mozilla Firefox Vulnerability Statistics. Retrieved from CVE Details: `https://www.cvedetails.com/vulnerability-list/vendor_id-452/product_id-3264/Mozilla-Firefox.html`
- MITRE. (February 13, 2024). kernel.org Added as CVE Numbering Authority (CNA). Retrieved from `https://www.cve.org/Media/News/item/news/2024/02/13/kernel-org-Added-as-CNA`
- Corbet, Jonathan. (February 14, 2024). *A turning point for CVE numbers*, LWN.net. Retrieved from`https://lwn.net/Articles/961978/`
- The kernel development community. (n.d.). CVEs. Retrieved from `https://docs.kernel.org/process/cve.html`
- Hughes, Maria H. (June 6, 2025). *The 2024 Red Hat Product Security Risk Report: CVEs, XZ Backdoor, SSCAs, AI...oh my!* Retrieved from `https://www.redhat.com/en/blog/2024-red-hat-product-security-risk-report-cves-xz-backdoor-sscas-aioh-my`
- Ubuntu. (n.d.). Is Ubuntu 16.04 LTS still supported? Retrieved from `https://ubuntu.com/16-04`
- CVE Details. (n.d.). Canonical Ubuntu Linux (Operating system): Versions. Retrieved from CVE Details: `https://www.cvedetails.com/version-list/4781/20550/1/Canonical-Ubuntu-Linux.html`
- Microsoft. (June 26, 2025). Windows 11 release information. Retrieved from `https://learn.microsoft.com/en-us/windows/release-health/windows11-release-information`
- Firefox. (n.d.). Billionaire-free for 20+ years. Retrieved from `https://www.firefox.com/`
- Gartner. (August 21, 2023). *How to Manage Cybersecurity Threats, Not Episodes.* Retrieved from `https://www.expresscomputer.in/guest-blogs/gartner-how-to-manage-cybersecurity-threats-not-episodes/103287/`

Get this book's PDF version and more

Scan the QR code (or go to `packtpub.com/unlock`). Search for this book by name, confirm the edition, and then follow the steps on the page.

UNLOCK NOW

Note: Keep your invoice handy. Purchases made directly from Packt don't require an invoice.

5

The Evolution of Malware

In *Chapters 3, Industry Vulnerability Disclosure Trends* and *4, Product Vulnerability Disclosure Trends*, I provided a deep dive into vulnerability management, vendor vulnerability trends, and product vulnerability trends because managing vulnerabilities is a cornerstone of a successful cybersecurity program. Understanding how enterprise vulnerability management and remediation teams operate, and the trade-offs they must make, are prerequisites for being a cybersecurity executive, such as a **chief information security officer** (**CISO**).

Another subject that cybersecurity executives need to be well-versed in is malware. One role I had during my time working at Microsoft was as a product manager in Microsoft's antimalware lab. In this role, I had the opportunity to work with some seriously talented malware researchers and analysts. At that time, when Microsoft decided they wanted to enter the enterprise antimalware business with their Forefront line of products, Microsoft hired some of the best researchers and analysts from other antimalware labs around the world, such as Symantec, McAfee, and CA, among others. As I discussed in *Chapter 2, What to Know About Threat Intelligence*, I co-authored 20+ volumes of the **Microsoft Security Intelligence Report** (**SIR**) with researchers and analysts from the **Microsoft Malware Protection Center** (**MMPC**). Over the years, I learned a lot about malware, malware analysis, and endpoint protection from these colleagues. What an education! My experience working on Microsoft's customer-facing incident response team, and then in its antimalware lab, prepared me for the later chapters in my career as a CISO. I'm happy to share some of what I learned in this chapter.

This chapter will provide a unique, detailed, data-driven historical perspective of how malware has evolved around the world. There are some very interesting differences in regional malware encounter rates and infection rates that I'll also dive into in this chapter. This view of the threat landscape will help CISOs and security teams understand how attackers change their malware ambitions over time. Not only is this data super interesting, but it can help take some of the

fear, uncertainty, and doubt (**FUD**) out of conversations about malware and how to manage the risks it poses.

I'll also provide a deep dive into how ransomware has changed over time to demystify this term, as it has largely been hijacked and overloaded in recent years. I'll explain how ransomware has always been one of the least prevalent categories of malware, but continues to strike fear into CISOs and security teams, and has become a fixture in the news.

The following topics will be covered in this chapter:

- The era of advanced threat begins
- The scope of the malware problem
- Why is there so much malware on Windows?
- Malware data sources
- About malware
- Measuring malware prevalence
- Global Windows malware infection analysis
- Regional Windows malware infection analysis
- Global malware evolution

The era of advanced threats begins

In 2003, when I worked on Microsoft's customer-facing incident response team, we began finding user-mode rootkits on compromised systems with some regularity, so much so that one of our best engineers built a tool that could find user-mode rootkits that were hiding from Windows. A user-mode rootkit runs like any other application that a normal user would run, but it hides itself. Then, one day, we received a call from a Microsoft support engineer who was helping troubleshoot an issue that an enterprise customer had on an Exchange email server. The symptom of the problem was that once every few days, the server would blue-screen. The support engineer couldn't figure out why and was doing a remote debug session, trying to find the code that caused the server to blue-screen. It took weeks, but once they found the code responsible for the blue screen, he couldn't explain what the code was, nor how it got installed on the server. That's when they called us for help.

When the server blue-screened and rebooted, this enabled us to look at a partial memory dump from the system. After a few days of analysis, we determined that the server was compromised in a way we had never seen before. A device driver on the system was hiding itself and other components. We had found the first *kernel-mode rootkit* that we had ever seen in the wild.

This was a big deal. Unlike a user-mode rootkit, developing and installing a kernel-mode rootkit required incredible expertise. This is because this type of rootkit runs in the most privileged part of the operating system, called the kernel, which few people really understand. At the time, although the concept of kernel-mode rootkits was discussed among security experts, finding one installed on a server running in an enterprise's production environment signaled that attackers were becoming far more sophisticated than ever. Graduating from user-mode rootkits to kernel-mode rootkits was a major leap forward in the evolution of malware.

To our incident response team, this was a call to action. We had to let the Windows kernel developers at Microsoft know that the thing that makes Windows a trusted computing base, its kernel, was being directly attacked by sophisticated authors of malware.

> **Note**
>
> Until then, a kernel-mode rootkit running in the wild was mythical. But now, we had evidence that these rootkits were real and were being used to attack enterprise customers.

We scheduled a meeting with the lead developers, testers, and program managers on the Windows kernel development team. We gathered in a room used for training, with an overhead projector, so that we could walk the developers through the memory dump we had from the compromised server to show them how the rootkit worked. We provided them with some context about the server, such as where it was running, the operating system version, the service pack level, a list of all the applications running on the server, and so on. We answered numerous questions about how we debugged the source of the blue screen, found the hidden driver, and discovered how it worked.

At first, the Windows kernel team was skeptical that we had found a kernel-mode rootkit running on a Windows server. But after we presented all the evidence and showed them the debug details, they gradually accepted the fact that it was indeed a kernel-mode rootkit. Our team expected adulation and respect for all the very technical work we had done, as well as our expertise on Windows kernel internals that allowed us to make this discovery. Instead, the kernel developers told us that our tools and our methods were as bad as the malware authors'. They warned us to stop using our tools to find rootkits, as the tools could make the Windows systems they ran on unstable unless rebooted. Finally, they offered to do nothing to harden the kernel to prevent such attacks in the future. It was a disappointing meeting for us, but you can't win them all!

After the successful large-scale worm attacks of 2003 and 2004, this tune changed. The entire Windows team stopped the development work they were doing on what would later become Windows Vista. Instead, they worked on improving the security of Windows XP and Server 2003, releasing Windows XP Service Pack 2 and Windows Server 2003 Service Pack 1. There was even talk of a new version of Windows, code-named Palladium, that had a security kernel to help mitigate rootkits like the one we discovered, but it never came to pass (Wikipedia, n.d.). Ultimately, our work on detecting kernel-mode rootkits did help drive positive change, as future 64-bit versions of Windows would not allow kernel-mode drivers, like the one we discovered, to be installed unless they had a valid digital signature.

As I mentioned earlier in this chapter, later in my career at Microsoft, I had the chance to work with world-class malware researchers and analysts in Microsoft's anti-malware research and response lab, who were protecting a billion systems from millions of new malware threats. Malware like the kernel-mode rootkit we had discovered 4 or 5 years earlier was now a commodity. Attackers were using large-scale automation and server-side polymorphism to create millions of unique malware every week. To win this war, the anti-virus industry needed to have bigger and better automation than large-scale purveyors of commodity malware, which has proven to be surprisingly difficult to accomplish. But the industry is now pushing new boundaries in malware research and response using **artificial intelligence** (**AI**) systems.

I have always thought of malware as a synonym for "attackers' automation." Purveyors of malware seek to compromise systems for a range of motivations, as I described in *Chapter 1, How Enterprises Get Hacked*. Any system that sends and receives email, is used to surf the internet, runs applications that connect to a network, or takes other forms of input can be attacked, regardless of whether it was manufactured in Redmond, Raleigh, Cupertino, Helsinki, or anywhere else. Simply put, if you don't trust the source of the code, don't run it. That might sound overly cautious or even pessimistic to some, but once you look at the growth of malware over the years, you will get a sense of the scope of this threat.

The scope of the malware problem

The AV-TEST Institute, one of the world's premier independent anti-virus testing labs, based in Germany, has one of the world's largest malware collections (AV-Test Institute, 2025). They have accumulated this collection for over 20 years. "Every day, the AV-TEST Institute registers over 450,000 new malicious programs (malware) and potentially unwanted applications (PUA). These are examined and classified according to their characteristics and saved" (AV-Test Institute, n.d.). Based on the data they published for the three years between 2023 and 2025, the rate of new malware is estimated to be 298,733 unique samples per day (AV-Test Institute, February, 2026). The statistics that they have published indicate that the total number of malware programs in their collection at the end of 2025 was approximately 1.3 billion (AV-Test Institute, February, 2026). If malware were a country, it would be the third-most-populated country in the world behind India and China.

Each year, the rate of growth in total malware is slightly different, with 2021 appearing to be the peak, with almost 162 million new malware programs detected that year, according to AV-Test. 2022 had the lowest growth level of the decade, with only 102 million new malware samples detected, a 37% decrease from the prior year. In the 11 years between 2015 and 2025, the average growth in new malware samples was approximately 112.2 million per year (AV-Test Institute, February, 2026). These growth rates are staggering when you consider that, if malware were a country, during the year with the lowest malware growth rate (2022), its population grew 10 times faster than the population of India grew in 2022.

> **Note**
>
> If malware were a country, it would become the most populated country in the world, overtaking India and China in the next two years.

You might wonder what all this malware was designed to attack. According to the data that AV-Test has published, during those 10 years, the number of malware programs designed to run on the Windows operating system grew 351% from 221,508,845 unique malware samples in 2015 to 997,878,296 malware samples in 2025 (AV-Test Institute, February, 2026). Looking at each individual year during that decade, the proportion of malware developed for Windows operating systems versus other operating systems targeted by malware ranged from as low as 74% of all malware detected to as high as 83% (AV-Test Institute, February, 2026). In the three years between 2023 and 2025, on average, 76% of all the malware samples AV-Test collected were designed for the Windows operating system.

The operating system with the next highest share of malware samples during those years was Google Android, with 3% of the total malware samples per year reported (AV-Test Institute,

February, 2026). The number of malware samples detected for Android surged in 2016, 2017, and 2018, with 18.7 million new malware samples collected during those three years, representing 50% of all the malware samples collected for Android between 2015 and 2025. In February 2026, AV-Test had 37,322,716 unique malware samples for the Android operating system (AV-Test Institute, February, 2026).

The total number of malware samples detected for Linux operating systems was 5,061,774 in February of 2026 (AV-Test Institute, February, 2026). The amount of malware detected for Linux in 2015 was just 54,827 samples. However, the amount of malware designed for Linux grew dramatically in 2021 and 2022, adding 1.5 million and 2.0 million new samples, respectively. The malware collected for Linux in these two years represents 70% of all the malware collected for Linux in the 11 years between 2015 and 2025. The proportion of malware designed for Linux operating systems represents a fraction of 1% of all malware detected each year during this period, ranging from 0.02% to 0.42% of the total.

macOS had the least amount of malware designed for it of any of the operating systems I've discussed. AV-Test had 998,817 malware samples for macOS as of February 2026 (AV-Test Institute, February, 2026), starting the 11-year period in 2015 with just 41,527 malware samples and ending it in 2025 with 997,932, a 2,303% increase. 2020 stands out as the single largest year of growth in malware for macOS, with 656,597 samples detected that year, 66% of all the malware collected for macOS between 2015 and 2025. Malware for macOS represented between 0.0034% and 0.08% of all malware AV-Test collected each year during those 11 years (AV-Test Institute, February, 2026).

Figure 5.1 is a pie chart that illustrates the relative proportions of AV-Test's malware sample collection for each operating system at the end of 2025:

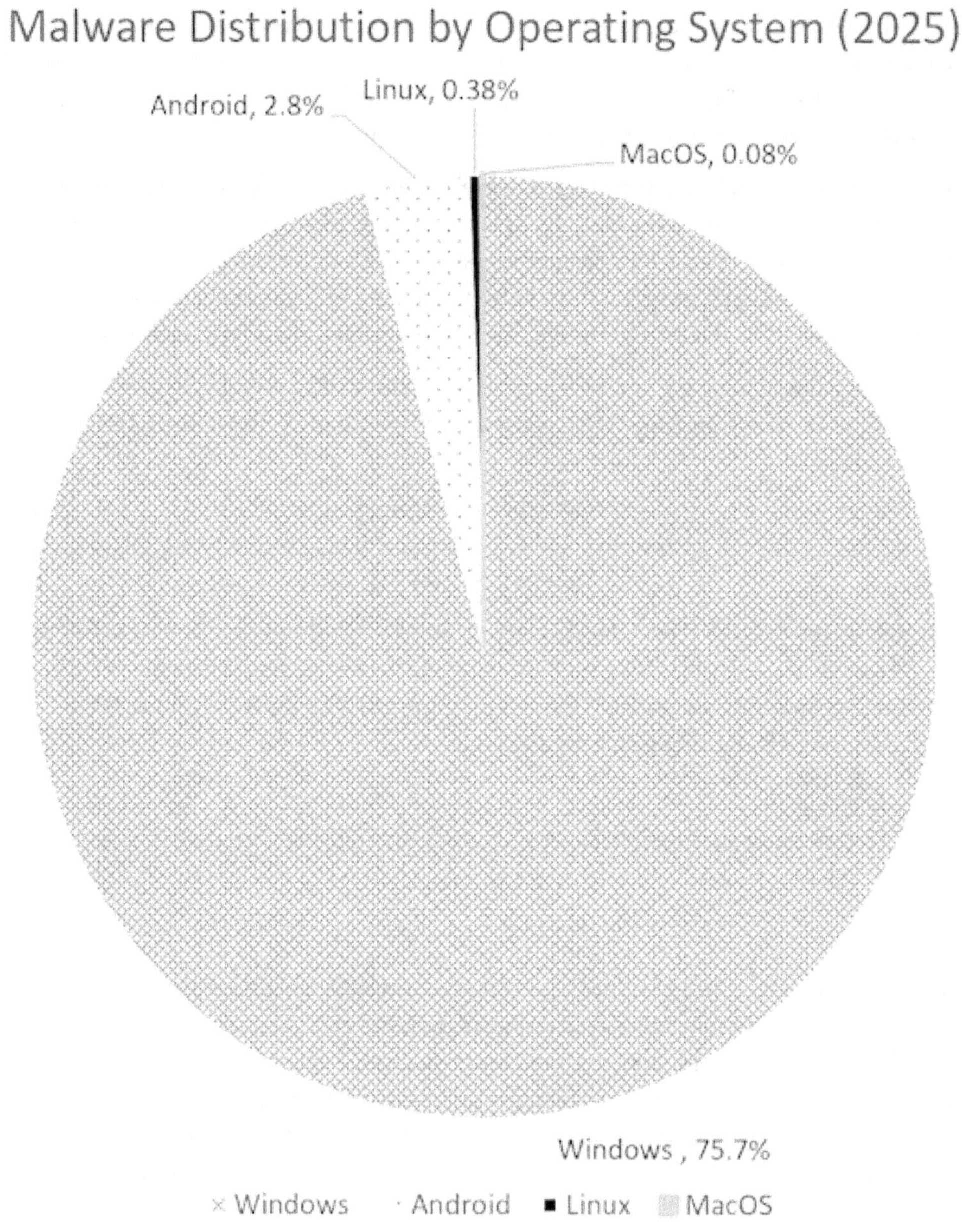

Figure 5.1 – Unique malware sample distribution by operating system (AV-Test Institute, February, 2026)

This data clearly suggests that the platform of choice for malware authors is the Windows operating system. That is, more unique malware is developed to attack Windows-based systems than any other platform. Once Windows systems are compromised, attackers will typically harvest software and game keys, financial information such as credit card numbers, and other confidential information they can use to steal identities, sometimes taking control of the system and its data for ransom. Many attackers will use compromised systems as platforms to perpetrate attacks from, using the anonymity that such systems provide.

Given that attackers have been targeting and leveraging Windows-based systems more than any other platform, and given the ubiquity of Windows, security experts need to understand how and where attackers have been using these systems. CISOs, aspiring CISOs, security teams, and cybersecurity experts can benefit from understanding how Windows-based systems are attacked in at least a few ways. The following are some advantages of this:

- Knowledge of malware and how it attacks systems can be useful to help recognize the fear, uncertainty, and doubt that some security vendors use to sell their products and services.
- Understanding how attackers have been using malware will help CISOs make better security-related investments and decisions and will help security teams do their jobs better.
- CISOs and security teams can take lessons from the Windows ecosystem and apply them to Linux-based systems and other platforms. Very often, the methods that malware authors use on the Windows platform will be adapted to attack other platforms, albeit usually on a smaller scale.

> **Tip**
>
> Unfortunately, CISOs don't get to tune out of Windows-based threats, even if they don't use Windows in their environments.

Finally, in my opinion, it will be difficult for cybersecurity *subject matter experts* to use this moniker if they are blissfully unaware of malware trends in an online ecosystem consisting of over a billion systems that support, at times, more than three-quarters of all the new malware in the world. It doesn't matter if there are more mobile devices, more IoT devices, or more secure operating systems. It is undeniable that Windows is everywhere. Subsequently, all cybersecurity experts should know a little about the largest participant in the global threat landscape.

Next, let's examine why there's so much malware designed to attack Windows-based systems.

Why is there so much malware on Windows?

The data we just looked at suggests that 76% of all new malware in 2025 was designed for the Windows operating system, and that 77% of all malware in AV-Test's malware collection was coded for Windows. Let's take a moment to consider why this is the case. After all, there are certainly more mobile internet-connected devices today than there are Windows-based systems. Mobile device adoption exploded as Apple, Google, Samsung, and others brought very popular products to the global marketplace. But if there are far more mobile devices, shouldn't there be far more families of malware developed for those platforms?

The answer to this question lies in how applications get distributed in these ecosystems. Apple's App Store was a game changer for the industry. Not only did it make it easy for iPhone users to find and install applications, but it also *almost completely eliminated malware* for iOS-based devices.

Apple was able to accomplish this by making the App Store the one and only place consumers could install applications from (jailbreaking aside). **Independent software vendors** (**ISVs**) who want to get their apps onto consumers' iOS-based devices, such as iPhones and iPads, need to get their apps into the App Store. To do this, their apps need to meet Apple's security requirements, which they verify behind the scenes. This makes the App Store a perfect choke point that prevents malware from getting onto Apple devices.

In contrast, Microsoft Windows was developed in more naive times, when no one could predict that, one day, there would be more malicious files in the Windows ecosystem than legitimate files. One of the big advantages of Windows, for developers, was that they could develop their software for Windows and sell it directly to consumers and businesses. This model was the predominant software distribution model for PCs for decades. Since software can be installed without regard for its provenance and with limited ability to determine its trustworthiness, malware flourished in this ecosystem and continues to do so. Microsoft has taken numerous steps over the decades to combat this "side effect" of its software distribution model, with limited success. It turns out that the flexibility to deploy software without using an App Store model is coveted by operators of enterprise IT estates.

Some would argue that the Android ecosystem has ended up somewhere in between these two extremes. Google also has an app store, called the Play Store. Google has also taken steps to minimize malware in this app store. However, third-party app stores for Android-based devices didn't all maintain Google's high security standards, subsequently allowing malware for these devices to get into the ecosystem. Zscaler's ThreatLabz reported that 77 malicious Android apps with more than 19 million installs were delivering multiple malware families to Play Store users (Toulas, Bill. August 25, 2025). However, the data from AV-Test suggests that the number of malware samples detected for Android-based devices was 27 times smaller than that of Windows-based devices at the end of 2025 (AV-Test Institute, February, 2025).

These differences in software distribution models, at least partially, help to explain why there is so much more malware developed for Windows than for other platforms. Cybersecurity professionals can take some lessons from this into their own IT environments. Controlling how software is introduced to an enterprise IT environment can help minimize the amount of malware in it.

> Tip
>
> Remember the mantra: if you don't trust the source of the code, don't run it.

Here is some basic advice for CISOs and security teams that manage large IT estates of Windows-based devices.

- **Restrict how many users run in local administrator context**: One mistake I've seen numerous IT teams make in trying to enable users to perform self-service IT functions, such as installing software, is giving large swaths of their user bases standing local administrator privileges or other elevated user contexts. Users with elevated privileges are targets for attackers, who seek to trick them into installing malware and remote-control software, as well as disabling security features. When these accounts get compromised, they are a gift to attackers, who use their escalated privileges to accelerate their attacks. Allowing users to run in local administrator context on systems that they use to surf the internet, send and receive emails, and access removable mass storage devices on is an attacker's dream come true. It's a bonus to them if these systems are also used to commit code. What could go wrong? Re-read that last line with a heavy dose of sarcasm in your mind. This level of naivete is exactly what attackers hope to find as they use the Cybersecurity Usual Suspects to initially compromise systems and then take advantage of the user's elevated privileges to steal more credentials, move laterally, stay persistent, access sensitive data and exfiltrate it, and deploy ransomware. For example, when attackers have local administrator privileges, it potentially enables them to "bring their own vulnerable driver" or to "bring their own **endpoint detection and response** (**EDR**)" that disables the legitimate endpoint protection software. Both tactics result in attackers disabling security software and controls to have complete control of systems. Restricting the number of user accounts that have standing administrator privileges has been a Microsoft best practice for more than 20 years.

- **Leverage Microsoft Software Center to enable users to install software on their own Windows systems**: In large enterprises, the top use case for giving users standing local administrator privileges is to enable them to install software on their systems themselves. Users do not require escalated privileges to install software from the Software Center. The IT team that manages user desktops will need to maintain the Software Center by ensuring the latest versions of the software their organizations have procured are published in it and available for users. This includes newer versions of that software as it becomes available. This centralized approach also ensures users aren't installing software that didn't go through their organization's legal and procurement processes, helping to avoid running pirated software. In large enterprise environments, this isn't a part-time job. It takes resources, time, and dedication to ensure users have access to the latest versions of the software they need to perform their roles, published in the Software Center. This is an important function that rarely gets the credit it deserves.
- **Consider whether a local privilege escalation tool will meet their needs instead of giving them persistent administrator privileges**: This applies to users who require escalated privileges to do their jobs. Examples of vendors that offer these tools include CyberArk, Delinea, BeyondTrust, and others. Microsoft announced a new Windows 11 platform security feature in 2025 called Administrator Protection with this same goal in mind (Microsoft, May 2025).
- **Leverage Continuous Integration (CI)/Continuous Deployment (CD) pipelines for applications developed in-house**: CI/CD pipelines can help enterprises restrict how software is introduced into their environments and ensure it meets security and compliance requirements before deploying it into production.
- **Block outbound user access to unneeded internet domains**: It turns out that most, if not all, the malware trying to get into enterprise IT environments is on the internet (USB mass storage devices excluded, of course). Do any of your users speak or read Russian, or a dialect of Chinese, Persian, or Arabic? Does your organization have customers, partners, or employees who live in foreign countries where these languages are used? If not, then why would your users need unfettered access to the country code top-level domains on the internet where these languages are predominant, such as *.ru*, *.cn*, and *.ir*? Blocking outbound user access to unneeded internet domains can provide high security ROI. Applying the principle of least privilege to internet access will result in mitigating many internet-based threats, such as phishing attacks and drive-by download attacks. If your users can't get to the sites hosting malware, credential theft attacks, and other threats, it makes it harder for malware and attackers to get into your IT environment. I've used this tactic with great success at very large

organizations. The key is to ensure users have access to the websites they need access to. I'll discuss this tactic more in *Chapter 14, Mitigating "Living Off the Land" Tactics.*

Now that we've briefly discussed how software distribution models can impact the distribution of malware, let's dive deep into malware. Security teams can learn a lot from studying malware developed for Windows operating systems, even if they don't use Windows themselves. The methods that malware authors employ on Windows can be and are used for malware developed for many different platforms, including Linux and macOS. Studying how malware works in the largest malware ecosystem can help us defend against it almost everywhere else. But before I dive right into the historical malware trend data, it's important for you to understand the sources of the data that I'm going to show you. As I discussed in *Chapter 2*, to truly understand threat intelligence, also known as **Cyber Threat Intelligence** (**CTI**), you need to understand the data sources.

Malware data sources

The primary source for the historical data in this chapter is the Microsoft **Security Intelligence Report** (**SIR**) and newer reports such as the Microsoft Digital Defense Reports (Microsoft Corporation, n.d.). As I mentioned earlier in the chapter, I worked on 20+ volumes of the SIR and understood the data sources we used intimately. In each volume of the SIR, we documented the data sources used in the appendix. Microsoft still uses many of these data sources to protect its customers today and inform their investments in security.

The data in these historical reports comes from Microsoft's anti-malware products that enterprises and consumers used, including the **Malicious Software Removal Tool**, **Microsoft Safety Scanner**, **Microsoft Security Essentials**, **Microsoft System Center Endpoint Protection**, **Windows Defender**, **Windows Defender Advanced Threat Protection**, **Windows Defender Offline**, **Azure Security Center**, and the **SmartScreen** filter built into Microsoft web browsers. Other non-security products and services that provide valuable data for volumes of this report include Exchange Online, Office 365, and Bing (Note that some of the names of these products and tools have changed since these reports were published). Let me explain in more detail how this eclectic group of data sources helps paint a well-rounded picture of the threat landscape.

The Malicious Software Removal Tool

The Malicious Software Removal Tool (**MSRT**) is an interesting tool that provides valuable data. In the wake of the Blaster worm attacks (there were variants) (Microsoft Corporation, n.d.) in the summer of 2003, Microsoft developed a free **Blaster Removal Tool** that was designed to help customers detect and remove the Blaster worm and its variants (Leyden, J., January 7, 2004). Remember that, at that time, very few systems ran up-to-date, real-time anti-virus software. The Blaster Removal Tool was free. This tool made a huge difference as tens of millions of systems ran it. Because of the tool's success and the constant barrage of malware attacks that followed it in history, such as Sasser, MyDoom, and many others, and the fact that so few systems had anti-virus software running, Microsoft decided to release a *malicious software removal tool* every month. The MSRT was born.

It was meant to be a way to detect infected systems and clean the most prevalent or serious malware threats from the entire Windows ecosystem. Microsoft's anti-malware lab decides what new detections to add to the MSRT every month. A list of all the malware it detects is published on Microsoft's website (Microsoft Corporation, n.d.). Between January 2005 and February 2026, 487 malware families were added to the detections for the MSRT. Keep in mind that there are at least hundreds of thousands, if not millions, of known malware families, so this is a very small subset of the total that real-time anti-malware software packages detect. The MSRT is released monthly (more or less) with security updates on "Patch Tuesday," the second Tuesday of every month. It gets automatically downloaded from Windows Update or Microsoft Update to every Windows system in the world that has opted to run it. During the time I was publishing data from the MSRT in the SIR, the MSRT was running on hundreds of millions of systems per month on average.

Once the MSRT's **End User License Agreement** (**EULA**) is agreed to, the MSRT runs silently without a user interface as it's a command-line tool. If it doesn't find any malware infections, it stops execution and is unloaded from memory. No data is sent to Microsoft in this case. But if malware is detected by the MSRT, then it will try to remove the malware from the system and report the infection to the user and to Microsoft.

Microsoft publishes the specific list of data fields that the MSRT sends back for analysis, including the version of Windows that the malware was detected on, the operating system locale, and which malware family was detected, among others (Microsoft Corporation, n.d.). Administrators can download the MSRT and run it manually; the MSRT can also be configured not to send data back to Microsoft. Most enterprises that I advised, who executed the MSRT on their Windows systems, typically blocked data sent to Microsoft at their firewall. Subsequently, my educated guess is that 95% or more of the hundreds of millions of systems returning MSRT data to Microsoft are likely consumers' systems.

The MSRT provides a great post-malware exposure snapshot of a small list of known, prevalent malware that is infecting consumers' systems around the world. When Microsoft's anti-malware lab adds a detection to the MSRT for a threat that's very prevalent, we should expect to see a spike in detections for that malware family in the data. This happens from time to time, as you'll see in the data shared later in this chapter. Keep in mind that the infected systems might have been infected for weeks, months, or years prior to the detection being added to the MSRT. Since the MSRT runs on systems all over the world and it returns the

Windows locale and country location of infected systems, it provides us with a way to see regional differences in malware infections. I will discuss this in detail later in this chapter.

Real-time anti-malware tools

Unlike the MSRT, which cleans Windows-based systems that have already been successfully infected with prevalent malware, the primary purpose of real-time anti-malware software is to block the installation of malware. It does this by scanning incoming files, monitoring systems for tell-tale signs of infection, scanning files when they are accessed, and periodically scanning storage. Real-time anti-malware software can also find pre-existing infections on systems when the real-time anti-malware package is initially installed. Real-time anti-malware software typically gets signature and engine updates periodically (daily, weekly, monthly, and so on). This helps it block new and emerging threats, as well as old threats it wasn't previously able to detect.

For example, if detection is added for a malware threat, but that malware threat has already successfully infected systems that are running the real-time anti-malware software, the update could potentially enable the anti-malware software to detect, and hopefully remove, the existing infection.

My point is that data from real-time anti-malware software provides us with a different view of the threat landscape compared to MSRT. Microsoft has offered different solutions for threat detection and rebranded its Windows anti-malware solution a few times over the years. Microsoft Defender Antivirus, Microsoft Defender XDR, Windows Defender, Microsoft Security Essentials, Microsoft System Center Endpoint Protection, and Windows Defender Advanced Threat Protection are all examples of real-time anti-malware software that are data sources. Microsoft Defender Antivirus is the default anti-malware package for Windows 11-based systems. Windows Defender was the default anti-virus solution on Windows 10-based systems until it was rebranded Microsoft Defender. In a blog post in August of 2025, Microsoft mentioned that *"Microsoft's Defender platform scans more than one billion monthly active devices through the company's Defender suite of products..."* (Microsoft Corporation, August 5, 2025).

This massive scale makes Microsoft's Defender-branded products a great source of threat intelligence data. Incidentally, Windows Defender was the original name of Microsoft's anti-spyware solution when personal computers required separate solutions for malware and spyware. I'll touch on this conundrum later when I discuss "potentially unwanted software." Also note that some of these real-time anti-malware solutions are for consumers and others are for enterprise customers. Enterprise customers demand methods to deploy, manage, and observe data from their anti-malware solutions that protect thousands of systems, as well as faster research and response. Today, enterprises leverage **Endpoint Detection and Response** (**EDR**) or **Extended Detection and Response** (**XDR**) that provide real-time antimalware protection as well as a range of other functions that go well beyond malware detection. I'll talk about these in more depth in *Chapter 14*.

During some of the threat intelligence briefings I've done, some attendees asserted that using Microsoft data sources for intelligence only provides a view of malware that Microsoft knows about. But this isn't quite true. The major anti-malware vendors share information with each other, including malware samples. So, while the first anti-malware lab that discovers a threat will have detections for that threat before anyone else, over time, all anti-malware vendors will have detections for it. Microsoft manages several security information-sharing programs, with the goal of helping all vendors better protect their shared customers (Microsoft Corporation, 2019). Additionally, Microsoft has expanded support for Microsoft Defender to non-Microsoft operating systems, such as Android, iPhone iOS, and macOS, which will give them even more data on threats across these platforms (Microsoft Corporation, n.d.).

Microsoft's web browsers have had the SmartScreen filter—think anti-malware software for the browser—built into them for many years. The SmartScreen filter gives us a view of phishing sites and malware hosted on the web (Microsoft Corporation, n.d.). As users browse the web, SmartScreen will warn them about known malicious websites they try to visit and scan files that are downloaded in the browser, looking for malware. The data on sites hosting malicious software, and the malicious files themselves, can give us a view of the most common threats hosted on the web, as well as where in the world threats are hosted most, and the regions that the victim populations are in. The current version of this feature is called Microsoft SmartScreen Defender and is built into Windows 10 (Creators Update and above) and Windows 11.

Non-security data sources

Sources of data, such as email services and internet search services, can provide an additional dimension to threat intelligence. For example, data from Microsoft 365 (formerly called Office 365) and Outlook.com provides visibility of the threats that flow through email, including the sources and destinations of those threats and their volumes. The volume of data that Microsoft has from Microsoft 365 is mind-boggling, with hundreds of millions of users all over the world and hundreds of billions of email messages flowing through it every month (Microsoft Corporation, 2018).

Bing, Microsoft's internet search engine service, is also a rich source of threat intelligence data. As Bing indexes billions of web pages so that its users can get quick, relevant search results, it's also looking for drive-by download sites, malware-hosting sites, and phishing sites. This data can help us better understand where in the world malware is being hosted, where it migrates to over time, and where the victims are.

When data from some select non-security data sources is combined with data from some of the security sources of data I discussed previously, we can get a more rounded view of the threat landscape. Microsoft 365 and Outlook.com receive emails sent from all sorts of non-Microsoft clients and email servers, and Bing indexes content hosted on all types of platforms. Certainly, the combination of this data does not provide us with perfect visibility, but the scale of these data sources gives us the potential for good insights.

Now that you know where I retrieved the historical malware-related data from that I'm going to share with you, let's take a quick look at the different categories of malware that are included in the data and analysis. These categories of malware have been fixtures in the global threat landscape for decades, meaning that CISOs and security teams should be very knowledgeable about these categories. I'm going to show you how attackers change the malware categories they use over time when those categories become less effective. Some people call this "evolution," but I call it old wine in new bottles because the data clearly shows us attackers moving from one known malware category to another known malware category. It's not very often that a novel category of malware is discovered—more often, attackers use variations on themes invented decades ago. This isn't to say that nothing has changed; as an example, we will examine the ways that ransomware has changed over time later in this chapter.

About malware

Before we dive into the historical threat data, I need to provide you with some definitions for terms I'll use throughout the rest of this chapter.

Malicious software, also known as malware, is software whose author's intent is malicious. The developers of malware are trying to impede the confidentiality, integrity, and/or availability of data and/or the systems that process, transmit, and store it.

As I discussed in *Chapter 1*, malware authors can be motivated by many different things, including hubris, notoriety, military espionage, economic espionage, and hacktivism, among others.

Most malware families today are blended threats. What I mean by this is that, many years ago, threats were discrete. That is, they were either a **worm** or a **backdoor**, but not both. Today, most malware has characteristics of multiple categories of malware. Analysts in anti-malware labs that reverse-engineer malware samples typically classify malware by the primary or most prominent way each sample behaves.

For example, a piece of malware might exhibit characteristics of a worm, a Trojan, and ransomware. An analyst might classify it as ransomware because that's its dominant behavior or characteristic.

> **Note**
>
> The volume of threats has grown dramatically over the years. Malware researchers in major anti-malware labs generally don't have time to spend weeks or months researching one malware threat, as they might have done 25 years ago. However, I have seen analysts in CERTs or boutique research labs do this for specific, sophisticated threats found in their customers' environments. Protecting vast numbers of systems from an ever-growing volume of serious threats means that some major anti-virus labs are spending less time researching and publishing detailed findings on every threat they discover. Also, most enterprise customers are more interested in blocking infections or recovering from infections as quickly as possible and moving on with business than diving into the inner workings of malware du jour.

Generally speaking, malware research and response is more about automation and science now than the art it once was. Don't get me wrong; if you can understand how a piece of malware spreads and what its payload is, then you can effectively mitigate it. But the volume and complexity of threats seen today will challenge any organization to do this at any scale. Instead, security teams typically must spend time and resources mitigating as many malware threats as possible, not just one popular category or family. As you'll see from the historical data I provide in this chapter, some attackers even use old-school file infectors (viruses).

All that said, AI is playing a bigger role in the categorization of malware in antimalware labs to help manage the massive volume and complexity. In August of 2025, Microsoft announced "Project Ire" in a blog post published on the Microsoft Research blog. The team working on this project described it this way:

> *"Today, we are excited to introduce an autonomous AI agent that can analyze and classify software without assistance, a step forward in cybersecurity and malware detection. The prototype, Project Ire, automates what is considered the gold standard in malware classification: fully reverse engineering a software file without any clues about its origin or purpose. It uses decompilers and other tools, reviews their output, and determines whether the software is malicious or benign...*
>
> *Based on these early successes, the Project Ire prototype will be leveraged inside Microsoft's Defender organization as Binary Analyzer for threat detection and software classification.*

> *Our goal is to scale the system's speed and accuracy so that it can correctly classify files from any source, even on first encounter. Ultimately, our vision is to detect novel malware directly in memory, at scale." (Microsoft Corporation, August 5, 2025)*

How malware infections spread

Malware isn't magic. It must get into IT environments somehow. Hopefully, you'll remember the Cybersecurity Usual Suspects, that is, the five ways that organizations are initially compromised, which I wrote about in detail in *Chapter 1*. To refresh your memory, the Cybersecurity Usual Suspects are as follows:

- Unpatched vulnerabilities
- Security misconfigurations
- Weak, leaked, and stolen credentials
- Social engineering
- Insider threats

Malware threats can use all the Cybersecurity Usual Suspects to compromise systems. Some malware is used to initially compromise systems so that threat actors achieve their objectives. Some malware is used in IT environments after the environment has already been compromised. For example, after attackers use one or more of the Cybersecurity Usual Suspects to initially compromise a network, they can use malware that will encrypt sensitive data and/or find cached administrator credentials and upload them to a remote server. Some malware is sophisticated enough to be used for both initial compromise and post-compromise objectives. As I mentioned earlier, I have always thought of malware as a synonym for "attackers' automation." Instead of the attacker manually typing commands or running scripts, malware is a program that performs illicit activities for the attacker, autonomously or in a semiautonomous fashion. Malware can help attackers achieve their objectives, whether their objective is destruction and anarchy or economic espionage.

The categories of malware I'll discuss in this chapter include different types of Trojans, browser modifiers, exploits, exploit kits, potentially unwanted software, ransomware, viruses, and worms. Microsoft provides definitions for these categories of malware and others (Microsoft Corporation, March 13, 2025). Your favorite anti-malware provider or threat intelligence provider might have different definitions than these. That's perfectly okay, but just keep in mind that there might be some minor, nuanced differences between definitions. I'll provide you with my own, less formal definitions to make this chapter easier to read and understand.

Trojans

I'll start with Trojans since, worldwide, they have been the most prevalent category of malware for the last 15 years or more. A **Trojan** is a program or file that represents itself as one thing when really it is another, just like the Trojan horse story that it's based on. The user is tricked into downloading it and opening or running it.

> Note
>
> Trojans don't spread themselves using unpatched vulnerabilities or weak passwords like worms do; they must rely on social engineering.

Backdoor Trojans and **remote access Trojans** are variations of this. Once the user is tricked into running the malicious program (scripts and macros can be malicious too), a backdoor Trojan gives attackers remote access to the infected system. Once they have remote access, they can potentially steal identities and data, software and game keys, install software and more malware of their choice, enlist the infected system into botnets so that they can do "project work" for attackers, and so on. Project work can include extortion, **Distributed Denial of Service** (**DDoS**) attacks, storing and distributing illicit and questionable content, or anything else the attackers are willing to trade or sell access to their network of compromised systems for.

Trojan downloaders and **droppers** are yet another variation on this theme. Once the user is tricked into running the malicious program, the Trojan then unpacks more malware from itself or downloads more malicious software from remote servers. The result is typically the same—malicious servitude and harvesting the system for all that it is worth. Trojan downloaders and droppers were all the rage among attackers in 2006 and 2007 and have made dramatic appearances in limited time periods since then.

A great example of a Trojan downloader and dropper is the notorious threat called **Zlob**. Users were tricked into installing it on their systems when visiting malicious websites that had video content they wanted to view. When they clicked on the video file to watch it, the website told them they didn't have the correct video codec installed to watch the video. Helpfully, the website offered the video codec for download so that the user could watch the video. The user was really downloading and installing Zlob (Microsoft Corporation, n.d.). Once installed, it would then expose the user to pop-up advertisements for free "security software" that would help them secure their system. Users who clicked on the ads to download and install the security software were giving the attackers more and more control over their systems. More recent examples of prevalent Trojans include *Agent Tesla* and *AsyncRAT*, which both rely on users being tricked into taking some action to infect their systems. Trojans remain popular with attackers and purveyors of malware because they are flexible weapons and can be distributed in many different ways, including email, drive-by download attacks, and watering hole attacks, among others.

Let's look at another type of threat that relies on social engineering, potentially unwanted software.

Potentially unwanted software

While I am discussing threats that use social engineering, another near-ubiquitous threat category is called **potentially unwanted software**, also known as potentially unwanted applications, potentially unwanted programs, and a few other names. Why does this category have so many seemingly unassuming names? This is a category of threats that lawyers invented. That's not necessarily a bad thing—it really is an interesting threat category. There are some shades of gray in malware research, and this category exposes those.

Let me give you a hypothetical example of potentially unwanted software that isn't based on any real-world company or organization. What would happen if a legitimate company offered consumers a free game in exchange for monitoring their internet browsing habits, all so that they could be targeted more accurately with online advertising? I think most people I know would think that's creepy and not give up their privacy in exchange for access to a free game. But if this privacy trade-off was only listed in the free game's **end user license agreement (EULA)**, where very few people would read it, how many people would simply download the free game and play it? In this case, let's say the free game ended up as a malware sample in an anti-malware company's threat collection. The analysts in the anti-malware lab could decide that the game company wasn't being transparent enough with the game's users and categorize the game as a Trojan. The anti-malware company would then update the signatures for its anti-malware products to detect this new threat. The anti-malware company's anti-malware solution would then detect and remove the game from every system where it was running. Did the anti-malware company help its customers by removing the game and its ability to track their internet browsing habits? Or, did it damage a legitimate company's business by deeming its product as malware and removing it from its customers' systems without permission?

The answer that the anti-malware industry came up with was to call it "potentially unwanted software" (or a similar name), flag it for users when it's detected, and ask the users to explicitly approve or disapprove its removal. This way, the game company's customer decides whether they want to remove the game company's product, not the anti-malware company. This helps mitigate the predictable damage claims and litigation that the anti-malware industry faces with potentially unwanted software.

Many, many variations of the example I described have been offered on the internet and are installed on systems all over the world. Some of them are legitimate companies with legitimate businesses, while others are threat actors pretending to be legitimate companies. Some families of this threat category start off as legitimate programs but later turn malicious when their supply chain is compromised, or their operators turn malevolent. Other examples of this category include fake anti-virus software, fake browser protector software, software bundles that contain a bunch of different software offerings and components, and so on. This is the most common "threat" found in the curated app stores and the mobile devices they support. My advice and mantra for many years has been don't trust the software if you don't trust the people who wrote it.

Viruses

Viruses have been around for decades. They are typically self-replicating file infectors. Viruses can spread when they are inadvertently copied between systems. Because they infect files and/or the **master boot record** (**MBR**) on systems, sometimes indiscriminately, they can be very "noisy" threats that are easy to detect, but hard to disinfect. Viruses are another malware category that seems to have periodic resurgences in popularity among some attackers. Modern attackers who develop viruses typically don't just infect files like their predecessors did decades ago; they can be more imaginative and malicious.

> Tip
>
> Remember, most threats are blended. Modern viruses have been known to download other malware once they infect a system, disable anti-malware software, steal cached credentials, turn on the microphone and/or video camera on a computer, collect audio and video data, open backdoors for attackers, and send stolen data to remote servers for attackers to pick up.

In modern times, viruses have not been anywhere near as prevalent as Trojans or potentially unwanted software, but there always seems to be some volume of detections. A great example of a family of viruses that has been around for many years is **Sality** (Microsoft Corporation, n.d.).

Browser modifiers

Browser modifiers are designed to modify browser settings without users' permission. Some browser modifiers also install malicious browser add-ons/extensions without permission, change the default search provider, modify search results, inject ads, and change the home page and pop-up blocker settings.

Browser modifiers typically rely on social engineering for installation. The motivation for browser modifiers is typically profit; attackers use them to perpetrate click fraud. But like all threats, they can be blended with other categories and provide backdoor access and download command and control capabilities for attackers. Next, let's look at exploits and exploit kits.

Exploits and exploit kits

Chapters 3 and *4* were dedicated to vulnerabilities. Remember that a vulnerability can allow an attacker to compromise the confidentiality, integrity, or availability of hardware or software. An exploit is a technique or piece of code that leverages a vulnerability in hardware or software to bypass security controls and execute malicious actions. You might also remember from my discussion of vulnerabilities in *Chapter 3* that not all vulnerabilities are the same. Some vulnerabilities, if exploited, have a higher potential impact on the system than others. Exploits for critical-rated vulnerabilities are highly sought after by attackers. This is because they give attackers the best chance to take full control of the vulnerable system and run arbitrary code of their choice. That arbitrary code can do anything that the user context it is running in can do. For example, it can download more malware from servers on the internet that will enable attackers to remotely control the system, steal identities and data, enlist the system into a botnet, and so on.

> **Note**
>
> Working exploits for vulnerabilities in web browsers, operating systems, and file parsers (for file formats such as `.pdf`, `.doc`, `.xlsx`, and so on) can be worth a lot of money because of the ubiquity of these products. Subsequently, a sophisticated marketplace has developed over the last two decades around the supply and demand for exploits.

Exploits must be delivered to their target. They can be delivered in several different ways, some of which rely on social engineering to succeed. For example, an attacker might deliver an exploit by developing a malformed `.pdf` file designed to exploit a specific unpatched vulnerability in a parser such as Adobe Acrobat Reader or Microsoft Word.

When a victim opens the `.pdf` file with a parser that isn't patched for the vulnerability that the attacker is using, and if no other mitigations are in place, then the vulnerability is exploited on the system, potentially running arbitrary code of the attacker's choice. But how does the attacker get the victim to run the exploit? One way is social engineering. The malformed `.pdf` file can be sent to the victim via email, with the sender masquerading as a co-worker or friend of the victim. Since the victim trusts their co-worker or friend, they open the email attachment, and the exploit is executed. Exploits can also be hosted on web pages as downloads for victims, sent via social networks, and distributed on USB drives and other removable media.

An exploit kit is a library of exploits with some management software. A kit's exploit library can contain any number of exploits for any number of products. An exploit kit might also provide attackers with web pages that make it easy to deliver the exploits. The management software built into the kit helps attackers understand which exploits are successful and which are not. This helps attackers make better decisions about which exploits to use and where to maximize their return on investment. This management software might also help attackers identify and replace exploits on their web pages that are no longer effective with new ones. Examples of exploit kits include **Angler** (also known as **Axpergle**), **Neutrino**, and the notorious **Blackhole** exploit kit. Examples of newer exploit kits include **Rig EK**, **Magnitude EK**, and **Fallout EK**. This approach underpins a business model and has led to the coining of a new phrase, **Malware as a Service** (**MaaS**). Exploit kits fall in and out of favor with attackers, but exploits don't.

Worms

A **worm** provides its own delivery mechanism so that it can automatically spread from system to system. Worms can use unpatched vulnerabilities, security misconfigurations, weak passwords, and social engineering to propagate themselves from system to system. A great example of a worm is **Conficker**. There were at least a few variants of this worm. It used unpatched vulnerabilities, such as MS08-067, a hardcoded list of weak passwords, and Autorun feature abuse (a feature in Windows) to spread from Windows system to Windows system (Microsoft, 2017). It could spread via removable drives, such as USB drives, as well as across networks. Successful worms can be very difficult to remove from an IT environment once they get into the environment. This is because they can *hide* in online and offline storage media and operating system images.

Other examples of successful worms include SQL Slammer and Microsoft Blaster, which both spread like wildfire around the world using unpatched vulnerabilities. There are also worms, such as MyDoom, that spread via email. It's interesting that millions of people were willing to double-click on an email attachment called MyDoom when it arrived in their inbox. Opening this attachment ran the worm that then sent a copy of itself to all the email addresses in the user's contact list. Worms are not a threat from the distant past. Since the days of Conficker (2007), there have been a few wormable vulnerabilities in Windows that were accessible through default exceptions in the Windows Firewall. In all of these cases, Microsoft was able to patch hundreds of millions of systems on the internet quickly enough so that large-scale worm attacks were avoided. But this is as dangerous a scenario as it can get for a world that relies so heavily on technology.

Recall the global malware attack scenario that I described in *Chapter 1*. I painted a picture of a worst-case worm scenario, based on my personal experience leading Microsoft's response to Blaster and Conficker.

Once a worm successfully spreads on the internet, it will continue until there's no fuel left for it. No more systems left unpatched with the vulnerabilities it knows how to exploit, no more weak passwords it attempts to use, no more users plugging USB drives into vulnerable systems, and so on. In other words, these worms continue to lurk on the internet and private networks for many years after the initial worm attack event. When governments use worms in cyber-attacks, as they did with Stuxnet, for example, they accept that there will be unintended consequences and collateral damage for years after the attacks. Worms combined with a ransomware payload can be devastating for their victims—WannaCry being the best example of this type of threat (Fruhlinger, Josh. August 24, 2022). Speaking of ransomware, let's discuss that next.

Ransomware

None of the other categories of malware strike fear into the hearts of CISOs and other executives like ransomware does. However, part of the reason for this is the litany of threats that this label is applied to by the industry and the media. For example, ransomware is used to describe all of these:

- A category of malware with many families
- Any attack where attackers deny the victim access to data and/or systems by leveraging encryption or any other method
- Any attack where attackers demand a ransom to stop the attack, including DDoS attacks
- Any attack where attackers steal data and demand a ransom not to publish it
- Any attack that involves extortion
- Any attack where the attackers' goal is destruction, not profit

The meaning of the term *ransomware* has become overloaded over time and is now a source of confusion among cybersecurity practitioners, business and government leaders, and public policy influencers. Labeling all these different types of attacks as *ransomware* isn't helpful in my view. I've seen confusing conversations among CISOs, security teams, their stakeholders, cybersecurity vendors, and even government agencies that provide cybersecurity guidance. I've been in so many meetings where one person is talking about the classic malware category that employs file encryption, while the others are discussing targeted attacks where sensitive data is stolen and attackers threaten to release it publicly (also known as **Doxware**). The ways they need to protect, detect, respond, and recover can be quite different depending on which of these threats they really intend to focus on. In such meetings, I found it helpful to provide a definition of ransomware to the participants so that everyone in the meeting was referring to the same thing. Then the group could have a productive, single-threaded conversation about the specific mitigations they had in mind. Being explicit about the type of threat helps scope the conversation, reduce confusion among its participants, and usually results in better outcomes. The use of "ransomware" has evolved so much over the past 40 years. Let's look at some of the ways this term and the threats associated with it have evolved.

Ransomware: the classic malware category

Ransomware still does refer to the classic category of malware first seen in the 1980s. Besides a couple of malware categories that are capable of self-propagating, such as worms and viruses, other malware categories generally must rely on humans and other malware to spread. Ransomware is no exception. Once ransomware malware gets onto a system via a human or other malware using one or more of the Cybersecurity Usual Suspects, it will then encrypt data (crypto ransomware) and/or lock the users out of the desktop of the system (locker ransomware). The locked desktop typically displays a message that demands a ransom to be paid and instructions on how to pay it. Successful ransomware attacks have made headlines around the world. Good examples of ransomware families include **Reveton** (Krebs, Brian., August 13, 2012) and **Petya** (Microsoft Corporation, February 5, 2018). In the case of Reveton, it was a blended threat that was primarily a Trojan married with a ransomware payload. Petya initially compromised its victims via the installation of a compromised legitimate application, after which it used an unpatched vulnerability and stolen credentials to further spread. Attackers who use ransomware are brazen in their attempts to extort all sorts of organizations, including hospitals and all levels of government.

Although ransomware gets headlines, it is actually one of the least prevalent malware categories, from a global perspective. Even old-fashioned viruses are typically more prevalent than ransomware malware. Many of the executives I briefed were skeptical when I told them this. After all, how could one of the least prevalent categories of malware garner so much attention and drive so much investment in cybersecurity programs? Remember that risk is composed of probability and impact. The thing that makes ransomware a high-risk threat isn't the probability of encountering it; it's the impact when it's encountered. Data that has been encrypted by ransomware that utilizes properly implemented strong encryption is gone forever without the decryption keys. Subsequently, many organizations decide to pay the ransom without any guarantee that they will be able to recover all of their data. Spending time and resources to implement a ransomware mitigation strategy is a good investment. Making offline backups of all datasets that are high-value assets is a good starting point. Backups are targets for attackers who use ransomware so keeping backups offline is an effective and necessary practice. I'll discuss this in more depth in *Chapter 10, Cybersecurity Strategies*.

Also, keep in mind that nothing stays the same for long, and ransomware is constantly evolving. There is nothing preventing authors of more prevalent and successful threats from incorporating ransomware tactics as the payloads in their malware. Ransomware has been used in targeted attacks for years. One thing that likely governs the use of ransomware tactics is just how criminal the attackers are; it's one thing to develop and anonymously release malware on the internet that disrupts people and organizations, but holding the assets of big corporations and government departments for a ransom and collecting that ransom is a different proposition, usually perpetrated by a different kind of criminal altogether. The world has changed in dramatic ways, enabling some attackers to work in the open without threat of consequence to them by local or international authorities. Attackers based in Russia, China, the Democratic People's Republic of Korea (North Korea), and Iran have little to fear when attacking targets in Western countries.

We will examine some data that helps us understand the prevalence of ransomware malware relative to other prevalent categories of malware. I'll explain the concept of prevalence in a little more detail later in the chapter. But before I show you prevalence data on ransomware from Microsoft, I must first explain one of the ways Microsoft measured the prevalence of malware over the years, called the malware **encounter rate** (**ER**). Microsoft defines ER as the following:

> *"The percentage of computers running Microsoft real-time security software that report detecting malware or potentially unwanted software, or report detecting a specific threat or family, during a period." (Microsoft Corporation, 2016)*

Put another way, of the systems running one of the real-time anti-malware software options from Microsoft (that I described earlier in this chapter), the ER represents the percentage of those systems where malware was blocked from being installed or where a malware infection was cleaned. The ER provides us with a good idea of how many Windows systems encountered ransomware out of the sheer number of Windows systems running Microsoft's real-time anti-malware software. Let's compare the ER for ransomware to the ER of other categories of malware. *Figure 5.2* illustrates the ER for Trojans and worms compared to that of ransomware over eight quarters between 2013 and 2016.

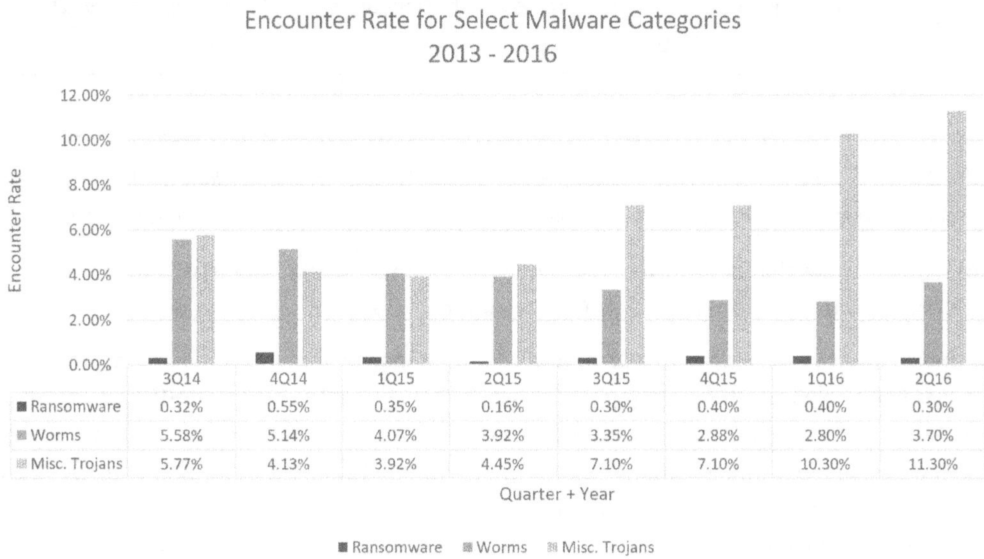

Figure 5.2 – ER for ransomware, worms, and Trojans between the third quarter of 2014 and the fourth quarter of 2017 (Microsoft Corporation, n.d.)

In the second quarter of 2016 (2Q16), ransomware was encountered on 0.30% of systems running Microsoft real-time anti-malware software, while worms were encountered on 3.7% of systems and Trojans on 11.30% of systems. During this quarter, Trojans were encountered almost 38 times more frequently than ransomware was. During the quarter where ransomware had its highest ER during this period, the fourth quarter of 2014 (4Q14), the ER of Trojans and worms were 18 times and 17 times that of ransomware, respectively.

Let's look at some slightly newer data that AV-Test published. *Table 5.1* contains data from the AV-Test Security Report 2018/19 (AV-Test Institute, April 2019) comparing the percentage of new Trojans developed for Windows to the percentage of new ransomware developed for Windows based on the samples that AV-Test collects.

Period	Development of New Trojans % of Total	Development of New Ransomware % of Total
Jan-18	69.46	0.26
Aug-18	71.12	0.54

Period	Development of New Trojans % of Total	Development of New Ransomware % of Total
Mar-19	55.25	0.39

Table 5.1 – New Trojans and new ransomware developed for Windows as a percentage of all new malware developed for Windows in January 2018, August 2018, and March 2019 (AV-Test Institute, April 2019)

This data indicates that new ransomware collected in January 2018, August 2018, and March 2019 was a fraction of a percent, while new Trojans constituted the majority of new malware.

The next year, the AV-Test Security Report 2019/2020 reported that new unique ransomware samples had tripled in 2019, reaching their highest level to date, with almost 910,000 samples (AV-Test Institute, April 2019). However, even after tripling the number of unique ransomware malware samples in 2019, the data AV-Test published reveals that ransomware comprised just 0.78% of overall malware distribution that year. Meanwhile, Trojans constituted 58.29% with 68,048,576 unique samples during the same period, 75 times the number of samples as ransomware (AV-Test Institute, April 2019). Just focusing on Windows in 2019, ransomware made up under 1% of the total distribution of malware.

Let's look at AV-Test's latest data from 2025 to see if the mix of malware threats has changed. In the two-week period between August 17, 2025, and August 31, 2025, the development of new Trojans trended between 66% and 80% of all new malware developed for Windows-based systems, totaling 1,712,160 samples. During the same period, just 1,674 new ransomware samples were collected, representing just 0.07% of all the malware developed and collected for Windows.

We've now looked at data from two credible sources across a 10-year period, and ransomware, the classic category of malware, didn't even reach 1% of encounters on hundreds of millions of systems running Microsoft real-time software, nor 1% of collected malware samples, among the millions of samples collected by one of the top independent anti-virus testing organizations in the world. This is also consistent with my experience publishing thousands of pages of CTI in the SIR during my time at Microsoft. Ransomware, the category of malware, simply isn't as prevalent as most other categories of malware. We could examine even more data from other credible sources that support the notion that the classic malware category called ransomware isn't anywhere near as prevalent as other malware categories. However, I think the explanation as to why this is the case is straightforward, and more data won't be necessary once that becomes clear.

Remember that *ransomware can't spread by itself*, as a worm or virus can. Like other malware, ransomware must rely on humans and other malware to spread. As I mentioned earlier, Trojans have been the highest-volume malware category for a very long time. Once attackers have initially compromised a system using a Trojan, they typically unpack or download more malware to the system that enables them to move forward with their objectives. If their objective is profit, destruction, or anarchy, deploying ransomware could be the second stage or payload of their attack.

What happens when the initial compromise attempt is unsuccessful? That is, when the Trojan isn't successful because it's detected and blocked by anti-malware software, the second stage of the attack involving ransomware doesn't have a chance to execute. When we use CTI data sources such as anti-malware software, the data will typically show the malware encounters for the Trojans, but not for the ransomware, because the ransomware was never encountered. The attack was stopped before the ransomware was unpacked or downloaded to the system by the Trojan. This is another reason why first-stage malware, such as Trojans, is so much more prevalent than second-stage malware, such as ransomware.

If ransomware really is far less prevalent than other malware categories, why, then, is it viewed as such a severe threat? Recall that risk is the combination of probability and impact. I don't think I have seen extinction events announced for organizations after they've encountered Trojans, despite how prevalent they have been. On the other hand, the probability of encountering ransomware might be low, but the impact could be super high. High-risk threats such as ransomware typically warrant some extra attention from security teams because their strategies to mitigate threats like this shouldn't be hope—playing the odds that their organizations simply won't encounter it. If the threat of ransomware really were limited to malware, then offline backups of critical data and pervasive endpoint protection would likely mitigate it sufficiently for most enterprises.

However, during the past decade, the threat of ransomware has grown dramatically, as evidenced by the proliferation of ransomware gangs and their victims. This growth isn't because the classic category of malware suddenly became more prevalent. The taxonomy changed. That is, the way the industry started using the term "ransomware" has evolved. Let's look at some of the key ways ransomware has evolved in order to understand what this threat really looks like.

The evolution of ransomware

Over the past few years, "ransomware" has been routinely used to describe any attack where extortion is involved. This includes the same types of targeted attacks we've seen over the past two and a half decades, even when ransomware (the classic category of malware) isn't used at all. Ransomware is now the label used for DDoS attacks where attackers demand a ransom to prevent or stop an attack. There's no ransomware malware involved in these DDoS attacks. The current trend is for attackers to simply steal sensitive data and demand a ransom not to publish it. There's no malware, no encryption, or DDoS attacks involved—just old-fashioned extortion.

> **Tip**
>
> As mentioned earlier, labeling all these different types of attacks as "ransomware" confuses conversations among CISOs, security teams, their stakeholders, cybersecurity vendors, and even government agencies that provide cybersecurity guidance and enforce regulatory compliance.

How did the concept behind a single relatively unpopular malware category evolve to become so muddy and so pervasive at the same time? At least part of the answer to this question lies in the ways ransomware malware evolved. There are at least five different ways ransomware has evolved over time. Let's look at each one briefly.

Delivery mechanisms

For decades, the classic category of malware was largely spread by humans and other malware. Prior to the advent of the internet, floppy disks and local area networks were really the only ways to spread this type of malware. Luck played a role in which systems would get victimized and which would not, because there wasn't really a targeted delivery system for malware. In the past 15 years, as ransomware became more popular with attackers, more blended malware was developed that enabled ransomware to spread more easily, such as worms that also encrypted data as they self-replicated from system to system. Today, ransomware is routinely leveraged in targeted attacks where humans, on their keyboards, are initially compromising their victims' IT environments (or buying access from an access broker), moving laterally, discovering valuable data and systems, and then using ransomware or other tools to deny access to the legitimate owners.

Some vendors have called this type of attack "human-operated ransomware." Targeted attacks have been commonplace for at least 20 years, but instead of trying to stay persistent and exfiltrating data to sell or trade, many attackers simply go for their victims' jugulars as quickly as possible by encrypting and/or exfiltrating data as soon as they can. This has resulted in a shift in some attackers' dwell times from several months to just a few hours; as soon as they find valuable enough data to extort their victims, they exfiltrate it, encrypt it, delete it, and so on, after which they aren't concerned whether their presence is detected. To facilitate this compressed "smash and grab" attack pattern, attackers have been using **commercial threat emulation tools** that accelerate their attacks, lower the barrier to entry for less technically sophisticated attackers, and act as a delivery mechanism for ransomware. These tools are designed to simulate real-world attacks. Attackers misuse these tools because they provide several advantages to them, including the following:

- Prebuilt attack chains (automated playbooks) they can leverage

- Automated exploitation workflows
- Continuous reconnaissance and lateral-movement logic
- Their operation can blend into legitimate red team activities

This is how a Sophos report puts it:

> *"Hacked Cobalt Strike suites have become the Saturday Night Specials of cybercrime: they are widely available on underground marketplaces and can be easily customized...As a result, most of the ransomware cases we've seen over the last year have involved the use of Cobalt Strike Beacons. While many malware operators use backdoors associated with the open source Metasploit framework, Cobalt Strike Beacons have become the favored tool of ransomware affiliates and access brokers who sell compromises to ransomware gangs and are often seen tied to ransomware execution." Sophos 2022 Threat Report*

Of course, there are those who aspire to collect rich ransom demands and do not have the requisite technical skills to develop sophisticated ransomware tools and attack patterns. For these people, access brokers and **Ransomware-as-a-Service** (**RaaS**) are available. Access brokers are people who sell the details of compromised networks to other criminals. In other words, they have knowledge of organizations that have been compromised and are willing to sell the *keys* to attackers who will use them to pursue their own motivations.

Attributing ransomware attacks to specific ransomware gangs and nation states started as a boutique cottage industry and has evolved into big business. All the big cybersecurity vendors tout their attribution capabilities to generate interest and sales of their products and services, and to help their customers defend themselves. These include Check Point, CrowdStrike, Microsoft, Palo Alto Networks, RecordedFuture, and Sophos, to name just a few. Examining the various security intelligence reports that these vendors published in the recent past reveals that most of these vendors have identified and tracked many of the same ransomware groups and associated families of malware. The ransomware gangs most often cited in these reports in 2024 included **3AM**, **Akira**, **Fog**, **LockBit**, **Medusa**, **Play**, **Qilin**, and **RansomHub**, among many others. The Check Point security vendor describes the scope of the gangs they track this way in their Check Point Cyber Security Report, 2025:

> *"This section presents data and insights drawn from over 140 ransomware Data Leak Sites (DLS) operated by more than 90 double-extortion ransomware groups. The details of more [sic] 5,200 companies have been published on data leak sites by cyber criminals who use these platforms to increase pressure on organizations that refuse to comply with ransom demands." (Check Point Cyber Security Report, 2025)*

Microsoft described the scope of ransomware gangs this way in the Microsoft Digital Defense Report 2023:

> *"Approximately 40 percent of the ransomware encounters we detected in June were human driven. Most of these attacks can be attributed to 123 tracked ransomware-as-a-service affiliates. The number of affiliates grew by 12 percent in the last year, setting up conditions for human-operated ransomware attacks to continue to grow in 2024." (Microsoft Digital Defense Report 2023)*

Of course, ransomware gangs aren't the only organizations that leverage ransomware and extortion as part of their attacks. Some nation-state-backed groups do as well. According to the Microsoft Digital Defense Report 2024, several nation-state threat actors Microsoft tracks leverage ransomware tactics and are motivated by extortion and/or profit; these threat actors include **Seashell Blizzard**, **Moonstone Sleet**, **Cotton Sandstorm**, **Mint Sandstorm**, **Octo Tempest**, **Storm-0501**, **Storm-0784**, and **Storm-0842**.

One of the reasons that cybersecurity teams generally like it when specific attacks can be attributed to specific groups is that it helps them understand the **tactics, techniques, and procedures** (**TTPs**) that attackers have used in the past. This gives them more confidence that they can prepare for their attacks, detect them earlier, and ferret them out. **Indicators of compromise** (**IoCs**) for specific threat actors help security teams determine whether the attackers are already present in their environment or have been in the past (with varying levels of confidence). This assessment typically includes information about how each threat actor achieved initial access into their victim's environments. This gives us insights into how delivery mechanisms have evolved from the luck that purveyors of the classic ransomware malware used to rely on. Conveniently, CTI providers typically supply TTPs and IoCs for the threat actors they track. You have plenty of choices about where you get TTPs and IoCs from, as we discussed in *Chapter 2*. CISA and its partner organizations, including the FBI, also publish details on many ransomware threat actors as part of their *#StopRansomware* effort. Let's look at some of the details they shared for a couple of the aforementioned ransomware threat actors.

Akira was one of the most active threat actors in 2024/2025. CISA published a joint cybersecurity advisory containing details about this organization, including TTPs and IoCs. They describe Akira this way:

> *"Since March 2023, Akira ransomware has impacted a wide range of businesses and critical infrastructure entities in North America, Europe, and Australia. In April 2023, following an initial focus on Windows systems, Akira threat actors deployed a Linux variant targeting VMware ESXi virtual machines. As of January 1, 2024, the ransomware group has impacted over 250 organizations and claimed approximately $42 million (USD) in ransomware proceeds." (CISA, April 18, 2024)*

The advisory goes on to describe the TTPs Akira has leveraged to gain initial access, to stay persistent and perform network and asset discovery, evade defensive measures, exfiltrate data, and encrypt their victims' data. To gain initial access, they are known to use the following TTPs (CISA, April 18, 2024):

- Login via VPN accounts that are not protected with MFA with weak, leaked, or stolen passwords
- Exploiting unpatched vulnerabilities in Cisco products (CVE-2020-3259 and CVE-2023-20269)
- Logging into internet-facing services such as **Remote Desktop Protocol** (**RDP**) with MFA with weak, leaked, or stolen passwords
- Spear phishing
- Abuse of valid credentials

> Note
>
> Notice that all these TTPs used for initial access are our Cybersecurity Usual Suspects. Threat actors such as Akira typically use brute force attacks on VPN and RDP services that are exposed to the internet. They are also known to simply buy leaked or stolen credentials from access brokers that possess them. Of course, spear phishing continues to be a mainstay in such attackers' arsenals.

Advanced threat actors such as Akira also have expertise in exploiting vulnerabilities in routing and switching equipment because they know, besides **supervisory control and data acquisition** (**SCADA**) equipment, it is typically not maintained as quickly or often as other types of IT equipment, such as workstations and servers. This includes routers, switches, firewalls, **web application firewalls** (**WAFs**), and other devices that perform route determination and packet switching. In large enterprises, these devices are typically supported by a different team than workstations and servers—a "networking" team. In enterprises, networking teams install, configure, and support the hardware and software that enable systems to communicate with each other, as well as systems on the internet. This includes routing and switching equipment. Routers and switches historically have not been able to run vulnerability management agents such as workstations and servers; this makes scanning and patching them more challenging. In fact, most enterprises continue to run routing and switching equipment well past their product end-of-support dates, and they can't be patched with security updates. Even when the hardware is supported, the operating systems running on these devices can be years out of date because it is time-consuming and disruptive to upgrade them regularly. Further, upgrading or replacing large swaths of old routing and switching equipment at one time (because they were all procured and deployed at the same time originally) can be very time-consuming, prohibitively expensive, and disruptive for most organizations. This can be so painful that many enterprise networking teams avoid this work until it becomes a crisis. For most CISOs and cybersecurity teams, routing and switching equipment represents the bottom of the iceberg that is rarely seen or talked about. Advanced threat actors know that routing and switching equipment is an Achilles' heel for defenders, and they take advantage of that.

Coveware is a firm that specializes in ransomware negotiations and related services. According to Coveware's May 1, 2025 quarterly report, the median organization size decreased 20% from the fourth quarter of 2024 to a median size of 228 employees (Coveware, May 1, 2025). According to the same report, organizations with between 101 and 1,000 employees comprised one-third of the ransomware victims in the first quarter of 2025, with organizations with 11 to 100 employees representing 36% of all victims. According to Coveware's report, 68% of all ransomware victims in Q1 of 2025 had less than 1,001 employees.

If there is a silver lining, it is that all these threat actors are still leveraging the Cybersecurity Usual Suspects to gain initial access, and the TTPs and IoCs that describe their modes of operation are widely circulated among enterprise security teams and law enforcement. Knowing their enemy gives defenders an advantage. The names of the gangs might change, but the TTPs largely haven't needed to change in 20 years—the same old targeted attack patterns are still effective today. However, defenders are faced with an ever-growing and metastasizing cadre of advanced criminal gangs and nation-state-backed attackers from all over the world. AI is only going to allow these threat actors to further compress their attack timelines and reduce barriers to entry into this modern extortion business model.

Let me summarize how delivery mechanisms for ransomware have evolved. The classic category of malware largely relied on luck to infect its victims. Ransomware had to rely on other categories of malware and/or humans to transport it to its victims. Consumers were victimized as much or more than enterprises. In contrast, today, ransomware gangs are highly organized and sophisticated and leverage affiliate criminal networks to deliver effective targeted attacks on organizations of all sizes, including hospitals, law enforcement organizations, judiciaries, and governments.

Execution mechanisms

Extortionists' modus operandi has also evolved over time. Most of the ransomware families in the classic category of malware either encrypted data on the local system's attached storage or locked out the desktop before making a ransom demand. Some malware developers failed to properly implement their encryption algorithms, which enabled security companies to help victims decrypt their data without paying the ransom in exchange for the decryption keys.

Sometimes extortionists' decryption mechanisms failed, only decrypted some of the data, or took inordinate amounts of time to decrypt. These failures made it less likely that future victims would pay ransoms. Over time, most purveyors of ransomware worked the bugs out of their encryption and decryption mechanisms and made them highly efficient.

As I mentioned earlier, today, human-operated ransomware has become commonplace. Human-operated ransomware attacks might or might not employ the classic ransomware category of malware. These attackers might not choose to encrypt data at all. Attackers have realized that victims are willing to pay for decryption keys, but many of them are also willing to pay to simply regain control of their data, whether it's encrypted or not. For example, in the cloud, the classic category of ransomware typically has a much harder time being successful because compute and mass storage devices are decoupled. That is, classic ransomware malware requires compute to run and typically encrypts the locally attached storage devices. In the cloud, compute can take many other forms, including serverless and AI/ML. Storage can also look and behave differently in the cloud compared to traditional compute with locally attached storage.

Subsequently, attackers had to devise other methods of getting leverage over their victims in the cloud. For example, after attackers initially compromise a cloud account and elevate their privileges (if necessary), they can change the cloud account's policies to deny the legitimate owner access to the account or limit their access to specific resources within the account. Then they demand a ransom to restore access to the account owner. The account owner knows that the attacker has control of their data in ways that will allow them to exfiltrate it, delete it, encrypt it, and so on. This creates a sense of extreme urgency for the victim and the willingness to pay a ransom to regain control of the account as quickly as possible.

> **Tip**
>
> Notice there was no malware or encryption involved in this attack scenario; unauthorized access was the only execution mechanism used.

Many victims are willing to pay attackers to keep their stolen data confidential after exfiltration. The brand damage from a public revelation that they suffered a data breach motivates them to pay such ransom demands. Fines and class-action lawsuits also increase the pain for victims after a breach. In the US, the **Securities and Exchange Commission** (**US SEC**) has even pursued at least one CISO with criminal charges after a breach (US SEC, October 30, 2023). Simply put, there are many incentives for paying ransom demands even when no encryption or decryption mechanisms were involved in a successful attack. In such attacks, unauthorized access and data exfiltration were the execution mechanisms used.

Keep in mind that since human-operated ransomware is all the rage these days, TTPs can and do change frequently as these gangs update the tools they use for their attacks. Unlike classic malware that is programmed to take a limited range of actions, humans can decide to change their tactics anytime based on a range of factors. Some of the most common malware and tools used by ransomware gangs in the first half of 2025 included **XMRig**, **njRAT**, **DCRat**, **XWorm**, **AsyncRAT**, **Redline**, **LummaC2**, **Stealc**, **Cobalt Strike**, and **Mirai** (Recorded Future, August 26, 2025). So, you can see that human-operated ransomware leverages a range of malware and tools that might not include classic ransomware malware or encryption.

Ransom payment methods

If there's any one area of advancement that has fueled the growth in attacks that involve extortion, it's payment methods. Payment methods used by the classic category of malware changed over time as new methods of transferring money or other valuables became available. Early on, schemes that required bank transfers typically employed *cash mules*, people hired to physically walk into a bank to do a cash withdrawal. This is risky business since the victim might decide against paying the ransom, instead partnering with law enforcement to arrest the person picking up the ransom. It's one thing to develop a program that encrypts disk drives and demands a ransom to decrypt them, but it's quite another to physically walk into a bank with the intention of committing fraud. Traditionally, these are two different types of criminals. Ransomware developers that didn't have the stomach to commit a crime in the real world had to partner with people who did have the guts to physically take possession of their ransom. These different roles comprise the so-called *affiliate network* that many ransomware gangs employ. The more people involved in a crime, the higher the risk of someone disclosing details or getting caught.

However, as other payment methods became available, ransomware developers had choices for their victims' payment methods. Premium SMS message scams and gift cards became the favorite payment methods of many purveyors of ransomware. The victim was forced to text a specific phone number at the rate of $20 per text until the ransom amount was met, or the victim was asked to mail a number of gift cards with equivalent value to the ransom demand. In both scenarios, the extortionists were able to collect their ransoms while maintaining their anonymity and without involving cash mules. However, the ransom demands were limited in size because of the relatively small amounts of cash these methods were capable of transferring.

The innovation that enabled ransomware gangs to dramatically increase their ransom demands to millions of dollars was cryptocurrencies. The proliferation of these financial tools enabled attackers to maintain their anonymity while collecting millions of dollars in illicit payments. Cryptocurrencies also helped foreign attackers target international victims across borders. For example, according to media reports, in the Colonial Pipeline attack, the attackers were paid 75 Bitcoin, the equivalent of $4.4 million at the time (Bussewitz, 2021).

However, things have changed in ways that help authorities better track and recover ransom payments made with cryptocurrencies. Cross-agency and cross-industry collaboration, more restrictive exchange regulations, and advances in blockchain forensics have buoyed international law enforcement efforts to combat ransomware gangs. For example, in 2024, Operation Cronos was a task force involving authorities in 10 countries that resulted in more than 200 cryptocurrency accounts being frozen, 2 arrests, 34 servers taken down, and law enforcement control of LockBit's infrastructure and victim leak site (Europol, n.d.). At that time, LockBit was recognized as the world's most prolific ransomware gang. Other ransomware gangs were successfully disrupted in 2025, including BlackBasta and RansomHub. Some of the disrupted gangs' members joined other ransomware gangs or formed new organizations, shifting the threat landscape (Recorded Future, August 26, 2025).

Despite the recent successful operational disruptions of some ransomware gangs, Coveware reports that the average ransom payment in Q1 of 2025 was $577,777, and the median payment was $200,000 (Coveware, May 1, 2025). It would be challenging to make such large payments using gift cards purchased from local participating outlets. The average ransomware payment resolution rate between Q4 of 2024 and Q1 of 2025 was 26%, meaning 26% of victims decided to pay the ransom demands during that 6-month period. Stated another way, during those 6 months, 74% of ransomware victims did not pay the ransom demands. The rate of victims paying ransoms to get decryption keys or suppress the release of stolen information was between 25% and 35%, going back to the third quarter of 2023. An average of 36% of victims paid ransom demands solely to suppress the release of their stolen data (no encryption involved) during the six months spanning the third quarter of 2024 and the end of the first quarter of 2025 (Coveware, May 1, 2025). Coveware described the decision to pay ransom demands this way:

> *"As expected, the highest payments were driven by decryption-motivated settlements to mitigate business interruption in the absence of valid backups. Only about one third of payments were driven by a desire to suppress the release of stolen data. Despite the big game hunting model that anticipates larger companies will pay larger ransoms, Coveware's data shows it is not the company size or sector but rather the impact of the incident that drives costs." (Coveware, May 1, 2025)*

Ransom demands and communications

Ransom demands and communications with victims, media, and governments have evolved over time. With the classic category of malware, the malware itself communicated the ransom demand to the user on the screen of the system after it was infected and encrypted. But as ransom payment methods evolved to enable ever-increasing demand amounts, ransomware gangs' communications became more and more brazen. Quiet ransom demands directly to victims have been complemented by very public victim-shaming exercises using blogs, web pages, and other public communications channels to persuade their victims to pay. Attackers are betting that large organizations that have strong brands and complicated regulatory compliance obligations are willing to pay millions of dollars to regain control of their sensitive data and avoid the financial, PR, legal, and regulatory fallout from the public revelation that they have had a data breach. This has led the US federal government and industries themselves to try to standardize data breach reporting requirements and ransomware payment notifications specifically. If there is a regulation that requires disclosure of a data breach or ransom payment, this is a disincentive for victim organizations to participate. The underlying theory is that sunlight is the best disinfectant—that is, organizations will be less willing to pay ransoms if they must disclose when they do this.

In the Colonial Pipeline attack, the ransomware gang reportedly sent their victims a URL to a "personal leak page." This page contained the victim's stolen data, which was poised to be published if the ransom demand was not paid by the deadline (Russon, 2021).

Russia was seen by some as complicit in the attack because it was thought that the perpetrators, identified as the **DarkSide** ransomware gang, were in Russia. The DarkSide gang took the extraordinary step of publicly communicating directly with the US government via their website, to assure them that their motive for the attack was profit and not an attack on critical infrastructure as an act of war or political statement. They wrote on their website, *"We do not participate in geopolitics, do not need to tie us with a defined government and look for... our motives...Our goal is to make money and not creating problems for society..."* (Russon, 2021). Presumably, they did this to de-escalate the political tension between the US and Russia in order to reduce the likelihood that they would be pursued by law enforcement in Russia. What a tangled web indeed!

Not only has extortionists' mode of demanding ransoms changed, but the number and nature of demands have changed as well. Not content with victimizing organizations just once, it has become a popular approach for attackers to make multiple ransom demands once they have a victim on the hook. One demand for a ransom to return control of the data and infrastructure to the victim, another in exchange for promising not to publicly release the victim's sensitive data, another in exchange for promising to delete the victim's exfiltrated data, another in exchange for promising not to sell access to the victim's compromised infrastructure to other attackers, and on and on. This is why so many security experts advise their clients not to pay ransoms; the only way to win this game is not to play—plan to be breached, prepare for it, and practice.

Ransomware gangs' victim shaming sites offer a glimpse into how many organizations each gang victimizes. These sites are public leak portals where ransomware gangs post stolen data to pressure victims into paying ransoms. Extortionists use them because the threat of public exposure increases leverage, inflicts reputational harm on victims, and potentially accelerates negotiations. According to Recorded Future's Cyber Threat Analysis report for the first half of 2025, the top 10 ransomware groups, ranked by the number of victims they claimed, victimized a total of 2,066 victims in those six months (Recorded Future, August 26, 2025). That's an average of 344 ransomware victims per month or 11.5 victims per day—roughly one ransomware victim every two hours. If you visit these victim-shaming sites (using a sandboxed browser, of course), you'll see the types of victims some of these gangs targeted include children's hospitals, hospices, schools, car dealerships, government departments, banks, and so many others. Once the threat actors decide to publish a victim's data publicly, the data sits on the ransomware gang's victim-shaming site for anyone to download, indefinitely. This helps explain why roughly a third of victims pay ransom demands to suppress the publication of sensitive information.

Business model

The evolution of delivery mechanisms, execution mechanisms, ransom payment methods, and ransom demands and communications has enabled attackers to change their business models over time. In decades past, before the internet was pervasive, purveyors of classic ransomware relied on luck to support very small-scale attacks—typically one personal computer at a time. Once the interest was established and became widely popular, attackers were able to leverage drive-by download attacks and worms to scale their attacks. However, the success of attacks still largely depended on luck as they did not have a precise targeting mechanism. Once payment methods enabled illicit payments in the millions of dollars, the so-called **Advanced Persistent Threat** (**APT**) actors capable of perpetrating successful targeted attacks against enterprises changed their modus operandi. Instead of trying to maximize their dwell times in order to steal valuable information to sell or trade, now they could simply extort the victim directly and quickly. In other words, they could get a much bigger payday much quicker than ever before.

Ransomware gangs develop and provide the tools required to perpetrate attacks, and their affiliates use those tools to victimize organizations. Under this RaaS business model, these two groups share the profits from successful ransomware attacks. RaaS lowers the barrier to entry for attackers and can make it harder for purveyors of CTI to perform strong attribution. If several groups of affiliates all use the same RaaS toolkit, attackers are much harder to distinguish from each other (SophosLabs, 2021). Advances in attacker automation, such as RaaS and commercial attack simulation tools, have lowered the bar to entry in this criminal industry and supercharged its growth.

Ransomware guidance

In ransomware briefings I've done with CISOs and security teams, at this point, someone typically asks, "What does this all mean?" What they are really asking is how does the evolution of ransomware change the work of cybersecurity strategists, architects, and operations teams? I think the answer to this question is straightforward. Clearly define ransomware for your organization. If your organization is mitigating ransomware as if it were just a category of malware, then you are going to have massive gaps in your strategy.

> **Note**
>
> Security teams that treat ransomware as if it were a category of malware typically employ a cybersecurity strategy that I call the "protect and recover" strategy, which focuses on preventing ransomware from spreading in their IT environment and then restoring backups when that fails. I will cover this strategy, as well as many others, in *Chapter 10*. There are better strategies to mitigate modern-day threats, such as human-operated ransomware, which I have been calling *targeted attacks* where extortion is involved.

An effective mitigation strategy needs an effective ransomware definition so that any confusion about what this threat is to your organization is cleared up for the entire stakeholder community, including the CISO, the security team, IT leadership, IT professionals, business stakeholders, and all the vendors you procure IT and cybersecurity capabilities from, and for your board of directors. Everyone in your organization needs a shared understanding of a high-risk threat you plan to spend budget and resources to mitigate. Today, I'd define ransomware as an *extortionist business model* that can employ a range of tactics, techniques, and procedures to deny victims access to their valuable data, IT infrastructure, or services, or to publicly publish sensitive stolen data unless the victims fulfill the attackers' ransom demands. This might or might not involve the use of the classic ransomware category of malware or encryption more generally.

> **Tip**
>
> Regardless of whether you plan to mitigate the ransomware category of malware, targeted attacks involving extortion more generally, or both, initial compromise will always use one or more of the Cybersecurity Usual Suspects that I discussed in detail in *Chapter 1*.

Once the threat has been defined, your strategy, architecture, CIRT, CSOC, and IT teams can approach it with the proper perspective in mind. For most organizations, a *ransomware strategy* is identical to an all-encompassing enterprise cybersecurity strategy. Put another way, a ransomware strategy is no narrower than a strategy that seeks to mitigate all targeted attacks. After all, in the modern lexicon, ransomware is any attack where extortion is involved. Don't approach it as if it is just malware because it can be much more sophisticated, with many moving parts that anti-malware solutions and backups by themselves cannot stop.

I have found it useful to further define the ransomware scenario that the cybersecurity team plans to spend resources to mitigate so that there's no confusion in the stakeholder community about what the planned ransomware recovery looks like or how long it might take. There are three scenarios I typically highlight for stakeholders that require increasing levels of funding and resources to mitigate:

- The classic ransomware category of malware that seeks to encrypt data and/or lock systems' desktops.
- Human-operated ransomware, also known as targeted attacks, where extortion is involved.
- The **wiper** scenario, where the attackers aren't motivated by profit. In this scenario, attackers are trying to irrevocably damage their victims' IT and/or OT infrastructures and data. For example, Russia allegedly used wiper malware to attack Ukraine as part of its ongoing military attack (Goodin, March 21, 2024). There is no decryption key to use to recover data or hard drives that have been encrypted—they are irrevocably damaged or damaged in such a way that the manufacturer is needed to repair them.

The first scenario is the easiest and least expensive to mitigate. Running up-to-date anti-malware or XDR software on every endpoint, backing up sensitive data offline, and mitigating all five of the Cybersecurity Usual Suspects gets you most of the way there. The worst-case scenario is the global worm attack I described in *Chapter 1*, where the worm uses zero-day vulnerabilities to spread, and its payload is ransomware. It's harder to mitigate unpatched vulnerabilities when vendors haven't distributed the updates to address them, but it is not impossible.

As I've already mentioned, the second scenario requires a holistic cybersecurity strategy to give you the best chance to mitigate it. Efforts to mitigate human-operated ransomware will also benefit from the mitigations mentioned in the first scenario. However, backing up sensitive data but not having a practiced disaster recovery strategy for broader human-made disasters that impact infrastructure, systems, and information workers is a big gap. There are some cybersecurity strategies that will be much more effective in this scenario than simply running anti-malware software and backing up sensitive data. We'll discuss these in *Chapter 10*.

The third scenario, the wiper scenario, is the most expensive and resource-intensive to mitigate. In order to *really* be prepared to recover from the catastrophic hardware and software failures that accompany an irreversible wiper attack in a reasonable period of time, much more preparation, investment, and resources are required. We'll dive into the relevant considerations for this scenario in *Chapter 10* when we discuss resilience as a cybersecurity strategy, but here are some of them for your reference:

- What do you really need to have on hand to replace damaged hardware?
- Do you know all the systems' dependencies that must also be restored, and the order they need to be restored in?
- Do you have all the system and hardware configurations backed up offline, as well as the data?
- How long would recovery take if your identity system, such as Active Directory, were destroyed?
- Do you have an offline identity system provisioned that enables you to get access to the backups?
- Do you have an inventory of replacement hardware? Does the manufacturer even produce your hardware anymore?
- Will the organization survive if it takes months or years to recover, or will it be an extinction event for the organization?

Most organizations choose not to prepare for the wiper scenario as they simply do not have the wherewithal to do so. Their limited resources are better spent focusing on preparing for the other two ransomware scenarios. However, cybersecurity teams that do invest in mitigating the wiper scenario effectively mitigate the first two scenarios as well. Organizations that are deemed critical infrastructure need to make this investment decision carefully. Do they need to plan to mitigate the ransomware wiper scenario, or do they adopt a strategy that helps them mitigate more common targeted attacks? I've worked for organizations that chose to mitigate the wiper scenario because they operate critical infrastructure. This strategy can literally be years of work, but even if they never get to the planned destination, these organizations typically have much better overall cybersecurity, are better prepared for ransomware attacks, and can recover from them faster. Getting alignment with all your stakeholders about which of these three ransomware scenarios your organization plans to prepare for will help you get the appropriate levels of investment and resources and properly set expectations about recovery times and recovery points.

That wraps up my introduction to categories of malware and a deep dive into the evolution of ransomware. As you've seen, ransomware isn't a prevalent category of malware, but so-called human-operated ransomware is a top threat to enterprises. Next, let's look at the most prevalent malware threats that CISOs and cybersecurity teams need to be prepared for.

Measuring malware prevalence

In this section, I provide a historical perspective on how malware infections evolved over time. This will help you understand how attackers change their attacks over time to continually adjust attacks towards the techniques and tactics that are successful at that time.

Before diving into that data, you'll need to understand two of the ways that the prevalence of malware can be measured. The first one is called **computers cleaned per mille** (**CCM**) (Microsoft Corporation, n.d.). The term "per mille" is Latin for "in each thousand." We used this measure at Microsoft to measure how many Windows systems were infected with malware for every 1,000 systems that the MSRT scanned. You'll remember that the MSRT runs on hundreds of millions of systems when it's released on the second Tuesday of every month with the security updates for Microsoft products. CCM is calculated by taking the number of systems found to be infected by the MSRT in a country and dividing it by the total number of MSRT executions in that country. Then, multiply it by 1,000. For example, let's say the MSRT found 600 systems infected with malware after scanning 100,000 systems; the CCM would be (600/100,000)*1,000 = 6 (Microsoft Corporation, 2016).

The CCM is helpful because it allows us to compare malware infection rates of different countries by removing the Windows install base bias. For example, it's fair to say there are more Windows systems running in the US than in Spain. Spain is a smaller country with a smaller population than the US. If we compared the raw number of systems found infected in the US with the raw number of infected systems in Spain, the US would likely look many, many more times infected than Spain. In actual fact, the CCM exposes that, for many time periods, the number of systems infected for every 1,000 scanned in Spain was much higher than the number in the US.

Before a system can get infected with malware, it must encounter it first. Once a system encounters malware, the malware will use one or more of the Cybersecurity Usual Suspects to try to infect the system. If the malware successfully infects the system, then the MSRT runs on the system, detects the infection, and cleans the system. This will be reflected in the CCM.

I introduced the next measure of prevalence earlier in this chapter when we examined the prevalence of ransomware—the malware **encounter rate** (**ER**). Of the systems running real-time anti-malware software from Microsoft that I described earlier in this chapter, the ER is the percentage of those systems where malware was blocked from being installed or where a malware infection was cleaned.

I'll use these two measures to show you how the threat landscape has changed over time. The only drawback to using this data is that Microsoft did not publish both of these measures for every time period. For example, they published CCM data from 2008 to 2016 and then stopped publishing CCM data. They started publishing ER data in 2013 and continued to publish some ER data into 2019. But as you'll see, they did not publish ER data for the second half of 2016, leaving a hole in the available data. Additionally, sometimes, data was published in half-year periods and other times in quarterly periods. I've done my best to compensate for these inconsistencies in the analysis I'll share with you next. As far as I can tell, Microsoft has stopped publishing this data altogether in recent years and has focused on providing insights into human-operated ransomware, nation-state threat actors, and threat actor attribution. While this analysis is limited to the data we have access to, it will illustrate a long-term trend that we can learn from.

> **Tip**
>
> One of the things I hope you take away from this section is how being intimately familiar with the data sources helps you accurately interpret data. There are many ways this data could be interpreted, but really understanding how the data sources generate data is key to interpreting the data accurately.

Global Windows malware infection analysis

I have aggregated data from over 20 volumes and special editions of the Microsoft SIR to provide a view of how the threat landscape evolved over a long period of time. The first measure we'll look at is the worldwide average CCM. This is the number of systems that the MSRT found to be infected with malware for every 1,000 systems it scanned around the world. *Figure 5.3* includes all the time periods that Microsoft published CCM data for in the SIR, each quarter between the third quarter of 2008 and the second quarter of 2016.

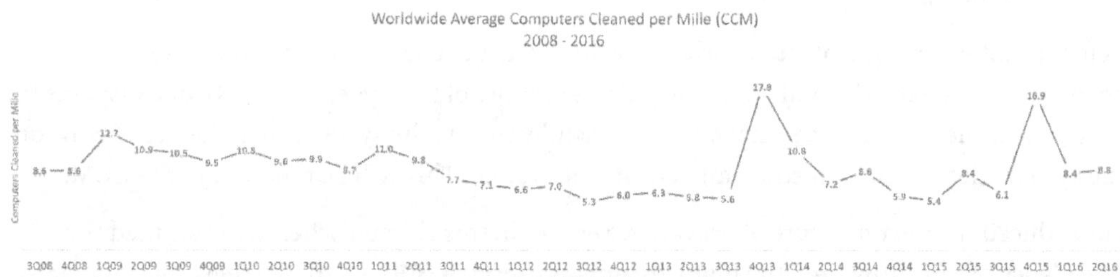

Figure 5.3 – Worldwide average malware infection rate (CCM) 2008–2016 (Microsoft Corporation, n.d.)

The horizontal axis illustrates the time periods represented by the quarter and year. For example, 3Q08 is shorthand for the third quarter of 2008, while 4Q13 is the fourth quarter of 2013. The vertical axis represents the worldwide CCM for each time period. For example, in the 1st quarter of 2009 (1Q09), the worldwide average CCM was 12.7.

The worldwide average CCM for all 32 quarters illustrated in *Figure 5.3* is 8.82. To make this number clearer, let's convert it into a percentage: 8.82/1000*100 = 0.882%. For the 8-year period between the third quarter of 2008 and the end of the second quarter of 2016, the worldwide average infection rate, as measured by the MSRT, is less than 1 percent. This will likely surprise some of you who have long thought that the Windows install base has always had really high malware infection rates. This is why comparing the infection rates of different countries and regions is interesting. Some countries have much higher infection rates than the worldwide average, and some countries have much lower CCMs. I'll discuss this in detail later in this chapter.

The other factor contributing to a lower malware infection rate than you might have been expecting is that the source of this data is the MSRT. Remember that the MSRT is a free ecosystem cleaner designed to clean largely unprotected systems from the most prevalent and serious threats. If you look at the dates when detections were added to the MSRT, you will see that it is really cleaning a tiny fraction of the known malware families. For example, according to the list, at the end of 2005, the MSRT had detected 62 malware families (Microsoft Corporation, n.d.). But it's certain that there were orders of magnitude more malware in the wild in 2005. In mid-2025, the MSRT was capable of detecting and cleaning 475 malware families, among the nearly 1 billion unique malware samples that AV-Test had in its collection for Windows.

While the MSRT is only capable of detecting a fraction of all malware families, it does run on hundreds of millions of systems around the world every month. This provides us with a limited, but valuable, snapshot of the relative state of computer populations around the world. When we cross-reference MSRT data with data from real-time anti-malware solutions and some of the other data sources I outlined, we get a more complete picture of the threat landscape.

Another aspect of the MSRT that's important to understand is that it measures which malware families have successfully infected systems at scale. Microsoft researchers add detections to the MSRT for malware families they think are highly prevalent. Then, when the MSRT is released with the new detections, the malware researchers can see whether they guessed correctly. If they did add detections for a family of malware that was really widespread, it will appear as a spike in the malware infection rate. Adding a single new detection to the MSRT can result in a large increase in the worldwide infection rate. For example, between the third and fourth quarters of 2015 (3Q15 and 4Q15 in *Figure 5.3*), the CCM increased from 6.1 to 16.9. This is a 177% change in the malware infection rate in a single quarter. Then, in the next quarter, the CCM went down to 8.4. What drove this dramatic increase and then decrease? Microsoft malware researchers added detections to the MSRT for a threat called Win32/Diplugem in October 2015 (Microsoft Corporation). This threat is a browser modifier that turned out to be installed on a lot of systems. When Microsoft added detection for it to the MSRT in October, it cleaned Diplugem from lots of systems in October, November, and December. Typically, when a new detection is added to the MSRT, it will clean lots of infected systems in the first month, fewer in the second month, and fewer yet in the third month. A lot of systems were cleaned of Diplugem in the three months of the fourth quarter of 2015. Once the swamp was mostly drained of Diplugem in 4Q15, the infection rate went down 50% in the first quarter of 2016.

This type of detection spike can also be seen between the third and fourth quarters of 2013 (3Q13 and 4Q13, in *Figure 5.3*) when the CCM increased from 5.6 to 17.8. This is a 218% change in the malware infection rate in a single quarter. Five new detections were added to the MSRT in the fourth quarter of 2013.

The detection rate spike in 4Q13 was a result of adding detection to the MSRT for a threat called Win32/Rotbrow (Microsoft Corporation, n.d.), which is a family of Trojans that can install other malware such as Win32/Sefnit (Microsoft Corporation, n.d.). After the big CCM increase that this detection produced, the CCM receded to lower levels over the next two quarters.

In order to see what's happening in a more recent time period, we'll have to use the malware ER instead of the CCM because Microsoft stopped publishing CCM data in 2016. *Figure 5.4* illustrates the ER for the period from the first quarter of 2013 (1Q13) to the fourth quarter of 2018 (4Q18). Microsoft didn't publish a worldwide average ER for the second half of 2016, so we are left without data for that period.

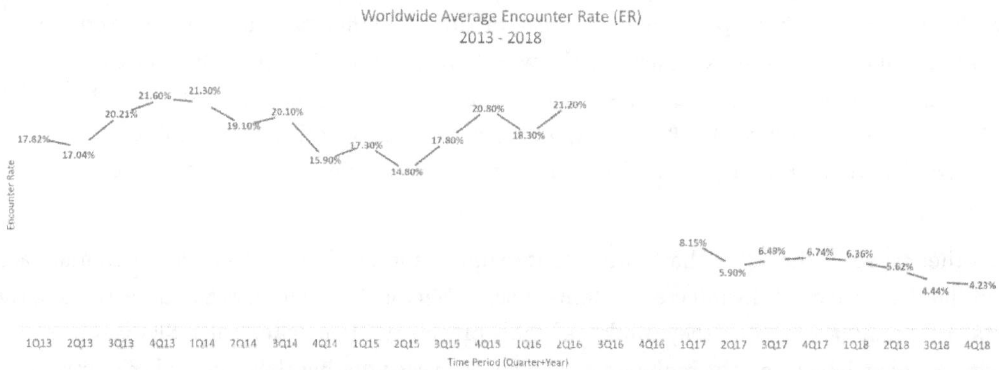

Figure 5.4 – Worldwide average encounter rate (ER) 2008–2016

The average ER for the period between 2013 and the end of the first half of 2016 was 18.81%. This means that about 19% of Windows systems that were running Microsoft real-time anti-malware software encountered malware. Almost all of these encounters likely resulted in anti-malware software blocking the installation of the malware. Some smaller proportion of encounters likely resulted in disinfection.

The ER dropped 62% between the second quarter of 2016 (2Q16) and the first quarter of 2017 (1Q17) and didn't go back up to normal levels. In 2017 and 2018, the worldwide average ER was only 6%.

That has given you a long-term view of malware trends on Windows operating systems from a global perspective. Many of the CISOs and security teams that I've briefed using similar data expressed surprise at how low the global ER and CCM numbers are, given all the negative press malware on Windows has generated over the years. In fact, during some of my speaking engagements at conferences, I would ask the attendees what percentage of Windows systems in the world they thought were infected with malware at any given time. Attendees' guesses would typically start at 80% and work their way up from there. CISOs, security teams, and security experts need to be firmly grounded in reality if they want to lead their organizations and the industry in directions that truly make sense. That's what makes this data helpful and interesting.

That said, I find regional perspectives much more interesting and insightful than the global perspective. Next, let's look at how malware encounters and infections differ between geographic locations around the world.

Regional Windows malware infection analysis

I started studying regional malware infection rates back in 2007. At first, I studied a relatively small group of countries, probably six or seven. But over time, our work in the SIR was expanded to provide malware CCM and ER data for all countries (over 100) where there was enough data to report statistically significant findings. Over the years, three loosely coupled groups of locations emerged from the data:

- Locations that consistently had malware infection rates (CCMs) lower than the worldwide average
- Locations that typically had malware infection rates consistent with the worldwide average
- Locations that consistently had malware infection rates much higher than the worldwide average

Figure 5.5 illustrates some of the locations with the highest and lowest ERs in the world between 2015 and 2018.

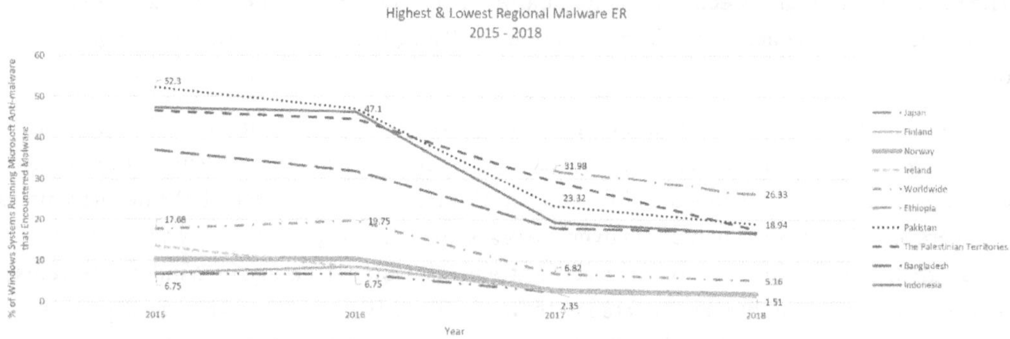

Figure 5.5 – Highest and lowest regional malware ERs (Microsoft Corporation, n.d.)

The dotted line represents the worldwide average ER so that you can see how much the other locations listed deviate from the average. Countries such as Japan and Finland tended to have the lowest malware encounter rates and the lowest malware infection rates in the world. Norway was also among the locations with low CCM and ER. Ireland was a relatively new addition to the list of least impacted locations. The CCM and ER for Ireland were typically lower than the worldwide average, but not one of the five or six lowest. For example, in 2008, the worldwide average CCM was 8.6, while Japan had a CCM of 1.7, and Ireland's CCM was 4.2 (Microsoft Corporation, 2009). It might be tempting to think, duh, a lower ER means a lower infection rate, right? Some locations have both low CCM and low ER. But that's not always the case.

Over time, I have seen plenty of examples of locations that have high ERs but still maintain low CCMs, and vice versa. One reason for this is that not all locations have the same adoption rate of anti-malware software. This is one reason Microsoft started giving real-time anti-malware software away as a free download and now offers it as part of the operating system. There were parts of the world with alarmingly low anti-malware adoption rates. If these locations became heavily infected, they could be used as platforms to attack the rest of the world. Countries with high anti-malware protection adoption can have high ERs but generally have much lower CCMs. This is because the real-time anti-malware software blocks malware from installing, thus increasing the ER and leaving less prevalent threats for the MSRT to clean, thereby lowering the CCM.

You might be wondering why there are regional differences in malware encounter rates and infection rates. Why do places such as Japan and Finland tend to have ultra-low infection rates, while places such as Pakistan and the Palestinian territories tend to have very high infection rates? Is there something that the locations with low infection rates are doing that other locations can benefit from? When I first started studying these differences, I hypothesized that language could be the key difference between lowly and highly infected locations. For example, Japan has a hard language to learn as it's sufficiently different from English, Russian, and other languages, so it could be a barrier for would-be attackers. After all, it's hard to successfully attack victims using social engineering if they don't understand the language you are using in your attacks. But this is also true of South Korea, yet it had one of the highest CCMs in the world back in 2012, with a CCM that ranged between 70 and 93 (one of the highest CCMs ever published in the SIR).

Ultimately, we tried to develop a model we could use to predict regional malware infection rates. If we could predict which locations would have high infection rates, then we were optimistic that we could help those locations develop public policy and public-private sector partnerships that could make a positive difference. Some colleagues of mine in Trustworthy Computing at Microsoft published a Microsoft Security Intelligence Report Special Edition focused on this work: *The Cybersecurity Risk Paradox, Impact of Social, Economic, and Technological Factors on Rates of Malware* (Burt, David., 2014). They developed a model that used 11 socio-economic factors in 3 categories to predict regional malware infection rates. The categories and factors included (Burt, David., 2014) the following:

- Digital access:
    - Internet users per capita
    - Secure network servers per million people
    - Facebook penetration
- Institutional stability:
    - Government corruption
    - Rule of law
    - Literacy rate
    - Regime stability
- Economic development:
    - Regulatory quality
    - Productivity
    - Gross income per capita
    - GDP per capita

The study found that as developing nations increased their citizens' access to technology, their CCM increased. But more mature nations that increased their citizens' access to technology saw decreases in their CCMs. This suggests that there is a tipping point for developing nations as they transition from developing to more mature across the aforementioned categories, where increasing access to technology no longer increases CCM; instead, it decreases it.

An example of a country that appeared to make this transition in 2011–2012 was Brazil. With some positive changes in some of the socio-economic factors in the digital access and institutional stability categories, Brazil's CCM decreased from 17.3 to 9.9 (a 42% reduction) between 2011 and 2012 (Burt, David., 2014).

Another nuance from the study is that the locations that had some of the highest CCMs and worst-performing socio-economic factors tended to be war-torn countries, such as Iraq. Another interesting insight is that in locations that don't have very good internet connectivity, whether it's because they are geographically isolated or perpetual military conflict has impacted the availability and quality of the internet, malware infects systems via USB drives and other types of removable storage media; that is, when the internet is not able to help attackers propagate their malware, malware that doesn't rely on network connectivity becomes prevalent. When internet connectivity and access improve, CCMs tend to increase in these locations until socio-economic conditions improve to the point that the governments and public-private sector partnerships start to make a positive difference to cybersecurity in the region. Strife and the poverty that can follow it can slow down technology refresh rates, making it easier for attackers to take advantage of people. This was a super interesting area of research.

Global malware evolution

Understanding the evolution of malware will help CISOs and security teams put the hysteria they read in the news into context. Keep the Cybersecurity Usual Suspects in the back of your mind as you read this section.

In the wake of the successful large-scale worm attacks of 2003 and early 2004, Microsoft introduced Windows XP Service Pack 2 in August 2004. Among other things, Windows XP Service Pack 2 turned on the Windows Firewall by default for the first time in a Windows operating system. Prior to this, it was an optional setting that was left to customers to turn on, configure, and test with their applications. This service pack also offered **Address Space Layout Randomization** (**ASLR**) and **Data Execution Prevention** (**DEP**) for the first time in a Windows operating system (Ladd, David., 2011). These three features blunted the success of future mass worm attacks that sought to use the same tactics as SQL Slammer and MSBlaster. A vulnerability in a service listening on a network port cannot be exploited if there's a host-based firewall blocking packets from getting to the port. The memory location of a vulnerability might not be the same on every system, making it harder to find and exploit.

Eighteen months after Windows XP Service Pack 2 was released and its adoption was widespread, the data shows us that worms and backdoors fell out of favor with attackers. As shown in *Figure 5.6*, the number of detections of these categories of malware saw dramatic reductions in 2006, 2007, and 2008.

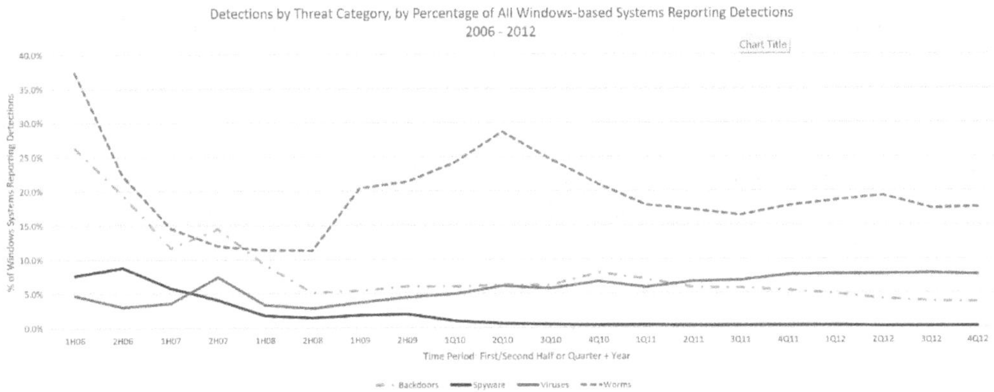

Figure 5.6 – Detections by threat category, including backdoors, spyware, viruses, and worms by percentage of all Windows-based systems reporting detections, 2006–2012 (Microsoft Corporation, n.d.)

A different type of worm, one that didn't just use unpatched vulnerabilities, became popular with attackers in 2009, 5 years after Windows Firewall, ASLR, and DEP were turned on in Windows operating systems.

Once worms were no longer effective for mass attacks, the data shows us that miscellaneous potentially unwanted software became popular in 2006, 2007, and 2008. You can see this marked increase in *Figure 5.7*.

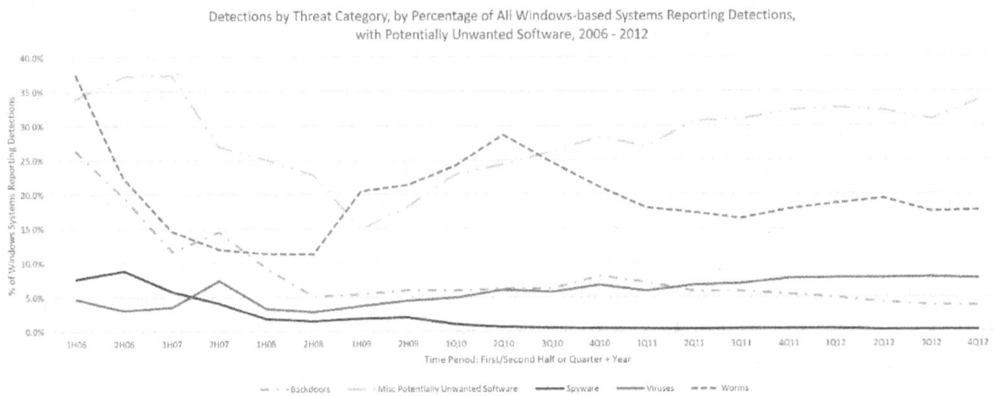

Figure 5.7 – Detections by threat category, including backdoors, spyware, viruses, worms, and Miscellaneous Potentially Unwanted Software by percentage of all Windows-based systems reporting detections, 2006–2012 (Microsoft Corporation, n.d.)

Tip

As I described earlier in this chapter, this category of threat typically relies on social engineering to infect systems. Fake anti-virus software, fake spyware detection suites, and fake browser protectors were all the rage during this period.

As the use of potentially unwanted software peaked in 2006 and more people were getting wise to it, detections trended down in 2007 and 2008. During this time, the data shows us that Trojan downloaders and droppers came into fashion. This is clearly reflected in *Figure 5.8*.

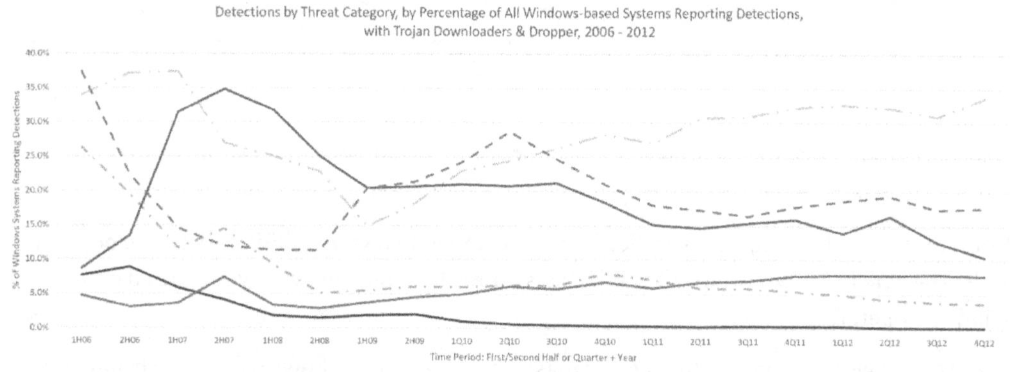

Figure 5.8 – Detections by threat category, including backdoors, spyware, viruses, worms, Miscellaneous Potentially Unwanted Software, and Trojan downloaders and droppers by percentage of all Windows-based systems reporting detections, 2006–2012 (Microsoft Corporation, n.d.)

This category of threat also primarily relies on social engineering to initially compromise systems. They trick the user into installing them and then unpack or download more malware to the system to give attackers further control. During this time, it was not uncommon for Trojan downloaders and droppers to enlist their victims' systems into botnets for use in other types of attacks.

As people caught on to the dirty tricks that attackers were using with Trojan downloaders and droppers, and anti-virus companies focused on eradicating this popular category of malware, the data shows the popularity of droppers and downloaders receding, while detections of miscellaneous Trojans peaked in 2008 and again in 2009. This category of threat also relies primarily on social engineering to be successful. The data also shows us that there was a significant increase in the detection of password stealers and monitoring tools between 2007 and 2011.

There was a resurgence in the popularity of worms in 2008, when Conficker showed attackers what was possible by combining three of the Cybersecurity Usual Suspects into a single worm.

In *Figure 5.9*, notice the slow but steady rise of exploits starting in 2009.

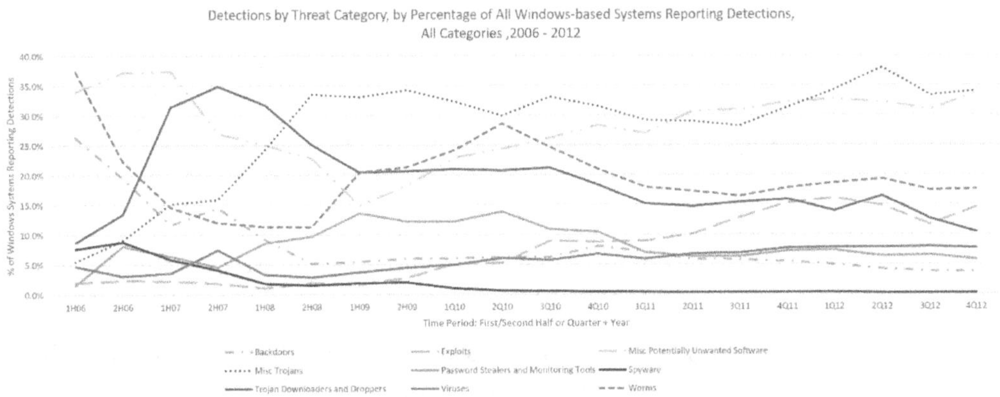

Figure 5.9 – Detections by threat category, all categories, by percentage of all Windows-based systems reporting detections, 2006–2012 (Microsoft Corporation, n.d.)

This trend peaked in 2012, when exploit kits were all the rage on the internet. Also, notice that there is no significant volume of ransomware throughout this entire period. As we leave this period at the end of 2012, the categories in the top-right corner of the graph, Trojans and potentially unwanted software, rely on social engineering to be successful.

Entering 2013, Microsoft started using the ER to measure threat detections. Note that the measure used between 2013 and 2017 is ER versus the detections measure used in the prior period. These are slightly different data points. Microsoft did not publish ER data in the third and fourth quarters of 2016, so there is a hole in the data for this period. The ER data confirms that miscellaneous Trojans was the most frequent threat category encountered in 2013. Unfortunately, I could not find a published data source for the ER of potentially unwanted software, so it's missing from *Figure 5.10*.

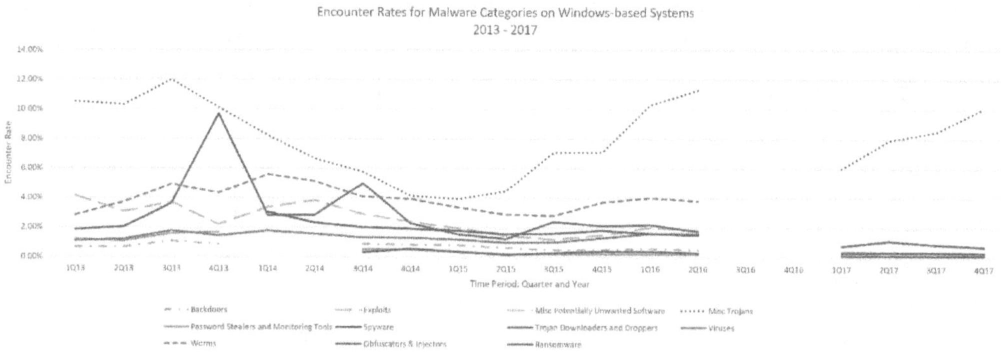

Figure 5.10 – Encounter rates by threat category on Windows-based systems reporting detections, 2013–2017 (Microsoft Corporation, n.d.)

The ER spike for Trojan downloaders and droppers in the second half of 2013 was due to three threats: **Rotbrow**, **Brantall**, and **Sefnit** (Microsoft, 2014).

At the end of this period, in the fourth quarter of 2017, ransomware had an ER of 0.13%, while miscellaneous Trojans had an ER of 10.10%, meaning miscellaneous Trojans were encountered 78 times more often than ransomware. It appears that the investments Microsoft made in memory safety features and other mitigations in Windows operating systems have helped drive down the global ER during this period, despite increasing numbers of vulnerability disclosures in Windows. If ER is an indicator, the one tactic that the purveyors of malware seem to get a solid **Return on Investment** (**ROI**) from is social engineering.

Now that you've seen the long-term historical trend and understand how attackers have evolved their attacks over time, you might be wondering what has been happening with malware more recently.

According to Sophos 2025 Annual Threat Report, based on data from their Sophos **Managed Detection and Response** (**MDR**) service, in 2024, nearly 60% of incidents observed did not involve ransomware (Sophos X-Ops., April 16, 2025). The top three categories of malware they detected in 2024 included Trojan downloaders and droppers, information stealers/spyware, and backdoor Trojans/remote access Trojans. Trojans continue to be attackers' favorite tool. Sophos shares this about the information stealer category that is popular with attackers at this time:

> *"Information-stealing malware is often the first step in the access broker's playbook, providing passwords, cookies, and other data that can be used for financial fraud, business email compromise, and ransomware attacks, among other schemes. Lumma Stealer, sold through Russian-speaking forums as a Malware-as-a-Service (MaaS),*

> *was the most frequently encountered information stealer in MDR incidents, and second in overall endpoint detection reports." (Sophos X-Ops., April 16, 2025)*

Data published by Check Point also suggests that information stealers are in vogue with attackers.

> *"As big botnets and banking malware decline, infostealers have emerged as the new Big Bad, now distributed through large-scale campaigns. A quick search on the Russian Market, one of the largest underground criminal marketplaces, reveals that over 10 million infostealer logs are currently available for purchase. ...*
>
> *Infostealer infection attempts also increased significantly, from 12% to 19% of organizations affected in 2024, a 58% increase. The rise in infostealer attacks, typically distributed in mass campaigns rather than targeting specific victims, reflects a maturing ecosystem and an increasing demand for stolen infostealer logs containing credentials, session cookies, and other personal information. Infostealers are used for multiple malicious activities, ranging from direct fraud via stolen financial credentials to leveraging stolen session cookies for breaching corporate networks." (Check Point, 2025).*

Recorded Future uses malware references in **Command and Control** (**C2**) server configurations to provide a slightly different view into the malware landscape than malware detections from endpoint protection software:

> *"Several of H1 2024 's top ten malware (Vidar, RedLine Stealer, and LokiBot, for example) have largely fallen off in 2025, owing in part to disruptive operations and law enforcement actions, while other malware families surged or emerged to take their place...H1 2025 's C2 detections also highlight the enduring presence of long-lived malware. Sality, a polymorphic botnet first seen in 2003, remains in the top tier after a major resurgence in 2024, demonstrating the resilience of legacy threats. Likewise, the Tofsee trojan (active for over a decade) appears among the top families." (Recorded Future., August 26, 2025).*

I was warning people about Sality and the resurgence of old-fashioned file infectors (viruses) back in 2013!

> *"Writing on the Microsoft Security Blog, Rains says, 'I have rarely seen the virus threat category found on more than 5 percent of systems with detections globally. But more recently I have noticed that viruses seem to be making a comeback. The relative prevalence of viruses has been trending up. The prevalence worldwide for the virus threat category was 7.8 percent in the fourth quarter of 2012...' Pointing to the success of Win32/Sality, a family of polymorphic file injectors found on 8,204,434*

> *computers worldwide, Rains says, 'Sality is one of the top five detections on Windows XP.'" (Waugh, Rob., May 21, 2013)*

I hope this makes it clear that malware goes in and out of vogue with attackers. Attackers use whichever types of malware are successful until they decline in effectiveness. Then they switch to other categories that provide a higher return on investment for them, and the cycle continues. Every once in a while, reports of advanced threat actor activity reveal truly novel malware, such as Win32/Flame and Win32/Conficker. But the millions of other malware threats that continue to get churned out are recycled and banal. This is good news for defenders.

Global malware evolution conclusions

The malware category data we examined shows us that purveyors of malware really are limited to only a few options when trying to initially compromise systems. Exploiting unpatched vulnerabilities is a reliable method for only limited periods of time, but this doesn't stop attackers from attempting to exploit old vulnerabilities for years after a security update has become available. Worms come in and out of fashion with attackers and require technical skills to develop. But the one tactic that is a mainstay tactic is social engineering. When the other four Cybersecurity Usual Suspects are not viable options, many attackers will attempt to use good old-fashioned social engineering.

This concludes my marathon discussion on malware, the global Windows threat landscape, and ransomware. I feel like I have only scratched the surface here, but we have so many other interesting topics to discuss! Please remember the best practices and tips on what makes good CTI that I shared in *Chapter 2* when consuming threat intelligence.

Summary

In this chapter, I tried to provide you with a unique long-term view of the threat landscape and some useful context. Now let's summarize the key takeaways from this chapter.

Malware uses the Cybersecurity Usual Suspects to initially compromise systems; these include unpatched vulnerabilities, security misconfigurations, weak, leaked, and stolen credentials, insider threats, and social engineering. Of these, social engineering is attackers' favorite tactic, as evidenced by the consistent prevalence of malware categories that leverage it. Malware can also be employed after the initial compromise to further the attackers' objectives.

Some successful malware families impact systems around the world quickly after release, while others start as regional threats before growing into global threats. Some threats stay localized to a region because they rely on a specific non-English language to trick users into installing them. Regions have different malware encounter and infection rates. Research conducted by Microsoft indicates that some socio-economic factors, such as GDP, could be influencing these differences. Regions with unusually high levels of strife and the socio-economic conditions that accompany it typically have higher malware encounter and infection rates.

Focusing on the cybersecurity fundamentals, which address the Cybersecurity Usual Suspects, will help mitigate malware threats. In addition, running up-to-date anti-malware solutions or **Extended Detection and Response** (**EDR** or **XDR**) endpoint solutions from a trusted vendor will help block the installation of most malware and disinfect systems that get infected.

> **Tip**
>
> Blocking information workers' access to regions of the internet that do not have legitimate business purposes can help prevent exposure to malware and compromised systems in these regions.

Ransomware has evolved over time, and now this term means different things to different people. Ensuring your organization has a shared understanding of what modern ransomware is will help align strategies and resources required to mitigate it. An effective ransomware strategy is the same as an all-encompassing enterprise cybersecurity strategy designed to mitigate targeted attacks. Mitigating wiper ransomware typically requires more investment and resources—something CISOs and their stakeholders should align on.

So far, we've examined the long-term trends for vulnerabilities and malware. In the next chapter, we'll explore the ways attackers have been using the internet and how these methods have evolved over time.

References

- AV-Test Institute (2017). *The AV-TEST Security Report* 2016/2017. Magdeburg, Germany: AV-Test Institute. Retrieved from: `https://www.av-test.org/fileadmin/pdf/security_report/AV-TEST_Security_Report_2016-2017.pdf`
- AV-Test Institute (2018). *The AV-TEST Security Report* 2017/2018. Magdeburg, Germany: AV-Test Institute. Retrieved from: `https://www.av-test.org/fileadmin/pdf/security_report/AV-TEST_Security_Report_2017-2018.pdf`
- AV-Test Institute (April 2019). *The AV-TEST Security Report* 2018/2019. Magdeburg, Germany: AV-Test Institute. Retrieved from AV-Test: `https://www.av-test.org/fileadmin/pdf/security_report/AV-TEST_Security_Report_2018-2019.pdf`

- AV-Test Institute (April 2019). *The AV-TEST Security* Report 2019/2020. Magdeburg, Germany: AV-Test Institute. Retrieved from AV-Test: `https://www.av-test.org/fileadmin/pdf/security_report/AV-TEST_Security_Report_2019-2020.pdf`
- AV-Test Institute (August, 2025). *About the AV-TEST Institute*. Retrieved from AV-Test: `https://www.av-test.org/en/about-the-institute/`
- AV-Test Institute (n.d.). *AV-Test Malware Statistics*. Retrieved from AV-Test: `https://www.av-test.org/en/statistics/malware/`
- AV-Test Institute (February 2026). *AV-Test Total Malware*. Retrieved from AV-Test: `https://www.av-test.org/en/statistics/malware/`
- Toulas, Bill. (August 25, 2025). *Malicious Android apps with 19M installs removed from Google Play*. Retrieved from BleepingComputer: `https://www.bleepingcomputer.com/news/security/malicious-android-apps-with-19m-installs-removed-from-google-play/`
- AV-Test Institute (April, 2020). *International Presence and Publications*. Retrieved from AV-Test Institute: `https://www.av-test.org/en/about-the-institute/publications/`
- Burt, David, P. N. (2014). *The Cybersecurity Risk Paradox*, Microsoft Security Intelligence Report Special Edition. Microsoft. Retrieved from `https://www.google.com/url?sa=t&rct=j&q=&esrc=s&source=web&cd=&ved=2ahUKEwicr_W8-saPAxWDIDQIHdG8DeAQFnoECBMQAQ&url=https%3A%2F%2Fdownload.microsoft.com%2Fdownload%2FE%2F1%2F8%2FE18A8FBB-7BA6-48BD-97D2-9CD32A71B434%2FCybersecurity-Risk-Paradox.pdf&usg=AOvVaw2lCrd8JXrrmZ1Vyfjl9P6L&opi=89978449`
- Check Point (2025). *Check Point Cyber Security Report*, 2025. Retrieved from `https://www.checkpoint.com/resources/items/report--cyber-security-report-2025-bf02?fw=18b74`
- CISA (April 18, 2024). *#StopRansomware: Akira Ransomware*. Retrieved from `https://www.cisa.gov/news-events/cybersecurity-advisories/aa24-109a`
- Coveware (May 1, 2025). *May 1, 2025 Quarterly Report: The organizational structure of ransomware threat actor groups is evolving before our eyes*. Retrieved from `https://www.coveware.com/blog/2025/4/29/the-organizational-structure-of-ransomware-threat-actor-groups-is-evolving-before-our-eyes`

- Ladd, David F. S. (2011). *The SDL Progress Report*. Microsoft. Retrieved from `http://download.microsoft.com/download/c/e/f/cefb7bf3-de0c-4dcb-995a-c1c69659bf49/sdlprogressreport.pdf`
- Europol. (n.d.). *Law enforcement disrupt world's biggest ransomware operation.* Retrieved from `https://www.europol.europa.eu/media-press/newsroom/news/law-enforcement-disrupt-worlds-biggest-ransomware-operation`
- Fruhlinger, Josh. (August 24, 2022). *WannaCry explained: A perfect ransomware storm.* Retrieved from CSO Online: `https://www.csoonline.com/article/563017/wannacry-explained-a-perfect-ransomware-storm.html`
- Goodin, Dan. (March 21, 2024). *Never-before-seen data wiper may have been used by Russia against Ukraine.* Retrieved from Ars Technica: `https://arstechnica.com/security/2024/03/never-before-seen-data-wiper-may-have-been-used-by-russia-against-ukraine/`
- Leyden, J. (January 7, 2014). *Microsoft releases Blaster clean-up tool.* Retrieved from The Register: `https://www.theregister.co.uk/2004/01/07/microsoft_releases_blaster_cleanup_tool/`
- Microsoft (2014). *Microsoft Security Intelligence Report Volume 16.* Retrieved from `https://go.microsoft.com/fwlink/p/?linkid=2036139&clcid=0x409&culture=en-us&country=us`
- Microsoft (December 14, 2016). *Microsoft Security Intelligence Report Volume 21.* Retrieved from `https://go.microsoft.com/fwlink/p/?linkid=2036108&clcid=0x409&culture=en-us&country=us`
- Microsoft Corporation (April 8, 2019). *Microsoft Security Intelligence Report Volume 6.* Retrieved from Microsoft Security Intelligence Report Volume 6: `https://go.microsoft.com/fwlink/p/?linkid=2036319&clcid=0x409&culture=en-us&country=us`
- Microsoft Corporation (July 7, 2016). *Microsoft Security Intelligence Report Volume 20.* Retrieved from Microsoft Security Intelligence Report Volume 20: `https://go.microsoft.com/fwlink/p/?linkid=2036113&clcid=0x409&culture=en-us&country=us`
- Microsoft Corporation (August 17, 2017). *Microsoft Security Intelligence Report Volume 22.* Retrieved from Microsoft Security Intelligence Report Volume 22: `https://`

go.microsoft.com/fwlink/p/?linkid=2045580&clcid=0x409&culture=en-us&country=us

- Microsoft Corporation (2018). *Microsoft Security Intelligence Report Volume 23*. Retrieved from Microsoft Security Intelligence Report Volume 23: https://go.microsoft.com/fwlink/p/?linkid=2073690&clcid=0x409&culture=en-us&country=us
- Microsoft Corporation (August 10, 2019). *Industry collaboration programs*. Retrieved from Microsoft: https://docs.microsoft.com/en-us/windows/security/threat-protection/intelligence/cybersecurity-industry-partners
- Microsoft Corporation (May 19, 2025). *Enhance your application security with administrator protection*. Retrieved from Microsoft Windows Blog: https://blogs.windows.com/windowsdeveloper/2025/05/19/enhance-your-application-security-with-administrator-protection/
- Microsoft Corporation (n.d.). *Diplugem description*. Retrieved from Microsoft Security Intelligence: https://www.microsoft.com/en-us/wdsi/threats/malware-encyclopedia-description?Name=Win32/Diplugem&threatId=
- Microsoft Corporation (March 13, 2025). *How Microsoft identifies malware and potentially unwanted applications*. Retrieved from Microsoft Corporation: https://learn.microsoft.com/en-us/unified-secops/criteria
- Microsoft Corporation (n.d.). *Malware encounter rates*. Retrieved from Microsoft Security Intelligence Report: https://www.microsoft.com/securityinsights/Malware
- Microsoft Corporation (n.d.). *Microsoft Security Intelligence Report*. Retrieved from Microsoft Security: https://www.microsoft.com/en-us/security/business/security-intelligence-report?msockid=31172e3ff77a656817c33ec5f6c964c4
- Microsoft Corporation (August 5, 2025). *Project Ire autonomously identifies malware at scale*. Retrieved from Microsoft Research Blog: https://www.microsoft.com/en-us/research/blog/project-ire-autonomously-identifies-malware-at-scale/
- Microsoft Corporation (n.d.). *Petya description*. Retrieved from Microsoft Security Intelligence: https://www.microsoft.com/en-us/wdsi/threats/malware-encyclopedia-description?Name=Ransom:DOS/Petya.A&threatId=-2147257025
- Microsoft Corporation (n.d.). *Remove specific prevalent malware with Windows Malicious Software Removal Tool*. Retrieved from Microsoft Corporation: https://support.microsoft.com/en-us/topic/remove-specific-prevalent-malware-with-

`windows-malicious-software-removal-tool-kb890830-ba51b71f-39cd-cdec-73eb-61979b0661e0`

- Microsoft Corporation (n.d.). *Microsoft Defender Online security, simplified.* Retrieved from `https://www.microsoft.com/en-us/microsoft-365/microsoft-defender-for-individuals`
- Microsoft Corporation (n.d.). *Zlob description.* Retrieved from Microsoft Security Intelligence: `https://www.microsoft.com/en-us/wdsi/threats/malware-encyclopedia-description?Name=TrojanDownloader:Win32/Zlob&threatId=16998`
- Microsoft Corporation (Sept 15, 2017). *Conficker description.* Retrieved from Microsoft Security Intelligence: `https://www.microsoft.com/en-us/wdsi/threats/malware-encyclopedia-description?Name=Win32/Conficker`
- Krebs, Brian. (August 13, 2012). *Inside a 'Reveton' Ransomware Operation.* Retrieved from Krebs on Security: `https://krebsonsecurity.com/2012/08/inside-a-reveton-ransomware-operation/`
- Microsoft Corporation (n.d.). *Rotbrow description.* Retrieved from Microsoft Security Intelligence: `https://www.microsoft.com/en-us/wdsi/threats/malware-encyclopedia-description?Name=Win32/Rotbrow`
- Microsoft Corporation (n.d.). *Sality description.* Retrieved from Microsoft Security Intelligence: `https://www.microsoft.com/en-us/wdsi/threats/malware-encyclopedia-description?Name=Virus%3aWin32%2fSality`
- Microsoft Corporation (n.d.). *Sefnit description.* Retrieved from Microsoft Security Intelligence: `https://www.microsoft.com/en-us/wdsi/threats/malware-encyclopedia-description?Name=Win32/Sefnit`
- Microsoft Corporation (n.d.). *SmartScreen: FAQ.* Retrieved from Microsoft Corporation: `https://support.microsoft.com/en-gb/help/17443/windows-internet-explorer-smartscreen-faq`
- Microsoft Corporation (n.d.). *Taterf description.* Retrieved from Microsoft Security Intelligence: `https://www.microsoft.com/en-us/wdsi/threats/malware-encyclopedia-description?Name=Win32/Taterf&threatId=`
- Microsoft Corporation (n.d.). *Virus alert about the Blaster worm and its variants.* Retrieved from Microsoft Corporation: `https://support.microsoft.com/en-us/help/826955/virus-alert-about-the-blasterworm-and-its-variants`

- Microsoft Corporation (n.d.). *Microsoft Security Intelligence*. Retrieved from `https://www.microsoft.com/en-us/wdsi/threats`
- NIST (n.d.). CVE-2019-0708 Detail. Retrieved from National Vulnerability Database: `https://nvd.nist.gov/vuln/detail/CVE2019-0708`
- Recorded Future. (August 26, 2025). *H1 2025 Malware and Vulnerability Trends.* Retrieved from `https://www.recordedfuture.com/research/h1-2025-malware-and-vulnerability-trends`
- US Department of Homeland Security (n.d.). *Critical Infrastructure Sectors.* Retrieved from CISA Cyber Infrastructure: `https://www.cisa.gov/critical-infrastructure-sectors`
- Waugh, Rob. (May 21, 2013). *Computer viruses "are making a comeback", says Microsoft.* Retrieved from `https://www.welivesecurity.com/2013/05/21/computer-viruses-making-comeback/`
- US SEC, (October 30, 2023). *SEC Charges SolarWinds and Chief Information Security Officer with Fraud, Internal Control Failures.* Retrieved from `https://www.sec.gov/newsroom/press-releases/2023-227`
- SophosLabs, (November 2021). *Sophos 2022 Threat Report.* Retrieved from `https://www.sophos.com/en-us/content/security-threat-report`
- Sophos X-Ops, (April 16, 2025). *Sophos Annual Threat Report appendix: Most frequently encountered malware and abused software.* Retrieved from `https://news.sophos.com/en-us/2025/04/16/the-sophos-annual-threat-report-appendix-most-frequently-encountered-malware-and-abused-software/#_Toc192600945`
- Bussewitz, Cathy. (2021, May 19). *Colonial Pipeline confirms it paid $4.4 million to hackers.* Associated Press: `https://www.pbs.org/newshour/economy/colonial-pipeline-confirms-it-paid-4-4-million-to-hackers`
- Russon, Mary-Ann. (2021, May 10). *US fuel pipeline hackers 'didn't mean to create problems'.* BBC News: `https://www.bbc.com/news/business-57050690`

Get this book's PDF version and more

Scan the QR code (or go to `packtpub.com/unlock`). Search for this book by name, confirm the edition, and then follow the steps on the page.

UNLOCK NOW

Note: Keep your invoice handy. Purchases made directly from Packt don't require an invoice.

6

Internet-Based Threats

In the last three chapters, I provided a deep examination of data and trends for vulnerability disclosures and malware. Both types of threats are constantly leveraged by attackers seeking to compromise organizations and consumers around the world. The ways that attackers deliver their weapons, whether they are exploits for vulnerabilities or malware that provides illicit backdoors for attackers, are varied.

The threats we've examined so far have the potential to enable attackers to compromise applications, clients, servers, consumer and **Internet of Things** (**IoT**) devices, routing and switching equipment, industrial control systems, and other systems that enterprises rely on. Whether these attacks are designed to victimize massive numbers of organizations and consumers or are targeted at specific organizations, attackers will use the Cybersecurity Usual Suspects to initially compromise IT systems. As a reminder, these include unpatched vulnerabilities, security misconfigurations, social engineering, insider threats, and weak, leaked, or stolen credentials.

It's rare that an attacker is physically sitting at the keyboard of the system they are attempting to compromise. The vast majority of attackers perpetrate their attacks remotely over networks, leveraging no network more than the internet. In the same way that the internet has allowed small businesses to compete with large multinationals, it also enables individuals and small groups to attack massive numbers of consumers and the world's largest organizations. In this chapter, we'll look at some of the ways attackers have been using the internet and how these methods have evolved over time. In this chapter, we'll look at the following topics:

- What a typical attack looks like
- How many people encounter malicious websites?
- Phishing attacks

- Drive-by download attacks
- **Distributed denial of service** (**DDoS**) attacks

Now, let's look at a typical attack pattern as an example of how attackers have learned to leverage the internet.

What a typical attack looks like

Let's take a fictional example. The attacker in this case is physically located in Australia, and the intended victim of the attack is headquartered in the United States. The attacker's motivation is profit, and they seek to steal valuable information from the organization they are targeting and sell it.

The intended victim is supported by a CISO and a security team. The attacker's constant vulnerability scans of the victim's perimeter reveal that they are proficient at vulnerability management, as vulnerabilities on internet-facing systems are quickly and efficiently patched. After doing some research on the victim organization, the attacker decides to use a multi-pronged approach to initially compromise the organization.

The attacker has always been successful, one way or another, using social engineering to trick non-technical businesspeople into making **poor trust decisions** that could be capitalized on. A poor trust decision in this context is where the victim decides to open an attachment or click on a URL in an email, lower their system's security settings, open host-based firewall ports, or take other such actions that enable the attacker to victimize them more easily. In this case, the attacker is going to use two different tactics to try to compromise a few information workers' laptops, with the goal of getting access to their email inboxes. Both tactics will leverage email as their delivery mechanism and rely on social engineering and sloppy security mitigation to succeed.

The first tactic is to send phishing emails to specific individuals the attacker has identified as working in the company's finance department, using the company's public website as a source of information. It didn't take long to get a list of email addresses for the people the attacker wanted to target. The goal of these phishing emails is to trick one or more of the targeted information workers into sharing their Microsoft 365 credentials, which the attacker can then use to access their email inbox.

The second tactic is to send emails that contain a malicious link to the same information workers through a drive-by download site. If the information workers take the bait and click on the link, their web browser will take them to a malicious web page that will expose them to several exploits for browser and operating system vulnerabilities. If their client isn't fully patched, there's a good chance that the attacker will be able to install a backdoor into their system that might allow them to get privileged access to the victim's laptop and, ultimately, to their email.

Of course, if the attacker does get privileged access to the victim's laptop, they might be able to harvest all sorts of other valuable information in addition to email. Examples include documents stored locally on the laptop, contact lists, access to social networking accounts, software license keys, expense and credit card information, banking information and credentials, as well as personal information that can be used for identity theft, and so on. If the laptop is passively managed by IT, attackers could use it to store illicit material, enrolled in a botnet, and used in attacks against other targets. For example, it could be used for spam and phishing campaigns, to host drive-by download attacks, malware, advertising click-fraud, DDoS attacks, or whatever "project" the attacker decides to undertake. Additionally, the attacker could sell or trade any of the information they pilfered, including account credentials.

This type of attack is all too typical. It involved three of the five Cybersecurity Usual Suspects, including social engineering, unpatched vulnerabilities, and stolen credentials. Let's now take a closer look at some of these methods, how they work, and how popular they really are. To do this, I'll draw on threat intelligence and data that has been published by industry leaders over the years.

How many people encounter malicious websites?

Let's look at a couple of good sources of data to get an idea of just how many people encounter threats that are hosted on the internet. Internet search engines and web browsers are great sources of data to help us understand the pervasiveness of phishing sites and drive-by download sites. After all, Google and Bing are constantly indexing billions of web pages on the internet so that internet searches can provide fast, accurate results. Additionally, many millions of people use Google Chrome and Microsoft web browsers to surf the internet. Browsers allow users to report sites that are suspicious or outright unsafe. Google and Microsoft employ capabilities in their browsers and internet search engines to look for phishing sites, malware-hosting sites, and other types of malicious websites. Then, they help users of their products and services avoid the malicious sites they find by integrating continuously updated lists of malicious URLs and IP addresses into their products and services. Both browsers and internet search engines, among other services, can warn users when they attempt to visit a known malicious website. All this web page scanning and user behavior in the browsers generates data on malicious websites that both Google and Microsoft periodically publish. Let's look at some of this data.

Google's technology that looks for malicious websites is called **Safe Browsing**. This is how Google describes it:

> *"Google Safe Browsing helps protect over five billion devices every day by showing warnings to users when they attempt to navigate to dangerous sites or download dangerous files. Safe Browsing also notifies webmasters when their websites are compromised by malicious actors and helps them diagnose and resolve the problem so that their visitors stay safer. Safe Browsing protections work across Google products and power safer browsing experiences across the Internet." (Google, n.d.)*

Figure 6.1 reveals the average number of warnings per week that Google Chrome web browser users received when they tried to go to malicious websites, during the four years between 2019 and 2022.

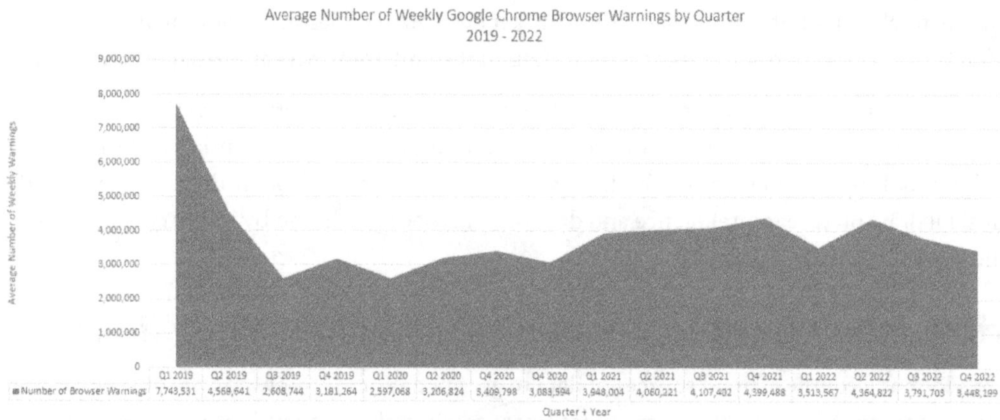

Figure 6.1 – Average number of malicious website warnings Google Chrome shared with users per week, each quarter between 2019 and 2022

The highest level during the period was during the first quarter of 2019, with 7,743,531 warnings per week on average, and the lowest was the first quarter of 2020, when 2,597,068 warnings were generated per week on average. The weekly average across all quarters and years was 3.87 million warnings.

Figure 6.2 shows us the average weekly volume of warnings presented next to malicious sites in Google Search results during the same period.

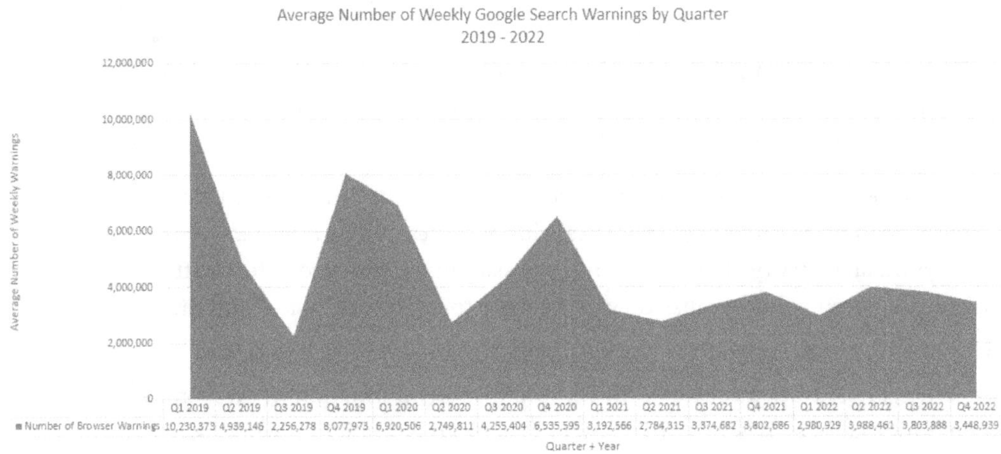

Figure 6.2 – Average number of malicious website warnings Google Search shared with users per week, each quarter between 2019 and 2022

Google Search shared more warnings with users than the Google Chrome browser did during the same period. Like the browser warnings, the highest level during the period was during the first quarter of 2019, with 10,230,373 warnings per week on average. The lowest weekly average was the third quarter of 2019, when Google search generated 2,256,278 warnings per week on average. The weekly average across all quarters and years was 4.58 million warnings.

If this data is from over five billion devices (the denominator), assuming all of them used the Google Chrome browser and Google Search, on average, a small fraction of 1% received warnings; 0.078% of Chrome browser users and 0.092% of Google Search users on those five billion devices received warnings about malicious websites each week. The quarter with the highest volume of warnings from Google Search was the first quarter of 2019, with 10,230,373 warnings per week on average. This represents just 0.21% of the five billion devices Google protects with Safe Browsing.

Next, let's look at each type of attack in more detail, starting with phishing.

Phishing attacks

Social engineering is a mainstay tactic for attackers around the world. **Phishing** is at the intersection of two of the Cybersecurity Usual Suspects: social engineering and weak, leaked, and stolen credentials. Many of the largest data breaches in history started with a phishing attack. In simple terms, phishing is a social engineering tactic where the attacker tries to trick their victim into sharing confidential information with them. Attackers use emails, websites, and advertising to entice people into disclosing account credentials, personal details, credit cards, and financial account information, among other things. In recent years, as phishing defenses improved, many attackers pivoted to using variations such as **SMS phishing** (**smishing**) and **voice phishing** (**vishing**) to achieve the same goals. The information that victims disclose in these attacks might be used to illegally access online accounts, conduct illegal financial transactions, and steal the victims' identities, among other purposes.

Some attackers cast an indiscriminate wide net for their phishing attacks to snare as many people as possible in order to increase the odds of success. Some attackers focus their phishing activities on an industry or group of targets. Spear phishing is used to focus attacks on individuals, presumably because they have access to information or wealth that the attacker desires.

Very often, after attackers successfully compromise an information worker's system, the victim's own contact lists are used to attack their friends, family, co-workers, and business contacts. For example, once a victim's social networking account has been compromised, attackers can use the victim's account to communicate with the victim's social network. Since the communications seemingly originate from a trusted source, others in the victim's social network are easily tricked by any phishing emails and websites shared via the victim's account.

When a corporate account is compromised, attackers will often look for ways to get access to more accounts and credentials to help them stay persistent, move laterally, and get access to more systems and data. The more accounts they have access to, the more fun the attack is for them. Sending phishing emails to victims' coworkers' corporate email accounts can be very effective. When was the last time you doubted the authenticity of an email you received from your coworkers? Trust in corporate email systems remains super high, even though so many of them have been compromised during cybersecurity incidents, including Microsoft's immensely popular hosted email services used by millions of information workers around the world (Microsoft, July 11, 2023). Attackers can use the inherent trust in corporate email systems to their advantage. Not only do email users trust email from senders in their own organizations, but data of all sensitivities makes its way into email. Email contents and attachments are some of the most confidential and sensitive information that organizations possess. Getting access to the right accounts and their corresponding email inboxes can be a boon to attackers. Additionally, emails sent between internal users (those that have an internal sender and an internal recipient) don't typically go through the same security rigor as emails from the internet do. I've seen attackers use internal URL shortening services to shorten URLs that take victims to attacker-controlled, malicious websites on the internet when clicked. When an email containing a shortened URL was sent by an internal email sender to an internal email recipient, those URLs weren't scanned by the layers of email security services that emails from the internet would go through. Unsuspecting users clicked on the links because they were from coworkers whom they are supposed to trust and were exposed to phishing attacks and drive-by download attacks that enabled the attackers to get access to more credentials and more systems.

Attackers do not limit themselves to attacking their target's corporate accounts and will seek to compromise the personal systems of information workers, knowing that these systems often have remote access to corporate assets. Some attackers install keyloggers or other types of malware to automate the collection of data from their victims' personal systems. Attackers use their victims' personal email and cloud storage accounts as additional ways to exfiltrate data, enable identity theft, and ensnare more victims.

Phishing attacks can also involve several technology components, including the victims' workstations and the infrastructure used to attack the victims – for example, the email servers from which phishing emails originate or the web servers on which phishing pages are hosted. Very often, these email and web servers are hosted on legitimate systems that have been compromised and are subsequently used for phishing campaigns. **Botnets**, which are networks of compromised systems that are illicitly remote-controlled, are commonly used for phishing campaigns. Using compromised systems for phishing campaign infrastructure reduces the costs for attackers, protects their identities, and helps them achieve a scale they likely could not achieve by other means. Additionally, the availability of phishing kits makes it easy for almost anyone to wage a phishing attack. Not only will attackers use compromised legitimate domains for their phishing attacks, but they will also use so-called *bulletproof hosting providers* who ignore abuse complaints and make taking down phishing sites more difficult.

Next, let's examine the scale of this problem by looking at the number of phishing sites on the internet, how many phishing emails are sent to ensnare victims, and how many victims there have been.

How many phishing websites are there on the internet?

The **Anti-Phishing Working Group** (**APWG**) publishes *APWG Phishing Activity Trends Reports* on a quarterly basis. These reports are chock-full of good data on phishing attacks. The APWG describes their data sources and unique phishing sites this way:

> *"Unique phishing sites. This is a primary measure of reported phishing across the globe. This is determined by the unique bases of phishing URLs found in phishing emails reported to APWG's repository. (A single phishing site may be advertised as thousands of customized URLs, all leading to basically the same destination.) Thus, APWG measures reported phishing sites, which is a more relevant metric than URLs. A synonym for sites is attacks." (APWG, November 2, 2023)*

Aggregating data from numerous APWG quarterly reports published between 2021 and 2024, *Figure 6.3* reveals how the average number of unique phishing sites identified each month grew and receded each quarter during those four years (APWG, n.d.).

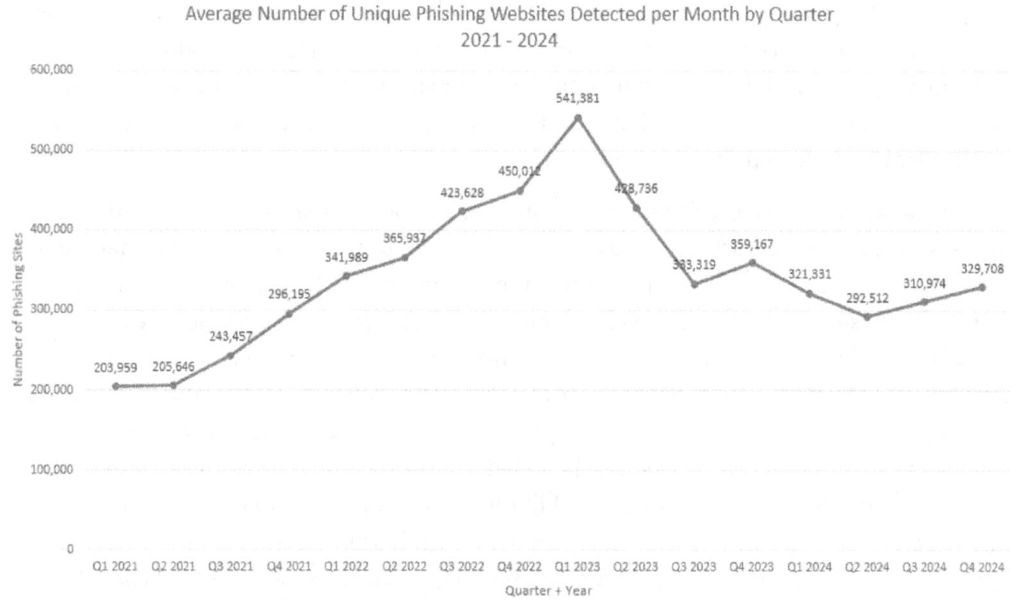

Figure 6.3 – The average number of unique phishing websites detected by APWG members per month, each quarter between 2021 and 2024 (APWG, n.d.)

Notice the trend of steady increases in unique phishing sites until its peak in the first quarter of 2023. The average number of phishing sites identified per month during the three months of that quarter by the APWG was 541,381. During that quarter, in March 2023, the APWG identified 619,060 unique phishing sites. But within two months of that peak, the number of unique phishing sites dropped to more typical levels, with 381,572 unique sites identified in May 2023. That's a 48% reduction in the number of unique phishing sites identified in just 60 days. Brian Krebs suggested that a contributing factor to this significant decrease in unique phishing sites was a lawsuit filed by Meta against a domain register located in the Netherlands called Freenom. Krebs published the following explanation on his blog:

> *"The number of phishing websites tied to domain name registrar Freenom dropped precipitously in the months surrounding a recent lawsuit from social networking giant Meta, which alleged the free domain name provider has a long history of ignoring abuse complaints about phishing websites while monetizing traffic to those abusive domains." (Krebs, Brian., May 26, 2023)*

The number of unique phishing sites identified each month after the decline appeared to stabilize, and the average number of unique phishing sites identified by the APWG each month in 2024 was 313,631.

Phishing emails

The highest volume method that phishers use to attract potential victims is email. Some threat intelligence vendors categorize attacks that leverage email into attack types that reflect the attackers' intent, such as credential theft, fraud, **business email compromise** (**BEC**), impersonation, and so on. **Credential theft** is the largest category, typically compromising a large majority of all phishing emails in each period.

The volume of phishing emails circulating is immense. According to Microsoft, "*between January and December 2024, Microsoft detected more than 30 billion phishing emails targeting customers*" (Microsoft Corporation, March 24, 2025). Combine that with all the other phishing emails blocked by other commercial phishing filters, such as Google Gmail, Abnormal Security, Darktrace, Proofpoint, Check Point, and others, and the number of emails sent for the purposes of victimizing people each year is many times the Earth's population.

According to Abnormal Security's *H2 2024 Threat Report*, the volume of phishing attacks increases and decreases over time, but the number of advanced attacks increased by 49.6% between mid-2023 and mid-2024 (Abnormal Security, 2024). *Figure 6.4* illustrates the increase in median attacks per 1,000 mailboxes during 6-month periods in 2022, 2023, and 2024.

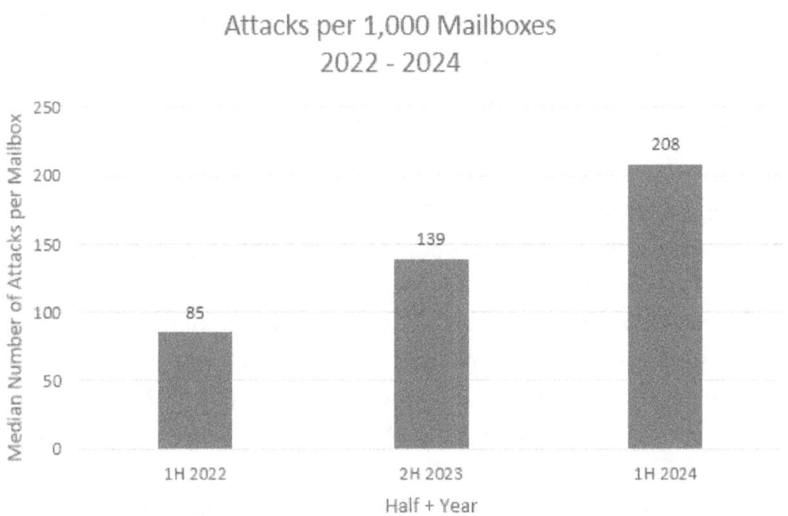

Figure 6.4 – Median attacks per 1,000 mailboxes from the first half of 2022, the second half of 2023, and the first half of 2024 (Abnormal Security, 2024)

Beyond the notable volume of phishing emails, here are some recent interesting data points that help us understand other characteristics of phishing emails, as published in the *KnowBe4 Phishing Trends Report* that focused on the period between September 15, 2024, and February 14th, 2025 (KnowBe4, March 2025):

- They saw a 57% increase in phishing attacks sent from compromised accounts during the period, with 11.4% sent from trusted senders in victims' supply chains
- The most impersonated brands they identified during the period were Microsoft, DocuSign, Adobe, PayPal, and LinkedIn
- The top five legitimate platforms used to send phishing emails during the period were DocuSign, PayPal, Microsoft, Google Drive, and Salesforce
- 81.9% of victims' email addresses were previously leaked in data breaches

According to data published in the *Microsoft Digital Defense Report 2024*, phishing emails leveraged URLs/links 56% of the time, QR codes 25% of the time, and attachments 19% of the time during the second half of 2024 (Microsoft Corporation, October 2023). Microsoft published an earlier *Microsoft Digital Defense Report* that revealed attackers were increasing their usage of URLs with open redirectors and open shorteners. Phishing emails with URL redirects were counted in the millions each month of the first half of 2023, and the count of URL shorteners used in phishing emails numbered hundreds of thousands per month during the same period.

> *"URL open redirectors are vulnerabilities found in web applications that enable attackers to manipulate URLs to redirect unsuspecting users to malicious websites. Here, they may be victim to phishing attacks, data breaches, account takeovers, or malware infections." Microsoft Corporation, October 2023*

Given the huge volume of phishing emails and all the tactics these attackers employ, you might wonder how many people get tricked into disclosing their credentials. Using data from Microsoft Defender SmartScreen that was published in the *Microsoft Digital Defense Report 2023*, Microsoft revealed that "*in April-June 2023 we alerted users of approximately 10,000 password entries per month into malicious sites*" (Microsoft Corporation, October 2023). This gives us some insight into the number of people running Windows 11 who were warned about phishing sites. However, according to StatCounter, in April to June 2023, Windows 11 was running on 24% of personal computers, while Windows 10 was running on 71% (StatCounter, n.d.). So, this particular Windows 11 SmartScreen data point gives us insight into only part of the total picture. And, of course, there are many other systems running on non-Windows platforms, including mobile platforms, that this data doesn't provide visibility into. Based on this, we can assume that the number of people tricked into entering their credentials into phishing sites is much larger than 10,000 per month.

Another source of data that can help us gain insight into the scale of the success of phishing is the number of victims who filed complaints with law enforcement. According to the US Federal Bureau of Investigation's Internet Crime Complaint Center's *Internet Crime Report 2024*, of the 859,532 total complaints filed with them in 2024, "phishing/spoofing" was the top crime type, with 193,407 complaints (Internet Crime Complaint Center, n.d.). Extortion was a distant second with 86,415 complaints. The losses associated with the phishing/spoofing complaints were $70,013,036. Typically, English-speaking countries such as Canada, the United Kingdom, and the United States endure more phishing attacks than non-English-speaking countries, but phishing is a global challenge. The number of victims is undoubtedly much higher than the numbers I discussed here.

Allow me to paint a picture of phishing using the 2023–2025 phishing data that I discussed:

- There were hundreds of thousands of phishing sites on the internet at any given time.
- There was an average of 2.5 billion phishing emails sent per month, trying to lure victims to those sites.
- There were 10,000 attempts from systems running Windows 11 to enter credentials into those phishing sites per month.
- Of the people who were victimized by phishing, fewer than 200,000 filed a complaint with the Federal Bureau of Investigation's Internet Crime Complaint Center in 2024. The financial losses associated with these complaints were about $70 million.
- 82% of victims' email addresses were previously leaked in data breaches.
- Vishing, smishing, and **quishing** (**QR code phishing**) are rapidly growing in popularity among attackers.

The number of victims seems surprisingly small given the massive number of lures that phishers are constantly deploying. However, remember that it takes just one compromised account to provide attackers with initial access to an enterprise IT or OT environment. Given this, the proportion of lures deployed to the number of people who click on them and enter their credentials isn't something security teams can really take comfort in.

> **Tip**
>
> Remember the foreword – you are in a submarine where everyone aboard has a shared destiny.

It's not all bad news, though. Microsoft, Google, and other organizations take a range of actions to disrupt and take down phishing sites. For example, in September 2025, Microsoft announced that it had seized 338 websites to disrupt the RaccoonO365 phishing service. Microsoft described the operation this way:

> *"Microsoft's Digital Crimes Unit (DCU) has disrupted RaccoonO365, the fastest-growing tool used by cybercriminals to steal Microsoft 365 usernames and passwords ("credentials"). Using a court order granted by the Southern District of New York, the DCU seized 338 websites associated with the popular service, disrupting the operation's technical infrastructure and cutting off criminals' access to victims. This case shows that cybercriminals don't need to be sophisticated to cause widespread harm—simple tools like RaccoonO365 make cybercrime accessible to virtually anyone, putting millions of users at risk...Since July 2024, RaccoonO365's kits have been used to steal at least 5,000 Microsoft credentials from 94 countries." (Microsoft Corporation, 2025)*

There are plenty of examples of such disruptive actions. Microsoft made more than 168,000 phishing site take-downs in 2021 (Microsoft Corporation, October 2021). In August 2022, they announced that they took down "*more than 531,000 unique phishing URLs and 5,400 phish kits between July 2021 and June 2022, leading to the identification and closure of over 1,400 malicious email accounts used to collect stolen customer credentials*" (Microsoft Corporation, August 2022).

Top phishing domains

You might be wondering where the most phishing sites are hosted. Of course, the answer to this question changes over time as attackers look for easy places (low oversight and inexpensive) to host their attacks. The **Spamhaus Project** is a good source of IP and domain reputation data. Looking at their most recent data (at the end of September 2025), the top five **country code top-level domains** (**ccTLDs**) associated with phishing activities based on the number of detections are as follows (Spamhaus Project, September 28, 2025):

1. `.pw`: The Republic of Palau
2. `.cc`: Cocos Islands
3. `.cn`: The People's Republic of China
4. `.su`: The Soviet Union
5. `.ru`: Russia

The top five **general top-level domains** (**gTLDs**) associated with the worst domain reputation scores, as calculated by the Spamhaus Project, were the following (Spamhaus Project, September 28, 2025):

1. `.xin`
2. `.pro`
3. `.cfd`

4. `.mobi`
5. `.icu`

You might be wondering where older, more mainstream gTLDs ranked on their list; `.com` was ranked 63rd, and `.org` was ranked 82nd.

The Cybercrime Information Center provides a TLD ranking based on the number of malicious phishing domains it found in each TLD. This gives us a slightly different view. The top five TLDs by the number of malicious phishing domains in the three months from November 2023 to January 2024 were as follows (Cybercrime Information Center, n.d.):

1. `.com`
2. `.top`
3. `.xyz`
4. `.sbs`
5. `.cn`

Regardless of where attackers host their phishing operations, organizations need to mitigate these attacks. However, knowing which TLDs host significant numbers of phishing attacks can be helpful. Next, let's discuss some of the mitigations that enterprises can employ to minimize successful phishing attacks.

Mitigating phishing

Phishing websites used to be easier for users to identify than they are today. If a web page was asking you for credentials or confidential information, but was not protecting that data in transit using HTTPS (the lack of the legitimate lock icon in the web browser indicates this), then why would you type anything into that page? But this is no longer an effective way to identify phishing sites, as they leverage TLS certificates routinely now.

In this section, I'll give you some advice on how to mitigate phishing, informed by my experience managing cybersecurity programs for large enterprises. As you can see from the data I provided in this chapter, phishing is a constant threat that never really recedes – at any moment, someone in your organization can fall victim to a phishing attack, providing attackers with initial access to your organization's network. There are several things you can do to protect people from these attacks and minimize the impact that a successful phishing attack has on your organization. Some of my favorite mitigations are somewhat unconventional; however, I hope you'll see the wisdom in them.

Multi-factor authentication

Mitigating phishing attacks that are focused on credential theft is both easy and difficult at the same time. For example, phishing attacks that seek to steal credentials can largely be mitigated by enforcing the requirement to use **multi-factor authentication** (**MFA**). NIST defines MFA this way:

> *"An authentication system that requires more than one distinct type of authentication factor for successful authentication. MFA can be performed using a multi-factor authenticator or by combining single-factor authenticators that provide different types of factors." (NIST, July 2025)*

Some examples of vendors and commercial products that enterprises use for MFA include Google Authenticator, Microsoft Authenticator, RSA SecurID, Cisco Duo, Auth0, PingID, Okta, and many others.

How effective is MFA at mitigating phishing? According to studies conducted by Microsoft:

> *"Your password doesn't matter, but MFA does! Based on our studies, your account is more than 99.9% less likely to be compromised if you use MFA." (Weinert, 2019)*

Requiring a second factor for authentication largely mitigates the risks associated with weak, leaked, and stolen passwords. If an attacker successfully tricks a user into disclosing their credentials in a phishing attack, but access to the account requires another factor, such as physical access to a token, access to the victim's mobile phone, or their authenticator application then the credentials by themselves won't give attackers access to the account. Of course, that doesn't stop attackers from trying to use those stolen credentials on hundreds of online financial and e-commerce sites, betting on the chance that the user used the same credentials multiple times; their scripts do this within seconds of obtaining leaked and stolen credentials. Reusing the same password across accounts is still too common but can be largely mitigated by leveraging MFA everywhere.

Unfortunately, this is more challenging to accomplish than it sounds. MFA isn't available everywhere, especially in enterprise environments with decades of legacy applications. In every operational cybersecurity program I managed, I started an "MFA Everywhere" initiative. The objective of these initiatives was to enforce MFA everywhere a username and password are used in enterprise IT environments. This includes device access (desktop computers, laptops, and mobile devices), VPN access, **Virtual Desktop Infrastructure** (**VDI**) access, and application access. Literally everywhere a password is used to authenticate for access to resources, MFA should be enforced. There are some exceptions where MFA can't easily be leveraged, but everywhere it can be leveraged, it should be enforced.

This starts by writing or updating an existing network access policy that requires MFA to be used everywhere passwords are used for access, unless an explicit exception is granted. Let's use VPN access as an example. Attackers commonly leverage VPNs to access their victims' networks. A very common scenario is for attackers to trick a user into disclosing their credentials in a phishing attack and then use their credentials to access their organizations network using the stolen credentials. If phishing-resistant MFA is enforced on every VPN connection, attackers will not be able to access the victim's network via VPN because they don't have access to the second authentication factor. In the case of VPN, examples of second authentication factors include a digital certificate installed on the organization's systems or having the user approve an MFA prompt in an authenticator application on their mobile phone.

Here are some useful recommendations for MFA:

- The organization's network access policy should require that MFA be enforced on every VPN connection to the organization's network. Be explicit and highlight that this includes user account access as well as point-to-point VPN connections that connect entire offices of users, and any other scenario where VPN is used.

  > **Tip**
  >
  > Remember that many IT workers become lawyerly when faced with policies they don't want to support. Ensure that your policy is explicit enough that it can't be willfully misinterpreted.

- The policy should also specify that the MFA control implementations be audited periodically to ensure that MFA doesn't get disabled in the future, unbeknownst to the security team.
- Security teams should configure monitoring and alertingon VPN MFA configuration changes so that their security operations centers are alerted quickly when configuration changes are made to these critical settings.
- If someone decides to disable the MFA requirement or give specific users or systems exceptions without going through proper governance channels, this should garner scrutiny very quickly. Without MFA, it's only a matter of time before the constant brute-force and password spray attacks that plague internet-facing VPN services succeed.

> **Note**
>
> A password spray attack is a type of brute-force attack where attackers attempt to log in across many different user accounts using a relatively small number of commonly used passwords.

You need to know with certainty that VPN access to your network can only succeed with MFA.

Even when MFA is available, it is typically viewed by consumers and enterprise information workers alike as a hassle, regardless of how effective it is. Many information workers and executives love to complain about the necessity of using a second authentication factor, even if it is as easy as pressing a button on their mobile device. To counter this perception, I happily share how many attacks MFA blocks each week or month with my stakeholder communities. Once they see the large volume and constant barrage of attacks on internet-facing VPN servers, for example, complaints tend to simmer down.

> **Note**
>
> Very often, executives will request exceptions to MFA policies. However, all senior executives and their delegates should use MFA everywhere and are the last people who should be exempt from MFA policies; after all, they are the primary targets of BEC and other social engineering attacks. Making executives' lives easier by giving them exceptions for the very security policies and controls that mitigate attacks against them specifically isn't prudent and is, very literally, a gift to attackers.

One effective tool I've seen used in cases where executives demand exceptions for security policies is risk acceptance letters. A **risk acceptance letter** or risk acknowledgment letter documents that the risks associated with the security policy exception have been explained to the executive, they understand these risks, and accept them on behalf of their entire organization. If accepted, that risk is entered into the cybersecurity risk register. Periodically, these risks in the cybersecurity risk register should be reviewed by the CISO, senior executives, and potentially the Board of Directors, to ensure that systemic, long-term risk has not been inappropriately accepted. When confronted with one of these risk acceptance letters, executives who want security policy exceptions typically pause at the last minute once they have time to reflect on the potential consequences to their organizations and their own careers. In the end, many such executives prudently decide not to demand security policy exceptions.

Phishing training and simulations

Of course, phishing isn't limited to credential theft. Attackers use phishing in their attempts to trick people into disclosing information that they otherwise would not share. MFA doesn't mitigate these types of attacks. In these cases, the best mitigation is *education*. Training information workers to recognize potential phishing attacks and other social engineering tactics isn't foolproof, but it can be very effective. Some organizations simply refuse to approve phishing exercises designed to train their information workers to recognize phishing attacks. In many cases, the justification is that they don't want to embarrass anyone. The management of these organizations does their employees a disservice with such decisions, in my opinion.

One of the tools that CISOs have, when faced with management teams that do not support this type of training, is *risk management*. Simplify the decision by using math. In my experience, CISOs who quantify risk for their management teams have a better chance of success; it helps put their efforts into context, even when nothing bad happens. Remember that *risk* is the combination of *probability* and *impact*. The fact that most of the largest and highest-profile data breaches in history started with a phishing email can help communicate the risk. So can the volume of phishing emails and the number of phishing sites that I provided in this chapter. Recall that Microsoft's data from 2024 revealed that 2.5 billion phishing emails are sent every month on average. Additionally, at least a few hundred thousand active phishing websites are online at any given time. Combine this with phishing data from your own organization to quantify the probability that information workers will receive phishing emails and visit compromised websites, how many, and how often.

Then, develop some quantitative impact estimates, ranging from no impact because phishing emails were filtered before they made it to information workers, to a successful compromise that involved data exfiltration and subsequent reputational damage and legal liability for the organization. Such figures can help make the decision to train people to recognize social engineering attacks that are less abstract and easier to compare to the other risks that management teams already manage.

In 2023, Microsoft published data related to phishing simulations. They examined Microsoft Defender for Office 365 attack simulation training data from tens of millions of users to better understand the impact of phishing training. Their data revealed that 45% of users who received phishing emails read them, 11% reported them, 8% clicked on the link in the phishing email, while 0.8% opened malicious attachments, and 2.3% supplied their credentials to attackers (Microsoft, October 2023). 2.3% might not sound like a big number, but again, remember that it only takes one user to get phished successfully to give attackers the initial access they need.

Not everyone agrees that phishing awareness training and simulations are effective. After studying 19,789 personnel for 8 months in 2023, a team of researchers from the University of

Chicago, the **University of California, San Diego** (**UCSD**), and UCSD Health concluded that the typical type of industry phishing training wasn't effective in preventing users from getting tricked by phishing emails:

> *"The big finding is that these standard, out-of-the-box industry trainings are not efficacious in preventing users from clicking on emails in the future," says Ariana Mirian, one of the co-authors and senior security researcher at Censys. She adds, though, that "there's a lot of nuance there." (Nelson, Nate, July 1, 2025)*

My own experience with phishing training and awareness is that there always seems to be 1–2% of email users who are willing to click the malicious links in emails and enter their credentials into phishing sites. Identifying those email users who consistently behave this way and targeting them with extra training and attention can make a difference. But frankly, the days when enterprises could simply trust their employees to make the right choices 100% of the time are long over. The stakes are too high with pervasive ransomware gangs seemingly always at the door. This is why the next two mitigations that I'm going to discuss are so important and actually a little less common than MFA and training.

Restricting inbound network traffic

Recall that when a user is tricked into entering their credentials into a phishing site, the very next thing to happen is that attackers attempt to use those credentials to gain initial access to the victim's network and internet-facing applications. Restricting the places from which authentication traffic can originate can make it harder for attackers. For example, it's common for attackers to attempt to use stolen credentials to access their victim's network by logging in via the victim's VPN service. Why allow attackers to even get to the VPN login portal to enter the credentials if they are doing so from a location that has no value to the victim? If the victim organization does not have any employees, supply chain partners, or customers in Russia, for example, why allow network traffic from Russia to get to the VPN login portal? Geo-blocking network traffic from entire countries and restricting inbound network traffic selectively will make it a little harder for some attackers to use the credentials they have stolen.

Many security experts and networking subject matter experts will be quick to point out that attackers will just stage their attacks from a location that does have access. That's correct, but security teams should make each step in attackers' kill chains as difficult as possible.

> **Tip**
>
> Don't make anything easy for them. Make every step difficult and awkward to execute. Break their scripts and automation wherever and whenever possible. If they are going to attack you, make them work and work and work. Make them stage their attacks from a location that you must allow network traffic from.

This will enable your organization to continue to function normally while reducing the number of places you can be attacked from. If your organization isn't doing business in Russia, the People's Republic of China, Iran, or the Democratic People's Republic of Korea (North Korea), why would you allow network traffic from these locations to your VPN service, your online email service, or other internet-facing applications?

Adding inbound network restrictions also makes it easier to detect unexpected changes in your organization's external attack surface. If network traffic from Spain is blocked because your organization has no business interests there, it makes it easy to spot login attempts from Spain to your internet-facing applications and VPN login portals. Simply stated, there should be zero login attempts from Spain because network traffic from Spain can't make it to the network port that the login services are listening on.

If you don't believe there's value in implementing these types of restrictions, go check out all the brute-force attacks and password spray attacks on your organization's VPN service and Microsoft 365 portal from locations where your organization has no business interests. You might be surprised to see a constant barrage of attacks from all over the world. There are 195–200 countries in the world, depending on how you count them (US Department of State, March 12, 2025). If your organization doesn't have business interests in all these places, why allow attackers to use them to stage their attacks against you? Of course, for global organizations that do business in nearly all these countries, the value of geo-blocking won't be as great. But even those organizations are likely to have countries they can't do business in because of international sanctions or other restrictions, such as the Democratic People's Republic of Korea (North Korea), for example. Blocking network traffic from such locations has security value.

For countries where your organization does have business interests, such as customers and supply chain partners, a blunt tool such as geo-blocking won't be useful. However, that doesn't mean you can't use inbound network restrictions to your advantage. To complement geo-blocking, use automation to temporarily block the IP addresses used in attacks. For example, let's say you are a US-based company with millions of customers in the US. You can't geo-block network traffic from the US, as it would negatively impact your organization. However, leveraging automation that blocks US-based IP addresses that are used for brute-force and password spray attacks against your VPN portal at the network level for a random period of time (1–4 hours) will blunt such attacks and frustrate attackers by forcing them to change IP addresses constantly. It should become clear to the attacker that this tactic increases the amount of time they need for their attack dramatically. Combined with lengthy passwords (15 characters) and MFA, their chances of success with brute-force and password spray attacks are very low. In my experience, these attackers move on to other targets. It's no fun for them if they can't even get through their big list of passwords for months or years.

You might wonder why I recommend using inbound network blocking if MFA has been implemented. The concept of "defense in depth" has fallen out of favor with many cybersecurity professionals. However, as I mentioned earlier, MFA is extremely effective – until it isn't. I've been burned more than once by unapproved changes to MFA settings, made by administrators and attackers alike. Some administrators can't help themselves but turn off security mitigations during troubleshooting exercises to simplify the variables they are dealing with. But often, these administrators fail to turn the security mitigations back on, either unintentionally or purposely. One of the first things many attackers do after initial access is identify the "MFA exception" group in Active Directory and add the accounts they are using to it. Alternatively, they simply add their own MFA second factors to the accounts they use so that they have both the credentials and the second factors to enable them to log in like any other user. During the subsequent intrusion reconstruction that the incident response team does, one of the findings is that the initial access would have been prevented had inbound connections to VPN been restricted.

Restricting outbound network traffic

Earlier, I mentioned that some mitigations that I was going to recommend were somewhat unconventional. This is one of them. Not only is it unconventional, but it's also unpopular among almost everyone, including users, executives, IT operators, cybersecurity practitioners, and, most importantly, attackers. But for CISOs who can manage skeptical stakeholder communities, this mitigation pays high dividends because it adds friction to so many attacker activities.

This mitigation involves embracing the principle of least privilege for outbound network access to the internet – that is, giving users on your network access to only the internet sites they actually need access to. This can involve a combination of technical controls, such as DNS sinkholing and egress firewall filters that block users' attempts to get to sites on the internet that aren't authorized to visit. DNS sinkholing redirects or blocks DNS name resolution requests for malicious or unwanted domain requests, while egress filtering on firewalls restricts outbound traffic to permitted sites. Let me provide a concrete example of how such restrictions can be helpful.

Recall how a phishing attack works. Let's use a phishing email example because it's the most popular lure based on the data we examined. The attacker sends an email to the intended victim with a link to a website that the attacker controls. On that website, the attacker has crafted a web page that looks just like a legitimate login portal that the victim uses, such as Microsoft 365, for example. The victim believes it's the legitimate login portal and enters their credentials. The attacker immediately starts using those stolen credentials for illicit purposes.

What if, when the user clicked the link in the phishing email, it was simply broken? That is, their browser opened and gave them an error message telling them the remote server didn't respond: `This site can't be reached. Try checking the connection. Try checking the proxy, firewall, and DNS configuration. (ERR_NAME_NOT_RESOLVED)`. Alternatively, the browser could display a custom error message telling the user that access to the website was restricted and point them to an internal internet access policy exception intake form to fill out if they really need access to the website.

Notice that, in this case, our phishing and awareness training failed, our email phishing filters failed, the rewritten URL provided by the phishing filters failed, and the web browser's built-in phishing protection didn't help, but we still prevented the user from getting to a malicious site and prevented attackers from stealing their credentials. Simply preventing the user from getting to the phishing site compensated for the failure or lack of other security controls. Some cybersecurity professionals are bound to ask: why not just remove URLs from email before they get to inboxes or just rewrite URLs so they can be checked when the user clicks on them? These mitigations have real efficacy, but they don't provide the "bonus" that outbound internet restrictions provide.

The bonus is that outbound restrictions can also make it harder for attackers to download their tools to the victim's network. They can also make it harder for attackers to remotely control compromised systems on their victim's network from the internet. It can also make it harder for attackers to perform data exfiltration from their victim's network to systems or sites they control on the internet. It turns out that many attackers rely heavily on broad outbound access to the internet for their attacks to succeed. When outbound access is materially restricted, attackers' scripts break, and they are potentially forced to spend significantly more time and effort on critical parts of their kill chain. More time and effort mean lower ROI for attackers. If the time and effort become practically insurmountable, they will move on to other easier targets.

Many of the detractors of this tactic are quick to point out that users won't like being restricted. This is certainly true. But if you do your job with a high level of competence, they should rarely even notice. I've implemented draconian outbound internet restrictions at a few companies during my career with great results. Some of these companies were quite large (200,000+ employees in 30 countries) and some smaller (15,000 employees). In every case, successful phishing attacks were virtually eliminated, the leakage/theft of credentials stopped, and incident response volumes dropped. It gave these organizations the time and space they needed to get other important mitigations in place, such as TLS inspection and **secure access service edge** (**SASE**).

Consider whether your organization's information workers really require unfettered access to the internet. Do they really need to visit websites with content in languages that they do not know how to read? I've had plenty of executives assert that their teams need unfettered access to the internet. I typically ask them how many people on their team can read Russian, or a dialect of Chinese, Persian, or Korean. That's when the look on their faces typically changes because they've never considered the non-English-speaking parts of the internet before. Is there really a legitimate business need to allow everyone in an organization to go everywhere on the internet? They typically quickly backtrack their demands for unfettered access and begin to consider the things their teams really need access to. Of course, global organizations will need access to huge swaths of the internet, but even they don't have a need for everyone to access everything on the internet.

If you decide to go down this path, you don't have to start from a place where no one has access to anything. Use DNS logs and firewall logs to identify the most popular sites for your user population. When you start restricting access to the internet, most of these sites should be on your allowlist and accessible. Everything listed on internal human resources websites should also be accessible. You'll need a process that enables users to request access to URLs that get added to the allow list over time – for example, a ServiceNow form that intakes requests and enables the firewall team to process them. Allow users to submit multiple URLs (hundreds) in each request to make it less frustrating for them. In my experience, once the allow list gets to about 70,000 sites, the complaints and volume of allow list requests drop significantly. Given that there are hundreds of millions of websites on the internet, access to only 70,000 or even 100,000 sites dramatically reduces the number of sites that can be used for phishing, malicious downloads, remote-controlling compromised systems, data exfiltration, and other parts of attackers' kill chains.

The objective is to give users and executives access to all the resources they need to do their work and to support a positive culture within the organization. I recommend allowing access to popular news sites, social media sites, and financial sites to support these objectives. The more sensitive sites that you want to limit access to, or block altogether, are those that enable data exfiltration, such as internet storage services, unapproved email services, unapproved instant messaging, and even legitimate businesses that enable their customers to upload files. I'll discuss outbound internet restrictions in more detail in *Chapter 14, Mitigating "Living Off the Land" Tactics.*

The combination of MFA, commercial phishing filters, URL rewriting, and outbound internet blocking will make successful phishing attacks much harder to accomplish and add friction into other parts of attackers' kill chains. If they are going to accomplish initial access, download their tools, remote-control systems, and exfiltrate data, they are going to have to find and compromise the accounts that enable all these activities.

Now, let's look at the second tactic the attackers used in our example of a typical attack, a drive-by download attack.

Drive-by download attacks

While phishing attacks are at the intersection of social engineering and weak, leaked, and stolen passwords, drive-by download attacks are at the intersection of social engineering and unpatched vulnerabilities. Drive-by attacks are typically performed by attackers using social engineering to trick users into visiting a malicious website. They can do this in several ways, including via email, online ads, putting links to malicious sites in the comments sections of web pages and social network posts, and many other tactics. Sometimes, attackers compromise a legitimate website and use it to host drive-by download attacks; the more popular the website, the better for the attackers, as it increases their chances of successfully compromising as many systems as possible.

Getting potential victims to malicious websites under the control of attackers is the first step in the attack. The next step is to exploit unpatched vulnerabilities on the victims' systems. To do this, attackers will attempt to run scripts that have embedded URLs, or they will use an **inline frame** (**IFrame**) to load another HTML document page unbeknownst to the user. IFrames have legitimate uses, making it complicated to distinguish between good ones and malicious ones. Attackers will place IFrames the size of a pixel on their malicious web pages so that users cannot see them. When these HTML documents load, they can, among other things, run scripts that detect the victim's operating system and browser versions, select and download corresponding exploits for common vulnerabilities for these versions, and, ultimately, download and install other malware that gives attackers illicit control of the compromised system. Such malicious IFrames can be placed on web pages of legitimate websites that have been compromised. This means that visiting a trusted website with a system that is not fully patched can result in a compromised system that attackers can control remotely, cripple with ransomware, and so on.

MITRE lists "drive-by compromise" as a known technique that attackers use in their enterprise ATT&CK framework, along with 43 "procedure examples" that illustrate how real-world attackers are known to have leveraged them (MITRE, April 15, 2025). However, drive-by download attacks have become less common over time. Let's look at some historical data from Microsoft.

Figure 6.5 reveals that, for the period between July 2012 and January 2020, the highest number of drive-by download pages discovered on the internet was in 2013, where more than one drive-by download page was found per thousand URLs indexed by Microsoft's Bing search engine.

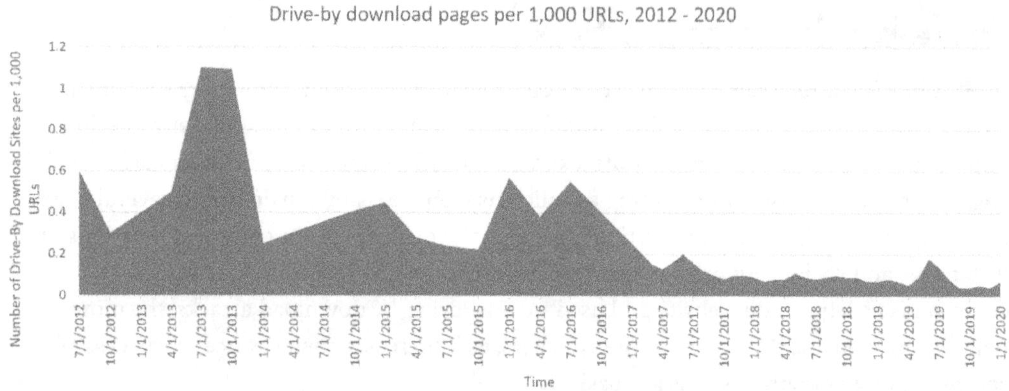

Figure 6.5 – Drive-by download pages per 1,000 URLs indexed by Microsoft's Bing search engine between 2012–2020 as published in the Microsoft Security Intelligence Report Volumes 14–21 (Microsoft Corporation, 2012–2017) and Interactive Microsoft Security Intelligence Reports (Microsoft Corporation, May 2020)

However, more recently, the worldwide average was 0.09 and 0.08 of these malicious sites per 1,000 URLs indexed in 2018 and 2019, respectively. That means the number of drive-by download sites per thousand URLs in 2013 was 14 times higher than the number in 2019.

> **Note**
>
> The data in *Figure 6.5* has been collated from Microsoft's *Security Intelligence Report* and the *Interactive Microsoft Security Intelligence Reports.* Microsoft appears to have stopped publishing this data regularly.

The components used in drive-by download attacks can be distributed, with several different remote systems hosting them. The scripts that run can be hosted on different "redirector" servers, the exploits used to exploit unpatched vulnerabilities can be hosted on separate exploit servers, and the malware that ultimately gets downloaded to the victims' systems can be hosted on separate malware-hosting servers. Distributing components of drive-by download attacks this way provides several advantages to attackers. It allows attackers to be more agile, enabling them to adjust their attacks quickly. This helps them optimize their attacks and makes it harder to find and dismantle all the components attackers use.

Subsequently, the infrastructure used to host the components of drive-by download attacks is distributed all over the world. *Table 6.1* provides the locations with the highest number of drive-by download URLs per 1,000 URLs indexed by Microsoft's Bing search engine in 2019 (Microsoft Corporation, 2020). I'm sharing data from this specific time period with you because it is especially interesting – note the top entry in the table:

Location	Number of drive-by download URLs per 1,000 URLs
Oman	687.3
French Polynesia	2.22
Gambia	1.89
Afghanistan	1.85
Saint Lucia	1.57
Myanmar	1.16
Libya	1.09
Colombia	0.48
Russia	0.45
El Salvador	0.43
Worldwide Average	0.08

Table 6.1 – Locations with the highest number of drive-by download sites in 2019 (Microsoft Corporation, 2020)

The number of drive-by download pages per 1,000 URLs in Oman in 2019 isn't a typo. According to data published by Microsoft, there were 687.3 drive-by download URLs for every 1,000 URLs in Oman, averaged across the 12 months of 2019 (Microsoft Corporation, 2020). That's 8,591.25 times higher than the worldwide average. In November 2019, Microsoft reported that there were 1,251.94 drive-by download URLs for every 1,000 URLs found by Bing in Oman (Microsoft Corporation, 2020). This means that on average, each URL Bing indexed in Oman triggered more than one drive-by download attempt. That suggests a very high concentration of drive-by download URLs in this ccTLD at the time. It might also be the case that a small set of URLs generated a disproportionately large number of malicious events.

Although this could be a simple error in the data, there could be another, less banal explanation. The ccTLD for Oman is `.om`. Attackers could have registered and used domain names in this ccTLD to catch web browser users who type `.om` instead of `.com`. This hypothesis seems plausible given how often people could make the trivial mistake of typing `google.om` instead of `google.com`, `apple.om` instead of `apple.com`, and so on. How many people would make mistakes like this every day? It seems it was enough to get the attention of attackers leveraging drive-by download sites. This is what some cybersecurity researchers were reporting back in 2016. It seems that this tactic was still in widespread use almost three years later in the last quarter of 2019:

> *"According to Endgame security researchers, the top level domain for Middle Eastern country Oman (.om) is being exploited by typosquatters who have registered more than 300 domain names with the .om suffix for U.S. companies and services such as Citibank, Dell, Macys, and Gmail. Endgame made the discovery last week and reports that several groups are behind the typosquatter campaigns."—(Spring, 2016)*

In more recent periods, drive-by attacks appear to have become less popular with attackers, so much so that it is hard to find credible sources of data to help quantify the likelihood that you'll encounter one.

> *"Although drive-by download attacks don't appear to be as popular with attackers as they used to be, that doesn't mean modern attackers don't leverage them. Every once in a while, the methods of a named attacker come to light, and drive-by downloads are in their toolkit. For example, on May 21st, 2025, Microsoft published a blog post outlining the delivery techniques for Lumma Stealer, a prolific information stealer family of malware. Their analysis revealed that Lumma was leveraging drive-by download attacks:*
>
> *Drive-by download on compromised websites: Threat actors were observed compromising groups of legitimate websites, typically through a particular vulnerability or misconfiguration. They modify site content by inserting malicious JavaScript. The JavaScript runs when sites are visited by unsuspecting users, leading to delivery of a payload, intermediary script, or displaying further lures to convince users to perform an action." (Microsoft Corporation, May 21, 2025)*

Mitigating drive-by download attacks

These attacks tend to rely on unpatched vulnerabilities to be successful. Attackers have exploit libraries that they leverage for their drive-by download attacks. Studies have shown that attackers have used between one and over 20 exploits on a single drive-by URL. If the underlying vulnerabilities that these exploits try to take advantage of are patched, these attacks won't be successful. Therefore, a well-run vulnerability management program will mitigate drive-by download attacks. Keeping systems that are used to access content on the internet up to date with security updates is a very effective mitigation.

Additionally, preventing exposure to malicious websites such as drive-by download sites can be helpful. Consider whether allowing information workers and system administrators unfettered access to the internet is required and worth the risk. Why do they need access to the `.om` ccTLD, for example, or any of the other ccTLD domains where there likely aren't legitimate business reasons to visit? Leveraging actively managed web filtering services can be helpful; blocking access to parts of the internet from corporate assets that don't have a clear business purpose can also be helpful.

Don't allow system administrators to visit the internet using web browsers from servers that process anything, or from systems that are important. Secure access workstations or privileged access workstations should be used for server administration to limit risk to important systems. Browsing sites on the public internet should be strictly forbidden on such systems and prevented with technical controls. In environments where this simply isn't possible, restrictive outbound internet access should be enforced to enable access to approved websites while preventing unfettered access to the internet.

Running up-to-date anti-malware software from a trusted anti-malware vendor can also be an effective mitigation. Drive-by download attacks typically result in malware being downloaded to the victim's system. If anti-malware software detects the exploit attempt and blocks the download and installation of such malware, a potential disaster is averted.

Next, let's discuss a couple of threats that compromised systems are used for after they are compromised – botnets and DDoS attacks.

Botnets and DDoS attacks

Once systems have been initially compromised via one or more of the Cybersecurity Usual Suspects, such as unpatched vulnerabilities and/or social engineering, as we discussed in this chapter, any information of value is siphoned from victims' systems to be sold or traded. At this point, attackers have full control of the systems they have compromised. Many times, victims' systems are enlisted into botnets and used to perform whatever illicit projects their operators desire, including DDoS attacks.

There's a lot that can be written about botnets, how they operate, and the projects they are typically employed on. In fact, entire books have been dedicated to botnets. I won't try to duplicate those here. But I do want to briefly mention a few things on this topic.

It goes without saying that botnets have garnered a lot of attention over the years. When I worked at Microsoft, the Microsoft **Digital Crimes Unit** (**DCU**) worked with law enforcement and industry experts to disrupt some of the largest botnets in operation. This work helped to dramatically reduce spam on the internet and degrade the attack power these botnets provided to their operators. Some of these botnets were composed of hundreds of thousands or millions of compromised systems and were capable of sending tens of billions of spam and phishing email messages per day. Rustock and Waledac are two examples of such botnets. To do this, the DCU had to approach the problem as a novel legal challenge in which they sought and were given legal control over the domains and physical infrastructure these botnets used (Microsoft Corporation, 2011).

In 2024, the top botnets identified by Recorded Future included Mozi Botnet, 7777-Botnet, Mirai, Hajime, and Moobot:

> *"In 2024, the top five botnets based on Insikt Group Botnet Validation data are Mozi Botnet, 7777-Botnet (also known as Quad7), Mirai, Hajime, and Moobot... Mozi Botnet and Hajime operate on a peer-to-peer model, offering greater resilience to takedowns but with increased complexity in implementation and management...In contrast, 7777-Botnet, Mirai, and Moobot use a client-server model with centralized control, simplifying management for their operators. While all botnets except the 7777-Botnet are primarily used for DDoS and occasionally spamming attacks, the 7777-Botnet has been observed for password spraying attacks..." (Recorded Future, February 28, 2025).*

The Mirai botnet gained notoriety back in 2016 when it was discovered that it was composed of online cameras, routers, and other IoT devices that leveraged ARC processors and a Linux-based operating system. The attackers behind the Mirai botnet leveraged an unchanged default username and password (a security misconfiguration) to grow it (CloudFlare, n.d.). Variants have flourished since then.

The Mozi botnet was the largest botnet, by number of identified bots tracked in 2024 by Recorded Future (Recorded Future, February 28, 2025). Like the Mirai botnet, the Mozi botnet targets IoT devices. Microsoft describes it this way:

> *"Mozi is a peer-to-peer (P2P) botnet that uses a BitTorrent-like network to infect IoT devices such as network gateways and digital video records (DVRs). It works by exploiting weak telnet passwords and nearly a dozen unpatched IoT vulnerabilities and it's been used to conduct distributed denial-of-service (DDoS) attacks, data exfiltration, and command or payload execution." (Microsoft Corporation, August 19, 2021)*

Attackers will drain anything of value from the systems they have complete control over, including cached credentials. Massive lists of leaked and stolen credentials have been found on the internet over the years, including a list with 16 billion passwords that had been amassed over the years that was discovered in June of 2025 (Sayegh, June 30, 2025). If the compromised systems or accounts have authenticated and authorized access to other systems in the environment, attackers will potentially have access and control over them as well, exacerbating the damage to organizations.

Accelerating detection and recovery activities can reduce the amount of time attackers control these assets, thus potentially reducing the damage they do to other victims and the costs associated with the recovery and restoration of normal operations. Threat intelligence can help organizations identify systems communicating with known botnet command-and-control infrastructures. Attackers know this and have been hosting some of their infrastructures in public web hosting and cloud environments in an effort to hide their operations among legitimate network traffic.

If you are interested in the granular details of attackers' internet-based infrastructures, I recommend reading the *Malicious Infrastructure Reports* published by Recorded Future's Insikt Group. They describe these reports this way:

> *"Building on Insikt Group's annual adversary infrastructure reports from 2022 and 2023, the 2024 Malicious Infrastructure Report provides a concise, data-based overview of malicious infrastructure observed throughout 2024. This year, it specifically emphasizes the synergy among passive infrastructure detection, higher-tier infrastructure insights powered by Recorded Future Network Intelligence, and victim identification. Overall, this report is for anyone interested in malicious infrastructure, offering a high-level overview of its current state as well as summaries of key findings to inform decision-making and provide a broad perspective in this highly dynamic environment." (Recorded Future, February 28, 2025)*

Their *2024 Malicious Infrastructure Report* can be downloaded from `https://www.recordedfuture.com/research/2024-malicious-infrastructure-report`.

One of the illicit purposes that botnets have been employed to perform over the years has been DDoS. Modern DDoS attacks use sophisticated techniques to overwhelm their targets with network traffic, thus depriving legitimate users of the services hosted by the victim.

Types of DDoS attacks

The three most common types of DDoS attacks include volumetric attacks, protocol attacks, and application attacks (Kesavan, November 15, 2016). There are many variations of attacks in these categories. Here is a non-exhaustive list of some examples:

- **Volumetric attack**: The attacker attempts to exhaust all available bandwidth to/from their victim's server by sending large volumes of requests to the server. Examples of types of volumetric attacks include UDP flood, reflection amplification attacks, and many others.

- **Hyper-volumetric**: L3/4 DDoS attacks that muster at least 1 **billion packets per second** (**Bpps**) or **terabits per second** (**Tbps**). Also included in this category are HTTP DDoS attacks that exceed 1 million requests per second (Cloudflare, July 15, 2025).
- **Protocol attacks**: These attempt to exploit weaknesses in TCP/IP and related protocols and their implementations. Examples include `SYN` flood and `RST` flood attacks (Kesavan, November 15, 2016).
- **Application attacks**: These attempt to exploit weaknesses at the application layer (layer 7) of the protocol stack. Examples include HTTP flood attacks and attacks that target DNS servers (Kesavan, November 15, 2016).
- **DNS flood attack**: These hammer DNS servers with high volumes of DNS queries to disrupt regular DNS service.
- **SYN flood attack**: Every TCP session starts with a three-way handshake (`SYN`, `SYN-ACK`, and `ACK`). This attack floods a server with `SYN` requests, but doesn't complete the three-way handshake, in an attempt to exhaust the server's memory and resources.
- **UDP flood attack**: Attackers send a high volume of UDP packets at the victim's server in an attempt to exhaust the server's resources and/or the network connection to the server.
- **RST flood attack**: The TCP protocol uses "reset" packets when a server needs to close a TCP session unexpectedly (when the connection can't close gracefully). Attackers flood the victim's server with TCP reset packets using spoofed sender IP addresses in an attempt to disrupt legitimate TCP sessions.
- **A ping or ICMP flood attack**: TCP/IP uses the **Internet Control Message Protocol** (**ICMP**) to test and manage connectivity to networking devices. Attackers flood the victim's server with ICMP requests in an attempt to disrupt connectivity to the server.

How large can DDoS attacks get? In February 2018, attackers launched an attack on GitHub. This DDoS attack is said to have peaked at 1.35 Tbps, which is the equivalent of more than 126 million packets per second (Kottler, 2018). This attack used a novel approach by abusing memcached instances that were not secured. This approach enabled attackers to amplify their attack by a factor of 51,000; put another way, for every 1 byte of network traffic that attackers sent, up to 51,000 bytes (51 KB) were sent to their target. This allowed attackers to overwhelm GitHub's network capacity with a massive amount of UDP traffic that interrupted network connectivity to the site for almost 10 minutes.

In January of 2022, Microsoft mitigated another record-breaking volumetric DDoS attack that threw 3.47 Tbps at their network, sending approximately 340 million packets per second.

> *"The attack Microsoft mitigated came from about 10,000 sources and from countries that include the United States, China, South Korea, Russia, Thailand, India, Vietnam, Iran, Indonesia, and Taiwan. Attack vectors were floods of User Datagram Protocol packets reflected over port 80 using SSDP, CLDAP, NTP, and Domain Name System servers." – (Goodin, Dan., January 2022)*

On June 1st, 2022, Google reportedly prevented the largest HTTPS DDoS attack ever recorded at the time, from denying service to one of their customer's internet services hosted in Google's cloud. This 69-minute attack peaked at 46 million requests per second using HTTPS-based requests. According to the Google product manager who was interviewed after the attack, it was like "*receiving all the daily requests to Wikipedia (one of the top 10 trafficked websites in the world) in just 10 seconds*" (Kan, August 18, 2022). A botnet was suspected of generating this attack.

Since that time, DDoS attacks have continued to get larger. On September 2nd, 2025, Cloudflare reported that they had blocked the largest volumetric DDOS attack in history. They reported that the attack originated from several cloud and IoT providers.

> *"Cloudflare's defenses have been working overtime. Over the past few weeks, we've autonomously blocked hundreds of hyper-volumetric DDoS attacks, with the largest reaching peaks of 5.1 Bpps and 11.5 Tbps," the company said in a Tuesday tweet." (Sergiu, Gatlan., September 2, 2025)*

Then, just three weeks later, Cloudflare reported blocking another record-setting DDoS attack that peaked at 22.2 Tbps and 10.6 Bpps (Toulas, September 23, 2025). This is a 1,544% increase in Tbps since that quaint 1.35 Tbps DDoS attack that I mentioned occurred in 2018. Recall that the attack generated 126 million packets per second compared to the attack in 2025, which generated 10.6 Bpps. 10.6 billion is 84 times more packets per second than 126 million.

Of course, not all DDoS attacks need to be that large or innovative to be disruptive. Cloudflare published some statistics, presented here, that reveal DDoS attack sizes and durations in the second quarter of 2025 (Cloudflare, July 15, 2025):

- 6 out of every 100 HTTP DDoS attacks exceed 1 million HTTP requests per second
- 5 out of every 10,000 Layer 3/Layer 4 DDoS attacks exceed 1 Tbps
- 92% of Layer 3/Layer 4 DDoS attacks and 75% of HTTP DDoS attacks end within 10 minutes

- Cloudflare blocked over 6,500 hyper-volumetric attacks in the quarter, which is an average of 71 per day
- The majority of DDoS attacks each year are Layer 3/Layer 4 DDoS attacks as opposed to HTTP DDoS attacks

Perhaps a less sophisticated but more interesting DDoS attack from the history books was the attack on critical infrastructure in Estonia in 2007. Some attributed this attack to Russia (Anderson, 2007). The reason this is interesting is that it perhaps gave us a preview of what to expect in future cyberwar conflicts – simultaneous kinetic and online attacks that overwhelm the defending state's ability to wage warfare physically and logistically. A modern version of this playbook was reportedly used just prior to Russia's military invasion of Ukraine, 15 years later in 2022. In mid-February of that year, DDoS attacks targeted military and financial institutions in Ukraine (Antoniuk, February 14, 2022). Eight days later, Russia crossed the border and started its invasion of Ukraine. These DDoS attacks were not record-setting but could have been much more disruptive had they not been effectively mitigated. The attack playbook used against Ukraine before and during the invasion is of high interest to many people, including other governments and DDoS mitigation vendors themselves.

Organizations have options to help them mitigate such attacks. There are many vendors that offer DDoS protection services, some of which include AWS Shield, Amazon CloudFront, Google Cloud Armor, Microsoft Azure DDoS Protection, Cloudflare, Akamai, and many others. In addition to protection services, the cloud offers techniques that can be used to scale infrastructure automatically as needed during DDoS attacks (Amazon Web Services, August 9, 2023).

To summarize, the key is to focus on the cybersecurity fundamentals, so your systems do not end up being part of a botnet and used to attack countless other organizations and consumers. As I will discuss in *Chapter 10, Cybersecurity Strategies*, investing in detection and response capabilities will help organizations minimize the damage and costs associated with botnets and the grief they bring with them to the internet.

Summary

This chapter focused on internet-based threats. We examined phishing attacks and drive-by download attacks. So many attacks leverage social engineering that CISOs and security teams must spend time and resources to mitigate it. For example, every week, tens of thousands of new phishing sites are connected to the internet, and every month, billions of phishing emails are sent to prospective victims.

Most phishing emails include a link to a phishing site, and most phishing sites leverage HTTPS (TLS certificates). Accounts are nearly 100% less likely to be compromised when MFA is enabled. Anti-social engineering training for information workers can also help organizations avoid falling victim to phishing attacks.

Drive-by download attacks leverage unpatched vulnerabilities to install malware unbeknownst to the user. According to data released by Microsoft, Oman's ccTLD hosted 8,591 times more drive-by download sites than the worldwide average in 2019 (Microsoft Corporation, 2020). This could indicate that attackers are using the `.om` domain to attack users who mistype URLs in the `.com` domain.

The number of drive-by download sites and phishing sites changes over time, sometimes dramatically. Subsequently, a cybersecurity strategy that doesn't include mitigations for these types of internet-based threats could have high-risk gaps.

A well-run vulnerability management program and running up-to-date anti-malware from a trusted vendor can be effective mitigations for drive-by downloads. Aggressive inbound and outbound internet access restrictions can help security teams mitigate phishing attacks, drive-by download attacks, complicate attackers' ability to command and control compromised systems, and their data exfiltration efforts. We'll discuss this in more detail in *Chapter 14*.

Systems compromised by phishing attacks, drive-by downloads, and other malicious websites can end up being enlisted into botnets and used to attack other organizations and consumers, including participating in DDoS attacks. There are different types of DDoS attacks, including volumetric and hyper-volumetric attacks, protocol attacks, and application layer attacks. DDoS attacks have been getting more intense and increasing in frequency over the years. DDoS mitigation is no longer optional for enterprise organizations. Many vendors offer DDoS protection services that enterprises can employ to mitigate even the largest DDoS attacks.

That wraps up our look at internet-based threats. I've exposed you to a lot of data, graphs, and tables in the last four chapters in an effort to provide a data-driven view of some of the threats that CISOs and security teams face every day. Another threat that CISOs and security teams need to be prepared for is attacks on **application programming interfaces** (**APIs**). Let's examine API security in the next chapter.

References

- APWG (n.d.). *APWG Phishing Activity Trends Reports* for various quarters between 2021 and 2024. Retrieved from `https://apwg.org/trendsreports/`
- APWG (November 2, 2023). *APWG Phishing Activity Trends Report 1st Quarter 2023*. Retrieved from `https://docs.apwg.org/reports/apwg_trends_report_q1_2023.pdf`

- Krebs, Brian. (May 26, 2023). *Phishing Domains Tanked After Meta Sued Freenom.* Retrieved from Krebs on Security: `https://krebsonsecurity.com/2023/05/phishing-domains-tanked-after-meta-sued-freenom/`
- Amazon Web Services (December, 2019). *AWS Best Practices for DDoS Resiliency.* Retrieved from Amazon Web Services: `https://docs.aws.amazon.com/whitepapers/latest/aws-best-practices-ddos-resiliency/aws-best-practices-ddos-resiliency.html`
- Anderson, N. (May 14, 2007). *Massive DDoS attacks target Estonia; Russia accused.* Retrieved from Ars Technica: `https://arstechnica.com/information-technology/2007/05/massive-ddos-attacks-target-estonia-russia-accused/`
- Google. (n.d.). *Google Safe Browsing.* Retrieved from `https://safebrowsing.google.com/`
- Google (May, 2020). *Safe Browsing site status.* Retrieved from Google Transparency Report: `https://transparencyreport.google.com/safe-browsing/search?hl=en`
- Google (August, 2022). *Safe Browsing.* Retrieved from Google Transparency Report: `https://transparencyreport.google.com/safe-browsing/search?hl=en`
- Google (May 9, 2020). *Where malware originates.* Retrieved from Google Transparency Report: `https://transparencyreport.google.com/archive/safe-browsing/malware?autonomous_scan_history=systemId:18779;dataset:0&lu=global_malware&global_malware=time:q`
- Internet Crime Complaint Center. (n.d.). *Federal Bureau of Investigation Internet Crime Report 2024.* Retrieved from `https://www.ic3.gov/AnnualReport/Reports/2024_IC3Report.pdf`
- Microsoft Corporation. (March 17, 2011). *Taking Down Botnets: Microsoft and the Rustock Botnet.* Retrieved from Microsoft Corporate Blog: `https://blogs.microsoft.com/on-the-issues/2011/03/17/taking-down-botnets-microsoft-and-the-rustock-botnet/`
- KnowBe4. (March, 2025). Phishing Threat Trends Report March 2025, Volume 5. Retrieved from: `https://www.knowbe4.com/hubfs/Phishing-Threat-Trends-2025_Report.pdf`
- Kottler, S. (March 1, 2018). *February 28th DDoS Incident Report.* Retrieved from The GitHub Blog: `https://github.blog/2018-03-01-ddos-incident-report/`

- Microsoft Corporation. (October 2024). *Microsoft Digital Defense Report 2024*. Retrieved from `https://www.microsoft.com/en-us/security/security-insider/threat-landscape/microsoft-digital-defense-report-2024`
- Microsoft Corporation. (October 2023). *Microsoft Digital Defense Report 2023*. Retrieved from `https://www.microsoft.com/en-us/security/security-insider/threat-landscape/microsoft-digital-defense-report-2023`
- Microsoft Corporation. (March 24, 2025). *Microsoft unveils Microsoft Security Copilot agents and new protections for AI*. Retrieved from `https://www.microsoft.com/en-us/security/blog/2025/03/24/microsoft-unveils-microsoft-security-copilot-agents-and-new-protections-for-ai`
- StatCounter. (n.d.). *Desktop Windows Version Market Share Worldwide - Apr - June 2023*. Retrieved from `https://gs.statcounter.com/windows-version-market-share/desktop/worldwide/#monthly-202304-202306`
- Microsoft Corporation. (September 16, 2025). *Microsoft seizes 338 websites to disrupt rapidly growing 'RaccoonO365' phishing service*. Retrieved from `https://blogs.microsoft.com/on-the-issues/2025/09/16/microsoft-seizes-338-websites-to-disrupt-rapidly-growing-raccoono365-phishing-service/`
- Spamhaus Project. (September 28, 2025). *Top 10 ccTLDs associated with phishing activities by number of detections*. Retrieved from `https://www.spamhaus.org/reputation-statistics/cctlds/phishing/`
- Spamhaus Project. (September 28, 2025). *Focusing on gTLDs associated with phishing activities*. Retrieved from `https://www.spamhaus.org/reputation-statistics/gtlds/phishing/`
- Cybercrime Information Center. (n.d.). *Ranking of TLDs by Malicious Phishing Domains (November to January 2024)*. Retrieved from `https://www.cybercrimeinfocenter.org/phishing-activity-in-tlds-november-january-2024`
- NIST. (July 2025). *NIST Special Publication, NIST SP 800-63-4, Digital Identity Guidelines*. Retrieved from `https://nvlpubs.nist.gov/nistpubs/SpecialPublications/NIST.SP.800-63-4.pdf`
- Nelson, Nate. (July 1, 2025). *We've All Been Wrong: Phishing Training Doesn't Work*. Retrieved from Dark Reading: `https://www.darkreading.com/endpoint-security/phishing-training-doesnt-work`

- US Department of State. (March 12, 2025). *Independent States in the World.* Retrieved from `https://www.state.gov/independent-states-in-the-world/`
- MITRE Corporation. (April 18, 2025). *Drive-by Compromise.* Retrieved from `https://attack.mitre.org/techniques/T1189/`
- Microsoft Corporation. (May 21, 2025). *Lumma Stealer: Breaking down the delivery techniques and capabilities of a prolific infostealer.* Retrieved from `https://www.microsoft.com/en-us/security/blog/2025/05/21/lumma-stealer-breaking-down-the-delivery-techniques-and-capabilities-of-a-prolific-infostealer/`
- Recorded Future. (February 28, 2025). *2024 Malicious Infrastructure Report.* Retrieved from `https://assets.recordedfuture.com/insikt-report-pdfs/2025/cta-2025-0228.pdf`
- CloudFlare. (n.d.). *What is the Mirai Botnet?* Retrieved from `https://www.cloudflare.com/learning/ddos/glossary/mirai-botnet/`
- Microsoft Corporation. (August 19, 2021). *How to proactively defend against Mozi IoT botnet.* Retrieved from `https://www.microsoft.com/en-us/security/blog/2021/08/19/how-to-proactively-defend-against-mozi-iot-botnet/`
- Microsoft Corporation. (July 11, 2023). *Microsoft mitigates China-based threat actor Storm-0558 targeting of customer email.* Retrieved from `https://msrc.microsoft.com/blog/2023/07/microsoft-mitigates-china-based-threat-actor-storm-0558-targeting-of-customer-email/`
- Microsoft Corporation (2012-2017). *Microsoft Security Intelligence Report.* Redmond: Microsoft Corporation
- Microsoft Corporation (2012-2017). *Microsoft Security Intelligence Report Volumes 14–21.* Redmond: Microsoft Corporation. Internet-Based Threats
- Microsoft Corporation (2015-2017). *Microsoft Security Intelligence Report Volumes 19–23.* Redmond: Microsoft Corporation. Retrieved from `www.microsoft.com/sir`
- Microsoft Corporation (2016). *Microsoft Security Intelligence Report Volume 21.* Redmond: Microsoft Corporation. Retrieved from `https://query.prod.cms.rt.microsoft.com/cms/api/am/binary/RE2GQwi`
- Microsoft Corporation (2018). *Microsoft Security Intelligence Report Volume 23.* Redmond: Microsoft Corporation. Retrieved from `https://query.prod.cms.rt.microsoft.com/cms/api/am/binary/RWt530`

- Microsoft Corporation (2019). *Microsoft Security Intelligence Report Volume 24*. Redmond: Microsoft Corporation. Retrieved from `https://info.microsoft.com/ww-landing-M365-SIR-v24-Report-eBook.html?lcid=en-us`
- Microsoft Corporation (May 8, 2020). *Drive-by download pages*. Retrieved from Microsoft: `https://www.microsoft.com/securityinsights/Driveby`
- Microsoft Corporation (May 15, 2020). *Help protect my PC with Microsoft Defender Offline*. Retrieved from `https://support.microsoft.com/en-us/windows/help-protect-my-pc-with-microsoft-defender-offline-9306d528-64bf-4668-5b80-ff533f183d6c`
- Microsoft Corporation (May 8, 2020). *Malware encounter rates*. Retrieved from Microsoft: `https://www.microsoft.com/securityinsights/Malware`
- Microsoft Defender ATP Research Team (August 9, 2018). *Protecting the protector: Hardening machine learning defenses against adversarial attacks*. Retrieved from Microsoft: `https://www.microsoft.com/security/blog/2018/08/09/protecting-the-protector-hardeningmachine-learning-defenses-against-adversarial-attacks/`
- Sayegh, Emil. (June 30, 2025). *Silent Breach Exposes 16 Billion Passwords: 5 Things You Must Do Now*. Retrieved from Forbes: `https://www.forbes.com/sites/emilsayegh/2025/06/30/silent-breach-exposes-16-billion-passwords-5-things-you-must-do-now/`
- Spring, Tom. (March 14, 2016). *Typosquatters Target Mac Users With New '.om' Domain Scam*. Retrieved from Threatpost: `https://threatpost.com/typosquatters-target-apple-mac-users-with-new-om-domain-scam/116768/`
- URLhaus (May 9, 2020). *About*. Retrieved from URLhaus: `https://urlhaus.abuse.ch/about/`
- URLhaus (August 24, 2022). *Statistics*. Retrieved from URLhaus: `https://urlhaus.abuse.ch/statistics/`
- Weinert, Alex. (July 9, 2019). *Your Pa$$word doesn't matter*. Retrieved from Microsoft Corporation: `https://techcommunity.microsoft.com/t5/azure-active-directory-identity/your-pa-word-doesn-tmatter/ba-p/731984#`
- Microsoft Corporation. (October, 2021). *Microsoft Digital Defense Report*. Retrieved from `https://query.prod.cms.rt.microsoft.com/cms/api/am/binary/RWMFIi`
- Ganacharya, Tanmay. (March 20, 2020). *Protecting against coronavirus themed phishing attacks*. Retrieved from Microsoft Security Blog: `https://www.microsoft.com/`

security/blog/2020/03/20/protecting-against-coronavirus-themed-phishing-attacks/

- JPCERT/CC (May 25, 2022). *Trends of Reported Phishing Sites and Compromised Domains in 2021.* Retrieved from JPCERT/CC Eyes: https://blogs.jpcert.or.jp/en/2022/05/phishing2021.html
- Microsoft Corporation. (August 2022). *Cyber Signals August 2022.* Retrieved from https://query.prod.cms.rt.microsoft.com/cms/api/am/binary/RE54L7v
- Kesavan, Archana. (November 15, 2016). *Three Types of DDoS Attacks.* Retrieved from Cisco Thousand Eyes blog: https://www.thousandeyes.com/blog/three-types-ddos-attacks#:~:text=Protocol-based%20attacks
- Kan, Michael. (August 18, 2022). *Google Fends Off Record-Breaking DDoS Attack.* Retrieved from PCMag: https://www.pcmag.com/news/google-fends-off-record-breaking-ddos-attack
- Goodin, Dan. (January 28, 2022). *Microsoft fends off record-breaking 3.47Tbps DDoS attack.* Retrieved from Ars Technica: https://arstechnica.com/information-technology/2022/01/microsoft-fends-off-record-breaking-3-47-tbps-ddos-attack/
- Sergiu, Gatlan. (September 2, 2025). *Cloudflare blocks largest recorded DDoS attack peaking at 11.5 Tbps.* Retrieved from https://www.bleepingcomputer.com/news/security/cloudflare-blocks-record-breaking-115-tbps-ddos-attack/
- Toulas, Bill. (September 23, 2025). *Cloudflare mitigates new record-breaking 22.2 Tbps DDoS attack.* Retrieved from https://www.bleepingcomputer.com/news/security/cloudflare-mitigates-new-record-breaking-222-tbps-ddos-attack/
- Antoniuk, Daryna. (February 14, 2022). *DDoS attacks hit Ukrainian government websites.* Retrieved from https://therecord.media/ddos-attacks-hit-websites-of-ukraines-state-banks-defense-ministry-and-armed-forces
- Cloudflare. (July 15, 2025). *DDoS threat report for 2025 Q2.* Retrieved from https://radar.cloudflare.com/reports/ddos-2025-q2

Get this book's PDF version and more

Scan the QR code (or go to packtpub.com/unlock). Search for this book by name, confirm the edition, and then follow the steps on the page.

UNLOCK NOW

Note: Keep your invoice handy. Purchases made directly from Packt don't require an invoice.

Get this book's PDF version and more

7

Application Programming Interface Security

We live in an **application programming interface** (**API**)-driven world. Whether you are banking, making travel arrangements, listening to music or watching a show or movie on a streaming service, checking the weather, counting steps with a fitness tracker, or using almost any application in any scenario, it is likely APIs are involved. Most modern applications use APIs to interact with other software systems. APIs have become ubiquitous as developers have put them everywhere to enable data exchanges and functionality sharing across digital platforms.

Of course, this involves considerable complexity. Although APIs simplify the knowledge of software systems that developers require to leverage them, there are a myriad of details that developers must tend to to protect the software they develop and the systems their software runs on from exploitation.

As the number of APIs that enterprises develop and rely on continues to proliferate, few organizations have paused to ask their CISOs about the resources needed to identify, protect, detect, and respond to threats against their APIs. These conversations typically happen only after an organization runs out of luck and gets burned by poor choices made during application development or vulnerabilities in their APIs. But by then, the challenge of securing APIs that are already in production is typically compounded by their numbers and their complexity. They also need to secure the APIs they are currently developing for release into production in the future. These are not insurmountable tasks, but they do need to be taken seriously if organizations want to avoid potentially expensive and embarrassing data breaches via insecure APIs.

It is important that CISOs and security teams understand the security and privacy challenges that developers have when developing and working with APIs. The choices that developers make turn out to be critical to the security of their software and the data it processes. Unfortunately, network and security infrastructure cannot compensate for many of the poor choices developers can make using APIs. A combination of security and privacy requirements during the development process, along with processes and technologies that identify, protect, detect, and respond to threats against APIs, is necessary.

In this chapter, we'll examine the most common vulnerabilities in APIs through a CISO lens. By the end of this chapter, you'll understand some of the most important aspects of API security and be able to discuss them with developers, vendors, and other stakeholders.

The following topics will be covered in this chapter:

- An API primer
- The web application and API threat landscape
- The security development lifecycle
- OWASP API Security Top 10

Let's start with a quick primer on APIs.

An API primer

The **National Institute of Standards and Technology** (**NIST**) defines an API as "*a system access point or library function that has a well-defined syntax and is accessible from application programs or user code to provide well-defined functionality*" (NIST, n.d.). As this relatively broad definition suggests, there are many different types of APIs. For example, when I worked at Microsoft in the Core Operating System Division, I worked with APIs for operating systems, programming languages, and software libraries. This chapter will focus on web APIs that enable applications running on internet-connected systems to communicate with each other.

As the web came to support different types of media over the decades, APIs evolved and became more sophisticated. Web APIs rely on a combination of data formats, protocols, and architectural styles, such as the following:

- **Extensible Markup Language** (**XML**)
- **Hypertext Transfer Protocol** (**HTTP**)
- **Representational State Transfer** (**REST**)
- **Simple Object Access Protocol** (**SOAP**)
- **JavaScript Object Notation** (**JSON**)

Basic system interaction involves four main components: clients, requests, servers, and responses. Software running on a client (such as a workstation, laptop, device, virtual machine, agent, etc.) sends a request over a network to an API running on a server. The server hosts the

API and receives the client's request. The server then processes the request according to how the developer of the API designed it. For example, it might include performing calculations, retrieving data from a database, or executing automation functions. Once the server processing is complete, the server sends a response back to the client. This could contain the data it requested, a status message, or an error code. The developer of the API determines what the API will return to the client and how it behaves. *Figure 7.1* illustrates a simplified example of how a web API works. In this example, the user uses a weather application on their mobile device to get the current weather forecast for their location. The application makes an API call to a weather service on the internet, which returns the weather forecast to the application for the user.

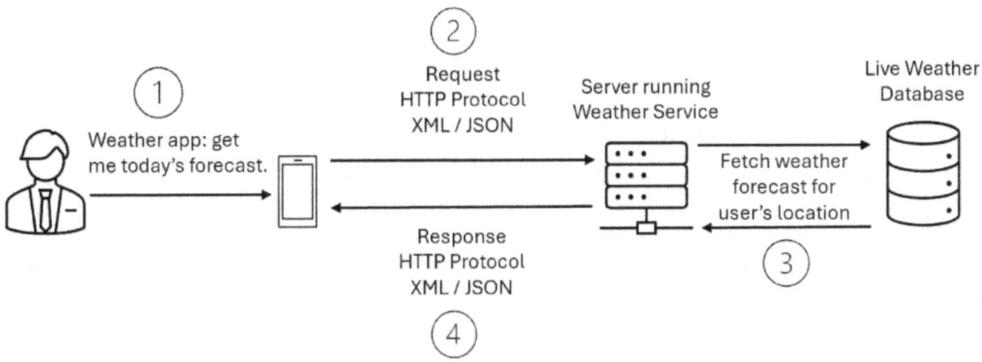

Figure 7.1 – An example of how a web API works

Let's take an example of a client running a web browser. The client sends an HTTP request to a web server requesting access to a specific web page specified by a **Uniform Resource Locator** (**URL**). If the web page exists and the user is authorized, the server returns the web page to the client in a format that it expects, and the browser reads and renders the web page for the user. If the web server doesn't have the requested web page, it returns an HTTP 404 (Not Found) error to the client, and the user's browser displays the error to them.

In this case, both the developers of the web server and the web browser needed to understand how the APIs they used were implemented. By using existing APIs, they saved on the time and effort it would have taken to implement their own TCP/IP stack, HTTP protocol, and so on. When a user enters a URL, developers use APIs to send that request to the server. The operating system and network manage most of the underlying details for the developer. Because of this, developers don't need deep expertise in the HTTP protocol, TCP/IP, authentication and authorization methods, web browsers, or web servers. This model simplifies and accelerates web development.

Developers can work with an API only when they understand how it's built, which means they rely on the API's specification to see how its endpoints, inputs, and behaviors are defined. API specifications are written in a standard, structured way. This helps developers understand and use APIs and makes testing easier.

Let's look at an example where a developer is developing an application that requests data from a web server that returns the requested data in JSON format. In this example, the client application asks the API on the remote server where a picture is and uses the response to display the picture.

First, the client sends a request to the API on the remote server using an `HTTPS GET` method. This request looks like a standard URL:

```
GET https://api.packt.com/picture
```

The URL is the API's endpoint for the resource requested – in this case, the picture. The `GET` requests a representation of the specified resource. In this example, the API does not require authentication.

The server processes the request and returns the requested data as a JSON object. The client application uses the returned data to locate and display the picture for the user:

```
{
  "date": "2025-10-31",
  "explanation": "This is the picture you requested...",
  "hdurl": "https://api.packt.com/images/610/picture_610.jpg",
  "media_type": "image",
  "title": "Your Picture",
  "url": "https://api.packt.com/images/610/picture_610.jpg"
}
```

In today's API-driven world, APIs have been built into everything to make leveraging services and accessing data over networks easy. Payment services offer payment APIs, map services offer mapping APIs, e-commerce platforms provide APIs that support shopping and inventory management, and social media platforms offer APIs that enable developers to interact with them.

Because APIs are so ubiquitous and play critical roles in modern applications, many threat actors focus on attacking APIs. The categories of attacks include the following:

- **Exploiting vulnerabilities**: We discussed vulnerabilities and their exploitation in detail in *Chapters 3, Industry Vulnerability Disclosure Trends* and *4, Product Vulnerability*

Disclosure Trends. In 2025, there were more than 48,500 vulnerability disclosures across the entire industry, equivalent to 133 new vulnerability disclosures per day on average. Many of these vulnerabilities were in APIs. We'll spend some time later in the chapter looking at the most common types of vulnerabilities in APIs.

- **Abuse of functionality**: This involves threat actors manipulating an API to perform an action or return data it was never intended to provide. Attackers probe APIs to learn about the business logic they support and then devise ways of abusing the APIs. Recall the "data breach via an insecure API" example attack we discussed in *Chapter 1, How Enterprises Get Hacked*. In this example, the attacker queried an API repeatedly, increasing the customer ID by 1 each time. This allowed them to get unauthorized access to customer account data. To do this, the attacker had to figure out the length and format of customer account numbers and study how the API worked. The attacker also took advantage of the lack of query rate limiting on the API, which allowed thousands of queries for different accounts from the same small group of systems – unlikely behavior of legitimate customers.
- **Access violations**: Managing authentication and authorization for APIs from so many possible devices and types of identities is a challenge many developers struggle with. Threat actors will take advantage of weaknesses in APIs' authentication and authorization controls if given the opportunity. Properly implemented authentication and authorization mechanisms are critical for API designs and implementations. I'll discuss authentication and authorization in detail later in this chapter.
- **Denial of service (DoS)**: If threat actors can consume all the resources on the server hosting an API or all the network bandwidth of the connection to the server, legitimate API transactions will fail. If attackers can deny service to legitimate API transactions for long enough, they can force the service offline and even demand a ransom from the victim to restore service.
- **Operational threats**: For years, the IT environments of many big enterprises have deployed large numbers of APIs ungoverned. Large enterprises rarely have full and accurate inventories of all the APIs they use. This makes it much harder to understand where sensitive data flows are occurring or to properly manage vulnerabilities in APIs. Over time, some APIs are abandoned as their owners change roles or when teams are reorganized. Documentation is lost; inventories begin to allow technical debt and risk to accumulate. Forgotten APIs can sit exposed on the external internet-facing attack surfaces of enterprises for years before anyone notices and decommissions them. Additionally, shadow IT plagues big enterprises, which leads to shadow APIs. These are undocumented APIs created and used without IT's knowledge. All these issues give an

advantage to attackers who are not encumbered by their victims' lack of management discipline.

We'll take a deeper look at each of these categories of threats and how they can be mitigated in the remainder of this chapter. If you don't recall the "data breach via an insecure API" example attack I provided in *Chapter 1*, I suggest that you review it now as I'll be referencing it in this chapter.

First, let's look at the web application and API threat landscape to understand how often attacks on APIs happen and what some of their impacts are. This will give you an idea of both the probability and impact sides of the risk equation regarding API threats. When your stakeholders ask why they should care about API security, you should be able to give them an answer based on data instead of just opinion.

The web application and API threat landscape

Let's get a sense of how often APIs are attacked. Akamai's *State of Web and API Security 2025* report gives us several insights. One insight is that attacks are happening at a massive scale and increasing:

> *"Organizations are confronting a marked increase in attacks that target web applications — Akamai observed more than 311 billion web application and API attacks in 2024 alone, representing a 33% year-over-year increase. This surge correlates directly with the accelerated adoption of cloud services, microservices architectures, and artificial intelligence (AI)–powered applications." (Akamai, State of Apps and API Security 2025, Vol. 11, Issue 02, 2025)*

These are a few other insights from Akamai's *State of Web and API Security 2025* report (Akamai, State of Apps and API Security 2025, Vol. 11, Issue 02, 2025):

- 33% increase in global web attacks year over year
- The most impacted industry, based on Akamai's data, was commerce organizations, with more than 230 billion attacks in 2025
- The number of Layer 7 DDoS attacks that targeted organizations in North America was 11.9 trillion between Q1 2023 and Q4 2024

Cloudflare's 2024 *API Security & Management Report* also contains data that helps us understand the nature of attacks on APIs. Here are some key findings from their report (Cloudflare, 2024):

- Successful API requests accounted for over half (57%) of dynamic HTTP traffic on the internet in 2024

- The most common API errors were "too many requests," "bad request," "not found," "unauthorized," and "forbidden"
- One prediction from the report was: "because GenAI usage dramatically increases API usage, GenAI services will also attract more API related attacks against their APIs"

Salt Security's Q1 2025 *State of API Security Report* also provides insightful data points (Salt, n.d.):

- "With 95% of attack attempts coming from authenticated sources, this underscores the growing risk of insider threats, compromised accounts, and attackers leveraging stolen credentials"
- "... 98% of attack attempts target external-facing APIs, reinforcing that public APIs are the primary attack surface for malicious actors"
- "When examining attack techniques, 80% of attempts align with the **Open Worldwide Application Security Project** (**OWASP**) API Security Top 10, indicating that attackers are actively exploiting known API vulnerabilities rather than relying on novel attack vectors"

There are some conclusions that I think we can draw from these insights. First, APIs are critical to web applications, given that more than half of the dynamic HTTP traffic on the internet is API traffic. One major cloud provider observed more than 311 billion attacks on web applications and APIs in 2024. That's an average of more than 850,000,000 attacks per day. If we extrapolate this data by assuming that the number of attacks observed by other major cloud providers is similar, the number of attacks each year on web applications and APIs is certainly several hundred billion, if not more.

These numbers could grow even more as generative AI services continue to expand the use and creation of APIs. Almost all of these attacks are from authenticated sources, and most of them are on internet-facing APIs. Attackers have been primarily using techniques reflected in the OWASP API Security Project, which we will examine in this chapter. This means that although the number of attacks is huge, the majority of them should be mitigatable.

However, this isn't as easy as putting your web applications behind a firewall or **web application firewall** (**WAF**). The data suggests that 20% of attacks are not reflected in OWASP's current list of top API vulnerabilities. 20% of such a huge number of attacks must also be mitigated. Identifying, protecting, detecting, and responding to threats against your organization's APIs will require the same effort it takes to do so for web applications. Application security starts with the development process, so let's discuss that next.

The security development lifecycle

I had the opportunity to work closely with the **Security Development Lifecycle** (**SDL**) team at Microsoft for several years, where I learned a lot about this approach to development. The SDL was mandated at Microsoft after devastating worm attacks in 2003 and 2004, including SQL Slammer and MSBlaster. Teams that develop code at Microsoft for enterprise customers are required to meet the requirements of the SDL. This includes web applications and APIs.

The objectives of the SDL are straightforward:

- Reduce the number of vulnerabilities in Microsoft products
- Reduce the severity of vulnerabilities in Microsoft products
- Make vulnerabilities in Microsoft products difficult or impossible to exploit

The SDL is a set of practices and supporting tools designed to achieve these objectives. The SDL can be applied regardless of whether you are developing software using a traditional waterfall approach or a more modern DevOps methodology. It can also help with developing more secure applications and APIs across platforms such as on-premises IT environments, cloud, hybrid infrastructures, and mobile platforms.

The example Microsoft provides has a four-stage development process underpinned by Zero Trust architecture and governance principles. The four stages illustrated in *Figure 7.2* are as follows (Microsoft, n.d.):

1. **Design**: The design should prevent attackers from easily getting unauthorized access
2. **Code**: Develop code in a way that prevents attackers from taking unauthorized actions or accessing data
3. **Build and deploy**: Secure **continuous integration and continuous deployment** (**CI/CD**) processes to prevent unauthorized changes to the code
4. **Run**: Security best practices should be adopted across the platforms where the code runs, including on-premises IT environments, cloud, hybrid, and mobile

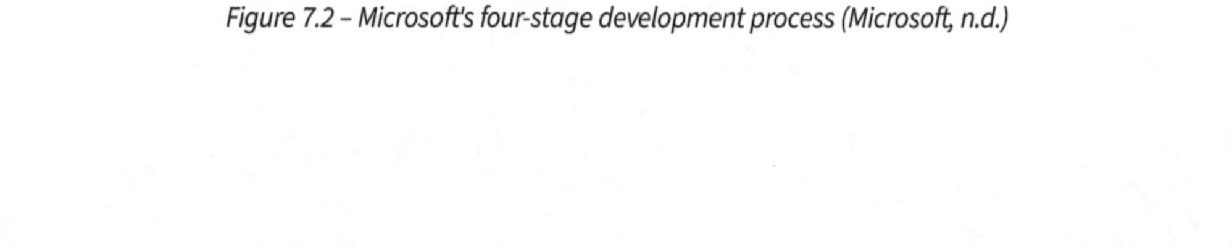

Figure 7.2 – Microsoft's four-stage development process (Microsoft, n.d.)

These stages of development should follow Zero Trust principles, including the following (Microsoft, n.d.):

- **Assume breach**: The system will be compromised at some point, so plan for that eventuality.
- **Explicitly verify trust**: Don't assume trusted relationships. Reauthenticate parties for every action and verify authorization.
- **Embrace the principle of least privilege**: Assign only the minimum privileges to identities required for any operation.

There are 10 key practices that integrate security into the development process (Microsoft, n.d.):

- Establish security standards, metrics, and governance
- Require the use of proven security features, languages, and frameworks
- Perform security design review and threat modeling
- Define and use cryptography standards
- Secure the software supply chain
- Secure the engineering environment
- Perform security testing
- Ensure operational platform security
- Implement security monitoring and response
- Provide security training

Microsoft provides details on each of these practices at `https://www.microsoft.com/en-us/securityengineering/sdl/practices`. I recommend that you take the time to review each practice in detail. Next, I'll highlight a few of these practices that I think have particularly high security return on investment for web applications and APIs.

Privacy by design

Some development teams spend time thoroughly thinking about security for their applications and APIs. But privacy is often overlooked, as it was in the "data breach via an insecure API" example attack I discussed in *Chapter 1*. In my experience, the lack of understanding and focus on privacy considerations during development projects is widespread, and as data breaches around the world have illustrated, it's a challenge for development teams everywhere. I examine privacy in more detail in *Chapter 8, Friend or Foe? The Roles Governments Play in Cybersecurity*. Let's discuss privacy by design here, in the context of API development, because it could help many developers avoid self-inflicted data breaches that can't be mitigated using traditional IT infrastructure, such as firewalls or WAFs.

One of the organizations that helped formalize this approach describes privacy by design this way:

> *"Privacy by Design is a methodology for proactively embedding privacy into information technology, business practices, and networked infrastructures. The Privacy by Design measures are designed to anticipate and prevent privacy invasive events before they occur." (Information and Privacy Commissioner of Ontario, January 2018)*

Privacy by design espouses seven principles (Information and Privacy Commissioner of Ontario, January 2018). Let's look at what these principles are:

- **Proactive not reactive**: Prevent problems before they occur. Don't wait for attackers to point issues out to you. Proactively anticipate data breaches involving sensitive data and try to prevent them.
- **Privacy as the default setting**: System users shouldn't have to take any actions, such as opting in, for their privacy to be protected. Privacy controls should be turned on by default.
- **Privacy embedded into design**: Design and configure systems with privacy in mind from the outset. Avoid designing systems and then attempting to add privacy controls and related configurations after the fact.
- **Full functionality**: It's not about privacy versus security. Instead of focusing on privacy and security trade-offs, look for ways that users can get both.
- **End-to-end security**: Data should be protected during its entire life cycle, so plan accordingly and embed the appropriate security measures to accomplish this.
- **Visibility and transparency**: Transparency helps build trust with users and other stakeholders. Leverage open privacy standards and plan to provide third-party attestations that the system is designed and operated in accordance with those standards.
- **Respect for user privacy**: Turn privacy controls on by default and provide users with appropriate notice when privacy-related controls change or other material changes to the system are implemented that impact users' privacy. In short, keep it user-centric.

As you can see from the principles, embedding privacy considerations into the development process doesn't necessarily require more resources or longer schedules. Developers need to be educated on these principles and trained in the development practices that help them to align with them. A little effort here can result in an outsized return on investment for data protection.

One of the key practices of Microsoft's SDL is "Establish security standards, metrics, and governance." Microsoft describes this practice as follows:

> *"This practice focuses on continually updating and communicating security requirements to reflect changes in functionality and to the regulatory and threat landscape.*
>
> *Clear guidance and rules are required to guide team members (product line leaders, product owners, developers, operations, and other roles) through what they need to do for security, how success is measured, and what resources are available to help them.*
>
> *The need to consider security and privacy is a fundamental aspect of developing highly secure applications and systems and regardless of development methodology being used. Security requirements must be continually updated to reflect changes in required functionality and changes to the threat landscape." (Microsoft, n.d.)*

Next, let's look at another practice that typically provides high security return on investment and helps organizations identify avoidable cybersecurity issues – threat modeling.

Threat modeling

Another SDL key practice I want to highlight for you is "Perform security design review and threat modeling." Microsoft describes this practice as follows:

> *"Threat modeling and security design reviews of threat models identify potential security threats so that designers can mitigate them early in the development process, resulting in systems that are Secure by Design. Adding security during the design process is much cheaper and less risky than adding it after the fact." (Microsoft, n.d.)*

Threat models help developers determine which security features and functionality their specific application requires. Without a threat model, developers are left to arbitrarily decide where to add appropriate security protection for the data flowing through their systems. For example, a threat model helps developers determine where they need to implement encryption for data at rest and data in transit. Without a threat model, developers might implement such protections at points in their application where they are not necessary or not implement appropriate security controls where they are necessary. For example, without a threat model, developers might decide to forgo authentication for low-value transactions to streamline users' experiences. This might be an appropriate trade-off when considering the confidentiality of the data, but they also need to consider potential impacts on the integrity of the data. Good threat models contemplate different types of threats to the systems they are associated with.

There are at least a few different threat-modeling frameworks available to leverage, including PASTA, LINDDUN, OCTAVE, and VAST. The framework I've used the most is **STRIDE**, which was the framework developed at Microsoft when I worked there. STRIDE stands for the following:

- **Spoofing**: Impersonating someone or pretending to be something to interact with the system for illegitimate purposes. For example, an attacker sends a login request impersonating a legitimate user by forging their authentication token.
- **Tampering**: Changing the system for illegitimate purposes, typically without authorization. For example, a threat actor makes a change to a configuration file to disable logging to avoid detection during an intrusion.
- **Repudiation**: Allows an entity, such as a user, to deny that they were responsible for making a change to the system, a transaction, or an event. For example, a user deletes audit logs and later plausibly denies it because the system lacks authentication and non-repudiation controls.
- **Information disclosure**: Making the system disclose data that it was not intended to. For example, an attacker is able to access confidential data by providing non-secret, easily guessable inputs to the system, such as phone numbers.
- **Denial of service**: Abusing system resources to deny legitimate use or operation. For example, an attacker floods an API endpoint with excessive requests, exhausting system resources and preventing legitimate users from accessing the service.
- **Elevation of privilege**: An unprivileged user gains privileged access to the system that enables unauthorized actions on the system. For example, a low-privileged user exploits a flawed access control check to gain administrative rights and performs actions reserved for administrators.

Developing a threat model generally requires the application to develop data flow diagrams first. So many development teams I've worked with over the years didn't take the time to develop detailed data flow diagrams or threat models before they started writing code. Data flow diagrams are like the blueprints of a system and illustrate how the developers envision data flowing through the system, including computing resources, storage, databases, and networks. A level 1 or level 2 data flow diagram typically has enough detail to develop a threat model for the system.

With data flow diagrams in hand, a threat model will take a short period of time (hours) to develop if the right people with knowledge of the system's design participate. System architects who have knowledge of the system's design, including storage, databases, network, and computing resources, working with developers and cybersecurity subject matter experts, can typically develop a threat model efficiently.

With a data flow diagram, the threat-modeling process involves identifying the trust boundaries between processes in the diagram. *Figure 7.3* illustrates how authentication boundaries are added to a simple data flow diagram. Then, the STRIDE framework is applied to each of those boundaries to identify potential threats to the system. Context is important as not every threat will be relevant to every part of the system.

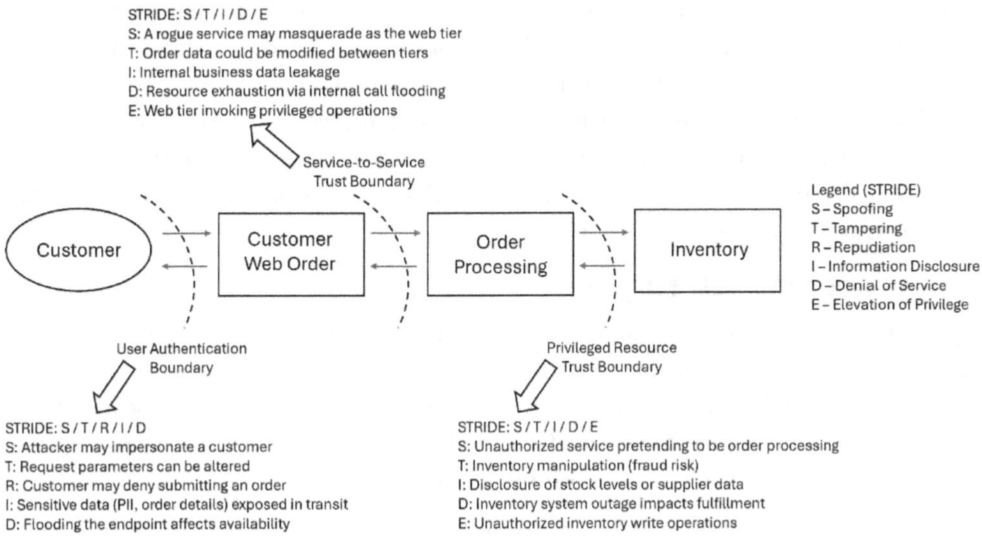

Figure 7.3 – An example of a threat model developed from a simple data flow diagram

For each threat identified, a corresponding mitigation or a list of potential mitigations should be developed. A list of potential mitigations gives the development team options on how to mitigate the threats identified and informs the design choices they make and the code they write.

Without a threat model, development teams tend to develop systems that meet functional specifications but are largely uninformed by threats to the system. Traditionally, if a post-development penetration test uncovered unmitigated threats, development teams would either go back and fix them or seek policy exceptions that preserved these risks to the system, usually until they were exploited. This is the most expensive and highest-risk approach to development, but also the most popular in my experience. Spending the few hours it typically takes to develop a threat model almost always has a high security return on investment.

> **Tip**
>
> If you are interested in learning more about threat modeling, numerous books are available. My favorite book on the topic was written by a former co-worker of mine at Microsoft: *Threat Modeling: Designing for Security* by Adam Shostack. Additionally,

> Microsoft offers a free Threat Modeling Tool to make threat modeling even easier; the tool is available at `https://learn.microsoft.com/en-us/azure/security/develop/threat-modeling-tool`.

Even with a threat model, typically not all threats identified get mitigated during the development of large complex systems. Real trade-offs between risks, schedules, budgets, customer expectations, the competitive nature of organizations' industries, and other factors exist. If development teams are making risk-based decisions, they ultimately decide whether to mitigate each identified risk, transfer it to another party, such as a cyber-insurance company, or accept it. This is where a cybersecurity risk register can be important for CISOs and security teams. Let's discuss this next.

Cybersecurity risk register

A cybersecurity risk register is a tool that security teams can use to track cybersecurity risks, their severity, who owns each risk, and dates for any planned threat mitigations. Recording the risk acceptance and risk transfer decisions in the cybersecurity risk register (a document, a spreadsheet, or a risk register tool) provides formal documentation of what each risk is, who accepted or transferred the risk, and any future mitigation plans.

If the risk is realized in the future, the cybersecurity risk register keeps the organization honest with itself and prevents stakeholders from pretending that the organization didn't know about the risks before they were exploited. It also helps CISOs avoid becoming scapegoats for risks that development teams and other executives had knowingly accepted on behalf of the entire organization, its boards of directors, and its shareholders. CISOs who review their cybersecurity risk register with their senior stakeholders periodically can insulate themselves from the "blame game" that ensues at many organizations when their stakeholders' risk choices are realized. For some organizations, leveraging a formal risk acceptance form that explains the risk and is signed by the risk owner is necessary to ensure everyone has the same understanding of the risk and its potential impact on the organization. Later, if the risk is realized, signed risk acceptance forms ensure everyone remembers the risk the same way.

A cybersecurity risk register also provides helpful context on each risk treatment decision, which can otherwise be lost as personnel changes over time. CISOs shouldn't rely on tribal knowledge for risk management. Recording the risks in a cybersecurity register, sharing it, and reviewing it with senior stakeholders periodically is strongly recommended. Share these risks often enough that the most severe risks in the register aren't surprises to senior stakeholders when they see them.

Some organizations have an enterprise risk register that captures risks to the entire enterprise. These risks include economic, financial, and legal risks, among others. Cybersecurity is likely in this register too. However, the altitude of enterprise risks tends to be much higher level than the granular security risks, such as risks to specific IT systems. For this reason, I recommend using a separate risk register to track the treatment of more granular security-related risks.

Security training

The final SDL practice I'll highlight is training. Organizations can't expect developers and architects to simply possess innate knowledge of cybersecurity threats and mitigations or risk management. They don't all need to be subject matter experts, but they do all need to understand the basics, as well as how the organization's SDL process works. Developing a repeatable process that improves itself over time and training development teams to use this process is key.

For organizations that are in hyper-competitive industries that need to move as fast as possible, such as high tech or finance, the key is to train as many people as possible. The traditional friction in the development process isn't security professionals pointing out security threats or design deficiencies that need attention; it's untrained developers and architects constantly pushing back on the notion that security threats exist. These threats exist, clearly. We have decades of data on cyber-attacks that is undeniable. As entertaining as it is to see smart developers assert that they are omniscient, this is what slows development teams down.

Training as many people as possible on your organization's SDL will minimize the friction and allow them to embed security into every phase of development. When organizations do this successfully, they can develop software as quickly as their resources allow them to. Security-related processes won't slow them down because they are baked into the software development process. Program managers and project managers will be able to more accurately plan the time it takes for software to make it through the entire development process. Security will be integrated into the schedule because it is built into the process, not added at the end. The key is to train people to stop objecting to doing basic security-related work and simply follow the organization's SDL process as the only way to release software. The more people who understand the process for releasing software, the more efficient it becomes. Greater awareness and adherence to the process reduces the likelihood of expensive, untreated security vulnerabilities and issues making their way into production.

Unfortunately, training isn't a one-time activity. As development tools and threats evolve, development teams must evolve with them. Training during onboarding and conducting annual refreshers are common practices I've seen in the industry.

There are numerous options for security training for development teams, including training from Avatao, Black Duck, Immersive, SANS Institute, Secure Code Warrior, SecureFlag, Microsoft, and Google.

I've only scratched the surface here.

> **Note**
>
> To learn more, review all 10 of the key practices Microsoft provides that integrate security into the development process at `https://www.microsoft.com/en-us/securityengineering/sdl/practices`.

Now that I've addressed how important the SDL, privacy concerns, threat modeling, a risk register, and training are to API security, let's shift focus and talk about the specific vulnerabilities that APIs suffer from and how to mitigate them.

OWASP API Security Top 10

OWASP is an international non-profit foundation that focuses on software security. OWASP projects are open source and managed by communities of volunteer members. There are many OWASP projects, including OWASP Top 10 Web Application Security Risks, OWASP GenAI Security Project, OWASP Mobile Application Security, and OWASP Software Assurance Maturity Model, to name a few. The OWASP Top 10 Web Application Security Risks has become an invaluable resource to application security teams and cybersecurity teams around the world who use it to identify and remediate code-level security issues, as well as monitoring and blocking related attacks on web applications.

The OWASP project most relevant to our discussion in this chapter is the **OWASP API Security Project**. OWASP typically publishes updated Top 10 lists every two or three years. OWASP published the second edition of the OWASP API Security Top 10 in mid-2023, called OWASP API Security Project 2023. It describes the top 10 list as follows:

> *"API Specific Risks*
>
> *The list is built to address security risks that are more specific to APIs.*
>
> *It does not imply that other generic application security risks don't exist in API based applications. For example, we didn't include risks such as "Vulnerable and Outdated Components" or "Injection", even though you might find them in API based applications. These risks are generic, they don't behave differently in APIs, nor [sic] their exploitation is different.*

> *Our goal is to increase the awareness of security risks that deserve special attention in APIs." (OWASP, 2023)*

This Top 10 list is comprised of the following risks (OWASP, 2023):

- API1:2023 – Broken Object Level Authorization
- API2:2023 – Broken Authentication
- API3:2023 – Broken Object Property Level Authorization
- API4:2023 – Unrestricted Resource Consumption
- API5:2023 – Broken Function Level Authorization
- API6:2023 – Unrestricted Access to Sensitive Business Flows
- API7:2023 – Server Side Request Forgery
- API8:2023 – Security Misconfiguration
- API9:2023 – Improper Inventory Management
- API10:2023 – Unsafe Consumption of APIs

Development teams can use this Top 10 list to learn about the common mistakes that developers make that create security risks and avoid them. Cybersecurity teams can use this Top 10 list to inform the types of web application and API attacks to monitor and block. Entire books have been written on OWASP Top 10 lists, and OWASP provides a lot of guidance on their website, so I won't try to duplicate that work in this chapter. But let's look at the top two risks in detail to give you insight into what they are and how to mitigate them.

Broken object-level authorization

According to OWASP, this API vulnerability is "extremely" common, thus it sits in the top spot on the Top 10 list.

Let's start with an example. An employee wants to check their work schedule for the week using their employer's web application. The employee installs their employer's app on their mobile device so they can check their work schedule from any place, at any time. The application also stores users' personal information, such as their full name, address, phone number, Social Security number, and banking information. Employees can use the application to change this information when they need to and make scheduling requests. When the employee starts the app on their mobile device, it prompts them for a username and password to log in. The app then sends an API request to the scheduling web application running on their employer's web server. The request contains the employee's employee ID so that the application can look up their schedule and share it with them.

This application seems simple enough, but let's see how attackers can use broken object-level authorization to get unauthorized access to data.

How do attackers use this type of vulnerability?

In this example, the web application running on the employer's web server accepts a request via an API from the employee's mobile device, with the "object ID" set to the employee's employee ID in the request. The web application uses that object ID to query a backend database for the schedule associated with that employee ID and then returns the schedule to the user's mobile app that requested it.

The issue here is that the application didn't first check whether the user using the mobile app was authorized to access the schedule for that particular employee. That is, the application didn't perform object-level authorization – the developers assumed that since the user had a valid username and password, any API request from their mobile app would be valid and authorized. In other words, the web application running on the employer's web server would happily process any API request for any employee's schedule, as long as the user was authenticated and the API request had a properly formatted object ID.

The risk is that an attacker who has access to one compromised user account for the application can manipulate the object IDs in API requests to get access to all employees' schedules. This type of attack is typically easy to perpetrate, especially when object IDs sent in API requests, in this case, employee IDs, are predictable. It wouldn't be difficult to predict employee IDs if they were all six digits long and issued in sequential order. An attacker with access to a compromised account could send a series of API requests incrementing the object ID by 1. Every time the object ID turns out to be a valid employee ID, the API will return the schedule for that employee to the attacker. Recall that this is exactly how the data breach via the insecure API happened in the scenario I described in *Chapter 1*.

Once attackers have fine-tuned the API request for their attack, they can choose to exfiltrate data from the insecure API very quickly or take a "low-and-slow" approach to minimize the chances of their illicit activity being detected and shut down. In such attacks, attackers might choose to exfiltrate data, or they could alter or delete it if the API allows it. Attacks on the integrity of data can be challenging to detect and recover from. This type of vulnerability could also enable the full takeover of impacted accounts, depending on the application.

You might wonder how the attacker got access to a compromised account in the first place. Remember, attackers typically gain initial access via the cybersecurity usual suspects. In this case, the attacker could have used social engineering, such as a smishing text message, to trick the user into disclosing their username and password. Or the user could have used the same password as they do for all their online accounts, and it has ended up on the large lists of compromised credentials from past breaches that attackers have accumulated. This dramatically increases the odds that attackers' password-spray attacks on the employer's web server will be successful. The attacker could be a disgruntled employee who has turned into an insider threat and sold their credentials to attackers or is perpetrating attacks themselves.

In my experience, when security teams flag this type of vulnerability for development teams before it is exploited, developers typically have two naive retorts as they resist the recommendation to fix their code:

- "*No one would do that type of attack*"
- "*Attackers wouldn't have the expertise to do that*"

However, there are reasons this type of vulnerability tops OWASP's Top 10 list – it's common and easy to exploit, making it popular with attackers. Next, I'll provide some guidance on how to prevent a broken object-level authorization vulnerability.

Mitigation

The following non-exhaustive list contains some of the ways that broken object-level authorization vulnerabilities and related attacks can be mitigated:

- **Implement proper authorization**: Applications should have authorization mechanisms that enable the application to check whether users are authorized to perform actions.
- **Authorization checks**: Every time an authenticated user attempts to perform some action in the application, the authorization mechanism should be used to check whether the user has permission to do so. Don't simply assume that since the user was authenticated or authorization was previously checked, the user is authorized to perform the action they are attempting, for example.
- **Least privilege**: Ruthlessly apply the principle of least privilege by ensuring every user has only the privileges to perform the functions required. To do this, every new user account should have the absolute least privileges in the application, and more privileges should be granted to those accounts as needed. This means the so-called "birthrights" of applications' users are designed with security in mind, not to minimize work for application administrators. **Role-based access control** (**RBAC**) is a mechanism that makes this easy for application administrators.
- **Avoid predictable values**: Don't use easy-to-predict or incremental values such as employee IDs or phone numbers in API requests; use **globally unique identifiers** (**GUIDs**) instead.
- **Constantly test security assumptions**: Don't "set and forget" this control. If your development teams are constantly updating their applications, test to ensure that the authorization mechanisms in applications are working as expected in production. This

minimizes the time between an update that inadvertently breaks the authorization and its detection and remediation. Don't wait until there's a security incident to discover the issue.

- **Enforce multi-factor authentication (MFA)**: The key to this attack was that the attacker was able to use a compromised account to send API requests. Enforcing phishing-resistant MFA on all user accounts makes this harder. It also provides mathematically provable non-repudiation for insiders who perpetrate this type of attack.
- **API motherhood and apple pie**: Always have API request monitoring and rate limiting configured. This won't stop this type of attack, but it will potentially slow it down and help operations and security teams detect it early. API management platforms offer rich sets of such capabilities.

> Tip
>
> OWASP offers a free authorization cheat sheet to help:
>
> `https://cheatsheetseries.owasp.org/cheatsheets/Authorization_Cheat_Sheet.html`

Next, let's look at broken authentication vulnerabilities.

Broken authentication

This is #2 on the OWASP API Security Top 10 list. Like broken object-level authentication, which we discussed earlier, this type of vulnerability is common and relatively easy to exploit. Broken authentication is a vulnerability category that includes several different vulnerabilities, any of which can help attackers gain complete control of users' accounts, exfiltrate their account information, and perform actions while impersonating them. The key is for developers and operations staff to implement controls that make it harder for attackers to attack the authentication mechanisms their applications rely on.

How do attackers use this type of vulnerability?

Attackers leverage a range of tactics to attack the authentication mechanisms that applications rely on, including the following:

- **Guess weak passwords**: Applications that allow users to set easily guessed passwords make it easy for attackers to compromise accounts.

- **Use default credentials**: Attackers compromise administrator accounts using default credentials that vendors release with their applications, and their customers don't change in production – for example, username "admin" and password "admin."
- **Brute-force attacks**: The application allows attackers to continually guess the password for a single account until a valid password is discovered. This type of attack is typically automated.
- **Credential-stuffing attacks**: The application allows attackers to use username and password pairs in continual login attempts until a valid username and password are found. This type of attack is typically automated. Massive lists of vulnerabilities, such as valid usernames and passwords from past breaches, are available on the internet for this purpose. This attack can be especially effective when users use the same passwords across multiple applications and internet services because attackers get valid passwords to all of them when one of them is breached.
- **Attack password reset mechanism**: The application doesn't confirm the current password before allowing users to change the current password, email addresses, and other mechanisms used to reset account passwords.
- **Exposed sensitive authentication details**: Applications that send user authentication details (tokens and passwords) in URLs make it easy for attackers to find and leverage this information to take over accounts.
- **Weak protection for authentication secrets**: Applications that leverage unencrypted, plaintext passwords or weak encryption keys can enable unauthorized access to applications.
- **Token validation issues**: Attackers take advantage of applications that don't validate the authenticity of tokens or their expiration dates or accept unsigned tokens.

This list is not exhaustive. There are many other tactics that attackers can use to overcome poorly implemented authentication mechanisms. These are likely the most common attacks on applications and systems. Remember the old saying: "*attackers don't break in, they log in.*" This is why broken authentication is #2 on OWASP's Top 10 list. Given this, let's discuss some of the ways to mitigate this type of vulnerability and some of the associated attacks.

Mitigation

The following non-exhaustive list provides several ways to mitigate broken authentication vulnerabilities and attacks that use them:

- Start by cataloging the authentication flows for your APIs. You have a better chance of success if you know all the ways API authentications happen, including web and mobile. Catalog the mechanisms each API leverages for authentication.

- Developers shouldn't develop their own authentication mechanisms – use industry-standard mechanisms. This practice prevents well-intentioned developers from unwittingly introducing new vulnerabilities into their authentication processes and allows them to invest their time in other areas that have not already benefited from decades of industry rigor.
- User accounts should be protected by MFA so that even if their passwords are known by attackers, they can't access user accounts without also possessing the other factors.
- Always have API query monitoring and rate limiting configured. This won't stop these types of attacks, but it will potentially slow them down and help operations teams and security teams detect them early. API management platforms offer rich sets of such capabilities.
- Consider using "advanced bot" protection offered by WAF vendors to detect and blunt password-spraying and brute-force attacks. These services typically leverage algorithms that detect and blunt automated attacks from botnets and attackers' malicious infrastructures.
- Passwords cannot be relied on to protect enterprises' data and systems by themselves, but if your application uses them, ensure it enforces long (15 characters), complex passwords, and does not allow the use of known compromised passwords or variants of old passwords.

I used to believe that account lockout mechanisms to slow down brute-force and password-spray attacks weren't needed if 15-character passwords were enforced. Mathematics tells us that attackers shouldn't be able to guess a password that long in any useful period of time. But it turns out that attackers have all sorts of shortcuts to dramatically reduce the amount of time required to derive users' passwords. Attackers have access to huge networks of systems with GPUs optimized for password-cracking calculations in the cloud. This enables them to crack the weakest passwords in stolen Active Directories (`ntds.dit` files) within minutes.

Predictable human behavior that leads some users to use the same passwords across internet services, reuse old passwords, or use simple variants of old passwords gives attackers a big head start in guessing their current passwords. Those huge lists of compromised passwords available on the internet, combined with other tools, such as *cracklib* and *passwdqc*, will likely enable attackers to overcome traditional assumptions about password strength for some subset of user accounts. Subsequently, I recommend enforcing account lockouts for a short duration after a small number of failed login attempts, as this will introduce friction into these attacks.

> **Tip**
>
> OWASP offers a free authentication cheat sheet to help:
>
> https://cheatsheetseries.owasp.org/cheatsheets/Authentication_Cheat_Sheet.html

I hope this dive into broken authentication and broken object-level authorization gave you a taste for the types of vulnerabilities APIs commonly have and the attacks that target them. Visit OWASP's website to learn more about the OWASP Top 10 API Security Risks and access more resources: `https://owasp.org/API-Security/editions/2023/en/0x11-t10/`.

Summary

This chapter examined API security through a CISO and enterprise risk lens, emphasizing why APIs have become one of the most critical, and most targeted, components of modern digital systems. It introduced APIs, explained how web APIs function, and highlighted how their ubiquity, scale, and complexity make them a prime attack surface for threat actors.

A central theme of this chapter was that you cannot bolt on API security after deployment. Instead, it must be embedded throughout the SDL, with strong alignment to Zero Trust principles, including assume breach, explicit verification, and least privilege. Key development practices such as privacy by design, threat modeling, security training, and the use of a cybersecurity risk register were presented as high-return investments that help organizations prevent self-inflicted vulnerabilities and manage unavoidable risks transparently.

We explored the API threat landscape, using recent industry data to show the scale, frequency, and nature of attacks against web applications and APIs. A key takeaway is that most API attacks exploit well-known weaknesses, not novel techniques, making them largely preventable with disciplined engineering and governance.

Finally, the chapter introduced the OWASP API Security Top 10, with a deeper dive into broken object-level authorization and broken authentication, the two most common and impactful API vulnerabilities. Through concrete examples, the chapter illustrated how these flaws are exploited and provided practical mitigation guidance that development, security, and operations teams can apply immediately.

In the next chapter, we'll examine what some CISOs and cybersecurity teams consider a cybersecurity threat – governments.

References

- NIST. (n.d.). *Application Programming Interface (API)*. Retrieved from NIST Glossary: https://csrc.nist.gov/glossary/term/Application_Programming_Interface.
- Akamai. *State of Apps and API Security 2025, Vol. 11, Issue 02, 2025*. Retrieved from https://www.akamai.com/site/en/documents/state-of-the-internet/2025/akamai-web-application-attacks-and-api-attacks-report.pdf.
- Cloudflare. (2024). *2024 API Security & Management Report*. Retrieved from https://cf-assets.www.cloudflare.com/slt3lc6tev37/34fZmoyhTkkjr06Z1zB8jb/9b9d8cbcac8472a510808642466e4ed3/Cloudflare-2024-API-Security-Management-Report.pdf.
- Salt. (n.d.). *State of API Security Report 2025*. Retrieved from https://content.salt.security/state-api-report.html.
- Microsoft Corporation. (n.d.). *Security Development Lifecycle (SDL) Practices*. Retrieved from https://www.microsoft.com/en-us/securityengineering/sdl/practices.
- Information and Privacy Commissioner of Ontario. (January 2018). *Privacy by Design*. Retrieved from https://www.ipc.on.ca/sites/default/files/legacy/2018/01/pbd-1.pdf.
- OWASP. (2023). *OWASP API Security Top 10 – Methodology and Data*. Retrieved from https://owasp.org/API-Security/editions/2023/en/0xd0-about-data/.
- OWASP. (2023). *OWASP Top 10 API Security Risks*. Retrieved from https://owasp.org/API-Security/editions/2023/en/0x11-t10/.

Get this book's PDF version and more

Scan the QR code (or go to `packtpub.com/unlock`). Search for this book by name, confirm the edition, and then follow the steps on the page.

UNLOCK NOW

Note: Keep your invoice handy. Purchases made directly from Packt don't require an invoice.

8

Friend or Foe? The Roles Governments Play in Cybersecurity

> Note
>
> **Chapter disclaimer**
>
> This chapter discusses cybersecurity governance, government policy, and risk management using publicly available sources and the author's professional judgment. References to governments, agencies, or organizations reflect reported information, legal interpretations, and opinion at the time of writing and should not be construed as allegations of unlawful conduct except where explicitly stated and attributed. This material is informational only and does not constitute legal advice.

I spent most of the preceding chapters of this book examining different types of cybersecurity threats in detail. These threats include vulnerabilities in software and hardware, malware such as Trojans and worms, various types of ransomware extortion schemes, internet-based threats such as phishing and **Distributed-Denial-of-Service** (**DDoS**) attacks, and attacks on **Application Programming Interfaces** (**APIs**) and web applications. CISOs and security teams manage their cybersecurity programs to measure and mitigate all of these threats. However, many CISOs and security teams also focus on one other type of cybersecurity threat—governments.

In this context, in the US, CISOs and security teams tend to focus on nation-state threat actors, sponsored by governments such as the **People's Republic of China** (**PRC**), the Russian

Federation, the Islamic Republic of Iran, and the **Democratic People's Republic of Korea (DPRK)**.

However, outside the US, some organizations view certain US government legal and intelligence authorities as presenting cybersecurity-related risks. CISOs of these organizations aren't typically worried about the risk of US government-sponsored threat actors attacking them the way they are with the PRC or DPRK. However, many organizations outside the US perceive US legal authorities—such as warrants, subpoenas, **National Security Letters (NSLs)**, **Foreign Intelligence Surveillance Act (FISA)** court orders, and the **Clarifying Lawful Overseas Use of Data (CLOUD)** Act—as mechanisms that can compel access to sensitive data under certain circumstances. This has led to a proliferation of regulations in the **European Union (EU)** and other countries that seek to control the flow of their data outside their borders, including to and from the US. This has also led to US-based companies being fined billions of dollars for insufficient compliance with EU regulations.

In this chapter, I'll explain the roles that governments play in cybersecurity and why they are viewed as threats by many organizations. I'll describe the cybersecurity tension that exists between the US and the EU, drawing on my experience working as a cybersecurity advisor at both Microsoft and **Amazon Web Services (AWS)**. During the years that I lived in Europe, I had thousands of conversations with representatives of governments and European-based firms about cybersecurity, regulatory compliance, data residency, data sovereignty, the PATRIOT Act, the CLOUD Act, and other related topics. From these conversations, I learned a lot about the European perspective on privacy. This is central to understanding why the US government's legal and intelligence authorities are considered to present cybersecurity-related risks by so many organizations outside the US. I'll also offer some guidance to CISOs who seek to protect their organization's data from the threat that governments pose.

Before we dig into these super interesting topics, let me provide a little background on my exposure to them.

Background information

In my career, among other experiences, I have been fortunate enough to work as one of the most senior cybersecurity advisors at both Microsoft and AWS. I led teams of cybersecurity advisors at both of these companies. In these roles, I met with literally thousands of organizations all over the world. I learned so much through these discussions.

When I worked as Microsoft's global chief security advisor, I traveled the world meeting with CISOs and security teams to give threat intelligence briefings and discuss how we could help their cybersecurity programs. I would spend weeks at a time in Europe, Africa, Asia, and South America. I also hosted the CISOs of Microsoft's biggest accounts at Microsoft headquarters in Redmond, Washington. I learned so much from spending time with these people and listening to how they thought about threats, risk, mitigations, and cybersecurity. Many of the things I learned from them have informed my own thinking about cybersecurity. The collective wisdom of these CISOs has been incredible.

Initially, I spent most of my time with private sector customers who were focused on protecting company data, assets, and, ultimately, their shareholders' value. Then I started meeting more and more public sector organizations and learned that their challenges were a lot more complex and arguably more important than developing products and services for markets, creating meaningful brands, maximizing profit, and driving growth. Some examples of public sector challenges include issues related to elections, taxation, education, food supply chain safety, and national defense.

When I joined AWS as their worldwide public sector security and compliance leader for **Europe, the Middle East, and Africa** (**EMEA**), my family and I moved to London, UK. In this role, my full-time job was advising federal and provincial/state governments, pan-European institutions, national security agencies, healthcare and educational institutions, non-profit organizations, federal banks, and other public sector verticals across EMEA. Over the next two and a half years, I traveled to two or three cities a week in EMEA to meet with public sector organizations to discuss cybersecurity. I spent a lot of time in cities that were the centers of government for their countries or regions, such as London, Paris, Brussels, The Hague, Berlin, Stockholm, Helsinki, and Bern. Later, I relocated back to AWS headquarters in Seattle, Washington, where I worked as AWS' worldwide public sector security and compliance leader. I led a geographically dispersed team that worked with governments in Asia, Oceania, South America, Europe, the Middle East, Africa, Canada, and the US.

In the next role I had in my career, as vice president of trust and cyber risk at T-Mobile, I had the opportunity to serve as a member of the president of the United States' **National Security Telecommunications Advisory Committee** (**NSTAC**). The subcommittee was tasked with developing recommendations for the president on improving national cybersecurity. We developed a report for President Biden focused on incentivizing and measuring the adoption of cybersecurity best practices among critical infrastructure providers. I had the opportunity to work with luminaries and senior leaders from across the cybersecurity industry, including the **Cybersecurity and Infrastructure Security Agency** (**CISA**). It was an amazing experience.

One of the things I learned from all these conversations is that governments play a myriad of roles in cybersecurity. CISOs and security teams cannot simply treat all governments as threats because they rely on them for many things.

> Note
>
> When it comes to cybersecurity, many of the CISOs I advised relied on governments to help them achieve their objectives by setting and regulating industry security

> standards, while others looked to governments as a source of threat intelligence, guidance, and protection; yet other CISOs viewed governments as threats to their organizations.

What role do governments really play in cybersecurity? After thousands of conversations with private and public sector organizations around the world about cybersecurity, I thought I'd share some insights that might help answer this question.

The following topics will be covered in this chapter:

- The roles governments play in cybersecurity
- Governments as cybersecurity threats
- The threat of lawful government access to data

The roles governments play in cybersecurity

Most federal, state, provincial, and large municipal governments organize themselves into departments, divisions, agencies, ministries, and other organizational units. These different parts of each government help them function by dividing roles and responsibilities among them.

It is important to be aware that some parts of a government might pursue their agendas in ways that potentially conflict with other parts of the government. For example, an agency with some responsibility for public safety might participate in industry efforts to reduce vulnerabilities in software and drive awareness among consumers to keep their systems up to date. Driving down the number of vulnerabilities in the products that consumers use and keeping consumers' systems patched means less criminal exploitation of citizens, less crime for law enforcement to manage, fewer criminal cases in the courts, less associated costs to society, and so on. But in another part of the same government that has some responsibility for national security, they are proactively trying to discover new vulnerabilities and buy new vulnerabilities from other security researchers. Instead of reporting vulnerabilities to the vendors that can fix them, like the public safety agency and the industry both recommend, some government agencies have acknowledged retaining undisclosed software vulnerabilities for intelligence or national security purposes, a practice that has generated ongoing public policy debate. It is important to recognize that both of these contrasting agendas are important and support citizens' pursuit of happiness.

Although it might seem innocuous, referring to a government as a simple, single entity instead of a group of individual departments or ministries with different, sometimes conflicting charters often leads to some overly simplistic conclusions in a cybersecurity context. In my experience, this tended to be especially true of statements made about the US government by security professionals outside the US. Once they deemed "the US government" to be a threat to their organization, that simplistic thinking meant that every government department and every private sector firm doing business with the government was suspect at best. It was guilt by association—software, hardware, cloud services, and encryption technologies—all suddenly became untrustworthy simply because the entire US government was labeled as untrustworthy and a threat. I had this conversation with so many CISOs in EMEA. I'll dive into this topic in more detail later in this chapter.

Let's take a closer look at some of the roles that governments play in cybersecurity.

Governments as cybersecurity market participants

The economies of most countries rely on governments as major sources of spending and employment. Governments require IT and cybersecurity. All government departments and agencies must have the people, processes, and technologies required to forward their charters and to protect, detect, respond to, and recover from modern-day threats. To do this, they must procure a lot of the same technologies as companies operating in the private sector. The combination of these factors typically gives governments immense purchasing power.

While governments procure lots of technologies and cybersecurity capabilities, they also require technical expertise to develop, deploy, and operate these capabilities. Governments are major employers of IT and cybersecurity professionals and compete with the commercial sector for professional talent.

Since governments' purchasing power is quite significant, they typically require their supply chain partners to comply with specific standards. Let's examine governments' roles as standards bodies next.

Governments as standards bodies

Because governments procure so many goods and services, it is important that they set and maintain standards to ensure measurable minimum levels of functionality and quality in their procurements. Sometimes governments accomplish this through formal standards bodies, and sometimes formal standards bodies aren't involved. Although governments are not formal standards development organizations, they often act as *de facto* standard setters by embedding technical requirements into procurement contracts and then reinforcing them through regulation. In cybersecurity, this happens when governments require vendors to meet specific security baselines, such as standardized incident reporting, supply chain controls, or maturity certifications, as a condition of selling to the state. In some cases, they use acquisition rules such as the US **Federal Acquisition Regulation** (**FAR**) to make those requirements mandatory across agencies. Because governments are among the largest buyers of technology, these procurement requirements effectively set market-wide norms, pushing private companies to adopt the same cybersecurity practices even outside government contracts. Over time, regulatory follow-through and enforcement further solidify these requirements into widely accepted "standards," even when they did not originate in a traditional standards organization.

Many CISOs and security teams rely on the **National Institute of Standards and Technology** (**NIST**) for cybersecurity standards. NIST is a non-regulatory federal science agency within the US Department of Commerce. NIST operates as a bureau of the Department of Commerce and is led by a director, who is appointed by the president and confirmed by the Senate. It is primarily funded through congressional appropriations as part of the Department of Commerce budget.

This is how NIST describes cybersecurity standards:

> *"The goal of cyber security standards is to improve the security of information technology (IT) systems, networks, and critical infrastructures. A cyber security standard defines both functional and assurance requirements within a product, system, process, or technology environment. Well-developed cyber security standards enable consistency among product developers and serve as a reliable metric for purchasing security products." (Scarfone, K., Benigni, D., and Grance, T., 2009)*

Most of the CISOs I advised over the years typically used NIST cybersecurity standards in at least three ways:

- First, if their organization did business with the US federal government or aspired to, they would select one or more NIST standards that were applicable to the product or service they wanted to sell, and work to comply with the requirements of those standards.
- Many CISOs leveraged NIST standards to ensure their security control sets were complete. They would compare the controls implemented in their IT estates and their settings to NIST standards to ensure that they didn't have obvious gaps. NIST **Special Publication** (**SP**) 800-53 is an example of a standard (control catalog) used in this manner. Security teams take their current control set, which includes technical controls, policies, procedures, and operational practices, and map them to the relevant SP 800-53 controls. NIST supports this exercise by publishing the control catalog in spreadsheet and machine-readable formats, explicitly to enable comparison, mapping, and analysis. Once this mapping is complete, CISOs review unmapped or weakly mapped controls to identify obvious gaps in coverage.

- Some organizations take this one step further and use compliance with standards as their enterprise cybersecurity strategy. I'll discuss this strategy, what I call "compliance as a security strategy," in detail in *Chapter 10, Cybersecurity Strategies*.
- CISOs also use NIST standards to prove that they are managing their security programs in a way that complies with stringent US government cybersecurity standards, whether they do business with the US government or not. If these CISOs experienced a data breach, they could point to their NIST standards compliance as evidence that they weren't an outlier and that they were managing their cybersecurity program responsibly and in alignment with others in the industry. This could help blunt the potential negative reputational and financial damage and regulatory outcomes that accompany data breaches so often today.

Of course, the US government isn't the only government that publishes cybersecurity standards. This is a good place to insert a joke for geeks: "The good thing about standards is that there are so many to choose from" (Tanenbaum, Andrew S. n.d.). Governments in other countries besides the US also have bodies that publish cybersecurity standards for organizations in their regions and their supply chain partners. A great example is the **Federal Office of Information Security** (known as the **BSI**) in Germany. I had the opportunity to meet with representatives of the BSI a few times over the years. Germany is the single largest market in the EU. This means that the standards published by the BSI are very influential in Germany and the EU. Subsequently, big global technology providers such as Microsoft and AWS, among others, as well as technology providers based in Western Europe, pay close attention to the guidance and standards that the BSI publishes. The BSI describes their mission this way:

> *"We assume responsibility for all issues related to information security. We protect the federal administration from cyber attacks and monitor the current cyber security situation nationally and internationally, investigate and assess existing security risks and anticipate the impact of new developments. Based on this knowledge, we support citizens, companies and authorities at federal, state and municipality level with services in the core areas of information, consulting, operational protection and development, including standardisation [sic] and certification." (BSI, n.d.)*

Most large, developed countries have some office or agency responsible for developing cybersecurity standards for their national government's use or more broadly across industries within their borders. However, in many cases, I've found that they are similar to NIST SP 800-53. This is another reason why so many of the CISOs I know adopt NIST SP 800-53 as the standard they try to conform to.

Next, let's examine governments' role as enforcers.

Governments as enforcers

Governments provide at least two different functions in their role as enforcers, in a cybersecurity context—regulators and law enforcement. Let's briefly look at both functions.

Regulators

We just discussed governments as standards bodies. As we discussed, standards are important not only for government procurement purposes but also for the broader markets. However, just because a standards body publishes some standards, it doesn't necessarily mean that private and public sector organizations will spend the time, effort, or budget to conform to those standards. Typically, there must be some sort of clear benefit or incentive for organizations to change the way they operate.

Sometimes, despite the right incentives, markets or industries are too slow to change by themselves, and a "market failure" occurs. In cases such as this, governments use the tools they have in their toolboxes; in the case of cybersecurity, this includes *regulation*. Regulations typically implement restrictions that industries must conform to. Examples of regulated standards for cybersecurity purposes include the **California Consumer Privacy Act** (**CCPA**), the **Federal Information Security Modernization Act** (**FISMA**) in the US, and the **General Data Protection Regulation** (**GDPR**) in the EU and the **European Economic Area** (**EEA**). To give you a sense of the teeth that the European Parliament put into GDPR, failure to comply with it could result in a fine of up to €20 million or up to 4% of annual worldwide revenue, whichever is larger. More than 2,600 administrative fines related to GDPR non-compliance have been levied since enforcement started in 2018, the largest of which were given to large high-tech companies such as Meta (€1.2 billion), Amazon (€746 million), and LinkedIn (€310 million) (GDPR Enforcement Tracker, n.d.). Avoiding these administrative fines is the incentive for private and public sector organizations to comply with this regulation.

Ransomware is another area where regulation is changing market behavior. In the wake of the Colonial Pipeline Company ransomware attack that shut down a pipeline system in the Eastern US for several days in May 2021, calls for new regulation resulted. Here are some examples of regulatory-related activity resulting from this one cyberattack:

- The US **Federal Energy Regulatory Commission** (**FERC**) renewed calls for mandatory cybersecurity standards for the US' pipeline infrastructure (Federal Energy Regulatory Commission, 2021).
- The US **Environmental Protection Agency** (**EPA**) issued a second emergency fuel waiver meant to further alleviate fuel shortages in US states impacted by the pipeline shutdown (U.S. Environmental Protection Agency, 2021). This waived requirements for low-volatility conventional gasoline and **Reformulated Gasoline** (**RFG**) in a dozen states.

- The Department of Homeland Security approved a temporary Jones Act waiver to ease oil supply constraints in targeted parts of the US eastern seaboard (U.S. Department of Homeland Security, 2021). This waiver enabled the transport of oil products between the Gulf Coast and the East Coast of the US.
- The US **Department of Transportation** (**DOT**) allowed states to use Interstate highways to transport overweight loads of gasoline and other fuels, to help address shortages (U.S. Department of Transportation, 2021).
- The President of the United States signed an *Executive Order on Improving the Nation's Cybersecurity* (The White House, 2021). This executive order had a profound effect on how the US federal government was expected to manage cybersecurity moving forward, including all its suppliers in its supply chain.

Typically, a cyberattack on a US-based company would not result in this significant regulatory activity. However, in this case, the convergence of a high-profile ransomware attack, a multi-million-dollar ransom demand that was paid potentially in violation of US Department of the Treasury's **Office of Foreign Assets Control** (**OFAC**) regulations, an attack on a company in an industry that was deemed US critical infrastructure, the interruption of nearly half the gas supply in the Eastern seaboard of the US, and the attackers' location in Russia contributed to this crescendo of government activity. At the core of all this activity was the uncertainty around the attackers' motivation—was it simply profit or was it a state-sponsored attack? Even after the attack was attributed to attackers in Russia using DarkSide ransomware, their motivations were still suspect. As I mentioned in *Chapter 5*, *The Evolution of Malware*, the attackers issued a statement to try to make their motivations clear and de-escalate the situation.

Notice how some of the regulatory activity that resulted from this ransomware attack were unintended consequences, easing or waiving regulatory restrictions to blunt the effects of the attack. What if the opposite was also possible? What if attackers could use regulations to attack their victims? For example, in a completely hypothetical scenario, suppose a criminal noticed that a large, multi-national company was recording personal information of their customers, which included residents of the EU, in an immutable blockchain ledger. Although the company could have completely legitimate business reasons for doing this, the immutable property of the database they chose to use makes it impossible for the company to delete customer information if an EU-based customer requested it. Realizing that this misstep likely violates GDPR, and it could cost the company tens of millions of dollars in administrative fines, the criminal issues a ransom demand to the company in exchange for their promise not to file a privacy complaint with a data protection authority in the EU. Interesting conundrum!

Law enforcement

The other function that governments perform in their role as enforcers is law enforcement. Law enforcement is intended to deter crime by imposing consequences, such as arrest and prosecution, that most people seek to avoid. However, just as the internet has leveled the playing field for individuals and small businesses to compete with large enterprises, it has also enabled crime at a scale and speed not previously possible. The internet allows individuals or small groups to simultaneously target vast numbers of people, businesses, and institutions with relative anonymity and low cost. This creates an unprecedented form of asymmetry, where small numbers of attackers can impact far larger organizations across jurisdictions. Traditional law enforcement mechanisms have proven far less effective as a deterrent to cybercrime under these conditions, and this structural mismatch may be one of the contributing factors.

AI makes this even easier for the criminally minded by reducing the technical skills they need to perpetrate such attacks. An individual can perpetrate a large DDoS attack or a drive-by download attack against very well-resourced organizations and be successful.

There are at least a few reasons why this is the case. First, the internet is a global network that allows attackers to perpetrate their attacks from almost anywhere in the world against victims located almost anywhere. Criminals have used borders to evade arrest and prosecution for centuries, and the internet enables this on a vast scale. For example, given the current situation with Russia invading Ukraine and all the sanctions placed on it, it is highly unlikely that Russia will prioritize investigating cybercrimes against organizations in Western countries. The same can be said for the DPRK (North Korea), Iran, and the PRC (China).

The second reason why traditional law enforcement has been a less effective deterrent to serious cybercrime is the challenge of strong attribution. If victims don't know who is attacking them, how can they determine what a proportional response is? Which government (national, regional, or municipal) should help with the response, and which specific ministry, department, or agency should lead? Is the attack a matter of national security where intelligence agencies and the military should be involved or a criminal matter? If it is a criminal matter, which law enforcement agencies should be involved—national police (such as the FBI in the US), regional (state/provincial) police, or municipal police? Which jurisdiction should lead the investigation—where the victims are located, where the attack originated from, or where it is suspected that the attackers are based?

Still, if law enforcement doesn't make a serious effort to investigate, arrest, and prosecute cybercriminals, then there really is no deterrent at all. Of course, law enforcement in most major countries takes cybercrimes very seriously because of the consequences for victims, their communities, industry, and society.

In the US, several federal agencies have authority to bring cybercrime-related law enforcement actions, including the **Federal Bureau of Investigation** (**FBI**), the **Securities and Exchange Commission** (**SEC**), the Secret Service, the US Attorney's Office, the **Internal Revenue Service** (**IRS**), the **Federal Trade Commission** (**FTC**), and US **Immigration and Customs Enforcement** (**ICE**). Because of the scale of the problem, none of these organizations can investigate all cybercrimes where US citizens are victimized. The FBI has published some guidelines for the voluntary sharing of cyber-incident information between **State, Local, Tribal, and Territorial** (**SLTT**) law enforcement organizations and the US federal government; these guidelines provide insight into the types of incidents that the FBI is willing to engage in:

> *"In particular, a cyber incident should be reported if it:*
>
> *May impact national security, economic security, or public health and safety.*
>
> *Affects core government or critical infrastructure functions.*
>
> *Results in a significant loss of data, system availability, or control of systems.*
>
> *Involves a large number of victims.*
>
> *Indicates unauthorized access to, or malicious software present on, critical information technology systems.*
>
> *Violates federal or SLTT law." (US Federal Bureau of Investigation, n.d.)*

The FBI's guidelines further note that "no matter which 'door' SLTT law enforcement uses, information is shared within the federal government to provide an appropriate response while protecting citizens' privacy and civil liberties under the law" (US Federal Bureau of Investigation, n.d.).

In 2020, the FBI discussed a new strategy to fight cybercrime that would "impose risk and consequences on cyber adversaries" (Wray, C. 2020). They further stated the following:

> *"We've got to change the cost-benefit calculus of criminals and nation-states who believe they can compromise U.S. networks, steal U.S. financial and intellectual property, and hold our critical infrastructure at risk, all without incurring any risk themselves..." (Wray, C. 2020)*

The pillars of this strategy include the following (US Federal Bureau of Investigation, n.d.):

- **Unique authorities**: Leverage both criminal and counterintelligence authorities to fight cyber-criminals and foreign threat actors to compromise US networks

- **World-class capabilities**: Adapt to cyber-threats by leveraging new, innovative investigative techniques, developing new tools, and recruiting a world-class workforce
- **Enduring partnerships**: Leverage the FBI's strengths to enable their partners to defend systems, perform attribution, impose sanctions on threat actors, and pursue adversaries overseas

Of course, other major countries also have ministries, departments, and agencies involved in law enforcement action resulting from cybercrimes. Most of the governments I advised had multiple agencies that shared the responsibility of investigating and responding to cybercrimes. Sometimes it was obvious that there were disagreements between agencies regarding jurisdictions and the scope of their various cyber operations.

Consequently, the way in which governments organize themselves to fight cybercrime is also new and evolving. In my experience, it was rare to find a federal or regional law enforcement organization or regulatory authority that wasn't trying to position itself to be more relevant in the fight against cybercrime, especially when new government agencies were being created for this specific purpose. Some open questions in many of these cases seemed to be, are new agencies needed because the old institutions aren't effective at fighting cybercrime? Do new approaches to crime require new approaches to law enforcement? How does AI change this? The answers to these questions are likely to continue to play out well into the future.

I realize I have barely scratched the surface of this subject, and I haven't discussed law enforcement as a potential cyber-threat yet. I'll discuss this later in this chapter. If you view governments, and law enforcement more specifically, as a cyber-threat, keep reading!

Next, let's look at governments as defenders.

Governments as defenders

The White House published a National Cybersecurity Strategy in March 2023. This strategy outlines how the federal government, together with its allies and partners, will build a "digital ecosystem together, making it more easily and inherently defensible, resilient, and aligned with our values" (The White House, March 2023). The strategy outlines five pillars that include the following:

- Defend critical infrastructure
- Disrupt and dismantle threat actors
- Shape market forces to drive security and resilience
- Invest in a resilient future
- Forge international partnerships to pursue shared goals

The strategy states that "criminal syndicates now represent a threat to the nation security, public safety, and economic prosperity of the United States and its allies and partners" (The

White House, March 2023). Let's look at three of the functions that governments provide when playing the role of defender in a cybersecurity context: **public safety**, **national security**, and **military**.

Public safety

Most major national governments have a department or ministry that is responsible for public safety. Sometimes, public safety is a subset of the work a government department does. Over the past 25 years, many countries have created national cybersecurity centers that include public safety, among other things, in their charters. Examples include the **National Cyber Security Centre** (**NCSC**) in the UK, the **National Cyber Security Centre of Ireland** (**NCSC**), the **French National Cybersecurity Agency** (**ANSSI**), the Canadian Centre for Cyber Security, the **Cyber Security Agency** (**CSA**) of Singapore, the Australian Cyber Security Centre, and CISA in the US. All of these government organizations are at least in part responsible for driving awareness of cybercrime and related threats among government departments, industries, and citizens. Some of them also provide cybersecurity advisory services to government departments to help protect critical infrastructure. Some of these organizations are responsible for managing incident response processes and managing **Cyber Threat Intelligence** (**CTI**) programs for government departments. Some of these centers were created by merging parts of **National Computer Emergency Response Teams** (**CERTs**), large government departments with cybersecurity charters, law enforcement, and intelligence agencies together. The combination of the capabilities that these stakeholder organizations bring together is much greater than any of them could develop only by themselves. Typically, the one function they lack within their departments is enforcement, which they partner with law enforcement agencies to perform.

Additionally, most of these cybersecurity centers offer educational opportunities to public and private sector organizations and to citizens. The idea here is that a better-educated society will be able to recognize cyberattacks more readily, report them, and hopefully help mitigate them. I had the opportunity to attend some of these events, such as the UK NCSC's CYBERUK security event.

National security

Another function governments fulfill in their role as defenders is national security. I've found this to be a loaded term that means different things to different people. Governments have been gathering intelligence and practicing military espionage to understand their adversaries' and allies' military capabilities for as long as governments have existed. Today, this includes both cyber-offensive and cybersecurity capabilities.

Intelligence gathering is typically a function of national security organizations. Since military secrets are highly classified, they are typically protected using encryption and key management technologies and processes. Therefore, intelligence agencies also have deep expertise in signals intelligence (gathering intelligence by intercepting signals between systems) and cryptography, so they might intercept and access classified information that they otherwise would not have access to, as well as protect their own governments' information more effectively.

Here's how the US **National Security Agency** (**NSA**) describes their mission:

> *"The National Security Agency/Central Security Service (NSA/CSS) leads the U.S. Government in cryptology that encompasses both signals intelligence (SIGINT) insights and cybersecurity products and services and enables computer network operations to gain a decisive advantage for the nation and our allies." (National Security Agency, n.d.)*

The NSA also provides combat support for the US military and its allies. We discussed governments as standards bodies earlier in the chapter. The NSA is another example of this, as they "set common protocols and standards so that our military can securely share information with our allies, NATO and coalition forces around the world. Interoperability is a key to successful joint operations and exercises" (National Security Agency, n.d.).

The NSA also focuses on cybersecurity:

> *"NSA Cybersecurity prevents and eradicates threats to U.S. national security systems, with an initial focus on the Defense Industrial Base (DIB) and the improvement of the nation's weapons' security. At its core, NSA Cybersecurity aims to defeat the adversary through the seven core missions and functions:*
>
> *- Provide intelligence to warn of malicious cyber threats and information U.S. Government (USG) policy*
>
> *- Develop integrated Nuclear Command & Control Systems threat, vulnerability, risk, and cryptographic products & services*
>
> *- Release integrated threat, assessment, and mitigation/protection products for the Department of Defense (DoD) and USG customers*
>
> *- Execute high-assurance cryptography and security engineering*
>
> *- Offer combined defense/offence operations with key government partners*
>
> *- Enable the defense of the agency's networks in coordination with NSA's Chief Information Officer*
>
> *- Promote information sharing to support the agency's cybersecurity mission"*

(National Security Agency, n.d.)

Of course, other countries have organizations dedicated to national security as well. In the UK, domestic intelligence and foreign intelligence services are provided by **Military Intelligence, Section 5** (**MI5**) and **Military Intelligence, Section 6** (**MI6**), respectively. There are numerous other stakeholders and participants, including **Government Communications Headquarters** (**GCHQ**), the NCSC, and the Home Office.

In Canada, national security organizations include the **Canadian Security Intelligence Service** (**CSIS**), the **Royal Canadian Mounted Police** (**RCMP**), the **Communications Security Establishment** (**CSE**), and the Canadian Centre for Cyber Security, among others.

The Israeli Intelligence Corps has Unit 8200. This is said to have a similar charter as the NSA in the US, specializing in **Signals Intelligence** (**SIGINT**). Many former Unit 8200 members have gone on to establish successful cybersecurity start-ups and to lead major companies.

There are also international partnerships that focus on the national security of partner countries. A great example of this type of organization is the **Five Eyes**. This is an alliance between Australia, Canada, New Zealand, the UK, and the US, focusing on intelligence sharing (Office of the Director of National Intelligence, n.d.). The idea here is that sharing intelligence across five countries provides these governments with better visibility of potential threats.

> Note
>
> Many of the CISOs and security teams I advised considered the aforementioned intelligence agencies as threats to their organizations. I discuss intelligence gathering, such as SIGINT, as cyber-threats later in this chapter.

One of the reasons governments have national security intelligence programs is to provide their military forces with information needed to deter war and defend their borders and their allies. Let's discuss this function next.

Military

The US **Department of Defense** (**DoD**), is the largest agency in the US government and the largest employer in the world, employing over 1.3 million people on active duty and 742,000 civilian personnel (US Department of Defense, n.d.). The president requested a $849.8 billion budget for the DoD in 2025 (Office of the Under Secretary of Defense (Comptroller)/Chief Financial Officer, March 2024). The armed forces of the US include the Army, Marine Corps, Navy, Air Force, Space Force, and Coast Guard. There are two reserve components—the Army National Guard and the Air National Guard. The stated mission of the DoD is to "provide the military forces needed to deter war and ensure our nation's security." This includes both offensive and defensive aspects of cybersecurity. With so many people, DoD performs a myriad of cybersecurity functions.

For example, **USCYBERCOM** is a unified **Combatant Command** (**CCMD**) of the DoD. It is responsible for coordinating military operations involving computer networks and digital infrastructure to defend DoD networks, support military missions, and protect US national interests from cyber threats. The DoD has 11 of these unified CCMDs organized around geographic locations or around specific functions. Cyber is one of those functions. USCYBERCOM is called a "joint command" because it is composed of several parts of the armed forces, including the Army, Navy, Air Force, and Marines. The NSA is also a partner in this joint command. The DoD's vision for USCYBERCOM is as follows:

> *"Achieve and maintain superiority in the cyberspace domain to influence adversary behavior, deliver strategic and operational advantages for the Joint Force, and defend and advance our national interests." (United States Cyber Command, April 2018)*

USCYBERCOM's strategy paper *Achieve and Maintain Cyberspace Superiority Command - Vision for US Cyber Command* really is a great read. It is very well written and describes the cybersecurity challenge through a military lens. I think the following two excerpts from this paper summarize their strategy. The first excerpt describes USCYBERCOM's view of the challenge that adversaries pose:

> *"The security of the United States and our allies depends on international stability and global prosperity. The spread of technology and communications has enabled new means of influence and coercion. Adversaries continuously operate against us below the threshold of armed conflict. In this 'new normal,' our adversaries are extending their influence without resorting to physical aggression. They provoke and intimidate our citizens and enterprises without fear of legal or military consequences. They understand the constraints under which the United States chooses to operate in cyberspace, including our traditionally high threshold for response to adversary activity. They use this insight to exploit our dependencies and vulnerabilities in cyberspace and use our systems, processes, and values against us to weaken our democratic institutions and gain economic, diplomatic, and military advantages...Aggressive non-state actors like terrorists, criminals, and hacktivists pose lesser threats than states but can still damage our military capabilities and critical infrastructure, as well as endanger American lives." (United States Cyber Command, April 2018)*

This second excerpt from the paper focuses on how USCYBERCOM operates to address these cyber threats to the US:

> *"Superiority through persistence seizes and maintains the initiative in cyberspace by continuously engaging and contesting adversaries and causing them uncertainty wherever they maneuver. It describes how we operate—maneuvering seamlessly between defense and offense across the interconnected battlespace. It describes where we operate—globally, as close as possible to adversaries and their operations. It describes when we operate—continuously, shaping the battlespace. It describes why we operate—to create operational advantage for us while denying the same to our adversaries...Through persistent action and competing more effectively below the level of armed conflict, we can influence the calculations of our adversaries, deter aggression, and clarify the distinction between acceptable and unacceptable behavior in cyberspace. Our goal is to improve the security and stability of cyberspace. This approach will complement the efforts of other agencies to preserve our interests and protect our values. We measure success by our ability to increase options for decision makers and by the reduction of adversary aggression." (United States Cyber Command, April 2018)*

Of course, the US isn't the only military force in the world that has been developing offensive and defensive capabilities. In 2013, cybersecurity firm Mandiant publicly attributed a series of cyber-intrusions affecting US organizations to a group it identified as Unit 61398 of China's **People's Liberation Army** (**PLA**), based on its analysis (CBS News, 2013). In 2014, the US Department of Justice indicted five members of Unit 61398 on charges related to intellectual property theft.

Unit 61398 is believed to be just one of many such PLA groups in China that focus on cybersecurity capabilities. Military units of various other countries allegedly conducting cyber operations have popped up in news feeds ever since. The DPRK (North Korea) and Iran are two such examples.

I hope that provides a little insight into some of the ways that some countries are leveraging their military forces for cybersecurity purposes. When viewed through this lens, it becomes obvious that governments have developed and are using offensive cyber capabilities as part of their national defense strategies.

Now that we've discussed the roles governments play, this makes conversations about governments as threats potentially much more productive. I've found that when security teams can articulate specific threats, only then can specific mitigations be developed with confidence. A cyberattack by the US military is quite a different risk than a law enforcement agency serving an organization with a search warrant. Getting specific about the threats and risks you really need to be concerned with helps you better prioritize resources and avoid investing in mitigating risks that are ridiculously vague or improbable.

Tip

The more specifically we can define a threat, the clearer it becomes as to whether we can mitigate, transfer, or accept the risk it poses to our organization.

Next, I'll dive into the two specific government cybersecurity threats that I discussed with CISOs most often: **nation-state threat actors** and **lawful government access to data**. Note that I'll be discussing legal concepts and mechanisms, regulations, and laws in this section of the chapter.

Note

I'm not an attorney, and I'm not offering legal advice. I recommend that you consult a qualified attorney for advice on the topics you read in this chapter. Additionally, what is written in this chapter and in the entire book are my own personal opinions and not those of my current employer or any former employers. With that said, let's get started!

Governments as cybersecurity threats

Governments weren't always viewed as cybersecurity threats by CISOs. However, 2013 was a turning point. Two widely publicized events happened during that year.

First, in February 2013, Mandiant published the aforementioned report that identified Unit 61398 of the PLA as the source of hundreds of cyberattacks on US companies (CBS News, 2013). Mandiant labeled the group **APT1**, short for **Advanced Persistent Threat 1**. They attributed cyberattacks to APT1 going as far back as 2006. They even published pictures of the building they alleged this group worked in, in Shanghai. Mandiant's report stated that APT1 had stolen hundreds of terabytes of data from 141 of the organizations they had attacked between 2006 and 2013 (Mandiant, Feb 1, 2013). APT1 maintained access to their victims' networks once they had it. The report states the following:

> *"...we found that APT1 maintained access to the victim's network for an average of 356 days. The longest time period APT1 maintained access to a victim's network was at least 1,764 days, or four years and ten months. APT1 was not continuously active on a daily basis during this time period; however, in the vast majority of cases we observed, APT1 continued to commit data theft as long as they had access to the network." (Mandiant, Feb 1, 2013)*

> **Note**
>
> The revelation that China was using its military to attack civilian businesses and organizations in the US changed the way people perceived China and their relationship with the Western world. Many organizations continue to view China through this lens.

Another dramatic event occurred in June 2013. At the time, I worked at Microsoft as the director of trustworthy computing. In those days, customers typically wanted threat intelligence briefings from me, and to discuss threats to their Windows system networks, but that all changed in June 2013. That's when Edward Snowden gave a trove of classified documents to journalists that revealed details about some of the US government's intelligence-gathering programs. After the first news stories were published, a global news cycle ensued. Predictably, numerous large international public and private sector organizations were suddenly interested in whether their data was safe in the hands of technology companies that were based in the US. At that time, the underlying question from international customers was whether US-based companies were obligated to give US intelligence agencies whatever data they wanted. Since then, many other details of US intelligence agencies' activities have come to light, and questions about the role of US-based technology firms in these activities have continued for years.

Fast-forward four or five years, and I was working for AWS, based in London, in the UK. My job was to advise public sector organizations on how to modernize their cybersecurity strategies and show them how cloud computing can help. One topic that public sector organizations across Europe and the Middle East wanted to talk about was government access to data, more specifically, US government access to data.

Meanwhile, when I'd go back to the US and talk to customers and colleagues there, they were largely unaware of the debate that had been going on in Europe about the trustworthiness of US technology providers. They simply didn't think that the US' closest allies in Europe would be concerned about using their tech products and services. After all, the US' position as the dominant technology innovation leader in the world meant that they would follow **World Trade Organization** (**WTO**) trade rules and never steal intellectual property from other countries in the way that China was accused of doing. If they crossed that line, they would have more to lose than any other country in the world. What was the big deal?

Until I lived in London and talked to European-based companies and public sector organizations every day, I too hadn't fully realized the extent to which the trustworthiness of the US had been severely tarnished. I came to learn about the collective consciousness among

Western Europeans that resulted from the cumulative impact of a series of revelations about US intelligence agencies' operations in Europe. Let me give you some examples:

- Classified documents leaked by Edward Snowden triggered a series of news cycles revealing the scope and scale of some US intelligence-gathering programs. The White House initially defended these programs but later apologized for their overreach (Gidda, 2013).
- Documents disclosed by Edward Snowden and subsequently reported by journalists prompted widespread scrutiny and criticism of US intelligence surveillance programs, including their scope and oversight (Ball, 2013).
- WikiLeaks published a series of classified reports that they called "Espionnage Élysée." The reports revealed that the NSA had allegedly intercepted the communications of three different French presidents, cabinet ministers, and the French ambassador to the US (James Regan, 2015). WikiLeaks also alleged that "the US has had a decade-long policy of economic espionage against France, including the interception of all French corporate contracts and negotiations valued at more than $200 million" (WikiLeaks, 2015).
- WikiLeaks published a series of classified documents that they called "Euro Intercepts" that alleged the NSA had intercepted the communications of senior German government officials, including the German chancellor at the time, Angela Merkel, her senior staff, as well as staff of former chancellors going back almost two decades. According to WikiLeaks, "WikiLeaks so far shows the NSA explicitly targeted for long-term surveillance 125 phone numbers for top German officials and did so for political and economic reasons, according to its own designations" (WikiLeaks, 2015).

These revelations, and others, damaged the relationship the US had with their European allies. Unfortunately, this is not limited to Europe; Brazil (WikiLeaks, 2015) and Japan (WikiLeaks, 2015) are two other examples. For US technology companies caught in the middle, this developed into a quagmire of distrust. Every time I walked into a meeting with a company or a public sector organization in France, Germany, or Switzerland, I knew this collective consciousness would be generating serious headwinds. Just how strong were those headwinds? During some of the public events I spoke at, I'd survey audiences with a question such as this:

Which one of these threats is your organization most concerned about? Select only one answer.

1. Attackers from China
2. Attackers from Russia

3. US government access to data using a valid warrant or subpoena
4. Other

In Western Europe, between 2017 and 2020, typically 80–90% of the people I surveyed selected answer 3. If this surprises you, you probably live in the US. If you live in Germany, France, or another location in the EU or the EEA, this likely will not surprise you at all.

The good news for CISOs, their security teams, compliance and risk management professionals, and other executives is that these dramatic revelations have led to levels of transparency that can help them quantify and manage the risk associated with government access to data. I'll explain how to do this, but first, we need to unpack this issue a bit more because typically, there are a lot of assumptions, generalizations, and misconceptions about it. In fact, there are a few different scenarios that are typically conflated in conversations about government access to data; these scenarios do not have the same risk (probability and impact) for every organization.

Thinking about the US government as a single entity with a single agenda isn't accurate and typically isn't helpful to CISOs, security teams, and executives who are serious about understanding and mitigating risks to their organizations. In the thousands of conversations I've had about governments as threats, many CISOs, security teams, and executives tended to conflate three different scenarios. Let's look at each of them in depth.

The signals intelligence scenario

The SIGINT scenario is where government agencies gather intelligence by intercepting and analyzing communications and electronic signals, potentially employing cryptanalysis on encrypted communications. SIGINT programs were the focus of many of the dramatic WikiLeaks announcements. The reality is that this type of intelligence gathering is employed by many major governments around the world (Wikipedia, n.d.). The US uses this type of intelligence gathering to get visibility into its adversaries' evolving military capabilities (National Security Agency Central Security Service, n.d.). Keep in mind that the US shares intelligence with the other members of NATO and the Five Eyes SIGINT sharing alliance (National Security Agency Central Security Service, n.d.).

Many of the executives I met expressed concern about the information leaked by WikiLeaks because it suggests that some of the targets of SIGINT have been world leaders, their staff, and the public at large via mass data collection programs. Getting them to put their personal outrage aside and articulate how they plan to manage the risk that such programs pose to their organizations was sometimes challenging.

Many executives told me that simply not using US-based technology providers was the way they planned to mitigate this threat. Since these US intelligence programs, their objectives, their targets, and their capabilities are all classified, managing such risks with so little information can be challenging. However, choosing not to use US-based technology providers would not mitigate the threat that these programs pose in any way because SIGINT doesn't depend on its targets using technology that is designed, manufactured, or operated by US-based technology firms.

Nation-state threat actors (unlawful government access to data)

Nation-state threat actors, also called state-sponsored threat actors, that perpetrate cyberattacks are involved in unlawful government access to data. Microsoft offers this definition:

> *"Nation-state actor*
>
> *A cyber threat actor sponsored or directed by a government, often targeting other countries for espionage, disruption, or influence." (Microsoft, 2025)*

The US CISA provides this description:

> *"As a nation, we are seeing continued cyber and physical threats targeting critical infrastructure Americans rely on every day. Nation-state actors and nation-states sponsored entitiespose [sic] an elevated threat to our national security. On the cyber front these adversaries are known for their advanced persistent threat (APT) activity:*
>
> *The Chinese government—officially known as the People's Republic of China (PRC)—engages in malicious cyber activities to pursue its national interests including infiltrating critical infrastructure networks.*
>
> *The Iranian government—officially known as the Islamic Republic of Iran—has exercised its increasingly sophisticated cyber capabilities to suppress certain social and political activity, and to harm regional and international adversaries.*
>
> *The North Korean government—officially known as the Democratic People's Republic of Korea (DPRK)—employs malicious cyber activity to collect intelligence, conduct attacks, and generate revenue.*

> *The Russian government—officially known as the Russian Federation—engages in malicious cyber activities to enable broad-scope cyber espionage, to suppress certain social and political activity, to steal intellectual property, and to harm regional and international adversaries." (CISA, n.d.)*

In this scenario, government agencies or their affiliates perpetrate cyberattacks to steal data from organizations or their supply chain vendors, as opposed to obtaining a valid court order to compel such information legally. Military and economic espionage are typical motivations that are associated with this scenario. Foreign political influence and disinformation campaigns are also employed in the pursuit of foreign policy objectives to confuse civilian populations and destabilize governments. In the case of the DPRK (North Korea), it is widely believed that they are using profits from ongoing cyberattacks to fund their nuclear weapons program, among other things (NCC Group, June 30, 2022).

Stuxnet is widely attributed by researchers and media reports to the US and Israeli intelligence agencies, though neither government has formally acknowledged involvement.

Various governments, security researchers, and courts have alleged that state-sponsored actors linked to China have engaged in cyber-enabled economic espionage, including the unauthorized acquisition of intellectual property. Of course, there are examples of other countries allegedly performing acts of espionage as well; examples include France (Ewing, 2014), the United Arab Emirates (Christopher Bing, 2019), Saudi Arabia (Mark Mazzetti, 2019), Israel (Mehul Srivastava, 2019), and Russia (US Department of Justice, June 28, 2010).

Microsoft has published data on the activities of the numerous nation-state threat actors it tracks. According to Microsoft, in the 12 months between July 2020 and June 2021, the top three countries most targeted by nation-state threat actors were the US, Ukraine, and the UK (Microsoft, October 2021). The most targeted sectors during this time included government, **Nongovernmental Organizations** (**NGOs**), a category called "other," and education. The top targets changed slightly three years later, in the 12 months between July 2024 and June 2025, which included the US, Israel, and Ukraine. The most targeted sectors during this period included IT, research and academia, and government.

Let me break this data down a little further for you, using data published in the Microsoft Digital Defense Report 2025. *Table 8.1* shows how each nation-state threat actor focused its attacks in the period of July 2024 to June 2025:

Country	Top 5 sectors targeted	Top 5 countries targeted	Summary of insights
China	Information technology	United States	Chinese nation-state threat actors are increasingly targeting IT, government, and NGOs to expand China's influence and counter Western interests, with a notable rise in activity focused on Thailand.
	Government	Thailand	
	Think tanks/ NGOs	Taiwan	
	Manufacturin g	Korea	
	Research and academia	Japan	
Iran	Information technology	Israel	Compromising the IT sector provides Iran with potential supply chain access to other industries. Israel is Iran's top rival in the region.
	Research and academia	United States	
	Government	United Arab Emirates	
	Transportatio n	India	
	Consumer retail	Greece	
Russia	Government	United States	Russia's targets are primarily NATO countries and Ukraine. The sectors they attack have intelligence value to them during wartime.
	Research and academia	United Kingdom	

Country	Top 5 sectors targeted	Top 5 countries targeted	Summary of insights
	Think tanks/ NGOs	Ukraine	
	Information technology	Germany	
	Energy	Belgium	
North Korea	Information technology	United States	The DPRK's targets reflect their objectives to generate revenue and collect intelligence.
	Research and academia	Italy	
	Think tanks/ NGOs	Australia	
	Consumer retail	United Kingdom	
	Finance	Switzerlan d	

Table 8.1 – The top sectors and countries each nation-state threat actor focused on between July 2024 and June 2025 according to the Microsoft Digital Defense Report 2025 (Microsoft, 2025)

IT was the primary target for most of these nation-state threat actors, presumably because of the valuable intellectual property it possesses, as well as that industry's unique position in so many organizations' supply chains. Compromising a major IT vendor could provide pathways into many other organizations. Research and academia were also common targets of these nation-state threat actors, presumably because of their valuable intellectual property.

Notably absent from these top sector target lists is the defense sector; this absence does not indicate a lack of importance, but rather reflects that it is well defended, politically sensitive, and strategically approached through indirect paths. Nation-state actors target the defense sector by exploiting IT and cloud providers, stealing research from academia, compromising the defense industrial base, and targeting people rather than core military networks (Defense

Counterintelligence and Security Agency [DCSA], 2025; Google Threat Intelligence Group, 2026).

How do CISOs manage the risks associated with adversaries that have massive or unlimited budgets, can sequester any technical expertise they need, and infiltrate their organizations from within? It turns out that these nation-state threat actors accomplish initial access using one or more of the Cybersecurity Usual Suspects that I outlined in *Chapter 1, How Enterprises Get Hacked*. Investing in the cybersecurity fundamentals to mitigate the Cybersecurity Usual Suspects helps organizations defend themselves whether the attackers are criminals or governments.

For organizations that are legitimately concerned about US-sponsored threat actors, there are both legal and technical mitigations available to them. An example of legal mitigation is the US Constitution. If a US law enforcement or intelligence agency simply steals data that is stored inside the US, if caught, they are subject to the laws of the US, including potential prosecution and prison time for those involved in the crime. But if the same data is stored outside the US, in the heart of Bavaria, Germany, for example, there is no US Constitution protection there. Non-US organizations that are serious about managing the risk of unlawful US government access to data actually circumvent some of the legal mitigations against this threat by demanding that their data stay resident in their countries. This is counterintuitive for many of the executives I've talked to because most executives intuitively equate "keeping data in my country" with "reducing foreign government risk," when in reality it often does the opposite for US-sponsored access concerns. However, if executives can remove the emotions that have permeated the collective consciousness of Western Europeans, they can devise risk management strategies that are much more effective.

In the case of unlawful government access to data, most private and public sector organizations have higher-priority risks to manage, but others, such as intelligence agencies, militaries, witness protection programs, and commercial organizations with high-value intellectual property that is seriously at risk from acts of espionage, unlawful government access to data is a priority risk that they will invest considerable resources into mitigating. Strong encryption and effective key management are crucial technical controls in this scenario that I'll discuss later in this chapter, as well as in *Chapter 10*.

Now, let's look at the third scenario that executives tend to conflate when discussing governments as threats.

Lawful government access to data scenario

Lawful government access to data is a scenario where a law enforcement or intelligence agency gets a valid court order compelling an organization or a vendor in its supply chain to provide specific evidence that is in their possession, for use in a criminal investigation.

For most of the large private and public sector organizations that I have discussed in relation to government access to data, the risk they fear isn't that they might receive a subpoena or warrant that compels them to provide evidence in a criminal matter. After all, most of these organizations have general counsels and legal departments that already manage such legal requests. Over time, some of these legal departments have developed processes to manage such requests and surface them to senior management, oversight committees, and their boards of directors. This allows them to manage the potential domestic legal risks posed by such law enforcement requests. It also helps them manage potential international legal consequences where obeying local laws could compel them to potentially break international laws or regulations such as GDPR. It also allows them to manage other risks, such as the reputational risk to their organization.

The risk that these organizations are actually worried about is that one of their partners or a vendor in their supply chain would receive a court order for evidence in a criminal matter and they wouldn't be notified. If they don't know that law enforcement is trying to compel the "production of data" that they are responsible for, then they can't employ their own attorneys and their own internal legal processes to manage the request; essentially, a risk to their organization exists that they don't know about and subsequently can't manage.

> **Note**
>
> The terms "production of data" and "production of evidence" are industry legal lingo that mean finding and turning over the requested data to the requester.

You might wonder how often a scenario such as this happens. In the US, gag orders prevented recipients of court orders from informing the target of the investigations about said order.

An example of an FBI gag order can be seen in the NSL served to Calyx Internet Access, which legally prohibited the recipient from disclosing the existence of the request (Boghani, 2015):

> *"In 2004, Merrill, then the CEO of a New York-based web-hosting firm called Calyx, received a so-called national security letter. The letter asked for what Merrill described as a significant array of information from the company, but because of a gag order, he was legally barred from even speaking about it." (Boghani, 2015)*

However, Microsoft filed a lawsuit against the US Department of Justice in April 2016 to stop the practice. As Brad Smith, Microsoft's general counsel and president, explained, "When we filed our case, we explained that in an 18-month period, 2,576 of the legal demands we received from the US government included an obligation of secrecy, and 68 percent of these appeared to be indefinite demands for secrecy. In short, we were prevented from ever telling a large number of customers that the government had sought to access their data" . As a result of this lawsuit, the US Department of Justice changed its practices so that such gag orders are the exception to the rule, not the norm.

It turns out that once I broke down these three different scenarios for the executives I was advising, they were then most concerned about lawful government access to data. Outside the US, they were always concerned about lawful *US government* access to data in particular. The prevailing view in Western Europe was that US legal instruments such as the PATRIOT Act and the CLOUD Act expanded the government's ability to compel access to data, a perception that contributed to heightened concern and mistrust.

The good news for CISOs faced with mitigating this threat for their organizations is that there is far more transparency and data available on the risk of lawful government access to data than just that of the previous two scenarios I have discussed. This makes it easier for CISOs and other executives to understand the risk and whether their organization should invest resources to mitigate it, transfer it, or accept it. I'll focus the bulk of the rest of this chapter on discussing the risk of lawful government access to data and provide some insights to help you manage it.

Before diving deep into the topic of lawful government access to data, there is one related scenario that straddles lawful and unlawful government access to data that's worth discussing: the commercial lawful intercept scenario.

The commercial lawful intercept scenario

One type of tool that many governments have used to collect evidence and conduct surveillance in serious criminal investigations is **commercial lawful intercept** solutions. Essentially, there is a commercial industry in which private companies develop and sell surveillance software to government agencies, typically for law enforcement or investigative purposes. Much of what is known about this industry and the software they produce is based on research conducted by The Citizen Lab, described as follows:

> *"The Citizen Lab is an interdisciplinary laboratory based at the Munk School of Global Affairs & Public Policy, University of Toronto, focusing on research, development, and high-level strategic policy and legal engagement at the intersection of information and communication technologies, human rights, and global security.*
>
> *We use a 'mixed methods' approach to research combining practices from political science, law, computer science, and area studies. Our research includes: investigating digital espionage against civil society, documenting Internet filtering and other technologies and practices that impact freedom of expression online, analyzing privacy, security, and information controls of popular applications, and examining transparency and accountability mechanisms relevant to the*

> *relationship between corporations and state agencies regarding personal data and other surveillance activities." (The Citizen Lab, n.d.)*

The Citizen Lab's research into the commercial lawful intercept software used by governments for surveillance has had a wide-ranging impact on the industry. According to that research, such software is typically installed on a targeted individual's mobile phone using either one-click or zero-click exploits that leverage previously unknown software vulnerabilities. In the one-click scenario, the target is typically sent an SMS text message with a URL that, when clicked, installs the malware on the phone. In the zero-click scenario, no user interaction is required; once the target mobile device is identified, the malware is installed on the individual's phone without any indication or their knowledge.

Once the commercial lawful intercept software is installed, it is reported to provide the software's operator with extensive access to the device, including passwords; emails; SMS text messages; location tracking; network details; device settings; browser history; contact details; social networks; the ability to monitor phone calls; calendar records; file retrieval capabilities; access to instant messaging, photos, and screenshots; and the ability to turn on the phone's microphone and camera to monitor conversations that occur in the presence of the phone. Infected devices transmit the information collected from the phone back to the software's operator (Marczak, Scott-Railton, et al., 2018).

In August 2016, forensics experts at The Citizen Lab were forwarded a suspicious URL that was originally sent to an award-winning human rights activist in the **United Arab Emirates** (**UAE**) (Marczak, Scott-Railton August 25, 2016). The Citizen Lab tested the URL and discovered that clicking on it could result in the installation of commercial lawful intercept software. Their subsequent investigation found that the installation process involved a chain of zero-day exploits that enabled the compromise of the target's iPhone and the installation of the commercial lawful intercept software (Marczak, Scott-Railton, August 25, 2016). They reported the vulnerabilities to Apple, and CVE IDs were subsequently assigned to the vulnerabilities, including CVE-2016-4657, CVE-2016-4655, and CVE-2016-4656. Apple fixed all three vulnerabilities in the release of iOS version 9.3.5.

Further, operators may seek to discover or acquire new zero-day exploits over time to maintain the operational effectiveness of their products. As a result, remediating these specific vulnerabilities would not, by itself, permanently prevent similar classes of commercial lawful intercept software from operating on iPhones. Apple introduced a new feature on the iPhone called Lockdown Mode to provide a layer of protection for people who may be targets of such attacks. Apple describes this feature as follows:

> *"Lockdown Mode is an optional, extreme protection that's designed for the very few individuals who, because of who they are or what they do, might be personally*

> *targeted by some of the most sophisticated digital threats. Most people are never targeted by attacks of this nature.*
>
> *When Lockdown Mode is enabled, your device won't function like it typically does. To reduce the attack surface that potentially could be exploited by highly targeted mercenary spyware, certain apps, websites, and features are strictly limited for security and some experiences might not be available at all.*
>
> *Lockdown Mode is available in iOS 16 or later, iPadOS 16 or later, watchOS 10 or later, and macOS Ventura or later. Additional protections are available starting in iOS 17, iPadOS 17, watchOS 10, and macOS Sonoma." (Apple, September 15, 2025)*

A question that might be raised is whether some government users of commercial lawful intercept tools consistently limit their use to investigations involving serious crime, terrorism, or clearly defined national security threats.

Both the US government and telecommunications vendors have publicly expressed concerns about the potential misuse of commercial lawful intercept software. In March 2023, President Biden signed an executive order titled *Executive Order on Prohibition on Use by the United States Government of Commercial Spyware that Poses Risks to National Security*. The executive order states the following:

> *"Foreign governments and persons have deployed commercial spyware against United States Government institutions, personnel, information, and information systems, presenting significant counterintelligence and security risks to the United States Government. Foreign governments and persons have also used commercial spyware for improper purposes, such as to target and intimidate perceived opponents; curb dissent; limit freedoms of expression, peaceful assembly, or association; enable other human rights abuses or suppression of civil liberties; and track or target United States persons without proper legal authorization, safeguards, or oversight." (The White House, March 27, 2023)*

The executive order restricts and, in most cases, prohibits US government agencies' use of commercial lawful intercept software and institutes some oversight and transparency of its use.

While many governments continue to assert that commercial lawful intercept software can serve legitimate national security and law enforcement purposes, ongoing reporting, litigation, and policy actions suggest that debates regarding regulation, oversight, and ethical constraints are likely to continue.

With that context established, we will now turn to the scenario for which the most empirical data is available: lawful government access to data.

The threat of lawful government access to data

Law enforcement agencies all over the world seek evidence for use in criminal cases. This is core to the function they play in government and society. Sometimes, the investigative trail they follow leads them to potential evidence that is located overseas. The challenge for law enforcement in these cases is that they need a way to compel the production of evidence from people who are not subject to their local legal jurisdiction. Put another way, the domestic legal mechanisms that law enforcement agencies use to collect evidence in their country won't be sufficient by themselves to enable investigators to collect evidence located in other countries. This challenge for law enforcement isn't a new one. Criminals have sought to cover their tracks and subvert legal processes by crossing jurisdictional boundaries for centuries. This challenge is exacerbated in a world where data can be transmitted across international legal boundaries in a fraction of a second and stored in almost any country in the world, using consumer-grade commodity technologies available to hundreds of millions of people, in many cases, for free. How are law enforcement agencies supposed to successfully conduct investigations into terrorism, espionage, child exploitation, and other serious crimes if they lack the legal tools to request evidence that is stored outside of their country?

To help address this challenge, one of the legal mechanisms that many governments have put in place is **Mutual Legal Assistance Treaties** (**MLATs**). The last time I counted, the US had signed more than 70 MLATs for use in criminal matters with countries around the world (US Department of Justice, April, 2022). Most of these are bilateral treaties, and a few are multilateral, such as with the EU. MLATs have been in place for many years. For example, the current MLAT between the US and Germany was signed in 2003 and entered into force in 2009. Similarly, the current MLAT between the US and France was signed in 2001, the MLAT between the US and the EU was signed in 2003, and the MLAT between Sweden and the US was signed in 2001. These MLATs have been put in place with the stated purpose of enabling cooperation in criminal investigations, as outlined in the letter of transmittal included within each MLAT, examples of which are displayed in the following figures:

108TH CONGRESS *2d Session* — SENATE — TREATY DOC. 108–27

MUTUAL LEGAL ASSISTANCE TREATY WITH GERMANY

MESSAGE

FROM

THE PRESIDENT OF THE UNITED STATES

TRANSMITTING

TREATY BETWEEN THE UNITED STATES OF AMERICA AND THE FEDERAL REPUBLIC OF GERMANY ON MUTUAL LEGAL ASSISTANCE IN CRIMINAL MATTERS, SIGNED AT WASHINGTON ON OCTOBER 14, 2003; AND A RELATED EXCHANGE OF NOTES

NOVEMBER 16, 2004.—Treaty was read the first time, and together with the accompanying papers, referred to the Committee on Foreign Relations and ordered to be printed for the use of the Senate

U.S. GOVERNMENT PRINTING OFFICE
39-118 WASHINGTON : 2004

LETTER OF TRANSMITTAL

THE WHITE HOUSE, *November 16, 2004.*

To the Senate of the United States:

With a view to receiving the advice and consent of the Senate to ratification, I transmit herewith the Treaty Between the United States of America and the Federal Republic of Germany on Mutual Legal Assistance in Criminal Matters, signed at Washington on October 14, 2003, and a related exchange of notes. I transmit also, for the information of the Senate, the report of the Department of State with respect to the Treaty.

The Treaty is one of a series of modern mutual legal assistance treaties being negotiated by the United States in order to counter criminal activities more effectively. The Treaty should be an effective tool to assist in the prosecution of a wide variety of crimes. The Treaty is self-executing.

The Treaty provides for a broad range of cooperation in criminal matters. Mutual assistance available under the Treaty includes: taking the testimony or statements of persons; providing documents, records, and articles of evidence; locating or identifying persons; serving documents; transferring persons in custody for testimony or other purposes; executing requests for searches and seizures; undertaking telecommunications surveillance, undercover investigations, and controlled deliveries; assisting in proceedings related to immobilization and forfeiture of assets, restitution to the victims of crime and collection of fines; and any other form of assistance not prohibited by the laws of the State from whom the assistance is requested.

I recommend that the Senate give early and favorable consideration to the Treaty, and give its advice and consent to ratification.

GEORGE W. BUSH.

Figure 8.1 – Left: the MLAT between the US and Germany signed in 2003 (U.S. GOVERNMENT PRINTING OFFICE, 2004); right: the Letter of Transmittal on page 3 of the MLAT between the US and Germany, which explains the purpose of the MLAT (U.S. GOVERNMENT PRINTING OFFICE, 2004)

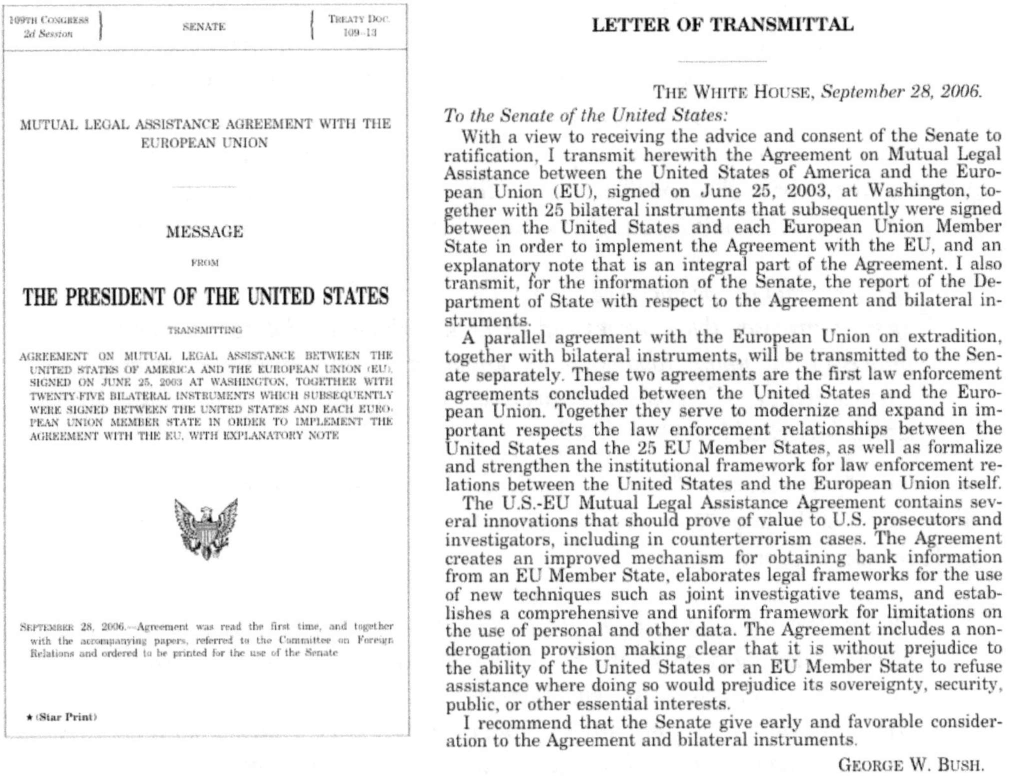

109TH CONGRESS 2d Session | SENATE | TREATY DOC. 109–13

MUTUAL LEGAL ASSISTANCE AGREEMENT WITH THE EUROPEAN UNION

MESSAGE

FROM

THE PRESIDENT OF THE UNITED STATES

TRANSMITTING

AGREEMENT ON MUTUAL LEGAL ASSISTANCE BETWEEN THE UNITED STATES OF AMERICA AND THE EUROPEAN UNION (EU), SIGNED ON JUNE 25, 2003 AT WASHINGTON, TOGETHER WITH TWENTY-FIVE BILATERAL INSTRUMENTS WHICH SUBSEQUENTLY WERE SIGNED BETWEEN THE UNITED STATES AND EACH EUROPEAN UNION MEMBER STATE IN ORDER TO IMPLEMENT THE AGREEMENT WITH THE EU, WITH EXPLANATORY NOTE

SEPTEMBER 28, 2006.—Agreement was read the first time, and together with the accompanying papers, referred to the Committee on Foreign Relations and ordered to be printed for the use of the Senate

★ (Star Print)

LETTER OF TRANSMITTAL

THE WHITE HOUSE, *September 28, 2006.*

To the Senate of the United States:

With a view to receiving the advice and consent of the Senate to ratification, I transmit herewith the Agreement on Mutual Legal Assistance between the United States of America and the European Union (EU), signed on June 25, 2003, at Washington, together with 25 bilateral instruments that subsequently were signed between the United States and each European Union Member State in order to implement the Agreement with the EU, and an explanatory note that is an integral part of the Agreement. I also transmit, for the information of the Senate, the report of the Department of State with respect to the Agreement and bilateral instruments.

A parallel agreement with the European Union on extradition, together with bilateral instruments, will be transmitted to the Senate separately. These two agreements are the first law enforcement agreements concluded between the United States and the European Union. Together they serve to modernize and expand in important respects the law enforcement relationships between the United States and the 25 EU Member States, as well as formalize and strengthen the institutional framework for law enforcement relations between the United States and the European Union itself.

The U.S.-EU Mutual Legal Assistance Agreement contains several innovations that should prove of value to U.S. prosecutors and investigators, including in counterterrorism cases. The Agreement creates an improved mechanism for obtaining bank information from an EU Member State, elaborates legal frameworks for the use of new techniques such as joint investigative teams, and establishes a comprehensive and uniform framework for limitations on the use of personal and other data. The Agreement includes a non-derogation provision making clear that it is without prejudice to the ability of the United States or an EU Member State to refuse assistance where doing so would prejudice its sovereignty, security, public, or other essential interests.

I recommend that the Senate give early and favorable consideration to the Agreement and bilateral instruments.

GEORGE W. BUSH.

Figure 8.2 – Left: the multilateral MLAT between the US and the EU signed in 2003 (U.S. GOVERNMENT PRINTING OFFICE, 2006); right: the Letter of Transmittal on page 3 of the MLAT between the US and the EU, which explains the purpose of the MLAT (U.S. GOVERNMENT PRINTING OFFICE, 2006)

MLATs between the US and other countries provide a way for law enforcement in participating countries to request evidence located in the US and vice versa. An important aspect of how these MLATs work is the legal standard applied to search and seizure requests. To understand this, we need to go back to the founding documents of the US and look at the initial amendments to the Constitution, otherwise known as the Bill of Rights (National Archives, n.d.). This is where civil rights and liberties are defined for citizens of the US. The Fourth Amendment to the US Constitution prohibits unreasonable search and seizure, as follows:

> *"[t]he right of the people to be secure in their persons, houses, papers, and effects, against unreasonable searches and seizures, shall not be violated, and no Warrants shall issue, but upon probable cause, supported by Oath or affirmation, and particularly describing the place to be searched, and the persons or things to be seized." (Cornell Law School, n.d.)*

The concept of "probable cause" has been the focus of much legal debate and numerous court cases since at least the late 1780s, when the Bill of Rights was proposed. One definition of probable cause is as follows:

> *"Probable cause is a requirement found in the Fourth Amendment that must usually be met before police make an arrest, conduct a search, or receive a warrant. Courts usually find probable cause when there is a reasonable basis for believing that a crime may have been committed (for an arrest) or when evidence of the crime is present in the place to be searched (for a search)." (Cornell Law School, n.d.)*

Whether it's a US law enforcement agency or a law enforcement agency in another MLAT country using an MLAT to request data, the standard applied to the request is the US legal standard of probable cause. Put another way, the US will not make an MLAT request or service an MLAT request unless it meets the probable cause standard; this means that MLAT requests must meet the highest legal standard in the world for search and seizure. This nuance provides additional protection for people under investigation in countries where the legal bar for search and seizure is lower than in the US. Subsequently, when foreign investigators submit an MLAT request to the US, it gets evaluated several times. Internationally recognized legal expert and law professor Peter Swire describes the process as follows, using France as an example:

> *"Each successful request is evaluated by the DOJ's Office of International Affairs (OIA), a US Attorney's office, a federal magistrate judge, and then again by the Federal Bureau of Investigation (FBI) and the OIA. The OIA, US Attorney's office, and magistrate judge each review to ensure that enough evidence exists for the type of information sought—a probable cause warrant for content, and a 2703(d) order showing a reasonable and articulable suspicion for much non-content data. After the magistrate judge approves the request, and the company produces the records,*

> *the FBI and OIA review the records so that only data responsive to the request is returned to France, and that no data is included that may violate the US First Amendment, such as prosecution of a political or speech crime."*

All these reviews and evaluations take time. According to White House legal experts, incoming valid MLAT requests to the US take, on average, *10 months* to fulfill, "with some requests taking considerably longer" . In some cases, multiple requests might be required to get the answers investigators are looking for. Using MLATs is simply too slow. I'm sure this is a view shared by the victims of serious crimes as well.

This is the problem that the CLOUD Act tries to solve. Let's examine this next.

The CLOUD Act and the PATRIOT Act

Unfortunately, this poorly chosen acronym has caused a lot of confusion in both the public and private sectors. The CLOUD Act does not just apply to **Cloud Service Providers** (**CSPs**). It applies to a variety of service providers, including email providers, telephone companies, social media sites, and other types of organizations. However, the acronym itself has led many of the executives that I have talked to believe that the CLOUD Act was specifically designed to give the US government unfettered access to data when it's in a US-based service provider's cloud service. This isn't true, but I've seen many foreign competitors of US-based CSPs try to use this confusion to their advantage, telling their customers that it doesn't apply to non-US-based service providers, despite the fact that the CLOUD Act applies to many, if not all, of them as well. *Figure 8.3* presents an excerpt from the CLOUD Act:

2201

DIVISION V—CLOUD ACT

SEC. 101. SHORT TITLE.

This division may be cited as the "Clarifying Lawful Overseas Use of Data Act" or the "CLOUD Act".

SEC. 102. CONGRESSIONAL FINDINGS.

Congress finds the following:

(1) Timely access to electronic data held by communications-service providers is an essential component of government efforts to protect public safety and combat serious crime, including terrorism.

(2) Such efforts by the United States Government are being impeded by the inability to access data stored outside the United States that is in the custody, control, or possession of communications-service providers that are subject to jurisdiction of the United States.

(3) Foreign governments also increasingly seek access to electronic data held by communications-service providers in the United States for the purpose of combating serious crime.

(4) Communications-service providers face potential conflicting legal obligations when a foreign government orders production of electronic data that

Figure 8.3 – The first page of the CLOUD Act (United States Congress, 2018)

The CLOUD Act was signed into law on March 23, 2018. Many of the European executives that I talked to in the first few years after the CLOUD Act was passed described it as the "USA PATRIOT Act 2.0." This was another misconception that non-US-based technology companies liked to play up. However, the 32-page CLOUD Act isn't an amendment or extension of the 10 titles of the **Uniting and Strengthening America by Providing Appropriate Tools Required to Intercept and Obstruct Terrorism** (**USA PATRIOT**) Act that was enacted in October 2001 in the wake of the 9/11 terrorist attacks. Both the PATRIOT Act and the CLOUD Act amend the Stored Communications Act in different ways for different purposes. Title II of the PATRIOT Act focused on enhanced surveillance procedures; it expanded the scope of wiretapping and surveillance orders and enabled the surveillance of packet-switched networks.

This is different from the CLOUD Act, which provides an international legal framework to expedite law enforcement agencies' lawful access to evidence stored overseas. This is referred to as the "production of evidence" in legal parlance, but it is easy to understand why some executives may conclude that the PATRIOT and CLOUD Acts are somehow related, especially if they live in Germany, France, Brazil, Japan, or other places where US intelligence has allegedly intercepted their government leaders' communications. I've seen some non-US-based managed service providers using the PATRIOT Act to convince organizations to buy their services instead of those from US-based providers. These arguments make little sense in this context, as most public and private sector organizations are not involved in terrorism or money laundering to support terrorism. Additionally, key surveillance authorities under Section 215 expired in 2020 (Electronic Frontier Foundation, December 29, 2020).

Among many of the executives and cybersecurity teams that I have met outside the US, there is no doubt that the PATRIOT Act was reviled. The information leaked by Edward Snowden and WikiLeaks did nothing to improve the US' reputation internationally, but CISOs and vendors weren't helping their organizations by perpetuating outdated arguments about ethereal risks; procuring non-US products and services doesn't mitigate the perceived risks. Then and now, CISOs need to get specific about the risks that their organizations really need to manage so that they can decide how to apply the limited resources they have to specific mitigations for those risks.

The CLOUD Act amends the Stored Communications Act, which was passed in 1986. The Stored Communications Act enabled US law enforcement to include electronic communications in their investigations, but it didn't cover internet-related scenarios because the internet was nascent when it was written. Subsequently, it didn't consider scenarios such as internet-based storage or global cloud services. The CLOUD Act modernizes some of the tools given to US law enforcement in the Stored Communications Act and makes it clear that organizations doing business in the US (whether they are based in the US or elsewhere) can be legally compelled to provide data for criminal investigations regardless of where it's stored.

> **Note**
>
> Like the PATRIOT Act, I've seen some non-US-based vendors sow fear, uncertainty, and doubt in the minds of their customers using the CLOUD Act. I've also seen public and private sector organizations based in Europe assert this themselves. The argument that these people make is that using a US-based cloud provider makes it easier for the US government to get access to data because of the CLOUD Act, but this characterization does not provide a complete picture of the Act because it conveniently omits a few key facts.

It is true that US-based telephone companies, email providers, social media companies, CSPs, and other such companies are required to follow the letter of the law in the US, including the CLOUD Act. However, US jurisdiction is not limited to US-based companies. The US has jurisdiction over any company that has "minimum contact" with it. This includes a range of scenarios. For example, a foreign-owned, foreign-based company that has a physical presence in the US, such as a branch office or US headquarters, is subject to US law. If the company has personnel or customers in the US, it's likely subject to US law. In fact, US courts have ruled in the past that simply having a non-US website that US customers visit can bring an organization under US legal jurisdiction. Considering these factors, organizations that are really trying to understand and manage the risks associated with being subject to US legal jurisdiction will need to examine all the vendors that they already have in their supply chains. For enterprises and federal government departments, chances are that the "local" IT vendors, consulting firms, and service providers that they have been using for decades also have a physical presence in the US and/or gain revenue from US customers, which makes them subject to US law, potentially including the CLOUD Act. It doesn't matter if these local vendors have data centers in the heart of Bavaria, Paris, or Stockholm. If they are subject to US jurisdiction because they have the minimum contact with the US, they can be legally compelled to turn over data stored in these data centers for US law enforcement investigations.

> **Note**
>
> When their executives face jail time and their US business interests are threatened because of a failure to comply with valid court orders, businesses tend to cooperate. Not many businesses would abandon their investments in the US market simply to defy a valid court order in a criminal investigation, especially when the legal bar being applied for the search and seizure exceeds their own country's legal standard.

Simply put, organizations that want access to US markets are required to follow the letter of US law, whether the data they have is in the US or not. We haven't seen a mass exodus of German, French, Swiss, or Swedish companies from the US, so European customers of these companies need to accept that the data residency protection arguments forwarded by them are largely hollow. However, this reality isn't necessarily a bad thing, since data residency does not equate to better data security. After all, the physical location of data does not mitigate any of the Cybersecurity Usual Suspects that I discussed at length in *Chapter 1*. Nearly 100% of attacks happen over a network. Whether the data is in a data center in Berlin, Bern, Beijing, or Boston makes no difference to attackers who will likely never have physical access to the infrastructure anyway. Strong encryption and effective key management, supported by other technologies and processes, mitigate unauthorized access to data, not data residency. I will discuss encryption and key management in more depth later in this chapter.

Of course, not everyone agrees that accelerating the production of evidence in criminal investigations by streamlining checks and balances is a good idea, but CISOs and security teams need to put their personal feelings aside and determine whether the CLOUD Act poses an incremental risk that their organizations should invest in mitigating. To answer this question, they need data to determine the probability and impact of law enforcement actions. But before looking at that, there's one more US legal instrument that European CISOs were always concerned about when I discussed cybersecurity with them: the Foreign Intelligence Surveillance Act. I'll explain that next.

FISA, GDPR, the EU-US Privacy Shield, and Schrems

The US FISA was enacted in 1978. Here is a description of it from the US Library of Congress:

> *"FISA provides a statutory framework for government agencies to obtain authorization to gather foreign intelligence by means of (1) electronic surveillance, (2) physical searches, (3) pen registers and trap and trace (PR/TT) devices (which record or decode dialing, routing, addressing, or signaling information), or (4) the production of certain business records...Following revelations regarding widespread privacy violations by the federal government during the Watergate era, Congress enacted FISA to govern foreign intelligence information collection. FISA currently defines foreign intelligence information as information relating to a foreign power or that generally concerns the ability of the United States to protect against international terrorism, potential attacks by foreign powers or agents of foreign powers, or international drug trafficking. Though Congress initially limited FISA to regulating government use of electronic surveillance, Congress has amended FISA to regulate other intelligence-gathering practices, such as physical searches, the use of PR/TT devices, and compelled production of certain types of business records." (Kuersten, Andreas, December 17, 2024)*

There are two FISA courts that adjudicate the government's requests to use FISA: the **Foreign Intelligence Surveillance Court** (**FISC**) and the **Foreign Intelligence Surveillance Court of Review** (**FISCR**). FISCR is an appeals court for FISC.

It turns out that FISA is problematic for organizations in member states in the EU and the EEA. If you live in the US, you might wonder why public and commercial sector organizations in the EU and EEA would be concerned about FISA orders. After all, if they aren't involved in terrorism, money laundering to fund terrorism, or espionage, why would they be concerned about US laws established to surveil such activities?

The answer to this question is a bit complicated, but I'll try to summarize the situation, which means I'll be glossing over a lot of detail. Since the answer to this question is intertwined with GDPR, let me start by giving you some background on GDPR that will help you understand how it is related to FISA.

GDPR regulates the cross-border transfer of personal information outside of the EU and the EEA. I've heard many American executives state that GDPR doesn't apply to them because they don't do business in the EU or EEA. However, GDPR is extra-territorial, meaning it doesn't just regulate data transfer between EU member states—it applies worldwide. It applies to both the commercial sector and the public sector. Subsequently, many countries have enacted their own similar local versions of GDPR to ensure their industries comply with it.

It is important to understand that the purpose of GDPR is to enable cross-border commerce while protecting people's personal information. Some of the security professionals in the US with whom I've discussed GDPR assume that it tries to prevent the transfer of data, but its purpose is to regulate the transfer of data:

> *"Directive 95/46/EC of the European Parliament and of the Council seeks to harmonise [sic] the protection of fundamental rights and freedoms of natural persons in respect of processing activities and to ensure the free flow of personal data between Member States." (The European Parliament and The Council Of The European Union, 2016)*

Under GDPR, the transfer of the personal data of EU data subjects to countries outside the EEA (called third countries) is not permitted, unless specific requirements are met or the third country has a GDPR **adequacy decision**. Data can be transferred between the EEA and the third country without any extra safeguards when the third country has an adequacy decision. The adequacy decision indicates that the third country has levels of data protection and privacy that meet the EU's standards. Only 14 countries in the world have one of these adequacy decisions, including Andorra, Argentina, Canada, the Faroe Islands, Guernsey, Israel, the Isle of Man, Japan, Jersey, New Zealand, the Republic of Korea, Switzerland, the United

Kingdom, the US (commercial organizations participating in the EU-US Data Privacy Framework), and Uruguay.

> **Note**
>
> You can see the current list of countries with adequacy decisions on the European Commission's website: `https://ec.europa.eu/info/law/law-topic/data-protection/international-dimension-data-protection/adequacy-decisions_en/`.

For organizations in countries that do not have an adequacy decision from the European Commission, the other two ways that EU data subject personal information could be transferred out of the EEA are **Standard Contractual Clauses** (**SCCs**) and the EU-US Privacy Shield. Failure to comply with GDPR could lead to administrative fines of up to €20 million or 4% of the organization's annual worldwide revenue from the previous year, whichever of these is larger; this gives this regulation enough potential to garner a lot of attention. Subsequently, every private sector and public sector customer I advised in Europe after May 2018, when enforcement of GDPR started, wanted to discuss the best practices for complying with GDPR. Since then, there have been thousands of GDPR administrative fines imposed. As I mentioned earlier in this chapter, American big tech companies, including Meta, Amazon, and LinkedIn, have levied some of the largest fines—in some cases, hundreds of millions of dollars (GDPR Enforcement Tracker, n.d.). The top GDPR violations cited for the fines include the following (GDPR Enforcement Tracker, n.d.):

- 785 fines levied for "Insufficient legal basis for data processing"
- 721 fines levied for "Non-compliance with general data processing principles"
- 514 fines levied for "Insufficient technical and organisational [sic] measures to ensure information security"
- 276 fines levied for "Insufficient fulfilment of data subjects rights"
- 202 fines levied for "Insufficient fulfilment of information obligations"

In the top fine category, over €3 billion in fines were collected because the organizations that were fined allegedly didn't have a legal basis to collect, use, or share personal data. GDPR Article 6 defines several lawful bases to process personal data, including the following (The European Parliament and The Council of The European Union, April 27, 2016):

- Individual consent
- Performance of a contract
- Legal compliance obligations

- Vital interests, such as protecting life
- Performance of a task carried out in the public interest or in the exercise of official authority
- Legitimate interests of the organization processing are not overridden by the interests or fundamental rights and freedoms of the data subject

In the category with the second most fines, over €2.5 billion in fines were levied on organizations that allegedly didn't handle the data in a manner consistent with GDPR's general data-processing principles (GDPR Article 5). These principles are as follows (The European Parliament and The Council of The European Union, April 27, 2016):

- Data must be processed legally, fairly, and openly
- Data can only be used for the specific, explicit purpose stated
- Data minimization is required to ensure the minimum necessary data is collected
- Personal data that is collected must be kept accurate and, where necessary, up to date
- Store data only as long as necessary for its purpose
- Data must be processed securely to ensure integrity and confidentiality
- The data controller is accountable and must comply and demonstrate compliance

Notice how these principles and rules could make it harder for organizations that collect and process personal data to do so without being very thoughtful about their approach to GDPR compliance. Large organizations with hundreds or thousands of systems that process personal data in the decades prior to May 2018, when GDPR enforcement started, would likely have a large and expensive undertaking to alter or replace systems that do not meet GDPR requirements. Ultimately, those big fines for GDPR non-compliance play a role in incentivizing organizations to modernize their approach to data privacy and security.

Now that we've discussed GDPR, we can answer the question I raised earlier: why are public and commercial sector organizations in the EU and EEA concerned about FISA orders?

In July 2020, the **Court of Justice of the European Union** (**CJEU**) invalidated the adequacy decision that underpinned the EU-US Privacy Shield. Until that time, the Privacy Shield was used as a legal framework to facilitate cross-border data transfers of EU data subjects' personal data for commercial uses between the EU and the US. By following the Privacy Shield program's data protection requirements, program participants' data transfers would be deemed compliant with EU law. The CJEU's legal decision to invalidate the Privacy Shield is referred to as Schrems II, named after the Austrian lawyer Maximillian Schrems, who filed the complaint against Facebook that led to the court's ruling, known as Data Protection Commissioner v. Facebook Ireland Limited. The CJEU's ruling found the following:

> *"...Privacy Shield [is] inadequate in part because it does not restrain U.S. intelligence authorities' data collection activities. According to the CJEU, U.S. law allows intelligence agencies to collect and use the personal data transferred under the Privacy Shield framework in a manner that is inconsistent with rights guaranteed under EU law. The CJEU focused on Section 702 of the Foreign Intelligence Surveillance Act, Executive Order 12333, and Presidential Policy Directive 28, which govern how the U.S. government may conduct surveillance of non-U.S. persons located outside of the United States." (Congressional Research Service, 2021)*

The CJEU essentially ruled that GDPR restricts transferring EU citizens' personal data to countries where government surveillance laws, such as the US FISA, allow access to that data without protections equivalent to those required under EU law. The court's finding directly referenced FISA Section 702 and Executive Order 12333. You might be wondering what these have to do with GDPR and data transfers.

The NSA describes FISA Section 702 in this way:

> *"In general, Section 702 authorizes the Attorney General and Director of National Intelligence to make and submit to the FISA Court written certifications for the purpose of acquiring foreign intelligence information. Upon the issuance of an order by the FISA Court approving such a certification and the use of targeting and minimization procedures, the Attorney General and Director of National Intelligence may jointly authorize for up to one year the targeting of non-United States persons reasonably believed to be located overseas to acquire foreign intelligence information." (National Security Agency/Central Security Service, n.d.)*

One issue that the CJEU cited was, "Section 702's limitations on judicial remedies for EU citizens as falling short of the GDPR's requirements" (Congressional Research Service, 2021).

That is, in some circumstances, FISA Section 702 could permit secret surveillance with no opportunity for judicial review for EU citizens. For example, if US authorities decided to use the evidence collected from FISA Section 702 surveillance to prosecute a non-US person for a crime, that person and their attorneys would, at some point, be given notice that this surveillance took place and be confronted with the evidence collected (Congressional Research Service, 2021). The court could then review the surveillance and its lawfulness, but if the authorities decided not to prosecute the target of the surveillance for a related crime, the target would likely never know that they had been under surveillance and would not have an opportunity to request judicial review of the surveillance and the personal information collected. The CJEU also found that EU citizens did not have enforceable rights under

Executive Order 12333 and that it didn't include sufficient protections to limit surveillance to a reasonable scope (Congressional Research Service, 2021).

At that time, with the EU-US Privacy Shield invalidated and no adequacy decision for the US, only SCCs remained to protect organizations that transfer the personal data of EEA data subjects outside the EEA. SCCs are contractual clauses that include EU pre-approved clauses that impose data protection standards on the organizations that use them. However, the technical implementation of the rather vague data protection standards and requirements in SCCs left their legal efficacy open to interpretation. This uncertainty left some organizations uncomfortable with using SCCs as the legal means to transfer the personal data of EEA data subjects outside the EEA. Keep in mind that for many of these organizations, the decision to use SCCs represents up to €20 million or 4% of their annual worldwide revenue in potential GDPR administrative fines.

This is one reason why so many CISOs in Europe were concerned about the risk that US national security orders pose to their organizations. Under the CJEU's interpretation, FISA Section 702 and Executive Order 12333 did not offer EU data subjects the same rights as US citizens where US intelligence surveillance is concerned. One of the risks envisioned is that if US authorities intercept an EU organization's cross-border data transfers, there is no legal protection for the EU data subjects impacted. This could be a violation of GDPR for the organization doing the transfer. With the potential of tens of millions of euros in fines and a ruined reputation across the EEA, many organizations were concerned.

In October 2022, US President Biden signed an Executive Order to implement a new **EU-US Data Privacy Framework** (**EU-US DPF**). The White House stated the following:

> *"The EU-U.S. DPF will restore an important legal basis for transatlantic data flows by addressing concerns that the Court of Justice of the European Union raised in striking down the prior EU-U.S. Privacy Shield framework as a valid data transfer mechanism under EU law...These steps will provide the European Commission with a basis to adopt a new adequacy determination, which will restore an important, accessible, and affordable data transfer mechanism under EU law. It will also provide greater legal certainty for companies using Standard Contractual Clauses and Binding Corporate Rules to transfer EU personal data to the United States." (The White House, October 7, 2022)*

This Executive Order strengthened privacy safeguards, enforced stricter rules for SIGINT collection, and required intelligence agencies to update their policies to reflect the new safeguards. It also created a binding redress system for individuals who believe their personal information was collected illegally. Finally, it established an independent Privacy and Civil Liberties Oversight Board.

By December 2022, the European Commission had drafted a new adequacy decision for the US based on the President's Executive Order. At that time, Maximillian Schrems, the Austrian lawyer who successfully challenged the EU-US Privacy Shield, said the following:

> *"We will analyze the draft decision in detail the next days. As the draft decision is based on the known Executive Order, I can't see how this would survive a challenge before the Court of Justice. It seems that the European Commission just issues similar decisions over and over again - in flagrant breach of our fundamental rights."*

In July 2023, the European Commission started allowing personal data transfers between the EU and the US based on the EU-US DPF. However, in September 2023, a French member of Parliament, Philippe Latombe, challenged several aspects of the EU-US DPF in the General Court of the EU. Ultimately, the court dismissed this challenge two years later in September 2025. Maximillian Schrems once again commented:

> *"'We are convinced that a broader review of U.S. law — especially the use of executive orders by the Trump administration should yield a different result,' Schrems added. 'We are reviewing our options to bring such a challenge. While the Commission may have gained another year, we still lack any legal certainty for users and businesses.'" (Duball, Joe, September 3, 2025)*

This was the third time in 10 years that the adequacy decision for personal data transfers between the EU and the US made it to the EU's highest court. In October 2025, Philippe Latombe confirmed he would appeal the court's decision (Krempl, Stefan, October 30, 2025).

If you live in the US, you might be wondering why there is so much tension between the EU and the US focused on the privacy of personal information. If large GDPR fines are any indication, US-based high-tech companies are on the front lines of this conflict. As I learned from many of the conversations I had with Europeans, the events of the 1930s in Germany and World War II deeply influenced the imperative for privacy in Germany and across the rest of Europe. The Holocaust irrevocably changed Europe, and privacy is viewed as a key tool to prevent anything like that from occurring there again. This view was reinforced by events in the Cold War era. The Soviets controlled East Germany, where the Stasi secret police maintained surveillance files on millions of East German citizens. Edward Snowden's and WikiLeaks' revelations about US surveillance programs largely polarized the collective consciousness among Western Europeans. For many of the Europeans I met with, the massive benefits of cross-border commerce with one of the largest commercial markets in the world and intelligence sharing with one of the world's biggest intelligence apparatuses no longer offset the risks they perceived in US intelligence data gathering. They also seemed to be willing to forgo the undeniable benefits that the US-based hyper-scale CSPs' services offer, along with other modern technologies that the US can provide, without further assurances about US government surveillance programs, data privacy, data residency, data sovereignty, and digital sovereignty.

Given that so many CISOs and organizations view lawful government access to data as a legitimate threat via law enforcement requests and court orders related to government surveillance and intelligence programs, let's examine the quantitative risk associated with lawful government access to data next.

Managing the risk of government access to data

With so many governments around the world working to find ways to facilitate and expedite the cross-border production of data for law enforcement purposes, what should CISOs do? First, it's important to recognize that not every organization needs to be concerned about government access to data, MLATs, and the CLOUD Act. Most of the executives I advised had not previously parsed the specific threats that are often lumped into the risk of government access to data. For some of them, once they recognized that SIGINT, unlawful access to data (nation-state threat actors), and lawful access to data are different threats, they adopted a less emotional, more pragmatic approach. However, others still wanted more clarity on the risks that these threats pose. Since the industry has very little authoritative data to inform risk calculations for communications that are intercepted by SIGINT, these risks are harder to quantify. Let's put this risk category aside for the moment and focus on lawful government access to data, as there is a lot of data available that will inform our risk calculations for this threat.

Note that the scenario is quite different if an organization is being investigated itself for criminal acts versus being asked to produce data they control for an investigation not related to them. I'll focus on the latter scenario. The question we want to try to answer is, in the context of lawful government access to data, what is the incremental risk of adding a particular vendor or vendor's service to our supply chain or IT portfolio? Put another way, since there is already a risk that law enforcement will ask organizations directly for access to data that they control, we want to figure out what the increased risk is of adding a service provider's product(s) to their IT portfolio. We'll examine the increased risk of using vendors because most enterprises are worried that adding a service provider can increase the number of independent parties that control or can be compelled to disclose the organization's data, thereby incrementally expanding exposure to lawful government access beyond the risk the organization already carries on its own.

Remember that risk is the combination of probability and impact; that is, the probability of a specific threat being realized and the impact on the organization if it is realized. There are several different ways to calculate risk. Some of the organizations I discussed risk management with used a quantitative approach to calculate risk, where they tried to assign numeric values to the probability and impact sides of the risk equation. Other organizations I talked with used a qualitative approach to calculate risk in a way that didn't assign numeric values to probability and impact; they used risk categories instead, such as *low*, *medium*, and *high*. Some organizations use a combination of qualitative and quantitative approaches. Whatever approach your organization uses, it is likely better than not using a risk-based approach at all. You might have to iterate to find which approach works best for your organization if it hasn't already adopted one. Ultimately, these approaches help determine which risks have the highest combined probability and impact on each organization.

Determining the potential impact of a court order demanding the production of specific data that an organization controls, related to a criminal investigation, will likely require the expertise of the organization's general counsel and legal team. For an enterprise-sized public or private sector organization, chances are their legal team has already managed such requests in the past, and this risk isn't new to them, even if it's the first time their CISO has contemplated it.

> **Note**
>
> I have found that legal teams rarely copy CISOs into such matters unless there is some compelling reason to do so. This is why most CISOs are unaware that their organization already processes law enforcement requests for information. Many CISOs I've advised had no idea that their legal departments had received such requests and were operating on the assumption that this was a new risk to the organization. However, senior management teams manage all sorts of risks from the day the company or agency comes into existence.

Even if the organization has never received a request for information from a law enforcement agency, the legal team is typically the team that will manage such requests and has the best insights into the potential impact on the organization. Depending on the type of organization, the business that they are in, and the nature of the request, it might also be prudent to get the advice of public relations experts as well, regarding potential impact on the company's reputation or brand.

Industry transparency reports and information request reports are valuable on the probability side of the risk equation. Most top-tier technology companies publish reports on the volume of warrants, subpoenas, NSLs, FISA orders, and other court orders that they receive. They do this because it helps their customers understand the risk of lawful government access to data associated with using their products and services. Here is a list of some of the transparency reports published by major vendors:

- Adobe law enforcement requests: `https://www.adobe.com/legal/lawenforcementrequests/transparency.html`
- Amazon information request reports: `https://aws.amazon.com/compliance/amazon-information-requests/`
- Apple Transparency Report: `https://www.apple.com/legal/transparency/`
- Cisco transparency and law enforcement requests for customer data: `https://www.cisco.com/c/en/us/about/trust-center/transparency.html`
- Google requests for user information: `https://transparencyreport.google.com/user-data/overview`
- Meta transparency report: `https://transparency.facebook.com/government-data-requests`
- Microsoft law enforcement requests report: `https://www.microsoft.com/en-us/corporate-responsibility/reports/government-requests/customer-data`
- Oracle Law Enforcement Requests Report: `https://www.oracle.com/legal/law-enforcement-requests-report/`

These vendors should be commended for listening to their customers and for their transparency.

It is difficult to estimate the probability of the risk related to using products from vendors that don't publish this data; it can be difficult to manage something you can't measure. If your organization is using managed service providers, have they been providing you with similar reports? If lawful access to data is a risk that your organization is interested in understanding, you should ask all the vendors in your supply chain for data that helps you understand and manage it.

> **Tip**
>
> Remember, many of these managed service providers, especially the big providers that have been in the industry for decades, are likely subject to US jurisdiction just like the US-based hyper-scale CSPs are.

Before I dive into some of the data in these reports, you'll need some definitions. There are no industry standards about the kind of data to publish and how it should be reported, but many of these reports include data that is similar. I helped develop the transparency reports published by Microsoft and AWS when I worked at these companies, so I have a few insights that can help with interpreting the data.

First, there are the concepts of **content** and **non-content**. In this context, content means the contents of files that are created and/or owned by the vendor's customers. Some examples include the content of an email, a picture, a spreadsheet, or a document. Law enforcement might request the contents of a specific email, as I described earlier in the chapter. This is typically referred to as "data," "content," or "user content" in these industry transparency reports.

Many times, law enforcement investigators don't know whether a specific file even exists or whether a suspect even has an account for a particular online service. Since they aren't omniscient and they can't lawfully request unfettered access to an online service to check whether the suspect has an account, they must submit a request via a warrant, subpoena, or court order to the service provider. Instead of user content, the request is limited to account details such as when the account was opened, the name and address associated with the account, and billing information. This is typically referred to as non-content or **metadata** in industry reports. Note that some information you might think should be considered content is categorized by the law as metadata. For example, the "To" and "From" fields in an email are considered non-content. This information is contained in the header of an email, like the envelope that a physical letter is posted in, and isn't considered confidential information. After all, it's on the outside of the envelope, so anyone who can see the envelope can see the addresses printed on it.

Many of these reports provide aggregate numbers, such as the total number of law enforcement requests they received in a specified period, typically a half-year or quarter, and the number of times or percentage of cases where this content was provided to law enforcement. Some of these reports also contain the number of accounts that were impacted, as well as a breakdown of the number of requests that were rejected or only partially fulfilled. Some vendors provide a breakdown of the number of warrants, subpoenas, NSLs, preservation requests, and other court orders they have received.

Additionally, you might see references to national security requests or similar labels in these reports. There are generally two types of orders that get lumped into this category: NSLs and FISA orders. Since FISA investigations are covert, court orders supporting those require a court that is not open to the public but still has appropriate oversight. FISC reviews applications and FISCR handles appeals . Also recall that President Biden's Executive Order on EU-US DPF established an independent Privacy and Civil Liberties Oversight Board. The two courts and the oversight board provide oversight to ensure that FISA is observed in the collection of intelligence.

The other type of national security order you might see in some industry reports is an NSL. The FBI and the Executive Branch of the US government can use NSLs to request some limited subscriber data (non-content) as part of national security investigations.

> **Note**
>
> Google has published a breakdown of the FISA orders and NSLs it has received, including copies of some lightly redacted NSLs they have received. If you are interested in seeing what an NSL looks like, visit `https://transparencyreport.google.com/user-data/us-national-security`. Microsoft also breaks out FISA orders and NSLs into separate reports from the normal law enforcement requests they receive. You can see this data here: `https://www.microsoft.com/en-us/corporate-responsibility/reports/government-requests/customer-data#tab-national-security-orders-report`.

US authorities do not permit vendors to publish the exact number of FISA orders or NSLs they receive; they can only publish ranges such as 0–499 or 500–999. There is a mandatory six-month delay, after which the newest data can be published. Presumably, they take these precautions so that foreign purveyors of espionage or terrorist organizations cannot reverse-engineer how many court orders are issued or get any clues about investigations. However, this means the newest data on FISA orders and NSLs in vendor transparency reports is at least six months old, or older in some cases.

The volume of law enforcement requests

It is helpful to understand how many law enforcement requests vendors receive in order to calculate the probability side of the risk equation. *Figure 8.4* provides the total number of law enforcement requests from around the world submitted to each vendor, not including NSLs, FISA orders, and non-account-related requests, such as requests for information on mobile devices.

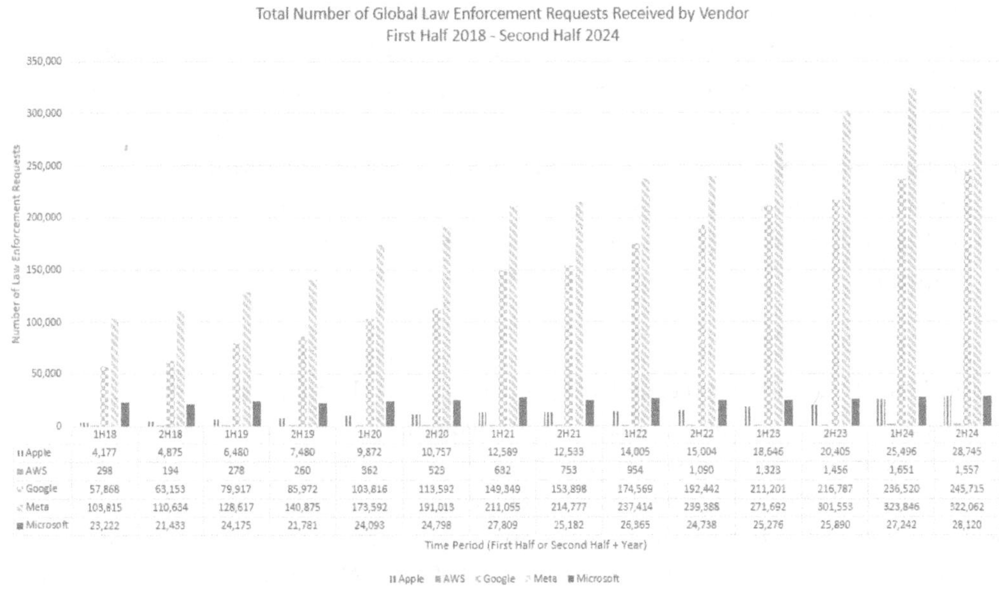

	1H18	2H18	1H19	2H19	1H20	2H20	1H21	2H21	1H22	2H22	1H23	2H23	1H24	2H24
Apple	4,177	4,875	6,480	7,480	9,872	10,757	12,589	12,533	14,005	15,004	18,646	20,405	25,496	28,745
AWS	298	194	278	260	362	523	632	753	954	1,090	1,323	1,456	1,651	1,557
Google	57,868	63,153	79,917	85,972	103,816	113,592	149,349	153,898	174,569	192,442	211,201	216,787	236,520	245,715
Meta	103,815	110,634	128,617	140,875	173,592	191,013	211,055	214,777	237,414	239,388	271,692	301,553	323,846	322,062
Microsoft	23,222	21,433	24,175	21,781	24,093	24,798	27,809	25,182	26,365	24,738	25,276	25,890	27,242	28,120

Figure 8.4 – Total number of law enforcement requests from around the world that each vendor reported receiving in each six-month period between the first half of 2018 (1H18) and the second half of 2024 (2H24) (Apple, n.d., Amazon, n.d.; Google, n.d.; Meta, n.d.; Microsoft, n.d.)

The period covered is the first half of 2018 (1H18) to the second half of 2024 (2H24). The sources of data for this table are the transparency reports, law enforcement requests reports, and so on that each vendor has published on their public website (Apple, n.d.; Amazon, n.d.; Google, n.d.; Meta, n.d.; Microsoft, n.d.).

There are significant differences in the number of requests that each of these vendors received. Vendors that operate popular consumer communications systems, such as email, chat, and social media, appear to have received more law enforcement requests on average. This could be because such two-way communication mechanisms enable law enforcement to connect victims and perpetrators and criminals with other criminals during their investigations.

> **Note**
>
> As you can see from this data, with a few exceptions, the volume of law enforcement requests increased over time. I think this trend was predictable. People and organizations are becoming more reliant on online services for a growing number of purposes—a trend that will likely continue, especially in the new era of AI and agentic AI applications. At the same time, more and more law enforcement agencies around the world are becoming increasingly aware of the use of online services by suspects in their criminal investigations and the fact that evidence of crimes can also be found online. As I mentioned earlier, many governments around the world have been working on ways to make it easier for law enforcement to get lawful access to data regardless of where it is stored. All of these factors lead me to believe that the volume of requests from law enforcement across the industry will likely continue to increase over time. This simply reflects that societies around the world are moving online, and criminals are coming with them.

We are kind of comparing apples and oranges in *Figure 8.4*. Although it is helpful to understand the total volume of law enforcement requests that each vendor receives, counting requests for data in consumer services isn't the same as requests for enterprise data. This contrast is clear when comparing the number of requests that a consumer service company such as Meta receives with that of AWS; the latter serves the private and public sector organizations almost exclusively. In the second half of 2024, AWS received 0.5% of the volume of requests that Meta received.

> **Tip**
>
> Remember, CISOs are concerned about law enforcement requests for their organizations' data, which is not the same as requests for pictures, emails, and texts for criminal investigations focused on crimes that individuals or consumers are involved in. Put another way, we want to understand the probability that one of these vendors receives a request for enterprise data. To do this more precisely, we shouldn't count requests for consumer data as part of that probability calculation.

I've seen some vendors emphasize interpretations of US surveillance and data access laws in their competitive positioning, occasionally leading to confusion among customers about the practical risks involved.

They'll point at the relatively large volume of law enforcement requests that Meta receives and paint the entire US technology industry with that brush. Some of these critics have argued that the CLOUD Act expands US law enforcement's ability to compel the production of data stored overseas, while supporters emphasize that such access remains subject to judicial oversight and legal standards. However, it is easier for Western European executives to buy into the critical view because of the erosion of trust in the US that I discussed earlier. If it were suddenly revealed that the head of your country's government was spied on for years by one of your closest allies, how would you feel about that? However, executives, CISOs, and security team members need to ask themselves whether they really need to be concerned with US-based consumer services as part of their own risk calculations. Do they plan to store their enterprise data on Facebook? As mentioned earlier, CISOs need to have specific clarity about the threats and risks to *their* organization's data and avoid being distracted by claims that the entire high-tech industry in the US is somehow corrupted. This polarized view isn't helpful in managing risk for private or public sector organizations.

Breaking the data down to provide the number of requests submitted on a country-by-country basis is another pivot that some vendors offer in their transparency reports. The more detail they provide in their reports, the more accurate the risk estimates can be. For example, many of the CISOs I talked to didn't care if their own country sent their vendors requests for information—it was really only the US requests that they were concerned about.

Additionally, many CISOs aren't overly concerned about non-content data because they consider such data as publicly available or easily discoverable, such as an email address, for example. If they can determine the number of requests made by US law enforcement where content was produced, that gives them a good insight into the specific threat that they are concerned about. Let's examine this data specifically to better understand the associated risk.

The probability of US law enforcement accessing enterprise data in the cloud

Many of the CIOs and CISOs that I advised over the years were worried that using US-based service providers would make it easier for the US government to get access to their data. Let's try to get a better idea of the probability side of the risk equation for this scenario. This will give us some insight into the risk of adding US-based hyper-scale CSPs' services to organizations' current on-premises IT. I'll only focus on **hyper-scale CSPs** that provide services for enterprise customers as opposed to consumer services. For this example, let's include three hyper-scale CSPs: **AWS**, **Google**, and **Microsoft**.

AWS law enforcement requests

Let's start with AWS. *Figure 8.5* illustrates the volume of law enforcement requests that AWS received in the four and a half years between the second half of 2020 and the end of 2024.

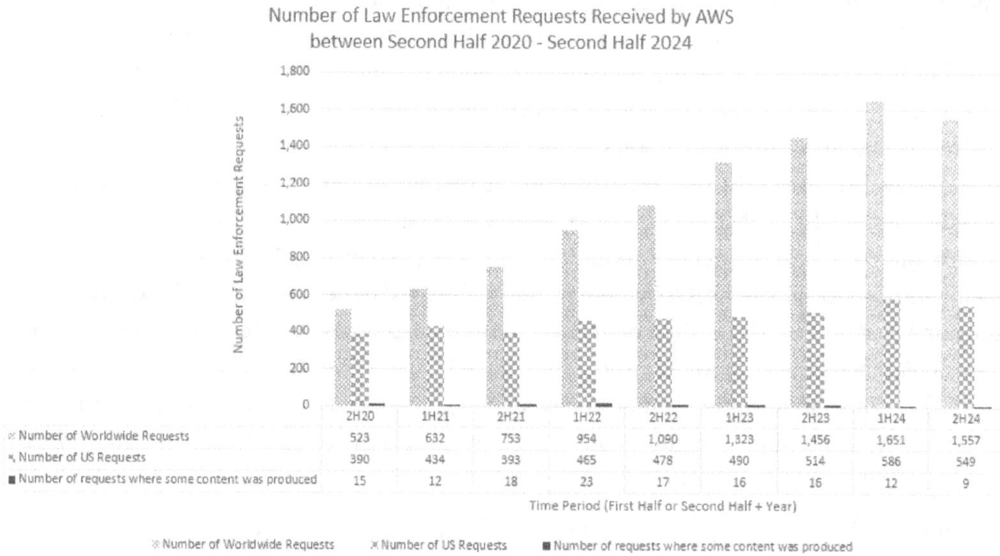

Figure 8.5 – The number of law enforcement requests AWS received from authorities worldwide and from authorities in the US in each six-month period between the second half of 2020 (2H20) and the second half of 2024 (2H24). The graph also illustrates the number of law enforcement requests where some content was produced in each period (AWS, n.d.)

AWS' customers are almost exclusively enterprises in the commercial sector and public sector, so they don't provide a breakdown of data specifically for enterprise customer accounts and consumer accounts the way Google and Microsoft do in their reports. AWS received the highest number of law enforcement requests in the first half of 2024 (1H24)—1,651 requests from countries around the world. Of those 1,651 requests, 586 came from US authorities, equivalent to 35.5% of the total. Besides the US, the highest volume of law enforcement requests during this period came from authorities in India, with 19.7% of the total, and 14.3% from Germany (AWS, n.d.). *Figure 8.5* also shows the number of worldwide requests that resulted in some content being produced for law enforcement. In 1H24, 12 requests, or 0.7% of the 1,651 total requests, resulted in content handover. AWS' reports don't provide a breakdown of the number of these requests by country. But even if you assume that all 12 content requests were in response to US law enforcement, that still only represents 2% of the total requests from the US. The six-month period with the highest number of requests resulting in production of content was 1H22, with 23 such requests. This represents 3% of all worldwide requests during that period and 5% of all US requests. During this period, US law enforcement requests represented 48.7% of all requests, with India's requests representing 17.4% and Germany's representing 10.4%. The period with the lowest number of requests that produced some content was 2H24 with 9 such requests, equivalent to 0.6% of all requests and 1.6% of all US requests.

Although AWS' reports don't break down the number of requests that resulted in content handover by country, they do provide one data point that helps CIOs and CISOs outside the US understand the risk of US government requests for content located outside the US. In the FAQ section of every Amazon information request report they published during this period, they stated the following:

> *"How many requests resulted in the disclosure to the U.S. government of enterprise or government content data located outside the United States? None." (Amazon Web Services, n.d.)*

Therefore, if you are a CIO or CISO concerned about the US government using search warrants and court orders to access your organization's data, and that data is in an AWS region outside the US, such as Europe, for example, the number of times this happened in the 4.5 years I examined is *zero*.

Next, let's look at law enforcement data that Google has published.

Google law enforcement requests

Google's requests for user information reports provide a breakdown of law enforcement request data for enterprise cloud customer accounts. This makes it easier to see how many US law enforcement requests for enterprise cloud customer account content resulted in the production of data. *Figure 8.6* illustrates the number of US law enforcement requests Google received between the second half of 2020 (2H20) and the end of 2024 (2H24) for Google Enterprise Cloud customer accounts.

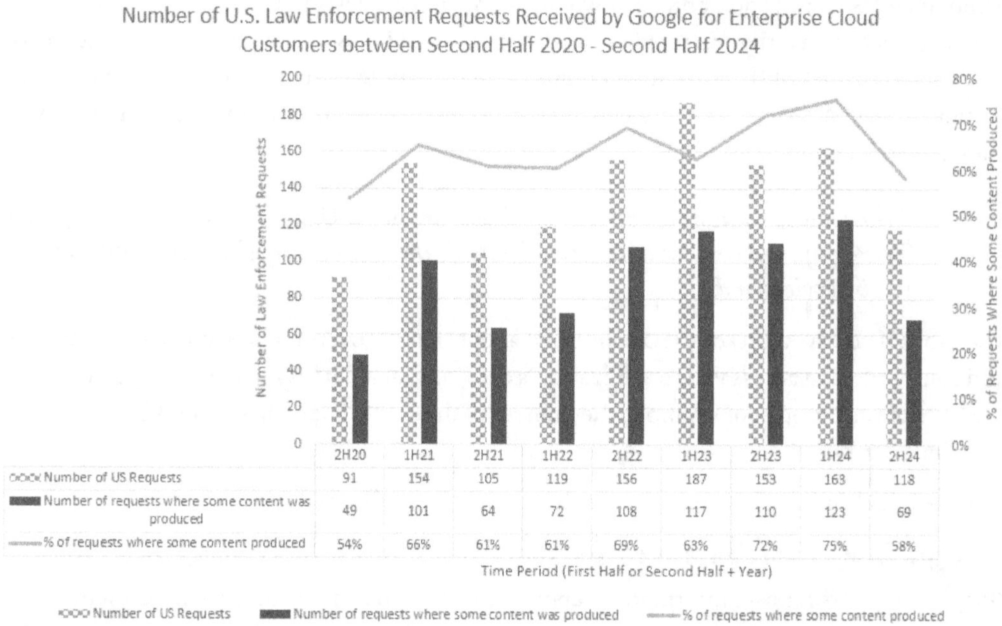

	2H20	1H21	2H21	1H22	2H22	1H23	2H23	1H24	2H24
Number of US Requests	91	154	105	119	156	187	153	163	118
Number of requests where some content was produced	49	101	64	72	108	117	110	123	69
% of requests where some content produced	54%	66%	61%	61%	69%	63%	72%	75%	58%

Figure 8.6 – The number of law enforcement requests Google received from US authorities in each six-month period between the second half of 2020 and the second half of 2024. The graph also illustrates the number of these requests where some content was produced in each period (Google, n.d.)

The figure also shows us how many of these US law enforcement requests resulted in the production of content and the percentage of all requests that those represent. For example, the six-month period with the most law enforcement requests during these 4.5 years was 1H23, with 187 requests made by US law enforcement agencies. Of the 187 requests, 117 resulted in the production of some content, equivalent to 63% of the total (Google, n.d.). In the most recent period for which Google published this data, 2H24, there were 118 US law enforcement requests for enterprise cloud accounts, 58% of which resulted in the production of some content.

> **Note**
>
> Note that these totals do not include law enforcement requests that typically aren't used to compel the production of data, such as subpoenas, other court orders, other legal orders, and preservation requests.

Besides the US, countries that submitted relatively high volumes of law enforcement requests during these 4.5 years include the UK, Brazil, and Japan. But the volume of these requests were fractions of the number of requests made by US law enforcement.

It appears that the percentage of law enforcement requests sent to Google where it is compelled to produce content is significantly higher than that of AWS. However, note that the absolute number of law enforcement requests for Google enterprise cloud customer accounts is significantly lower than the number of requests sent to AWS in every six-month period I examined. In both cases, the number of requests where some content was produced is minuscule compared to the number of customers these hyper-scale CSPs have.

As I mentioned earlier, in some cases, law enforcement requests have multiple accounts in their scope. That is, one request can impact more than one account. Google's requests for user information reports include the number of accounts that were subject to government requests. As *Table 8.2* shows us, the number of accounts potentially impacted is not significantly higher than the number of law enforcement requests:

Period	Number of US requests	Max number of enterprise cloud customer accounts subject to requests
2H20	91	94
1H21	154	172
2H21	105	118
1H22	119	121
2H22	156	165
1H23	187	195
2H23	153	156
1H24	163	166
2H24	118	129

Table 8.2 – The number of law enforcement requests Google received from US authorities in each six-month period between the second half of 2020 and the second half of 2024. The table also illustrates the number of enterprise cloud customer accounts that were subject to the requests in each period (Google, n.d.)

This will be a relief to those CISOs who believe US authorities are using law enforcement requests to vacuum up bulk data from vast numbers of accounts in the cloud. The FAQ in Google's reports suggests many of these accounts were likely double counted for various reasons, so the number of accounts impacted is likely even smaller than the table suggests.

Next, let's look at the law enforcement requests that Microsoft received during this period.

Microsoft law enforcement requests

Microsoft's government requests reports provide slightly different data than AWS and Google. *Figure 8.7* reveals the volume of law enforcement requests for enterprise accounts associated with enterprise cloud customers from law enforcement organizations around the world.

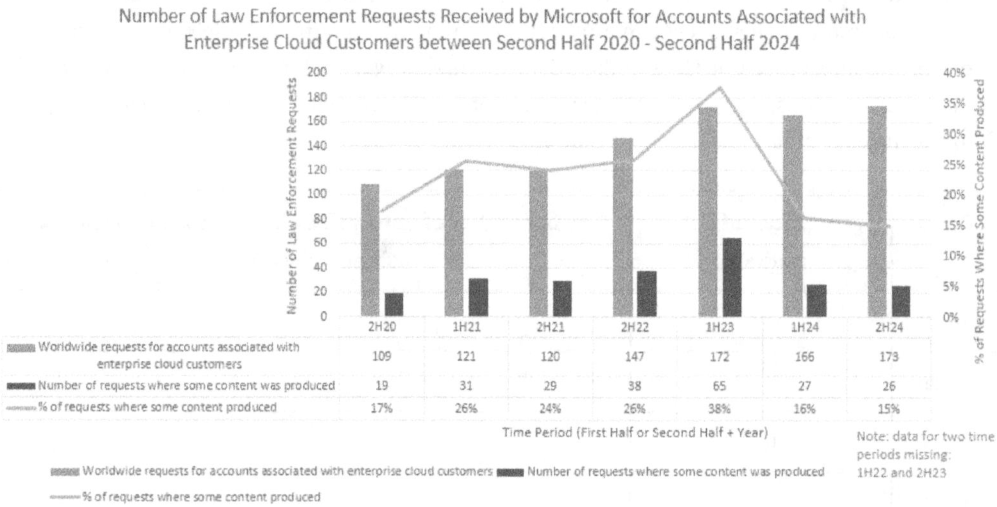

Figure 8.7 – The number of law enforcement requests Microsoft received from law enforcement authorities around the world associated with enterprise cloud customers in each six-month period between the second half of 2020 (2H20) and the end of 2024 (2H24). The graph also illustrates the number of these requests where some content was produced in each period (Microsoft, n.d.)

The figure also shows the number of requests that resulted in the production of some content. Note that I was unable to find these specific data points for two of the six-month periods, 1H22 and 2H23. The six-month period with the highest number of requests was the most recent period, 2H24, during which Microsoft received 173 requests. Of these 173 requests, 26 of them, equivalent to 15%, resulted in the production of some content (Microsoft, n.d.).

I was only able to find data on the number of US law enforcement requests Microsoft received for accounts associated with enterprise cloud customers for four six-month periods, shown in *Table 8.3*. This data shows us that US authorities, as well as authorities in other countries, are compelling the production of content in volumes consistent with the other hyper-scale CSPs:

Period	Worldwide requests for accounts associated with enterprise cloud customers	Number of requests where some content was produced	Number of requests where some content was produced for US authorities
2H22	147	38	33
1H23	172	65	22
1H24	166	27	16
2H24	173	26	20

Table 8.3 – The number of law enforcement requests Microsoft received from US authorities in four six-month periods between the second half of 2022 (2H22) and the second half of 2024 (2H24) (Microsoft, n.d.)

Table 8.4 provides insights into the volume of requests to Microsoft from US law enforcement resulting in the disclosure of enterprise content stored outside the US, and disclosures involving Azure enterprise customers for content belonging to commercial, public sector, or educational customers:

Disclosure detail	2H20	1H21	2H21	1H22	2H22	1H23	2H23	1H24	2H24
Number of warrants from US law enforcement resulting in the disclosure of enterprise content data stored outside the US	1	2	3	0	4	4	5	1	5
Number of disclosures involving Azure enterprise customers for content belonging to commercial sector, public sector, or educational customers	No data	No data	No data	0	0	0	0	1	1

Table 8.4 –The number of law enforcement requests Microsoft received from US authorities resulting in the disclosure of enterprise content data stored outside the US in each six-month period between the second half of

2020 (2H20) and the second half of 2024 (2H24). Also included is the number of disclosures involving Azure enterprise customers belonging to commercial sector, public sector, and educational customers (Microsoft, n.d.)

These data points provide further transparency into the volume of US law enforcement requests that potentially impact customers who store data outside the US, and the potential impact on enterprises leveraging Microsoft Azure.

The law enforcement data we have looked at for these three hyper-scale CSPs should help inform the probability side of organizations' risk calculations related to leveraging US-based CSPs. The number of law enforcement requests worldwide is tiny relative to other cybersecurity threats, such as attackers leveraging unpatched vulnerabilities, malware, and internet-based attacks against web applications and APIs. This data should provide non-US CIOs and CISOs with some confidence that the frequency at which US law enforcement targets foreign companies and public sector organizations with warrants seeking their data is truly anomalous relative to the number of enterprise customers these hyper-scale CSPs have. Additionally, this data enables CIOs and CISOs to recognize and be cautious of vendors who try to spread fear, uncertainty, and doubt about US law enforcement agencies accessing data in the cloud.

Now that we have some insight into the volume of law enforcement requests, let's examine the volume of US intelligence agencies' national security orders that these three US-based CSPs receive.

The probability of US intelligence accessing data in the cloud

You might recall that US national security orders include NSLs and US FISA orders that are lumped into ranges such as 0–499. Let's look at the volume of these requests that Microsoft, Google, and AWS have received to help us understand the probability of government access to data for national security purposes.

Microsoft provides the following context for why they are only permitted to publish the volume of FISA orders and NSLs in ranges:

> *"Prior to 2014, U.S. technology providers were not allowed to report any information regarding U.S. national security demands. As a result of litigation that Microsoft and other technology companies filed against the U.S. government in 2014, the government agreed for the first time to permit technology companies to publish data about FISA orders. This reporting structure was then codified as part of the USA FREEDOM Act. While there remain constraints on what we can publish, this report presents the most comprehensive, legally permissible picture of the types of requests that we receive from the U.S. government pursuant to its national security authorities." (Microsoft, n.d.)*

Note that both Microsoft and Google make it clear in their respective reports that NSLs cannot be used to request customer content. Microsoft states the following:

> *"National Security Letters may require the disclosure of basic subscriber information such as the name, address and length of service of a customer who has subscribed to one of our services. NSLs may not be used to require the disclosure of the content of a customer's communications or data. NSLs may only be used to request basic subscriber information that is relevant to U.S. national security and cannot be used for criminal, civil, or administrative investigations." (Microsoft, 2021)*

Google's description of how NSLs are used, published in their Google Transparency Report, is consistent with Microsoft's. Google described their use in this way:

> *"Using a NSL, the FBI can seek 'the name, address, length of service, and local and long distance toll billing records' of a subscriber to a wire or electronic communications service. The FBI can't use NSLs to obtain anything else from Google, such as Gmail content, search queries, YouTube videos or user IP addresses." (Google, n.d.)*

Given this, I'll focus my examination on the volume of FISA orders that resulted in the disclosure of some content. Both Microsoft and Google provide the volume of national security requests under FISA for both content and non-content requests. AWS doesn't break their data down this way, but the data they publish still helps us understand the volume of FISA orders they potentially receive. Let's start by looking at AWS.

AWS FISA order volumes

This data comes from numerous Amazon information request reports. *Table 8.5* shows us the volume of FISA orders received by AWS in six-month periods between the second half of 2020 and the end of 2024:

Time period	Number of FISA orders (range)
2H20	0–249
1H21	0–249
2H21	0–249
1H22	0–249
2H22	0–249
1H23	0–249

Time period	Number of FISA orders (range)
2H23	0–249
1H24	0–249
2H24	0–249

Table 8.5 – The number of possible FISA orders that AWS received from US authorities in each six-month period between the second half of 2020 (2H20) and the second half of 2024 (2H24), expressed as a range between 0 and 499 (AWS, n.d.)

The table tells us that AWS might not have received any FISA orders in any of the six-month periods examined because the low end of the range is 0. The maximum number of orders they could have received in each half-year period was 249.

Note

AWS didn't disclose how many accounts were in scope of those orders, or whether any of them were seeking content, the way that Google and Microsoft have in their reports.

Even if we consider the maximum number of FISA requests, compared to the millions of enterprise users AWS has, the estimated probability of US authorities using FISA orders to get access to content is a tiny fraction of 1%. If we had an accurate number of active users and the number of FISA orders that were seeking content, the probability would be even smaller. Keep in mind that the probability could be zero if we focus on the possibility that AWS didn't receive any FISA orders during these periods.

Let's look at the volume of requests sent to Google next.

Google FISA order volumes

Google publishes data in the *United States national security requests for user information* section of their transparency report. The data in *Table 8.6* is from this report:

Time period	Number of FISA orders (range)	Number of accounts
2H20	0–499	80,000–80,499
1H21	0–499	89,000–89,499
2H21	0–499	95,500–95,999

Time period	Number of FISA orders (range)	Number of accounts
1H22	0–499	103,000–103,499
2H22	0–499	106,000–106,499
1H23	0–499	115,000–115,499
2H23	0–499	118,000–118,499
1H24	0–499	127,000–127,499

Table 8.6 – The number of possible FISA orders that Google received from US authorities in each six-month period between the second half of 2020 (2H20) and the first half of 2024 (1H24), expressed as a range between 0 and 499. The table also includes the number of accounts that were subject to a government request for user information (Google, n.d.)

They break down the potential range of FISA orders that included demands for users' content, such as email, documents, and photos. *Table 8.6* shows us the range of FISA orders with content requests published by Google for each six-month period between the second half of 2020 and the first half of 2024. Data for the second half of 2024 hadn't been published at the time I wrote this. Google's data includes the number of accounts that were subject to government requests for user information (Google, n.d.).

According to this data, Google potentially received up to twice as many FISA orders as AWS did during the same period. Conversely, the range suggests that they might have received zero FISA orders. Regarding what we can glean from the number of accounts published, if we assume Google received the maximum number of potential orders for the maximum number of accounts for a given time period, such as 1H24, on average, 255 accounts were subject to each order they received. Large enterprises often have at least dozens of cloud accounts and, in many cases, 100 or more cloud accounts in their cloud portfolios, because accounts are security boundaries and can also help simplify billing practices. Again, the probability side of the risk equation seems minute given the millions of enterprise customers Google serves and the hundreds of millions of accounts in use.

Let's look at the volume of FISA orders that Microsoft receives next.

Microsoft FISA order volumes

Microsoft publishes FISA order data in the *U.S. National Security Orders Report* section of their *Government Requests for Customer Data Report*. This is where the data in *Table 8.7* is from. Like Google, Microsoft reported receiving 0–499 FISA orders during every six-month period between the second half of 2020 and the end of 2024. The number of accounts Microsoft reports were "impacted by orders seeking content" is significantly lower than the numbers Google published. This data is shown in *Table 8.7*:

Time period	Orders seeking disclosure of content	Accounts impacted by orders seeking content
2H20	0–499	15,000–15,499
1H21	0–499	15,000–15,499
2H21	0–499	21,000–21,499
1H22	0–499	21,000–21,499
2H22	0–499	20,500–20,999
1H23	0–499	24,000–24,499
2H23	0–499	22,000–22,499
1H24	0–499	26,000–26,499
2H24	0–499	26,000–26,499

Table 8.7 – The number of possible FISA orders that Microsoft received from US authorities in each six-month period between the second half of 2020 (2H20) and the second half of 2024 (2H24), expressed as a range between 0 and 499. The table also includes the number of accounts that were subject to a government request for user information (Microsoft, n.d.)

In 2H24, for example, if we assume Microsoft received 499 FISA orders and 26,499 accounts were impacted by these orders, that's equivalent to 53 accounts impacted per order on average. Once again, relative to the number of enterprises using Microsoft's cloud services and the number of cloud accounts in use, the probability of being impacted by a FISA order seems very small.

Given the reported figures, it is possible that none of the three US-based CSPs have received a FISA order in recent years. However, because US authorities prohibit vendors from releasing the exact number of FISA orders they receive, we are left to decide which figure to use for our risk calculation—whether to use zero or the maximum number in the range. We could simply use the maximum number in each reported range to ensure we don't underestimate the probability.

To calculate the probabilities, let's divide the number of requests by the number of active customers that use these services. It is likely that we won't be able to find exact numbers or even estimates of the number of customers that were actively using each CSP's services during each time period, but since these are some of the biggest high-tech companies in the world, we know anecdotally that they have millions of active enterprise customers each. Let's purposely use a low number. If we use just 2 million enterprise customers as the base of our division calculation, this will render a higher probability than if we used a larger, more accurate customer base number. This will make it less likely that we underestimate the probabilities.

AWS reported receiving 0–249 in every six-month period examined. Given this, we can expect 0.0125% of their customers to be impacted in each six-month period: ***249 / 2,000,000 = 0.0125%***. This percentage gets lower if we assume that the number of customers is higher, which is likely. Also, since AWS doesn't break down the number of FISA orders they received specifically seeking content, the probability of being impacted by one of those orders is potentially even lower. Google and Microsoft reported receiving 0–499 FISA orders in every six-month period examined. Given this, we can expect 0.025% of their customers to be impacted in each six-month period: ***499 / 2,000,000 = 0.025%***.

As this data illustrates, in the most recent time periods for which we have data, the estimated probability of realizing the threat of US authorities using FISA orders to get access to content from the three US-based hyper-scale CSPs is between ***0.0125%*** and ***0.025%***. These hyper-scale CSPs undoubtedly have more than 2 million enterprise customers using their cloud services, so the actual percentages are likely even lower.

You might be wondering whether these probabilities are good or bad. The answer really depends on two things.

First, since the risk is the combination of probability and impact, CIOs and CISOs need to discuss the potential impact with their general counsel and legal team.

> **Tip**
>
> Remember that some threats can be super-low probability, but if they are realized, the impact can be high.

Although the probability of both US law enforcement requests and FISA orders is very low, CIOs and CISOs really need to understand the potential impact on their organizations. For instance, a 0.0125% probability of a potential maximum fine equivalent to €20 million or 4% of annual revenue might still be too high a risk for organizations that are extremely risk averse. Additionally, some of the executives I met in Western Europe told me that *any chance* that their organization's reputation could be tarnished was too high. Put another way, if the probability wasn't zero, it was unacceptable to them. Of course, risk decisions need to be made on an organization-by-organization basis.

> **Tip**
>
> Keep in mind that voluntarily imposing dramatic restrictions on the ability of organizations, industries, or groups of countries to compete or fulfill their charter effectively also has associated risks and consequences. There are opportunity costs for not taking risks in life. In the case of the EEA and cloud computing, instead of being at the forefront of new technologies as they have been for decades, they are at risk of being left behind. These tiny probabilities related to FISA orders are slowing the adoption of new technologies and subsequently slowing progress everywhere new technologies could be leveraged.

The second factor to consider when interpreting these probability figures is that risks are relative. Most organizations have limited resources, so they must prioritize their investments. This applies to managing risk too. CIOs and CISOs should stack-rank US law enforcement requests and FISA order risks with all the other risks that their organization has identified. These risks likely include financial risks, economic risks, legal risks, HR risks, and other cybersecurity risks such as ransomware. Stack-ranking each threat by its probability and impact on the organization will help CIOs and CISOs prioritize risks as per their organization's needs. Some organizations use limits or thresholds (anything above a specified risk score) to determine which risks will be mitigated and which risks are accepted. If the risk of lawful government access to data is a priority risk for the organization, then the CIO, CISO, security team, and legal team should identify a list of possible mitigations and their costs to the organization. The company's risk management stakeholder community or board can then decide whether to mitigate the risk, try to transfer it somehow, or accept it. This risk treatment decision should be revisited periodically to determine whether any changes are prudent based on new information or changing circumstances.

There are some organizations that are legally required to prevent all forms of unauthorized access to their data, including requests from law enforcement and intelligence agencies. These organizations typically have sovereign immunity. These include law enforcement agencies, intelligence agencies, national security agencies, arms of the military, and organizations responsible for the economies of nations, such as federal reserves and judiciaries. There are also commercial sector companies that must protect their most sensitive intellectual property, trade secrets, and customer information, or they face extinction. However, the vast majority of private and public sector organizations I've talked to over the years won't spend extra time or resources trying to mitigate government access to data because they have higher-priority risks to mitigate.

> **Note**
>
> Most organizations simply accept the risk of government access to data because its probability is much lower than that of the other risks they face. After all, you rarely see news reports that a company went out of business after receiving a request for specific data in their possession for a criminal investigation unrelated to the company itself—but you do see headlines nearly every week about ransomware crippling organizations and costing them millions.

Despite the near-zero probabilities associated with lawful government access to data, it is a risk that some organizations still choose to mitigate. Let's look at what this entails next.

Mitigating government access to data

The security controls used to mitigate lawful government access to data may or may not also be effective in mitigating unlawful government access to data and SIGINT threat scenarios; it's difficult to determine with so little insight and publicly available data on these activities. However, from a cybersecurity strategy perspective, all three of these scenarios essentially represent the same type of threat—the threat of unauthorized access to data. For security professionals, this is a simple but powerful construct. Many of the same controls they are already familiar with will help mitigate unauthorized access to data regardless of who is trying to access it.

Now that we have some idea of how low the probability of US government access to data is, we can better grasp why some organizations will choose to accept the risk, while others will choose to mitigate it. Next, we'll step through some high-level guidance that will help CIOs and CISOs mitigate the risk of US government access to data when they leverage US-based CSPs' services.

Understanding the scope and defining it

If you *really* want to protect data from unauthorized access, precisely identifying the data you are trying to protect is a crucial first step. Trying to protect *some* or *all* data is a theoretical or academic exercise. I have discussed this with so many CISOs and executives who initially refused to pivot from their emotional, theoretical objections to real-world solutions. Walking them through the data from transparency reports and the associated probability calculations typically helped take the emotion out of these conversations. The smaller the scope, the better your chance of success. Further, developing a repeatable pattern from this exercise that can be applied to other larger datasets is a best practice.

It is critical to identify how your target data flows through your organization, including through its supply chain. This involves identifying where and how the target data is transmitted, stored, and processed on your network and third-party networks that your organization leverages. Understanding these data flows enables you to apply people, processes, and technologies to protect against and detect unauthorized access attempts and respond as quickly and efficiently as possible. Typically, this is a challenging task with complicated legacy solutions running in large, complex IT environments. Again, get as specific as possible when identifying all storage, networks, databases, and compute resources involved in the target data flows. Once target data flows are well understood, you can develop a plan to address any gaps where the target data is not appropriately protected.

For organizations that already have effective security development practices, this work might have already been completed as part of the application development process. A very effective early step in a security development life cycle is the development of a threat model. A former Microsoft co-worker of mine, Adam Shostack, wrote an excellent book on this topic that I recommend reading: *Threat Modeling: Designing for Security* .

Setting realistic objectives

An important part of planning is setting objectives. An example of a realistic objective for mitigating government access to data is to ensure all access to the target data is first approved by the company's own access request processes. For governments potentially seeking access to the target data, this means ensuring the only course of action they have is to come through the company's front doors in the light of day with a valid court order so that the company's general counsel and legal team can manage their requests. Your legal team should ensure court orders are valid and binding and challenge orders that are overbroad. An example of an overbroad order is a court order that demands all customer emails, files, and metadata across an entire platform for a multi-year period, even though the investigation concerns one specific individual or account and a narrow time window, because it compels disclosure far beyond what is relevant or necessary to the stated investigation.

However, your teams can't manage target data access requests that they aren't aware of. As we discussed earlier with respect to gag orders and US FISA orders, if government requests go to an organization's supply chain partners instead of directly to them, the government could get access to the target data without giving the organization any opportunity to oppose that action.

> **Note**
>
> CISOs and executives who attempt to mitigate a risk with a probability of 0.025% (or lower) by simply refusing to use US-based CSP services pay severely disproportionate opportunity costs because their organizations give up using cloud services that are

> likely many years ahead of what they can possibly accomplish in their legacy on-premises IT environments, if at all. I'll discuss this in more depth in *Chapter 13, Modern Approaches to Security and Compliance.*

Security professionals can't prevent governments from making lawful requests for their target data, but they can do their best to ensure that such requests go directly to their organizations instead of their supply chain partners. In other words, securing the target data so supply chain partners cannot access it to fulfill government demands will force governments seeking data to request it directly from its owner/controller. For example, organizations can encrypt sensitive data with keys that they alone control so that suppliers cannot decrypt it, forcing any lawful government access request to be made directly to the data owner rather than through the supply chain.

This should be the primary objective of mitigating the risk of government access to data.

One important consideration is whether all the vendors in an organization's supply chain are willing and able to challenge legal requests for data. The US-based hyper-scale CSPs have all publicly stated that their attorneys review the requests they receive and ensure that they follow the letter of the law and are not overreaching. Their cloud businesses depend on trust. For them, losing their customers' trust means losing their share of a rapidly growing *trillion-dollar* industry. Therefore, they are willing to defend their customers' privacy by challenging requests when it is appropriate to do so. However, it's likely that not every technology provider in an organization's supply chain will be willing and able to resist these legal requests. If this is a risk that an organization is serious about, then they should choose their vendors with this in mind.

Planning data protection controls

Now that we have identified the target data we want to protect, we understand how it flows through our organization's systems and those of our supply chain partners. We have a clear objective, and we can design processes and technologies, managed by people and systems, to restrict access to the target data. There are numerous legal, administrative, and technical controls that could be employed to do this. I won't reprint NIST SP 800-53 here. The rest of this book is dedicated to examining security strategies, and some of them can be used to protect data. However, I will draw your attention to one capability that I consider to be the ultimate control for preventing unauthorized access to data in the public cloud: **client-side encryption**. Regardless of where my advisory conversations with CISOs and executives started, they would almost always end with discussions about encryption and key management options. Together with some supporting controls, client-side encryption can protect your target data in the cloud from attackers, CSPs, supply chain partners, and governments alike. However, it does have its own limitations and opportunity costs that I'll discuss.

Client-side encryption

Encryption can help maintain the confidentiality and integrity of your data. Depending on the requirements, encryption can also help organizations meet some of their compliance obligations. If encryption really can help with all these things, then why haven't organizations been encrypting everything everywhere? Historically, encryption and key management introduced friction into the operationalization of data. Put another way, there has been a tension between the security benefits that encryption and key management provide and the operational requirements most organizations have for their data. For example, historically, encryption created friction by adding complexity to key management and access control, making everyday activities such as data access, sharing, recovery, and system integration slower and more operationally fragile. Given this, most organizations that employ encryption do so relatively sparingly, attempting to balance security risks with operational risks such as costs, lack of expertise, and business consequences.

Some organizations are interested in protecting their target data in the cloud from unauthorized access, including unauthorized access attempts by the CSPs themselves. AWS, Google, and Microsoft have all developed impressive encryption and key management capabilities for use with their cloud services. They want to help their customers protect data that is in transit and at rest. They have taken slightly different approaches to these challenges, but the common denominator is that they have tried to make using encryption and key management as frictionless as possible. They have designed systems that can perform lightning-fast encryption and decryption operations that help protect millions of customers' data at massive scales.

For protecting data *at rest*, there are two general options these CSPs offer: server-side encryption and client-side encryption. Server-side encryption is managed by the CSP after the customer has transferred their data to the service. For example, when a customer saves new data to a cloud storage service, it is protected by **Transport Layer Security** (**TLS**) as it moves to the cloud. Once it gets into the cloud storage service, server-side encryption can be employed to protect it. The customer brings the data, and the CSP services encrypt it and then decrypt it as customers access it; the cloud storage service is responsible for managing the keys as well in this case. The complexity of the encryption, decryption, and key management is abstracted from the customer. Put another way, the customer has delegated the responsibility for encryption and key management to the CSP.

Some CISOs are quick to point out that when server-side encryption is used, the CSPs have access to the keys used for encryption and decryption processes because they are managing them. This is true, but the CSPs have designed and implemented key management services that are backed by **Hardware Security Modules** (**HSMs**). HSMs are designed to make it hard or impossible to remove key material from them, even by their system administrators. These HSMs are typically tamper-evident, meaning if someone tried to physically break into one of them, this would be obvious to anyone inspecting the HSM. Given how HSMs are designed, physical access would not enable easy access to key material. By doing this, the CSPs mitigate the risk of insider threats to the key material and earn the trust of their customers. However, some organizations still do not want to use server-side encryption, and so they let their CSP manage keys on their behalf. Remember, they are trying to mitigate an already tiny risk; they want mitigation options that result in a near-zero risk of unauthorized access to their target data.

This is a scenario where client-side encryption can help. This means that the developer of the application, in this case, the CSP's customer, is responsible for implementing encryption algorithms, managing keys, and performing encryption and decryption operations. Using this approach, before data is transmitted anywhere, it is first encrypted by the client application handling the data. Because the customer can decide where and how their keys will be used, and they perform all the encryption and decryption operations themselves, they can choose to never share their keys or cleartext data with their CSP.

Once a customer uses client-side encryption, their encryption application can generate encryption keys or retrieve them from the customer's own on-premises key management infrastructure, such as an HSM. Once the data has been encrypted in the customer's own on-premises data center, the application transfers the encrypted data to the CSP's storage service. Now, an encrypted copy of the original data is in the cloud storage service. The cleartext data and the encryption keys were never transferred outside the customer's own on-premises data center. Because the CSP doesn't have access to the original cleartext data or the keys, there is no risk that they can access the data using the encrypted copy stored in their cloud storage service.

There are a few different ways that client-side encryption can be leveraged in a storage scenario such as this one. Here are some of the options the customer has; note that this is not an exhaustive list of options:

- Instead of running the application performing the encryption in the on-premises data center, it could be run on a **Virtual Machine** (**VM**) running in the cloud. When the application needs to, it can reach back into the on-premises data center via a VPN connection or dedicated connection to retrieve keys to perform encryption and decryption operations, after which it destroys the keys in the memory of the VM. The CSP still does not have access to cleartext data or keys.
- Instead of running the key infrastructure in the on-premises data center, it can be run on VMs in the cloud. These VMs can be managed by the customer or a trusted third

party, such as a vendor or non-commercial agency, that provides key infrastructure services. The CSP still does not have access to cleartext data or keys.

- Instead of leveraging a key management infrastructure themselves, the customer can delegate *some* of this responsibility to the CSP. For example, AWS Cloud HSM is a service that enables customers to provision their own single-tenant HSM instance in the cloud that is FIPS-validated. The CSP manages the hardware, and the customer is responsible for managing most other aspects of this infrastructure themselves, including backups. The customer gets the benefits of using an HSM without the costs and complexity of buying and maintaining their own hardware. The CSP cannot access the key material in the HSM because it is specifically designed to prevent this.

Instead of provisioning and managing key infrastructure themselves, the customer can delegate this *entirely* to the CSP. All the CSPs offer fully managed key vault solutions that are backed by HSMs. These key management services are integrated into the CSPs' other services to enable seamless encryption and decryption operations at scale in the cloud as data moves from service to service. The CSP secures and manages the keys. There are some options that allow customers to import key material from their own key management infrastructures to the CSP's managed key services, giving the customer more control over the durability and lifetime of the keys.

> **Note**
>
> Note that some governments define their own cryptographic standards and certification schemes, meaning they do not rely on US encryption standards and may not accept US-based cryptography validation programs.

All of these options provide customers with flexibility in how they mitigate the risk of unauthorized access to data. However, client-side encryption is not a panacea; it does have some limitations that need to be carefully considered. The confidentiality and integrity that client-side encryption provides come at a cost. Organizations that adopt this approach must have the technical expertise to manage their own encryption and decryption operations at the application level, in addition to managing their own key infrastructures. This isn't as fun as it sounds; I've never met anyone involved in managing HSMs who looked forward to doing so. There's also the integrity of the data to be concerned with. If there's a mistake in the client-side encryption code or in managing the keys, the organization's data could be lost forever. Overall, it's a huge responsibility for organizations. Organizations should acquire validated cryptography libraries and modules instead of developing their own. Additionally, client-side encryption typically introduces higher costs. Moving data between on-premises data centers and the cloud for encryption and decryption operations typically has transfer costs associated with it, and HSMs are not inexpensive to procure or manage either.

In the storage scenario I described, client-side encryption is relatively straightforward. Client-side encryption can also be used with databases that support it, and this is much more complex than a simple storage scenario. Encrypting data at the field level to prevent unauthorized access while preserving database indexing and search functionality requires planning and expertise.

Moreover, client-side encryption can't be used with all cloud services. For example, leveraging fully managed services in the cloud typically means the CSP needs to process cleartext data and subsequently cannot process encrypted data without access to the keys. Until homomorphic encryption or other solutions that enable the processing of encrypted data are widely adopted, client-side encryption isn't going to be a helpful option in all scenarios.

Some of the customers I advised, who had very stringent data protection requirements, started their journey to the cloud leveraging client-side encryption. Initially, they viewed it as the best option to mitigate the risk of unauthorized access to data in the cloud. However, over a period of years, as they became more comfortable with how cloud services are designed and operated, with the identity and access management capabilities in the cloud, and with the monitoring and audit capabilities, they started using HSMs provided by their CSP and, in some cases, the CSP's fully managed key vault solutions. Many of these customers concluded that using partially managed or fully managed HSMs in the cloud mitigated the same risks as client-side encryption, but without the added complexity and costs.

This concludes this brief introduction to client-side encryption. If you are interested in taking a deeper dive into client-side encryption and server-side encryption, please watch this video I recorded on the topic when I worked at AWS: *AWS Security Webinar: The Key to Effective Cloud Encryption*, available at `https://www.youtube.com/watch?v=78qFK-r7WBI`. Several newer resources have been published since I recorded that video, including this article: `https://aws.amazon.com/blogs/storage/understanding-amazon-s3-client-side-encryption-options/`.

Sovereign cloud regions

One final note about encryption and key management. Did you know it can help meet data residency requirements? Encryption and effective key management can help reduce an organization's attack surface. It shifts the responsibility of protecting all the organization's data, wherever it is, for decades to just protecting the keys used to encrypt and decrypt it. It is typically much easier to protect keys because the attack surface and the size of keys are both much smaller than protecting all the cleartext data itself. This reduced attack surface can also help your organization meet data residency requirements. The process of employing properly implemented strong encryption transforms data into something that resembles random noise. This means encrypted data is not the original cleartext data any longer and it never will be again without the decryption keys. Given this, shouldn't the encrypted version of the data, resembling random noise, be permitted to be transmitted and stored anywhere? If the encryption/decryption keys never leave their origin country or region, neither does the original cleartext data, regardless of where the encrypted data travels, right?

So many security professionals that I discussed data residency with struggled with this concept. Many of them clung to the notion that the physical location of their data somehow made it more secure. That's one of the cool things about math—it works the same everywhere in the world. That is to say, the mathematical security guarantees of correctly implemented encryption are universal, meaning they remain valid and unchanged regardless of the country in which the data is stored or processed. Arguments about nascent quantum computing capabilities aside, if properly implemented strong encryption protects the confidentiality and integrity of data in Germany, it also protects it when it travels across borders to the US. Keep this in mind when thinking through your organization's data residency requirements so that you don't pay an excessive opportunity cost for mitigation—data residency in this case—that has little or no cybersecurity value.

Despite this, there was enough fear, confusion, and friction in cloud sales cycles in Western Europe that all the hyper-scale CSPs built "sovereign cloud regions" to address European regulatory compliance requirements, as well as data residency and data sovereignty requirements. Of course, encryption and key management play a key role in these offerings. These offerings also rely on EU-only data centers and, in some cases, trusted national or regional partners staffed by EU citizens to operate the services and act as designated data custodians.

AWS describes their AWS European Sovereign Cloud in this way:

> *"The AWS European Sovereign Cloud is a new, independent cloud for Europe entirely located within the European Union (EU), designed to help customers meet their evolving sovereignty requirements. Launching in 2025, the AWS European Sovereign Cloud will be the only fully featured, independently operated sovereign cloud backed by strong technical controls, sovereign assurances, and legal protections designed to meet the needs of European governments and enterprises."* (AWS, n.d.)

Microsoft describes the "customer value" of their Microsoft Sovereign Cloud as follows:

> *"Compliance confidence: Align with local and sector-specific regulations.*
>
> *Operational control: Decide where data resides and who can access it.*

> *Security assurance: Use confidential computing and advanced encryption.*
>
> *Innovation access: Use the same Azure and Microsoft 365 services as the global cloud, with added sovereignty controls.*
>
> *Local partnership and ecosystem development: Use domestic partner participation to accelerate national digital capability, support local compliance interpretation, and foster a resilient regional supply and skills ecosystem." (Microsoft, n.d.)*

The combination of strict data residency boundaries and controls that restrict the movement of EU customers' data within the EU, encryption, key management, and EU-based staff operating the data centers provides a higher level of security and privacy assurances to organizations in the EU that choose to use these sovereign cloud regions.

Many of the executives I discussed government access to data with became far more comfortable using US-based CSPs and technology companies once they understood some of the nuances and the risks associated with it. They were also better prepared to ask the non-US-based vendors in their current supply chains whether they are subject to US jurisdiction, the same way US providers are. This exercise helps them understand the current risks of government access to data that they've likely been accepting for years or even decades.

> **Note**
>
> Some of the executives that I have advised still wanted to mitigate this risk to ensure that their own legal teams and processes are used to manage requests from law enforcement. Encryption and key management can be very effective at mitigating unauthorized access to data, whether it's attackers or governments trying to gain access to it. Of course, there are many other possible mitigations as well. These are topics I'll discuss in other chapters.

The topic of government access to data has been evolving, especially in Western Europe, and especially in light of the rapid adoption of AI. For many executives, CISOs, and security teams that are responsible for protecting the data of public or private sector organizations, this evolving narrative can be distracting, but they cannot ignore it because other executives in their organization who read these headlines will examine their organization's cybersecurity strategy using this lens. This is another great reason to have a well-thought-out cybersecurity strategy. With it, CISOs will be able to answer questions about how they are managing the risk of government access to data, using mitigations that work.

Summary

Governments typically pledge to provide their citizens with national security, law enforcement, judicial systems, and other essential functions that provide security and support citizens' pursuit of happiness. To do this, governments organize themselves into different departments, ministries, and agencies. In this chapter, we explored the different roles governments play in providing cybersecurity for their citizens and some real-world examples of how they do this. Here's a high-level summary:

- Governments are cybersecurity market participants that invest heavily in cybersecurity products, services, and talent
- Governments are standards bodies that set efficacy standards for cybersecurity
- Governments play the role of enforcers in at least two different capacities:
  - **Regulators**: Governments regulate industries to ensure they function properly
  - **Law enforcement**: Governments provide security and justice for their citizens, leveraging law enforcement bodies
- Governments also play the role of defenders in a few different capacities:
  - **Public safety**: Help protect citizens from threats such as disasters, crime, and cybersecurity threats
  - **National security**: Protect residents, institutions, and their sovereignty from internal and external threats to provide stability and prosperity
  - **Military**: Provide national defense and emergency response

We also spent significant time in this chapter looking at governments as potential cybersecurity threats. There are three different scenarios related to government access to data that often get conflated:

- **The SIGINT scenario**: Government agencies gather intelligence by intercepting and analyzing communications and electronic signals, potentially employing cryptanalysis
- **Nation-state threat actors (the unlawful government access to data scenario)**: A government agency steals data from an organization or a vendor in their supply chain, as opposed to getting a valid court order to compel it; military espionage and economic espionage are typical motivations
- **The lawful government access to data scenario**: A law enforcement or intelligence agency gets a valid court order compelling an organization or a vendor in their supply chain to provide specific evidence that is in their possession, for a criminal or national security investigation

Encryption and effective key management are important controls for mitigating all three of these threats and other types of unauthorized access to data. Client-side encryption enables organizations to encrypt sensitive data before they put it in the cloud, keeping the cleartext data and keys on-premises. Without the keys, no one can access the data stored in the cloud. Major CSPs offer some of their customers sovereign cloud regions with controls that help increase assurances that local regulations, data residency, and data sovereignty requirements are met.

Using available data from the transparency reports published by major US-based vendors, the probability of a US government request for data in the cloud is typically a fraction of 1%. Stack-ranking this risk with the other risks that organizations manage can help determine whether any resources should be invested to mitigate this threat.

This concludes my in-depth examination of government access to data. We've spent most of the first half of this book examining threats. Now, we'll shift our focus to cybersecurity strategies. In the next chapter of this book, we will explore the ingredients for a successful cybersecurity strategy.

References

- US Department of Defense. (2022). *About | US Department of Defense.* Retrieved from `https://www.defense.gov/About`
- Germany Federal Office of Information Security. (n.d.). *What do we do?* Retrieved from `https://www.bsi.bund.de/EN/Das-BSI/Leitbild/leitbild_node.html`
- Scarfone, K., Benigni, D., and Grance, T. (2009). *Cyber Security Standards,* Wiley Handbook of Science and Technology for Homeland Security, John Wiley & Sons, Inc., Hoboken, NJ, [online], `https://tsapps.nist.gov/publication/get_pdf.cfm?pub_id=152153` (accessed November 22, 2025)
- NIST. (n.d.). *About NIST.* Retrieved from `https://www.nist.gov/about-nist`
- GDPR Enforcement Tracker. (n.d.). *Statistics: Fines imposed over time.* Retrieved from `https://www.enforcementtracker.com/?insights`
- US Federal Bureau of Investigation. (n.d.). *Law Enforcement Cyber Incident Reporting, A Unified Message for State, Local, Tribal, and Territorial Law Enforcement.* Retrieved from `https://www.fbi.gov/file-repository/law-enforcement-cyber-incident-reporting.pdf/view`
- Wray, Christopher. (September 16, 2020). *Tackling the Cyber Threat Through Partnerships and Innovation.* Retrieved from `https://www.fbi.gov/news/speeches-and-`

testimony/cisa-cybersecurity-summit-addressing-threats-through-partnerships

- US Federal Bureau of Investigation. (n.d.). *What We Investigate*. Retrieved from https://www.fbi.gov/investigate/cyber#
- Federal Energy Regulatory Commission. (May 10, 2021). *Statement from FERC Chairman Richard Glick: Chairman Glick and Commissioner Clements Call for Examination of Mandatory Pipeline Cyber Standards in Wake of Colonial Pipeline Ransomware Incident.* Retrieved from https://www.ferc.gov/news-events/news/statement-ferc-chairman-richard-glick-chairman-glick-and-commissioner-clements
- U.S. Environmental Protection Agency. (May 11, 2021). *EPA Issues Fuel Waiver for Twelve States and the District of Columbia Impacted by Colonial Pipeline Shutdown*. Retrieved from https://www.epa.gov/newsreleases/epa-issues-fuel-waiver-twelve-states-and-district-columbia-impacted-colonial-pipeline
- U.S. Department of Homeland Security. (May 12, 2021). *Statement by Secretary Mayorkas on the Approval of a Jones Act Waiver in Response to Eastern Seaboard Oil Supply Constraints*. Retrieved from https://www.dhs.gov/news/2021/05/12/statement-secretary-mayorkas-approval-jones-act-waiver-response-eastern-seaboard-oil
- U.S. Department of Transportation. (May 11, 2021). *USDOT Announces Additional Measures to Help States in Areas Affected by the Colonial Pipeline Incident*. Retrieved from https://www.transportation.gov/briefing-room/usdot-announces-additional-measures-help-states-areas-affected-colonial-pipeline
- The White House. (May 12, 2021). *Executive Order on Improving the Nation's Cybersecurity*. Retrieved from https://bidenwhitehouse.archives.gov/briefing-room/presidential-actions/2021/05/12/executive-order-on-improving-the-nations-cybersecurity/
- The White House. (May 12, 2021). *FACT SHEET: President Signs Executive Order Charting New Course to Improve the Nation's Cybersecurity and Protect Federal Government Networks.* Retrieved from https://bidenwhitehouse.archives.gov/briefing-room/statements-releases/2021/05/12/fact-sheet-president-signs-executive-order-charting-new-course-to-improve-the-nations-cybersecurity-and-protect-federal-government-networks/
- National Security Agency. (n.d.). *About NSA/CSS*. Retrieved from https://www.nsa.gov/about/

- Office of the Director of National Intelligence. (n.d.). *Five Eyes Intelligence Oversight and Review Council (FIORC)*. Retrieved from `https://www.dni.gov/index.php/who-we-are/organizations/enterprise-capacity/chco/chco-related-menus/chco-related-links/recruitment-and-outreach/217-about/organization/icig-pages/2660-icig-fiorc`
- National Security Agency. (n.d.). *National Security Agency/Central Security Service*. Retrieved from `https://www.nsa.gov/Cybersecurity/Overview/`
- Office of the Under Secretary of Defense (Comptroller)/Chief Financial Officer. (March 2024). *Defense Budget Overview*. Retrieved from `https://comptroller.war.gov/Portals/45/Documents/defbudget/FY2025/FY2025_Budget_Request_Overview_Book.pdf`
- US Department of Defense. (n.d.). United States Department of Defense LinkedIn page. Retrieved from `https://www.linkedin.com/company/deptofwar`
- United States Cyber Command. (April, 2018). *Achieve and Maintain Cyberspace Superiority: Command Vision for US Cyber Command*. Retrieved from `https://www.cybercom.mil/Portals/56/Documents/USCYBERCOM%20Vision%20April%202018.pdf?ver=2018-06-14-152556-010`
- The White House. (March 2023). *National Cybersecurity Strategy*. Retrieved from `https://www.cybercom.mil/Portals/56/Documents/Mission%20and%20Vision/National-Cybersecurity-Strategy-2023.pdf`
- CBS News. (February 19, 2013). *China military unit behind many hacking attacks on U.S., cybersecurity firm says*. Retrieved from `https://www.cbsnews.com/news/china-military-unit-behind-many-hacking-attacks-on-us-cybersecurity-firm-says/`
- Mandiant. (Feb 1, 2013). *Mandiant, APT 1: Exposing One of China's Cyber Espionage Units*. Retrieved from `https://nsarchive.gwu.edu/document/21484-document-83`
- Gidda, M. (Aug 21, 2013). *Edward Snowden and the NSA files – timeline*. Retrieved from The Guardian: `https://www.theguardian.com/world/2013/jun/23/edward-snowden-nsa-files-timeline`
- Ball, J. (Oct 25, 2013). *NSA monitored calls of 35 world leaders after US official handed over contacts*. Retrieved from The Guardian: `https://www.theguardian.com/world/2013/oct/24/nsa-surveillance-world-leaders-calls`

- James Regan, M. J. (June 23, 2015). NSA spied on French presidents, WikiLeaks. Retrieved from Reuters: https://www.reuters.com/article/us-france-wikileaks/nsa-spied-on-french-presidents-wikileaks-idUSKBN0P32EM20150623
- Brookings. (May 22, 2014). *Unit 61398 Indictment Exposes Real Faces and Names Behind Shanghai Keyboards Used to Steal from U.S. Businesses.* Retrieved from https://www.brookings.edu/blog/brookings-now/2014/05/22/unit-61398-indictment-exposes-real-faces-and-names-behind-shanghai-keyboards-used-to-steal-from-u-s-businesses/
- WikiLeaks. (July 8, 2015). *All the Chancellor's Men.* Retrieved from WikiLeaks: https://wikileaks.org/nsa-germany/index.de
- WikiLeaks. (July 4,). *Bugging Brazil.* Retrieved from WikiLeaks: https://wikileaks.org/nsa-brazil/
- WikiLeaks. (June 29, 2015). *Espionnage Élysée.* Retrieved from WikiLeaks: https://wikileaks.org/nsa-france/
- WikiLeaks. (July 31, 2015). *Target Tokyo.* Retrieved from WikiLeaks: https://wikileaks.org/nsa-japan/
- Wikipedia. (n.d.). *Signals intelligence by alliances, nations and industries.* Retrieved from Wikipedia: https://en.wikipedia.org/wiki/Signals_intelligence_by_alliances,_nations_and_industries
- EWING, P. (May 22, 2014). *Gates: French cyber spies target U.S..* Retrieved from Politico: https://www.politico.com/story/2014/05/france-intellectual-property-theft-107020
- Christopher Bing, J. S. (2019, January 30). *Inside the UAE's Secret Hacking Team of American Mercenaries.* Retrieved from Reuters: https://www.reuters.com/investigates/special-report/usa-spying-raven/
- Mark Mazzetti, A. G. (Mar 21, 2019). *A New Age of Warfare: How Internet Mercenaries Do Battle for Authoritarian Governments.* Retrieved from New York Times: https://www.nytimes.com/2019/03/21/us/politics/government-hackers-nso-darkmatter.html
- Mehul Srivastava, R. S. (May 14, 2019). *Israel's NSO: the business of spying on your iPhone.* Retrieved from Financial Times: https://www.ft.com/content/7f2f39b2-733e-11e9-bf5c-6eeb837566c5

- US Department of Justice. (June 28, 2010). *Ten Alleged Secret Agents Arrested in the United States*. Retrieved from `https://www.justice.gov/archives/opa/pr/ten-alleged-secret-agents-arrested-united-states`
- NCC Group. (June 30, 2022). *The Lazarus group: North Korean scourge for +10 years*. Retrieved from`https://www.nccgroup.com/the-lazarus-group-north-korean-scourge-for-plus10-years/`
- Microsoft. (2025). *Microsoft Digital Defense Report 2025*. Retrieved from `https://www.microsoft.com/en-us/security/security-insider/threat-landscape/microsoft-digital-defense-report-2025`
- Microsoft. (October, 2021). *Microsoft Digital Defense Report 2021*. Retrieved from `https://www.microsoft.com/en-us/security/security-insider/threat-landscape/microsoft-digital-defense-report-2021`
- CISA. (n.d.). *Nation-State Threats*. Retrieved from `https://www.cisa.gov/topics/cyber-threats-and-advisories/nation-state-cyber-actors`
- Smith, B. (October 23, 2017). *DOJ acts to curb the overuse of secrecy orders. Now it's Congress' turn*. Retrieved from Microsoft On the Issues: `https://blogs.microsoft.com/on-the-issues/2017/10/23/doj-acts-curb-overuse-secrecy-orders-now-congress-turn/`
- Marczak, B., Scott-Railton, J., McKune, S., Abdul Razzak, B., and Deibert, B. "Hide and Seek: Tracking NSO Group's Pegasus Spyware to Operations in 45 Countries," Citizen Lab Research Report No. 113, University of Toronto, September 2018. Retrieved from `https://utoronto.scholaris.ca/server/api/core/bitstreams/d4c5b5f4-96bd-45e3-a5a9-c60c8228dff3/content`
- Marczak, B., Scott-Railton, J. (August 24, 2016). *The Million Dollar Dissident*. Retrieved from `https://citizenlab.ca/2016/08/million-dollar-dissident-iphone-zero-day-nso-group-uae/`
- The Citizen Lab. (n.d.). *Who We Are*. Retrieved from `https://citizenlab.ca/about/`
- Deibert, R. "Chasing Shadows with Ronald Deibert and Ellen Nakashima." Interview by Ellen Nakashima. April 18, 2025. Video, 1:08:25. `https://www.youtube.com/watch?v=iFIG0dP87hw`
- The White House. (March 27, 2023). *FACT SHEET: President Biden Signs Executive Order to Prohibit U.S. Government Use of Commercial Spyware that Poses Risks to National Security*. Retrieved from `https://bidenwhitehouse.archives.gov/briefing-room/`

statements-releases/2023/03/27/fact-sheet-president-biden-signs-executive-order-to-prohibit-u-s-government-use-of-commercial-spyware-that-poses-risks-to-national-security/

- Apple. (September 15, 2025). *About Lockdown Mode.* Retrieved from https://support.apple.com/en-us/105120
- Atwood, K., Lyngaas, S. (December 3, 2021). *US State Department phones were hacked with NSO Group spyware.* Retrieved from https://www.cnn.com/2021/12/03/politics/state-department-nso-spyware
- US Department of Justice. (April, 2022). *Mutual Legal Assistance Treaties of the United States.* Retrieved from US Department of Justice: https://www.justice.gov/criminal/criminal-oia/file/1498806/dl
- U.S. GOVERNMENT PRINTING OFFICE. (2004). *MUTUAL LEGAL ASSISTANCE TREATY WITH GERMANY.* Retrieved from United States Congress: https://www.congress.gov/108/cdoc/tdoc27/CDOC-108tdoc27.pdf
- U.S. GOVERNMENT PRINTING OFFICE. (2006, 10 28). *MUTUAL LEGAL ASSISTANCE AGREEMENT WITH THE EUROPEAN UNION.* Retrieved from United States Congress: https://www.congress.gov/109/cdoc/tdoc13/CDOC-109tdoc13.pdf
- Cornell Law School. (n.d.). *Fourth Amendment.* Retrieved from Legal Information Institute: https://www.law.cornell.edu/wex/fourth_amendment
- Cornell Law School. (n.d.). *Probable Cause.* Retrieved from Legal Information Institute: https://www.law.cornell.edu/wex/probable_cause
- U.S. GOVERNMENT PRINTING OFFICE. (2000). *TREATY WITH FRANCE ON MUTUAL LEGAL ASSISTANCE IN CRIMINAL MATTERS.* Retrieved from United States Congress: https://www.congress.gov/106/cdoc/tdoc17/CDOC-106tdoc17.pdf
- Swire, P., Hemmings, J. D., Vergnolle, S. (2016, 11 15). *A Mutual Legal Assistance Case Study: The United States and France.* Retrieved from Peterswire.net: http://peterswire.net/wp-content/uploads/mutual-legal-assistance-case-study-US-France.pdf
- Richard A., Clarke, M. J. (2013, December 12). *LIBERTY AND SECURITY IN A CHANGING WORLD.* Retrieved from Obamawhitehouse.archives.gov: https://obamawhitehouse.archives.gov/sites/default/files/docs/2013-12-12_rg_final_report.pdf

- United States Congress. (March 21, 2018). *CLOUD Act Resources*. Retrieved from Justice.gov: `https://www.justice.gov/criminal/cloud-act-resources`
- Electronic Frontier Foundation. (December 29, 2020). *Section 215 Expired: Year in Review 2020*. Retrieved from EFF.org: `https://www.eff.org/deeplinks/2020/12/section-215-expired-year-review-2020`
- Kuersten, Andreas. (December 17, 2024). *Foreign Intelligence Surveillance Act (FISA)*. Retrieved from Congress.gov: `https://www.congress.gov/crs-product/IF11451`
- The European Parliament and The Council of The European Union. (2016, 04 27). *REGULATION (EU) 2016/679 OF THE EUROPEAN PARLIAMENT AND OF THE COUNCIL*. Retrieved from EUR-Lex: `https://eur-lex.europa.eu/legal-content/EN/TXT/PDF/?uri=CELEX:32016R0679&from=EN`
- Congressional Research Service. (2021). *EU Data Transfer Requirements and U.S. Intelligence Laws: Understanding Schrems II and Its Impact on the EU-U.S. Privacy Shield*. Congressional Research Service. Retrieved from `https://www.congress.gov/crs_external_products/R/HTML/R46724.web.html`
- Congressional Research Service. (2021). *Foreign Intelligence Surveillance Act (FISA): An Overview*. Retrieved from Congressional Research Service: `https://www.congress.gov/crs_external_products/IF/PDF/IF11451/IF11451.2.pdf`
- National Security Agency/Central Security Service. (n.d.). *Foreign Intelligence Surveillance Act of 1978 (FISA)*. Retrieved from National Security Agency/Central Security Service: `https://www.nsa.gov/Signals-Intelligence/FISA/`
- The White House. (October 7, 2022). *FACT SHEET: President Biden Signs Executive Order to Implement the European Union-U.S. Data Privacy Framework*. Retrieved from `https://bidenwhitehouse.archives.gov/briefing-room/statements-releases/2022/10/07/fact-sheet-president-biden-signs-executive-order-to-implement-the-european-union-u-s-data-privacy-framework/`
- Duball, J. (September 3, 2025). *European General Court dismisses Latombe challenge, upholds EU-US Data Privacy Framework*. Retrieved from IAPP: `https://iapp.org/news/a/european-general-court-dismisses-latombe-challenge-upholds-eu-us-data-privacy-framework`
- NOYB. (December 13, 2022). *Statement on EU Comission [sic] adequacy decision on US*. Retrieved from NOYB: `https://noyb.eu/en/statement-eu-comission-adequacy-decision-us`

- Krempl, S. (Oct 30, 2025). *Data transfer to US: lawsuit against EU data protection framework goes to ECJ*. Retrieved from Heise Online: `https://www.heise.de/en/news/Data-transfer-to-US-lawsuit-against-EU-data-protection-framework-goes-to-ECJ-10965203.html`
- Shostack, A. (2014). *Threat Modeling: Designing for Security*. Wiley
- AWS. (n.d.). AWS European Sovereign Cloud. Retrieved from `https://aws.eu/`
- Microsoft. (n.d.). *What is Microsoft Sovereign Cloud?*. Retrieved from `https://learn.microsoft.com/en-us/industry/sovereign-cloud/overview/microsoft-sovereign-cloud`
- Boghani, P. (2015, December 1). *Gag Order Gone, Secrets of a National Security Letter are Revealed*. PBS Frontline. `https://www.pbs.org/wgbh/frontline/article/gag-order-gone-secrets-of-a-national-security-letter-are-revealed/`

Transparency reports, law enforcement request reports, and related data:

- Apple. (n.d.). Transparency reports. Retrieved from `https://www.apple.com/legal/transparency/report-pdf.html`
- Amazon Web Services. (n.d.). Law Enforcement Information Requests. Retrieved from `https://www.amazon.com/gp/help/customer/display.html?nodeId=GYSDRGWQ2C2CRYEF`
- Google. (n.d.). Transparency report. Retrieved from `https://transparencyreport.google.com/?hl=en`
- Google. (n.d.). *United States national security requests for user information*. Retrieved from`https://transparencyreport.google.com/user-data/us-national-security?hl=en`
- Google. (n.d.). *Is the number of "accounts" a comprehensive count of the total number of users implicated by government requests for user information?*. Retrieved from`https://support.google.com/transparencyreport/answer/9713961#zippy=%2Cis-the-number-of-accounts-a-comprehensive-count-of-the-total-number-of-users-implicated-by-government-requests-for-user-information`
- Meta. (n.d.). *Government Requests for User Data*. Retrieved from `https://transparency.meta.com/reports/government-data-requests/`
- Microsoft. (n.d.). *Government Requests for Customer Data Report*. Retrieved from `https://www.microsoft.com/en-us/corporate-responsibility/reports/government-requests/customer-data`

- Microsoft. (n.d.). *Microsoft Government Requests Report H2*. Retrieved from `https://cdn-dynmedia-1.microsoft.com/is/content/microsoftcorp/microsoft/msc/documents/presentations/CSR/MSFT-GRR-Enterprise-One-Pager-H2-2024.pdf`
- Microsoft. (n.d.). *Microsoft Government Requests Report*. Retrieved from `https://cdn-dynmedia-1.microsoft.com/is/content/microsoftcorp/microsoft/msc/documents/presentations/CSR/MSFT-GRR-Enterprise-One-Pager-H1-2024.pdf`
- Microsoft. (April 21, 2022). *Microsoft releases biannual digital trust reports*. Retrieved from `https://blogs.microsoft.com/on-the-issues/2022/04/21/microsoft-releases-biannual-digital-trust-reports-2022/`
- Microsoft. (n.d.). *About our practices and your data*. Retrieved from `https://blogs.microsoft.com/datalaw/our-practices/`
- Condon, S. (April 15, 2021). *Microsoft reports increase in US law enforcement data requests in 2020*. Retrieved from `https://www.zdnet.com/article/microsoft-reports-increase-in-us-law-enforcement-data-requests-in-2020/`
- Microsoft. (October 21, 2021). *Microsoft releases biannual digital trust reports*. Retrieved from `https://blogs.microsoft.com/on-the-issues/2021/10/21/microsoft-biannual-digital-trust-reports-2021/#:~:text=Law%20enforcement%20requests,-When%20Microsoft%20receives&text=We%20disclose%20customer%20data%20only,we%20received%205%2C682%20legal%20requests`
- Microsoft. (n.d.). *U.S. National Security Orders Report*. Retrieved from`https://www.microsoft.com/en-us/corporate-responsibility/reports/government-requests/customer-data#tab-national-security-orders-report`
- Defense Counterintelligence and Security Agency. (2025). *Targeting U.S. Technologies: A Report of Threats to Cleared Industry* (DCSA-TA-26-001). U.S. Department of Defense. `https://www.dcsa.mil/Portals/128/Documents/CI/DCSA-TA-26-001%20Targeting%20US%20Technologies%20FY25.pdf`
- Google Threat Intelligence Group. (2026, February 10). *Beyond the Battlefield: Threats to the Defense Industrial Base*. Google Cloud Blog. `https://cloud.google.com/blog/topics/threat-intelligence/threats-to-defense-industrial-base/`

Get this book's PDF version and more

Scan the QR code (or go to `packtpub.com/unlock`). Search for this book by name, confirm the edition, and then follow the steps on the page.

Note: Keep your invoice handy. Purchases made directly from Packt don't require an invoice.

Part 3

Cybersecurity strategies

In this section, you'll learn how to build a cybersecurity strategy that is both effective and executable. You'll understand the core ingredients of a successful strategy—governance, risk management, fundamentals, high-value asset protection, business alignment, and security culture—and how to apply them in real organizations. You'll compare common cybersecurity strategies, evaluate their strengths using the Cybersecurity Fundamentals Scoring System (CFSS), and learn how to choose and combine approaches that fit your environment.

You'll then move into practical implementation, learning how to apply the Intrusion Kill Chain strategy, modernize it for today's networks, map controls, identify gaps, and integrate complementary frameworks like MITRE ATT&CK®. Finally, you'll see how to measure whether your strategy is working through data-driven methods such as vulnerability metrics, intrusion reconstructions, and attack-centric evaluations.

By the end, you'll know how to design, implement, and continuously improve a cybersecurity strategy that stands up to real-world threats.

This part of the book includes the following chapters:

- *Chapter 9, Ingredients for a Successful Cybersecurity Strategy*
- *Chapter 10, Cybersecurity Strategies*
- *Chapter 11, Cybersecurity Strategy Implementation*
- *Chapter 12, Measuring Performance and Effectiveness*

9

Ingredients for a Successful Cybersecurity Strategy

Given the rapid evolution of the threat landscape, CISOs increasingly recognize that their teams can no longer keep pace by simply reacting to vulnerabilities and attacks. The expanding number of endpoints, systems, and threat actors has dramatically increased the scope of what must be defended. At the same time, resource constraints and unpredictable economic conditions continue to pressure cybersecurity budgets and staffing. In this environment, organizations need well-designed, threat-adapted strategies and the ability to execute them consistently with clear, measurable outcomes.

There are several ingredients that are necessary for a cybersecurity program to have the best chance of being successful; for example, business objective alignment, understanding the risk appetite of the organization, and fostering a strong cybersecurity culture can have very positive impacts on cybersecurity programs. This chapter will help you understand what a cybersecurity strategy looks like and some tips for success based on my experience managing cybersecurity programs of various sizes and complexities.

This chapter covers the following topics:

- What is a cybersecurity strategy?
- Other ingredients for a successful strategy

Let's begin with a couple of fundamental questions that we'll need to answer before discussing cybersecurity strategies in any detail: what is a cybersecurity strategy, and why do we need one?

What is a cybersecurity strategy?

A cybersecurity strategy is an intentional, long-term plan that defines how your organization protects its most important assets, reduces risk, and adapts to evolving threats. It aligns security priorities with business objectives, establishes the principles and capabilities you will rely on, and guides how people, processes, and technology work together to achieve measurable security outcomes. Having a well-developed cybersecurity strategy has helped me as a cybersecurity leader in at least a few different ways.

First, having a well-developed strategy helped me compensate for the lack of strong pre-existing cybersecurity cultures at some of the organizations I worked at. Cybersecurity cultures take time to develop, and a solid strategy can give you some of the time needed.

Many of the cybersecurity programs I worked on were using various cybersecurity-related frameworks, models, and standards in disjointed ways. Frameworks and models such as NIST CSF, MITRE ATT&CK, and others can work in concert. I found that a well-developed cybersecurity strategy can help coalesce and harmonize disparate frameworks, models, and standards.

Additionally, having a strategy that makes it easy to measure progress helped me communicate the efficacy of the cybersecurity program to my stakeholders. That is, a coherent strategy helped me explain what the Cybersecurity team was doing and why, and describe its progress, to C-level executives, the Board of Directors, and other interested third parties such as vendors, regulators, and others.

Let's dig into each one of these benefits in a little more detail.

Cybersecurity culture

Organizations that have a super-strong cybersecurity culture essentially have cybersecurity baked into them. For everyone else, there's strategy. For example, for militaries and law enforcement agencies, each member's security competency can be the difference between life, death, and jail time. These are strong incentives to follow established procedures and always be security-minded. For these organizations, their shared beliefs, customs, and traditions result in their members exhibiting natural behaviors that tend to lead to favorable security outcomes. For example, evidence-handling discipline in law enforcement is critical. The procedures and practices law enforcement personnel follow are key to their success and become second nature to people in these organizations. Officers instinctively bag, seal, and label evidence the moment it's collected, even before thinking about paperwork. They maintain an almost reflexive awareness of who touched what, when, and why. Evidence is never left unattended in vehicles, hallways, or interview rooms, not because of a checklist, but because it violates professional norms and risks the integrity of the case. These behaviors are self-reinforcing because they provide consistent feedback loops for both positive and negative actions. For example, a lack of rigor in evidence handling discipline can lead to very poor outcomes for law enforcement organizations and the personnel who work at them, so leadership and personnel in these organizations constantly encourage disciplined behaviors.

While this culture absolutely helps law enforcement organizations enforce the law more successfully, it doesn't mean that a strong cybersecurity culture is a given in these organizations. After all, evidence handling discipline and effective practices around physical security don't prevent someone from clicking on links in a phishing email and entering their credentials. A culture that helps people make such trust decisions is what I mean when I refer to cybersecurity culture; the discipline not to click on links or open attachments unless absolutely necessary, the discipline not to visit websites that aren't absolutely necessary, the discipline not to reuse passwords across services, and so on. When these behaviors become as natural for information workers as evidence handling discipline is for law enforcement, their organizations' cybersecurity benefits.

For enterprises, a strong cybersecurity culture doesn't make them un-hackable, but when everyone is conscious about the potential security outcomes of their actions, fewer bad outcomes occur. Simply put, when everyone working at an organization is consciously trying to help the CISO and Security team be successful, the CISO and Security team have a better chance of success.

In my experience, most organizations don't have this type of security culture—they rely on hiring smart people and their employees' best judgment, supported by annual training, corporate policies, processes, and procedures. In my experience, organizations such as these can develop lower morale if their employees are encumbered with too many procedures and processes, and red tape. These same organizations are under constant attack via all the threats we discussed earlier in this book, including exploitation of unpatched vulnerabilities, malware, ransomware extortion schemes, **Distributed Denial of Service** (**DDoS**) attacks, drive-by download attacks, attacks on web applications and APIs, and so many others.

An effective cybersecurity strategy can help these organizations compensate for the lack of a super-strong cybersecurity culture. As I've told so many executives over the years, cybersecurity isn't a self-cleaning oven that you can set and forget. Their organizations are under constant attack from every direction, and their approach to cybersecurity needs to reflect this. Confidence, enthusiasm, and hope, by themselves, are not going to fend off nation-state attackers, ransomware gangs, or other highly capable adversaries. Enterprises need a way to keep up with the proliferation of attackers and their constantly evolving tactics. Some organizations may never develop the shared beliefs and habits that naturally produce strong cybersecurity outcomes. However, cybersecurity is an existential threat for all organizations today; every organization needs a successful cybersecurity program, whether they have a strong cybersecurity culture or not. This is what a cybersecurity strategy seeks to accomplish.

Coalesce cybersecurity frameworks, models, and standards

Cybersecurity and compliance professionals sometimes use the term "strategy" when they are referring to frameworks, models, or standards. There are lots of these in the industry and many organizations use them – for example, ISO standards, NIST standards, the NIST Cybersecurity Framework, OWASP Top 10, CIS Benchmarks, STRIDE, PASTA, risk management frameworks, SOC 2, PCI DSS, HIPAA, the Cloud Security Alliance Cloud Controls Matrix, the AWS Cloud Adoption Framework Security perspective, the AWS Well-Architected Framework security pillar, and many more. All of these can be helpful tools for organizations seeking to improve their security postures, comply with regulations, and demonstrate that they meet or exceed industry standards. In my career, I have met many CISOs who have adopted some of these as their enterprise cybersecurity strategy—some with remarkable success. However, there has been a proliferation of cybersecurity frameworks, standards, and regulations over the decades, making it challenging for CISOs and cybersecurity teams to evaluate and adopt them in a coherent way.

Ultimately, a CISO's job is to operate cybersecurity programs that help meet their organization's objectives. For many CISOs, this typically involves a combination of data protection objectives and complying with some level of industry standards and regulations, at a minimum. Many CISOs try to accomplish this by adopting "off-the-shelf" frameworks and by implementing "best practices" and industry standards. However, these are all typically based on someone else's threat model. Using best practices and industry standards without grounding them in your organization's specific requirements increases the likelihood of critical gaps. For example, was FedRAMP based on your organization's specific requirements? Probably not. That doesn't mean it can't be helpful, but it's important to recognize the limitations of using someone else's model or standard.

A strong cybersecurity strategy aligns directly with your organization's high-value assets and the specific requirements, threats, and risks that surround them, giving you a far greater chance of achieving meaningful security outcomes. You can still use combinations and permutations of your favorite cybersecurity frameworks, models, and standards, but wrapped in a strategy that helps to rationalize these choices. I'll provide an example of this for you later in this chapter.

Communicating the efficacy of the cybersecurity program

One job I was fortunate enough to work in during my career was as a director of corporate communications for cybersecurity at Microsoft. In this job, I learned firsthand how important communications are. Without effectively communicating your strategy, how your investments align with it, and your progress executing on it, CISOs invite criticism from other executives, members of the board of directors, and from vendors that are trying to sell their products and services.

Reflecting on my years as a cybersecurity advisor at Microsoft and Amazon Web Services, I can recall only a handful of CISOs who were able to clearly articulate their cybersecurity strategy. Many of them were well spoken and had more experience managing operational cybersecurity teams than I did, but they couldn't explain the big picture—how all the pieces of their program fit together in a rational way that resulted in better cybersecurity. The CISOs who could describe a coherent picture of their cybersecurity program orchestration were impressive. They were able to explain what each of their teams did and why, and how they integrated together with the other teams in their organizations to address their organizations' top risks, industry and regulatory compliance requirements, and their boards' biggest cybersecurity concerns, while helping to drive their businesses forward. They knew where their gaps were and could explain why they existed and whether they'd be addressed in the future.

CISOs who clearly articulate their strategies tend to build strong credibility with stakeholders. They demonstrated they knew more about effective cybersecurity practices at *their* organization than anyone else could. It also enabled their teams to understand and repeat this strategy, which became self-reinforcing. Everyone on their teams knew how their functions fit into the big picture; no one was left to wonder what their contribution or opportunity looked like.

Asserting that an industry framework, control set, or standard is your organization's cybersecurity strategy is difficult to defend, given how many organizations have tried and failed using the very same approaches. Many enterprises breached in recent years were operating under ISO, NIST, PCI DSS, or similar standards at the time. These aren't bad by any means; in fact, they can materially improve an organization's security posture. But they are almost always built around someone else's threat model. Relying on best practices that weren't designed for your specific requirements makes it far more likely that critical gaps will emerge. PCI DSS, for example, was created to protect the payment card ecosystem, not your entire enterprise IT estate. It can still be valuable, but only if you recognize the limitations of adopting a model optimized for someone else's risks.

I'm not suggesting that your organization is a unique snowflake, because it likely isn't. But it does have its own combination of requirements based on its leadership's risk appetite, how fiercely it must compete in the marketplace, its culture, and the risks with the highest probabilities and impacts associated with them. In cases where CISOs use industry frameworks as their cybersecurity strategies, a vendor deeply familiar with that framework may be able to point out gaps that aren't aligned with the organization's actual risks. If cybersecurity were as easy as being really good at implementing and operating an industry framework, it wouldn't be a $271 billion industry (in 2025) with an estimated **Compound Annual Growth Rate** (**CAGR**) of 11.9% (Grand View Research, 2025). The mission would be accomplished already. Unfortunately, enterprise cybersecurity is a much harder challenge than that.

Simply stated, CISOs who can articulate a coherent cybersecurity strategy for their organizations and can provide data that shows progress executing on it have a much easier time in their roles than CISOs who can't. To do this, they need an effective cybersecurity strategy, and they must be able to articulate it in whole and in part, in both verbal and written communication when needed. As a cybersecurity executive, I do this constantly because it provides clarity for people who need it to help us achieve better cybersecurity, whether they are on my team, on an adjacent team, other executives, board members, regulators, auditors, lawyers, or vendors. The strategy isn't meant to be a secret; it is designed to help orchestrate resources to address the most urgent risks organizations face. In a world where most cybersecurity teams have limited resources, a strategy that helps do this is critical. CISOs' ability to communicate their strategies and get stakeholder buy-in is the critical path for a successful cybersecurity strategy.

Compensating for the lack of a pre-existing strong cybersecurity culture, coalescing cybersecurity frameworks and standards, and communicating the efficacy of the cybersecurity program are some of the benefits I have derived from having a well-developed cybersecurity strategy. Let me make the concept of a cybersecurity strategy a little more concrete by providing you with an example of one.

Cybersecurity strategy example

It is said that a picture is worth a thousand words. *Figure 9.1* offers a clear example of how a framework can be used to shape a basic cybersecurity strategy tailored to your organization. Documenting what your program is doing today in each area, and what you intend to do next, provides the foundation for a practical, actionable strategy execution plan.

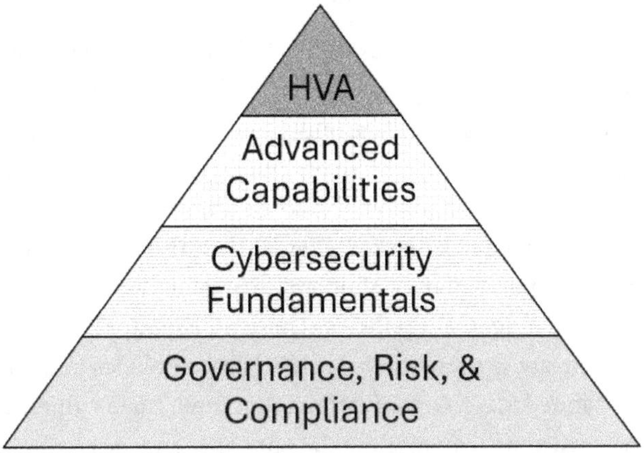

Figure 9.1 – An illustrative example of a cybersecurity strategy

This cybersecurity strategy is illustrated as a pyramid. There are a few reasons I selected this shape. First, it helps us understand that the strategy relies on its foundation. Without a solid foundation, the strategy will fail. Building a solid foundation gives the strategy the best chance for long-term success. Second, each part of the strategy relies on and benefits from the parts it rests on. For example, cybersecurity fundamentals rely on and benefit from a solid foundation provided by **governance, risk, and compliance** (**GRC**). Without effective GRC, the cybersecurity fundamentals will fail. **High-value assets** (**HVAs**), the most important assets the organization has, are at the top of the pyramid, benefiting from all the other parts of the strategy, but also reliant on them. If the other parts of the strategy fail, ultimately, efforts at protecting the highest value assets will also fail. CISOs and security teams that adopt this strategy will seek to orchestrate the resources they have to develop and support each part of this strategy. Let's dive into each part of this strategy in more detail next.

Governance, risk, and compliance

Let's start by discussing the foundation of this strategy, GRC. For many of the enterprises I advised, GRC was often an undervalued part of their cybersecurity programs, especially for highly technical cybersecurity teams. Highly technical cybersecurity teams tend to try to mitigate every risk and solve every problem using technical controls—this is their forte. But this approach is like bailing water out of a sinking boat; water keeps pouring in regardless of how much water gets bailed out. If the hole in the hull were addressed, the amount of water bailed would be dramatically reduced or unnecessary. Let me explain.

Governance

The governance function aligns the cybersecurity strategy with business objectives and executive priorities. This is where an organization's appetite for risk and its culture manifest themselves in policies, standards, and procedures.

Let's use vulnerability management as an example. I discussed vulnerability management in detail in *Chapter 3, Industry Vulnerability Disclosure Trends* and *Chapter 4, Product Vulnerability Disclosure Trends*. Recall my discussion concerning how much risk vulnerability remediation **service-level agreements** (**SLAs**) represent to organizations. Enterprises that have relatively short vulnerability remediation SLAs, such as hours or days after a vendor publishes an update for a critical vulnerability, reduce risk markedly faster than those enterprises that patch such vulnerabilities once per month or quarter. Vulnerability remediation SLAs are defined in enterprises' vulnerability management policies. These policies apply to technology asset owners and operators who are expected to comply with the policies and remediate vulnerabilities within defined SLAs. Organizations that don't have vulnerability management policies or have policies without remediation SLAs or consequences for non-compliance may be carrying far more risk than their leadership intends. Defining vulnerability remediation SLAs in a policy that reflects the risk appetite of the organization's management, including the board, and has real consequences for non-compliance, can help control the incoming volume of vulnerabilities by dictating how quickly vulnerabilities should be remediated. When governance mechanisms aren't in place, cybersecurity teams face a constant influx of issues that are difficult to manage effectively.

There are plenty of other examples where governance can help organizations achieve better cybersecurity, such as acceptable use policies, remote access policies, password policies, incident response policies, data classification and protection policies, third-party risk policies, and others. In other words, governance can help reduce the range of cybersecurity risks by setting expectations that everyone needs to meet. Adopting standards and following policies designed to reduce cybersecurity risks can dramatically reduce the volume of high-priority threats that cybersecurity teams manage. When everyone embraces cybersecurity policies and standards, it can also reduce the number and complexity of technical cybersecurity controls needed. Some highly technical CISOs may emphasize technical controls more than governance mechanisms, simply because those controls are where they have the deepest expertise. It's hard for these CISOs to give up hiring another offensive security engineer or incident responder in favor of hiring a security governance lead. But policies and standards can be a powerful tool to help them achieve better cybersecurity for their organizations.

Risk

Another typically underappreciated function in cybersecurity programs is risk management. I typically use my risk management team to perform at least two important functions: managing the cybersecurity risk register and quantifying the top risks.

Managing the cybersecurity risk register involves tracking cybersecurity risks that have been discovered and that cannot be remediated quickly. Each risk in the risk register is assigned to a risk owner and has a risk treatment plan and a remediation target date if appropriate. For example, suppose a system is past its end-of-life date, as defined by the vendor that developed and sold it, and it no longer receives security updates. This is a known risk that should be entered into the risk register along with the name of the person or group that owns it and details of their remediation plan, including its planned decommission date. The Risk Management team is responsible for overseeing the remediation plans in the risk register, ensuring that each action is carried out with the appropriate level of urgency and completed by the target date when remediation is required. The Risk Management team also ensures the risk register is reviewed at least quarterly by a Risk Board or the appropriate group of executives. These reviews are important so that senior executives are aware of the known cybersecurity risks, approve of their risk treatment plans, and ensure risks don't become permanent fixtures in the register.

Quantifying the top risks to the organization involves identifying the most probable and potentially impactful risks to the organization and quantifying the estimated cost for each risk if it is realized. This data can help inform the cybersecurity strategy, priorities, as well as budget and resource allocations. It helps senior executives and boards of directors understand the organization's cybersecurity strategy and why the CISO is investing in and prioritizing specific work items. This data is also very helpful when making a business case for funding new capabilities or tools. For example, if the quantitative risk analysis reveals that a top risk would cost the organization $20 million if it were realized, but it only costs $100,000 a year to manage, it makes spending decisions easier for senior executives. For Risk Management teams that aren't sophisticated enough to develop their own risk quantification dollar cost estimates, identifying the top risks to their organizations based on probability and impact scores is still very helpful data they can provide.

Compliance

Finally, the compliance component of GRC is responsible for ensuring adherence to cybersecurity industry standards, regulations, and laws. Examples include the **Payment Card Industry Data Security Standard** (**PCI-DSS**), the **Health Insurance Portability and Accountability Act** (**HIPAA**), the **California Privacy Rights Act** (**CPRA**), the **General Data Protection Regulation** (**GDPR**), **Sarbanes-Oxley** (**SOX**), NIST and ISO standards, and many others. The applicability of each law, regulation, and standard can depend on the industry each organization is in, the locations they do business in, and the type of data they collect, among other factors. For example, some regulations, such as GDPR, are designed to have a broad global scope, while SOX applies only to issuers of securities registered with the SEC. Compliance teams help their organizations by reducing exposure to fines, legal penalties, and reputational damage. Cybersecurity Compliance teams typically work closely with Legal teams, Enterprise Compliance, and Audit teams to provide management and the boards of directors with a complete picture of the compliance status of the organization. Fines, legal penalties, and potential reputational damage can be strong incentives for IT teams and business units to comply with regulated and industry standards, which can help achieve better cybersecurity. When compliance teams are under-resourced, organizations miss out on the full benefits those programs can deliver. I'll discuss compliance again later in this chapter, as well as in *Chapter 10, Cybersecurity Strategies.*

Without effective GRC, CISOs, cybersecurity teams, and their allies typically have a much harder time trying to provide security for ungoverned environments where the risks are not well understood, and complying with industry standards and regulations is not taken seriously. As they say, cybersecurity is a team sport, and without the help of all the stakeholders, the chances of success over time are slim to none. Organizations that make effective use of GRC can establish a foundation that the rest of their cybersecurity strategies can depend on.

Let's discuss the next part of our example strategy, the cybersecurity fundamentals.

The cybersecurity fundamentals

With the solid foundation that GRC can provide, the next part of the strategy is the cybersecurity fundamentals. The cybersecurity fundamentals are parts of the strategy that focus on mitigating the Cybersecurity Usual Suspects, or the five ways enterprises get initially compromised. You'll recall that I discussed the Cybersecurity Usual Suspects in detail in *Chapter 1, How Enterprises Get Hacked.* The Cybersecurity Usual Suspects are as follows:

- Unpatched vulnerabilities
- Security misconfigurations
- Weak, leaked, and stolen credentials
- Social engineering
- Insider threats

Cybersecurity strategies must be informed by the Cybersecurity Usual Suspects and be effective at mitigating them—this is what the cybersecurity fundamentals do. I consider these concepts to be critical ingredients of effective cybersecurity strategies. Strategies that do not focus on the fundamentals and therefore do not address the Cybersecurity Usual Suspects need to be complemented by other strategies that do, or the approach will have gaps that attackers can take advantage of. Remember, all attackers use one or more of the Cybersecurity Usual Suspects to initially compromise enterprise environments. While it's true that not all attackers need to initially compromise their target, because someone else already has and provides them with access, initial access was originally achieved by leveraging the Cybersecurity Usual Suspects. This is true whether attackers are a notorious ransomware gang, a nation-state threat actor, or a commercial penetration testing firm hired to test defenses. Investing in protection, detection, and response capabilities that help mitigate the Cybersecurity Usual Suspects typically provides the highest cybersecurity return on investment for organizations. It also provides a foundation for other, more advanced capabilities, which I'll discuss next.

Advanced cybersecurity capabilities

Advanced cybersecurity capabilities are investments that organizations should make as they become very proficient at the fundamentals. If your organization isn't *really* good at the fundamentals, then that's the place they should invest in first before investing in advanced cybersecurity capabilities. Investing in the cybersecurity fundamentals will provide the best return on investment for most organizations.

For organizations that are really good at the cybersecurity fundamentals, advanced capabilities are the second line of defense. It is likely that no matter how good they are at vulnerability management, identity management, and cybersecurity training for their staff, they won't be able to keep up with the volume of threats or prevent credential leakage, or they'll simply make a mistake somewhere along the way. This is where advanced capabilities can help. Designed properly, they can help prevent initial compromise or detect it quickly enough for automated and manual response processes to disrupt or stop the attack. Advanced capabilities can help reduce attackers' dwell times in their victims' environments, thus reducing potential damage and the cost of recovery.

Advanced capabilities are not optional for organizations that leverage large inventories of APIs, AI, and agentic AI solutions. As I discussed in *Chapter 7, Application Programming Interface Security*, investing in capabilities that help your organization to inventory and manage the security of APIs during and after development is critical to protect data. Newer AI technologies bring with them new attack surfaces that traditional cybersecurity processes and technologies do not fully cover. I'll discuss AI in detail in *Chapter 15, Artificial Intelligence: Security of AI Systems and Using AI for Better Cybersecurity*.

Let's discuss the top of the strategy pyramid next—high-value assets.

High-value assets

HVAs are also known as "crown jewels." There are many definitions for these terms. But when I use them, I mean the organization will fail or be severely disrupted if the asset's confidentiality, integrity, or availability is compromised. HVAs are rarely the computers that the organization's information workers use. Yet I've seen so many organizations focus on the security of desktop systems as if they were HVAs. Given the importance of HVAs, it would be easy to focus on them to the exclusion of lower-value assets. But keep in mind that attackers often use lower-value assets as an entry point to attack HVAs. For example, those old development and test environments that were never decommissioned properly typically aren't HVAs. But they are often found to be a source of compromise.

One of the first things a CISO needs to do when they start a cybersecurity program or assume management of an existing program is to identify the organization's HVAs. This might be more challenging than it sounds, as the crown jewels might not be obvious to people who don't possess expertise specifically related to the business they are supporting. Interviewing members of the C-suite, other executives, and senior technical staff can help to identify assets that would truly cause the business to fail or be severely disrupted if they became unavailable for an extended period.

Working backward from the organization's objectives can also help identify its HVAs. As security teams do this analysis, they should be prepared for some nuances that weren't initially obvious. For example, could the business still meet its objectives without power, water, heating, air conditioning, and life-safety systems? Depending on the business and the type of building(s) it uses, if elevators aren't available, is there any point in letting employees and customers through the front door? Customers might be willing to walk up a few flights of stairs, but would they be willing to walk up 40 flights of stairs if that were necessary? Probably not.

If this disruption were sustained for days, weeks, or months, how long could the business survive? Where are the control systems for these functions? And when was the last time the security posture of these systems was assessed? Identifying an organization's HVAs doesn't mean that CISOs can ignore everything else. Understanding which assets are truly HVAs and which aren't helps CISOs prioritize their limited resources and focus on avoiding extinction events for the organization.

Once the CISO has identified their organization's crown jewels, the next step is to ensure that the internal stakeholder community (IT, Legal, Finance, Procurement, and others), the C-suite, and the board of directors understand and agree with that list. This clarity will be very helpful when the time comes to request more resources or different resources than the organization has leveraged in the past. When the organization needs to make hard decisions about reductions in resources, clarity around HVAs will help with risk-based decisions. The time and effort spent getting the senior stakeholder community on the same page will make the CISO's life easier moving forward. Getting buy-in on the list of crown jewels might be easy in some organizations, but CISOs need to be prepared to defend their list. Some stakeholders will want their assets on the list even when they aren't crown jewels, while others will want their assets removed from the list to avoid potential extra scrutiny and work. Using a structured methodology or at least defining principles or a scoring system that is used to determine what is and what is not a crown jewel, is strongly recommended.

After the list of crown jewels is approved by stakeholders, they represent a priority list. These assets get the benefits of all the parts of the cybersecurity strategy, and given their relative importance to the organization, the security of these assets should be assessed first. The underlying IT assets that compose each HVA should be inventoried and recorded. Inventory details such as names of the HVA owners and operators, as well as the purpose of the system, should be recorded.

With a complete and accurate asset inventory, the HVAs can then be scanned for unpatched vulnerabilities every day. This is where governance plays an important role. If you have specific SLAs for HVAs in the vulnerability management policy, the owners and operators need to ensure their HVAs are being patched within those SLAs. The configuration of the underlying assets can be compared to an existing internal standard or to an industry standard such as the appropriate **Center for Internet Security** (**CIS**) benchmark. The status of critical controls, such as MFA, should be assessed and remediated where possible. Security control gaps that are identified during these assessments, that cannot be addressed quickly, should be entered into the risk register with their owners and treatment plans.

A complete and accurate asset inventory for each HVA also enables other important parts of a security assessment to be completed. For example, each HVA should have a threat model to identify unmitigated threats to the system. To develop a threat model, a data flow diagram will be needed. If this doesn't exist already, it will need to be developed. An incident response plan for each HVA should also be developed. This will save the incident response team valuable time in the early hours of an incident by providing important details that they'd otherwise have to spend time finding after the incident starts. This can include details about the asset inventory, the owners and operators, data flow diagrams, threat models, and other details that will give the incident response team a head start if an incident occurs.

Organizations that take the time to identify their crown jewels and their underlying IT assets can ensure their HVAs get the benefits of all the parts of their cybersecurity strategy. This also enables crown jewels to get extra attention via periodic security assessments to ensure their security postures are still well understood and supported by all parts of their cybersecurity strategy.

Now that we've examined an example of a cybersecurity strategy, let's look at some other ingredients that will give such a strategy the best chance of success.

Other ingredients for a successful strategy

There is some management-related work that needs to be done to ensure the CISO, the Security team, and the rest of the organization can effectively execute a cybersecurity strategy. Examples include business objective alignment and understanding the organization's risk appetite. This section outlines some of the ingredients that give a strategy the best chance of success.

Business objective alignment

I've met many CISOs who were struggling in their roles. Some of them simply weren't properly supported by their organizations. It's easy to find groups of executives that think cybersecurity threats are overblown and that everything their CISO does is a tax on what they are trying to accomplish. To these folks, cybersecurity is just another initiative that should stand in line behind them for resources. After all, the company won't get to that next big revenue milestone via a cost center, right?

Working with executives who don't understand the cybersecurity threats their organization faces and really don't have the time to pay attention isn't uncommon. Most CISOs must work with other executives to get things done, even if those executives don't realize they have a shared destiny with the CISO; when the CISO fails, they all fail. But the best CISOs I've met tend to thrive in such environments.

Whether a CISO works in an environment like the one I described, or they are lucky enough to work with people who care if they are successful, to be successful, CISOs need to align with the business they support. Those who don't understand and embrace the objectives of the organizations they support generate friction. There is only so much friction senior leaders are willing to tolerate before they demand change. Deep understanding of the business and how it works gives enlightened CISOs the knowledge and credibility required to truly support their organizations. Put another way, "purist" CISOs who try to protect data without regard for the people, business processes, and technologies that their organization relies on to succeed are only doing part of the job they were hired to do.

A cybersecurity strategy will only be successful if it truly supports the business. Developing a strategy that helps mitigate the risks that the Security team cares most about might give the team the satisfaction that they have a buttoned-up plan that will make it difficult for attackers to be successful. But if that strategy also makes it difficult for the business to be competitive and agile, then the security team must do better.

The best way to prove to your C-suite peers that you are there to help them is to learn about the parts of the business they manage, what their priorities are, and to earn their trust. None of this is going to happen in your **security operations center** (**SOC**), so you are going to have to spend time in their world, whether that's on a factory floor, in a warehouse, in a truck, or in an office. Walk a mile in their shoes and they'll have an easier time following your counsel and advocating for you when it's important.

Lastly, remember it's the CISO's job to discover, communicate, manage, and mitigate risk to the business, not to decide what the organization's risk appetite is. The board of directors and senior management have been managing risk for the organization since it was founded. They've been managing all sorts of risks, including financial risks, economic risks, HR risks, legal risks, and many others. Cybersecurity risks might be a newer type of risk to them, but if the CISO can communicate cybersecurity risks in the same way that the other parts of the business do, the business will do the right thing for its customers and shareholders, or they will pay the price—but that's the business's decision, not the CISO's.

That said, accountability, liability, and empowerment go hand in hand. Many CISOs face the harsh reality that they are made accountable for mitigating risks accepted by the business, but sometimes are not empowered to make the necessary changes or implement countermeasures. Simply put, a CISO's job is a hard one. This might help explain why CISO tenures are typically so short compared to those of other executives.

Having a clear and shared vision of where cybersecurity fits into an organization's wider business strategy is not only important within the upper echelons of an organization; the organization as a whole should have a clear stance on its vision, mission, and imperatives for its cybersecurity program. We'll take a look at this next.

Cybersecurity vision, mission, and imperatives

Taking the time to develop and document a vision, mission statement, and imperatives for the cybersecurity program can be helpful to CISOs. A shared vision that communicates what the future optimal state looks like for the organization from a cybersecurity perspective can be a powerful tool to develop a supportive corporate culture. It can inspire confidence in the cybersecurity team and the future of the organization. It can also generate excitement and goodwill toward the security team that will be helpful in the course of their work. Vision statements are supposed to be bold and aspirational. Here's an example of a vision statement:

"To be a trusted protector of digital assets, enabling innovation and resilience by proactively defending against evolving threats, fostering a culture of cybersecurity awareness, and ensuring compliance with the industry's most stringent standards—so our organization can flourish securely in an AI-driven world."

Similarly, a well-written mission statement can become a positive cultural mantra for organizations. A good mission statement can communicate what the security team is trying to accomplish while simultaneously demonstrating how the security team is aligned with the business, its customers, and shareholders. The mission statement will help communicate the security team's objectives as it meets and works with other parts of the organization. Here's an example of a mission statement:

"Our mission is to protect and defend the organization's digital ecosystem by identifying and mitigating cyber threats. We work to ensure confidentiality, integrity, and availability of data and technology through proactive cybersecurity, continuous monitoring, and collaboration across the organization. By cultivating cybersecurity awareness and compliance, we enable rapid innovation while supporting our stakeholders, customers, and employees."

Finally, business imperatives are the major goals that the cybersecurity team will undertake over a 2- or 3-year period. These goals should be ambitious enough that they can't be achieved in a single fiscal year. Imperatives support the strategy and are aligned with the broader business objectives. When the strategy isn't aligned with broader business objectives, this can show up as an imperative that is out of place—a square peg in a round hole. Why would the business support a big multi-year goal that isn't aligned with its objectives? This should be a message to the CISO to realign the strategy and rethink the imperatives. These multi-year goals become the basis for the projects that the cybersecurity group embarks on. An imperative might be accomplished by a single project or might require multiple projects. Remember, a project has a defined start date, end date, and budget. Here are some examples of cybersecurity imperatives that align with the aforementioned vision and mission statements. Notice how broad these examples are; each one represents a multi-year effort.

- Protect HVAs
- Enable business resilience and continuity
- Foster a culture of cybersecurity awareness and compliance

Developing a vision, mission statement, and imperatives for an organization's cybersecurity program isn't always easy or straightforward. The vision cannot be actioned without the support of stakeholders outside of the cybersecurity group and convincing them of the value of the program can be time-consuming. The future rewards from this work, for the CISO and the Cybersecurity team, typically make the effort worthwhile. We'll briefly discuss securing this support next, as one of the important ingredients of a successful cybersecurity strategy.

Senior executive and board support

Ensuring that the senior executives and the board of directors understand and support the organization's cybersecurity strategy is an important step for a successful security program. If the senior executives understand the strategy and participate in developing and approving it, they are more likely to show more ownership and support for it moving forward. But if they don't have a connection to the strategy, then the activities that are executed to support it will be potentially disruptive and unwelcome. They won't understand why changes are being made or why the governance model behaves the way it does.

Two of the important questions CISOs should ask when they are interviewing for a new CISO job are who the CISO role reports to and how often the CISO will be meeting with the board of directors or the board audit committee. If the CISO isn't meeting with the board quarterly or twice per year, that's a red flag. It might be that the role that the CISO reports to, such as the CIO, meets with the board instead of the CISO to discuss cybersecurity. But unless that role is steeped in the strategy and the daily operations, they should be sharing or delegating the job of meeting with the board to the CISO. This gives the CISO firsthand experience of discussing priorities with the board. It also allows board members to get their updates directly from the CISO and ask them their questions directly. I'd be hesitant to take an operational CISO job where the role didn't meet directly with the board audit committee at least a couple of times per year.

This experience is important and demonstrates that the CISO is a legitimate member of the organization's C-suite. If the CISO doesn't have the opportunity to ask the board for help when they need it, that can make the job even more challenging. Adding a management layer between the CISO and the board can be a tactic that senior management uses to delay, influence, or deter the CISO from making progress with their security program. It can also provide shelter for CISOs that don't have the business acumen or corporate maturity to interact directly with the board.

If the executive management team is truly supportive of the CISO and the cybersecurity strategy, they should welcome the opportunity for the CISO to get the help they need as quickly as possible without instituting more bureaucracy. Besides, the executive team should already know what the CISO is going to tell the board prior to meeting with them, as they should be getting regular updates from the CISO. CISOs need to be prepared for interactions with the board and its members and recognize it as a privilege that doesn't get extended to most other executives.

If the CISO is successful at getting the board on board with the cybersecurity strategy, this will make it easier for the board to understand why the security team is doing what they are doing. It will also make it easier for the CISO to elicit help when needed and report results against the strategy. If the CISO can effectively communicate a data-driven view of results against the same strategy that the board reviewed, these conversations can be very helpful for all stakeholders. Additionally, results from internal and external audits typically provide boards with some confidence that the CISO is doing their job effectively.

After talking with so many executives at organizations around the world about cybersecurity, I can tell you that there are real differences in how much risk organizations are willing to accept. In addition to gaining support from senior executives and the board, it is important to have a good understanding of their appetite for risk, as we'll discuss next, since this could significantly impact cybersecurity strategy.

Understanding your organization's risk appetite

Some organizations are in hypercompetitive industries where innovation, speed, and agility are top priorities; these organizations tend to be willing to accept more risk when faced with security and compliance decisions that will potentially slow them down or otherwise impede their ability to compete. For these companies, if they don't take calculated risks, they won't be in business long enough to make decisions in the future. For example, they might be willing to adopt a quarterly vulnerability remediation schedule for their on-premises IT estate to avoid potentially disruptive server reboots.

Other organizations I've talked to are very risk averse. That doesn't mean they necessarily move slowly, but they demand more certainty when making decisions. They are willing to take the time to really understand factors and nuances in risk-based decisions in an effort to make the best possible decision for their organization. For example, they are meticulous about system configuration changes and have developed rigorous change control processes that take more time, resulting in fewer security incidents caused by security misconfigurations.

Of course, there are also organizations in the spectrum between these two examples.

CISOs who understand the risk appetite of the senior management in their organizations can help them make faster, better decisions. I've seen many CISOs over the years decide to play the role of "the adult in the room" and try to dictate how much risk the organization should accept. In most cases, this isn't the CISO's job. Providing context and data to help the business make informed risk-based decisions is a function that CISOs should provide. Sometimes, they also have to educate executives and board members who do not understand cybersecurity risks. But I find it useful to always keep in mind that, in established organizations, senior executives were managing many types of risks for the organization long before cybersecurity risks became relevant to them. Note, this could be different for start-ups or in organizations where the CISO also has deep expertise in the business they support; in these scenarios, the CISO might be expected to make risk decisions for the organization more directly. But in all cases, understanding how much risk the organization is willing to accept in the normal course of business is important for CISOs.

The organization's appetite for risk will show up in its governance model and governance practices, or lack thereof. In many cases, organizations that accept more risk in order to move faster will streamline their governance practices to minimize friction and blockages. Organizations that want to take a meticulous approach to decision-making will typically implement more governance controls to ensure decisions travel fully through the appropriate processes. For this reason, it's important that CISOs validate their understanding of their organization's risk appetite instead of making assumptions about it. This is where their knowledge of the business and their peers' priorities will help. Some organizations develop official risk appetite statements that their boards of directors approve. These insights can be helpful to CISOs and security teams as they try to optimize their programs by adding or removing cybersecurity-related people, processes, and technologies to support the business. When Cybersecurity teams add too much friction, based on the organization's appetite for risk, discontent and calls for change typically follow. When there's too little friction, this can be an indicator that the GRC program and Cybersecurity team are not meeting expectations, because too much risk is being accepted. Some organizations establish a risk council or board to ensure the amount of risk the organization accepts is commensurate with the risk appetite of the organization, and this is maintained over time.

In addition to a knowledge of business priorities, it's important to have a realistic idea of the organization's current capabilities and technical talent. We'll discuss that next.

A realistic view of current cybersecurity capabilities and technical talent

Many of the CISOs I know aspire to have a world-class cybersecurity team designing, implementing, and operating sophisticated and effective controls. However, being honest with themselves about their current state of affairs is the best starting point.

Until recently, the industry has suffered from a shortage of cybersecurity talent for many years. This problem grew worse as more and more organizations came to the realization that they needed to take cybersecurity seriously or suffer potential non-compliance penalties and negative reputational consequences. Several high-profile ransomware attacks reinforced this reality.

Assessing the talent that a security team has helps CISOs, as well as CIOs, identify critical gaps in expertise. For example, if a security team is understaffed in a critical area such as vulnerability management or incident response, CIOs and CISOs need to know this sooner rather than later. If you have people who are untrained in some of the hardware, software, or processes that they are responsible for or are expected to use, identifying those gaps is the first step in addressing them. It also helps CIOs and CISOs identify professional growth areas for the people on the security team and spot potential future leaders. Cross-pollinating staff across teams or functions will help develop them in ways that will potentially be useful in the future.

The key is for CIOs and CISOs to be as realistic in their assessments as they can be so that they have a grounded view of the talent in the organization. Don't let aspirations of greatness paint an inaccurate picture of the talent the organization has. This will make it easier to prioritize the type of talent required and give the organization's recruiters a better chance of attracting the right new talent.

Cartography, or doing an inventory of your current cybersecurity capabilities, is another important exercise. The results will inform the development of the cybersecurity imperatives that I discussed earlier, as well as helping to identify critical gaps in capabilities. It can also help identify over-investments in capabilities. For example, it's discovered that the organization procured three identity management systems and only one of them is actually deployed. This is the case while the organization doesn't have enough vulnerability scanners to do a competent job of scanning and patching the infrastructure in a reasonable amount of time. They've over-invested in one area at the expense of another critical area.

In most big, complex IT environments, this won't be an easy task. It might turn out to be relatively easy to get a list of entitlements from the procurement department or a deployed software inventory from IT. But knowing that a particular appliance, piece of software, or suite of capabilities has been deployed only answers part of the question the CISO needs answered. Really understanding the maturity of the deployment and operation of those capabilities is just as important but is typically much harder to determine. Just because an identity management product is in production doesn't mean all of its capabilities have been implemented or enabled, the product is being actively managed, and the data it produces is being consumed by anyone.

Discovering these details can be challenging, and measuring their impact on your strategy might be too difficult to realistically contemplate. But without these details, you might not be able to accurately identify gaps in protection, detection, and response capabilities, and areas where over-investment has occurred.

If CIOs and CISOs can get an accurate view of the current cybersecurity talent and capabilities they have, it makes it much easier and less expensive for them to effectively manage cybersecurity programs for their organizations.

In my experience, there can be a lot of conflict and friction in organizations when Cybersecurity teams and Compliance teams do not work well together. Let's explore this dynamic next.

Compliance program and control framework alignment

I've seen Cybersecurity and Compliance teams end up in conflict over which control frameworks and configurations to follow. When this happens, it's usually a sign that the organization's cybersecurity strategy and compliance strategy are no longer aligned. For example, the CISO may decide that the Cybersecurity team will anchor its program to NIST SP 800-53 as the control catalog they measure themselves against, while the Compliance team is focused on demonstrating conformity with ISO/IEC 27001. The result is a series of recurring debates about frameworks, mappings, and configurations. Some organizations reconcile these differences quickly, but others struggle to harmonize the two efforts, creating friction that slows progress on both sides.

A common area for misalignment between Cybersecurity and Compliance teams is when controls in an internal standard and an industry standard differ. Internal standards are typically informed by the specific risks and controls that are most applicable to each organization. But differences between an internal standard and an industry standard can happen when the internal standard is newer than the industry standard or vice versa. For example, the industry standard states that an account lockout policy must be set to a maximum of five incorrect password entries. The Cybersecurity team knows that this control isn't strictly required in an environment that enforces complex 15-character passwords, and especially on systems that have MFA enabled. But in order to meet the industry standard, they might be forced to turn on the account lockout policy, thus enabling attackers to lock accounts out at any time they want to with a denial-of-service attack.

I've seen compliance professionals argue with CISOs on the efficacy of such dated control standards, who are simply trying to successfully comply with an industry standard without considering that they are actually increasing risk for the entire organization. I've even seen some of these compliance professionals, in the course of their work, claim that they can accept risk on behalf of the entire organization where such decisions are concerned, which is rarely, if ever, the case.

The reality is that industry and regulated standards typically take years to be developed, refined, approved, and published. Subsequently, they're often going to be behind the times in terms of risks and risk mitigation.

It should be recognized and acknowledged that both compliance and security are important to organizations. Compliance is driven by the regulation of liability, and security is driven by prevention, detection, and response. CISOs should foster normalization and the alignment of applied frameworks for security and compliance. Compliance professionals need to recognize that any organization that places compliance as a priority will eventually be compromised because industry and regulated standards are almost always based on someone else's threat model.

Cybersecurity and Compliance teams should work together to find ways to meet standards while also protecting, detecting, and responding to modern-day threats. These different, but overlapping, disciplines should be coordinated with the common goal of helping to manage risk for the organization. As I mentioned earlier, the cybersecurity strategy should be informed by the organization's HVAs and the specific risks they care about, such as unauthorized access to proprietary models, disruption of revenue-critical systems, or insider misuse of sensitive data. The Compliance team is the second line of defense designed to ensure the Cybersecurity team is doing its job effectively by comparing controls against internal, industry, and/or regulated standards. But they need to be prepared to assess the efficacy of controls where there are differences or where they conflict, instead of blindly demanding a standard be adhered to.

Typically, the decision to accept more risk by meeting a dated industry standard, for example, should be made by a risk management board or the broader internal stakeholder community instead of by a single individual or group. Internal and external audit teams are the third line of defense that helps to keep both the Cybersecurity team and the Compliance team honest by auditing the results of their work. No one wins when these teams fight over control frameworks and standards, especially when the frameworks or standards in question are based on someone else's threat model, as is almost always the case with industry and regulated standards. Some organizations try to solve this problem by moving the CISO to report to the compliance organization. This might work for some organizations that are in heavily regulated industries.

However, simply put, cybersecurity and compliance are different disciplines. Compliance focuses on demonstrating that the organization is successfully meeting internal, industry, and/or regulated standards. Cybersecurity focuses on protecting, detecting, and responding to modern-day cybersecurity threats. Together, they help the organization manage risk. I'm going to discuss compliance as a cybersecurity strategy in detail in *Chapter 10*.

Next, we'll talk about the importance of Cybersecurity and IT teams maintaining a happy and productive relationship with one another.

An effective relationship between cybersecurity and IT

An effective relationship between Cybersecurity and IT teams is typically a critical ingredient for a successful cybersecurity strategy. Unfortunately, in my experience, CISOs and their IT partners all too often have dysfunctional or even acrimonious relationships. This is the top reason cybersecurity strategies fail. CISOs who have a great cybersecurity strategy, top cybersecurity talent, an appropriate budget, and support from their boards of directors can still be undermined by the lack of an effective working relationship with their IT groups. Both groups bring essential expertise, and both operate under real-world constraints such as technical debt, resource limitations, operational pressures, and the need to support business growth. When these teams work in concert, organizations are far better positioned to manage risk and respond to emerging threats.

CISOs who have a good working relationship with their business's IT organizations are typically happier and more effective in their jobs. An ineffective relationship with IT can make a CISO's life miserable. It's also true that CISOs can make the jobs of CIOs and the leadership of IT disciplines frustrating. I've seen many cybersecurity groups and IT organizations interact like oil and water, when the only way to be successful is to work together. After all, they have a shared destiny. So, what's the problem? There's a range of reasons for these poor working relationships. Before discussing the reasons behind this, it's important to understand how Cybersecurity teams and IT teams are organized to work with each other, as this plays a role.

The two most common ways I've seen cybersecurity groups integrated, which are typically newer than IT departments in large, mature organizations, are as follows:

- The CISO reports to the CIO or CTO in IT and shares IT resources to get work done.
- The CISO reports outside of IT to the CEO, Legal, Compliance, the CFO, or a "Transformation Office." There are at least two flavors of this model:
    - The CISO has their own cybersecurity resources but needs IT resources to get work done.
    - The CISO has their own cybersecurity and IT resources and can get work done independently of IT.

The scenario where the CISO reports to the IT organization, historically, has been very common. But this reporting line has evolved over time in many organizations. Estimates vary, but I think roughly 60%–70% of the CISOs I've met recently report to the CIO of their organization. One of the reasons for reporting lines changing for CISOs is that all too often, CIOs prioritize IT priorities over cybersecurity. In many cases, cybersecurity is treated like any other IT project in that it must queue up with other IT projects and compete with them for resources to get things done. However, attackers live in that balance. Simply stated, if technology can't be implemented and operated securely, don't do it. The data on threats I discussed in the first half of this book makes it clear that the probability and impact of encountering modern-day threats are dramatically higher than they were five or ten years ago. The volume of threats overwhelms even reasonably staffed Cybersecurity teams. AI is only going to compound this challenge by increasing attack surfaces in enterprises, providing attackers with better tools, and further compressing the time Cybersecurity teams have to respond and contain attackers.

It took years for many CIOs to realize that every IT project has security requirements. Deprioritizing or slowing down cybersecurity initiatives means that every IT project that has a dependency on cybersecurity capabilities will either be delayed or will need an exception to sidestep these requirements. The latter tends to be much more common than the former. When CEOs and other executives began losing their jobs and directors on boards were being held accountable because of data breaches, many organizations were counseled by outside consultants to have their CISOs report to the CEO or directly to the board of directors. This way, cybersecurity would not be deprioritized without the most senior people being involved in making those risk decisions.

A new challenge is introduced when the CISO reports outside of IT to the CEO, the board of directors, or another part of the company. Where is the CISO going to get the IT staff required to get things done? When the CISO reported to IT, it was likely easier to get access to IT resources, even if they had to queue up for them. CISOs who sit outside the IT organization only have a few options. They can get resources from IT and become their customer, or they must hire their own IT resources. Becoming a customer of IT sounds like it could make things easier for CISOs, but only when they have a good relationship with IT that leads to positive results. Otherwise, it might not be sufficiently different from the model where the CISO reports to IT.

As expedient as hiring their own resources sounds, there are challenges with this approach. For example, change control can become more complex because IT isn't the only group of people that can make changes in the environment. Many times, this results in IT engineers watching cybersecurity engineers making changes in their shared environment and vice versa. Using twice as many resources to ensure things get done in a timely manner is one way to approach this problem. But most organizations can find better uses for their resources. Duplicating resources is typically a significantly more expensive approach. When IT and cybersecurity budgets are held flat or reduced, this approach can become unrealistic.

I've seen a better approach in action. When CISOs, CIOs, and CTOs have mutual respect and sincerely support each other, the work is easier, things get done more efficiently, and top talent is easier to attract and retain for all of them. Instead of a relationship defined by resource contention or assertions of authority, CISOs need to have good, effective working relationships with their IT departments to ensure they can do their jobs. Building such relationships isn't always easy, or even possible, but I believe this is a critical ingredient for a successful cybersecurity strategy. Ideally, these relationships blossom into a security culture that the entire organization benefits from. Understanding why there's tension between stakeholders and the Cybersecurity team can be helpful in achieving this. Since dysfunctional relationships between Cybersecurity and IT teams are the top reason cybersecurity strategies fail, let's dig into the most common reasons I've seen poor relationships between CISOs and IT.

Defensiveness

Many IT teams often perceive their Cybersecurity teams' efforts to find and address security gaps as essentially pointing out quality issues with their work. Every time a security gap is found, the CISO feels like they added value and made it harder for attackers to be successful, but CIOs and CTOs often feel embarrassed or disappointed that their teams didn't find the gap first or do a better job. To avoid this trap, CIOs, CTOs, and CISOs need to establish and maintain a relationship based on trust and shared objectives. CISOs need to be thoughtful about how they communicate risks they discover to their IT teams and to their stakeholders; they should consciously avoid intimating questions of competence or blame.

This is where GRC can be helpful. If IT teams have cybersecurity policies and standards they work to meet, it is easier for them to prove they are successfully meeting standards. But in the absence of those, Cybersecurity teams and their stakeholder communities shouldn't have any expectations. IT teams shouldn't be held accountable for their inability to read their

Cybersecurity teams' minds and keep pools of resources ready for ad hoc work in a resource-constrained world. CISOs need to give credit where credit is due when IT teams quickly and decisively address gaps; this motivates them to continue this behavior in the future. The point for everyone to celebrate isn't that a security gap was found; it's that a security gap was addressed. As we've seen from the threats I discussed in the first half of this book, IT and cybersecurity teams don't have the time for dysfunction. They need to work together in order for their organization to be resilient enough to endure the modern threat landscape.

Lack of accountability for non-compliance with policies and standards

Many IT teams prefer to operate without oversight or complying with policies and standards because it gives them the most flexibility and leeway to do their jobs and meet expectations. To do this, many IT teams operate as if policies and standards only apply to them when instances of non-compliance are identified by their Cybersecurity teams. They view their CISOs and Cybersecurity teams largely as internal police forces responsible for finding and telling them about instances of non-compliance. Only after an instance of non-compliance is discovered will they do the work to address the shortcoming. They do this knowing that cybersecurity corporate policies and standards apply to them. Many IT teams rely on the time it takes their Cybersecurity teams to identify their non-compliance with policy SLAs because it gives them more time to get the work completed. If they aren't held accountable for consistent non-compliance with policies, there's no incentive to change their behavior or identify the root causes for their inability to comply. This makes it unlikely they will increase headcount or budget levels to address a problem they own.

The reality is that complying with corporate policies is *everyone's responsibility*, whether they appreciate the responsibility or not. If CISOs are required to constantly verify that the work of their IT partners complies with corporate cybersecurity policies and standards, their organizations pay a meaningful and perhaps devastating opportunity cost. Every minute Cybersecurity teams spend trying to get their IT partners to meet their organizations' expectations and remediate risks in their work that don't meet these expectations, it is time not spent improving their ability to protect, detect, and respond to modern threats. Remember, GRC can be an effective foundation for cybersecurity strategies, but this requires real accountability.

Risk-reward trade-offs are viewed differently

CISOs and their IT partners often approach risk with quite different priorities. For IT executives, "risk" usually refers to threats to IT project delivery and operational performance – delays to major initiatives, downtime, system instability, or potential data loss. For CISOs, risk is usually defined as the likelihood and impact of cybersecurity threats. These concerns often overlap with IT risks; issues in IT can create security exposure, and security failures can disrupt

IT operations. But the difference in how Cybersecurity teams and IT teams interpret risk can easily become a source of tension between them. Those differing perspectives shape how each group approaches its work, and if the gap isn't recognized and addressed, it can lead to a strained or dysfunctional working relationship.

For example, in a fictional scenario, an IT team has agreed to deploy a new cybersecurity product in their environment that will enable the Cybersecurity team to monitor and identify insider threats. The IT team that manages clients, such as Windows and Apple devices, has agreed to deploy an agent on clients across the organization, while the IT Networking team has agreed to configure the network in ways that will enable those agents to communicate with a cloud instance used for monitoring, alerting, and reporting purposes. The teams develop a project plan with a schedule that includes time for planning, analysis, design, implementation, and support phases. One of the final phases is the implementation phase, where the agent will be installed on the clients, and the network will be configured to allow access to the cloud instance. IT leadership wants to ensure proper testing is completed, pilots are performed, and the risks of disruption to the business are minimized by ensuring they have a thorough understanding of all the requirements before deploying something new in their production IT environment. If delays are introduced into the project, the amount of time before the agents get deployed is extended. Success for IT executives is deploying the new agents without any negative impact on IT or business operations.

Meanwhile, the CISO is questioning why the deployment is going to take so long. After all, every day that passes where the Cybersecurity team doesn't have capabilities that enable them to detect and stop insider threats is equivalent to the organization simply accepting the associated risks. Cybersecurity teams that perform deployments like this prefer to reduce risk every day, rather than waiting until the end of a lengthy project to accomplish this. For example, let's say they need to deploy the insider threat agent to 1,000 clients and want to do this in 60 days. Calculating 1,000/60 days shows us that to achieve this goal, 17 agents would need to be deployed each day on average, including weekends. At the end of 60 days, all 1,000 clients would have agents installed, and risk would have been reduced a little every single day because 17 agents were deployed every day. There are only 43 business days in a 60-day period, so unless the teams plan to work weekends, it's likely prudent to plan to deploy an average of 23.26 agents per business day. Given the choice, CISOs typically prefer risk reduction every day versus waiting months for any reduction in the associated risk. The typical IT project ends up maximizing the cybersecurity risks by addressing all the IT risks prior to any cybersecurity risk reduction, because deployment happens near the end of the project instead of throughout it. Success for CISOs is getting the new insider threat capability deployed as quickly as possible before the risk of insider threats can be realized, which can potentially happen any day.

These different success criteria can drive a wedge between IT executives and CISOs. Many IT executives don't want to compromise on longstanding processes that are associated with IT excellence. Meanwhile, CISOs are forced to recognize that a lack of protection, detection, and response capabilities can result in catastrophic consequences for their organizations. If there is a "right" approach, it is typically dictated by each organization's corporate culture. Will the organization tolerate IT disruptions while its IT groups practice more aggressive approaches to reduce cybersecurity-related risks? Is the organization willing to potentially get hacked while it gives its IT group the time it needs to minimize the chances of IT disruptions? Which risk is deemed more impactful to the organization, the risk of disruptions to IT systems or the risk of a catastrophic cybersecurity event?

This is another area where GRC can help. Those risk quantification calculations I mentioned earlier can help stakeholders decide whether the costs associated with potential IT disruptions are greater than the potential costs associated with cybersecurity exposures. CIOs and CISOs who recognize how they make different risk-reward trade-offs and work together to find ways that harmonize them will be happier and more effective.

Speaking of happier and more effective people, let's discuss another important ingredient of a successful cybersecurity strategy – culture.

Security culture

Someone famous recently said, "Culture eats strategy for breakfast." I agree wholeheartedly. Organizations that are successful at integrating security into their corporate cultures are in a much better position to protect, detect, and respond to modern-day threats. For example, when everyone in the organization understands what a social engineering attack looks like and is on the lookout for such attacks, it makes the Cybersecurity team's job much easier and gives them a greater chance of success. Contrast this with work environments where employees are constantly getting successfully phished and vulnerabilities are constantly being exploited because employees are double-clicking on attachments in emails from unknown senders. In these environments, the Cybersecurity team is spending a lot of their time and effort reacting to threats that have been realized. A strong security culture helps reduce exposure to threats, decrease detection and response times, and thus reduce the associated damage and costs.

Culture transcends training. It's one thing for employees to receive one-time or annual security training for compliance purposes, but it is quite another thing for the concepts and calls to action that employees learn in training to be constantly sustained and reinforced by all employees and the work environment itself. This shouldn't be limited to front-line information workers. Service desk personnel, developers, operations staff, and IT infrastructure staff all benefit from a culture where security is included. A security culture can help employees make better decisions in the absence of governance or clear guidance.

One note on the gamification of cybersecurity training: I've seen good results when organizations shift some of their cybersecurity training away from reading and videos to more interactive experiences. For example, I've facilitated "game days" and "executive security simulations" focused on helping organizations learn about threat modeling and cloud security. I've seen many groups of executives and security teams embrace these sessions and provide glowing feedback.

Changing a corporate culture to become more security focused or friendly typically requires sustained investment from the very top of the company. During the time I worked at Microsoft, we introduced the **Security Development Lifecycle** (**SDL**), which ushered in new requirements for developers, testers, and program managers in product teams and other roles across the company. Initially, many development teams took issue with the new requirements, but since the executive sponsor of the SDL was the CEO of the company, everyone had to comply. To do this, they created a centralized team responsible for security, privacy, and reliability governance, called Trustworthy Computing. I worked on this team for almost a decade. We published the requirements and tracked product teams' compliance with them. This was the start of real cultural change at Microsoft, and it absolutely required unwavering support from the top executives at the company.

CISOs have a better chance of success when everyone in their organizations helps them. I encourage CISOs, with the help of other executives, to invest some of their time and resources in fostering a security culture, as it will most certainly pay dividends. Real, corporate-wide security culture change requires senior executives to invest in it; without this, any change will likely be shallow and temporary.

One final important ingredient for a successful security strategy that I'll discuss is putting your organization's constraints in proper perspective.

Understanding constraints

Next, I'll discuss one simple truth about cybersecurity that is painfully obvious to CISOs and Cybersecurity teams, but typically non-obvious to non-security roles within organizations. Your organization's constraints are not attackers' constraints, and attackers exploit that asymmetry. For example, attackers don't care if security features weren't added to a product because they weren't in scope or weren't funded; they don't care if a system is a test system running in a non-production environment; they also don't care if vulnerabilities in a system can't be patched because the system is past the vendor's end-of-life date and is out of support —they are happy to attack it anyway.

Essentially, attackers don't care what defenders' constraints are or why they exist. Whether defenders have properly funded and resourced their cybersecurity programs and are otherwise prepared for cybersecurity attacks is meaningless to attackers. Defenders' constraints represent opportunities to attackers, and they rely on them to be successful.

Your organization's constraints are not shared by attackers, and it's profoundly unhelpful to pretend they are. Pointing this out to stakeholders who do not have an appropriate sense of urgency where cybersecurity matters are concerned can help get things moving. Organizations that do not have the will to prioritize cybersecurity appropriately will be victimized.

Developing a cybersecurity strategy is really a starting point, but as I discussed in this chapter, operationalizing that strategy in a resource-constrained world can be challenging. I hope you gained some insights from the tips I shared in this chapter. In the next chapter, I'll discuss cybersecurity strategies.

Summary

In this chapter, I explored what constitutes an effective cybersecurity strategy and the essential elements that drive its success. A successful strategy starts with a solid foundation in **Governance, Risk, and Compliance** (**GRC**). Governance aligns security with business objectives and sets policies that reflect the organization's risk appetite. In this context, risk management involves maintaining a cybersecurity risk register to track known risks and quantifying top cybersecurity risks to inform priorities and resource allocation. Compliance programs help to ensure adherence to relevant laws and standards, reducing exposure to penalties and reputational harm.

The next layer of the cybersecurity strategy we examined focuses on cybersecurity fundamentals, which address the five primary ways organizations are initially compromised: unpatched vulnerabilities; security misconfigurations; weak, leaked, or stolen credentials; social engineering; and insider threats. Mastery of these fundamentals provides the highest return on investment and forms the basis for more advanced capabilities.

Advanced cybersecurity capabilities become critical as organizations mature, especially those leveraging APIs and AI. These capabilities help protect, detect, and respond to threats that bypass basic controls. At the top of the strategy pyramid are **high-value assets** (**HVAs**)—the "crown jewels" whose compromise would severely disrupt or destroy the organization's ability to continue to operate. Subsequently, identifying, inventorying, and prioritizing protection for HVAs is vital.

Other key ingredients for success include aligning cybersecurity with business objectives, developing clear vision and mission statements, securing senior executive and board support, understanding the organization's risk appetite, and maintaining a realistic view of current capabilities and talent. Effective collaboration between Cybersecurity and IT teams is crucial, as dysfunctional relationships are a leading cause of cybersecurity strategy failure.

A strong security culture, sustained by leadership and reinforced through training and engagement, further enhances resilience. Finally, this chapter emphasized that attackers do not share organizational constraints—defenders must recognize and address this reality to avoid victimization.

We've spent the first nine chapters of this book discussing threats, background information, and context that will help us examine some popular cybersecurity strategies. In upcoming chapters, we will examine numerous different strategies, dive into an implementation example of one of them, and discuss how to measure the effectiveness of cybersecurity strategies.

References

- Kiwicon (2009), Hackers don't give a shit [Poster]. Retrieved from `https://www.kiwicon.org/site_media/poster_shit.pdf`
- Grand View Research (2025), *Cyber security market size & share: Industry report*, 2033. Retrieved from `https://www.grandviewresearch.com/industry-analysis/cyber-security-market`

10

Cybersecurity Strategies

I discussed some of the ingredients for a successful cybersecurity strategy in *Chapter 9, Ingredients for a Successful Cybersecurity Strategy*. These include what I consider to be a critical ingredient, the Cybersecurity Usual Suspects, that is, the five ways that organizations get initially compromised. I have spent most of the preceding chapters in this book discussing the most common threats that CISOs and security teams are typically concerned about, including vulnerabilities, exploits, malware, ransomware, internet-based threats like phishing attacks, attacks on APIs, and government access to data. In this chapter, I will combine all these concepts into an examination of some of the cybersecurity strategies that I have seen employed in the industry over the past 25 years. You have probably seen some of these before and perhaps have used some of them. My objective for this chapter isn't to show you a bunch of strategies so that you can select one to use. My objective is to provide you with a framework for determining the efficacy of cybersecurity strategies, including strategies that I won't discuss in this chapter but that you might encounter in your career. In other words, I hope to teach you how to fish instead of giving you a one-size-fits-all strategy that I know will only help a fraction of organizations that use it.

Additionally, in this chapter, I'll give you a slightly contrarian view that is meant to be food for thought. If your organization already has a cybersecurity strategy and it uses industry frameworks, this chapter will give you some questions to ask yourself about the effectiveness of your current strategy. If your organization doesn't have a cybersecurity strategy that you can articulate, this chapter will give you some ideas about some of the strategies that other organizations have used, their advantages and disadvantages, and a way to measure their potential effectiveness.

In this chapter, we'll cover a sampling of cybersecurity strategies that have been employed over the past two decades. The following topics will be covered:

- Measuring the efficacy of cybersecurity strategy

- Protect and recover strategy
- Endpoint protection strategy
- Physical control and security clearances strategy
- Compliance as a cybersecurity strategy
- Application-centric strategy
- Identity-centric strategy
- Data-centric strategy
- Attack-centric strategy
- Zero trust
- Resilience as a cybersecurity strategy

Let's begin by discussing which strategy is the right approach for your organization.

Measuring the efficacy of cybersecurity strategies

The right strategy for your organization is the one that helps mitigate the most important risks to your organization. Risk is relative; therefore, no one strategy can be a silver bullet for all organizations. I'll resist the temptation to simply tell you to use the NIST Cybersecurity Framework (NIST, n.d.), ISO/IEC 27001 (ISO, n.d.), or any of the other great frameworks that are available. Your organization has likely already embraced one or more of these frameworks, which is unavoidable for enterprise-scale organizations from a **Governance, Risk, and Compliance (GRC)** perspective; that is, your organization must prove it's doing what the rest of the industry is doing, or it will be seen as an outlier. GRC frameworks are typically designed to help insulate organizations from liability after an incident, and subsequently, many organizations prioritize them. However, the pace of data breaches hasn't slowed down, despite the number of great frameworks available. For example, the **European Data Protection Board (EDPB)** published a report on the results of the **General Data Protection Regulation (GDPR)** after the first nine months that GDPR became enforceable in 2018. Almost 65,000 data breach notifications were filed with the EDPB in those first nine months. The volume of data breach reporting to European authorities has dramatically increased since then. More recent data published in the seventh annual edition of DLA Piper's GDPR Fines and Data Breach Survey reveals the average number of breach notifications reported to European authorities was 363 per day in 2024 (de Souza, Rachel., January 21, 2025).

> *The average number of breach notifications per day increased slightly to 363 from 335 last year, a 'levelling off' consistent with previous years, likely indicative of organisations [sic] becoming more wary of reporting data breaches given the risk of*

> *investigations, enforcement, fines and compensation claims that may follow notification.*
>
> *A recurring theme of DLA Piper's previous annual surveys is that there has been little change at the top of the tables regarding the total number of data breach notifications made since the GDPR came into force on 25 May 2018 and during the most recent full year from 28 January 2024 to 27 January 2025. The Netherlands, Germany, and Poland remain the top three countries for the highest number of data breaches notified, with 33471, 27829 and 14,286 breaches notified respectively (de Souza, Rachel, January 21, 2025).*

The vast majority of these organizations were likely compliant with their own security policies, thus illustrating the difference between cybersecurity and compliance. This is likely the tip of the iceberg, but it gives us some indication that organizations, both large and small, need help with cybersecurity strategy.

> Note
>
> As you saw in *Chapter 9*, where I described what a cybersecurity strategy is, I'm purposely simplifying the descriptions of these strategies. I have talked to some CISOs that had incredibly dense cybersecurity strategies that few people in their organization could fully comprehend or repeat. Keeping the strategy simple to understand makes it easier for the stakeholder community and the people doing the work to understand the strategy and explain it to their teams (repeat it). If the strategy requires a secret decoder ring or knowledge of a specific technical industry standard to understand, it is unlikely that senior stakeholders who don't have cybersecurity backgrounds will understand it and really have confidence in it. It's likely that there are only a few teams within IT and the cybersecurity group that are responsible for understanding and executing the full strategy. You can reserve the super complicated version of the strategy, with overlays for GRC, product development, recruiting, supporting local cybersecurity educational programs, succession planning, and other components, for stakeholders that need and appreciate all that detail and ambition.

Regardless of how sophisticated a cybersecurity strategy is, its success relies on the ingredients I described in *Chapter 9* and, crucially, how well it addresses the cybersecurity fundamentals. Measuring how that strategy performs over time is important so that adjustments can be made to improve it.

Let me reacquaint you with two concepts that I introduced in *Chapter 1* and mentioned again in *Chapter 9*. We are going to use these two concepts to measure the potential efficacy of the strategies that we examine: the *Cybersecurity Usual Suspects* and the cybersecurity fundamentals.

Remember that the five ways that organizations get initially compromised, called the Cybersecurity Usual Suspects, are:

- Unpatched vulnerabilities
- Security misconfigurations
- Weak, leaked, or stolen credentials
- Social engineering
- Insider threats

Once an IT environment has been initially compromised, there are many, many **tactics, techniques, and procedures (TTPs)** that attackers can use to move laterally, steal credentials, compromise infrastructure, remain persistent, steal information, destroy data and infrastructure, and so on. Most of these TTPs have been around for years. Occasionally, the industry will see attackers employing novel approaches. Organizations that focus on getting really good at the cybersecurity fundamentals make it much harder for attackers to be successful. Even if an environment is already compromised, the organization still needs to focus on the cybersecurity fundamentals in order to prevent even more attackers from getting a foothold, and to prevent the attackers already inhabiting the environment from getting back into it if they can ever be driven from it. Whatever strategy an organization employs, it needs to incorporate the cybersecurity fundamentals.

Put another way, if an organization's cybersecurity strategy doesn't include being excellent at the cybersecurity fundamentals, it is setting itself up for failure. Still, there will be some organizations that are willing to take large risks so that they can compete in fast-moving, competitive industries. This is where some of the executives I've met felt like they must make a choice between cybersecurity and moving fast. But moving fast and managing risk are not mutually exclusive; this isn't a choice that they have to make, as they can get both cybersecurity efficacy AND business speed, agility, and scalability if they have a strategy that enables them to do so.

Once an organization hones its ability to manage the cybersecurity fundamentals and establishes a foundation that it can build on, then it makes sense to invest in advanced cybersecurity capabilities—capabilities that will help the organization when it fails to manage the cybersecurity fundamentals perfectly over time. Your strategy needs a solid foundation, even if it has advanced cybersecurity capabilities, because the platforms these advanced capabilities rely on for information and their own security can be undermined by unpatched vulnerabilities, security misconfigurations, social engineering, insider threats, and weak, leaked, and stolen credentials.

In fact, being excellent at addressing all the cybersecurity fundamentals in both Production and Development/Test environments is a requirement for successfully deploying and operating advanced cybersecurity capabilities in your IT environment. If an organization doesn't have a plan to find and correct security vulnerabilities and misconfigurations in the hardware and software they deploy as part of their advanced cybersecurity capabilities, they shouldn't bother deploying them. This is because, over time, such hardware and software will just increase the organization's attack surface.

You might be wondering why you must invest in advanced cybersecurity capabilities at all if your organization is really good at the cybersecurity fundamentals. Because you must plan for failure. You must assume that the organization will be breached – it's not a matter of *if*, only a matter of *when* and *how often* it will happen. This "assume breach" philosophy is important for at least two reasons:

- First, history has taught us that planning to achieve 100% perfect protection for large on-premises IT environments for a sustained period of time is a wildly optimistic ambition. People in your organization and supply chain will make mistakes, and some of these will be security related.
  For example, consider your applications; whether development is done in-house or through vendors, applications will have bugs in them. Some of these bugs will be security vulnerabilities. Some of these vulnerabilities will be exploitable. You need to plan for this eventuality. You need to plan for the mistakes that administrators make that lead to security misconfigurations. You need to plan for the scenario where the trusted vendors in your supply chain get compromised or turn malevolent. This is an area where **Red Teams** can ground strategy in reality, as they specialize in taking advantage of unrealistic assumptions.
- The second reason organizations need to adopt an "assume breach" philosophy is that it gives their security teams permission to think about some key questions that security teams who believe they can achieve 100% effective protection, forever, never ask themselves. For example, how would they know when they have been compromised? What will they do when they get compromised? These are questions that many security teams never ask themselves because they will not or cannot adopt an "assume breach" philosophy.

> Note
>
> Some corporate cultures will not tolerate failure, so the idea that they plan for failure makes no sense to them; it's like admitting that they aren't good enough to do their jobs. In other organizations, senior executives will not support a plan for failure. I've met many executives who do not understand that they are in a submarine under

> immense pressure, surrounded by attackers. Some of the executives I've talked to believe they are in a winnable battle. They believe that if they are smart enough, hire the right people, and buy the right protection capabilities, they will win the battle. But cybersecurity is a journey, not a destination. It doesn't have a beginning and an ending the way a battle does. It's constant, like pressure on the hull of a submarine. Planning for failure is the antithesis of their world view, so they refuse to support CISOs who know they need to embrace a more modern approach to cybersecurity. This is one reason why I've always tried to spend time with cybersecurity strategy stakeholders other than the CISO and the security team. Very often, the security team understands everything I've written here, but one or two executives or board members have uninformed views.

Advanced cybersecurity capabilities are the part of your strategy that will help you identify, protect, detect, respond, and recover (NIST, n.d.). This is the part of your strategy that helps augment and identify shortcomings in the cybersecurity fundamentals. You need to focus on both the cybersecurity fundamentals and advanced capabilities for the strategy to be successful. The **high-value assets (HVAs)** component of the strategy acknowledges the importance of HVAs. As I mentioned in *Chapter 9*, if the confidentiality, integrity, or availability of an HVA is compromised for an extended period, this typically means the organization itself will fail. The sustained compromise of an HVA could be an extinction event for a company (Ashford, 2016) and drive public sector organizations back to using pencils, paper, and the processes they used before they invested in IT.

Planning and investing in security specifically focused on HVAs, in addition to the cybersecurity fundamentals and advanced cybersecurity capabilities, will help organizations manage the risk to their most important assets. *Figure 10.1* illustrates how the framework I've been discussing in this section can be used to develop a basic cybersecurity strategy.

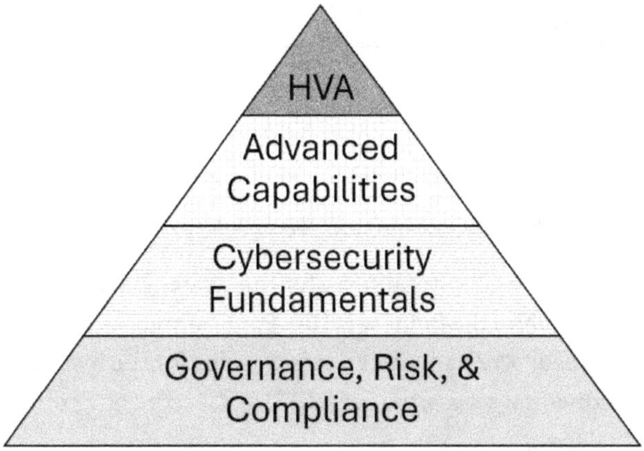

Figure 10.1 – An illustration of a cybersecurity strategy

Regardless of organizations' HVAs and which advanced cybersecurity capacities they decide to invest in (which is highly variable between organizations), the entire strategy model I've outlined here relies on the foundation that the cybersecurity fundamentals provide. Essentially, any cybersecurity strategy that an enterprise pursues needs to focus on the cybersecurity fundamentals at a minimum. Given this, I'm going to introduce a simple method to help determine a strategy's potential efficacy by estimating how well it incorporates the cybersecurity fundamentals and mitigates the Cybersecurity Usual Suspects.

I will estimate the potential efficacy of the cybersecurity strategies we examine by using a simple scoring system. I call this system the **Cybersecurity fundamentals scoring system (CFSS)**. This system assigns a score between 0 and 10 for each of the Cybersecurity Usual Suspects, based on how well the strategy mitigates the risk. Higher scores mean that the strategy is more effective at mitigating each particular Cybersecurity Usual Suspect. For example, a score of 20 means the strategy fully mitigates the risk associated with a specific Cybersecurity Usual Suspect. A low score, such as a score of 1, for example, means that the strategy's ability to mitigate the risk is relatively low. The CFSS includes a separate score for each of the five Cybersecurity Usual Suspects, as shown in *Table 10.1*.

Cybersecurity Usual Suspect	**Score**
Unpatched vulnerabilities	0–20
Security misconfigurations	0–20
Weak, leaked, or stolen credentials	0–20

Cybersecurity Usual Suspect	Score
Social engineering	0–20
Insider threat	0–20

Table 10.1 – Cybersecurity Fundamentals Scoring System (CFSS) summary

The total of all five scores is the CFSS total score for the strategy. The lowest possible CFSS total score for a strategy is zero, while the highest is 100. For example, as shown in *Table 10.2*, let's say we have a strategy called "XYZ" and we estimate scores for the five measures in the CFSS. When we add up the individual scores, we get a CFSS total score of 23 out of a possible 100 points.

XYZ Strategy Example	Score
Unpatched vulnerabilities	10
Security misconfigurations	10
Weak, leaked, or stolen credentials	2
Social engineering	0
Insider threat	1

Table 10.2 – An example of the CFSS applied to a strategy called "XYZ"

The goal is to find a strategy that gives us a perfect 100 score, although this is likely more aspirational than probable. However, this type of scoring system gives us a way to estimate a strategy's ability to not only mitigate all five ways organizations get initially compromised but also a way to compare strategies across the cybersecurity fundamentals. Potentially, this approach can help us identify a combination of strategies that gives us a perfect score, or a high score, across the Cybersecurity Usual Suspects if no single strategy does this. Finally, it can also help us determine where the gaps are in an organization's current strategy. If you know where the weaknesses or gaps are, then you can develop a plan to address these inadequacies.

Before we start measuring strategies using this framework, I want to point out a couple of hidden risks in using this type of rating. Like most risk-based approaches, it is based on the assumption that CISOs and security teams will be able to accurately estimate the level of risk and identify effective mitigations. In my experience, I have seen some CISOs overestimate their mitigation capabilities, while simultaneously underestimating the risks themselves and the effectiveness of the cybersecurity fundamentals. A second risk is that this approach assumes all five of the Cybersecurity Usual Suspects are equally important to the organization. Since each organization is different, mitigations can have different values for different organizations.

Now that we have a cybersecurity strategy concept in mind and a scoring system to help us determine the relative efficacy of different approaches, let's examine several cybersecurity strategies in more detail.

The following list contains many of the strategies that I have seen in use over the last two decades in the industry. I'm going to examine each of these strategies in detail and provide an estimated CFSS score for each one. The CFSS scores that I provide are my own subjective opinion and are subject to my own assumptions and biases. I provide you with some context on why each Cybersecurity Usual Suspect was scored the way it was so that you can understand my approach and agree or disagree with it.

> **Note**
>
> As I mentioned in *Chapter 9*, some of the cybersecurity professionals I have met have a negative reaction when the term "strategy" is used in a cybersecurity context. This is a word that can be used in at least a few different ways. Security and compliance professionals sometimes use the term "strategy" when they are referring to frameworks, models, or standards. I explained what I mean when I use this term, in detail, in *Chapter 1*. If you haven't read that chapter already, I recommend that you read it because it provides a lot of context that I won't repeat here. You'll see me use the terms **framework**, **approach**, and **model** interchangeably throughout all the chapters. Please feel free to associate whatever term makes the most sense to you when I use any of these terms.

I invite you to think through your own CFSS score estimate for each of these strategies:

- Protect and recover strategy
- Endpoint protection strategy
- Physical control and security clearances strategy
- Compliance as a cybersecurity strategy
- Application-centric strategy
- Identity-centric strategy
- Data-centric strategy
- Attack-centric strategy
- Zero trust

- DevSecOps
- Resilience as a cybersecurity strategy

Even if your organization doesn't use any of these strategies that we will review, please ask yourself if your supply chain vendors use any of them. If you don't know about the strategies they are using to manage the risk to their organizations and to their customers, then you might want to ask them how they are mitigating the Cybersecurity Usual Suspects. This is the minimum they should be doing for themselves and for their customers. Many enterprises already use security questionnaires, some of which have hundreds of questions, to get a better idea of whether potential vendors' security policies meet their standards. In these cases, it could be valuable to add a few questions about the strategy to these questionnaires to gauge the security maturity of the vendor.

Finally, let's examine some cybersecurity strategies!

Protect and recover strategy

Let's start with a relatively old strategy that I call the *protect and recover* strategy. It's also known as the *perimeter security* strategy. As the cliché goes, it's typically described as having a hard outer shell and a soft, gooey center. This analogy indicates that once an organization's perimeter defenses (hard outer shell) are penetrated, little or nothing impedes attackers from moving laterally in the environment and staying persistent indefinitely. The organization is left trying to recover the original data and IT environment (soft center), usually with mixed success. It is considered an old-fashioned strategy by today's standards, but I find a surprising number of organizations still cling to it, perhaps unwittingly.

As the name suggests, the focus of this strategy is to prevent attackers from being successful by investing in protection technologies such as firewalls, **demilitarized zones (DMZs)**, proxy servers, and network segmentation. Let's go back to 2003 for a great example of why this strategy became so popular. By 2003, there had already been successful mass worm attacks on the internet, such as Code Red and Nimda, that exploited Microsoft vulnerabilities. The risk of such attacks was no longer theoretical, as many people had argued it was at the time. The industry was just starting to understand that software had vulnerabilities and that some of these were exploitable.

> Note
>
> At that time, I was working on Microsoft's customer-facing Security Incident Response Team. Many of the organizations I helped blamed Microsoft for not doing more to protect Windows from such attacks. There was a widespread belief among enterprise customers that if they replaced Microsoft Windows with another operating system, then they'd be secure. Microsoft was the manufacturer of the world's most used

> operating system and subsequently garnered a lot of attention from legitimate security researchers and attackers alike. Of course, now, all these years later, I think everyone understands that all vendors have vulnerabilities in their software and hardware. If you still have any doubts about this, please go back and re-read *Chapters 3 and 4*, that focus on vulnerability disclosure trends.

In 2003, the mitigation for the risk that unpatched vulnerabilities posed was the firewall. Microsoft turned on Windows Firewall by default in Windows XP Service Pack 2 in hopes that this would prevent the exploitation of vulnerabilities in Windows services and applications listening on the network.

Windows Firewall, together with several other security mitigations, including automatic updates, successfully blunted the mass worm attacks of the era. Many enterprise-scale organizations already had corporate firewalls in place at the perimeter of their networks in 2003. But most of them had exceptions for all traffic going to and from ports 80 and 443 so that HTTP and HTTPS traffic could flow freely; these are the so-called "universal firewall bypass ports." For the next few years, enterprises that didn't already have DMZs put them in place to enforce better control of network traffic coming from and going to the internet.

This evolution in security strategy was an important and effective step for the industry. But somewhere along the way, the original benefits of perimeter security were distorted. Ultimately, perimeter security was supposed to provide organizations with two things:

- First, it protected resources that were supposed to be private from public access
- Second, blocking anonymous inbound network traffic to vulnerable services listening on the network gave organizations more time to test and deploy security updates

But the idea that firewalls, DMZs, and network segmentation could somehow provide a long-term solution to vulnerability management or the other four Cybersecurity Usual Suspects, five to ten years before application layer capabilities were built into some of these products, was misguided.

The underlying assumption of the protect and recover strategy is that the organization will be able to deploy and operate adequate protection technologies and processes. If these fail, then recovery is their plan. It is assumed that because the organization will be so good at protection, it doesn't really need to invest in detection and response capabilities. Most of the organizations that embraced this approach also invested in backup and recovery capabilities, but not necessarily for security purposes; rather, these capabilities mitigated the risk of data loss. When their protection strategy ultimately failed, their backup and recovery capabilities were their backstop. So, although these two components weren't necessarily meant to be parts of a coherent cybersecurity strategy, they have been so commonly deployed in enterprise environments that they complement each other very well. If the assumption that the organization can effectively protect itself 100% of the time, forever, turns out to be untrue, then it can restore itself from backup.

This approach is characterized by investments primarily in perimeter and network protection, as well as backup and recovery. Professionals with networking expertise could extend their expertise into the security domain. This made a lot of sense since nearly 100% of attacks happened using networks. For many enterprises, their networking groups extended the scope of their charters to include network security, DMZs, and managing firewalls.

The protect and recover strategy has some advantages. Technologies and disciplines like TCP/IP, routing and switching, firewall configuration, and operations are areas that traditionally have had a larger trained workforce compared to other security disciplines such as application security, malware reverse engineering, or red and blue teaming. Because it's a relatively mature strategy, there is a very well-developed vendor and consulting ecosystem that has decades of experience supporting it. A trained workforce and this ecosystem make this strategy a natural choice for organizations that constrain themselves to primarily using IT staff and vendors they already have commercial contracts with for cybersecurity.

Of course, this strategy also has some disadvantages. Historically, organizations relying solely on this strategy have experienced poor results. The reason this approach has failed time and again is that its underlying assumption is deeply flawed. The assumption that the organization will never be compromised because it will be 100% successful at protecting itself is wildly optimistic. Today, enterprises that don't invest in detection and response capabilities, in addition to protection and recovery capabilities, could be considered negligent.

Reducing the time between compromise and detection is seen as a modern cybersecurity mantra that the Protect and Recover Strategy was not designed to embrace. Subsequently, organizations that use this strategy can have very long periods between compromise and detection, sometimes hundreds of days or spanning years. This strategy doesn't recognize that attackers have a disproportionate advantage over defenders; defenders need to be perfect 100% of the time, which is an unrealistic aspiration, while attackers only need to be good or lucky once.

Further, this strategy relies on developers, administrators, vendors, partners, and users not making any mistakes or poor trust decisions that could lead to compromise. But as we've seen for decades, users will unwittingly bring threats through layers of perimeter defenses themselves. Without detection and response capabilities, once an organization is penetrated, attackers can typically persist indefinitely, making recovery aspirational and expensive.

The good news is that many of the organizations that used the protect and recover strategy in the past have matured their approach over time. They still employ this strategy but use it in combination with other strategies. They've also upgraded the technologies and products they rely on. Today, next-generation firewalls go far beyond filtering TCP and UDP ports and can perform deep packet inspection. But a question these organizations still need to consider is whether their business partners and supply chain partners still employ this old strategy. For many years, attackers have been targeting small, less mature partners and suppliers in order to get access to their large customers' infrastructures and data. Small legal firms, marketing and advertising firms, and even heating and air conditioning vendors have been targeted for this purpose. Many small firms like these, in countries around the world, still use the protect and recover strategy. In many cases, they have not invested in relatively expensive cybersecurity expertise that could help them modernize their approaches.

CFSS score

How well does the Protect and Recover Strategy mitigate the cybersecurity usual suspects? *Table 10.3* contains my CFSS score estimates.

Cybersecurity Fundamentals	Score (0–20)
Unpatched vulnerabilities	10
Security misconfigurations	10
Weak, leaked, or stolen credentials	0
Social engineering	5
Insider threat	0
CFSS Total Score (max = 100)	25

Table 10.3 – The CFSS score estimate for the Protect and Recover strategy

As you might have gleaned from my description of this strategy, although it has some benefits, it doesn't address the cybersecurity fundamentals very well.

For unpatched vulnerabilities, I gave this strategy 10/20. This score reflects that firewalls and network segmentation can only make it harder for attackers and malware to access exploitable vulnerabilities listening on network ports. If network traffic can't make it to the vulnerable service's port, then the vulnerability can't be exploited. However, this mitigation isn't a permanent condition for an exploitable vulnerability. As soon as an administrator changes the rule for the firewall filter blocking the port, the vulnerability could potentially become instantly exploitable, unbeknownst to the administrator.

Typically, filters will block unsolicited inbound traffic to a port, but they will allow inbound traffic resulting from legitimate outbound traffic on the same port. Under the right conditions, the service or application could be enticed to make an outbound connection to a destination under the control of attackers. Firewalls only provide temporary mitigation to unpatched vulnerabilities, giving vulnerability management teams more time to find and patch vulnerabilities. The vulnerable software needs to be uninstalled from the system (which can't be easily done for most operating system components), or it needs to be patched. The protect and recover strategy doesn't focus on vulnerability management. The same is true for security misconfigurations. This strategy doesn't help us fully mitigate these two Cybersecurity Usual Suspects—the best it can do is delay exploitation. For this reason, I gave it partial marks in these two areas.

This strategy does nothing to address weak, leaked, or stolen credentials or insider threats. Therefore, both received a score of zero.

Finally, I gave this strategy's ability to mitigate social engineering partial marks. Firewalls and DMZs can filter connections based on URLs and IP addresses. They can prevent users who are tricked into clicking on malicious links from connecting to known malicious servers and unauthorized sites. Outbound traffic can be blocked and flagged, as well as inbound replies to such outbound traffic. The challenge has been keeping up with attackers who use compromised systems all over the world to host complex multicomponent attacks and constantly change sources and destinations for attacks. History has taught us that this approach does not mitigate social engineering attacks very effectively. This is because it still relies on users and administrators to make sound trust decisions, which has always been challenging. Nonetheless, I gave it partial marks for social engineering.

With a CFSS total score of 25 out of a possible 100, clearly, this strategy must be used in combination with other strategies in order to really address the cybersecurity fundamentals, as well as provide a foundation that an enterprise can build on. Many organizations have already come to this conclusion and have evolved their approaches. But some of the smaller organizations likely still use this strategy in their supply chain because they lack the expertise and resources to evolve. How many small businesses and independent consultants still rely on the firewalls built into their wireless access points for protection?

Protect and recover strategy summary

The CFSS total score for this strategy is 25/100. It must be used in combination with other strategies.

The following are its advantages:

- Large vendor ecosystem to help organizations implement and operate
- Relatively large, trained workforce with years of experience

The following are the disadvantages:

- History has shown this to be a poor strategy by itself; failing to invest in detection and recovery capabilities gives attackers an unnecessary advantage
- Attackers have a disproportionate advantage over defenders because defenders must be perfect
- It relies on developers, administrators, and users not making mistakes or poor trust decisions that lead to compromise – individuals bring threats through the perimeter and host-based defenses themselves
- Once penetrated, attackers can persist indefinitely, making recovery aspirational because of a lack of investment in detection and response capabilities

Now, let's examine a strategy that doesn't focus on the network perimeter: the endpoint protection strategy.

Endpoint protection strategy

This is what I call a "proxy" strategy. Endpoints, such as personal computers, mobile devices, some types of IoT devices, and so on, are used to process, store, and transmit data. Therefore, if we protect these endpoints, we are, by proxy, protecting the data, which is the whole point of data protection. Stated another way, the data will be compromised if the endpoints or devices are compromised, so the endpoints must be protected. Once upon a time, many organizations used this strategy by itself to protect their assets. The underlying assumption of this strategy is that protecting endpoints and devices is an effective proxy for protecting the organization's data.

The endpoint protection strategy is characterized by investments in host protection technologies like asset inventorying and vulnerability management solutions, anti-malware solutions, file integrity monitoring, host-based firewalls, application whitelisting, web browser protections, mobile device management, enterprise configuration management, endpoint hardening, IoT device management, **Endpoint Detection and Response (EDR)**, and **Extended Detection and Response (XDR)**, among many others. Many of these capabilities are already built into Windows, macOS, and Linux operating systems, but that doesn't stop endpoint protection vendors from offering better implementations of these features that typically have integrated management and reporting capabilities.

It's important to understand that different operating system manufacturers allow different levels of system access to third-party **Independent Software Vendors (ISVs)**, which can have a big impact on what their solutions are capable of. Further, vendors that sell endpoint protection solutions have their own definitions of what an endpoint is that support their specific value propositions. This used to be a short list of major antivirus vendors, but in recent years, the list has grown, and the vendors have become far more diverse. There are dozens of different vendors that are actively marketing endpoint protection platform solutions. Some examples include the following (in alphabetical order): **Check Point, Cisco, CrowdStrike, ESET, Fortinet, F-Secure, Kaspersky, McAfee, Malwarebytes, Microsoft, Palo Alto Networks, Panda Security, SentinelOne, Sophos, Symantec, Trellix, Trend Micro, VMware Carbon Black**, **Webroot**, and many others. There are several other vendors in this space, including regional vendors in China, among others.

Some of these vendors have antivirus labs with decades of experience, while others are leveraging security company acquisitions and innovations from other areas to try to disrupt the endpoint protection market. Many vendors include analytics, response, cloud, and **artificial intelligence (AI)** capabilities as part of their solutions.

Having worked in an anti-malware lab for many years and on a security incident response team, I have an appreciation for this approach. Endpoints are where most of the action happens during a data breach. No matter how good firewall and IDS vendors' products get, they simply do not have the same vantage point as the endpoint device typically has itself. Solutions installed directly on the endpoints enable continuous monitoring and a range of automated actions when triggers are hit. Endpoint protection scanning engines are some of the most impressive feats of programming in the world. These engines are designed to unpack numerous file compression and obfuscation formats that can be nested by attackers, in virtual computing environments that simulate real operating systems, in order to determine if files are malicious in near real time.

Threats can be file-based, macros, scripts, polymorphic viruses, boot viruses, rootkits, and so on, across different operating systems and filesystems. Of course, they have a lot more functionality, like heuristics, behavioral analysis, browser protections, malicious IP address filtering, anti-tampering mechanisms, and much, much more. When you dig into the functionality of some of these endpoint protection solutions and consider how hard it is to develop them and keep them current, you will find they are super impressive.

However, engineering alone is not enough. These solutions are only as good as the research and response labs that care for and feed them. Maintaining critical masses of great researchers, analysts, and supporting staff is an important function that these vendors provide. The combination of impressive engineering and a world-class research and response lab is the key to selecting an effective endpoint protection vendor. The large vendor ecosystem that I described earlier is very positive. This is because it creates healthy competition, and these vendors keep each other honest by supporting third-party testing (av-test.org and av-comparatives.org, among others) and industry conferences (annual Virus Bulletin International Conference (Virus Bulletin, n.d.)), where they discuss how to govern their industry, among other things.

But of course, this approach also has challenges. History has taught us that the endpoint protection strategy, by itself, is insufficient. Have any of the victims in massive data breaches from the last 15 years not been running endpoint protection solutions? First, relying on a patient to diagnose and cure itself is an optimistic approach. Once the trusted computing base of a system has been compromised, how can endpoint protection solutions reliably use it to detect threats on the system and clean them? Further, endpoint protection solutions themselves have been targets for attackers and their malware for decades. One of the first things many families of malware do after they initially compromise a system is attempt to disable or subvert the endpoint protection solution. This is where remote attestation services can help, but in my experience, few organizations use such services because of their complexity. Some vendors use virtualization and other techniques to protect their solutions from attackers. But rest assured that attackers will continue to research ways to subvert endpoint protection solutions; they always have.

The playing field is never level in this game. Attackers can buy all the endpoint solutions available on the market and test their malware and tools prior to using them in attacks to ensure no solution can detect or clean them. The endpoint protection vendors don't have this same advantage. But more fundamentally, can the patient really be trusted to cure itself? Some organizations will clean compromised systems with endpoint solutions and allow them to continue running in production, while others have policies to flatten and rebuild any system that has been compromised.

Virtualization has made this easier, and the cloud, as I'll discuss in detail later, makes this even easier and more effective. But the key to this approach is still accurate threat detection. Keep in mind that although the aspirational goal for all these solutions is to detect, block, and, if necessary, clean 100% of threats, this isn't realistic. The internal goals of research and response labs are typically more realistic and attainable. For example, detection for 100% of threats in the "zoo" (their private malware library) or 100% detection for "in the wild" malware (commonly found threats) are likely common goals among these vendors. But detection goals for emerging threats might be 80%. After all, it takes time for research and response labs to get samples of threats, process them, and deploy appropriate protections to their customers, especially when attackers are using mass automation to generate millions of them constantly. Now that some labs are using AI to analyze and classify malware threats, perhaps their internal efficacy goals are more aggressive, but purveyors of malware can also use AI to attempt to stay one step ahead.

Would you set sail in a submarine that had the goal of keeping only 80% or 90% of the water outside the hull? Probably not. But as I wrote in *Chapter 5, The Evolution of Malware*, if you don't use endpoint protection because it doesn't protect the endpoint from 100% of threats, then you aren't protecting the endpoints from the millions of threats that endpoint protection solutions do protect against. But should endpoint protection be organizations' sole cybersecurity strategy? Let's try to answer this question using the CFSS.

CFSS score

Let's look at how the endpoint protection strategy helps organizations address the cybersecurity fundamentals. *Table 10.4* contains my CFSS score estimates.

Cybersecurity Fundamentals	Score (0–20)
Unpatched vulnerabilities	15
Security misconfigurations	15
Weak, leaked, or stolen credentials	15
Social engineering	10
Insider threat	15
CFSS Total Score (max = 100)	70

Table 10.4 – The CFSS score estimate for the endpoint protection strategy

> **Tip**
>
> Remember that these are just estimates based on my experience, and they don't reflect the state of the art in endpoint protection. Please feel free to develop your own estimates if you think I'm way off base with mine.

I gave this strategy partial marks for mitigating unpatched vulnerabilities and security misconfigurations because endpoint protection solutions can't be installed everywhere. I'll discuss this more in a moment. The combination of inventorying, scanning, updating, hardening, and monitoring can be very effective. For weak, leaked, and stolen credentials, I estimated endpoint protection mitigating 15/20. Organizations that use Secure Access Workstations or Privileged Access Workstations (endpoints hardened for attacks specifically looking for cached administrator credentials) as part of their endpoint strategy can mitigate this type of threat to a large extent, but not completely. Endpoint protection solutions can also help partially mitigate social engineering, as well as insider threat, by making it harder for users and administrators to make some of the common mistakes and poor trust choices that lead to compromise. Insider threat solutions for endpoints have become more sophisticated over time and can now be relied on to more reliably detect malicious insiders and to aid with incident response investigations. For this reason, I gave this strategy a score of 15/20 for insider threat.

Where this strategy typically fails is on network routing and switching infrastructure. You don't typically find endpoint protection on routing and switching devices. Instead, defenders rely on IDS/IPS and other network detection mechanisms to detect threats on their networks. But predictably, this can lead to large inventories of routing and switching equipment that haven't been inventoried, patched for vulnerabilities, or otherwise managed for security purposes. Once such equipment is compromised, it can be much harder to detect attackers and respond to them. Unfortunately, according to public reporting, attackers demonstrated they could leverage such gaps to their advantage by compromising some large US telecommunications systems in 2023 and 2024, in attacks attributed to Salt Typhoon, Chinese state-sponsored hackers. This attack took advantage of unpatched vulnerabilities in routing and switching equipment to initially compromise and remain persistent in large telecommunications environments (Sayegh, Emil, August 30, 2025). In my experience, routing and switching equipment is typically an under-managed layer of defenders' IT estates from a security perspective, and the lack of endpoint protection for these devices isn't helpful.

Although the endpoint protection strategy is insufficient by itself, it would be hard to imagine a successful enterprise cybersecurity strategy that didn't use it in combination with other strategies. It seems like the industry agrees with this assessment, as more and more organizations I have talked to have adopted or plan to adopt more sophisticated endpoint solutions over time.

Endpoint protection strategy summary

The CFSS total score for this strategy is 70/100. It must be used in combination with other strategies.

Here are the advantages:

- Superior visibility and control running on most of the endpoints
- Large vendor ecosystem providing decades of experience
- Constant threat research, response, and evolving technologies to stay ahead of attackers

Here are the disadvantages:

- Historically, organizations relying solely on this strategy have experienced poor results.

- Users resist systems that are too restrictive or impact productivity; individuals bring threats through defenses themselves in many cases. This approach can only partially mitigate the mistakes or poor trust decisions that developers, administrators, and users make that lead to compromise.
- Speed is a factor. Relatively slow and complicated vulnerability management processes give attackers an advantage. Organizations that have a good endpoint strategy but deploy security updates and other protections relatively slowly accept more risk.
- Endpoint protection suites have inconsistent performance histories and aspirational performance goals. Organizations that don't understand the internal goals of the endpoint protection vendors might not fully understand the associated risks.
- Managing endpoint security relies on accurate and timely asset inventorying and management capabilities. This has been notoriously hard in on-premises environments. I will discuss how the cloud can make this easier later.
- Many organizations allow employees and partners to use personal unmanaged or partially managed laptops, desktops, and mobile devices, known as the **Bring Your Own Device** (**BYOD**) strategy. Subsequently, the risk associated with the transmission, storage, and processing of corporate data on these devices might not be fully understood.
- Routing, switching, storage, IoT, and other hardware devices might not be integrated into an organization's endpoint protection strategy. This has been a gap in enterprise cybersecurity for decades because most of these devices aren't designed to run endpoint protection software and don't have such capabilities built into them.

That's the endpoint protection strategy. Now, let's move on to security strategies involving physical controls and security clearances.

Physical control and security clearances as a security strategy

I see this strategy in widespread use, especially in public sector organizations. I call this strategy the *physical control and security clearances* strategy. As is evident from the name, it relies on having physical control of the infrastructure used to transmit, store, and process data, as well as data classification and associated security clearances. The idea behind this strategy is that not all data has the same relative value to the organization that controls it. By classifying the data into different categories that reflect the relative value of the data, we can ensure the most valuable data is protected in ways that are commensurate with that value.

There are many different data classification schemes in use in the public and private sectors; many organizations have developed their own data classification schemes. We don't have to look any further than the US federal government to see a good example of a data classification scheme that has been deployed on a massive scale. Executive Order 13526 (United States Government Publishing Office, 2009) defines a three-tier system for classifying national security information, namely Top Secret, Secret, and Confidential. Another similar example is the UK government's **Government Security Classifications Policy (GSCP)** (U.K. Cabinet Office, October 18, 2013). It also defines three classifications that indicate the sensitivity of the information. These categories include Top Secret, Secret, and Official. There are many other examples of data classification schemes.

Data classification policies such as these can dictate the people, processes, and technologies that must be employed to handle data in each category. As such, the number and nature of the categories in the data classification schemes that organizations adopt can have a huge effect on organizations' cultures, recruiting practices, IT investments, and budgets, among other things.

This is where security clearances can become a factor. For some organizations, in order for personnel to be granted access to information that has been classified into a specific category, they must have a current security clearance for that category. For example, someone who doesn't have clearance for data that has been classified as secret will not be granted access to it. In order to get the necessary security clearance, there can be background checks involved, some of which are much deeper and more involved than others. Because positions with higher national security impact demand greater assurance of reliability, their background checks probe more deeply into an individual's history and potential risk factors.

For example, some security clearances require a criminal history check. Other, deeper background checks require a criminal history check, an employment background check, and a financial credit score check, in addition to the applicant providing personal references who will be interviewed as part of the background check process. Some security clearances even have specific citizenship requirements. Some clearances have a one-time process that applicants go through, while other clearances need to be periodically renewed. Some technology vendors give their customers insight into the background checks they subject their employees to. Microsoft is an example; they've published a personnel management overview that states the following.

> *"Background checks on employment candidates generally include review of the following components, to the extent permitted by law:*
>
> *Identity check*
>
> *Education verification*
>
> *Employment verification*

Criminal record review

Sex offender registry review

Global sanctions list review" (Microsoft Corporation, 2025)

You might be wondering why employers simply don't perform all these checks periodically. This is because different countries and jurisdictions have local labor laws and statutory regulations that protect the privacy and rights of employees. For example, in the US, too many credit checks can lower an individual's credit score. Allowing employers to institute administrative procedures that potentially negatively impact current or potential employees isn't generally viewed as a benefit of employment.

> **Note**
>
> Note that many data classification schemes don't require security clearances because they are designed to simply provide a way for the staff who handle data to understand how it should be handled.

From a security perspective, organizations that are serious about this approach are essentially trying to create a closed system for their data that has a high level of security assurance. People who handle data, especially sensitive data, will be vetted to minimize the likelihood that they have malicious intent or could be easily bribed or blackmailed to break their organization's policies. This concept of assurance also extends to their processes and technology. For example, some organizations have policies that dictate that data will only be transmitted, stored, and processed by hardware and software that has gone through their certification processes. All other electronics are never allowed in their on-premises environments. This includes anything that has a power cord or a battery.

Additionally, the business processes that these vetted employees use to operate their certified systems are carefully engineered to ensure auditability and that multiple people participate to keep each other honest. The underlying assumptions that make this closed system work are that the organization has end-to-end control of its entire infrastructure and that its supply chain is subject to security clearances and certification processes. Numerous trusted IT suppliers participate in these types of supply chains in countries all over the world.

The essence of this strategy can be traced back decades, if not centuries, as it has been heavily employed by militaries and national security organizations throughout the world. Of course, there have been national security failures throughout history, which tells us this approach isn't foolproof. In modern times, this model has been evolving. It works well on a small scale, but it gets incrementally harder to manage as it scales up. As their operations scaled, it became harder for these organizations to manage all their IT in-house. The types of organizations that use this model face the same IT resource and recruiting challenges as other industries. Subsequently, many of them have outsourced much of their IT to cope with these challenges. In many cases, this means that the contractors they use to manage their IT have physical access to the data centers and servers processing their data.

More specifically, in the course of their work, these contractors have access to the operating systems and hypervisors running on those servers, the virtualized workloads, and the data in those workloads. However, the organization that owns the data must maintain its closed system to protect it—that's its strategy. Because the contractors potentially have access to classified data, they require the same security clearances as the organization's regular personnel. The contractors' datacenters and the IT infrastructure in them also must go through the organization's certification processes. Despite all of the effort dedicated to clearances, history has taught us that they don't mitigate insider threats completely. Since this is all complicated and very expensive to accomplish, to make it economically viable, the contracts between organizations and qualified contractors tend to be very long-term, sometimes 10, 20, or even 30 years in duration. This managed service provider model is the way that IT has been outsourced to these organizations for the last 25+ years. Of course, there are a bunch of advantages and disadvantages to using managed service providers; I'll touch on a few of these in *Chapter 13, Modern Approaches to Security and Compliance.*

Note

To recap, the focus of the physical control and security clearances strategy is the security assurance of hardware and software, and periodic background checks of datacenter staff and administrators. It is characterized by investments in people, processes, and technologies that help maintain physical security, assurance, and confidence in the character of datacenter staff and administrators. Data classification also typically plays a critical role in helping protect the most important data. This approach has numerous benefits. Some governments literally have hundreds of years of practice using this type of strategy. It can help partially mitigate insider threats by identifying potentially risky job candidates and personnel who could have access to sensitive data. Furthermore, third-party verification or attestation of the trustworthiness of hardware and software contributes to security assurance and helps demonstrate due diligence. There is a large vendor ecosystem to help organizations that want to pursue this type of strategy.

Of course, the physical control and security clearances strategy also has some important disadvantages and limitations. First, data classification is challenging for most organizations. Data classification schemes are notoriously difficult to successfully institute in large organizations.

> **Note**
>
> In my experience, the organizations that have the most success with data classifications are those where security is deeply embedded in the culture. Military and paramilitary organizations, law enforcement agencies, national defense departments, and intelligence agencies are examples of organizations where data classification is deeply ingrained into the culture, people, processes, and supporting technologies. In these organizations, failure to comply with data classification policies and other policies can put human life at risk and lead to jail time in some cases. These powerful motivations generally help GRC programs become successful for these types of organizations.

Many commercial organizations have tried and failed—some, multiple times—to institute data classification schemes. The typical challenge for these organizations is finding a way to classify data that doesn't make it hard or impossible for information workers to get work done. Organizations that allow the same people who create the data to classify the data usually end up with large amounts of data that have been over-classified or under-classified, depending on the consequences to employees. For example, in military organizations, under-classifying data could lead to severe consequences such as loss of life or criminal charges. Conversely, data in these organizations tends to get over-classified because workers are better safe than sorry; they'll rarely get into trouble for over-classifying data, despite the immense extra costs when everyone in a large organization does this habitually.

In organizations where there aren't life-or-death consequences or national security concerns, data can be under-classified more easily, making it easier for information workers to get their work done. Some executive demand broad access to data regardless of how it is classified. This is one reason they are often the targets of Business Email Compromise schemes and other social engineering attacks. They can get access to any data and often, they are exempt from the inconvenient security controls that mitigate such attacks. It is a recipe for disaster that is often realized.

Of course, in neither of these scenarios where data is under- or over-classified does data classification fulfill its promise. In fact, some commercial and public sector organizations have decided not to institute data classification schemes because their past attempts to do so have failed or have not achieved their desired objectives. Essentially, these organizations have concluded that data classification is too complex and expensive to be worthwhile. For them, it's easier and more effective to treat all their data as if it's the same value. On the other hand, some of them will employ less formal, very simple data classification schemes by marking some documents and data as confidential or internal only, but the data protection requirements are the same for all their data.

Keep in mind that in many organizations, the one system that typically stores, processes, and transmits the data of all classifications is email. It's relatively rare for organizations to have two separate email systems—one email system for unclassified data and one for classified data. Subsequently, data of all classifications can end up in emails, which can become a source of data leakage. Even when organizations maintain separate email systems for classified and unclassified data, classified material can still be mistakenly sent over the unclassified system. In such cases, administrators may need security clearances so they can locate and remove that data from the unclassified environment.

To support rapid adoption of AI productivity tools, vendors such as Microsoft and Google introduced automated data-classification software. Platforms like Microsoft Purview can scan and label data across SharePoint, OneDrive, email, and other repositories, and enforce policies based on each item's sensitivity. I'll discuss this in more detail in *Chapter 15, Artificial Intelligence: Security of AI systems and using AI for better cybersecurity*.

Data residency is often a requirement for organizations that embrace this security strategy. That is, they require that all datacenters that process and store their data must be located in a specific country or jurisdiction. For example, all the data for a federal government department must stay within the national borders of their country. There are a few different reasons for data residency requirements, but the most common one cited is that data residency provides better security for the data and that the organization requires data sovereignty, which they likely will not have within the borders of another country. In order to maintain their closed system, they cannot risk putting a datacenter in a location that another government has sovereign control over.

Data residency doesn't mitigate any of the Cybersecurity Usual Suspects. This is because the overwhelming majority of the attacks happen remotely over the network, regardless of the physical location of the datacenter. Attackers don't care where the datacenter is physically located because it's not an effective mitigation for the vast majority of attacks.

This is why many organizations that embrace the Physical Control and Security Clearances Strategy put *air gaps* into their networks. Put another way, their networks are not directly connected to the internet. I've seen organizations try to accomplish air gaps in a few ways. Some simply don't procure internet connectivity from an ISP. Some use data diodes that are certified to only allow network traffic flow in one direction (PA Consulting, n.d.). Some organizations call a network "air-gapped" when it's behind a DMZ with very specific firewall rules. Truly air-gapping a network can be incredibly difficult to accomplish and maintain over time. The ubiquity of mobile devices, IoT devices, and common office equipment, like copiers that want to phone home with inventory and service information, makes it challenging to keep a disconnected network disconnected. Some organizations maintain two networks, one for classified information and the other for non-classified information. Information workers in these environments typically have two computers on their desks, one connected to each of these networks. Some of the organizations that use air-gapped networks require all mobile devices, laptops, and electronics to be kept in lockers at the front door of their facilities. I've visited many of these types of facilities around the world over the years, advising public sector customers.

Organizations that achieve and maintain air-gapped networks can make it much harder for attackers to leverage the Cybersecurity Usual Suspects to initially compromise their networks. However, as the Stuxnet attack and so many other attacks on air-gapped networks over the years have proven, it's not an insurmountable challenge for attackers. Moreover, data residency is far less effective than other available controls that help mitigate the risks that these organizations have in mind with their data residency requirements. Encryption and effective key management are primary among these controls, as I discussed in *Chapter 8, Friend or Foe? The roles governments play in cybersecurity*. By leveraging modern encryption and key management technologies, organizations can achieve very strong data protection while operationalizing data so that it can help them make better decisions faster.

Perhaps the biggest challenge for the physical control and security clearances strategy is that the world has changed in some key ways, all of which will make this strategy harder to pursue and less effective as time goes on. For example, most organizations today want to take advantage of **machine learning (ML)** and AI. They'll be challenged to do this in a scalable way in their accredited on-premises, air-gapped IT environments or via their traditional managed service providers' datacenters. In order to keep up with their adversaries, who aren't encumbered by the same certification and accreditation processes, organizations will have to change the way they procure and operate IT services. To do this, they will have to give up some of the end-to-end control they have had for decades. Their closed systems will have to evolve. For some of these organizations, this kind of change is super hard because it's initially uncomfortably different from how they've done GRC for the last few decades. This doesn't mean they have to settle for a less secure IT environment, but they do have to re-evaluate how to mitigate the risks they care about in a world where they don't own the infrastructure end-to-end. Additionally, increasing on-premises IT costs to maintain the status quo, in the face of tsunami after tsunami of innovation in the cloud, means that organizations that employ this type of strategy will either successfully evolve or become increasingly irrelevant.

CFSS score

Let's look at *Table 10.5*. How well does the physical control and security clearances strategy help address the cybersecurity fundamentals? I'll estimate scores for two flavors of this strategy: one with an air-gapped network and one without an air-gapped network. As you'll see, this makes a big difference in terms of the scores. Let's start by scoring this strategy for use on an air-gapped network.

Cybersecurity Fundamentals	Score (0–20)
Unpatched vulnerabilities	10
Security misconfigurations	10
Weak, leaked, or stolen credentials	15
Social engineering	10
Insider threat	10
CFSS Total Score (max = 100)	55

Table 10.5 – The CFSS score estimate for the physical control and security clearances strategy with an air-gapped network

None of this strategy's attributes, such as data classification, security clearances, or end-to-end control of certified hardware, help to fully mitigate unpatched vulnerabilities, security misconfigurations, and weak, leaked, or stolen passwords. Like the Protect and Recover Strategy, an air-gapped network can give security teams more time to address these Cybersecurity Usual Suspects, but they still must be addressed. Weak, leaked, and stolen credentials are harder to use if there is no remote network access to the target network. Applying the principle of least privilege accurately and consistently can make it harder to achieve unauthorized access to sensitive data.

As I discussed earlier in this section, data classification and security clearances can help mitigate insider threats, particularly malicious insiders. However, they don't fully mitigate users and administrators who make mistakes or poor trust decisions that lead to compromise. Because of this, I gave this strategy partial marks for insider threat and social engineering. This approach seems to be optimized to mitigate unlawful government access to data, such as military espionage. For many of the organizations that I have advised who use this strategy, this is definitely a real risk for them—perhaps their highest priority risk. But clearly, this isn't the only high-priority risk they need to mitigate.

I've seen organizations use this strategy without implementing an air-gapped network. Without the air-gapped network, relying on data classification, security clearances, and end-to-end certified hardware is far less effective at addressing the cybersecurity fundamentals, as *Table 10.6* reveals:

Cybersecurity Fundamentals	Score (0–20)
Unpatched vulnerabilities	0
Security misconfigurations	0
Weak, leaked, or stolen credentials	0
Social engineering	10
Insider threat	10
CFSS Total Score (max = 100)	20

Table 10.6 – The CFSS score estimate for the physical control and security clearances strategy without an air-gapped network

To really mitigate the Cybersecurity Usual Suspects, whether an air-gapped network is used or not, this approach needs to be used in combination with other cybersecurity strategies. I've met with many organizations that already know this and have been pursuing complementary strategies for years. However, the cultures of many of these organizations make it difficult for them to adopt new approaches and technologies. The internet, the cloud, and now AI have democratized IT, giving everyone capabilities that they didn't have before. The challenge for organizations that have used this strategy for years or decades is adapting their current approach quickly enough, all to enable them to mitigate a larger number of well-resourced adversaries than they've ever had in the past. Remember, defenders' constraints are not attackers' constraints.

Physical control and security clearances strategy summary

The CFSS total estimated score for this strategy, using air-gapped networks, is 55/100. For organizations that use this strategy but without an effective air-gapped network, my estimate of the CFSS total score is 20/100. My conclusion is that this strategy must be used in conjunction with other cybersecurity strategies in order to fully address the cybersecurity fundamentals.

The following are its advantages:

- Militaries and governments have hundreds of years of practice using similar approaches
- Air-gapped networks can help partially mitigate some of the Cybersecurity Usual Suspects.
- Helps partially mitigate insider threat, including unlawful government access to data, by making it harder for malicious insiders to succeed.
- Third-party verification/attestation of hardware contributes to security assurance and demonstrates due diligence.
- Has a large vendor ecosystem to help organizations that pursue this approach

The following are its disadvantages:

- Enormous costs are usually associated with the type of certified infrastructure typically leveraged with this approach
- The underlying assumption that data residency provides better security is not valid.
- Since most attacks are perpetrated remotely without physical access to hardware and regardless of the physical location of data, the success of this approach depends heavily on network air gaps to partially mitigate the Cybersecurity Usual Suspects.
- Data in highly restrictive, air-gapped environments can be harder to operationalize
- Doesn't fully mitigate insider threat because it focuses on mitigating malicious insiders, which does not include the mistakes that non-malicious insiders make, leading to poor security outcomes.
- Gives attackers an advantage because they can use newer technologies faster than defenders

Now, let's move on and consider how some organizations use compliance as a security strategy.

Compliance as a cybersecurity strategy

Compliance and cybersecurity are two different, slightly overlapping disciplines. Compliance typically focuses on proving that an organization meets requirements defined in regulated, industry, and/or internal standards. Compliance can be helpful in numerous ways, chief among them being for cybersecurity insurance purposes and demonstrating due diligence to limit liability. This is different from cybersecurity, which focuses on identifying, protecting, detecting, responding, and recovering (NIST, n.d.). However, I have seen some organizations conflate these different disciplines because they overlap each other, as I've illustrated in *Figure 10.2*.

Figure 10.2 – Compliance and security disciplines overlap, but are different

I've seen similar illustrations where compliance is a subset of cybersecurity or vice versa. I think arguments can be made for all of these approaches. The approach that some organizations I have discussed this with have taken is to rotate the two circles in *Figure 10.2* on top of each other and pretend that they are the same thing.

That's not to say that organizations can't align their efforts in order to pursue both compliance and cybersecurity. This is what most organizations need to do, but many fail to do so.

I've discovered that there are a variety of reasons that organizations conflate compliance and cybersecurity:

- First, some regulated standards have non-compliance penalties or fines associated with them. This provides an incentive for organizations to prove that they are meeting these standards and invest in compliance programs. But since most organizations have resource constraints, many of them believe they are forced to decide whether to use their resources on compliance or cybersecurity.
- In some cases, organizations end up using this strategy because their well-resourced, well-intentioned compliance organization over-functions. That is, they extend their efforts beyond proving they meet applicable standards to performing functions that you'd typically see a security team perform. There's nothing wrong with this per se, but we need to recognize that their area of expertise and the center of gravity for their program is compliance.
- Some of the organizations that I have seen using this strategy do so simply because their compliance program is older and more mature than their cybersecurity program; they have had compliance obligations for years or decades in their industry, and cybersecurity is a relatively new investment for them.

The underlying assumption of this strategy is that meeting compliance obligations is sufficient for protecting the organization's data. Subsequently, the focus is on meeting the organization's regulatory, industry, and internal compliance obligations and demonstrating this in internal and third-party audits.

These could include standards like PCI, HIPAA, GDPR, NIST standards, ISO standards, or an organization's own internal IT security standards, among others. This strategy is characterized by investments in people, processes, and technologies that help organizations meet their compliance obligations. This typically manifests itself as well-defined control sets and repeatable processes that are periodically audited.

This strategy can be very advantageous, healthy, and positive for organizations that do not have a cybersecurity strategy or mature governance practices. Most of the regulated security-related standards that have been instituted in industries provide a minimum set of requirements that organizations should work to achieve. The steps that organizations typically need to take to get their IT governance, infrastructure, and operations in shape to be audited for the first time against an industry standard can dramatically improve their security posture and their overall cybersecurity program.

> **Tip**
>
> Organizations should not underestimate the effort and potential change related to complying with regulated standards and industry standards. This effort is typically rewarded with much better security than where they started, as well as a foundation they can potentially extend and continue to build on.

The challenge for many organizations is to recognize that most regulated security-related standards are minimum requirements, not some sort of certification that means they can't be compromised. Although regulatory compliance is required for many organizations, it's insufficient to protect their systems and data from modern-day threats. This is where compliance as a security strategy tends to fall short. History has taught us that this is a poor strategy. There is no shortage of examples of large, well-funded organizations that met regulated standards but were breached all the same. Think about all the financial institutions, retailers, and restaurants that met their industries' regulated standards but were breached anyway. Think about all the organizations in the healthcare industry around the world that worked hard to comply with stringent regulated industry data protection standards and still lost control of patient data to attackers.

> **Note**
>
> My own personal data has been compromised multiple times in data breaches in all of these industries over the years. This doesn't mean that regulated security-related standards are worthless. As I mentioned, they are very positive for many, many

> organizations. I'd rather use my credit card in a restaurant that tries to comply with PCI DSS than one that doesn't.

Regulated security-related standards are insufficient by themselves. There are at least a couple of reasons for this. First, standards like these typically have a defined scope, such as credit card holder information or patient information. The control sets to support these standards are designed for the infrastructure and data that are in the defined scope. But what about the other HVAs that organizations have? If an organization uses its limited resources to address only the scope that's audited and subject to penalties, it is likely not paying enough attention to other HVAs and their broader infrastructure.

The second reason regulated standards are insufficient is that they are almost certainly based on someone else's threat model, not yours. This means they are certain to leave you with gaps if they are your sole approach to cybersecurity.

The final reason regulated standards are insufficient is that they rarely keep pace with the threat landscape or advances in technology. This has more to do with how quickly standards can be adopted in industries and their economic impact than with the standards bodies themselves. Using PCI DSS as an example, deploying updated security-related standards requirements to millions of retailers and restaurants around the world takes years. Subsequently, organizations typically need a broader cybersecurity strategy that embraces compliance but supplements its shortcomings in material ways. Simply put, enterprises need to do both.

Let's see how well compliance as a cybersecurity strategy addresses the Cybersecurity Usual Suspects.

CFSS score

My CFSS score estimates for compliance as a cybersecurity strategy reveal that this strategy can partially mitigate all the Cybersecurity Usual Suspects, as seen in *Table 10.7*. Remember, the goal is to find a strategy or combination of strategies that gives us a perfect 100/100 CFSS total score. Subsequently, this strategy will need to be used in combination with other strategies to fully address the Cybersecurity Usual Suspects.

Cybersecurity Fundamentals	**Score (0–20)**
Unpatched vulnerabilities	10
Security misconfigurations	10

Cybersecurity Fundamentals	Score (0–20)
Weak, leaked, or stolen credentials	10
Social engineering	10
Insider threat	10
CFSS Total Score (max = 100)	50

Table 10.7 – The CFSS score estimate for compliance as a security strategy

I gave this strategy partial marks across the board because it can help organizations mitigate all these threats, but it's typically used with limited scope and is slow to adapt to changes in the threat landscape. This strategy can and does create a foundation, albeit incomplete, that many organizations can build on with complementary approaches.

Compliance as a cybersecurity strategy summary

The CFSS total estimated score for this strategy is 50/100. This strategy can be very beneficial for organizations as a starting point for a broader cybersecurity strategy. Organizations that integrate their compliance requirements into a more holistic cybersecurity strategy can potentially reduce complexity and costs and achieve better security.

The following are its advantages:

- It can be very positive for organizations that do not have a security strategy or have immature governance practices
- Third-party verification/attestation by auditors is valuable to demonstrate due diligence
- Large vendor and audit firm ecosystem to help
- It can reduce complexity and costs and achieve better security when integrated with cybersecurity efforts
- Complying with some regulated standards, like GDPR, for example, can help organizations achieve better data protection

The following are the disadvantages:

- History has shown this to be a poor strategy as many organizations that complied with standards were breached anyway
- Typically relies on compliance and audit teams, as well as third-party auditors, to arbitrate the organization's security posture

- Focuses on implementing control sets specified in regulated standards with a specific scope that typically does not include all HVAs
- Regulated standards typically based on someone else's threat model, not yours
- Only attains minimum requirements specified by regulations when they were last published; rarely reflects modern-day risks and mitigations
- Attackers have a disproportionate advantage over defenders. This is because they have complete visibility into the control sets required to comply, and those control sets rarely keep pace with changes in the threat landscape.
- In some cases, regulatory compliance consumes resources that could otherwise be used for more effective cybersecurity.

Now, let's look at the application-centric strategy.

Application-centric strategy

This is another *proxy strategy*. The underlying assumption is that applications process, store, and transmit data; if we protect the application, then by proxy, we are protecting the data. This approach focuses on protecting applications by reducing the number and the severity of vulnerabilities in them. It also endeavors to make the vulnerabilities that are inevitably left in applications really difficult, if not impossible, to exploit. These are the same principles that underpin the vulnerability improvement framework that I introduced in *Chapter 3, Industry Vulnerability Disclosure Trends*. An underlying assumption of this approach is that it is much less expensive to fix bugs and mitigate vulnerabilities before an application is released into production. This involves investments in people, processes, and technologies, which can include threat modeling, security development life cycles, static and dynamic code analysis tools, penetration testing, mobile device management, mobile application management, bug bounties, and others.

I'm a big believer in this strategy; after all, would you set sail in a submarine where someone is drilling holes in the hull from the inside? This continues to be an underestimated risk, as many enterprises still don't seem to select vendors or solutions based on their secure development practices.

I led marketing communications for Microsoft's **Security Development Lifecycle (SDL)** (Microsoft Corporation, n.d.) for several years and saw how it could help development teams first-hand. However, you don't have to have a massive development organization like Microsoft to benefit from this strategy. As the saying goes, a rising tide lifts all boats. CISOs, security teams, compliance professionals, and development organizations can all help raise the security tide mark for their organization over time by implementing security development education, policies, and processes that are supported by tools to help improve the quality of the software both developed in-house and procured from third parties. For example, requiring that every in-house-developed application has a threat model prior to developers writing any code can help improve the design and mitigate potential vulnerabilities. Similarly, requiring static code analysis at specific milestones in development can help reduce the number and severity of vulnerabilities that make it into production. Organizations that don't enforce security requirements in every phase of the development process typically pay a higher price for this decision after their applications have been deployed.

But like all the other strategies we've examined, this one has drawbacks and limitations as well. The same operating system features, tools, IDEs, development libraries, and frameworks (C++, the JRE, .NET, and so on) that are used to protect applications can also be a persistent source of vulnerabilities. The **Java Runtime Environment (JRE)** was a perennial example for many years. It saved development teams a lot of time and expense, but the opportunity cost was that their application could inherit vulnerabilities that needed to be patched in the JRE itself. The time between vulnerabilities being discovered in these frameworks and being fixed represents a risk to the users of their applications.

Another drawback of this strategy that I've seen organizations grapple with numerous times is that, although fewer vulnerabilities and lower severity vulnerabilities are measurable metrics, they are hard to translate into business value. Arguing that attacks didn't happen because of the investment in application security can be a tough argument for CISOs and development organization leaders to make and for other executives to understand. What seems like common sense to CISOs and vulnerability management teams can remain nebulous for other stakeholders.

As I wrote in *Chapter 3*, using data from your vulnerability management program to provide visibility on the state of the environment can help you make the case for application security. Trying to drive the number of unpatched vulnerabilities to zero and using data to help other executives understand the progress against this goal and the associated costs can help them understand why it is important to prevent new vulnerabilities from being introduced into the environment via third-party and in-house applications.

CFSS score

All that said, let's see how the application-centric strategy scores on the CFSS.

Cybersecurity Fundamentals	Score (0–20)
Unpatched vulnerabilities	20
Security misconfigurations	20

Cybersecurity Fundamentals	Score (0–20)
Weak, leaked, or stolen credentials	10
Social engineering	10
Insider threat	10
CFSS Total Score (max = 100)	70

Table 10.8 – The CFSS score estimate for the application-centric strategy

I gave this strategy full marks for its ability to mitigate unpatched vulnerabilities and security misconfigurations. I realize this is a little optimistic for most organizations, but there are some scenarios where this could be possible. I gave this strategy partial marks for its ability to mitigate insider threat, social engineering, and weak, leaked, or stolen credentials. For example, designing applications that require MFA and provide rich logging and audit capabilities can help partially mitigate these threats.

Application-centric strategy summary

All organizations can benefit from this approach. However, by itself, its CFSS total estimated score is 70/100. I recommend that organizations embrace this strategy and supplement it with other approaches that will help fully address all the cybersecurity fundamentals.

The following are its advantages:

- It can reduce the number and severity of vulnerabilities in software that the organization procures and develops in house.
- It can lower maintenance costs, minimize business disruptions, and measurably improve application security.
- Leverages mitigations that are integrated into operating systems, IDEs, development libraries and frameworks (C++, the JRE, .NET, and so on), and containers. This reduces complexity, costs, and effort for development teams while potentially improving security.
- Large existing vendor ecosystem to help

The following are the disadvantages:

- It relies on developers to produce vulnerability-free source code and/or makes it impossible for vulnerabilities to be exploited; history teaches us that this is optimistic.

- Success is also subject to vulnerabilities in operating systems, IDEs, development libraries, frameworks, containers, and other technologies.
- Business ROI can be difficult to communicate effectively.

Onward now to the identity-centric strategy.

Identity-centric strategy

You'll remember that one of the Cybersecurity Usual Suspects is weak, leaked, and stolen credentials. Credentials and the assets that they protect have been the currency for attackers for decades. Many people reuse passwords across applications, systems, and services. When one of those is compromised and the credentials are stolen, attackers immediately try those credentials on other systems and services across the internet, such as major online banking portals, e-commerce sites, social networks, and so on. The industry has long wanted to deprecate passwords in favor of better authentication methods and to use data from authentication and authorization systems to make better resource access decisions. These concepts are central to the *identity-centric* strategy.

Although the concept of identity and proving your identity is ancient, the identity-centric strategy is a relatively new strategy that gained popularity rapidly. The idea behind this strategy is that during most successful data breaches, at some point, attackers will use legitimate credentials. There's a saying in the cybersecurity industry, "attackers don't break in – they log in." How can we use this to our advantage to protect, detect, and respond to attacks? Well, authentication and authorization processes can potentially generate some useful metadata. For example, if we can ascertain the approximate location that an authentication or authorization request is coming from, we might be able to calculate a level of confidence in its legitimacy. Similarly, if we can compare some key attributes of the request to characteristics of past requests from the same account, this too might help provide us with some level of confidence that the request was legitimate. There's a bunch of metadata like this that can help organizations protect, detect, and respond to attacks. Here's a partial list of such data:

- Strength of the credential used for the request (older protocols versus newer protocols)
- Location and temporal data
    - Origin location of request
    - Time of day of request
    - Time between requests from different locations—is it impossible to travel between those locations in the time between the requests?
- Trustworthiness of the device the request comes from:
    - Presence of a valid digital certificate installed by the organization

    - Corporate-managed device or unmanaged personal device
    - Latest operating system version installed on the device
    - Knowledge of unpatched vulnerabilities in the hardware or operating system
- User behavior
    - Number of times the user entered incorrect credentials
    - Time of last **Multi-Factor Authentication (MFA)** prompt and result

The underlying assumption of this strategy is that organizations can better protect data, detect compromises, and respond faster by better protecting the identities used to access data, and by using identity metadata to look for indicators of compromise. The focus of this approach is protecting the credentials used to access the organization's data, especially the credentials of privileged accounts, such as administrators. Incident response teams, forensics experts, as well as Red and Blue teams all know that privileged account credentials are like gold to attackers. When I worked on Microsoft's customer-facing **Cybersecurity Incident Response Team (CIRT)**, attackers' modus operandi was very consistent; once the attackers initially compromised an IT environment using one or more of the Cybersecurity Usual Suspects, within seconds, their scripts were running, trying to harvest cached credentials on the compromised system. They would use those credentials to move laterally through the environment if they could, looking for more cached credentials along the way. Finding cached credentials for privileged accounts made it much easier for attackers to penetrate the environment even deeper and then get access to more resources and data. If attackers were able to exfiltrate a copy of the victim's Microsoft Active Directory, they would perform an offline attack, using rainbow tables and/or other tools to get access to more credentials relatively quickly (Wikipedia, n.d.). Once attackers got to this stage, recovery was aspirational. I met numerous organizations over the years that found themselves in this scenario. Some of were forced to "share" their IT environment with attackers because recovery was too difficult. Others decided to rebuild their infrastructure from scratch or used the compromise as the impetus to start fresh in the cloud. Since attackers try to harvest credentials as a matter of course, many organizations focus on protecting credentials and use identity metadata to accelerate detection.

The Identity-Centric Strategy is characterized by investments in MFA, enforcing the principle of least privilege, identity management technologies, credential vaulting and hygiene practices, and detecting credentials that are being misused (Pass-the-Hash and Golden Ticket attacks are examples). For example, to counter attacks on Microsoft Active Directory, Microsoft has taken numerous steps to make it harder for attackers to succeed. In addition to engineering improvements in their products, they have published guidance on how to harden Active Directory (Microsoft Corporation, May 21, 2025).

They also published content on an enterprise access model that shows how privileged access fits into an overall enterprise access model (Microsoft Corporation, 2025). These types of architectures help protect privileged account credentials and make it much harder for attackers to get access to them. However, these advanced architectures and configurations are not for the faint of heart. Meeting and maintaining the requirements of these environments can be challenging. Protecting credentials in distributed environments has never been easy.

The identity space has exploded over the past couple of decades. There are vendors that specialize in access management, privileged access management, identity governance, and several other areas. Some vendors that sell technologies that support an identity-centric strategy call identity the "new perimeter" to highlight the importance of protecting credentials and credential hygiene. It's also important to note that identity plays a central role in cloud computing as well as Zero Trust strategies, where many of the same concepts are leveraged. I'll discuss this type of strategy later in the chapter. There are several vendors in the identity space that can help make protecting credentials easier and provide access to valuable metadata to accelerate anomaly detection. Some of the vendors that I have seen organizations leverage include BeyondTrust, CyberArk, Delinea, Google, Microsoft, Okta, Ping Identity, and others.

Let's see how well the identity-centric strategy helps us mitigate the Cybersecurity Usual Suspects.

CFSS score

How does the identity-centric strategy score in the CFSS? It doesn't fully address any of the cybersecurity fundamentals, as *Table 10.9* illustrates.

Cybersecurity Fundamentals	Score (0–20)
Unpatched vulnerabilities	5
Security misconfigurations	5
Weak, leaked, or stolen credentials	15
Social engineering	10
Insider threat	10
CFSS Total Score (max = 100)	45

Table 10.9 – The CFSS score estimate for the identity-centric strategy

This strategy doesn't mitigate unpatched vulnerabilities or security misconfigurations. But some vulnerabilities and security misconfigurations require authenticated access in order to be exploited. Organizations that focus on enforcing the principle of least privilege and practice good credential hygiene can make reliable exploitation of vulnerabilities and misconfigurations much more difficult and "limit the blast radius." Subsequently, I gave this strategy partial marks for these two cybersecurity fundamentals. I couldn't give it full marks for mitigating weak, leaked, and stolen credentials because legacy applications tend to fall through the cracks with this strategy; MFA typically can't be deployed everywhere, and metadata isn't always going to be available. Similarly, this approach can help partially mitigate insider threat by implementing **Just-in-Time (JIT)** and **Just-Enough-Administration (JEA)** models, credential vaulting, and other mitigations. Social engineering can be partially mitigated with MFA and least privilege, among other controls, but can't be completely mitigated. I'm sure some readers would give this strategy a higher score than I did – please use your own estimates where warranted.

Identity-centric strategy summary

This strategy needs to be used in combination with other strategies to fully mitigate the Cybersecurity Usual Suspects. Although it didn't score particularly high, it's certainly a valuable, modern, complementary approach to improving protection, detection, and containment capabilities. However, that might be understating the importance of identity in a modern cybersecurity strategy. Identity will remain central to an effective cybersecurity strategy, helping to address the cybersecurity fundamentals and provide advanced capabilities. Investments in this area can pay big dividends for CISOs.

The following are its advantages:

- Focuses on improving governance and technologies with a historically poor track record
- A large vendor ecosystem to help
- Can help manage risk related to weak, leaked, and stolen passwords
- Helps make MFA ubiquitous
- Help build confidence in the legitimacy of authentication requests through the strength of a credential, the location of a login attempt, the trustworthiness of the device, and MFA controls
- Can quickly identify authentication/authorization anomalies

- Can add friction to the authentication/authorization processes, which makes it harder for attackers to infiltrate
- Can bolster containment efforts and make it harder for attackers to move laterally and contain the "blast radius" of some attacks

The following are its disadvantages:

- Traditionally, federated identity systems have been complex, expensive, and hard to govern and manage; simply put, identity has always been hard
- Legacy applications have been challenging to govern and secure using a modern Identity-Centric Strategy; simply put, legacy applications have always been hard. There are typically far more legacy applications than modern applications in large, complex, mature enterprise IT environments.
- MFA is typically not implemented everywhere, leaving gaps and opportunities for attackers
- It can be complicated, time-consuming, and expensive to fully implement in enterprise on-premises environments

Next, let's look at a strategy that has had a resurgence in popularity—the data-centric strategy.

Data-centric strategy

The *data-centric* strategy has been growing in popularity for several reasons, including numerous high-profile data breaches, revelations about government data collection programs, the dramatically increased frequency of ransomware attacks, the increasing threat of intellectual property theft, and the hype surrounding quantum computing. There are also increasing regulatory demands that aim to help protect consumer privacy and have significant noncompliance fines associated with them, such as GDPR, for example. In addition, because of the challenges we discussed with the Protect and Recover Strategy, the Endpoint Protection Strategy, the Application-Centric Strategy, the popularity of BYOD, IT environments, and the emergence of IoT, some organizations have decided to stop using strategies that rely solely on proxies to protect their data. Instead of relying on the security provided by firewalls, endpoints, and applications, their strategy is to protect the data, no matter where it is.

Whether their data is inside their perimeter, accessed from a managed device, or processed by an application that meets their security development requirements, the data still needs to be protected. Some CISOs assume that endpoints cannot be fully trusted and that data can move in unexpected ways without their knowledge. They want to ensure that even in scenarios where they are not in control of their data, it's still protected.

This is where the data-centric strategy can help. There are several underlying assumptions for this approach. First, data, not the systems that process it, transmit it, or store it, is the HVA. Instead of focusing on the security of hardware and software that handles data, the focus should be on the data itself. Another assumption is that data will move without the organization's approval or knowledge, and therefore it must be protected, regardless of where it is. Some CISOs go so far as to assume that some of the systems that process their data are compromised and that the data must be protected in a compromised environment. Finally, organizations still require that their data can be shared appropriately within their organization and with authorized partners, such as outside manufacturing, marketing, PR, and law firms. That is, although the data must be secure, it still must be accessible and usable internally and externally. The focus of this strategy is to protect data wherever it is transmitted, processed, and stored, preferably forever, but for a reasonably long period of time. The period that data needs to be protected is based on the value of the data and the expected lifetime of sensitivity. This approach is characterized by investments in encryption and key management technologies, **Data Loss Prevention (DLP)**, and potentially, data classification.

A simplified example of this is encrypted PDF files, which can be read by authorized users but whose content cannot be copied and pasted. A more complicated example is the extreme data-centric solutions offered by blockchain platforms that implement data protection mechanisms as part of the data itself.

The heart of this strategy is encryption and key management; if data is encrypted everywhere all the time, the attack surface area can be dramatically reduced. For example, instead of trying to protect all files everywhere they currently are and will be in the future for the sensitivity lifetime of the data, encryption can help make this more manageable.

Encryption and key management can help maintain the confidentiality and integrity of the data it protects. Encrypting large numbers of files reduces the attack surface by shifting the focus from protecting all these files to potentially protecting a much smaller number of encryption keys. If strong, properly implemented encryption is employed, the primary focus can shift from the security of the encrypted files to managing the keys that are used to encrypt and decrypt them. Of course, if the owner of the data doesn't have access to the encrypted files, they can't decrypt them, and the data is lost—for example, when encrypted files are encrypted again during a ransomware attack. This means we shouldn't be cavalier with our data just because it's encrypted. However, the mathematical properties of properly implemented strong encryption can help reduce risk.

Besides reducing the attack surface, encryption buys organizations time. That is, properly encrypted data looks the same as random noise, and without the keys to decrypt the data, it will likely take many years of effort for attackers to decrypt a portion of the data. The confidentiality and integrity of the data are preserved during that time. But it is still prudent to assume that encrypted data has a finite lifespan. Periodically rotating keys and re-encrypting data can help extend this lifespan, but at some point, the algorithms or key lengths used will no longer provide adequate protection in the face of new technologies and advances in cryptanalysis. For example, for many years, there have been industry-wide efforts to develop post-quantum or quantum-safe encryption algorithms that can be used to preserve the confidentiality and integrity of data after quantum computers can be used to defeat current encryption methods. A thoughtful approach to managing encryption, decryption, and keys is required; this is not a "set it and forget it" solution to data protection.

You might be wondering, given that various types of encryption have been around for millennia, if encryption and key management are so powerful, then why haven't organizations always been encrypting everything, everywhere? Why have there been so many data breaches involving unencrypted data? Traditionally, there's been a tension between securing information and operationalizing information. Let me give you an example of this tension. I'll use a completely fictional scenario, where there are life-and-death consequences for unauthorized access to information – a witness protection program.

In this fictional scenario, the list of witnesses that the program is protecting is handwritten on paper. The list hasn't been digitized in any way; it only exists on paper. No one person has ever seen the entire list, as parts of the list are managed by separate program managers and are physically compartmentalized. The list is put into a fireproof filing cabinet that has a combination lock and steel bars locked across its drawers. The keys to these locks are given to separate program officers, requiring all of them to be present to open the filing cabinet.

The filing cabinet is in a vault, in a secured area in the middle of police headquarters, surrounded by on-duty police officers, with armed guards at the one fortified entrance to the building 24 hours a day. Of course, the building has an extensive security system, including video surveillance, mantraps, and card key access points. The vault can only be opened by following a specific protocol that requires the participation of two additional senior law enforcement officials under specific conditions.

I hope you agree that the list in this scenario has been secured in a way that mitigates many potential risks and that unauthorized access to the list would require extraordinary measures. Ethan Hunt from Mission Impossible might be able to breach all these controls, but I'm sure you'll agree that it would be difficult for most other people. However, an additional consequence of these controls is that legitimate, authorized access to the list has been encumbered, making it a complicated and slow process. In this scenario, since there can be life-and-death consequences to unauthorized access, access is purposely designed to be slow, cumbersome, and meticulous. However, if there were an emergency or some other need for quick access or repetitive access to the list, this process would frustrate those needs.

In another fictional scenario, a company that specializes in providing real-time advice on trading stocks has a different challenge. This company will go out of business if it can't access information, process it, and provide valuable advice to its large customer base in near real time. The information it has typically loses its value within minutes. Security controls are important to the company, as it has very aggressive competitors and regulators who would like to understand what its secret to success is. However, if security controls encumber the near real-time distribution of information inside the company or to its customers, the company will fail to keep its promises to its customers and go out of business in a hyper-competitive market. This company purposely prioritizes speed and agility over security. If it doesn't, it won't be in business very long.

These two scenarios demonstrate the tension between the need for data security and the need to operationalize information, which has traditionally challenged organizations. Combine this tension with the fact that encryption and key management have traditionally required specific, relatively hard-to-find, and expensive expertise, and this begins to explain why organizations don't simply encrypt all their data all the time.

Because of this tension and the traditional challenges associated with encryption, many organizations decide to encrypt only their most sensitive data. This reduces complexity and costs, while still ensuring their most valuable data is protected. To do this, many organizations have adopted data classification schemes in order to identify and more effectively protect high-value data. But as I mentioned earlier in this chapter, data classification policies are notoriously difficult for organizations to implement and adhere to. Many of the organizations I have talked to, particularly those that tried to implement data classification policies and failed, have concluded that it is more efficient to treat all data as if it's the same value. For them, this approach is less complicated and less expensive than trying to consistently identify the relative value of individual datasets and applying different security control sets based on that value. But these organizations are still faced with the challenge of managing encryption and key management.

Wouldn't it be great if CISOs didn't have to make these trade-offs? That is, they could have it all—uncompromising data security, the operational capabilities that enable organizations to move fast, the ability to share data when needed, and better visibility and control. Who wouldn't want that? This is what the data-centric strategy seeks to enable. Instead of just managing the security of the hardware and software that handles data, secure the data itself using encryption, key management, authentication, and authorization. In a world where data breaches have become common, this strategy can provide an effective line of defense when most other protection mechanisms fail. In addition, if encryption and decryption functions require authentication and authorization, the metadata generated from these activities can provide useful information on where the data is and who is trying to access it.

From a high level, the technologies used to support these capabilities include client-side or server-side encryption libraries or applications, **Public Key Infrastructures (PKIs)**, federated identity systems with authorization capabilities, as well as logging and reporting capabilities. A good example of a service that combines all these components is Microsoft Purview Information Protection. Microsoft Purview Information Protection protects sensitive data by automatically discovering, classifying, labeling, and encrypting it across organizations' digital estates (Microsoft Corporation. June 6, 2024). I'll discuss Microsoft Purview in *Chapter 15*.

One critical ingredient that enables a data-centric approach is identity. An identity strategy, like the Identity-Centric Strategy I described earlier in this chapter, is required for the data-centric strategy to be successful. Without authentication and authorization capabilities, the data-centric strategy isn't scalable.

DLP can also be employed in a data-centric strategy. DLP is a powerful tool to help prevent data from leaving an organization in an unauthorized way, including malicious and non-malicious data theft and leakage. DLP can monitor data that moves via the network, email, USB drives, and other removable media. But increasingly ubiquitous encryption can make it more difficult for DLP to achieve complete visibility. Additionally, DLP policy violations rarely result in consequences for the employees and executives that break them; this provides little incentive to pay attention to DLP-related policies. Finally, DLP can only slow down malicious insiders as they steal information, not stop them completely. They will almost always find a way to smuggle information out of an IT environment, like using the camera on their mobile phone to take a picture of it right off the screen of a secure workstation, for example. However, DLP combined with the Physical Control and Security Clearances Strategy—an air-gapped network in a facility that enforces a policy prohibiting all outside electronics including mobile phones, has physically removed USB and peripheral ports on computers in the facility, and searches employees as they enter and leave the facility—has a much better chance of preventing data theft. But few organizations outside those responsible for national security impose these types of controls.

Let's see how well the data-centric strategy addresses the Cybersecurity Usual Suspects.

CFSS score

Perhaps unexpectedly, the data-centric strategy does not earn a great CFSS score by itself, as shown in *Table 10.10*. After all, if the underlying infrastructure used for encryption, key management, authentication, authorization, logging, DLP, and other functions is compromised using one or more of the Cybersecurity Usual Suspects, then attackers can potentially get access to the data before it gets encrypted, or they could get access to credentials or decryption keys. Protecting the data is a powerful mitigation, but it requires that the components that make it possible are also protected.

Cybersecurity Fundamentals	Score (0–20)
Unpatched vulnerabilities	5
Security misconfigurations	5
Weak, leaked, or stolen credentials	0
Social engineering	15
Insider threat	15
CFSS Total Score (max = 100)	40

Table 10.10 – The CFSS score estimate for the data-centric strategy

I gave this approach partial marks for unpatched vulnerabilities and security misconfigurations because it can protect the confidentiality and integrity of the data, while vulnerability management teams scan and update systems. Like the protect and recover strategy, this approach can give vulnerability management teams more time to get this done.

It can also protect data for a period of time after the exploitation of vulnerabilities and misconfigurations. But it doesn't prevent the attackers from destroying the data or encrypting it themselves using ransomware. Crucially, it doesn't prevent attackers from exploiting vulnerabilities in the infrastructure, moving laterally, collecting credentials, persisting, and collecting data before it gets encrypted in web browsers and email clients, and so on. Of course, most credentials in Microsoft Active Directory and other modern directory services are encrypted, but that's not the focus of the data-centric strategy. It offers nothing new to protect passwords, as it relies on identity systems and federated identities. Subsequently, I gave it 0 out of 20 for weak, leaked, and stolen passwords.

This strategy can mitigate some forms of social engineering when used with the principle of least privilege and a meaningful separation of duties. This is also true of insider threats. Encrypted data can remain confidential, even when administrators make mistakes that lead to poor security outcomes, but there are limits. Malicious insiders will potentially have a harder time with a meaningful separation of duties that limits their access to encryption key material. Thus, I gave both social engineering and insider threat partial marks.

Data-centric strategy summary

Despite its relatively low CFSS score, I am a fan of the data-centric strategy. Although it doesn't mitigate the cybersecurity usual suspects by itself, it does act as an advanced capability, providing an important extra layer of protection and detection. Authenticated, authorized encryption and decryption operations can be very effective for protecting data. Using the metadata that I described can also be very helpful to security teams. For CISOs who try to protect everything as if it has the same value to the organization (which can be a recipe for disaster), dramatically reducing the attack surface area that they must focus on can be very helpful.

For many organizations, data classification can help determine which datasets they need to focus on protecting. But data classification is notoriously hard to implement and adhere to. Modern approaches to encryption and key management make it much easier and less expensive to encrypt everything all the time, especially in the cloud.

The following are its advantages:

- It potentially reduces the surface area to protect by focusing on data on the endpoint, email, network, proxy servers, and cloud.
- It can help protect data, detect data breaches, and respond to incidents more quickly than traditionally possible.
- It can effectively protect data from unauthorized access for relatively long periods, allowing security teams to focus on cybersecurity fundamentals and other advanced capabilities with more confidence.
- Encryption can help make data destruction easier for data owners when needed; destroying the keys effectively destroys the data they protect.
- DLP can be a powerful tool to help prevent data from leaving an organization and to help detect data leakage

The following are the disadvantages:

- Many organizations find data classification policies and technologies hard to implement and use consistently over time. Subsequently, many organizations have tried and failed to do data classification in a meaningful way.
- Key management can be challenging for some organizations. An on-premises PKI is not for the faint of heart and requires technical expertise. A failed PKI can have disastrous implications; the cloud makes this much easier.
- Many organizations terminate encrypted communications to inspect data and apply DLP policies as it moves. Increasing the use of encryption for data in transit and at rest has made it more challenging for DLP to be effective.

- Enforcing DLP policy violations can be challenging for some CISOs; how often is a senior executive reprimanded for breaking DLP policies? Many organizations do not adequately enforce policy violations when they're flagged by DLP.
- Relying on a sound identity strategy and federated identity implementation can be challenging to architect, implement, operate, and govern

Moving on to the next cybersecurity strategy that I will discuss: the attack-centric strategy.

Attack-centric strategy

The idea behind the *attack-centric* strategy is that the ways security teams protect systems, detect compromises, and respond to attackers should be informed by the TTPs that attackers actually use. Put another way, understanding how attackers operate and planning defenses around that makes those defenses more effective. The underlying assumption of this approach is that forcing attackers to be successful multiple times during intrusion attempts makes it much harder for them and decreases detection and recovery times. The focus of this approach is making each attacker tactic and technique ineffective. Lowering attackers' return on investment by increasing the time, effort, and costs associated with their attack will force attackers to rethink or abandon their attack. This approach is characterized by investments in numerous areas to block or impede attackers at each stage of their attack.

Two consummate examples of this approach are Lockheed Martin's Intrusion Kill Chain (Eric M. Hutchins, Michael J. Cloppert, and Rohan M. Amin, Ph.D.) and MITRE ATT&CK® (MITRE). These complementary approaches are informed by the steps attackers take to attack their victims and the specific tactics, techniques, and procedures they use. For example, the Intrusion Kill Chain approach defines seven phases or stages during an attack: **Reconnaissance, Weaponization, Delivery, Exploitation, Installation, Command and Control**, and **Actions on Objectives** (Eric M. Hutchins, Michael J. Cloppert, and Rohan M. Amin, Ph.D.). Attackers could use some or all of these phases in their attacks. Knowing this, organizations can layer their defenses to detect, deny, disrupt, degrade, deceive, and destroy at every stage of the attack. This will make it much harder for attackers to succeed because they must potentially defeat multiple layers of defenses, specifically designed around their modus operandi.

Similarly, MITRE ATT&CK® is designed to be a knowledge base of attackers' TTPs. Over the past decade, this framework has been evolving. MITRE described it this way in a 2020 whitepaper:

> *"ATT&CK focuses on how external adversaries compromise and operate within computer information networks. It originated out of a project to document and categorize post-compromise adversary tactics, techniques and procedures (TTPs)*

> *against Microsoft Windows systems to improve detection of malicious behavior. It has since grown to include Linux and macOS, and has expanded to cover behavior leading up to the compromise of an environment, as well as technology-focused domains like mobile devices, cloud-based systems, and industrial control systems." (Strom, Applebaum, Miller, Nickels, Pennington, and Thomas, 2020).*

ATT&CK can be used in several different ways, including the following (Strom, Applebaum, Miller, Nickels, Pennington, and Thomas, 2020):

- Emulating adversaries
- Red team/Blue team exercises
- Developing behavioral analytics
- Identifying gaps in defensive capabilities
- **Security Operations Centers** (**SOC**) maturity assessments
- Enriching **Cyber Threat Intelligence** (**CTI**)

Like the Intrusion Kill Chain, ATT&CK seeks to define the tactics (unordered steps or goals) that attackers can take or want to achieve in their attacks, and the specific actions (techniques and sub-techniques) they use to accomplish each tactic. The tactics in this framework include **Reconnaissance, Resource Development, Initial Access, Execution, Persistence, Privilege Escalation, Defense Evasion, Credential Access, Discovery, Lateral Movement, Collection, Command and Control, Exfiltration**, and **Impact**.

This framework provides a list of the specific techniques attackers are known to have used in each of the defined tactics. For example, in the Reconnaissance tactic, the step in an attack where attackers are researching their target(s), the framework currently provides 11 techniques that attackers use to perform this research. One of those 11 techniques is "Gather Victim Org Information." This technique currently has 4 sub-techniques associated with it, such as "Business Relationships" for example. This sub-technique indicates that attackers can gather information about business relationships that their targets have to evaluate whether these relationships can be leveraged in their attacks in some way. The framework also provides examples of procedures attackers can use in each sub-technique, along with mitigation and detection advice.

Let me give you another example. Let's say an attacker has accomplished the initial compromise and now wants to move laterally. Of course, defenders want to make that hard or impossible. According to ATT&CK, the Lateral Movement tactic has 9 techniques. For defenders, knowing there are 9 techniques is helpful because they can try to put mitigations for each one in place. One of those techniques is Internal Spearphishing. Attackers could decide to use spearphishing, leveraging the victim organization's own email system to trick targeted information workers into disclosing information and credentials that will enable them to move laterally. ATT&CK provides examples of procedures that specific attackers have used in the past to do this, as well as mitigation and detection recommendations. For example, one procedure example's name is Kimsuky, and it's described as follows: "Kimsuky has sent internal spearphishing emails for lateral movement after stealing victim information" (MITRE ATT&CK®, n.d.).

For some techniques, the ATT&CK framework offers mitigations and detection strategies. In this case, the framework doesn't offer any mitigations and instead states: "This type of attack technique cannot be easily mitigated with preventive controls since it is based on the abuse of system features" (MITRE ATT&CK®, n.d.). However, the framework does offer one detection strategy with 5 "analytics". Analytics are detection methods that map observed security data (log entries, alerts, behaviors) to the TTPs. In this case, one analytic provides a series of specific event IDs from Windows Event Logs and Microsoft 365 logs that are associated with internal emails sent from a recently compromised user account. Looking for this specific series of event IDs in logs during threat hunts can help detect if internal spearphishing attacks have occurred in the past. This information might also be helpful in configuring detection rules and alerts capable of identifying this type of attack in near real-time.

Understanding the tactics, each technique, and each sub-technique helps defenders design and implement layers of capabilities that make accomplishing each tactic much harder or impossible. The number of tactics, techniques, and sub-techniques can potentially change over time when new ones are discovered. Subsequently, ATT&CK is a living framework that will continue to be updated. According to the FAQ on their website, they plan to update it biannually (MITRE ATT&CK®, n.d.).

You might have noticed that the tactics defined in ATT&CK are similar to the steps defined in the Intrusion Kill Chain approach but are a little more granular. MITRE includes the following question and answer in the FAQ on their website:

> *"What is the relationship between ATT&CK and the Lockheed Martin Cyber Kill Chain®?*
>
> *ATT&CK and the Cyber Kill Chain are complementary. ATT&CK sits at a lower level of definition to describe adversary behavior than the Cyber Kill Chain. ATT&CK Tactics are unordered and may not all occur in a single intrusion because adversary tactical goals change throughout an operation, whereas the Cyber Kill Chain uses ordered phases to describe high-level adversary objectives." (MITRE ATT&CK®, n.d.).*

ATT&CK's tactics closely mirror the Intrusion Kill Chain, but at a more granular level. This overlap has led to efforts to unify the two, such as the Unified Kill Chain, which extends and integrates Lockheed Martin's Cyber Kill Chain® with MITRE's ATT&CK™ (The Unified Kill

Chain, n.d.). As ATT&CK has evolved, it has become a very popular approach for cybersecurity teams. This approach makes a lot of sense to me because it can be used to mitigate the Cybersecurity Usual Suspects and provide advanced capabilities as well. The cybersecurity industry has coalesced around this framework, with numerous vendors offering products, services, and professional services offerings to support organizations that want to embrace it.

Let's see how the attack-centric strategy scores using the CFSS.

CFSS score

Based on my evaluation, the attack-centric strategy has the highest CFSS score of any of the individual strategies I've examined in this chapter. In fact, my estimates of how capable it is of addressing all the cybersecurity fundamentals give it a near-perfect score, as shown in *Table 10.11*.

Cybersecurity Fundamentals	Score (0–20)
Unpatched vulnerabilities	20
Security misconfigurations	20
Weak, leaked, or stolen credentials	20
Social engineering	15
Insider threat	20
CFSS Total Score (max = 100)	95

Table 10.11 – The CFSS score estimate for the attack-centric strategy

The reason this approach scores so well is that it focuses on the ways that attackers initially compromise IT environments and the methods and tools they use after initial compromise. That is, it covers all the bases. The reason I didn't give it a perfect 100/100 is that social engineering is nearly impossible to completely mitigate in enterprises. Sooner or later, someone will make a mistake or a poor trust decision that leads to a suboptimal security outcome.

Despite the industry's best efforts to educate information workers, executives, and IT administrators, and to design software and hardware to make it harder for social engineering attacks to be successful, the data suggests that attackers are relying on it as much as they ever have. In an environment where mitigations for the Cybersecurity Usual Suspects are well managed, attackers are forced to turn to the one tactic they know has the best chance of succeeding: social engineering. They will continue to rely on humans to make mistakes and poor trust decisions.

Attack-centric strategy summary

The attack-centric strategy garnered a very high CFSS score. It can help CISOs and their teams focus on the cybersecurity fundamentals. This strategy is also capable of helping security teams go beyond the fundamentals and thoughtfully implement advanced cybersecurity capabilities and help protect their HVAs. That said, for most organizations that have limited resources, it isn't easy or inexpensive to design, procure, implement, operate, and support layers and layers of cybersecurity capabilities. Many organizations that aspire to use this approach realize they don't have the technical expertise or budget to truly embrace it in the long term.

Depending on the previous strategy or strategies that an organization has leveraged, they might have only invested in protection but not necessarily detection and response. Subsequently, if they start using the attack-centric strategy, they will likely increase investment in detection and response capabilities.

The following are its advantages:

- It potentially levels the playing field between attackers and defenders as they both understand attackers' TTPs
- It forces attackers to be successful multiple times instead of just once or twice, which is how many of the other cybersecurity strategies are designed
- It is designed to help detect intrusions as early in the attack as possible in order to reduce remediation and recovery time and costs.
- There is a vast ecosystem of vendors to assist.

The following are the disadvantages:

- This approach requires most organizations to increase investments in detection and response capabilities, thus typically increasing complexity and costs.
- Typically relies on technology from multiple vendors to work in concert to identify, protect, detect, and respond to threats. This could require technical expertise across multiple vendors' technologies, which might not be a realistic requirement for many organizations with limited resources and technical talent.
- Because of all the layers that this approach requires, it can be challenging to architect, deploy, and operate.
- This can be a relatively expensive strategy to pursue

Next, let's look at a strategy that is currently extremely popular in the industry: zero trust.

Zero trust

One of the underlying assumptions of all the strategies I've discussed in this chapter is that once a user or system has authenticated access to the IT environment, it is then trusted. The popularity of this convenient capability is evidenced by the ubiquity of **Single Sign-On (SSO)** requirements among enterprises. It's interesting that this assumption is as old as the oldest strategies I have examined. This assumption hasn't changed much since enterprises started procuring their first PCs. Some will argue that this assumption is one reason the industry has seen so many data breaches over the decades. I think it's fair to say that champions of the *zero trust* model would agree with this. Although this approach is regarded by many as relatively new, it was first conceived almost 25 years ago by a group of CISOs, according to industry lore.

The concept behind this approach is that all resources, including those inside the perimeter, should be untrusted. This makes a lot of sense in a world where less and less IT infrastructure and fewer and fewer information workers are behind corporate firewalls. For example, the ongoing proliferation of IoT devices should easily outnumber the number of desk-bound PCs and servers in datacenters, the same way that mobile devices have dramatically eclipsed them over the past two decades. Additionally, as I discussed in my examination of the protect and recover strategy, history has taught us that the old-school perimeter security approach, by itself, is a failure because its underlying assumptions have been proven to be wildly optimistic. You'll remember that one of those assumptions was that security teams could achieve perfect protection forever, and they didn't require investments in detection and response capabilities.

If we assume that all network traffic, systems, devices, and users cannot be trusted, regardless of whether they are behind an enterprise perimeter, this could potentially change a security team's approach in a substantial way. Authenticating and authorizing applications, network connections, devices, and users for each operation they attempt, instead of just at the time of first access, can make it harder for attackers to initially compromise an environment, move laterally, stay persistent, and gain access to sensitive data. Don't trust and always verify.

However, by itself, applying a design principle that requires near-constant authentication and authorization for users, systems, and devices doesn't address unpatched vulnerabilities, security misconfigurations, social engineering, or non-malicious insider threats. Remember the cliché, attackers don't break in, they log in. If an attacker has valid credentials, what does authenticating them every time they try to access a resource actually help mitigate? This approach requires strong identity verification and for the principle of least privilege to be religiously enforced, just like some of the other strategies I discussed. Consequently, zero trust needs a bunch of other elements to evolve into a full-blown cybersecurity strategy.

Marry the rigor of near-constant authentication and authorization with the capabilities of the identity-centric strategy that I discussed earlier, and this approach can help make better authentication and authorization decisions in real time. This approach might also benefit from many of the capabilities of the Endpoint Protection Strategy to provide the visibility and control needed on endpoints. Some vendors are resurrecting and integrating **Network Access Control (NAC)** and **Network Access Protection (NAP)** type capabilities into their Zero Trust product offerings to ensure endpoints meet corporate policies, such as being fully patched and running up-to-date anti-malware protection, among other requirements. Put another way, these capabilities enable the enterprise to treat its own endpoints as untrusted, keeping them disconnected from the internal corporate network until they prove they should be trusted by meeting security standards.

In fact, zero trust could borrow something from all the strategies I discussed in this chapter in order to address all the cybersecurity fundamentals and add advanced capabilities. This is, in fact, what's been happening. Almost every cybersecurity vendor today offers some sort of Zero Trust product or product line to support organizations that want to embrace the concept of treating everything as if it is untrusted. I once used Google to search for "zero trust security," which resulted in 334,000,000 results. Given there's so much interest in the concept, but the concept itself can be implemented in a myriad of ways, vendors and other interested parties, such as governments, provide their own visions of what zero trust means and how it should be implemented. Here are some examples.

Amazon Web Services (`https://aws.amazon.com/security/zero-trust/`):

> *"Zero trust is a security model centered on the idea that access to data should not be solely made based on network location. It requires users and systems to strongly prove their identities and trustworthiness, and enforces fine-grained identity-based authorization rules before allowing them to access applications, data, and other systems. With zero trust, these identities often operate within highly flexible identity-aware networks that further reduce surface area, eliminate unneeded pathways to data, and provide straightforward outer security guardrails." (Amazon Web Services, n.d.).*

Cisco (`https://www.cisco.com/c/en/us/solutions/collateral/enterprise/design-zone-security/zt-frameworks.html`):

> *"Security is not a one-size-fits-all and Zero Trust is more than network segmentation. To help understand the architecture, Cisco has broken it down into three pillars:*
>
> - *User and Device Security: making sure users and devices can be trusted as they access systems, regardless of location*

> • *Network and Cloud Security: protect all network resources on-prem and in the cloud, and ensure secure access for all connecting users*
>
> • *Application and Data Security: preventing unauthorized access within application environments irrespective of where they are hosted" (Cisco, May 18, 2023).*

Google (`https://cloud.google.com/learn/what-is-zero-trust?hl=en`):

> *"Zero trust is a security model used to secure an organization based on the idea that no person or device should be trusted by default, even if they are already inside an organization's network. A zero-trust approach aims to remove implicit trust by enforcing strict identity authentication and authorization throughout the network, not just at a trusted perimeter. In this model, every request to access resources is treated as if it comes from an untrusted network until it has been inspected, authenticated, and verified." (Google, n.d.).*

Microsoft (`https://www.microsoft.com/en-us/security/business/zero-trust`):

> *"Zero Trust is a modern security strategy based on the principle of never trust, always verify. Instead of assuming everything behind the corporate firewall is safe, the Zero Trust model assumes breach and verifies each request as though it originates from an open network...*
>
> *The three main pillars of Zero Trust are:*
>
> *1. Verify explicitly: always authenticate and authorize based on all available data points, including user identity, location, device health, service or workload, data classification, and anomalies.*
>
> *2. Use least-privilege access: limit user access with just-in-time and just-enough access, risk-based adaptive policies, and data protection to help secure data and improve productivity.*
>
> *3. Assume breach: verify end-to-end encryption and use analytics to gain visibility, detect threats, and improve defenses." (Microsoft, n.d.)*

The White House – Executive Order on Improving the Nation's Cybersecurity (`https://bidenwhitehouse.archives.gov/briefing-room/presidential-actions/2021/05/12/executive-order-on-improving-the-nations-cybersecurity/`):

> *"...the term "Zero Trust Architecture" means a security model, a set of system design principles, and a coordinated cybersecurity and system management strategy based on an acknowledgment that threats exist both inside and outside traditional network boundaries. The Zero Trust security model eliminates implicit trust in any one element, node, or service and instead requires continuous verification of the operational picture via real-time information from multiple sources to determine access and other system responses. In essence, a Zero Trust Architecture allows users full access but only to the bare minimum they need to perform their jobs. If a device is compromised, zero trust can ensure that the damage is contained. The Zero Trust Architecture security model assumes that a breach is inevitable or has likely already occurred, so it constantly limits access to only what is needed and looks for anomalous or malicious activity. Zero Trust Architecture embeds comprehensive security monitoring; granular risk-based access controls; and system security automation in a coordinated manner throughout all aspects of the infrastructure in order to focus on protecting data in real time within a dynamic threat environment. This data-centric security model allows the concept of least-privileged access to be applied for every access decision, where the answers to the questions of who, what, when, where, and how are critical for appropriately allowing or denying access to resources based on the combination of sever [sic]."*

The last definition I provided from Executive Order 14028, published by the White House, had a real-world impact. Zero trust is mentioned eleven times in that Executive Order, instructing branches of the US government to implement Zero Trust to improve their cybersecurity. By doing this, this Executive Order also instructed every IT and cybersecurity vendor in the world that already sells products and services to the US government, or aspires to, to support this definition of Zero Trust or elements of it. As I mentioned in *Chapter 8*, when the largest standards body and IT consumer in the world sets requirements, the entire industry pays attention as they all want their share of that business. However, many questions remain about how to implement such an architecture, especially at massive scales suggested by Executive Order 14028.

How do we score Zero Trust using the CFSS?

CFSS score

Given the number of descriptions and definitions of zero trust, I'm not sure I can give it a single CFSS score. It seems like the score is a function of the specific implementation used. For example, how does this approach address unpatched vulnerabilities? Simply increasing the frequency of authentication and authorization events for a user, system, or device does nothing to mitigate this Cybersecurity Usual Suspect. However, if you extend this principle to endpoints, treat them like they are untrusted, and force them to be fully patched before getting access to any corporate resources, then you could almost completely mitigate the threat that unpatched vulnerabilities pose. This approach could also dramatically reduce the scale and scope of your vulnerability management program because endpoints would have to scan themselves for missing security updates and install them before getting access to the network. Getting the endpoints to do that work instead of a centralized vulnerability management program can help reduce the pressure on the program while reducing risk to the enterprise. The Vulnerability Management team could reduce the frequency of scanning systems that do their own patching, to perhaps weekly or monthly to identify systems that aren't being updated as expected.

Of course, trusting endpoints to prove their own integrity is riddled with challenges. Are the endpoints untrusted or not? Do we trust them just enough to tell us if they are secure enough to connect to the corporate network? Wouldn't *zero* trust mean that some sort of remote attestation service running on separate hardware from the endpoints is required to determine if the endpoints meet security standards? Where do we draw the line? It appears the answer to this question is left to each individual organization and vendor. If we are honest with each other, Zero Trust still requires organizations to trust a bunch of technologies in order to test whether other technologies should be trusted. So, in this case, "zero" doesn't mean none.

Google offers an interesting point of view here:

> *"One of the most used buzzwords in cybersecurity today is undoubtedly "Zero Trust." It's been used to describe a wide range of approaches and products, leading to a fair bit of confusion about the term itself and to what it actually means. Some attempts to explain or simplify zero trust assert that "zero trust means trust nothing" or "zero trust is about delivering secure access without a VPN." This conventional wisdom is mostly incorrect and limiting. At the core of a Zero Trust approach is the idea that implicit trust in any single component of a complex, interconnected system can create significant security risks. Instead, trust needs to be established via multiple mechanisms and continuously verified. While end-user access is a domain to which this model can be applied to gain significant security improvements, it can just as readily be applied to domains such as the end-to-end process of running production systems and protecting workloads on cloud-native infrastructure." (Brewer, E. and Venables, P., 2021).*

My conclusion is that I can't provide a CFSS score for zero trust. It's not a cybersecurity strategy; it's a design principle or philosophy that can be applied as prudently as necessary. It could be applied to the mechanisms used to mitigate all the Cybersecurity Usual Suspects or not at all.

Looking for implicit trust assumptions in threat models can lead to positive improvements in many organizations' security postures. I don't think there's any doubt about that. For example, it might challenge some developers to try to design e-commerce applications capable of doing transactions on systems that are assumed to be compromised. The result should be better than assuming the system will never be compromised.

However, the success of this approach will depend on its implementation. For example, I mentioned that some vendors are using NAC/NAP in their zero trust solutions. The reason NAC/NAP failed the first time they became popular in the industry is because of the horrible user experience they imposed on users. All VPN users that connected to their office, where NAC/NAP were implemented, had the same dreaded experience at one time or another; they just wanted to check their emails, download a presentation, or quickly get access to some information, only to be quarantined and forced to slowly download and install security updates, antivirus signatures, endure reboots, and so on. Despite the positive advantages of ensuring systems were patched before connecting to the corporate network, it degraded the user experience so much that users would avoid connecting to the network for as long as they could. When they finally had to connect to the network, the user experience was even worse because of the backlog of updates the system required. This had the opposite effect on security than what was intended. Those vendors that offer Zero Trust solutions that leverage this same approach are doomed to the same fate. Users will only deal with so much overhead in their daily work before they actively try to avoid it or work around it. The user experience shouldn't be worse in environments with zero trust implementations – it needs to be better. This one factor will likely decide the effectiveness and fate of zero trust.

Let's examine one final cybersecurity strategy: resilience as a security strategy.

Resilience as a security strategy

This strategy has become popular in recent years due to the specter of high-impact ransomware attacks. The underlying assumption of this strategy is that successful cyber-attacks are inevitable. Subsequently, it makes sense to engineer systems to be resilient to such attacks.

NIST provides a good explanation in NIST Special Publication (SP) 800-160, Volume 2, Revision 1.

> *"NIST Special Publication (SP) 800-160, Volume 2, focuses on cyber resiliency engineering—an emerging specialty systems engineering discipline applied in conjunction with systems security engineering and resilience engineering to develop survivable, trustworthy secure systems. Cyber resiliency engineering intends to architect, design, develop, implement, maintain, and sustain the trustworthiness of systems with the capability to anticipate, withstand, recover from, and adapt to adverse conditions, stresses, attacks, or compromises that use or are enabled by cyber resources. From a risk management perspective, cyber resiliency is intended to help*

> *reduce the mission, business, organizational, enterprise, or sector risk of depending on cyber resources." (Ron Ross, Victoria Pillitteri, Richard Graubart, Deborah Bodeau, Rosalie McQuaid., December 2021).*

The key to this strategy is the ability to "anticipate, withstand, recover from, and adapt to adverse conditions, stresses, attacks, or compromises that use or are enabled by cyber resources." The difference between this strategy and others we've examined is that this strategy focuses on withstanding attacks and adapting to the adverse conditions that can accompany them, rather than just trying to identify, protect, detect, respond, and recover systems. This strategy seeks to enable organizations that are attacked to continue critical operations, minimize damage, recover quickly, and potentially evolve stronger after incidents.

Recovery plays a prominent role in this strategy because even if a system can be engineered to limit the impacts of a cyber-attack, recovering components of the system as well as data might still be necessary. Parts of this strategy look similar to traditional **disaster recovery (DR)** strategies. However, most DR strategies are designed to recover systems from natural disasters such as earthquakes, tornadoes, fires, floods, and so on. In the context of cybersecurity, defenders are attempting to recover systems and data from human-made disasters such as ransomware, and they will likely need to do this while attackers are actively working to prevent them from recovering. Many of the processes and technologies that IT teams use to design systems for traditional DR, like data replication for example, can actually help attackers scale their attacks and be more successful. This too must be considered when determining the best way to engineer systems to be resilient.

CISOs and security teams are typically required to protect both new systems as well as legacy systems. Most enterprise organizations cannot afford to replace all their legacy systems with new systems that were redeveloped or reimplemented with these resilience objectives as requirements. The result is that CISOs and CIOs who want more resilient systems need to embrace new development and implementation requirements for new systems, but they also need to find ways to improve the resilience of systems already in production and legacy systems. To make systems more resilient to cyber-attacks as well as IT outages, cybersecurity and IT teams need a deep understanding of how system components and dependencies operate and interact. This information enables them to perform a "cyber resiliency analysis" on systems to identify and prioritize opportunities for improvement.

I've used this approach at least a couple of times during my career with mixed success. The list below contains the high-level steps you can use if you choose to embrace this strategy.

1. **Identify target systems:** choose the system(s) you want to make more resilient to cyber-attacks. These systems can be your organization's HVAs, also called "crown jewels." However, it might be more useful to define a "minimum viable company" or "minimum viable product." These represent the business functions, processes, and

underlying IT systems that absolutely need to continue operating during or after a cyber-attack, such as a ransomware attack. This typically helps limit the scope of an organization's resilience efforts to a set of systems and data, as opposed to all systems and data, increasing the odds of success.

2. **Set recovery objectives:** work with the stakeholder community for the target systems to determine **Restore Point Objectives (RPOs)** and **Restore Time Objectives (RTOs)**. These will help determine how quickly systems need to be restored in the wake of a successful cyber-attack. They will also become inputs into the estimate for the budget and resources required to develop and operate the more resilient solutions. Generally speaking, the more aggressive the RPO and RTO, the more expensive the solution becomes.
3. **Decompose the underlying IT assets:** identify the IT assets of the target systems and map all their dependencies. For example, let's say you wanted to make Microsoft Active Directory more resilient to cyber-attacks. If a ransomware gang encrypted it during a traditional network intrusion attack, it would impact several HVAs and disrupt the entire organization. Decomposing Active Directory to map all its dependencies would reveal that, in order for it to operate, it requires a TCP/IP network, the **Domain Name System (DNS)** service, the **Network Time Service (NTS)**, the **Distributed File Replication Service (DFRS)**, and numerous other dependencies. Some dependencies are sure to have their own dependencies. The number of tiers of dependencies that get mapped is typically determined by the level of recovery assurance required. Higher levels of assurance might bring more layers of dependencies into scope.
4. **Cyber resilience analysis:** determine how you can make every dependency more resilient to cyber-attacks. This might involve implementing replicas of important databases or implementing full cold, warm, or hot sites.
5. **Recovery analysis:** develop a plan that enables you to fully restore the system—not just the data, but the required hardware, firmware, operating systems, management software, configurations, and so on. This must be designed to enable recovery within the defined RPOs and RTOs. Develop documentation on how to restore the complete system, including the order in which each dependency needs to be restored for the system to become operational. Recovering a system or dependencies might involve third parties, and the analysis should include these as well.
6. **Develop recovery infrastructure:** implement processes and technologies required to execute the recovery plan. This will potentially involve leveraging a "clean room," which is essentially an isolated recovery environment. A clean room is used to store backups of the materials required to recover the environment, including immutable copies of critical data, application and database backups, backups of system

configurations, virtual machine templates, baseline operating system images, offline copies of critical credentials, and automation scripts. The clean room should also store the forensic, threat-hunting, and incident-response tools and playbooks required for security operations. The cloud is an ideal place to put a clean room since it has independent identity and access management controls built into it. Automating as much of the recovery process as possible will enable faster recovery times. Consider what automation can be run from the clean room environment and what needs to run on-premises.

> **Tip**
>
> An important consideration is determining which identities will be used for recovery. If Active Directory or its dependencies have been encrypted and are permanently offline, which identities will you use to execute the recovery plan? You might require an offline identity store for emergencies.
>
> Training the people required to perform the recovery plan is an important aspect of preparation. Don't wait for an emergency to discover your recovery plan is too complicated to execute because no one was trained ahead of time.

7. **Practice:** car manufacturers don't crash clay cars together when they are crash-testing their cars. Resilience requires testing production systems to ensure they behave the way you think they should during an attack. Do not spend all this time, effort, and budget only to wait for an attacker to reveal whether your resilience strategy actually works. The more you exercise your production systems and work the problems out of them, the easier achieving your resilience objectives will be. There are many resilience testing tools available to help do this, including Chaos Monkey, Gremlin, LitmusChaos, Chaos Mesh, and Simian Army.

Let's see how resilience as a security strategy scores using the CFSS.

CFSS score

My estimated CFSS score for resilience as a security strategy is shown in *Table 10.12*.

Cybersecurity Fundamentals	Score (0–20)
Unpatched vulnerabilities	20
Security misconfigurations	20

Cybersecurity Fundamentals	Score (0–20)
Weak, leaked, or stolen credentials	5
Social engineering	5
Insider threat	15
CFSS Total Score (max = 100)	65

Table 10.12 – The CFSS score estimate for resilience as a security strategy

It turns out that the things required to build and operate more resilient systems can also address some of the Cybersecurity Usual Suspects. I gave this strategy high marks for unpatched vulnerabilities and misconfigurations because this approach should result in processes that address potential deficiencies in systems that could lead to disruption, such as unpatched vulnerabilities and configuration drift. Although this strategy doesn't focus on identities or social engineering per se, some of the process improvements that get introduced will have positive effects. The risks associated with insider threats should be reduced, but not completely mitigated, by the improved administrative processes and higher levels of automation.

Resilience as a security strategy summary

Although this strategy didn't score as well as the attack-centric strategy, it has become popular among organizations that have concluded that they are likely to suffer successful cybersecurity attacks in the future. With this assumption in mind, they seek to engineer their most critical systems to withstand cyberattacks and be in a position to restore them quickly.

The following are its advantages:

- It has perhaps the most realistic underlying assumption of any of the strategies we examined
- It enables organizations to build and operate systems that are designed to withstand attacks and can actually be recovered from human-caused disasters.
- This strategy makes it harder for attackers whose objective is to disrupt or destroy their victims' operations.
- There is a large ecosystem of vendors to assist.

The following are the disadvantages:

- This approach requires most organizations to increase investments in resilience engineering and DR capabilities. For large organizations with significant numbers of legacy IT systems, this strategy can be prohibitively expensive to pursue.
- It requires significant technical expertise and time to decompose systems, identify dependencies, engineer for resilience, and develop DR processes.

We have covered quite a bit of ground! Let's conclude our examination of cybersecurity strategies by summarizing what we have been discussing.

Cybersecurity strategies summary

We have reviewed the following popular cybersecurity strategies:

- Protect and recover strategy
- Endpoint protection strategy
- Physical control and security clearances strategy in an air-gapped environment
- Physical control and security clearances strategy without an air-gapped environment
- Compliance as a cybersecurity strategy
- Application-centric strategy
- Identity-centric strategy
- Data-centric strategy
- Attack-centric strategy
- Resilience as a cybersecurity strategy

We also discussed zero trust, which I concluded is not a strategy in the same way as the others on the list are.

A summary of my CFSS score estimates for these strategies is provided in *Table 10.13*. As you can see, I gave the attack-centric strategy the highest estimated CFSS score. In my view, it is the only strategy that has the greatest potential to help organizations address the cybersecurity fundamentals, mitigate the Cybersecurity Usual Suspects, and potentially implement advanced capabilities.

Cybersecurity strategy	Unpatched vulnerabilities	Security misconfigurations	Weak, leaked, or stolen credentials	Social engineering	Insider threats	Total score
Protect and recover strategy	10	10	0	5	0	25
Endpoint protection strategy	15	15	15	10	15	70
Physical control and security clearances strategy with air gap	10	10	15	10	10	55
Physical control and security clearances strategy without air gap	0	0	0	10	10	20
Compliance as a cybersecurity strategy	10	10	10	10	10	50
Application-centric strategy	20	20	10	10	10	70
Identity-centric strategy	5	5	15	10	10	45
Data-centric strategy	5	5	0	15	15	40
Attack-centric strategy	20	20	20	15	20	95
Resilience as a cybersecurity Strategy	20	20	5	5	15	65

Table 10.13 – CFSS score estimate summary

The reality is that most organizations that I have advised use a combination of some of these strategies. For example, it would be bold for an enterprise not to have both a perimeter security strategy and an endpoint security strategy, even as the industry offers newer technologies. Many organizations have some regulatory compliance requirements that they must meet. It can be helpful for organizations that already use some of these approaches to deliberately and thoughtfully reconcile where there has been over-investment and under-investment, and where gaps currently exist. This is another advantage that the attack-centric strategy has over these other strategies and combinations of them—investment and gap analysis are built right into it. I will discuss this in more detail in *Chapter 12, Measuring Performance and Effectiveness*.

Today, I see many organizations using a combination of the endpoint strategy, the identity-centric strategy, the attack-centric strategy, and resilience as a cybersecurity strategy. If they have the wherewithal to execute the combination of these strategies, they will be in a strong position versus many of the other possible combinations. In addition to these strategies, I also see continued use of the data-centric strategy among some public sector and financial services organizations that tend to have relatively large budgets and are deemed critical infrastructure.

You might disagree with my CFSS score estimates for some or all of these strategies. That's good. I encourage you to use the CFSS to perform your own scoring estimates for all the approaches I examined in this chapter and others I didn't cover. Security professionals all have different experiences, which could lead them to score one or more of these strategies higher or lower than I have. Frankly, this is to be expected as I've never met a security professional who didn't have an opinion. Despite this, most organizations do not have a cybersecurity strategy that their CISOs or other executives can articulate. My objective for this chapter is to provoke critical thought about the ways that organizations have been approaching cybersecurity and perhaps hold a mirror for CIOs, CISOs, and security teams to look into.

Now, let's look at a very popular approach that is different in some important ways from the more classical strategies I discussed in this chapter.

DevOps and DevSecOps

DevOps represents a change in the way that organizations have traditionally approached application development and deployment. Traditionally, developers and operations staff were managed as separate disciplines that rarely worked together. Developers would write code to specifications and when they wanted to deploy it, they "threw it over the fence" to the operations team. Sometimes, the operations team encountered issues deploying the application, so they would send it back to the development team with the issues that were preventing successful deployment. Developers and operations would iterate this process, typically at a slow and frustrating pace. Because these groups only communicated with each other periodically, the developers often lacked the operational and environmental context that would help them develop applications that could be deployed and operated in a real IT environment. Similarly, the operations teams often didn't have the technical details on the application to help them perform successful deployments. The feedback loop between teams was slow, leading to milestone delays, slow development cycles, and quality issues.

DevOps tries to address these challenges by tightly integrating developers and operations staff. They can give each other feedback more efficiently and quickly when they work with each other day in and day out. Operations staff can inform the design and functionality choices that the developers make while they are developing the application. The developers can get constant feedback on the viability and supportability of their ideas from the operations staff. This can lead to faster development and deployment cycles, better quality applications, less rework, and happier teams.

DevOps includes functions such as continuous testing, **Continuous Integration** (**CI**), **Continuous Delivery** (**CD**), continuous deployment, and continuous performance monitoring. This goes beyond the technologies, services, and products that support these functions because most organizations have had to make significant changes to their development philosophies, cultures, and processes to embrace DevOps. Today, the entire industry has shifted to leverage this approach for new software development. It is rare to find a development team not using DevOps and its accouterments today.

DevSecOps is DevOps with the explicit acknowledgment that security must be embedded in the philosophies, cultures, processes, and supporting technologies of development for this approach to be successful. Some argue that the "Sec" in DevSecOps is gratuitous because DevOps cannot be done properly without embedding security in it. I agree wholeheartedly. If your organization is currently doing DevOps and has decided that it will evolve into a DevSecOps approach later, then you are likely already doing DevOps wrong. Remember that "culture eats strategy for breakfast." This is why DevOps has been so powerful and transformational for IT organizations.

The value of DevOps is extended when it is used together with containers and cloud computing. For example, since infrastructure is code in the cloud, infrastructure is deployed, configured, and supported using code. This means that provisioning and managing infrastructure in the cloud can benefit from the virtues of DevOps. Developers can specify the hardware, software, and configuration for infrastructure in the code they write, informed by the requirements and continuous feedback provided by operations teams. This approach enables organizations to provision infrastructure faster than traditional approaches and at virtually any scale desired.

From a security perspective, DevOps offers a powerful model for building and deploying applications and infrastructure. This is where CI/CD pipelines are useful. A pipeline typically handles functions like checking code into a repository, automated building, automated testing, and deploying the tested code into production. The pipeline itself can be composed of a combination of tools, products, and services from one or multiple vendors. Some organizations that have embraced DevOps deploy all applications and all infrastructure via CI/CD pipelines. Put another way, nothing gets into their production environments unless it goes through a pipeline. Enforcing pipeline policies like this offers organizations at least a few advantages compared to legacy approaches. For example, when applications and infrastructure are required to go through a pipeline and the pipeline has automated checks to ensure regulatory, industry, and internal security standards are met, then everything that makes it into production is in this known good state.

This assurance makes short-lived environments possible by enabling infrastructure to be discarded and redeployed in a known good state every few hours. If that infrastructure gets compromised, attackers will only have control of that asset for a relatively short time before it gets blown away and replaced. This can make it harder for attackers to get a foothold in an environment and remain persistent. It can also help dramatically reduce the amount of work for vulnerability management teams. Instead of constantly performing inventories of systems, scanning them for security vulnerabilities, patching, and rebooting them, they can scan and patch the relatively small number of "gold images" used for infrastructure deployments. Gold images are fully configured, security-hardened master system images that serve as the organization's authoritative baseline for deploying systems. When a short-lived infrastructure is discarded and replaced, the new infrastructure is based on the up-to-date gold image. Verifying the patch status of a short-lived infrastructure is less work for vulnerability management teams and less disruptive to the business. There are similar advantages for compliance teams, as well as internal and external auditors. Constantly exercising the infrastructure this way results in less brittle environments that are naturally more resilient.

There are many security advantages in leveraging CI/CD pipelines, including the automation of many security controls, consistent policy enforcement, reduced attack surface, potentially faster incident response, and the ability to validate third-party dependencies. All this, in addition to accelerating software delivery, represents a win-win for developers and their cybersecurity teams.

Of course, DevOps isn't a panacea. DevOps and CI/CD pipelines done poorly can be a bad thing for organizations. Some of the organizations I've discussed DevOps with only use it in parts of their IT environment, and the rest of the organization is still chained to legacy models. Developers can become enamored with CI/CD pipelines. For example, developers who embrace CI/CD pipelines can end up spending more of their time developing tools and automation for their pipelines than working on applications and infrastructure. Organizations can also end up with too many CI/CD pipelines. Predictably, some attackers see potential victims leveraging DevOps and using CI/CD pipelines, so they target the pipeline infrastructure itself; CI/CD pipelines could end up becoming HVAs for some organizations and require more security rigor than they were initially prepared for.

I think the security and non-security advantages of DevOps and CI/CD pipelines outweigh any challenges they present. This is the reason the entire industry has moved to this model and will continue to leverage it for many years to come.

Summary

CISOs and security teams should select their organization's cybersecurity strategy based on how well it addresses the cybersecurity fundamentals, as the minimum bar. Without examining how their strategy mitigates all the Cybersecurity Usual Suspects, they could be lulling themselves into a false sense of security. The CFSS can help security teams determine how well their current or future strategies address the cybersecurity fundamentals.

Of the strategies examined in this chapter, the attack-centric strategy was deemed the strategy most capable of mitigating the Cybersecurity Usual Suspects and enabling advanced cybersecurity capabilities. The endpoint protection strategy and the application-centric strategy rounded out the top three strategies in this evaluation but will need to be used in combination with other strategies to fully address the cybersecurity fundamentals. The Zero Trust approach holds the potential to raise the security waterline for the entire industry. But how this approach is implemented and the user experience it imposes will determine its effectiveness and its fate. Resilience as a cybersecurity strategy used in combination with the attack-centric strategy seems to be a potentially highly effective combination for organizations that have the wherewithal to manage it.

DevOps is a holistic approach that leads to changes in development philosophies, cultures, and processes for the organizations that embrace it. This approach might not be as beneficial for legacy IT environments, where the more traditional cybersecurity strategies that I examined might be used during the transition to modern architectures like the cloud.

That completes my examination of cybersecurity strategies. In the next chapter, we will dive deep into an implementation example of the strategy that had the highest CFSS-estimated total score, the attack-centric strategy.

References

- Amazon Web Services. (n.d.). *Zero Trust on AWS*. Retrieved from: `https://aws.amazon.com/security/zero-trust/`
- Ashford, W. (August 3, 2016). *One in five businesses hit by ransomware are forced to close, study shows*. Retrieved from ComputerWeekly: `https://www.computerweekly.com/news/450301845/One-in-five-businesses-hit-by-ransomware-are-forced-to-close-study-shows`
- Brewer, E., Venables, P. (August 25, 2021). *A unified and proven Zero Trust system with BeyondCorp and BeyondProd*. Retrieved from: `https://cloud.google.com/blog/products/identity-security/applying-zero-trust-to-user-access-and-production-services`
- Cisco. (May 18, 2023). *Zero Trust Frameworks Architecture Guide*. Retrieved from: `https://www.cisco.com/c/en/us/solutions/collateral/enterprise/design-zone-security/zt-frameworks.html`
- de Souza, Rachel. (January 21, 2025). *EU: DLA Piper GDPR Fines and Data Breach Survey: January 2025*. Retrieved from `https://privacymatters.dlapiper.com/2025/01/eu-dla-piper-gdpr-fines-and-data-breach-survey-january-2025/`

- Hutchins, E.M., Cloppert, M.J., Amin, R.M.., Ph.D. (n.d.). *Intelligence-Driven Computer Network Defense Informed by Analysis of Adversary Campaigns and Intrusion Kill Chains.* Retrieved from Lockheed Martin: `https://lockheedmartin.com/content/dam/lockheed-martin/rms/documents/cyber/LM-White-Paper-Intel-Driven-Defense.pdf`
- ISO. (n.d.). *ISO/IEC 27001:2022.* Retrieved from `https://www.iso.org/standard/27001`
- Google. (n.d.). *What is zero-trust security?* Retrieved from: `https://cloud.google.com/learn/what-is-zero-trust?hl=en`
- Microsoft Corporation. (September 29, 2025). *Personnel Management Overview.* Retrieved from: `https://learn.microsoft.com/en-us/compliance/assurance/assurance-human-resources`
- Microsoft Corporation. (September 2, 2022). *Privileged access: Strategy.* Retrieved from `https://learn.microsoft.com/en-us/security/compass/privileged-access-strategy`
- Microsoft Corporation. (n.d.). *Microsoft Security Engineering.* Retrieved from `https://www.microsoft.com/en-us/securityengineering/sdl/`
- Microsoft Corporation. (May 21, 2025). Best practices for securing Active Directory. Retrieved from: `https://learn.microsoft.com/en-us/windows-server/identity/ad-ds/plan/security-best-practices/best-practices-for-securing-active-directory`
- Microsoft Corporation. (June 6, 2024). *Protect your sensitive data with Microsoft Purview.* Retrieved from: `https://learn.microsoft.com/en-us/purview/information-protection`
- Microsoft Corporation. (n.d.). *Microsoft Security.* Retrieved from `https://www.microsoft.com/en-us/security/business/zero-trust#FAQs`
- MITRE ATT&CK®. (n.d.). *MITRE ATT&CK Frequently Asked Questions.* Retrieved from `https://attack.mitre.org/resources/faq/`
- MITRE. (n.d.). *MITRE ATT&CK®.* Retrieved from `https://attack.mitre.org/`
- Strom, B.E., Applebaum, A., Miller, D.P., Nickels, K.C., Pennington, A.G., & Thomas, C.B. (March 31, 2020). *MITRE ATT&CK®: Design and Philosophy.* MITRE Corporation. Retrieved from `https://www.mitre.org/news-insights/publication/mitre-attck-design-and-philosophy`

- NIST. (n.d.). *Cybersecurity Framework.* Retrieved from `https://csrc.nist.gov/Projects/cybersecurity-framework/nist-cybersecurity-framework-a-quick-start-guide`
- NIST. (n.d.). *Cybersecurity Framework.* Retrieved from `https://www.nist.gov/cyberframework`
- PA Consulting. (n.d.). *Oak Door Data Diode.* Retrieved from `https://www.paconsulting.com/services/productdesign-and-engineering/data-diode/`
- Ron Ross, Victoria Pillitteri, Richard Graubart, Deborah Bodeau, Rosalie McQuaid. (December 2021). NIST Special Publication 800-160, Volume 2, Revision 1. *Developing Cyber-Resilient Systems: A Systems Security Engineering Approach.* Retrieved from: `https://nvlpubs.nist.gov/nistpubs/SpecialPublications/NIST.SP.800-160v2r1.pdf`
- Sayegh, Emil. (August 30, 2025). *U.S. and Allies Declare Salt Typhoon Hack a National Defense Crisis.* Retrieved from: `https://www.forbes.com/sites/emilsayegh/2025/08/30/us-and-allies-declare-salt-typhoon-hack-a-national-defense-crisis/`
- The White House. (May 2021). *Executive Order on Improving the Nation's Cybersecurity.* Retrieved from: `https://bidenwhitehouse.archives.gov/briefing-room/presidential-actions/2021/05/12/executive-order-on-improving-the-nations-cybersecurity/`
- U.K. Cabinet Office. (October 18, 2018). *Government Security Classifications.* Retrieved from: `https://www.gov.uk/government/publications/government-security-classifications`
- United States Government Publishing Office. (December 29, 2009). *Executive Order 13526 of December 29, 2009.* Retrieved from GovInfo: `https://www.govinfo.gov/content/pkg/DCPD-200901022/pdf/DCPD-200901022.pdf`
- Virus Bulletin. (n.d.). *Virus Bulletin.* Retrieved from Virus Bulletin: `https://www.virusbulletin.com/`
- Wikipedia. (n.d.). *Rainbow table.* Retrieved from Wikipedia: `https://en.wikipedia.org/wiki/Rainbow_table`

Get this book's PDF version and more

Scan the QR code (or go to `packtpub.com/unlock`). Search for this book by name, confirm the edition, and then follow the steps on the page.

UNLOCK NOW

Note: Keep your invoice handy. Purchases made directly from Packt don't require an invoice.

11

Cybersecurity Strategy Implementation

In the previous chapter, I discussed numerous cybersecurity strategies. In this chapter, I'll take one of those strategies and illustrate how it can be implemented in a real IT environment. The objective is to take the theoretical and make it a little more real for you. I'll also provide some tips and tricks I've learned in my career along the way.

You might recall from the last chapter that the Attack-Centric Strategy had the highest **Cybersecurity Fundamentals Scoring System** (**CFSS**) estimated total score. It earned nearly a perfect score with 95 points out of a possible 100. It earned a high score because it is capable of almost fully addressing all the Cybersecurity Usual Suspects, with the exception of social engineering, which can't really be fully mitigated.

Two popular examples of attack-centric frameworks used by security professionals in the industry include the Intrusion Kill Chain (Hutchins, Cloppert, Amin, n.d.) and the MITRE ATT&CK® model (MITRE, n.d.).

> **Note**
>
> All MITRE ATT&CK content in this chapter is reproduced under Creative Commons Attribution 4.0 International License.

In this chapter, I'll provide an example of how an attack-centric strategy can be implemented. The model I will focus on is the Intrusion Kill Chain framework, first pioneered by Lockheed Martin.

The CFSS score mentioned above suggests that the Attack-Centric Strategy can nearly fully mitigate the Cybersecurity Usual Suspects. Regardless of what this approach's champions or detractors say about it, *Chapter 10, Cybersecurity Strategies* gave you the CFSS method to decide its potential efficacy for yourself. I recommend making use of this tool when faced with disparate opinions about cybersecurity strategies. Additionally, keep in mind that this approach can be used in on-premises, cloud, and hybrid environments. Another strength of this approach is that it is technology-neutral, meaning it isn't limited to a specific technology or vendor and can be used by most organizations now and into the future as they evolve their IT strategies.

However, I do believe there is a better, more modern cybersecurity strategy for cloud environments. I'll discuss this in *Chapter 13, Modern Approaches to Security and Compliance.*

In this chapter, we will cover the following:

- What is the Intrusion Kill Chain?
- Some ways that the traditional Kill Chain model can be modernized
- Factors to consider when planning and implementing this model
- Designing security control sets to support this model

Since the MITRE ATT&CK® framework is also popular, very useful, and complementary to the Intrusion Kill Chain, I'll point out some of the areas where it is helpful. Let's start by discussing the details of the Intrusion Kill Chain framework.

What is the Intrusion Kill Chain?

The Intrusion Kill Chain framework is based on Lockheed Martin's paper Intelligence-*Driven Computer Network Defense Informed by Analysis of Adversary Campaigns and Intrusion Kill Chains* (Hutchins, Cloppert, Amin, n.d.). In my opinion, this paper is required reading for all cybersecurity professionals. Some of the concepts in this paper might seem obvious or even dated now, but when it was first published, it introduced concepts and ideas that changed the cybersecurity industry. Some might argue that this model has seen its best days and that there are now better approaches available, like the MITRE ATT&CK model. This isn't quite true, as ATT&CK is meant to be complementary to the Intrusion Kill Chain approach. The MITRE Corporation, which developed and maintains the ATT&CK framework, describes the relationship between the two approaches this way.

> *"What is the relationship between ATT&CK and the Lockheed Martin Cyber Kill Chain®?*
>
> *ATT&CK and the Cyber Kill Chain are complementary. ATT&CK sits at a lower level of definition to describe adversary behavior than the Cyber Kill Chain. ATT&CK Tactics are unordered and may not all occur in a single intrusion because adversary tactical goals change throughout an operation, whereas the Cyber Kill*

Chain uses ordered phases to describe high level adversary objectives." (MITRE, n.d.).

> **Note**
>
> I have found that security professionals either love or hate this model. I've actually had the opportunity to do some big-budget implementations of it, so I have some first-hand experience with it. As I contemplated these implementations, I realized an Intrusion Kill Chain could probably be implemented in several different ways. I'll describe one way this framework can be implemented, fully recognizing that there are other ways it can be implemented, and that mine might not be the best way.

An Intrusion Kill Chain describes the stages or phases that can be used in attacks by attackers. The phases provided in Lockheed Martin's paper include:

- Reconnaissance
- Weaponization
- Delivery
- Exploitation
- Installation
- Command and Control (C2)
- Actions on Objectives

Although you can probably tell from the name of each of these phases what they encompass, let me quickly summarize them for you. Note that this is based on my own interpretation of Lockheed Martin's paper, and other interpretations are possible.

Attackers select their target in the *Reconnaissance* phase (Hutchins, Cloppert, Amin, n.d.). Certainly, many attackers select targets opportunistically, often by coincidence, as evidenced by all the commodity malware present on the internet.

Other attackers might spend time and effort researching whom they should target based on their motivations for the attack. They will likely spend time in this phase discovering the IP address space their target uses, the hardware and software they use, the types of systems they have, how the business or organization works, which vendors are in their supply chain, and who works there. They can use a range of tools to conduct this research, including technical tools to do DNS name lookups, IP address range scans, and the websites where the organization advertises job openings that typically include technical qualifications based on the hardware and software they use, among many others. In the case of a mass malware attack, the attacker typically decides to attack everyone. However, they still need to make that decision, and it occurs in this stage of an attack.

> Note
>
> **Artificial** intelligence **(AI)** is now helping attackers with target selection and reconnaissance. It saves them time and can help automate their attacks. With new agentic AI capabilities in attackers' hands, we are poised to enter an era of fully autonomous attacks where humans do not play active roles in attacks. I'll discuss this in more detail in *Chapter 15, Artificial Intelligence: Security of AI systems and using AI for better cybersecurity*.

Once attackers have selected their target and have some understanding of where they have points of presence on the internet and the technologies they use, they then figure out how they are going to attack the victim. This phase is called *Weaponization* (Hutchins, Cloppert, Amin, n.d.). Attackers can build, buy, or partner with other miscreants to attain the weapons they plan to use. For example, suppose an attacker finds out that their target uses Adobe products. So, they plan to initially compromise the environment by exploiting potentially unpatched vulnerabilities for Acrobat Reader. To do this, they construct a malformed .pdf file that is capable of exploiting a particular vulnerability (CVE ID) when a victim opens it. Of course, this attack will only work if the vulnerability they are using has not been patched in the target's environment. Ultimately, the weapons the attackers use for initial access will be one or more of the Cybersecurity Usual Suspects.

After attackers have decided how they are going to try to initially compromise the target's environment, and they've attained the weapons they plan to use, next they have to decide how they will deliver the weapons to the target. In the *Delivery* phase, they decide if they are going to send the malformed .pdf file as an email attachment, use it as part of a watering hole attack, put it on USB drives and throw them into the organization's parking lot, and so on.

Once a weapon has been delivered to a potential victim, attackers need a way to activate the weapon. In our malicious .pdf example, the attacker hopes that the victim tries to open the malformed file so that their exploit runs on the victim's system. This phase is aptly called the *Exploitation* phase (Hutchins, Cloppert, Amin, n.d.). If the victim's system isn't patched for the specific vulnerability that the exploit is designed to take advantage of, then the attacker's exploit will successfully execute.

When the attacker's exploit is executed, it could download more malware to the victim's system or unpack malware from within itself. Typically, this will give the attacker remote access to the victim's system. This phase is called *Installation* (Hutchins, Cloppert, Amin, n.d.).

Once the attackers have successfully installed their tools on the victim's system, they can send commands to their tools or to the system itself. The attackers now control the system fully or partially, and they can potentially run arbitrary code of their choice on the victim's system. This phase of the attack is the *Command and Control (C2)* phase (Hutchins, Cloppert, Amin, n.d.). They might try to further penetrate the environment by attempting to compromise more systems.

Actions on Objectives is the final phase of the Intrusion Kill Chain. Now that attackers control one or more compromised systems, they pursue their objectives. As I discussed in *Chapter 1, How Enterprises Get Hacked*, their motivations could include profit, economic espionage, military espionage, notoriety, revenge, anarchy, and many others. Now, attackers are in a position to achieve the specific objectives to satisfy their motivation. They might steal intellectual property, stay persistent in order to collect information, attempt a kinetic attack to physically damage their victim's operations, destroy systems, and so on.

Note that I have written that these are phases that attackers *can* use in an attack. I didn't write that each of the phases *is always used in attacks*. This is a nuance that some of the detractors of this framework typically miss. They often argue that attackers don't have to use all seven phases that are listed in Lockheed Martin's paper. They only use the phases they have to use. Therefore, the model is flawed and shouldn't be used. I will admit that I have never understood this argument, but I hear it often when discussing this framework. It's helpful to keep the intended purpose of this framework in mind—to make it harder for attackers to succeed. Also, remember the tip I gave you in *Chapter 5, The Evolution of Malware*, about claims of omniscience. This argument relies on omniscience. We can't predict, with high confidence, everything attackers do. Because we can't perfectly predict what attackers will do in the present or the future, we must be prepared to protect, detect, and respond to whatever they choose to do. That is, we need to be grounded in the reality that attackers can use any of these phases.

For example, some environments are already compromised, making it easier for attackers to potentially penetrate such environments without going through the first three or four phases. That doesn't mean that an attacker didn't successfully go through these phases in a previous attack, and it doesn't mean attackers won't use them in the future.

> **Note**
>
> There is a difference between the Intrusion Kill Chain framework and the ATT&CK framework that is often pointed out. ATT&CK provides tactics that attackers might or might not use. These tactics are different from the ordered steps or stages in the Intrusion Kill Chain. Despite this difference, they both have the same limitation in that they cannot be used to predict the future. They provide ways to visualize the steps attackers could take in their attacks and organize defenses around them. The number

> and order of those steps cannot be predicted because of the large number of combinations and permutations of the states of IT environments, and the choices attackers can make. Spirited discussions among security team members as to which approach to use are likely a good use of time. However, those who argue that neither of these approaches should be used without offering a viable cybersecurity strategy themselves aren't helpful. The key to using either of these approaches is to measure the performance of the cybersecurity capability investments you choose to make and make changes where prudent. Using either of these approaches or both of them together still requires that you measure the efficacy of your particular implementation. This is the topic of *Chapter 12, Measuring Performance and Effectiveness.*

Knowing what the attacker's full Intrusion Kill Chain could look like can help defenders make it much harder for attackers to be successful. By significantly increasing the effort required for attackers to be successful, we reduce their return on investment and potentially their determination. To do this, the authors of the Intrusion Kill Chain paper suggest that defenders use a **Courses of Action Matrix** (Hutchins, Cloppert, Amin, n.d.). This matrix allows defenders to map out how they plan to detect, deny, disrupt, degrade, deceive, and destroy the attacker's efforts in each of the seven phases of their Intrusion Kill Chain. An example of this is illustrated in *Table 11.1.*

Kill Chain Phase	**Detect**	**Deny**	**Disrupt**	**Degrade**	**Deceive**	**Destroy**
Reconnaissance						
Weaponization						
Delivery						
Exploitation						
Installation						
Command and Control (C2)						
Actions on Objectives						

Table 11.1 – A Course of Action Matrix (Hutchins, Cloppert, Amin, n.d.)

By layering controls into this matrix, the objective is to make it much harder, or impossible, for attackers to progress through their Intrusion Kill Chain. Multiple complementary capabilities can be included in each of the cells in the matrix. For example, in the Delivery phase, email and file scanning, as well as web and content filtering, can all be deployed. Stopping attackers as early in their Intrusion Kill Chain as possible reduces the potential damage and associated recovery time and costs. Instead of attackers being successful after they defeat a firewall or a single set of controls, they must overcome the layered defenses in the Courses of Action Matrix for each step in their attack.

Modernizing the kill chain

One consideration before implementing this framework is whether defenders should use the original Intrusion Kill Chain framework or an updated version of it. There are several ways this framework can be modernized. The ATT&CK framework is an example of a modernized intrusion kill chain. At the time of writing, the current version (ATT&CK version 18.0) provides 14 tactics instead of the 7 stages provided by the original Intrusion Kill Chain framework. Although tactics and stages are slightly different, the concept is the same – understanding how attackers initially compromise and penetrate enterprise IT environments enables defenders to better protect, detect, and respond to those attacks.

I'll give you some ideas about how the original Intrusion Kill Chain can be modernized in this section. However, don't be afraid to embrace the notion of iterative improvement based on your organization's experiences with this framework or others.

Mapping the Cybersecurity Usual Suspects

I hope I have imparted the importance of mitigating the five ways that organizations are initially compromised. The Intrusion Kill Chain framework can be modified or reorganized to mitigate the Cybersecurity Usual Suspects and make it easier to identify gaps in an organization's security posture. This can be done in a couple of different ways. First, they can be integrated into the original Intrusion Kill Chain framework. That is, the controls used to mitigate the Cybersecurity Usual Suspects can be spread across the Courses of Action Matrix like all the other controls are. The challenge with this approach is that it can make it difficult to identify over-investment, under-investment, and gaps in those specific areas, especially if your matrix is large. To compensate for this, a column could be added to the matrix where the Cybersecurity Usual Suspects that each control mitigates are tracked. Some rows won't have an entry in this column because many controls will be advanced cybersecurity capabilities, not necessarily focused on the Cybersecurity Usual Suspects.

Another way to make it easier to ensure the Cybersecurity Usual Suspects are fully mitigated is to use two separate lists. Inventory the controls that mitigate the Cybersecurity Usual Suspects in one list and everything else in a separate Courses of Action Matrix. This way, you'll have complete, unobscured visibility into all controls. Note that this might lead to some duplication of controls in these lists, which makes it more complicated to track changes over time.

I prefer the second approach, that is, using two separate lists. I like clear visibility into the controls that mitigate the Cybersecurity Usual Suspects. Put another way, there is one list for controls focused on protecting, detecting, and responding to attempts to initially compromise an IT environment, and another list for post-compromise controls. This approach makes it easier to keep track of the controls that represent the foundation of the cybersecurity strategy. However, feel free to use either approach or a different one that works best for your organization. This is the approach I will use in the example provided in this chapter. I've already discussed the Cybersecurity Usual Suspects and the Cybersecurity Fundamentals extensively in other chapters. The example I'll provide here will focus on the advanced cybersecurity capabilities component of the strategy.

Updating the matrix

Another modification to this approach worth considering is whether to update the phases and the actions in the Courses of Action Matrix. For example, the Reconnaissance phase of the Intrusion Kill Chain can be split into two separate phases. This separation recognizes that there are potentially at least two different times in an intrusion attempt when attackers typically perform reconnaissance. Prior to the attack, attackers might spend time selecting their target and researching ways that they could be attacked. After one of the Cybersecurity Usual Suspects is used to initially compromise the victim, then the attackers might perform some reconnaissance again to map out the victim's network and where the **High-Value Assets** (**HVAs**) are and where potentially valuable data is stored. Separating these two phases can be helpful because the tools, techniques, tactics, and procedures used by attackers can be different before and after initial compromise. Updating the matrix by replacing the Reconnaissance phase with the Reconnaissance I and Reconnaissance II phases will enable security teams to map different controls to stop attackers in each of these phases. Keep in mind that, in both cases, attackers might use non-intrusive reconnaissance tactics or choose to use intrusive reconnaissance tactics.

This same type of modification has been implemented in the ATT&CK framework in the Reconnaissance and Discovery tactics. The former focuses on informing targeting, while the latter focuses on learning about the compromised environment.

Another potential update to the phases is dropping the Weaponization phase. This might seem like a significant change to the original framework, but in my experience, it doesn't change the controls defenders typically use. This phase of an attack is where the attackers, after having decided how they are going to attack the victim, plan to reuse old weapons or build and/or buy new weapons to use in their attack. Most of this activity happens out of the view of defenders. Subsequently, very few of the attacker's activities in this phase can be influenced by controls available to defenders. If attackers are cavalier about the sources they procure weapons from, threat intelligence vendors or law enforcement could get tipped off about their activities and perhaps their intentions. This could be helpful if the weapon is a zero-day vulnerability that the intended victim could deploy workarounds to mitigate, but frankly, focusing on the other attack phases will likely have a much higher return on investment for defenders, as they potentially have more visibility and control. The Weaponization phase is too opaque for most organizations to realistically influence.

> Tip
>
> CISOs typically do not have very effective controls for protection and detection prior to the Delivery phase; prioritizing investments in mitigations that have clear, measurable value is important.

This is reflected in the ATT&CK framework as well. In ATT&CK parlance, this weaponization concept is called Resource Development. It has fewer (8) techniques associated with it than any of the other tactics in the framework. The mitigation ATT&CK offers for all eight of these techniques is "This technique cannot be easily mitigated with preventive controls since it is based on behaviors performed outside of the scope of enterprise defenses and controls" (MITRE, n.d.).

The Courses of Action Matrix can also be updated to include some different actions. For example, Destroy could be dropped in favor of some more realistic actions, such as Limit and Recover. Using Limit as an action recognizes that defenders want to make it hard or impossible for attackers to move freely during their attack. For example, limiting the delivery options available to attackers and limiting the scope of the infrastructure that attackers can control both make it harder for attackers to be successful. Using a Recover action helps organizations plan their recovery if all the other mitigations layered in the model fail to perform as expected. For both Limit and Recover, not every cell in the matrix will necessarily have controls. For example, there likely is no control that will help Recover during the Reconnaissance I phase because the environment hasn't been attacked yet. There will potentially be several cells in the matrix without entries—this is to be expected. An example of the updated Courses of Action Matrix is illustrated in *Table 11.2*.

Kill Chain Phase	Detect	Detect Maturity Index (1-5)	Detect Data Consumer	Detect Consumer PoC	Deny	Deny Maturity Index (1-5)	Deny Data Consumer	Deny Consumer PoC
Reconnaissance I								
Delivery								
Exploitation								
Installation								
Command and Control (C2)								
Reconnaissance II								
Actions on Objectives								

Table 11.2 – Example of an updated Courses of Action Matrix

Of course, these updates are completely optional. Implementing the original Intrusion Kill Chain model can be an effective way for many organizations to improve their security posture. I suggest that before CISOs get serious about implementing this model, they spend some time thinking through whether any modifications to the original model would be advantageous. Then, they should update the Courses of Action Matrix before moving forward with this model, as this will save time, expense, and potentially frustrating rework.

Intrusion Kill Chain or ATT&CK?

Another decision to make is whether to use the Intrusion Kill Chain framework or the ATT&CK framework, or a combination of these approaches. In my experience, the relatively small number of high-level stages that the Intrusion Kill Chain offers makes it easier for Strategy and Architecture teams to visualize attacks and design and implement layered defenses for them.

Besides being a simpler model, this approach is also aligned with how cybersecurity vendors tend to market and sell their products and services. This makes it easier for the teams that negotiate deals with cybersecurity vendors, such as Procurement and Legal teams, to do their work. For example, an Endpoint Detection and Response vendor might highlight the various benefits of their product, such as high malware detection rates, low false positive detection rates, and advanced heuristics. In ATT&CK parlance, the same vendor would highlight that they have the best lsass.exe injection detection in the industry. Notice how the altitude of these benefits is different?

Lastly, I've found that the Intrusion Kill Chain framework is easier for senior stakeholders, namely IT leadership, senior executives, and members of the Board of Directors, to understand.

> **Tip**
>
> Remember one piece of advice I provided in *Chapter 9, Ingredients for a Successful Cybersecurity Strategy*: getting support from these stakeholders can be critical to the success of your strategy. If they can't understand the strategy, they might not fully support it.

In contrast, the ATT&CK taxonomy with tactics, techniques, sub-techniques, mitigations, detections, and so on is harder for senior executives and Board of Directors members to understand. This is another reason I have found the Intrusion Kill Chain framework valuable – it can be easier to get support for.

Where I have found the ATT&CK framework to be more helpful than the Intrusion Kill Chain is in doing security control validation and testing, designing and testing enterprise detection strategies, and attack simulations—any place where knowledge of the attackers' granular techniques could be helpful. The knowledgebase aspect of ATT&CK is really helpful in these scenarios, but the Intrusion Kill Chain largely leaves it up to strategy and architecture teams to figure these things out for themselves.

Subsequently, leveraging a combination of these approaches can make sense. Using the Intrusion Kill Chain framework to make things more straightforward for Strategy, Architecture, Procurement, Legal, and other stakeholders, such as senior executives and members of Boards, and using ATT&CK to inform the details for security teams can be a powerful combination for some organizations.

Ofcourse,someorganizationssimplystandardizeontheATT&CKframeworkandtrytouseitconsistentlyeverywhere this is also a great approach. Whichever route your organization goes down, remember that the best approach is the one that is going to be most successful for your organization, not someone else's. Remember that *best practices* are based on someone else's threat model.

I'll mention one caveat here. Both of these approaches can be used in the cloud. The question for CISOs is, can your organization manage two separate cybersecurity strategies, one for cloud and one for on-premises? Or should you use the same strategy in both environments to make things simpler and more consistent? In my role as a cybersecurity advisor, I found a surprising number of CISOs who expressed a preference to operate separate strategies for the cloud and their on-premises environments. I'll discuss this more in *Chapter 13*.

Getting started

Existing IT environments, especially those already under the management of a CISO, will likely have some cybersecurity controls already deployed in them. If the Attack-Centric Strategy and the Intrusion Kill Chain approach are new to an organization, chances are that the existing controls were deployed in a way that isn't necessarily consistent with the Courses of Action Matrix. Mapping currently deployed cybersecurity controls to the Courses of Action Matrix will help determine where potential gaps exist. It can also help identify areas of over-investment and under-investment. For example, after mapping their current cybersecurity capabilities to this matrix, the security team realizes that they have invested heavily in capabilities that deny the delivery of the attacker's weapons but have not invested in detecting delivery attempts; in fact, they now realize they have underinvested in detection capabilities across the entire Kill Chain. Thus, this mapping exercise can help expose optimistic assumptions about organizations' security capabilities. Some security professionals call this type of exercise *cartography*.

This exercise can be illuminating but also challenging to execute, especially in large, complex environments. Most organizations I've advised didn't have a complete, up-to-date list of tools, products, services, and configurations that are useful in an exercise like this one. Even organizations that have asset inventories and configuration management databases often find their data to be incomplete, out of date, and inaccurate. I've seen industry estimates suggesting that the average on-premises IT environment has 20% undocumented assets and services, and even higher estimates in some industries, like healthcare. Experience tells me these estimates are low.

Some organizations try to use procurement artifacts to determine what their IT department bought, but this is usually different from what was actually deployed. Faced with the challenge of getting an accurate, up-to-date inventory of the cybersecurity capabilities they have running in their environment, most organizations start with the data they have and manually verify what has been implemented. This isn't necessarily a bad thing because it can provide an accurate and current view but also includes qualitative insights that can't be rendered from an asset inventory database.

Maturity of current cybersecurity capabilities

I have had the opportunity to do this mapping exercise in some large, complicated IT environments. Let me share some of the things I've learned to save you some time if you are faced with the same challenge.

As you map current cybersecurity capabilities to the Courses of Action Matrix, one factor to be aware of is the maturity of the implementation of each control or capability. That is, an item on a software inventory list might not offer any clue as to whether the control is fully implemented or partially implemented. Understanding the maturity of each control's implementation is key to understanding where gaps exist and where under- and over-investment has occurred.

For example, suppose an organization procures a suite of cybersecurity capabilities from a top-tier industry vendor. This suite is capable of providing several important functions including file integrity monitoring, anti-malware scanning, and data loss prevention for desktops and servers. When mapping capabilities to the Courses of Action Matrix, it is easy to look at the capabilities of the suite and include all of them in the inventory of the organization's current capabilities. However, the question is, how many of the suite's capabilities have actually been deployed and enabled? A related question is, who is responsible for operating and maintaining these controls? These can be difficult questions to answer in large, complicated IT environments. However, without uncovering the truth about the maturity of the current implementation, the confidence of the mapping and the potential efficacy of the strategy can be undermined as well. Remember the submarine analogy I've used throughout this book; would you really be keen to set sail in a submarine if you didn't really know if all the critical systems were fully operational? Probably not.

Many organizations aspire to have a world-class cybersecurity team. To support this aspiration, a principle some of them use when evaluating and procuring cybersecurity capabilities is that they only want the best of breed technologies. That is, they only want the best products and won't settle for less than that. For most organizations, this is highly ambitious because attracting and retaining cybersecurity talent is a challenge for the entire industry. Adopting a "best of breed" procurement philosophy makes this challenge even more acute because it potentially narrows the number of people who have experience with these expensive and relatively rare "best of breed only" implementations. This approach can also be dangerous for organizations that are cash rich and believe they can simply buy effective cybersecurity instead of developing a culture where everyone participates. Most of the organizations that I've seen with this philosophy end up buying a Ferrari and using only its ashtray. They simply do not have the wherewithal to architect, deploy, operate, and maintain only the best of breed, so they only use a fraction of the available capabilities. In some cases, such organizations over-invest in an area by procuring the same or similar capabilities, often procuring products they cannot successfully deploy and operate themselves. Conducting the mapping exercise in such organizations can be especially hard because it uncovers hard truths about overly optimistic ambitions and assumptions, as well as cybersecurity investments with marginal returns. However, this process can be a necessary evil for organizations with the courage to look in the mirror and the willingness to make positive, incremental changes to their current security posture. There's nothing wrong with being ambitious and aiming high if those ambitions are realistically attainable by the organization.

It can be challenging to quantify how much of a cybersecurity suite or set of capabilities has been successfully deployed. One approach I've tried, with mixed results, is to break down the functionality of the set of capabilities into its constituent categories and use a maturity index to quantify how mature the deployment is using a scale between 1 and 5, where 5 is most mature. This can help determine whether more investment is required in a particular area. In large, complex environments, this is easier said than done, and some might wonder if it's worth the time and effort as they struggle through it. However, the more detail security teams have about the current state of their affairs, the more confidence they'll have moving forward with this strategy.

Pervasiveness of current cybersecurity capabilities

Another data point to consider collecting as you map current cybersecurity capabilities to the Courses of Action Matrix is the pervasiveness of the implementation of each control or capability. For example, suppose a server operations team procures a tool that helps them detect and block exploitation of vulnerabilities on the servers it's installed on. How many servers is this tool actually installed and running on? Is it installed on all servers running Windows and different flavors of Linux? In some IT environments, it is not safe to assume the tool is running on all servers. Determining the percentage of servers the tool is actually running on will help you get a more accurate picture of existing cybersecurity capabilities.

In some environments, different teams manage IT and make decisions independently. In scenarios like this one, the pervasiveness of cybersecurity capabilities might be limited to specific networks or specific parts of the organization. For example, while the company might have a total inventory of 100 security tools, only 20% of them are deployed in any one IT environment. This is important to understand for accurate cybersecurity capability inventories. Including a pervasiveness percentage estimate in your spreadsheet for each capability can be very helpful.

Who consumes the data?

One principle I have found helpful in mapping the current security capabilities of an IT environment to the Courses of Action Matrix is that the data generated by every control set needs someone or something to consume it. For example, a security team performing this mapping discovers that the network management team implemented potentially powerful IDS/IPS capabilities that were included with a network appliance they procured last fiscal year. Although these capabilities are enabled, they discover that no one in the network management team is actively monitoring or reviewing alerts from this system and that the organization's **Security Operations Center (SOC)** wasn't even aware that they existed. The net result of these capabilities is equivalent to not having them at all, since no one is consuming the data they generate. A human doesn't necessarily have to consume this data; orchestration and automation systems can also take actions based on such data. However, if neither a human nor a system is consuming this data, then security teams can't really include these capabilities in their mappings of currently implemented controls unless those deficiencies are addressed.

As security teams perform this mapping, for each control they identify, they should also record who or what consumes the data it generates. Recording the name of the person who is the point of contact for the consumption of this data will pay dividends to security teams. A point of contact might be a manager in the SOC or in the **Network Operations Center (NOC)**, an Incident Response team member, or a vendor. This information is valuable in building confidence in the organization's true cybersecurity capabilities. However, it is also very valuable in measuring the efficacy of your strategy, which I will discuss in detail in *Chapter 12*.

As shown in *Table 11.3*, as the Courses of Action Matrix is updated, it expands quickly.

Kill Chain Phase	Detect	Detect Maturity Index (1-5)	Detect Data Consumer	Detect Consumer PoC	Detect Renewal Date	Deny	Deny Maturity Index (1-5)	Deny Data Consumer	Deny Consumer PoC	Deny Renewal Date
Reconnaissance I										
Delivery										
Exploitation										
Installation										
Command and Control (C2)										
Reconnaissance II										
Actions on Objectives										

Table 11.3 – An example of a partial Courses of Action Matrix, which includes a maturity index, who or what is going to consume data from each control, and a point of contact (PoC)

I have used a spreadsheet to do this mapping in the past. I'll admit that this isn't the most elegant way to perform such mappings. One mapping I did was over 120 pages of controls in a spreadsheet; navigating that spreadsheet wasn't much fun. Additionally, a spreadsheet is not the most scalable tool, and reporting capabilities are limited. If you have a better tool, use it! If you don't have a better tool, rest assured that the mapping exercise can be done using a spreadsheet or a document. However, the bigger and more complex the environment is, the more challenging this becomes.

Cybersecurity license renewals

Most software and hardware that is procured from vendors has licensing terms that include a date when the licenses or agreements expire. When a license expires, it must be renewed, or the product must be decommissioned. Accordingly, another update to the Courses of Action Matrix to consider, which can be very helpful, is to add a column to track the contract renewal date for each capability listed. If you are taking the time to inventory the software and hardware used for cybersecurity, you might as well record the expiry/renewal date for each item also. This will give you an idea of the time each item on the list has before its license expires and renewal is required. Embedding this information into the control mapping itself will give you visibility of the potential remaining lifetime for each capability and can help remind the security team when to start reevaluating each product's effectiveness and whether to renew or replace existing capabilities.

Another similar date that can be helpful to track is the end of life/support date for products; typically, after this date, manufacturers stop supporting products and no longer offer security updates for them. Over time, these products increase the attack surface in IT environments as vulnerabilities in them continue to be disclosed publicly, even after their end of support date. Tracking these dates can help us avoid surprises. However, tracking these dates as part of a modified Courses of Action Matrix is optional.

CISOs and security teams shouldn't rely on their Procurement departments to flag renewal dates for them; it should work the other way around. Many of the CISOs I've talked to want to have visibility into this "horizon list," how it impacts their budgets, and key milestone dates when decisions need to be made. What CISO wouldn't want some advance notice that their network IDS/IPS was going to be turned off because their license was about to lapse? The more lead time these decisions have, the fewer last-minute surprises for security teams. Additionally, when I discuss measuring the efficacy of this strategy in the next chapter, you'll see that having this information at your fingertips can be helpful.

Of course, this update to the matrix is optional. Renewal dates can be tracked in a separate document or database. However, being able to cross-reference the renewal dates and the cybersecurity capabilities in your mapping should be something CISOs can do easily. They need sufficient lead time to determine whether they want to keep the products and services they already have in production or replace them.

An example of an updated Courses of Action Matrix with columns for renewal dates is shown in *Table 11.4*.

Kill Chain Phase	Detect	Detect Maturity Index (1-5)	Detect Data Consumer	Detect Consumer PoC	Detect Renewal Date	Deny	Deny Maturity Index (1-5)	Deny Data Consumer	Deny Consumer PoC	Deny Renewal Date
Reconnaissance I										
Delivery										
Exploitation										
Installation										
Command and Control (C2)										
Reconnaissance II										
Actions on Objectives										

Table 11.4 – An example of a partial Courses of Action Matrix, which includes a maturity index, who or what is going to consume data, a point of contact (PoC), and the renewal date for each control.

Implementing this strategy

By the end of the mapping process, CISOs and security teams should have a much better inventory of the cybersecurity capabilities and controls that have been deployed, as well as how the data from these are being consumed by the organization. This is a great starting point for implementing the Intrusion Kill Chain framework. However, do not underestimate how challenging it can be for organizations with large, complex IT environments to accomplish this.

For some organizations, it will be easier to divide mapping work into smaller, more achievable projects focused on parts of their environment than to try to map their entire environment. As mentioned earlier, moving forward with this strategy without an accurate, current mapping can easily lead to overinvestments, under-investments, and gaps in security capabilities. Although these can be corrected over time, it will likely make it more expensive and time-consuming than it needs to be. I've provided an example of what the first two actions (Detect and Deny) across an updated set of phases look like in *Table 11.5*.

Kill Chain Phase	Detect	Detect Description	Detect Maturity Index (1-5)	Detect Data Consumer	Detect Consumer PoC	Detect Renewal Date	Deny	Deny Description	Deny Maturity Index (1-5)	Deny Data Consumer	Deny Consumer PoC	Deny Renewal Date
Reconnaissance I												
Delivery	control_name	Network IDS/IPS	3	SOC	Leonard Nimoy	9/15/2028	control_name	email spam filter	2	eMail Administrator	Bruce Willis	1/1/2028
Delivery	control_name	System image agent	1	IR Team	Bruce Dern	6/3/2030	control_name	USB disable policy	2	Server Support	Bruno Mars	n/a
Exploitation	control_name	Windows Error Reporting	1	No one	No one	n/a	control_name	Anti-virus suite	4	SOC	Leonard Nimoy	4/15/2026
Exploitation	control_name	System Integrity Monitor	2	SOC	Leonard Nimoy	9/9/2030	control_name	File Integrity Monitoring	2	SOC	Leonard Nimoy	6/15/2030
Exploitation	control_name	Anti-virus suite	4	Desktop Support	Kathy Bates	4/15/2026	control_name	ASLR	5	Desktop Support	Kathy Bates	n/a
Installation	control_name	File Integrity Monitoring	2	Desktop Support	Kathy Bates	6/15/2030	control_name	Anti-virus suite	4	Desktop Support	Kathy Bates	4/15/2026
Installation	control_name	File Integrity Monitoring	2	Server Support	Bruno Mars	6/15/2030	control_name	Anti-virus suite	4	Server Support	Bruno Mars	4/15/2026
Installation	control_name	Anti-virus suite	4	SOC	Leonard Nimoy	4/15/2026						
Installation	control_name	Anti-virus suite	4	IR Team	Bruce Dern	4/15/2026						
Command and Control (C2)	control_name	Network IDS/IPS	3	NOC	Keanu Reeves	9/15/2028	control_name	Network IDS/IPS	3	NOC	Keanu Reeves	9/15/2028
Command and Control (C2)	control_name	Network IDS/IPS	3	SOC	Leonard Nimoy	9/15/2028						
Reconnaissance II	control_name	Network IDS/IPS	3	NOC	Keanu Reeves	9/15/2028	control_name	Network IDS/IPS	3	NOC	Keanu Reeves	9/15/2028
Reconnaissance II	control_name	Network IDS/IPS	3	SOC	Leonard Nimoy	9/15/2028						
Actions on Objectives	control_name	File Integrity Monitoring	2	Server Support	Bruno Mars	6/15/2030	control_name	File Integrity Monitoring	2	Server Support	Bruno Mars	6/15/2030
Actions on Objectives	control_name	File Integrity Monitoring	2	Desktop Support	Kathy Bates	6/15/2030	control_name	File Integrity Monitoring	2	Desktop Support	Kathy Bates	6/15/2030
Actions on Objectives	control_name	Deception technology	2	SOC	Leonard Nimoy	5/31/2025						

Table 11.5 – An example of a part of an updated Courses of Action Matrix that contains a mapping of an organization's current cybersecurity capabilities

An actual mapping for a large organization could potentially be much larger, but I want to give you an idea of what a mapping looks like. In an actual mapping, *control_name* will be the names of the specific products, services, features, or functionality that detect, deny, disrupt, and so on for each phase of an attack. The *Description* field is meant to be a short description of what each control does. I suggest providing more detail in this field than I have here so that it's clear what each control's function and scope are.

There is a *Maturity Index* for each control, ranging from 1 to 5, with 5 indicating that the implementation is as full and functional as possible. A maturity index of 1 or 2 indicates that while the product or feature has a lot of functionality, relatively little of it has been deployed or is being operated. This index will help inform our assumptions about how effective each control currently is versus its potential. This helps avoid the trap of assuming a control is operating at peak efficiency when in reality it isn't fully deployed, or it is not being actively operated or monitored. Color coding this field or entire line items based on this field can make it even easier to understand the maturity of each control.

I have not included a *Pervasiveness* column in *Table 11.5*, but had I, it would contain a percentage representing the estimated amount of the environment each control is installed and running on. Alternatively, I could have included two columns for *Pervasiveness*, one representing the low end of the estimated percentage range, and a second one for the high end of the range. For example, 30% in the low column and 50% in the high column indicates that the control is installed and running on between 30% and 50% of the environment in scope. Having two columns will allow you to filter the data in potentially more interesting ways later when you are analyzing the data and rationalizing the Courses of Action Matrix.

The *Data Consumer* for each action is the specific group or department in the organization that is using data from the control to detect, deny, disrupt, degrade, and so on. The Consumer PoC column contains the names of each point of contact in the group or department that is consuming the data from each control. This can make it easier to periodically verify that the data from each control is still being consumed as planned. After all, there's no point in deploying mitigations if no one is actually paying any attention to them. The time, effort, and budget spent on such controls can likely be used more effectively somewhere else in the organization.

Finally, the *Renewal Date* column for each action provides visibility into the potential expiry date of each control. It does this to help minimize potential unexpected lapses in the operational status of each control. This helps avoid the revelation that a mitigation you thought was fully operational has actually been partially or entirely disabled because of a lapse in licensing or a product going out of support. These surprises can burn CISOs and security teams.

Rationalizing the matrix: gaps, under-investments, and over-investments

As mentioned throughout our discussion, without mapping current cybersecurity capabilities to the Courses of Action Matrix, it can be very easy to over-invest or under-invest in cybersecurity products and have gaps in protection, detection, and response capabilities. But what exactly do I mean by over-investments, under-investments, and gaps?

Identifying gaps

Performed correctly, mapping can reveal key areas where organizations haven't invested at all —a gap. For example, in *Table 11.5*, the *Reconnaissance I* row doesn't have any entries in it; this can be a clear indication that the organization has a gap in its control set, which could make this phase of the attacker's Intrusion Kill Chain easier for them. It isn't uncommon for organizations to fail to invest in this area. A gap like this is a clear opportunity for improvement.

Identifying areas of under-investment

Under-investments in an area can be more subtle in the Courses of Action Matrix. An under-investment can appear as a relatively small number of entries for an activity or phase in the matrix. This is where the maturity index, pervasiveness percentage, and descriptions can help.

A single entry in the matrix with a maturity index of 5 might be all the investment that is needed for that action. But an entry with a maturity index of 5 and a pervasiveness percentage of 10% might be a different story. The combination of the maturity index, pervasiveness percentage, and the description should help make this determination. However, the entry's description should be verbose enough for the security team to understand if the functionality and scope of the capability will really break attackers' Kill Chains or if more investment is warranted in that area of the matrix. For example, if IDS/IPS is deployed and operational, but only on a specific part of the organization's network, that's worth capturing in the notes to make the lack of pervasiveness clear. The right control might be deployed, but if it's only partially implemented or partially operational, it might not be sufficient to break a Kill Chain or be effective in all scenarios. Further investment into maturing that control or expanding where it operates might be solutions to this problem. Another possible solution is investing in a different control to supplement the current mitigation. From this perspective, the Courses of Action Matrix becomes an important document to help during an incident and is the center of negotiations over budgets and resources with non-technical executives.

Identifying areas of over-investment

Over-investing in areas is a common problem that I've seen both public and private sector organizations suffer. It can occur slowly over time or quickly in the wake of a data breach. In the Courses of Action Matrix, an over-investment can appear as a lot of entries in one or two areas that perform the same or similar functions. For example, I've seen organizations procure multiple **identity and access management (IAM)** products and fully deploy none of them. This can happen for a range of reasons. For example, they may have been unrealistic about their ability to attract and retain the talent required to deploy these products.

Another example is that in the wake of a successful intrusion, it's not uncommon for a victimized organization to decide that it's time to make a big investment in cybersecurity. With a newfound sense of urgency and exuberance, they don't take the time to get an inventory of current capabilities and their maturity before they go on a cybersecurity shopping spree. Mergers and acquisitions can also leave organizations with over-investments in some areas of the matrix. Suddenly, after a merger, the organization has twice as many cybersecurity tools as it had before the merger, and performing cybersecurity capability inventories can be especially challenging after a recent merger or acquisition.

Finally, simply put, some salespeople are really good at their jobs. I've seen entire industries and geographical areas where everyone has literally procured the same SIEM or endpoint solution during the same 1 or 2 fiscal years. There's nothing wrong with this, but it's unlikely they all started with the same IT and OT environments, comparable cybersecurity talent, and the same licensing renewal dates for their current products. When a good salesperson is exceedingly successful, this can sometimes lead to over-investments in areas.

For organizations that haven't performed a cybersecurity capabilities inventory using a Courses of Action Matrix before, one area that seems to almost always be over-invested in is the intersection of Deny and Exploitation in the Courses of Action Matrix. There's good reason for this; stopping attackers before they get past this point in their Kill Chain can limit their scope of control and minimize damage and recovery costs. This is the stage in attacks that many security professionals refer to as "left of boom." In other words, stop them before they successfully complete the Exploitation phase of their attack and move to the Installation phase. Subsequently, it is not uncommon to see major over-investments in this one area in enterprise IT environments.

In recent years, the intersection of Detect and Exploitation in the Courses of Action Matrix has also become crowded as the industry has pivoted toward deploying detection capabilities instead of just relying on protective capabilities. Don't panic if the first time you complete a Courses of Action Matrix for an organization, the entire matrix is relatively empty except for Detect and Deny for Exploitation. It can be rewarding to see an overconfident CISO's expression change when they see their organization's Courses of Action Matrix for the first time and realize they have been over-investing in the same two areas for years. This is fairly typical the first time this Attack-Centric Strategy is embraced. It also means there are lots of opportunities for improvement.

Planning your implementation

It's important to identify gaps, under-invested areas, and areas of over-investment, as these will inform the implementation plan. Hopefully, many of the areas that the organization has already invested in won't require changes. This will allow the security and IT teams to focus on addressing gaps and shortcomings in their current security posture. At the point where these teams have a current mapping and have identified gaps, areas of under-investment, and areas of over-investment, they can start planning the rest of their implementation.

Security teams often ask where to start with a Courses of Action Matrix. For many organizations, the highest ROI comes from closing known gaps, though budgets and available cybersecurity talent inevitably shape what's possible. The overarching goal is to break attackers' Kill Chains, and doing so earlier in the chain generally reduces cost and damage. But assuming you can reliably stop every attack before Exploitation or Installation is unrealistic and sets teams up for failure. That's why several CISOs I've spoken with choose to invest modestly across all parts of the matrix, even though this approach is also constrained by resources.

Most CISOs I've talked to have limited budgets. For those that don't, they are typically still limited by their ability to architect, deploy, and operate new capabilities quickly. The renewal date for each item in the matrix can help inform a timeline used to address gaps and investment issues. Choosing not to renew licenses for less effective products in areas of over-investment might help free up some of the budget that can be used to address gaps and areas of underinvestment. Not every organization has over-investments, and many are chronically under-invested across the matrix. For organizations in this category, taking advantage of as many of the "free" controls in operating systems and integrated development environments as possible can be helpful.

For example, **Address Space Layout Randomization (ASLR)** and **Data Execution Prevention (DEP)** can help make the Exploitation phase of an attack harder to accomplish and inconsistent. ASLR is a memory safety feature that can make exploiting vulnerabilities harder for attackers by randomizing address space locations. Therefore, attackers are unable to consistently predict the memory locations of vulnerabilities they wish to exploit. ASLR should typically be used in combination with DEP (Matt Miller, 2010). DEP is another memory safety feature that stops attackers from using memory pages meant for data to execute their code (Matt Miller, 2010).

These features are built into most modern operating systems from major vendors today, although not all applications take advantage of them. Still, thoughtfully using such free or low-cost controls can help organizations with limited budgets pursue this strategy.

Another way I've seen CISOs plan their implementation is to use results from Red Team and Blue Team exercises and penetration tests. Penetration tests typically focus on confirming the effectiveness of security controls that have been implemented, whereas Red Team exercises focus on outrunning and outsmarting defenders. This is a direct way of testing the effectiveness of the people, processes, and technologies that are part of your current implementation. Just as important as identifying gaps, these exercises can identify controls and mitigations that are not performing as expected and help inform the maturity indexes in your mapping and prioritize items in your implementation plan in a practical, less theoretical way. The ATT&CK framework can also be very helpful in planning attack simulations that reveal areas for improvement and subsequent investment.

Finally, one other way I've seen CISOs decide to implement frameworks like this one is to invest in high ROI areas first. They do this by identifying where they get the biggest bang for their investment. This is done by identifying controls that provide mitigations in multiple parts of the matrix. For example, if the same control potentially helps break the attacker's Kill Chains in the Delivery, Exploitation, and Command and Control phases, they'll prioritize that one over controls that only potentially break one phase of an attack. Put another way, they look for areas where they can use two or three mitigations for the price of one. The more detailed their matrix is, the more of these opportunities they can identify.

I will revisit many of the factors that I discussed in this section in *Chapter 12*.

Designing control sets

With a current control set mapping, identified gaps, areas of under-investment, areas of over-investment, and a plan for which of these areas will be addressed, security teams can start designing control sets. This part of the process can be challenging, but a lot of fun as well. After all, designing controls to make it as hard as possible for attackers to succeed is fun! For some people, spending money on cybersecurity technologies is fun too, and there is an opportunity to lay the groundwork to do that in this exercise.

There are more combinations and permutations of possible control sets than I can cover in this book. This section is meant to provide you with more detail on each part of the updated Courses of Action Matrix that I outlined and to provoke some thought about ways that security teams could design control sets for their organization.

> **Note**
>
> This isn't a blueprint that should be followed; it's really just a high-level example. I didn't receive any promotional payments for any products or companies I mentioned in this section, and I don't endorse them or make any claims or warranties about them or their products. Please use whatever companies, products, services, and features meet your requirements. If you'd like professional recommendations, I recommend consuming the reports and services of industry analyst firms such as Forrester, Gartner, and IANS, among others. This is where CISO councils, professional societies, and gated social networks can be very helpful. Getting first-hand accounts of the efficacy of strategies, products, and services directly from other CISOs can be very helpful. Analyst firms can't be too publicly critical of a company or its products, but I haven't met many CISOs that weren't willing to be candid in private conversations behind closed doors.

Additionally, this is another place where the ATT&CK framework can help. The mitigations listed for each technique and sub-technique under the equivalent tactic or tactics in the ATT&CK framework can provide many ideas for effective controls. Using ATT&CK for this purpose can save security teams a lot of time designing control sets. ATT&CK can also inform testing for these control sets and attack simulations to ensure they all work as expected.

Reminder: the stages and actions in the modified Courses of Action Matrix that I'll cover in this section are illustrated in *Table 11.6*. In other words, I'll be giving you ideas about the cybersecurity capabilities that can be used to populate the cells in *Table 11.6*.

Kill Chain Phase	Detect	Deny	Disrupt	Degrade	Deceive	Limit	Recover
Reconnaissance I							
Delivery							
Exploitation							
Installation							
Command and Control (C2)							
Reconnaissance II							
Actions on Objectives							

Table 11.6 – Modified Courses of Action Matrix

Attack phase – Reconnaissance I

In this attack phase, attackers are selecting their targets, performing research, mapping and probing their targets' online presence, and doing the same for the organizations in their intended victims' supply chain. Attackers are seeking answers to the basic questions of what, why, when, and how. Their research isn't limited to IP addresses and open TCP/UDP ports; people, processes, and technologies are all potential pawns in their attacks.

The challenge for defenders in this stage is that reconnaissance activities blend in with legitimate network traffic, emails, telephone calls, employees, and so on. It can be very difficult to identify the attacker's reconnaissance activities when they aren't anomalous. Still, it can be worthwhile to invest in cybersecurity capabilities in this stage because, as I mentioned earlier, breaking the attacker's Kill Chains as early as possible typically has the highest ROI.

Categorizing reconnaissance activities into *passive* and *active* groups (Sanghvi, Dahiya, 2013) can help security teams decide where investments are practical. For example, it might be prohibitively expensive to try to identify attackers performing passive research by reading an organization's job postings website just to identify the types of hardware and software it uses. However, it might be practical to detect and block IP addresses of systems that are actively scanning for vulnerabilities on corporate firewalls. Many passive reconnaissance activities can be conducted out of the sight of defenders and subsequently won't generate log entries or alerts that defenders can use. However, many threat intelligence vendors offer services to their customers that scrape social media sites and illicit marketplaces, all to look for chatter in the dark web about their IP address ranges, domains, known vulnerabilities, credentials for sale, and imminent attacks. Active reconnaissance activities tend to interact directly with the victims and their supply chains, potentially providing defenders with a more direct glimpse of them.

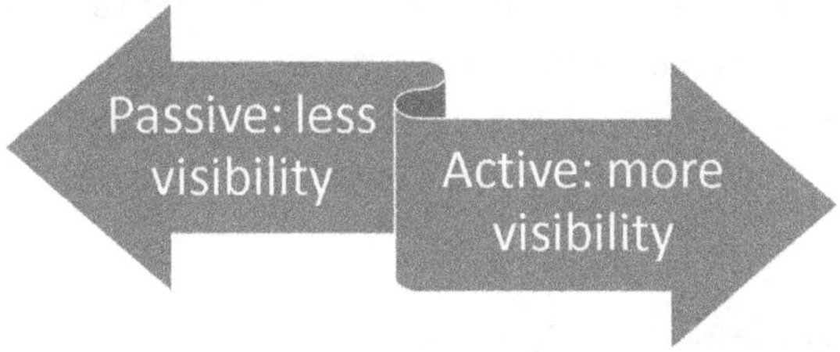

Figure 11.1 – Reconnaissance activity categories

Some cybersecurity capabilities that can help in this phase of an attack include the following:

- **Cyber threat intelligence (CTI) services** can help detect passive reconnaissance activities, potentially giving defenders notice of known vulnerabilities in their defensive posture and imminent attacks. Ideally, this can give them some time to address these known vulnerabilities and better prepare themselves for an attack. Some examples of threat intelligence vendors that currently offer such services are as follows:
    - Cisco Talos
    - CrowdStrike
    - IBM X-Force
    - Mandiant
    - Recorded Future
    - Palo Alto Networks Unit 42
    - Proofpoint
    - Many, many others, including smaller boutique firms
- **Web Application Firewalls (WAF)** can detect application layer attacks like SQL injection, cross-site scripting, and so on. A WAF can help detect, deny, disrupt, and degrade application layer attacks. Here are some examples of WAFs:
    - Akamai
    - Amazon Web Services
    - Barracuda
    - Cloudflare
    - F5
    - Imperva
    - Radware
    - Many, many others

- **Firewalls:** there are at least a few different flavors of firewalls. Firewalls can detect, deny, disrupt, and degrade some active network reconnaissance activities. There are too many examples of vendors that offer firewall products to list, but here are some:
    - Barracuda
    - Cisco
    - Check Point Software Technologies
    - Juniper Networks
    - Palo Alto Networks
    - SonicWall
    - Many, many others
- **Deception technologies** can be employed to deceive attackers performing active reconnaissance. Deception technology systems present systems as the legitimate infrastructure of the intended target or vendors in their supply chain. Attackers spend time and resources performing reconnaissance on these systems instead of production infrastructure and systems. Examples of deception technology vendors include the following:
    - Acalvio Technologies
    - Illusive Networks
    - Rapid7
    - TrapX Security
    - Many, many others
- **Automation** can be combined with threat intelligence and detection capabilities to enable dynamic responses to reconnaissance activities. For example, if a WAF or firewall detects probes from known malicious IP addresses, automation could be triggered to dynamically adjust the lists of blocked IP addresses for some period of time, or automation could try to degrade reconnaissance and waste the attacker's time by allowing ICMP network traffic from malicious IP addresses and blocking TCP traffic to ports 80, 443, and other open ports. This would allow attackers to see systems online but not connect to services running on them. This type of automation might be harder to accomplish in legacy on-premises environments, but it's baked into the cloud by default and relatively easy to configure. I'll discuss cloud capabilities in more detail in *Chapter 13*.

Next, let's put these controls into a Courses of Action Matrix to make it easier to understand where they add value and where we might still have gaps.

Example controls for Reconnaissance I

The following are examples of controls that can be used in the Reconnaissance I phase:

- **Deception** technology: Can help detect the attacker's reconnaissance activities and trick attackers into spending time performing recon on fake assets instead of real ones
- **Web Application Firewall** (**WAF**): Can detect application layer attacks like SQL injection, cross-site scripting, and so on
- **Firewalls**: Can detect network probes and some reconnaissance activity
- **Threat intelligence reconnaissance services**: Can help detect passive reconnaissance activities, giving defenders notice of known vulnerabilities in their defensive posture and imminent attacks
- **Automation**: Use automation when reconnaissance activities are detected to adjust firewall rules and other controls in ways that can deny, disrupt, degrade, or limit their activities

Table 11.7 illustrates how these example control ideas could provide coverage in our modified Courses of Action Matrix for the Reconnaissance I phase of attacks. It only scratches the surface of what's possible, but it illustrates the kinds of actions defenders can take during the first stage of an attack. You'll also notice there are no entries for the Recover action. Because reconnaissance rarely causes damage or compromise, there is nothing in this phase that requires recovery. Note that the controls don't necessarily have to be technologies; they can include people and processes as well.

People, Process, Technology	Detect	Deny	Disrupt	Degrade	Deceive	Limit	Recover
Deception Technology	■				■		
WAF	■	■	■	■			
Firewalls	■	■	■	■			
Threat intelligence reconnaissance services	■						
Automation		■	■	■		■	

Table 11.7 – A summary of control ideas for the Reconnaissance I phase

As noted earlier, Excel isn't the ideal tool for building a Courses of Action Matrix, but it's workable. The downside is that the resulting tables are far too large to print in a book and still be readable. To address this, I'm providing lists of example controls for each section of a sample matrix instead. To keep things simple, I've also left out the organization-specific modifications discussed earlier. This list isn't exhaustive; it's a set of foundational examples you can use as a starting point for developing your own matrix. You'll also notice some controls appear multiple times, reflecting their ability to serve several roles across the matrix.

As noted earlier in this chapter, ATT&CK is designed to complement the Intrusion Kill Chain rather than replace it. Now let's look at how the two frameworks reinforce each other in practice.

Insights from ATT&CK

ATT&CK can be very helpful in identifying specific types of reconnaissance techniques attackers have been using, as well as potential mitigations and detection methods for them. Under the Reconnaissance tactic in the current version of ATT&CK (v18.0), there are 11 techniques (MITRE, April 25, 2025):

- Active scanning
- Gather victim host information
- Gather victim identity information
- Gather victim network information
- Gather victim organization information
- Phishing for information
- Search closed sources
- Search open technical databases
- Search open websites/domains
- Search victim-owned websites
- Search threat vendor data

The first nine of the listed techniques have multiple sub-techniques associated with them. For example, active scanning is a technique that has three sub-techniques associated with it. These include scanning IP blocks, vulnerability scanning, and wordlist scanning (MITRE, April 25, 2025). The only mitigation listed for many of the techniques and sub-techniques is, "this technique cannot be easily mitigated with preventive controls since it is based on behaviors performed outside of the scope of enterprise defenses and controls. Efforts should focus on minimizing the amount and sensitivity of data available to external parties" (MITRE, April 25, 2025). However, two mitigations are listed for the Phishing for Information sub-technique and two for Search Open Websites/Domains (MITRE, April 25, 2025):

- "Use anti-spoofing and email authentication mechanisms to filter messages based on validity checks of the sender domain (using SPF) and integrity of messages (using DKIM). Enabling these mechanisms within an organization (through policies such as DMARC) may enable recipients (intra-org and cross domain) to perform similar message filtering and validation."

- "Users can be trained to identify social engineering techniques and spearphishing attempts."
- "Application developers uploading to public code repositories should be careful to avoid publishing sensitive information such as credentials and API keys."
- "Scan public code repositories for exposed credentials or other sensitive information before making commits. Ensure that any leaked credentials are removed from the commit history, not just the current latest version of the code."

Full details on this ATT&CK tactic are available at: `https://attack.mitre.org/tactics/TA0043/`

Attack phase – Delivery

At this point in an attack, the attackers have already decided which organization to target, done some research to help them execute their attack, and potentially done some active reconnaissance scanning and probed the intended victim's internet presence. Based on this information, they've also gone through some Weaponization stage or process where they procured and/or built weapons that will help them initially compromise their targets and enable their illicit activities afterwards. This Weaponization process typically happens out of the sight of defenders. However, as I mentioned in the Reconnaissance I phase, some threat intelligence vendors' services can sometimes get an insight into these activities.

The attacker's weapons can include people, processes, and technologies. With all this in hand, attackers must deliver these weapons to their targets; this is the objective of the Delivery phase. Attackers have a range of options to deliver their weapons to their targets and the vendors in their supply chains. Some examples of delivery mechanisms include malicious email attachments, malicious URLs in emails, malicious websites that attract the victims' attention, malicious insiders, self-propagating malware such as worms, leaving malicious USB drives on victims' premises, and many others.

The following are some investments that can help in this phase of an attack:

- **Education/training**: Recall the threat intelligence research I provided in *Chapter 5*. It's clear that different types of malware go in and out of vogue with attackers, but their mainstay approach has always been social engineering. Therefore, educating information workers and training them to spot common social engineering attacks can be very helpful in detecting the delivery of the attacker's weapons. IT service desks have been the origin of initial compromises in several high-profile attacks. The challenge is that social engineering training isn't a one-time activity; it's an ongoing investment. When training stops, current employees start to forget these lessons and new employees don't get trained. Note that the training itself needs to be kept up to date in order to continue being effective. The combination of training and simulations, such as phishing simulations, can be an effective way to help information workers spot and report social engineering when they see it.

> **Note**
>
> Some organizations simply don't have a culture that supports social engineering training that includes simulated phishing campaigns and other social engineering attacks against employees. However, organizations that don't do this type of training miss the opportunity to let their employees learn from experience and from failure. A culture where everyone tries to help the CISO is much more powerful than those where the security team is always reacting to uninformed, poor trust decisions that untrained information workers will make every day. Sometimes, senior executives or their direct reports simply don't want to be embarrassed if they make a poor choice in a phishing simulation. These executives need to check their egos and their pride at the door when they come to work, in order to give their organizations the best chance at spotting and stopping attackers' favorite tactics. Besides, they are the very targets for **Business Email Compromise (BEC)**, which has become a popular and profitable endeavor among attackers. They are the last people who should get exceptions or avoid such training.

- **Microsoft Defender for Office 365**: Email is a major vector for social engineering attacks. The volume of email-based attacks is relatively huge in any period of time. Offering information workers email inboxes without effective protection is setting the organization up for failure. Cloud-based services like Microsoft Defender for Office 365 help inoculate all their users by blocking threats that any of their users are exposed to. Services this large can easily identify the IP addresses that botnets and attackers use for spam, phishing, and other email-based attacks, and block them for all their users. There are numerous third-party solutions that can be used as alternatives to Microsoft Defender for Office 365 or complement it, including:
    - Abnormal Security
    - Barracuda
    - Check Point Software Technologies
    - Mimecast

    - Proofpoint
    - Many others

- **Deception technology**: I'm a big fan of deception technology. This technology goes beyond honeypots and honey-nets, offering full-blown environments that attract attackers, signal their presence, and waste their time, driving down their return on investment. Using deception technology to present vulnerable systems to attackers—systems that are critical infrastructure or systems that store or have access to potentially valuable data—can divert their efforts from legitimate systems. Deception technology can also be effective at detecting malicious insiders who are attracted by the bait it offers.
- **Anti-malware and endpoint security suites**: Anti-malware software and other types of endpoint security software can detect and block the attempted delivery of different types of cyber weapons. As I discussed in *Chapter 5*, anti-malware software isn't optional in a world where the number of malicious files easily outnumbers legitimate files. Some of the anti-malware and endpoint security vendors that offer products include:
    - CrowdStrike
    - Carbon Black
    - F-Secure
    - Kaspersky
    - McAfee
    - Microsoft
    - Trellix
    - Trend Micro
    - Many others
- **Web browser protection technologies**: Blocking access to known bad websites and insecure content, as well as scanning content before the browser downloads it, can help prevent exposure to drive-by download attacks, phishing attacks, malware hosting sites, and other malicious web-based attacks.
- **File Integrity Monitoring** (**FIM**): Detecting, blocking, disrupting, and degrading the delivery phase by maintaining the integrity of operating system and application files can help prevent attacks.
- **IDS/IPS**: Detecting, blocking, disrupting, and degrading the delivery phase by using IDS/IPS systems from vendors including Cisco, Juniper Networks, and many others can help prevent attacks.

- **Short-lived environments**: Creating environments or virtual machines that only live for a few hours can disrupt and degrade the attacker's ability to deliver their weapons, especially more complicated multi-stage delivery scenarios. The cloud can make leveraging short-lived environments relatively easy; I'll discuss this concept more in *Chapter 13*.
- **Recover**: I've met with many organizations over the years that rely on blocking mechanisms like anti-malware software to detect and block delivery but will rebuild systems if there is any chance they were compromised. If delivery is successful, even if exploitation and installation are blocked, some organizations want to flatten and rebuild systems or restore data from backups to ensure that everything is in a known good state.

Next, we'll look at what the Courses of Action Matrix for the Delivery phase looks like, based on the capabilities I discussed in this section.

Example controls for Delivery

The following are examples of controls that can be used in the Delivery phase:

- **Education/training**: Information worker education and training to spot social engineering attacks
- **Microsoft Defender for Office 365**: Detection and blocking of delivery of malicious email and files
- **Deception Technology**: Can attract attackers and detect weapon delivery to deception assets
- **Anti-malware suites**: Can detect and block delivery of malicious content from storage media, the network, and web browsers
- **FIM**: Can detect and block attempts to replace system files
- **IDS/IPS**: Can detect and potentially disrupt or stop delivery of malicious content delivered via the network
- **USB drive prohibit policy**: Blocking USB and removable media from mounting on systems can prevent delivery of malware and other malicious content. This can also help block data exfiltration.
- **Web browser protection technologies**: Blocking users from visiting known malicious websites can prevent exposure to phishing, exploits, malware, and other internet-based attacks.
- **Short-lived environments**: Environments or virtual machines that are replaced every few hours can make the Delivery phase harder for attackers

- **IAM technologies**: Enforcing the principle of least privilege and meaningful separation of duties can help limit weapon delivery in an IT environment
- **Backups**: Restore from backups as needed when weapon delivery cannot be stopped
- **Images and containers**: Rebuild infrastructure as needed when weapon delivery cannot be stopped

Note that the same control ideas in the list can apply to Disrupt and Degrade in the Delivery attack phase. *Table 11.8 illustrates* how these example control ideas could provide coverage in our modified Courses of Action Matrix for the Delivery phase of attacks.

People, Process, Technology	Detect	Deny	Disrupt	Degrade	Deceive	Limit	Recover
Education/training	■						
Microsoft Defender for Office 365	■	■					
Deception Technology	■				■		
Anti-malware suites	■	■	■	■			
FIM	■	■	■	■			
IDS/IPS	■	■	■	■			
USB drive prohibit policy		■					
Web browser protection technologies		■					
Short-lived environments			■	■			
IAM technologies					■	■	
Backups							■
Images and containers							■

Table 11.8 – A summary of control ideas for the Delivery phase

The examples I have provided here are simple, but I hope they give security teams some ideas. Layering capabilities into the mix that break the Delivery phase, regardless of the delivery vector, is key.

Insights from ATT&CK

The Initial Access tactic in the ATT&CK framework provides 11 techniques with 11 sub-techniques that attackers have been using to "gain their initial foothold within a network" (MITRE, April 25, 2025):

- Content injection
- Drive-by compromise
- Exploit public-facing application
- External remote services
- Hardware additions
- Phishing:
  - Sub-technique: Spearphishing attachment
  - Sub-technique: Spearphishing link

    - Sub-technique: Spearphishing via service
    - Sub-technique: Spearphishing voice
- Replication through removable media
- Supply chain compromise:
    - Sub-technique: Compromise software dependencies and development tools
    - Sub-technique: Compromise software supply chain
    - Sub-technique: Compromise hardware supply chain
- Trusted relationship
- Valid accounts:
    - Sub-technique: Default accounts
    - Sub-technique: Domain accounts
    - Sub-technique: Local accounts
    - Sub-technique: Cloud accounts
- Wi-fi networks

ATT&CK suggests numerous mitigation and detection capabilities to make these techniques harder or impossible for attackers to rely on. For example, for the exploit public-facing application technique, mitigations include application isolation, web application firewalls, network segmentation, privileged account management, updating software regularly, and vulnerability scanning, among others (MITRE, April 25, 2025).

Full details on this ATT&CK tactic are available at `https://attack.mitre.org/tactics/TA0001/`

Attack phase – Exploitation

After attackers deliver their weapon, it must be activated. In some cases, such as drive-by downloads, Delivery and Exploitation occur almost simultaneously. A user clicks a malicious link, the browser loads the page, and embedded scripts fingerprint the system and attempt to exploit unpatched vulnerabilities. If successful, attackers immediately download additional malware, install tools, and continue their Kill Chain.

In other attacks, especially email-based ones, delivery may occur minutes, days, or even months before a user opens a malicious attachment or link. In these cases, Delivery and Exploitation are clearly separate events (Hutchins, Cloppert, Amin, n.d.). Some attackers want instant results, while others prefer a slow, patient approach.

Defenders must be prepared for attacks across this spectrum. They cannot assume that the Delivery and Exploitation phases will always occur at nearly the same time, but they must be prepared for such scenarios. Breaking the Exploitation phase of the attacker's Kill Chain is critical, because if attackers successfully complete this phase of their attack, they could potentially have a foothold in the environment from which they can further penetrate it. After this phase in an attack, managing defenses can become harder for defenders. Because many attacks are automated, post-Exploitation phase activities can happen very quickly. Breaking the attacker's Kill Chains "left of boom," as the saying goes, is a prudent goal for security teams.

Scanning as frequently as operationally feasible, ideally daily, helps surface unpatched vulnerabilities quickly. Scanning all IT assets every day helps identify where unpatched vulnerabilities and security misconfigurations exist in the environment, thus surfacing the residual risk so that it can be mitigated, transferred, or accepted consciously. This helps security and remediation teams understand whether they are exceeding remediation **service level agreements (SLAs)** and accepting more risk than the organization planned to. When a system with an unpatched Log4j vulnerability magically appears in the environment, scanning everything every day means it is spotted within 24 hours of appearing and can be remediated appropriately. In addition to scanning everything every day, the following list provides you with some example controls that can be used to break attacker activities in the Exploitation phase of an attack. Hopefully, this will give you some ideas on how to make the Exploitation phase much more challenging for attackers.

- **Containerization and supporting security tools**: Using container technologies such as Docker and Kubernetes has many advantages, not least in helping to reduce the attack surface area for systems and applications. Of course, containers are software too and subsequently have vulnerabilities of their own. There are vendors that offer tools to help detect and prevent exploitation in environments that leverage containers. Some examples include:
    - Aqua Security
    - CrowdStrike
    - Dynatrace
    - Palo Alto Networks
    - Wiz
    - Others
- **IAM controls**: Strictly following the principle of least privilege can make vulnerability exploitation harder. Sometimes, the attacker's code runs under the account context of

the user who executed it, instead of under elevated privileges. Limiting user privileges can make it harder for exploitation to succeed or have the intended effect.

- **Short-lived environments**: Environments or virtual machines that only live for a few hours and are replaced with fully patched systems can make it much harder for exploitation to succeed

Example controls for Exploitation

The following are examples of controls that can be used in the Exploitation phase:

- **Anti-malware and endpoint security suites**: Anti-malware can detect and block exploitation of vulnerabilities
- **Containerization and supporting security tools**: Containerization can reduce attack surface area and supporting security tools can help detect and prevent exploitation
- **FIM**: can detect some exploitation attempts
- **Log reviews**: Reviewing various system logs can reveal indicators of exploitation
- **ASLR**: Using operating systems' ASLR can make exploitation inconsistent or impossible
- **DEP**: Using operating systems' DEP can make exploitation inconsistent or impossible
- **IAM controls**: Strictly following the principle of least privilege can prevent exploitation in some scenarios
- **Short-lived environments**: Environments or virtual machines that are replaced every few hours can make exploitation harder
- **Deception technology**: Can attract attackers and deceive them into attacking fake environments
- **Honeypots**: Can attract attackers and expose the exploits they use
- **Backups**: Restore from backup as necessary when exploitation cannot be stopped
- **Images and containers**: Rebuild infrastructure as necessary when exploitation cannot be stopped

A summary illustration of the example controls for the Exploitation phase is provided in *Table 11.9*.

People, Process, Technology	Detect	Deny	Disrupt	Degrade	Deceive	Limit	Recover
Anti-malware and endpoint security suites	■	■	■	■			
Containerization and supporting security tools	■	■	■	■			
FIM	■						
Log reviews	■						
ASLR		■	■	■		■	
DEP		■	■	■		■	
IAM controls		■					
Short-lived environments				■			
Deception technology					■		
Honeypots					■		
Backups							■
Images and containers							■

Table 11.9 – A summary of control ideas for the Exploitation phase

Spending time carefully layering controls to break the Exploitation phase of an attacker's Kill Chain is time well spent. An entire chapter in this book could be devoted to exploitation; I have only scratched the surface here, but I encourage CISOs and security teams to spend more time researching and considering how to implement this particular phase of this framework in their environments.

Insights from ATT&CK

The Execution tactic in the ATT&CK framework "consists of techniques that result in adversary-controlled code running on a local or remote system" (MITRE, April 25, 2025). This tactic has 17 techniques with 29 sub-techniques, and 41 sub-techniques when variants are included (MITRE, April 25, 2025):

- Cloud administration command
- Command and scripting interpreter:
    - Sub-technique: PowerShell
    - Sub-technique: AppleScript
    - Sub-technique: Windows Command Shell
    - Sub-technique: Unix Shell
    - Sub-technique: Visual Basic
    - Sub-technique: Python
    - Sub-technique: JavaScript
    - Sub-technique: Network Device CLI
    - Sub-technique: Cloud API
    - Sub-technique: AutoHotKey & AutoIT
    - Sub-technique: Lua

    - Hypervisor CLI
    - Container CLI/API
- ESXi Administration Command
- Hypervisor CLI
- Container CLI/API
- Container administration command
- Deploy container
- Exploitation for client execution
- Inter-process communication:
    - Sub-technique: Component Object Model
    - Sub-technique: Dynamic Data Exchange
    - Sub-technique: XPC Services
- Native API
- Scheduled task/job:
    - Sub-technique: At
    - Sub-technique: Cron
    - Sub-technique: Scheduled Task
    - Sub-technique: Systemd Timers
    - Sub-technique: Container Orchestration Job
- Serverless execution
- Shared modules
- Software deployment tools
- System services:
    - Sub-technique: launchctl
    - Sub-technique: Service Execution
    - Sub-technique: Systemctl
- User execution:
    - Sub-technique: Malicious link
    - Sub-technique: Malicious file
    - Sub-technique: Malicious image

  - Sub-technique: Malicious copy and paste
  - Sub-technique: Malicious library
- Windows Management Instrumentation

ATT&CK offers 27 mitigations for these techniques and sub-techniques. Some of these mitigations apply to a single technique, and some are used to mitigate multiple techniques. *Table 11.10* contains the top five mitigations that appear most often and therefore potentially have the biggest return on investment (MITRE, April 25, 2025).

ATT&CK Mitigation ID	Mitigation Name	Instances
M1038	Execution Prevention	38
M1017	User Training	38
M1021	Restrict Web-Based Content	7
M1048	Application Isolation and Sandboxing	4
M1050	Exploit Protection	4

Table 11.10 – The top five mitigations for ATT&CK Execution techniques with the number of times each was identified as a mitigation for a technique or sub-technique

Details associated with these Mitigation IDs, along with full details on the ATT&CK Execution tactic, are available at: `https://attack.mitre.org/tactics/TA0002/`

Attack phase – Installation

Simply successfully exploiting a vulnerability isn't the goal for most modern-day attackers, as it was back in 2003. Notoriety has been replaced by much more serious and sinister motivations. Once attackers successfully deliver their weapons and exploitation is successful, they typically seek to expand their scope of control in their victims' environments.

To do this, they have a range of options available to them, such as unpacking malware or remote-control tools from within the weapon itself or downloading them from another system under their control.

More recently, "living off the land" has regained popularity with attackers who seek to use tools, scripts, libraries, and binaries that are native and pre-installed with operating systems and applications. This tactic allows them to further penetrate compromised environments, all while evading defenders who focus on detecting the presence of specific files associated with malware and exploitation. Be aware that "living off the land" tactics can be used in several phases of an attacker's Kill Chain, not just in the Installation phase. Also, note that although it has been modernized somewhat, this tactic is as old as I am and relies on the knowledge of past defenders being lost in time.

When I worked on Microsoft's Incident Response team in 2003, every attacker "lived off the land." We saw a lot of creative tactics being used by attackers in those days. One lesson I learned was that removing all the built-in support tools native to the operating system, such as `ping.exe`, `tracert.exe`, and many others that attackers relied on, forced attackers to bring more of their own tools. Finding any of those tools on systems in the supported IT environment was an indicator of compromise. In the meantime, Desktop and Server Support personnel could download their own tools from a network share for troubleshooting purposes and remove them when they were done. Today, attackers are more sophisticated, using system binaries and libraries that can't really be removed without potentially damaging the operating system. However, leaving attackers with as little land to live off as possible can help defenders in multiple phases of an attack. These tactics have become so common in traditional network intrusions that I have dedicated an entire chapter topic, *Chapter 14, Mitigating "Living Off the Land" tactics.*

Attackers also relied on a lot of tricks to stay hidden on systems. For example, they would run components of their remote-control or surveillance software on a victim's system by naming it the same as a system file that administrators would expect to be running on the system but running it from a slightly different directory. The file and the process looked normal, and most administrators wouldn't notice it was running from the system directory instead of the system32 directory. This tactic was so common that I developed some popular support tools for Windows that could help detect such shenanigans, including Port Reporter, Port Reporter Parser, and Portqry (Microsoft Corporation, n.d.).

Portqry and Port Reporter are still available on the Microsoft Download Center for free download, although I doubt that they will run properly on Windows 11-based systems today, as many Windows APIs have changed since I developed these tools. Of course, I had to have some fun when I developed these tools; my name appears in the Port Reporter log files and when the hidden /dev switch is run with Portqry.

Figure 11.2 – Easter egg fun with Portqry version 2.0

Some of the capabilities that will help break the Installation phase of attacks include the following:

- **Anti-malware and endpoint security suites**: Anti-malware software can detect and block the attempted installation of different types of weapons. Keep anti-malware and endpoint security suites up to date; otherwise, they can increase the attack surface themselves.
- **File Integrity Management (FIM)**: I'm a fan of FIM. When it works properly, it can help detect installation attempts and, ideally, stop them. It can also help meet compliance obligations that many organizations have. FIM capabilities are built into some endpoint protection suites and can be integrated with SIEMs. Some of the FIM vendors/products I've seen in use include:
    - McAfee
    - Qualys
    - Tripwire
    - Many others
- **IAM controls**: Adhering to the principle of least privilege can make it harder for installation to succeed
- **Windows Device Guard**: Locking down Windows 10 systems to prevent unauthorized programs from running (Microsoft Corporation, 2017). This can help prevent exploitation and installation during an attack.
- **Mandatory Access Control, Role-Based Access Control on Linux systems**: These controls help enforce the principle of least privilege and control access to files and processes, which can make installation much harder or impossible

Example controls for Installation

The following are examples of controls that can be used in the Installation phase:

- **Anti-malware and endpoint security suites**: Modern endpoint protection platforms (EDR/XDR) can detect exploitation behaviors.
- **FIM**: Can detect and prevent changes to systems and application files
- **Log reviews**: Reviewing various system logs can reveal indicators of installation
- **Short-lived environments**: Replacing environments or virtual machines every few hours can make installation harder
- **Windows Device Guard**: Making it harder for unauthorized programs to run
- **Mandatory Access Control, Role-Based Access Control (RBAC), Attribute-Based Access Control (ABAC)**: Making it harder for unauthorized programs to run
- **IAM controls**: Strictly following the principle of least privilege makes installation much harder or impossible
- **Deception technology**: Can attract attackers and deceive them into attacking fake environments
- **Backups**: Restore from backups as necessary when installation cannot be stopped
- **Images and containers**: Rebuild infrastructure as necessary when installation cannot be stopped

Note that many of the same control ideas in the list below can apply to Deny, Disrupt, and Degrade in the Installation attack phase. *Table 11.11* illustrates how these example control ideas could provide coverage in our modified Courses of Action Matrix for the Installation phase of attacks.

People, Process, Technology	Detect	Deny	Disrupt	Degrade	Deceive	Limit	Recover
Anti-malware and endpoint security suites	■	■	■	■			
FIM	■	■	■	■		■	
Log reviews	■						
Short-lived environments		■	■	■			
Windows Device Guard		■	■	■		■	
Mandatory Access Control, Role-Based Access Control (RBAC), Attribute-Based Access Control (ABAC)		■	■	■			
IAM controls		■				■	
Deception technology					■		
Backups							■
Images and containers							■

Table 11.11 – A summary of control ideas for the Installation phase

There are lots of other controls that can help detect, deny, disrupt, degrade, deceive, and limit attackers during the Installation phase of their attack. If attackers are successful in this phase, most organizations will not rely on anti-malware or host-based restore points to recover; they will format the system and rebuild it from scratch, using images, backups, or new virtual machines. The cloud makes this much easier, as I discussed earlier, with short-lived environments, autoscaling, and other capabilities.

Insights from ATT&CK

There are three tactics in the ATT&CK framework that could potentially be included in the Installation stage of attackers' Kill Chains, depending on how security teams want to categorize them: Persistence, Privilege Escalation, and Defense Evasion. Let's take a closer look at two of them.

Persistence is a tactic that "consists of techniques that adversaries use to keep access to systems across restarts, changed credentials, and other interruptions that could cut off their access. Techniques used for persistence include any access, action, or configuration changes that let them maintain their foothold on systems, such as replacing or hijacking legitimate code or adding startup code" (MITRE, April 25, 2025). The Privilege Escalation tactic "consists of techniques that adversaries use to gain higher-level permissions on a system or network. Adversaries can often enter and explore a network with unprivileged access but require elevated permissions to follow through on their objectives. Common approaches are to take advantage of system weaknesses, misconfigurations, and vulnerabilities" (MITRE, April 25, 2025). Between the two of these tactics, there are 37 techniques, 198 sub-techniques, and 151 mitigations.

There are 23 techniques and 103 sub-techniques associated with Persistence (MITRE, April 25, 2025). Since this list is quite long, I am not reproducing it here: you can get these details directly from the MITRE ATT&CK website at: `https://attack.mitre.org/tactics/enterprise/`.

Some of the mitigations apply to a single technique, and some are used to mitigate multiple techniques. The most cited mitigations are in *Table 11.12*.

ATT&CK Mitigation ID	Mitigation Name	Instances
M1026	Privileged Account Management	33
M1047	Audit	31
M1018	User Account Management	31

ATT&CK Mitigation ID	Mitigation Name	Instances
M1022	Restrict File and Directory Permissions	23
M1032	Multi-factor Authentication	22

Table 11.12 – The top 5 mitigations for ATT&CK Persistence techniques, with the number of times each was identified as a mitigation for a technique or sub-technique

Details associated with these mitigations, along with full details on the ATT&CK Persistence tactic, are available at: `https://attack.mitre.org/tactics/TA0003/`

The Privilege Escalation tactic has 14 techniques and 95 sub-techniques mitigations associated with it. The techniques and sub-techniques include the following (MITRE, April 25, 2025). Since the list is quite long, I am not reproducing it here. You can get these details directly from the MITRE ATT&CK website at: `https://attack.mitre.org/tactics/enterprise/`.

The most frequently referenced mitigations for Privilege Escalation techniques are shown in *Table 11.13*.

ATT&CK Mitigation ID	Mitigation Name	Instances
M1018	User Account Management	39
M1026	Privileged Account Management	31
M1022	Restrict File and Directory Permissions	27
M1047	Audit	20
M1038	Execution Prevention	19

Table 11.13 – The top 5 mitigations for ATT&CK Privilege Escalation techniques, with the number of times each was identified as a mitigation for a technique or sub-technique

Details associated with its techniques, sub-techniques, and mitigations are available at `https://attack.mitre.org/tactics/TA0004/`.

Attack phase – Command and Control (C2)

If attackers are successful in the Installation phase of their attack, they typically seek to establish communication channels with the compromised systems. These communication channels enable attackers to send commands to the systems they have compromised, allowing them to take a range of actions in the next phases of their attacks. A botnet is a great illustrative example. Once attackers have compromised systems and installed their C2 software on them, they can use those "zombie" systems for a plethora of illicit purposes, including identity theft, intellectual property theft, DDoS attacks, and so on.

There are numerous techniques that attackers can employ for C2 communications. Some are more innovative and interesting than others. Communicating across the network is the most straightforward approach, and attackers have developed many different methods and protocols to facilitate C2 communications. These range from simply listening on a predefined TCP or UDP port number for commands to using more elaborate protocols like RPC and DNS, custom-built protocols, and employing proxies to further obfuscate their communications.

All these techniques can potentially help attackers remotely control compromised environments while evading detection. They want their network traffic to blend in with other legitimate network traffic. Some attackers have developed impressive domain generation algorithms that allow them to dynamically change IP addresses used for C2 communications. Conficker was the first big worm attack to use this method, almost 20 years ago. Some attackers have developed obfuscated and encrypted protocols that make it harder for defenders to detect and stop the attackers' commands.

By detecting, denying, disrupting, degrading, deceiving, and limiting C2 communications, defenders can minimize damage and expense to their organizations and accelerate recovery, all while increasing the expense to attackers. This is an area where vendors that have extensive networking expertise and capabilities, married with threat intelligence, can really add value. Some of the ways that defenders can do this include:

- **IDS/IPS**: These systems can detect and block C2 communications at several places on networks. Many organizations run IDS/IPS in their DMZs and inside their corporate networks. Many vendors offer IDS/IPS systems, including:
    - Check Point
    - Cisco
    - Palo Alto
    - Trellix
    - Fortinet
    - Many others

- Network micro-segmentation: This can provide granular control by enabling organizations to apply policies to individual workloads. This can make it harder for attackers to use compromised systems for C2 communications.
- Log reviews: Analyzing logs, NetFlow data, and DNS queries in an environment can help detect C2 communications. Since there can be too much data for humans to do this manually, many organizations now employ AI and/or **machine learning (ML)** to do this for them.

Example controls for C2

The following are examples of controls that can be used in the C2 phase:

- **IDS/IPS**: Can detect and stop attackers' communications
- **Firewalls and proxy servers**: Can detect and block communication with remote networks
- **Log reviews**: Reviewing various system logs, including DNS queries, can reveal indicators of C2 communications
- **Short-lived environments**: Replacing environments or virtual machines every few hours can make C2 communications harder to achieve and inconsistent
- **IAM controls**: Strictly following the principle of least privilege can make some C2 communications techniques much more difficult
- **Network micro-segmentation**: Enforcing rules that restrict communications can make some C2 communications techniques much more difficult
- **Deception technology**: Attackers communicating with fake environments waste time and energy

Note that the same control ideas in the list below can apply to Disrupt, Degrade, and Limit in the C2 attack phase. *Table 11.14* illustrates how these example control ideas could provide coverage in our modified Courses of Action Matrix for the C2 phase of attacks.

People, Process, Technology	Detect	Deny	Disrupt	Degrade	Deceive	Limit	Recover
IDS/IPS	■	■	■	■		■	
Firewalls and proxy servers	■	■	■	■		■	
Log reviews	■						
Short-lived environments		■	■	■		■	
IAM controls		■	■	■		■	
Network micro-segmentation			■	■		■	
Deception technology					■		

Table 11.14 – A summary of control ideas for the C2 phase

A critical aspect of detecting and preventing C2 communications is threat intelligence. Keep the tips I provided in *Chapter 2, What to Know About Threat Intelligence*, on how to identify credible threat intelligence in mind while evaluating vendors to help in this phase of the framework. Providing old intelligence, commodity intelligence, and false positives is rarely helpful but seems to be a common challenge many vendors have. I've also found that unless C2 communications or other malicious network traffic can be traced back to a specific identity context in the compromised environment, it can be less actionable. Subsequently, C2 detection and prevention systems that are integrated with identity systems seem to have an advantage over those that do not have such integrations. The value of these systems seems to be a function of the time and effort spent fine-tuning them, especially to minimize false positives.

Insights from ATT&CK

The ATT&CK framework provides a great list of techniques attackers use for C2 communications (MITRE, April 25, 2025). This is another good example of how the ATT&CK framework and the Intrusion Kill Chain framework complement each other. The ATT&CK Command and Control tactic "consists of techniques that adversaries may use to communicate with systems under their control within a victim network. Adversaries commonly attempt to mimic normal, expected traffic to avoid detection" (MITRE, April 25, 2025). This tactic has 18 techniques and 27 sub-techniques (MITRE, April 25, 2025):

- Application Layer Protocol:
  - Sub-technique: DNS
  - Sub-technique: File Transfer Protocols
  - Sub-technique: Mail Protocols
  - Sub-technique: Web Protocols
  - Sub-technique: Publish/Subscribe Protocols
- Communication Through Removable Media
- Content Injection
- Data Encoding:
  - Sub-technique: Non-standard Encoding
  - Sub-technique: Standard Encoding
- Data Obfuscation:
  - Sub-technique: Junk Data
  - Sub-technique: Protocol or Service Impersonation
  - Sub-technique: Steganography

- Dynamic Resolution:
    - Sub-technique: DNS Calculation
    - Sub-technique: Domain Generation Algorithms
    - Sub-technique: Fast Flux DNS
- Encrypted Channel:
    - Sub-technique: Asymmetric Cryptography
    - Sub-technique: Symmetric Cryptography
- Fallback Channels
- Hide Infrastructure
- Ingress Tool Transfer
- Multi-Stage Channels
- Non-Application Layer Protocol
- Non-Standard Port
- Protocol Tunneling
- Proxy:
    - Sub-technique: Domain Fronting
    - Sub-technique: External Proxy
    - Sub-technique: Internal Proxy
    - Sub-technique: Multi-hop Proxy
- Remote Access Tools
    - Sub-technique: IDE Tunneling
    - Sub-technique: Remote Desktop Software
    - Sub-technique: Remote Access Hardware
- Traffic Signaling:
    - Sub-technique: Port Knocking
    - Sub-technique: Socket Filters
- Web Service:
    - Sub-technique: Bidirectional Communication
    - Sub-technique: Dead Drop Resolver
    - Sub-technique: One-Way Communication

ATT&CK provides numerous mitigations for these techniques and sub-techniques. Some of these mitigations address a single technique, and some are used to mitigate multiple techniques. The mitigations in *Table 11.15* appear most often and therefore potentially have the biggest return on investment (MITRE, April 25, 2025).

ATT&CK Mitigation ID	Mitigation Name	Instances
M1031	Network Intrusion Prevention	32
M1037	Filter Network Traffic	16
M1021	Restrict Web-Based Content	7
M1042	Disable or Remove Feature or Program	4
M1020	SSL/TLS Inspection	4

Table 11.15 – The top 5 mitigations for ATT&CK C2 techniques, with the number of times each was identified as a mitigation for a technique or sub-technique

Details associated with these Mitigation IDs, along with full details on the ATT&CK Command and Control tactic, are available at: `https://attack.mitre.org/tactics/TA0011/`

Attack phase – Reconnaissance II

One of the things that attackers often command the compromised systems that they control to do is help them map out their victim's network. Attackers often want to explore networks to look for valuable data, valuable intellectual property, and high-value assets that they can steal, damage, or demand a ransom for their return. They also look for information, accounts, infrastructure, and anything else that might help them gain access to the aforementioned list of valuables. Again, they are trying to blend their reconnaissance activities into the common, legitimate network traffic, authentication, and authorization processes that occur on their victims' networks. This helps them evade detection and stay persistent on the network for longer periods.

Detecting reconnaissance activities can help defenders discover compromised systems in their environment. Additionally, making this type of reconnaissance difficult or impossible for attackers to perform might help limit the damage and expense associated with a compromise. This can be easier said than done, especially in legacy environments with lots of home-grown applications and older applications whose behavior can be surprising and unpredictable in many cases. Many SOC analysts have spotted a sequential port scan on their network, only to find some home-grown application using the noisiest possible way to communicate on the network. This behavior can usually be traced back to a developer trying to solve a problem while making their life easier. The world is full of applications like this, which make detecting true anomalies more work.

This is another phase where attackers routinely "live off the land." Whether they are running scripts to perform reconnaissance or doing it manually, when defenders leave most of the tools attackers need installed by default on systems, it makes the attacker's job easier. Removing or restricting the use of these common tools everywhere possible inconveniences attackers and will make it easier to detect when these tools, or others like them, are used in the environment. However, it's unlikely that security teams will be able to remove all the binaries and libraries that attackers can use from their environments.

Some of the other capabilities included in the control lists are the following:

- **Deception technology**: Whether the party performing reconnaissance inside the network is an attacker or an insider, deception technology can be helpful in detecting their presence. When someone starts poking at assets that no one in the organization has any legitimate business touching, this can be a red flag. Additionally, if attackers take the bait offered by deception technologies, like stealing credentials, for example, and use those credentials somewhere else in the environment, that's a very good indication of reconnaissance activities.
- **User Behavior Analytics (UBA)**: UBA, or Entity Behavioral Analytics, can help identify when users and other entities access resources out of the norm. This can indicate an insider threat or stolen credentials being used by attackers and uncover reconnaissance activities. There are many vendors that provide products that do this type of detection, including:
    - Exabeam
    - IBM
    - Microsoft
    - Secronix
    - Varonis
    - Others
- **SAW/PAW**: **Secure administrator workstations** (**SAWs**) or **privileged access workstations** (**PAWs**) make it much harder for attackers to steal and use credentials for administrator accounts and other accounts with elevated privileges. Monitored and audited SAWs/PAWs help detect unusual use of privileged credentials.

- **Active Directory hardening**: Makes it harder for attackers to access or steal credentials.
- **Encryption everywhere**: Protecting data while it travels across the network and everywhere it rests can be a powerful control for preventing effective reconnaissance.

Example controls for Reconnaissance II

The following are examples of controls that can be used in the Reconnaissance II phase:

- **Deception technology**: Deception technologies can help detect the attacker's reconnaissance activities and trick attackers into spending time performing reconnaissance on fake environments instead of real ones.
- **Log reviews**: Reviewing various system logs, including DNS queries, can reveal indicators of compromise
- **UBA**: Detecting anomalous behavior
- **SAW/PAW**: Monitored and audited SAWs/PAWs help detect unusual use of privileged credentials. This can make it much harder for attackers to steal and use credentials for administrator accounts and other accounts with elevated privileges.
- **Network micro-segmentation**: Enforcing rules that restrict network traffic can make reconnaissance more difficult.
- **IAM controls**: Strictly following the principle of least privilege can make it harder to perform reconnaissance.
- **Encryption everywhere**: Encrypting data in transit and at rest can protect data from attackers
- **Active Directory hardening**: This makes it harder for attackers to access and steal credentials

Note that the same control ideas in the list below can apply to Deny, Disrupt, Degrade, and Limit in the Reconnaissance II attack phase. *Table 11.16* illustrates how these example control ideas could provide coverage in our modified Courses of Action Matrix for the Reconnaissance II phase of attacks.

People, Process, Technology	Detect	Deny	Disrupt	Degrade	Deceive	Limit	Recover
Deception technology							
Log reviews							
UBA							
SAW/PAW							
Network micro-segmentation							
IAM controls							
Encryption everywhere							
Active Directory hardening							

Table 11.16 – A summary of control ideas for the Reconnaissance II phase

There are many more ways to detect and make reconnaissance harder for attackers; however, it seems that only after a successful compromise, during the response, are the tell-tale signs of reconnaissance spotted. Investments in this phase of the framework can have big returns for security teams.

Insights from ATT&CK

This is another good example of anintegrationpointbetweentheATT&CKframeworkandtheIntrusionKillChainframework.ATT&CKprovid it doesn't assume attacks are sequential discrete steps – attackers can choose to do many things and iterate between tactics as needed. Let's take a closer look at the Discovery tactic.

Discovery has 34 techniques and 15 sub-techniques (MITRE, April 25, 2025):

- Account Discovery:
  - Sub-technique: Cloud Account
  - Sub-technique: Domain Account
  - Sub-technique: Email Account
  - Sub-technique: Local Account
- Application Window Discovery
- Browser Bookmark Discovery
- Cloud Infrastructure Discovery
- Cloud Service Dashboard
- Cloud Service Discovery
- Cloud Storage Object Discovery
- Container and Resource Discovery
- Debugger Evasion
- Domain Trust Discovery

- File and Directory Discovery
- Group Policy Discovery
- Local Storage Discovery
- Log Enumeration
- Network Service Discovery
- Network Share Discovery
- Network Sniffing
- Password Policy Discovery
- Peripheral Device Discovery
- Permission Groups Discovery:
    - Sub-technique: Cloud Groups
    - Sub-technique: Domain Groups
    - Sub-technique: Local Groups
- Process Discovery
- Query Registry
- Remote System Discovery
- Software Discovery:
    - Sub-technique: Security Software Discovery
    - Sub-technique: Backup Software Discovery
- System Information Discovery
- System Location Discovery:
    - Sub-technique: System Language Discovery
- System Network Configuration Discovery:
    - Sub-technique: Internet Connection Discovery
    - Sub-technique: Wi-Fi Discovery
- System Network Connections Discovery
- System Owner/User Discovery
- System Service Discovery
- System Time Discovery

- Virtual Machine Discovery
- Virtualization/Sandbox Evasion:
  - Sub-technique: System Checks
  - Sub-technique: User Activity Based Checks
  - Sub-technique: Time Based Checks

For these 49 techniques and sub-techniques, ATT&CK offers numerous mitigations. Some are unique, and some are used multiple times across techniques and sub-techniques. The most frequently cited mitigations include the mitigations listed in *Table 11.17*.

ATT&CK Mitigation ID	Mitigation Name	Instances
M1018	User Account Management	8
M1028	Operating System Configuration	4
M1030	Network Segmentation	4
M1047	Audit	2

Table 11.17 – The top mitigations for ATT&CK Discovery techniques, with the number of times each was identified as a mitigation for a technique or sub-technique

Information on all the techniques, sub-techniques, and mitigations is available at `https://attack.mitre.org/tactics/TA0007/`.

Attack phase – Actions on Objectives

Remember that there are many possible motivations for attacks, including notoriety, profit, military espionage, economic espionage, revenge, anarchy, and many others. Once attackers make it to this phase in their attack, their objectives are potentially within their reach. In this phase, they might lock administrators out of systems, exfiltrate data, compromise the integrity of data, encrypt data, damage infrastructure, make systems unbootable, or simply stay persistent to watch their victims and collect data. What attackers do in the Actions on Objectives stage of their attacks depends on their motivations.

In some cases, this is the defender's last chance to detect and stop attackers before recovery becomes more expensive and potentially aspirational. However, the fact that attackers made it to this phase in their Kill Chain does not automatically mean they have access to all resources and are in full control of the IT environment; their objective might be much more tightly scoped, or the security controls that have been deployed to impede their progress might have had the intended effect. This could mean that many of the controls used to break other phases of the Kill Chain can still be helpful in this phase. If attackers were able to defeat or bypass controls in earlier phases of their attack, this doesn't mean they can do so everywhere in the IT environment at any time. Detecting and denying attackers is ideal, but disrupting, degrading, deceiving, and limiting their attacks is highly preferable to recovering from them.

Some of the controls to consider when mitigating this phase of an attack include:

- **Data backups**: If attackers choose to destroy data by damaging storage media or firmware, wiping storage media, encrypting data, or otherwise tampering with the integrity of data, backups can be very helpful. Offline, immutable backups are highly recommended as attackers will happily encrypt online backups if they can with their ransomware or cryptoware
- **SAW/PAW**: SAW or PAW can make it much harder for attackers to use privileged accounts to lock administrators out of the systems they manage
- **Encryption everywhere**: Remember that encryption not only provides confidentiality but can also safeguard the integrity of data; encryption can help detect that data has been altered.
- **IAM controls**: Identity is central to security. If attackers already own the Active Directory in the environment, then it's going to be very hard or impossible to expel them. However, if they only have access to some accounts, IAM controls can still help limit the scope of their attack.

Example controls for Actions on Objectives

The following are examples of controls that can be used in the Actions on Objectives phase:

- **Anti-malware suites**: Anti-malware detects and blocks malware.
- **FIM**: Can detect and prevent changes to systems and application files
- **Log reviews**: Reviewing various system logs can reveal indicators of compromise
- **User Behavior Analytics**: Can detect anomalous behavior
- **Deception technology**: Can detect the attacker's actions on assets and deceive them into attacking fake environments
- **SAW/PAW**: Monitored and audited SAWs/PAWs help detect unusual use of privileged credentials
- **Short-lived environments**: Environments or virtual machines that are replaced every few hours help make it harder for attackers to persist in compromised IT environments.
- **Windows Device Guard**: Can make it harder for unauthorized programs to run

- **Mandatory Access Control, Role-Based Access Control (RBAC), Attribute-Based Access Control (ABAC)**: Can make it harder for unauthorized programs to run
- **IAM controls**: Strictly following the principle of least privilege can make it harder for attackers to achieve their objectives
- **Encryption everywhere**: Encrypting data in transit and at rest can protect data from attackers
- **Backups**: Restore from backups as necessary
- **Images and containers**: Rebuild infrastructure as necessary
- **Disaster recovery processes and technologies**: Recover IT systems efficiently to minimize downtime and data loss

Note that the same control ideas in *Table 11.18* can apply to Deny, Disrupt, Degrade, and very similar controls for Limit in the Actions on Objectives attack phase.

People, Process, Technology	Detect	Deny	Disrupt	Degrade	Deceive	Limit	Recover
Anti-malware suites	■	■	■	■		■	
FIM	■	■	■	■		■	
Log reviews	■						
User Behavior Analytics	■						
Deception technology	■				■		
SAW/PAW	■						
Short-lived environments		■	■	■			
Windows Device Guard		■	■	■		■	
Mandatory Access Control, Role-Based Access Control (RBAC), Attribute-Based Access Control (ABAC)		■	■	■		■	
IAM controls		■	■	■		■	
Encryption everywhere		■	■	■			
Backups							■
Images and containers							■
Disaster recovery processes and technologies							■

Table 11.18 – A summary of control ideas for the Actions on Objectives phase

Insights from ATT&CK

Actions on Objectives is another phase where there's great potential integration between the Intrusion Kill Chain model and the ATT&CK framework. There are at least two ATT&CK tactics that can be used by attackers in the Actions on Objectives stage of their attacks: Exfiltration and Impact (MITRE, n.d.). Let's take a quick look at both of these tactics.

The ATT&CK Exfiltration tactic "consists of techniques that adversaries may use to steal data from your network. Once they've collected data, adversaries often package it to avoid detection while removing it. This can include compression and encryption. Techniques for getting data out of a target network typically include transferring it over their command and control channel or an alternate channel and may also include putting size limits on the transmission." (MITRE, April 25, 2025). This tactic has 9 techniques and 10 sub-techniques (MITRE, April 25, 2025):

- Automated Exfiltration:
    - Sub-technique: Traffic Duplication
- Data Transfer Size Limits
- Exfiltration Over Alternative Protocol:
    - Sub-technique: Exfiltration Over Asymmetric Encrypted Non-C2 Protocol
    - Sub-technique: Exfiltration Over Symmetric Encrypted Non-C2 Protocol
    - Sub-technique: Exfiltration Over Unencrypted Non-C2 Protocol
- Exfiltration Over C2 Channel
- Exfiltration Over Other Network Medium:
    - Sub-technique: Exfiltration Over Bluetooth
- Exfiltration Over Physical Medium:
    - Sub-technique: Exfiltration over USB
- Exfiltration Over Web Service:
    - Sub-technique: Exfiltration to Cloud Storage
    - Sub-technique: Exfiltration to Code Repository
    - Sub-technique: Exfiltration to Text Storage Sites
    - Sub-technique: Exfiltration over Webhook
- Scheduled Transfer
- Transfer Data to Cloud Account

For these 19 techniques and sub-techniques, ATT&CK offers several mitigations. Some are unique, and some are used multiple times across techniques and sub-techniques. The most frequently cited mitigations are included in *Table 11.19*.

ATT&CK Mitigation ID	**Mitigation Name**	**Instances**
M1057	Data Loss Prevention	10
M1031	Network Intrusion Prevention	7
M1037	Filter Network Traffic	5

ATT&CK Mitigation ID	Mitigation Name	Instances
M1042	Disable or Remove Feature or Program	4
M1030	Network Segmentation	4
M1021	Restrict Web-Based Content	4

Table 11.19 – The top mitigations for ATT&CK Exfiltration techniques, with the number of times each was identified as a mitigation for a technique or sub-technique

Information on all the techniques, sub-techniques, and mitigations for the Exfiltration tactic is available at `https://attack.mitre.org/tactics/TA0010/`.

The ATT&CK Impact tactic "consists of techniques that adversaries use to disrupt availability or compromise integrity by manipulating business and operational processes. Techniques used for impact can include destroying or tampering with data. In some cases, business processes can look fine but may have been altered to benefit the adversaries' goals. These techniques might be used by adversaries to follow through on their end goal or to provide cover for a confidentiality breach." (MITRE, April 25, 2025). This tactic has a total of 15 techniques and 18 sub-techniques. These include (MITRE, April 25, 2025):

- Account Access Removal
- Data Destruction
  - Sub-technique: Lifecycle-Triggered Deletion
- Data Encrypted for Impact
- Data Manipulation:
  - Sub-technique: Runtime Data Manipulation
  - Sub-technique: Stored Data Manipulation
  - Sub-technique: Transmitted Data Manipulation
- Defacement:
  - Sub-technique: External Defacement
  - Sub-technique: Internal Defacement
- Disk Wipe:
  - Sub-technique: Disk Content Wipe
  - Sub-technique: Disk Structure Wipe

- Email Bombing
- Endpoint Denial of Service:
    - Sub-technique: Application Exhaustion Flood
    - Sub-technique: Application or System Exploitation
    - Sub-technique: OS Exhaustion Flood
    - Sub-technique: Service Exhaustion Flood
- Financial Theft
- Firmware Corruption
- Inhibit System Recovery
- Network Denial of Service:
    - Sub-technique: Direct Network Flood
    - Sub-technique: Reflection Amplification
- Resource Hijacking
    - Sub-technique: Compute Hijacking
    - Sub-technique: Bandwidth Hijacking
    - Sub-technique: SMS Pumping
    - Sub-technique: Cloud Service Hijacking
- Service Stop
- System Shutdown/Reboot

For these 33 techniques and sub-techniques, ATT&CK offers several mitigations. Some of these mitigations address a single technique, and some are used to mitigate multiple techniques. The most frequently cited mitigations are shown in *Table 11.20*.

ATT&CK Mitigation ID	Mitigation Name	Instances
M1053	Data Backup	10
M1037	Filter Network Traffic	8
M1018	User Account Management	5
M1022	Restrict File and Directory Permissions	4
M1041	Encrypt Sensitive Information	3

ATT&CK Mitigation ID	Mitigation Name	Instances
M1030	Network Segmentation	3

Table 11.20 – The top mitigations for ATT&CK Impact techniques, with the number of times each was identified as a mitigation for a technique or sub-technique

Information on all the techniques, sub-techniques, and mitigations for the Impact tactic is available at `https://attack.mitre.org/tactics/TA0040/`.

At this point, we've covered all the phases in our modified Intrusion Kill Chain. We've discussed numerous ideas for effective controls for each phase and complemented these ideas with insights from the ATT&CK framework. Note that we didn't include every tactic that is included in the ATT&CKMatrixforEnterpriseinourKillChaindesign there are many more tactics, techniques, and mitigations to inform your Intrusion Kill Chain control set design.

You can get a complete, up-to-date list of tactics at `https://attack.mitre.org/tactics/enterprise/`.

The complete list of techniques and sub-techniques is available at `https://attack.mitre.org/techniques/enterprise/`.

The complete list of all the mitigations is available at `https://attack.mitre.org/mitigations/enterprise/`.

That's one way to implement the Intrusion Kill Chain framework. Obviously, there are other possible interpretations and approaches to implementing this model. I've seen some very well-thought-out and sophisticated approaches to this framework at conferences and documented on the internet, but the best way is the one that addresses the specific HVAs and risks that your organization is concerned about.

> **Tip**
>
> Remember that best practices are based on the threats and assets that someone else has in mind, not necessarily your own.

This might be obvious, but the Intrusion Kill Chain framework can help CISOs and security teams take a structured approach to managing traditional network intrusions. Arguably, traditional network intrusions are the most serious threats for most organizations because of their potential impact, but there are other threats that CISOs need to address. DDoS attacks, for example, typically don't involve intrusion attempts or require a Kill Chain framework to address.

Additionally, the Intrusion Kill Chain approach has become a little dated in a world where the cloud has disrupted and improved upon traditional approaches to IT and cybersecurity. Although this approach still has the potential to be highly effective in on-premises and hybrid environments, a framework designed to break Intrusion Kill Chains and stop so-called **Advanced Persistent Threat (APT)** actors isn't as relevant in the cloud. Used effectively, CI/CD pipelines, short-lived environments, autoscaling, and other capabilities the cloud offers significantly reduce opportunities for APT actors or other attackers to get a foothold in order to move laterally and remain persistent. Simply put, the cloud gives CISOs the opportunity to change the playing field dramatically. I'll discuss the cybersecurity benefits the cloud offers in more detail in *Chapter 13*.

Given that the industry will continue to transition from the old-fashioned on-premises IT world to the cloud for many years, the Intrusion Kill Chain framework still seems well poised to help organizations as a transitional Attack-Centric cybersecurity strategy. It can help organizations on-premises and in the cloud as they modernize their workforces to take advantage of DevOps, as well as Zero Trust methods, as these come to fruition.

It can also help CISOs who want to leverage a single cybersecurity strategy across their entire IT estate, including legacy on-premises and cloud environments. I have provided a head start on developing a Kill Chain approach for on-premises environments in this chapter. Additionally, I co-authored a whitepaper when I worked at AWS that will give security teams a big head start on implementing an Intrusion Kill Chain in AWS. This paper is titled "Classic intrusion analysis frameworks for AWS environments" (Rains, et al. 2022), and at the time of writing, it is still available for public download on the AWS website. This paper contains 70 pages of AWS services and security controls mapped to the Intrusion Kill Chain framework. This will potentially save security teams weeks or months of work trying to do this mapping themselves.

Finally, employing this strategy is potentially far superior to not having a cybersecurity strategy or using many of the other strategies I examined in *Chapter 10*. If your organization doesn't have a cybersecurity strategy or it does but no one can articulate it, you could likely do far worse than to embrace the Intrusion Kill Chain strategy. To do so, in many cases, you'll have to get far more detailed and specific than the high-level example that I have provided here. However, I think I have provided you with a head start on the best scoring cybersecurity strategy that we have examined. This is not a bad thing to have!

Summary

CISOs and security teams have numerous cybersecurity strategies, models, frameworks, and standards to choose from when developing their approach to protecting, detecting, and responding to modern-day threats. One attack-centric strategy that we examined in *Chapter 10*, the Intrusion Kill Chain, deserves serious consideration as it garnered the highest CFSS estimated total score. It earned nearly a perfect score with 95 points out of a possible 100. This chapter sought to provide you with an example of one way this model can be implemented.

The Intrusion Kill Chain model was pioneered by Lockheed Martin; the Kill Chain phases provided in Lockheed Martin's paper on this topic include Reconnaissance, Weaponization, Delivery, Exploitation, Installation, Command and Control, and Actions on Objectives (Hutchins, Cloppert, Amin, n.d.). One consideration before implementing this framework is whether defenders should use the original Intrusion Kill Chain framework or update it.

There are several ways this framework can be modernized. It can be modified or reorganized around the Cybersecurity Usual Suspects to ensure that they are mitigated and to make it easier to identify gaps in an organization's security posture. Split the Reconnaissance phase into two phases instead of one: the one attackers can use before initial compromise and the one after compromise. The Weaponization phase can be dropped, as CISOs typically do not have very effective controls for protection and detection prior to the Delivery phase. The Destroy phase can be replaced with more pragmatic phases such as Limit and Recover. Adding a maturity index to capture and communicate how much or how well each cybersecurity capability mitigates threats can help identify areas of under-investment and potential gaps in defenses. Including an estimate of how pervasively a control has been deployed can also be helpful. Adding a point of contact for each mitigation to make it clear who is consuming the data generated by cybersecurity capabilities will help ensure there are no unmanaged mitigations in the environment. Tracking cybersecurity license renewals and support deadlines will help prevent lapses in capabilities.

The Intrusion Kill Chain approach can be complemented with the ATT&CK framework, published and maintained by MITRE. ATT&CK has many uses. For example, the tactics, techniques, and sub-techniques provided by ATT&CK can be leveraged to inform the control set design and testing for your Kill Chain.

Rationalizing mitigations can help identify gaps and areas of underinvestment and over-investment. Where to start with an implementation can be informed by many factors, including budget, resources, gaps, and areas of under-investment and over-investment. Implementing controls that help break attackers' Kill Chains in multiple places might offer security teams higher ROIs.

That concludes my example of how a cybersecurity strategy can be implemented. I hope the tips and tricks I have provided are helpful to you. In the next chapter, I'll examine how CISOs and security teams can measure whether the implementation of their strategy is effective. This can be an important, yet elusive goal for security teams.

References

- Hutchins, E.M., Cloppert, M.J., Amin, R.M. Ph.D. (n.d.). *Intelligence-Driven Computer Network Defense Informed by Analysis of Adversary Campaigns and Intrusion Kill Chains.* Retrieved from Lockheed Martin: `https://lockheedmartin.com/content/dam/lockheed-martin/rms/documents/cyber/LM-White-Paper-Intel-Driven-Defense.pdf`
- Sanghvi, H. P., Dahiya, M. S. (2013). *Cyber Reconnaissance: An Alarm before Cyber Attack.* International Journal of Computer Applications (0975–8887), Volume 63, No. 6, pages 2-3. Retrieved from `https://research.ijcaonline.org/volume63/number6/pxc3885202.pdf`
- Matt Miller, M. (December 8, 2010). *On the effectiveness of DEP and ASLR.* Retrieved from Microsoft Security Response Center: `https://msrc-blog.microsoft.com/2010/12/08/on-the-effectiveness-of-dep-and-aslr/`
- Microsoft Corporation. (n.d.). *PortQry Command Line Port Scanner Version 2.0.* Retrieved from Microsoft Download Center: `https://www.microsoft.com/en-us/download/details.aspx?id=17148&msockid=31172e3ff77a656817c33ec5f6c964c4`
- MITRE. (n.d.). *MITRE ATT&CK®.* Retrieved from MITRE ATT&CK®: `https://attack.mitre.org/`
- MITRE. (n.d.). *MITRE ATT&CK® FAQ.* Retrieved from MITRE ATT&CK®: `https://attack.mitre.org/resources/faq/`
- MITRE. (April 25, 2025). *Reconnaissance.* Retrieved from MITRE ATT&CK®: `https://attack.mitre.org/tactics/TA0043/`
- MITRE. (April 25, 2025). *Initial Access.* Retrieved from MITRE ATT&CK®: `https://attack.mitre.org/tactics/TA0001/`
- MITRE. (April 25, 2025). *Execution.* Retrieved from MITRE ATT&CK®: `https://attack.mitre.org/tactics/TA0002/`
- MITRE. (April 25, 2025). *Persistence.* Retrieved from MITRE ATT&CK®: `https://attack.mitre.org/tactics/TA0003/`

- MITRE. (April 25, 2025). *Privilege Escalation*. Retrieved from MITRE ATT&CK®: `https://attack.mitre.org/tactics/TA0004/`
- MITRE. (April 25, 2025). *Command and Control*. Retrieved from MITRE ATT&CK®: `https://attack.mitre.org/tactics/TA0011/`
- MITRE. (April 25, 2025). *Discovery*. Retrieved from MITRE ATT&CK®: `https://attack.mitre.org/tactics/TA0007/`
- MITRE. (April 25, 2025). *Exfiltration*. Retrieved from MITRE ATT&CK®: `https://attack.mitre.org/tactics/TA0010/`
- MITRE. (April 25, 2025). *Impact*. Retrieved from MITRE ATT&CK®: `https://attack.mitre.org/tactics/TA0040/`
- Rains, Walker, Ryland, Scott-Cowley, Evans, Lyle, Samuel, Hodges, Alexander, Gera, and Vyas. (2022). *Classic Intrusion Analysis Frameworks for AWS Environments: Application and Enhancement*. Retrieved from `https://docs.aws.amazon.com/whitepapers/latest/classic-intrusion-analysis-frameworks-for-aws-environments/classic-intrusion-analysis-frameworks-for-aws-environments.html`

12

Measuring Performance and Effectiveness

The challenge with operational cybersecurity roles is that the job never ends, and when it seems to get easier, that's only temporary. Developing a cybersecurity strategy and deploying people, processes, and technologies to support that strategy is just the beginning. The work of cybersecurity teams includes constantly identifying assets and opportunities to improve, protecting assets and people, detecting potential adverse events, responding to cybersecurity incidents, and recovering from them when necessary. There's also all the work that goes into **governance, risk, and compliance (GRC)** functions. Given organizations and attackers are constantly evolving, the status quo isn't good enough for very long. The wolf is always at the door.

Given cybersecurity is a journey, not a destination, how do we know if the cybersecurity strategy we've employed is working? How do we know if the CISO and the security team are being effective? This chapter will focus on measuring the effectiveness of cybersecurity strategies.

In this chapter, we'll cover the following topics:

- The importance of cybersecurity metrics
- Using vulnerability management data
- Measuring performance and efficacy of cybersecurity strategies
- Examining an attack-centric cybersecurity strategy as an example
- Using intrusion reconstruction results
- Leveraging MITRE ATT&CK®

Let's begin this chapter with a question: ***Why do CISOs need to measure anything?***

The importance of cybersecurity metrics

There are many reasons why cybersecurity teams need to measure things. Compliance with regulatory standards, industry standards, and their own internal security standards is usually chief among them.

There are hundreds of metrics related to governance, risk, and compliance that organizations can choose to measure themselves against. Anyone who has studied for the **Certified Information Systems Security Professional (CISSP)** certification knows that there are eight security domains, including Security and Risk Management, Asset Security, Security Architecture and Engineering, Communication and Network Security, **Identity and Access Management (IAM),** Security Assessment and Testing, Security Operations, and Software Development Security (ISC2, April 15, 2024). The performance and efficacy of the people, processes, and technologies in each of these domains can be measured in many ways. In fact, the number of metrics and the ways they can be measured are dizzying. However, metrics must be context-specific and continuously adapted to be meaningful. To help security teams with this task, the National Institute of Standards and Technology published NIST SP 800-55 Vol. 2: Measurement Guide for Information Security: Volume 2 — Developing an Information Security Measurement Program (NIST, 2024). This document is well worth reading for teams that want to develop a formal measurement program.

Besides measuring things for compliance reasons, cybersecurity teams also try to find meaningful metrics to help prove they are adding value to the businesses they support. This can be challenging and a little unfair for CISOs. **Key performance indicators (KPIs)** and **objectives and key results (OKRs)** typically measure performance against targets or objectives. For security teams, it's failing to achieve an objective that tends to do the damage. While salespeople are tasked with achieving sales targets, the absence of severe cybersecurity incidents and the disruption they do to the business is the ultimate measure of success. However, it can be tough to find meaningful data that helps prove that the investments and efforts of the CISO and cybersecurity team are the reasons why the organization's IT infrastructure hasn't been compromised or had a data breach. Was it the cybersecurity team's work that prevented attackers from being successful? Or did the organization simply "fly under the radar" of attackers, as I've heard so many non-security executives suggest? This is where that submarine analogy that I introduced in the preface can be helpful. There is no flying under the radar on the internet where cybersecurity is concerned; there's only constant pressure from all directions. Besides, hope is not a strategy; it's the abdication of responsibility.

Nevertheless, CISOs need to be able to prove to their peers, the businesses or citizens they support, and shareholders that the results they've produced aren't a byproduct of luck or the fulfillment of hope. They need to show that their results are the product of successfully executing their cybersecurity strategy.

I've seen many CISOs try to do this through opinion and anecdotal evidence. But without data to support opinions and anecdotes, these CISOs tend to have a more difficult time defending the success of their strategy and cybersecurity program. It's only a matter of time before an auditor or consultant offers a different opinion that challenges the CISO's description of the current state of affairs.

Data is key to measuring the performance and efficacy of a cybersecurity strategy. Data helps CISOs manage their cybersecurity programs and investments and helps them prove that their cybersecurity program has been effective and constantly improving. In this chapter, I'll provide suggestions to CISOs and security teams on how they can measure the effectiveness of their cybersecurity strategy. To do this, I'll use the best scoring strategy I examined in *Chapter 10, Cybersecurity Strategies*, and *Chapter 11, Cybersecurity Strategy Implementation*, the Attack-Centric Strategy, as an example. I'll also draw on concepts and insights that I provided in the preceding chapters of this book. I will not cover measuring things for compliance or other purposes here, as there are many books, papers, and standards that already do this. Let's start by looking at the potential value of vulnerability management data.

Using vulnerability management data

I discussed vulnerability management in depth in *Chapter 3, Industry Vulnerability Disclosure Trends* and *Chapter 4, Product Vulnerability Disclosure Trends*. It is a cornerstone of a successful cybersecurity program and will be for the foreseeable future. It's also probably the most quantitative data CISOs have in their cybersecurity programs. I provided some advice on vulnerability management reporting in *Chapter 4*. But let's dig into this topic in a little more detail, given its importance in measuring the performance and effectiveness of vulnerability management programs.

For organizations that are just bootstrapping a cybersecurity program, or for CISOs who have assumed leadership of a program that has been struggling to gain traction in their organization, vulnerability management data can be a powerful tool. Even for well-established cybersecurity programs, vulnerability management data can help illustrate how the security team has been effectively managing risk for their organization and improving over time. Despite this, surprisingly, I've met some CISOs of large, well-established enterprises who do not aggregate, analyze, or otherwise use data from their vulnerability management programs. This surprises me when I come across it, because this data represents one of the most straightforward and easy ways available for CISOs to communicate the effectiveness of their cybersecurity programs.

A challenge for CISOs and IT executives is developing a performance overview based on data that aligns with the way business executives measure and communicate performance. The impact of such data can also be entirely different for CISOs.

For example, when a product production site is behind target, additional resources and action plans will kick in to help compensate. But for CISOs, additional resources are rarely the result of being behind target; for the most part, security programs are supposed to be like a utility—there when you need it, but out of sight until then.

As I discussed at length in earlier chapters, unpatched vulnerabilities and security misconfigurations are two of the five Cybersecurity Usual Suspects that are managed via a vulnerability management program. Subsequently, a well-run vulnerability management program is not optional. As I discussed in *Chapter 9, Ingredients for a Successful Cybersecurity Strategy*, asset inventories that are complete and up to date are critical to the success of vulnerability management programs and cybersecurity programs overall. After all, it's difficult for security teams to manage assets that they do not know exist.

Vulnerability management teams should scan everything in their inventories every single day for vulnerabilities and misconfigurations. This can help minimize the amount of time that unmitigated critical and high-severity vulnerabilities and misconfigurations are present and exploitable in their environments. Remember that vulnerabilities and misconfigurations can be introduced into IT environments in multiple ways: newly disclosed vulnerabilities (on average, 110 per day in 2024), software and systems built from old images or restored from backup, legacy software and systems that go out of support, and orphaned assets that become unmanaged over time, among other ways.

Every day that a vulnerability management team scans all their assets, they will have a new snapshot of the current state of the environment that they can stitch together with all the previous days' snapshots. Over time, this data can be used in multiple ways by the cybersecurity team. Let me give you some examples of how this data can be used.

Assets under management versus total assets

The number of assets under the management of a vulnerability management team versus the total number of assets that an organization owns and operates can be an interesting data point for some organizations. The difference between these two numbers potentially represents risk, especially if there are assets that are not actively managed for vulnerabilities and misconfigurations by anyone. I've seen big differences between these two numbers in organizations where IT has been chronically understaffed for long periods, and there isn't enough automation, documentation, or tribal knowledge to inform accurate asset inventories. Consequently, there can be large swaths of IT assets that are not inventoried and are not actively managed as part of a vulnerability management program. An example of this can be seen in *Figure 12.1*.

I've also seen big differences in these numbers when CISOs do not have good relationships with IT leadership; in cases like this, inaccurate IT inventories seem common and represent a real risk to an organization. In some of the cases I've seen, IT knows where all or most of the assets are but won't proactively work with the CISO to ensure they are all inventoried, enrolled in the vulnerability management program, and patched. As I wrote in *Chapter 9*, CISOs must work to have good relationships with their stakeholder communities, especially with their IT organizations. CIOs and CTOs also need to realize that their roles have a shared destiny with the CISO; when the vulnerability management program fails, they all fail and should share the "glory." The days when the CISO is the sole scapegoat for IT security failures are largely in the past—regulators, boards, and shareholders know better after decades of data breaches across industries and around the world. CISOs that find themselves in this scenario should work to improve their relationship with their IT partners in an effort to maximize the effectiveness of their cybersecurity programs.

In the fictional example scenario illustrated in *Figure 12.1*, the vulnerability management program continues to manage vulnerabilities and misconfigurations for the same number of IT assets throughout the year. They are blissfully unaware that there are network subnets with IT assets they are not managing. They are also not actively managing the new IT assets that have been introduced into the environment during the year. The space between the two lines in the graph represents the risk to the organization.

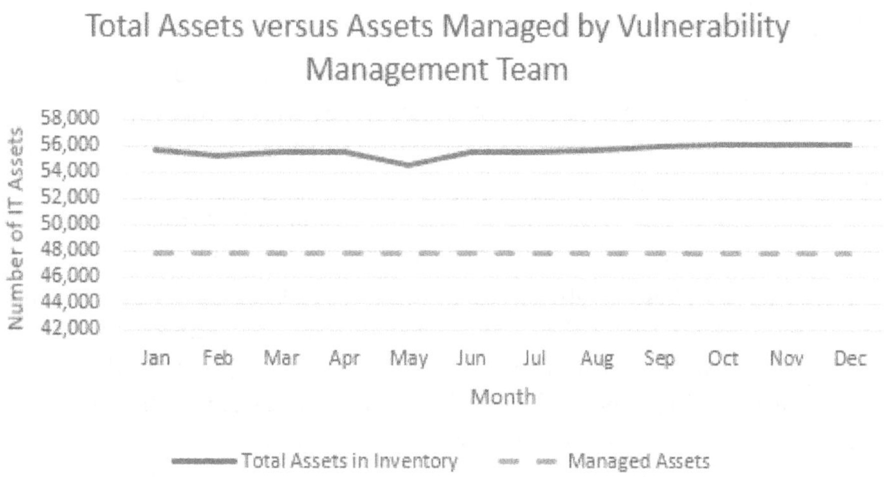

Figure 12.1 – An example of trend data illustrating the difference between the total number of IT assets in inventory and the number of assets enrolled in the vulnerability management program

The total number of IT assets and the total number of assets that are actively managed for vulnerabilities and misconfigurations every day should be identical to minimize risk. However, there might be good reasons, in large complex environments, for there to be exceptions to this rule. But exceptions still need to be known, understood, and tracked by the teams responsible for managing vulnerabilities; otherwise, the risk to the organization does not get surfaced at the right management level in the organization. Put another way, if the organization is going to have unpatched systems, the decision to do this and for how long needs to be accepted by the highest appropriate management layer and revisited periodically.

The appropriate management layer for decisions like this might not be in IT at all—it depends on the organization and the governance model it has adopted. Remember, a decision to allow an unpatched system to run in the environment is a decision to accept risk on behalf of the entire organization, not just the owner or manager of that asset. I've seen project managers all too enthusiastic to accept all manner of risks on behalf of their entire organization in order to meet the schedule, budget, and quality goals of their projects. This is despite the fact that the scope of their role is limited to the projects they work on. If a risk is never escalated to the proper management level, it could remain unknown and potentially unmanaged forever. This is where the cybersecurity risk register that I discussed in *Chapter 9*, can be helpful. Tracking exceptions to a vulnerability management policy in the cybersecurity risk register will ensure the risk is tracked with its owner and remediation plan, and periodically revisited. However, this can turn into an unwieldy exercise if risk exceptions are granted too often and for large numbers of requests. In these cases, the underlying reason for the exceptions needs to be investigated and solved. This could be increasing resources for patching systems, changing vulnerability remediation SLAs, or both.

In environments where the total number of IT assets and the total number of assets that are actively managed for vulnerabilities are meaningfully different, this is an opportunity for CISOs and vulnerability program managers to show how they are working to close that gap and thus reduce risk for the organization. They can use this data to educate IT leadership and their board of directors on the risks posed to their organizations. To do this, they can use partial and inaccurate asset inventories and talk about the presence of unmanaged assets. CISOs can provide stakeholders with regular updates on how the difference between the number of assets under the remit of the vulnerability management team and the total number of assets that the organization owns and operates trends over time, as IT and their cybersecurity team work together to reduce and minimize it. The trend data illustrates how the CISO and their vulnerability management team have managed it over time. If this number trends in the wrong direction, it is the responsibility of senior leadership and the management board to recognize this and to help address it.

Figure 12.2 illustrates that the fictional CISO and vulnerability management team have been working with their IT partners to reduce risk. This is a positive trend that the CISO can use to communicate the value of the cybersecurity program.

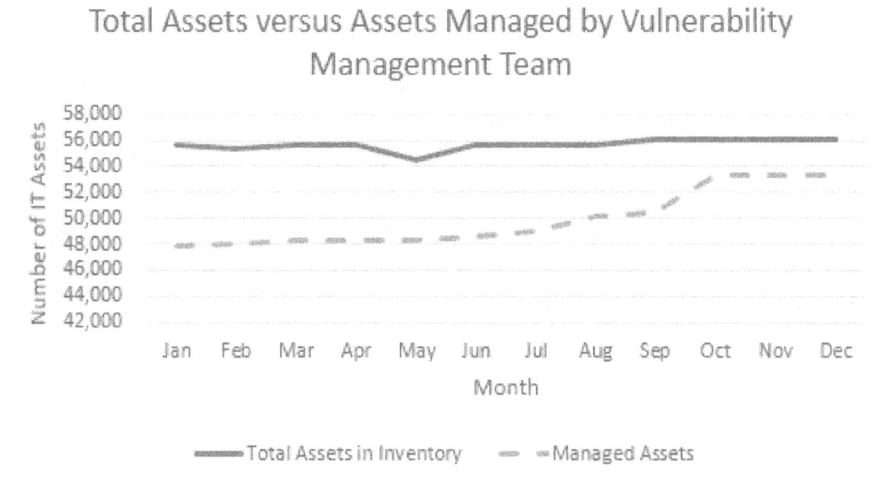

Figure 12.2 – An example of trend data illustrating an improving difference between the total number of IT assets in the inventory and the number of assets enrolled in the vulnerability management program

Known unpatched vulnerabilities

Another key data point from vulnerability management programs is the number of known unpatched vulnerabilities that are present in an environment. Remember that there are many reasons why some organizations have unpatched systems in their IT asset inventories. To be perfectly frank, the most frequently cited reason I have heard for this is a lack of investment in vulnerability management programs; understaffed and under-resourced programs simply cannot manage the volume of new vulnerabilities in their environments. Testing security updates and deploying them requires trained people, effective processes, supporting technologies, time, and, most importantly, the will to meet vulnerability management SLAs.

Regardless of the reasons, it is still important to understand which systems are unpatched, the severity of the unpatched vulnerabilities, and the mitigation plan for them. Regularly sharing how the number of unpatched vulnerabilities is reduced over time can help communicate how the CISO and cybersecurity team are contributing to the success of the business. One nuance for rapidly changing environments to consider is how the number of vulnerabilities was reduced, despite material changes to infrastructure or increases in the number of IT assets. To communicate this effectively, CISOs might have to educate some of their stakeholder community on the basics and nuances of vulnerability management metrics, as well as their significance to the overall risk of the organization. There are typically only one or two members on a board of directors who have a background in cybersecurity, and even fewer executives with that experience in the typical C-suite. In my experience, educating these stakeholders is time well spent and will help everyone understand the value that the cybersecurity team is providing. In cases where the vulnerability management team is under-resourced, this data can help build the business case for increased investment in an easy-to-understand way.

Figure 12.3 illustrates a fictional scenario where a vulnerability management team successfully minimized increases in unpatched vulnerabilities in their environment, despite modest increases in the number of IT assets enrolled in their program. However, the acquisition of a smaller firm that closed in October introduced a large number of new IT assets that the vulnerability management team was expected to manage. This was somewhat disruptive to the program for a short period and led to a dramatic increase in the number of unpatched vulnerabilities, which the team was able to reduce to more typical levels by the end of the quarter.

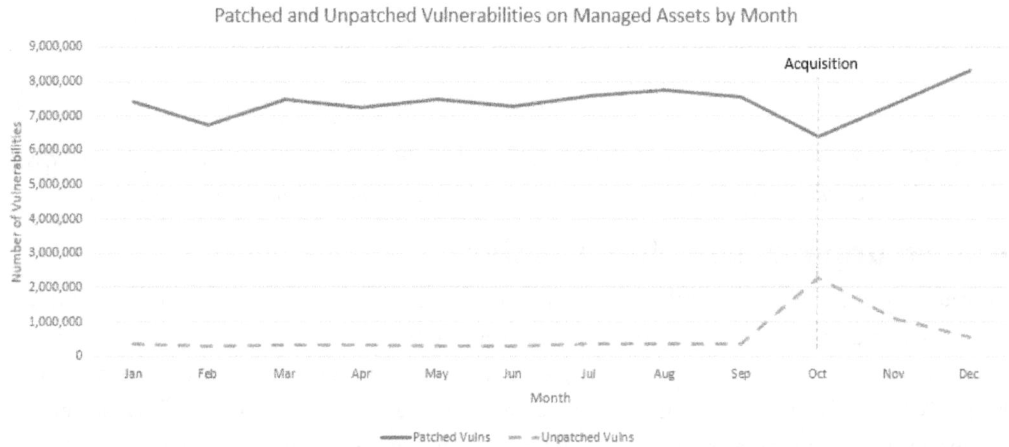

Figure 12.3 – An example of trend data illustrating the number of patched vulnerabilities and the number of unpatched vulnerabilities on assets enrolled in an organization's vulnerability management program before and after the organization acquired a company.

With data like this, the CISO and cybersecurity team look like heroes. Without data like this, it would be much harder to describe the scope of the challenge that the acquisition brought with it for the vulnerability management team, the subsequent increased workload, and the positive results. It's not all positive news, though, as this organization has a significant number of unpatched vulnerabilities in its environment, and with a larger number of assets to manage, it will be challenged to keep unpatched vulnerability counts low over time. The CISO should be able to articulate the plan to reduce the number of unpatched vulnerabilities to as close to zero as possible, using this same data to ask for more resources to accelerate that effort. Note that the figures I used in this example are completely fictional; actual data can vary wildly, depending on the number of assets, hardware, software, applications, remediation policies, governance practices, and so on.

Reducing the number of unpatched vulnerabilities can be easier said than done for some organizations. Some known vulnerabilities simply can't be patched. There are numerous reasons for this. For example, many vendors will not offer security updates for software that goes out of support. Unsupported operating systems and applications can be challenging to eliminate from large legacy on-premises environments. Some vendors go out of business and, subsequently, security updates for the products their customers have deployed cannot be offered. Another common example is legacy applications that have compatibility issues with specific security updates for operating systems or web browsers. In cases like this, often there are workarounds that can be implemented to make exploitation of specific vulnerabilities unlikely or impossible, even without installing the security updates that fix them. Typically, workarounds are meant to be short-term solutions until the security update that fixes the vulnerabilities can be deployed. However, in many environments, workarounds become permanent tenants. Reporting how known unpatched vulnerabilities are being mitigated using workarounds, instead of security updates, can help communicate risk and how it's being managed. Providing categories such as workarounds in progress, workarounds deployed, and no workaround available can help business sponsors see where decisions need to be made. The number of systems with workarounds deployed on them, as well as the severity of the underlying vulnerabilities that they mitigate, provides a nuanced view of risk in the environment. Marry this data with the long-term mitigation plan for the underlying vulnerabilities and CISOs have a risk management story they can share with stakeholders.

It's worth pointing out two important points about leveraging workarounds for vulnerabilities. First, leveraging a workaround such as a specific system configuration means that the system is potentially one configuration change away from compromise. Remember, any configuration change that administrators make, attackers can undo if they possess valid administrator credentials or escalate their privileges on the system. This is why keeping workarounds in place long-term is a bad idea.

The second point is that many vendors that offer workarounds for vulnerabilities do so without comprehensive testing to ensure the workaround is 100% as effective as the code change that fixes the vulnerability. How could they? Every one of their customers' system configurations and environments could be different. Did they test every possible combination of Windows registry entries, file system ACLs, and firewall exceptions? Workarounds are rarely published with a matrix of possible system and network configurations for administrators to consider. When faced with these nuances, many IT operations teams that resist installing security updates will assert that their specific system configuration makes the vulnerability in question unexploitable. Attackers love to prove these people wrong and often do. Such assertions typically rely on information provided by the vendor releasing the security update. IT operations teams typically don't have any expertise in exploit research themselves. All the execution paths to a vulnerability are rarely mitigated by simply blocking TCP and UDP ports or editing the Windows registry. Attackers are more than willing to use combinations of vulnerabilities to compromise systems, which makes the effectiveness of such workarounds much harder to predict. With these two nuances in mind, it should be clear that patching security bugs in the code is typically the most effective and most permanent way to address vulnerabilities.

Unpatched vulnerabilities by severity

Another potentially powerful data point is the number of vulnerabilities unpatched in an environment, categorized by severity. As I discussed at length in *Chapter 4*, critical and high-severity vulnerabilities that are known to be actively exploited represent the highest risk because of the probability and impact of their exploitation. *Figure 12.4* illustrates the *9-Box* format I discussed at length in *Chapter 4*. It maps the current inventory of unpatched vulnerabilities in the environment to vulnerability remediation policy SLAs.

	Highest Probability of Exploitation	Biggest Impact if Exploited	
	Internet-facing + Critical + High+ KEV **8 vulnerabilities** **2 assets**	**Crown Jewels + Critical + High+ KEV** **8 vulnerabilities** **2 assets**	Everything Else Critical + High + KEV 404 vulnerabilities 370 assets
5 week trend			
	Internet-facing + Critical + High+ KEV **100 vulnerabilities** **2 assets**	**Crown Jewels + Critical + High+ KEV** **150 vulnerabilities** **40 assets**	Everything Else Critical + High 2,205 vulnerabilities 303 assets
5 week trend			
	Internet-Facing All Severities 1,005 vulnerabilities 350 assets	Crown Jewels All Severities 1,200 vulnerabilities 75 assets	All Vulnerabilities 10,500 vulnerabilities 2,550 assets
5 week trend			
			Least Risk

Figure 12.4 – An example of a "9-Box" vulnerability reporting format designed for executives to understand what their unpatched vulnerability inventory looks like.

Tracking the volume of unpatched critical and high-severity vulnerabilities, including those in CISA's KEV catalog, and segmenting them by SLA non-compliance and age bands (1 year, 2+ years, and 5+ years) provides a sharp view of the organization's vulnerability-remediation posture. Capturing these aged, unpatched vulnerabilities in the cybersecurity risk register, along with accountable owners and documented reasons for deferral, gives senior leaders a transparent understanding of the organization's current risk exposure during periodic risk-register reviews.

Understanding how many of these vulnerabilities are present in the environment at any time, how long they have been present, and the time to remediation are all important data points to help articulate the risk they pose. Longer term, this data can help CISOs understand how quickly these risks are being mitigated and uncover the factors that lead to relatively long lifetimes in their environments. This data can help vulnerability management program managers and CISOs build the business case for more resources and better processes and technologies. This data can also be one of the most powerful indicators of the value of cybersecurity and remediation teams and how effectively they have been managing risk for the organization, because the risk these vulnerabilities pose is among the most serious and is easy to articulate to executives and boards.

Don't discount the value of medium-severity vulnerabilities in IT environments for attackers. Because of the monetary value of critical and high-rated vulnerabilities, attackers will use combinations of medium-severity vulnerabilities to compromise systems. CISOs and vulnerability management teams need to manage these vulnerabilities aggressively to minimize risk to their environments. This is another opportunity to show value to the businesses they support and communicate progress by constantly patching these vulnerabilities.

Vulnerabilities by product type

Another potentially useful dataset is vulnerabilities categorized by product type. Let's face it—most of the action occurs on user desktops because they bring threats through perimeter defenses into IT environments. Just as eyes are the windows to the souls of people, so too are browsers to operating systems. Attackers are constantly trying to find and exploit vulnerabilities in web browsers and operating systems.

The data illustrated in *Figure 12.5* is also touched upon in *Chapter 3*. The data shows us that more than 92% of vulnerabilities in products disclosed over time have been in operating systems, while 7% have been in web browsers. Other application vulnerability figures start to appear as the number of products is expanded from the top 25 to the top 50.

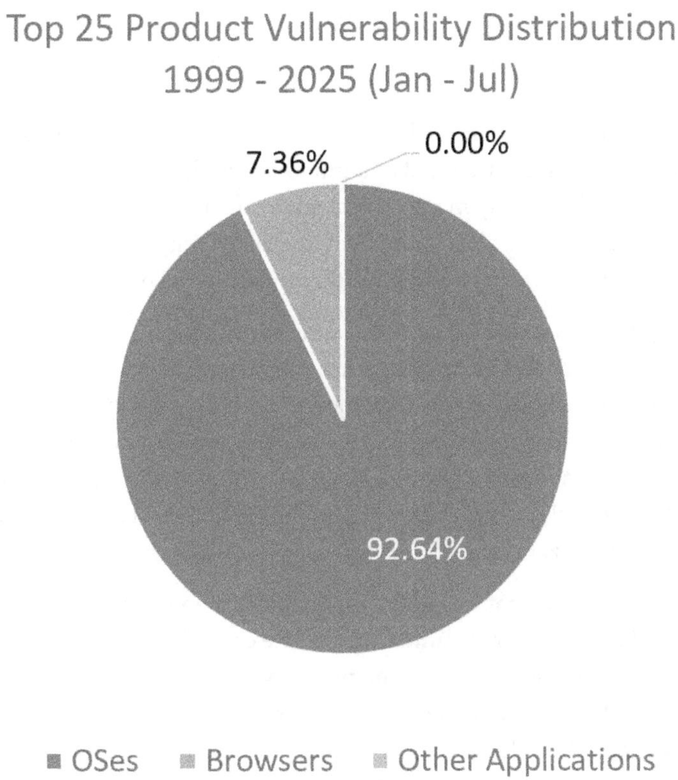

Figure 12.5 – Vulnerabilities in the 25 products with the most CVEs, categorized by product type (1999–2025, CVE Details, July 2025)

Vulnerability management teams can develop similar views for their environments to illustrate the challenge they have and their competence and progress in managing it. Data like this, combined with the previous data points I discussed, can help illustrate where the risk is for an organization and help optimize its treatment. The number of critical-, high-, and medium-severity unpatched vulnerabilities in operating systems, web browsers, and applications in an environment, along with the number of systems not managed by a vulnerability management program, can help CISOs and their stakeholders understand the risk in their IT environment. Of course, depending on the environment, data pertaining to cloud-based assets, mobile devices, hardware, firmware, appliances, routing and switch equipment, and other technologies that are in use in each IT and **operational technology (OT)** environment will provide a more complete view. The mix of these technologies and their underlying vulnerabilities is unique to each organization.

Providing executive management teams and board members with quantitative data like this helps them understand reality versus opinion. Without this type of data, it can be much more difficult to make compelling business cases and communicate progress against goals for cybersecurity programs. This data will also make it easier when random executives and other interested parties, such as overly aggressive vendors, ask cybersecurity program stakeholders about the "vulnerability du jour" that makes it into the news headlines. If senior stakeholders know that their CISO, vulnerability management team, and remediation teams are managing vulnerabilities and misconfigurations in their environment competently and diligently, a lot of noise that could otherwise be distracting to CISOs can be filtered out.

This reporting might sound complicated and intimidating to some. The good news is that there are asset management and vulnerability management products available that provide rich analytics and reporting capabilities. CISOs aren't limited to the ideas I've provided in this chapter, as asset management and vulnerability management vendors have lots of great ways to help measure and communicate progress. The key is to use analysis and reporting mechanisms to effectively show stakeholders how your vulnerability management program is reducing risk for the organization and to ask for resources when they are needed.

I've found one "proxy" metric that simplifies vulnerability management data in a way many stakeholders appreciate. The average time to remediate critical and high severity vulnerabilities versus vulnerability management policy SLAs can be used as a proxy to understand how well the program is performing compared to expectations. For example, if the policy SLA requires critical and high severity vulnerabilities to be remediated within 30 days but the actual average remediation time is 90 days, that single number (90 days) immediately communicates program effectiveness. A 90-day remediation cycle tells stakeholders they are taking three times longer than their target, giving them a clear sense of the environment's performance without overwhelming them with detail. This helps stakeholders understand the state of the environment in a concise way without letting all the details potentially confuse them.

Although data from vulnerability management programs can be very helpful for CISOs, it only helps them manage two of the five Cybersecurity Usual Suspects. There is potentially much more data that can help CISOs understand and manage the performance and efficacy of their cybersecurity strategies. Let's explore this next using the example I discussed at length in *Chapter 11*—an attack-centric strategy known as the Intrusion Kill Chain framework (Hutchins, E.M., Cloppert, M.J., Amin, R.M., n.d.).

Measuring performance and efficacy of an attack-centric strategy

As I mentioned in *Chapters 10* and *11*, the Intrusion Kill Chain framework has many attributes that make it an attractive cybersecurity strategy. First, it earned the highest **Cybersecurity Fundamentals Scoring System (CFSS)** estimated total score.

This means it had the greatest potential to fully mitigate the Cybersecurity Usual Suspects. Additionally, this approach can be used in on-premises, hybrid, and cloud environments. Perhaps the thing I like most about this framework is that its performance and efficacy can be measured in a relatively straightforward way. Let's examine this in detail.

Performing intrusion reconstructions

This will likely seem odd when you read it, but when it comes to measuring the performance and efficacy of a cybersecurity strategy, intrusion attempts are gifts from attackers to defenders. They are gifts because they test the implementation and operation of defenders' cybersecurity strategies. But in order to derive value from intrusion attempts, every successful, partially successful, and failed intrusion attempt must be decomposed and studied. In doing this, there are two key questions to be answered. First, how far did attackers get with their Intrusion Kill Chain before they were detected and ultimately stopped? Second, how did attackers defeat or bypass the layers of mitigating controls that the cybersecurity team deployed to break their Intrusion Kill Chain? Put another way, if attackers made it to phase four of their Intrusion Kill Chain, how did they get past all the mitigations layered in phases one, two, and three?

These are the central questions that intrusion reconstructions should help answer. In seeking the answers to these two questions, intrusion reconstructions should also answer many other questions that will help measure the performance and efficacy of each implementation of this approach. As you'll see as I describe this process, the underlying theme of these questions is whether the people, processes, and technologies that are working to break attackers' Intrusion Kill Chains are effective. We want to discover if any changes are required in each phase of our Attack-Centric Strategy. Let's get started.

The concept of intrusion reconstructions is discussed in Lockheed Martin's paper on Intrusion Kill Chains (Hutchins, E.M., Cloppert, M.J., Amin, R.M., n.d.). Again, I recommend reading this paper. The approach I'll describe in this chapter is slightly different from the approach described in Lockheed Martin's paper. There are at least a few ways intrusion reconstructions can be done; I'll describe one way that I've used with some success in the past.

This approach assumes that defenders will not be able to perform attribution with any confidence, so it doesn't rely on attribution the way that other approaches might. The goal of this approach to intrusion reconstructions is to identify areas where the implementation of the Intrusion Kill Chain framework can be improved, not to identify attackers and take military or legal action against them.

Let me offer some advice on when to do intrusion reconstructions. Do not perform reconstructions while incident response activities are underway. Using valuable resources and expertise that have a role in your organization's incident response process during an active incident is an unnecessary distraction. The reconstruction can wait until periods of crisis have passed. Ideally, reconstructions can be done while the details are still fresh in participants' minds in the days or weeks after the incident has passed. However, if your organization is always in crisis mode, then ignore this advice and get access to people and information when you can. Maybe you can help break the crisis cycle by identifying what deficiencies are contributing to it.

To perform an intrusion reconstruction, I strongly suggest that you have at least one representative from all the teams that are responsible for cybersecurity strategy, architecture, protection, detection, response, and recovery. In really large environments, this can be scoped to the relevant teams that were responsible for the areas involved in the intrusion attempt. Once the organization gets good at doing reconstructions, the number of participants can likely be reduced even more. But you need the expertise and visibility that each team has to reconstruct what happened during each failed, partially successful, and fully successful intrusion attempt. Remember that one of the modifications we made to the Courses of Action Matrix (Hutchins, E.M., Cloppert, M.J., Amin, R.M., n.d.) in *Chapter 11*, was adding a "data consumer point of contact" for each mitigation. This information can be helpful in identifying the right people from different teams to participate in reconstructions.

A decision should be made regarding whether to invite vendors to participate in these meetings. I have found it helpful to have trusted representatives from some of the cybersecurity vendors we use participate in intrusion reconstructions.

There are at least a couple of benefits to this approach. First, vendors should be able to bring expertise about their products and services and provide insights that might otherwise be missed. Second, it's important to share the "gifts" that attackers give you with the vendors that you've selected to help you defend against them. These exercises can inform your vendors' efforts to make better products, which your organization and others can benefit from. But it also gives you the opportunity to see how helpful your vendors really are willing to be, and whether they are willing to be held accountable for their shortcomings. I found that some of the vendors I used, who I thought would have my back during security incidents, folded up like a circus tent and left town when I really needed them. During intrusion reconstructions, these same vendors had the courage to participate but typically blamed their customers for their products' failure to perform as expected. If you do enough reconstruction exercises with vendors, you'll likely be able to determine whether they really have the desire and capability to help your organization in the way you thought they would. This knowledge comes in handy later when their product license renewal dates approach. I'll discuss this more later in this chapter.

All that said, inviting vendors to participate in reconstructions also has risk associated with it. Simply put, some vendors are really poor at keeping confidential information confidential. My advice is to discuss including vendors in these meetings, on a case-by-case basis, with the stakeholders who participate in the reconstruction exercises. If a vendor adds enough value and is trustworthy, then there is a case for including them in these exercises. Discussing this idea with senior leadership for their counsel is also a prudent step prior to finalizing a decision to include vendors in these exercises.

If your organization has a forensics team or uses a vendor for forensics, these experts can be incredibly helpful for intrusion reconstruction exercises. The tools and skills they have can help determine if systems in the reconstruction have been compromised, when, and likely how. In my experience, I've come across two flavors of forensics teams.

The first is the traditional forensics team, which has certified forensics examiners who follow strict procedures to maintain the integrity of the evidence they collect. In my experience with organizations that have this type of forensics team, they need a full-time team of experts who can preserve evidence, maintain the chain of custody, and potentially testify in court in the criminal matters they help investigate. More often, organizations outsource this type of work.

The other flavor of forensics team, which I see much more often, performs a different function and is sometimes simply referred to as incident responders. They too seek to determine if systems have been compromised. But these teams typically do not have certified forensics professionals, do not maintain the integrity of evidence, and do not plan to testify in a court of law. In fact, many times, their efforts to determine if a system has been compromised result in destroying what would be considered evidence in a criminal proceeding. This is where I've encountered interesting and sometimes provincial attitudes among certified forensics experts, as many of them wouldn't call these efforts forensics at all because they destroy evidence rather than properly preserve it. But these folks need to keep in mind that not every organization wants to spend time and effort tracking down attackers and trying to prosecute them in a court of law. Organizations need to decide which flavor of forensics professionals they need and can afford. Both types of forensics experts can be worth their weight in gold when they help determine if systems have been compromised and participate in intrusion reconstruction exercises.

Who should lead reconstruction exercises? I recommend that the individual or group responsible for cybersecurity strategy lead these exercises. This individual or group is ultimately responsible for the performance and efficacy of the overall strategy. They are also likely responsible for making adjustments as needed to ensure the success of the strategy. An alternative to the strategy group is the **incident response (IR)** team. The IR team should have most, if not all, of the details required to lead an intrusion reconstruction. If they don't, you've just identified the first area for improvement.

The IR team manages incidents, so they really should have most of the information related to partially and fully successful intrusion attempts at their fingertips. But they might not be involved in failed attempts that don't qualify as incidents. In these cases, SOC personnel, operations personnel, and architects likely have key information for the reconstruction.

Keep in mind that the goal isn't to triage every port scan that happens on the organization's internet-facing firewalls. I suggest getting agreement among the groups that will participate in reconstruction exercises most often on a principle that is used to determine the types of intrusions that reconstructions should be performed on. That is, define the characteristics of intrusion attempts that determine whether a formal reconstruction is performed. As shown in *Table 12.1*, using our updated Courses of Action Matrix from *Chapter 11*, an effective principle could be that any intrusion that makes it further than the Deny action in the Delivery phase should be reconstructed. A much less aggressive principle could be that any intrusion attempt that results in a Restore action should be reconstructed. There are numerous other options in the range between these two examples.

The goal of such a principle is to impose consistency that helps appropriately balance risk and the valuable time of reconstruction participants. This principle doesn't need to be permanent—it can change over time. When an organization first starts performing reconstructions, it can have a relatively aggressive principle that enables it to learn quickly. Then, once lessons from reconstructions have "normalized" somewhat, a less aggressive principle can be adopted. But getting agreement among the stakeholders for these reconstruction exercises on the principle used to initiate them is important for their long-term success and, therefore, the success of the cybersecurity strategy. Too few reconstructions relative to intrusion attempts could mean the organization isn't paying enough attention to the gifts it's being given by attackers and is potentially adjusting too slowly to attacks. Too many reconstructions can be disruptive and counterproductive. The agreed-upon principle should strike the right balance for the stakeholder community over time.

Once the appropriate participants, or their delegates, have been identified, and an intrusion reconstruction leader is ready to facilitate, a reconstruction meeting can be scheduled. Providing participants with enough lead time and guidance to gather the appropriate data for reconstruction will help save time and frustration. In my experience, some reconstruction exercises are straightforward because the intrusion attempt was detected and stopped in an early phase. In these cases, the number of participants and the amount of data they need to reconstruct the intrusion attempt can be relatively minor. Subsequently, the amount of time typically needed for this exercise is relatively short, such as 45 minutes or an hour, for example. If you are just starting to do reconstructions in your organization, you'll naturally need a little more time than you'll need after becoming accustomed to them. For more complicated intrusion attempts, especially when attackers make it to the later stages of their Kill Chain, more participants with more data might be required, increasing the amount of time needed for reconstruction exercises.

A Courses of Action Matrix, introduced in *Chapter 11*, helps defenders map how they intend to disrupt an attacker's progress at each phase of the Intrusion Kill Chain. *Table 12.1* provides an example. This same tool is invaluable during intrusion reconstructions because it captures what the security team expected to occur at every phase of an attack. Comparing those intended actions with what actually happened makes it easier to pinpoint failures, gaps, and breakdowns in execution.

Kill Chain Phase	Detect	Deny	Disrupt	Degrade	Deceive	Limit	Recover
Reconnaissance I							
Delivery							
Exploitation							
Installation							
Command and Control (C2)							
Reconnaissance II							
Actions on Objectives							

Table 12.1 – An example of an updated Courses of Action Matrix (Hutchins, Cloppert, Amin, n.d.)

Many of the organizations I've worked with label security incidents with code names. All subsequent communications about an incident use its code name. This way, if an email or other communications are seen by someone who has not been read into the incident, its context and significance are not obvious. Communications about, and invitations to, intrusion reconstructions should use incident code names when organizations label incidents with them. If you decide to use incident code names, be thoughtful about the names you use, avoiding labels that are potentially offensive. This includes names in languages other than English.

Consider the potential impact on the reputation of an organization if the code name ever became public knowledge. Stay away from themes that are inconsistent with the organization's brand or the brand it aspires to build in the minds of its customers. There really is no compelling business reason to use anything but benign code names. These are boring but effective on multiple levels.

Now we have a code name for our reconstruction exercise, participants who are going to bring relevant data, potentially some trustworthy vendors who will participate, and a leader to facilitate the exercise. The point of the exercise is to reconstruct the steps that attackers took in each phase of their Kill Chain. It might not be possible to do this with complete certainty, and some assumptions about their tactics and techniques might be necessary. But the more detail the reconstruction can include, the easier it will be to identify areas where people, processes, and technologies performed as expected or underperformed. Be prepared to take detailed notes during these exercises. A product of intrusion reconstruction exercises should be a report that contains the details of the intrusion attempt, as well as the performance of the defenses that the cybersecurity team had in place. These artifacts will potentially have value for many years as they will provide helpful continuity of knowledge about past attacks, even when key staff leave the organization. Put another way, when the lessons learned from these intrusion attempts are documented, they are available for current and future personnel to learn from. This is another reason I call intrusion attempts "gifts."

Our updated Kill Chain framework has seven phases. Where should a reconstruction exercise start? In the first phase, or perhaps the last phase? The answer to this question is, it depends. Sometimes, an intrusion is straightforward and can be charted from beginning to end in sequential order. However, with complicated intrusions or intrusions that started months or years earlier, it might not be prudent or possible to approach a reconstruction that way. Start with the phase that you have the best information on and the most certainty about. This could be late in the Kill Chain. From your starting point, build a timeline in both directions, using the data and insights that the reconstruction participants can offer. It might not be possible to build the entire timeline because of a lack of data or uncertainty.

The more details the reconstruction uncovers, the better, as this will help identify opportunities for improvement, gaps, and failures in defenses. In my example, I will simply start at the first phase and work forward through the Kill Chain. But just be aware that this might not be possible for every intrusion. Let's start with the Reconnaissance I phase.

Reconnaissance I phase

It might not be possible to attribute any particular threat actor's activities in the Reconnaissance I phase prior to their attack. With so much network traffic constantly bombarding all internet-connected devices, it is typically challenging to pick out specific probes and reconnaissance activities conducted by specific attackers. But it's not impossible. This is an area where the combination of **artificial intelligence (AI)**, machine learning **(ML)**, good threat intelligence, and granular logs is very promising. Using AI/ML systems to churn through massive amounts of log data, such as network flow data, DNS logs, authentication and authorization logs, API activity logs, and others, in near real time to find specific attackers' activities can be very effective. Cloud services do this today at scale.

Delivery phase

Collecting data and insights from the Delivery phase of an attack is obviously super-important. The key questions are—***how did the attackers defeat or bypass the layers of mitigations that the cybersecurity team deployed to break this phase of their Kill Chain; How did they successfully deliver their weapon; What people, processes, and technologies were involved?***

To answer these questions, I have found it useful to draw system flow charts on a whiteboard during the reconstruction exercise with the participants' help. Start by drawing the infrastructure that was involved with as much detail as possible, including perimeter defenses, servers, clients, applications, system names, IP addresses, and so on. Draw a map of the infrastructure involved and chart how data is supposed to flow in this infrastructure, the protocols used, authentication and authorization boundaries, the identities involved, storage, and so on. Then, draw how the attackers delivered the weapon during their intrusion attempt and what happened during delivery.

What enabled the attacker's success in this phase? The answer to this question involves asking and answering numerous other questions. Let me give you some examples. A useful data point in an intrusion reconstruction is how long it took for the attack to be detected. Building an attack timeline can be a useful tool to help determine how an attack was executed. In the context of the Delivery phase, was the delivery of the weapon detected, and what control detected it? If delivery wasn't detected, document which controls were supposed to detect it. If there is a clear gap here in your implementation of the Kill Chain framework, document that. This information will be very useful later when you remediate deficiencies in the implementation of the strategy.

Were there any controls that should have detected delivery but failed to do so? Why did these controls fail to operate as expected? Did they fail because they simply did not do what the vendor said they would do? Did they fail because of integrations or automation between controls or systems not working as intended? This is where log data and other sources of data from systems in the reconstruction flow chart can be very helpful. Try to piece together how the weapon was delivered, step by step, through data in logs of various systems in the flow chart. Does it look like all these systems performed as expected? If not, identify anomalies and weak links. In some cases, log data might not be available because logging wasn't turned on or aggressive data retention controls deleted the log data. ***Is there a good justification for not enabling logging on these systems and storing logs to help in the future?***

Was there enough data to determine how the weapon was delivered? Sometimes, it's simply not possible to determine how the weapon was delivered with the data that is available. Some IR teams refer to the first system that was compromised in an intrusion as "patient zero." In some intrusions, the attacker's entry point is very obvious and can be tracked back to an email, a visit to a malicious website, a USB drive, malware, and so on. In other cases, if the initial compromise was achieved weeks, months, or years earlier, and attackers were adept at covering their tracks, finding patient zero is aspirational and simply might not be possible. Think about what would have helped you in this scenario. ***Would increasing the verbosity of logging have helped? Would archiving logs for longer periods or shipping logs offsite have helped? Is there some capability that you don't currently have that would have helped fill this gap?***

Did the data consumers for the Delivery phase mitigations get the data they needed to detect and break this phase? For example, did the SOC get the data it needed to detect intrusion? Did the data consumers identified in the updated Courses of Action Matrix receive or have access to the data as intended? If not, what went wrong? Did the data delivery mechanism fail, or was the required data filtered out at the destination for some reason? Was it tagged with the right priority level? There could have been multiple failures in the collection, delivery, and analysis of the data. Dig into this to identify the things that did not work as planned and document them.

Did the controls, automation, and integrations work as expected, but people or processes were the sources of the failure? This scenario happens more than you might think. The architecture was sound, the systems worked as expected, the technologies performed as expected, the weapon was detected, but no one was paying attention, or the alert was noticed but dismissed. Unfortunately, people and process failures are as common, if not more common, than technical control failures. Failures in SOC processes, poor decision-making, vendors that make mistakes, and sometimes just laziness among key personnel can lead to failures to detect and break attacks.

Did attackers and/or defenders get lucky anywhere in this phase of the attack? Some security professionals I've met have told me they don't believe in luck. But I attribute this belief to naivety. I've seen attacks succeed because of a comedy of errors that likely could not be repeated or duplicated. Combinations of people, processes, technologies, and circumstances can lead to attack scenarios almost as unlikely as winning a lottery. Don't discount the role that luck can play. Remember that not all risks can truly be identified.

Exploitation phase

Once the reconstruction team understands how the Delivery phase of the attack was accomplished and this has been documented, we can move on to the next phase of the attack, the Exploitation phase (Hutchins, E.M., Cloppert, M.J., Amin, R.M., n.d.). Here, the reconstruction team will repeat the process, using data to try to determine if exploitation was attempted, detected, and stopped. The same questions we asked for the Delivery phase apply in this phase as well. What controls failed to prevent and detect exploitation? Where did gaps in protection and detection controls contribute to attacker success in this phase of their attack?

Did vendors' cybersecurity mitigations work as advertised? Did data consumers get the data they required to detect and break this phase? Did the IR process start and work as planned? What can we learn from attackers' success in this phase to make such success harder or impossible in the future? Document your findings.

Other phases

Continue to perform this investigation for all the phases of the Kill Chain. There might be phases where nothing occurred because attackers were stopped prior to those phases. Note where and when the attack was successfully detected and successfully broken. ***If the attack had not been broken in the phase it was, would the mitigations layered in later phases have successfully detected and stopped the attack?*** Be as candid with yourselves as possible in this assessment; platitudes, optimism, and plans in the undefined future may not be enough to break the next attacker's Intrusion Kill Chain. However, sober determination to make it as difficult as possible for attackers can be helpful. Remember to document these thoughts.

Now the reconstruction is complete, and you have asked and answered as many questions as needed to uncover what happened, ideally in every step of the attack. Next, let me provide some examples of the specific actionable things the reconstruction should have identified in the wake of failed, partially successful, and fully successful attacks.

Using intrusion reconstruction results

First, recall the discussion on identifying gaps and areas of over- and under-investment in *Chapter 11*. An intrusion reconstruction can confirm some of the analysis on gaps and under-investments that were done while planning the implementation of this strategy. For example, if a gap in detection in the Delivery phase was identified during planning and later intrusion reconstruction data also illustrates this same gap, this is strangely reassuring news. Now, the CISO has more data to help build the business case for investment to mitigate this gap. It's one thing for a CISO to say they need to invest in detection capabilities or bad things can happen, but such requests are much more powerful when CISOs can show senior executives and the Board of Directors that attackers have been actively using known gaps.

It counters any notion that the risk is theoretical when CISOs can provide evidence that the risk is real. It also helps build a sense of urgency where there was none before. If the intrusion attempt led to unplanned expenses related to response and recovery activities, this will help illustrate the current and potential future costs related to the gap. This data can inform both the probability and the impact sides of the risk equation, making it easier to compare to other risks. Using data like this, CISOs can give their management boards updates on gaps and under-investment areas at every cybersecurity program review meeting until they are mitigated.

When reconstruction exercises uncover previously unknown gaps or areas of under-investment, this truly is a gift from attackers. In doing so, attackers provide CISOs valuable insights into deficiencies in the implementation of their strategies, as well as a clear call to action to implement new mitigations or improve existing ones. Intrusion reconstruction data can also help to inform cybersecurity investment roadmaps. Remember that stopping attackers as early in the Intrusion Kill Chain as possible is highly preferable to stopping them in later phases. Reconstruction data can help cybersecurity teams identify and prioritize mitigations that will help make it harder or impossible for attackers to make it to later phases of their attack. Helping cybersecurity teams understand deficiencies and areas for improvement in the Delivery and Exploitation phases is a key outcome of intrusion reconstruction exercises. This data can then be used to plan the investment roadmap that charts the people, processes, and technologies an organization plans to deploy and when. Since most organizations have resource constraints, reconstruction data and the investment roadmaps they inform can become central to a cybersecurity team's planning processes.

Remember those cybersecurity imperatives and their supporting projects I discussed in *Chapter 9*? An imperative is a big, audacious, multi-year goal that should be aligned with an organization's business objectives. Upgrading to a much-needed modern identity system or finally getting rid of VPNs in favor of modern remote access solutions for thousands of Information Workers are two examples. Reconstruction data can help provide supporting data for cybersecurity imperatives and provide a shared sense of purpose for the staff that work on them. Conversely, reconstruction data might not always support the notion that planned imperatives are the right direction for the organization.

There's no expectation that these will necessarily align, especially in large organizations with complex environments and multiple imperatives. But when lightning strikes and reconstruction data suggest that an imperative is critical to the organization, it can supercharge the project teams that are working on it. This type of positive momentum can be beneficial by helping to maintain project timelines and getting projects across their finish lines.

Identifying lame controls

Another potential action area stemming from an intrusion reconstruction is correcting mitigations that failed to perform as expected. These are controls that have been deployed and are actively managed, but did not protect, detect, or help respond to the intrusion attempt as designed. To state the obvious, CISOs and security teams can't rely on controls that don't work the way they should. There is a range of possible root causes for controls that fail.

A common root cause for failure is that the control doesn't actually perform the function that the security team thought it did. Mismatches between security controls' functions and security teams' expectations are, unfortunately, very common. Some controls are designed to mitigate very specific threats under specific circumstances. But such nuances can get lost in vendors' marketing materials and sales motions. This is a critical function that architects play on many cybersecurity teams: to really understand the threats that each control mitigates and how controls need to be orchestrated to protect, detect, and respond to threats to their organizations. They should be thoughtfully performing the cybersecurity capabilities inventories I discussed in *Chapter 11*, and making changes to those inventories to minimize gaps and areas of under-investment. The maturity of the controls' implementation is an important factor, as is the consumption of the data generated by controls. This is something architects can have a hand in, that is, inventorying and planning, but data consumers, operations personnel, and SOC engineers, among others, need to help complete this picture. Otherwise, mismatches between control functions and expectations can burn cybersecurity teams.

Another common cause for mitigations failing to perform as expected is that they simply don't work the way vendors say they work. I know this is a shocking revelation for a few people, and it's an all-too-common challenge for security teams. If vendors kept all their promises, then there wouldn't be a global cybersecurity challenge, nor would there be a multi-billion-dollar cybersecurity industry. This is one reason it is prudent to have layers of defenses, so that when one control fails, other controls can help mitigate the threat. This is an area where CISOs can share and learn a lot from other CISOs. Professional experience with specific vendors and specific products is often the best reference to have.

Another common reason for mitigations failing to protect, detect, or respond is that the trusted computing base they rely on has been compromised. That is, attackers have undermined the mitigations by compromising the hardware and/or software they depend on to run. For example, one of the first things many attackers do once they use one or more of the Cybersecurity Usual Suspects to compromise a system is try to disable the endpoint protection software running on it. A less obviously visible tactic is to add directories to the endpoint security software engine's exceptions list so that the attacker's tools do not get scanned or detected. Once attackers or malware initially compromise systems, it is common for them to undermine the controls that have been deployed to protect systems and detect attackers. Therefore, becoming excellent at cybersecurity fundamentals is a prerequisite to deploying advanced cybersecurity capabilities. Don't bother deploying that expensive attacker detection system that uses AI to perform behavioral analysis unless you are also dedicated to managing the cybersecurity fundamentals for that system. Attackers will undermine those advanced cybersecurity capabilities if unpatched vulnerabilities, security misconfigurations, and weak, leaked, or stolen credentials enable them to access the systems they run on. I discussed this at length in earlier chapters, but I'll reiterate it here again. No cybersecurity strategy, not even a high-scoring strategy like the Attack-Centric strategy, will be effective if the cybersecurity fundamentals are not managed effectively.

Additionally, it's important that the cybersecurity products themselves are effectively managed with the cybersecurity fundamentals in mind. Endpoint security software and other common mitigations have been sources of exploitable vulnerabilities and security misconfigurations in the past. They too must be effectively managed so that they don't increase the attack surface area instead of decreasing it.

Another action item related to failed controls that can emerge from reconstruction exercises is addressing control integrations that failed. For example, an intrusion attempt wasn't detected until relatively late in an attacker's Kill Chain because, although a control successfully detected it in an earlier phase, that data never made it to the SIEM. Broken and degraded integrations like this example are common in large, complex IT environments and can be difficult to detect. It would be ideal if cybersecurity teams could simply rely on data consumers to identify anomalies in data reporting from cybersecurity controls, but in many cases, the absence of data isn't an anomaly. Technical debt in many organizations can make it challenging to identify and remediate poor integrations. Many times, such integrations are performed by vendors or professional services organizations who have limited knowledge of their customers' IT environments. This is where SOC engineers can be valuable; they can help ensure integrations are working as expected and improve them over time.

Learning from failure

In addition to identifying gaps and suboptimal controls and integrations, intrusion reconstructions can help CISOs and cybersecurity teams confirm that they have the right investment priorities. Data from reconstructions can help reprioritize investments so that the most critical areas are addressed first. Not only can this data help rationalize investment decisions, but it can also help CISOs justify their investment decisions, especially in the face of criticism from CIOs and CTOs who have different opinions and possibly differing agendas. Investing in areas that break attackers' efforts instead of new capabilities that IT has dependencies on might not be a popular choice among IT leadership, but using reconstruction data to defend such decisions will make it harder for others to disagree.

Besides identifying technologies that didn't work as expected, reconstructions can provide an opportunity to improve people and processes that performed below expectations. For example, in cases where lapses in governance led to poor security outcomes, this can be good data to help drive positive changes in governance processes and associated training. If complying with an internal standard or an industry standard wasn't helpful in protecting, detecting, or responding to an attack, reconstructions might be an impetus for change.

Allowing people in an organization to learn from failure is important. After spending time and effort to understand and recover from failures, organizations can increase their return on these investments by disseminating lessons from failures to the people in the organization who will benefit most from them. Reconstruction data can help build a case for social engineering training for executives or the entire organization, for example.

Identifying helpful vendors

Vendors are important partners for organizations as they typically provide technologies, services, people, and processes that their customers rely on. Intrusion reconstruction data can help identify vendors that are performing at or above expectations. It can also help identify vendors that are failing to perform as expected. This includes how vendors participate in intrusion reconstruction exercises themselves. Reconstruction exercises can help reveal those vendors who tend to blame their customers for failures in their products' and services' performance, which is rarely helpful. This, along with data on how vendors' products and services performed, can help inform vendor product license renewal negotiations. Once security teams get a taste of how the vendors' products really perform and how helpful they are willing to be during intrusions, they might be willing to pay much less for them in the future, or not willing to use them at all. If your organization doesn't already do this, I suggest maintaining a license renewal and end-of-life "horizon list" that shows you when key dates related to renewals and products' end of life are approaching.

Ensure an organization gives itself enough prior notice so it can spend a reasonable amount of time re-evaluating whether better mitigations now exist. After deploying and operating vendors' products, the organization likely has better data on its current vendors' performance to inform product evaluations than it did when it originally procured them.

Reward the vendors who are helpful and consider replacing vendors that don't understand their core value is supposed to be customer service. Looking at all the vendors I mentioned in *Chapter 11*, in addition to all the vendors I didn't mention, there is no shortage of companies competing for your organization's business. Don't settle for vendors that blame your organization for their failures. Even if it is true, they should be helping you overcome these challenges instead of playing the blame game. Intrusion reconstruction exercises are their opportunity to prove they are invested in your success, instead of being an uninterested third party on the sidelines, waiting for the next license renewal date. If they have been trying to help your organization get more value out of its products but your organization hasn't been receptive, then this should be reconciled prior to making rash decisions. Replacing good vendors that have been constantly swimming upstream to help your organization doesn't help you and could set your cybersecurity program back months, or even years. But their products either work as advertised and they are willing to help you get them into that state in a reasonable period, or they should be replaced. Otherwise, they just increase the attack surface area while using resources that could be used elsewhere to better protect, detect, and respond to threats.

Reconstruction data is likely the best data you'll have to truly gauge your cybersecurity vendors' performance. Use it in license renewal negotiations to counter marketing fluff and sales executives' promises that the latest version or the next version solves all your challenges, including their inability to provide essential levels of customer service. Sometimes, desperate vendors, sensing they are going to lose business, decide to go around the CISO and cybersecurity team by appealing directly to other executives or the Board of Directors. This can turn out to be suboptimal for CISOs who get saddled with products that don't help them.

But it's harder for executives and the board to award more business to such vendors when the CISO has been briefing them on intrusion reconstruction results and showing them how helpful or unhelpful some of their vendors have been. If executives still decide to award more business to vendors who, the data indicates, have not been performing to expectations, they have decided to accept risk on behalf of the entire organization. CISOs get stuck managing this type of risk all the time. But as the data continues to mount, it will become harder for everyone to simply accept the status quo. Data, instead of opinion alone, should help organizations make better decisions about the cybersecurity capabilities they invest in.

Informing internal assessments

The last potential action item area stemming from the results of intrusion reconstructions that I'll discuss is penetration testing and Red/Blue and Purple Team exercises. Organizations often invest in penetration testing and Red, Blue, and Purple Team exercises to simulate attacks in a structured, controlled manner. Insights from intrusion-reconstruction work should feed directly into these exercises. When reconstruction reveals weaknesses or seams that attackers could exploit in the current cybersecurity strategy, those areas should be retested through targeted Red or Purple Team activity until the underlying issues are fully resolved. When professional penetration testers and Red and Blue Teams are provided with intrusion reconstruction results, it can help them devise tests that will ensure these weaknesses have been properly mitigated. Ideally, penetration testers and Red/Blue and Purple Teams find implementation deficiencies before attackers get the chance to.

Adversary emulations leveraging MITRE ATT&CK

Making the most of all the "gifts" that attackers give your security team by testing your defenses is important. However, the objective is to break their Kill Chains as early as possible. To do this, it is prudent for security teams to test and assess the implementation of their cybersecurity strategies on an ongoing basis. Large, complex enterprise IT environments are constantly changing, sometimes in unexpected ways. At the same time, attackers are evolving their attacks and potentially becoming more effective. AI is only going to accelerate this. Don't wait for attackers to show you where underperforming controls and gaps are—find them before they do to minimize potential damage and costs.

You might recall in *Chapter 10*, that I mentioned several different ways that the ATT&CK framework can be used. ATT&CK can be leveraged for cyber threat intelligence purposes, threat detection, assessments, and emulating attackers. Subsequently, ATT&CK can be an invaluable tool for testing and assessing how strategy implementations are working.

Fortunately, MITRE published a series of blog posts that provide guidance on how to get started using ATT&CK for each of these purposes. If you are planning to use ATT&CK for any of these purposes, these blog posts are recommended reading. They provide a security team maturity model (just starting, mid-level, and advanced) and guidance for teams at each level in the model.

- *Getting Started with ATT&CK: Threat Intelligence* (`https://medium.com/mitre-attack/getting-started-with-attack-cti-4eb205be4b2f`)
- *Getting Started with ATT&CK: Detection and Analytics* (`https://medium.com/mitre-attack/getting-started-with-attack-detection-a8e49e4960d0`)
- *Getting Started with ATT&CK: Adversary Emulation and Red Teaming* (`https://medium.com/mitre-attack/getting-started-with-attack-red-29f074ccf7e3`)
- *Getting Started with ATT&CK: Assessments and Engineering* (`https://medium.com/mitre-attack/getting-started-with-attack-assessment-cc0b01769cb4`)

These blog posts reference numerous ATT&CK resources that you should be aware of. In the context of emulating attackers, MITRE provides "adversary emulation plans." The purpose of these plans is to "allow defenders to more effectively test their networks and defenses by enabling red teams to more actively model adversary behavior, as described by ATT&CK" (MITRE, n.d.). You can find these adversary emulation plans here: `https://attack.mitre.org/resources/adversary-emulation-plans/`. Other emulation and Red Teaming resources are available here: `https://attack.mitre.org/resources/get-started/adversary-emulation-and-red-teaming/`.

Test security assumptions

The last piece of advice I'll give you on measuring the performance of your strategy involves testing your assumptions about your cybersecurity controls. I've been burned more than a few times in my career from cybersecurity incidents that I thought should have been prevented. This revelation tends to come too late, after the root cause of an incident has been identified and the subsequent attack path becomes clear. Security controls that I thought were set and operating effectively turned out to be broken or only partially implemented. Specific security gaps identified long before the incident that I thought had been fixed weren't. Parts of the internet I thought were blocked weren't. The sensitivity of detection mechanisms I was relying on proved unworthy of my faith. I've learned the hard way that security controls simply can't be trusted to continue to be effective over time. Sometimes they don't work as they were described to, and attackers point this out for you. Sometimes they weren't configured properly. Sometimes they were deployed and configured properly, but the configuration drifted unchecked over time. Sometimes they worked as implemented perfectly, but the scope that needed their protection had expanded over time without anyone's knowledge. One way or another, security controls tend to fail to operate as expected over time unless you pay attention to them.

Based on these hard lessons, my strong recommendation to you is to establish security testing capabilities that enable you to test your most important assumptions about your security controls. For example, if you've implemented controls to prevent outbound network connections from your network to servers hosted in high-risk parts of the internet, like Iran (.ir), develop some automation to test that the control works as expected periodically. The more critical the control, the more frequently it should be tested. Here's another example: if you don't permit outbound VPN connections from workstations on your network to random VPN servers on the internet, periodically test that this isn't possible from different parts of your network using different VPN clients and VPN protocols. You might be surprised how often conditions change that make your most important assumptions false. Here's one more example: if you don't permit unapproved **remote monitoring and management (RMM)** tools to be installed and run on systems in your environment, periodically test whether some of these tools can be installed and/or executed in your environment. This gives you different information than just querying your SIEM to find if any of these tools are executed in your environment using log data. The absence of log data isn't the same as actually testing what is possible. That is, threat hunts and security testing are two different but complementary things.

I recommend automating as many of your security tests as possible so you can do as many of them as needed and as often as needed to increase your confidence that your most important security controls are indeed working as expected. Write down a list of your most fundamental and important assumptions about your security controls, and test them periodically to ensure your assumptions stay true over time.

This concludes our discussion of measuring the performance and effectiveness of cybersecurity strategies.

Summary

Cybersecurity teams need to measure many different things for a range of purposes, including complying with regulatory, industry, and internal standards. However, this chapter focuses on how CISOs and cybersecurity teams can measure the performance and efficacy of the implementation of their cybersecurity strategy, using an Attack-Centric Strategy as an example.

Data helps CISOs manage their cybersecurity programs and investments and helps them prove that their cybersecurity program has been effective and constantly improving; it can also help illustrate the effectiveness of corrective actions after issues are detected. A well-run vulnerability management program is not optional; leveraging data from it represents one of the easiest ways for CISOs to communicate effectiveness and progress. Vulnerability management teams should scan everything in their inventories every single day for vulnerabilities and misconfigurations. This can help minimize the amount of time that unmitigated vulnerabilities and misconfigurations are present and exploitable. Valuable trend data can emerge from vulnerability management scanning data over time. Some examples of valuable data include the following:

- The number of assets under the remit of the vulnerability management team versus the total number of assets that the organization owns and operates
- The number of vulnerabilities unpatched in the environment by vulnerability severity
- Vulnerabilities by product type can help illustrate where the most risk exists in an environment; the number of unpatched critical-, high-, and medium-severity vulnerabilities in operating systems, web browsers, and applications in an environment, along with the number of unmanaged systems, can help CISOs and their stakeholders understand the risk in their IT environment.
- The average time to remediate critical and high-severity vulnerabilities versus vulnerability management policy SLAs can be used as a proxy to understand how well the program is performing compared to expectations.

Attack-centric strategies, like the Intrusion Kill Chain, make it relatively easy to measure performance and efficacy; to do this, intrusion reconstructions are used. Intrusion reconstruction results can help CISOs in many different ways, not least by identifying mitigations that failed to perform as expected. To derive value from intrusion attempts, every successful, partially successful, and failed intrusion attempt must be decomposed and studied to answer two key questions:

1. How far did attackers get with their Intrusion Kill Chain before they were detected and ultimately stopped?
2. How did attackers defeat or bypass all the layers of mitigating controls that the cybersecurity team deployed to break their Intrusion Kill Chain before they were stopped?

Organizations that have the resources should test and assess the effectiveness of their strategy implementation on an ongoing basis. This can help security teams discover and address shortcomings before attackers have a chance to do so.

As good as the Attack-Centric strategy is at addressing the Cybersecurity Usual Suspects, there are better strategies for modern IT environments. In the next chapter, we'll explore some modern approaches to cybersecurity and compliance.

References

- CVE Details (2022). *Top 50 Products* by *Total Number* of *"Distinct" Vulnerabilities*. Retrieved from CVE Details: `https://www.cvedetails.com/top-50-products.php`
- Hutchins, E.M., Cloppert, M.J., Amin, R.M., Ph.D. (n.d.). *Intelligence-Driven Computer Network Defense Informed by Analysis of Adversary Campaigns and Intrusion Kill Chains*. Retrieved from Lockheed Martin: `https://lockheedmartin.com/content/dam/lockheed-martin/rms/documents/cyber/LM-White-Paper-Intel-Driven-Defense.pdf`
- National Institute of Standards and Technology. (2024). *Measurement guide for information security: Volume 2, Developing an information security measurement program (NIST Special Publication 800-55, Version 2)*. `https://doi.org/10.6028/NIST.SP.800-55v2`
- ISC2. (April 15, 2025). *CISSP Certification Exam Outline Summary*. Retrieved from ISC2: `https://www.isc2.org/certifications/cissp/cissp-certification-exam-outline`
- Strom, B., Schulz, T., Nickels, K. (July 17, 2019). *Getting Started with ATT&CK: Adversary Emulation and Red Teaming*. Retrieved from `https://medium.com/mitre-attack/getting-started-with-attack-red-29f074ccf7e3`
- MITRE. (n.d.). *Adversary Emulation Plans*. Retrieved from MITRE ATT&CK: `https://attack.mitre.org/resources/adversary-emulation-plans/`

Get this book's PDF version and more

Scan the QR code (or go to `packtpub.com/unlock`). Search for this book by name, confirm the edition, and then follow the steps on the page.

Note: Keep your invoice handy. Purchases made directly from Packt don't require an invoice.

Part 4

Modern approaches to cybersecurity and compliance

In this section, you'll learn how to strengthen your defenses against some of the most modern and complex challenges in cybersecurity. You'll see how cloud computing, APIs, and automation are reshaping both security and compliance, and how to use these capabilities to modernize your program and improve resilience. You'll gain a clear understanding of **Living Off the Land (LOTL)** techniques, how attackers exploit trusted tools to stay hidden and learn practical methods to detect, disrupt, and mitigate these stealthy behaviors.

You'll also explore the rapidly evolving world of artificial intelligence in cybersecurity. You'll learn the safety and security risks of generative and agentic AI systems, how adversaries are already using AI to enhance their attacks, and what it takes to securely deploy enterprise AI tools like Microsoft Copilot.

By the end of this section, you'll be equipped to navigate cloud-era security, counter stealthy attacker tradecraft, and apply AI responsibly and effectively within your organization.

This part of the book includes the following chapters:

- *Chapter 14, Mitigating "Living Off the Land" Techniques*
- *Chapter 15, Artificial Intelligence: Security of AI systems and using AI for better cybersecurity*

13

Modern Approaches to Security and Compliance

> *"We are chameleons, and our partialities and prejudices change places with an easy and blessed facility, and we are soon wonted to the change and happy in it." (Mark Twain, 1906)*

In the previous chapters of this book, I introduced you to the Cybersecurity Usual Suspects, and we discussed **Cyber Threat Intelligence (CTI)**, industry and vendor vulnerability disclosures, various threats such as malware and internet-based threats, and the roles governments can play in cybersecurity, including governments as cybersecurity threats. We also discussed ingredients that can help support a successful cybersecurity strategy, evaluated some cybersecurity strategies, took a close look at how the best scoring strategy could be implemented, and discussed how to measure the performance of that strategy.

Based on my analysis in *Chapter 10, Cybersecurity Strategies*, the Attack-Centric cybersecurity strategy was deemed potentially the most effective strategy for mitigating the Cybersecurity Usual Suspects. This strategy relies on granular knowledge of the tactics, techniques, and procedures that attackers leverage. With this knowledge, cybersecurity teams can use frameworks such as the **Intrusion Kill Chain** model and MITRE ATT&CK® framework to make it much harder for attackers to successfully perform traditional network intrusion attacks. The underlying assumption of this approach is that forcing attackers to be successful multiple times during intrusion attempts makes it much harder for attackers and decreases detection and recovery times. The focus of this approach is understanding how attackers operate and making each tactic and each technique they use ineffective. Lowering an attacker's return on investment by increasing the time, effort, and costs associated with their attack will force attackers to rethink or abandon their attack. This approach is characterized by investments in numerous areas to block or impede attackers at each stage of their attack.

But what if our assumptions about the types of technologies and processes that cybersecurity teams are asked to defend could evolve significantly? What if, instead of assuming that they need to defend physical servers running for months or years without interruption, that paradigm was literally turned upside down?

> *"Paradigm shift: an important change that happens when the usual way of thinking about or doing something is replaced by a new and different way" (Merriam-Webster, 2025)*

What if there were a cybersecurity strategy where Intrusion Kill Chains weren't as relevant because new technologies and processes no longer enabled attackers to use the **tactics, techniques, and procedures (TTPs)** that helped them perpetrate traditional network intrusions with the same success rate?

Now we are going to take a closer look at how newer, more modern technologies, such as cloud computing, can help security and compliance teams modernize their methods. This was my full-time job between 2012 and 2022. During this period, I discussed the security and compliance advantages of the cloud with thousands of private and public sector enterprise customers in my roles at Microsoft and **Amazon Web Services (AWS)**—two of the three preeminent **Cloud Service Providers (CSPs)** in the world. At Microsoft, I worked as the Global Chief Security Advisor, among other roles, and at AWS, I was the Global Security and Compliance Lead for Public Sector. Often, I was the very first person customers would talk to about the cloud once they decided to seriously evaluate it. I feel so fortunate to have had the opportunity to work with so many brilliant people at these CSPs, and to have helped so many enterprise customers around the world modernize their IT and improve their security and compliance programs. I'll share some of the things I learned along the way and some key insights in this chapter. Please note that all the views and opinions written in this chapter, as well as the rest of this book, are my own personal opinions and not those of any of my past or present employers.

This chapter will cover some concepts that will help put the cloud into context for CISOs and security and compliance professionals. It will also provide security and compliance teams with some food for thought on effective approaches to cybersecurity and compliance in cloud environments that they might not already be leveraging.

In this chapter, we'll cover the following topics:

- How is cloud computing different?
- Security and compliance game changers
- Using cybersecurity strategies in the cloud
- Encryption and key management

I will cover some of the new artificial intelligence **(AI)** capabilities, services, and features available in the cloud in *Chapter 15, Artificial Intelligence: Security of AI systems and using AI for better cybersecurity*.

Let's begin by looking at how the cloud is different from what IT and security teams have been doing in on-premises IT environments.

How is cloud computing different?

The three most popular CSPs in the world are AWS, Microsoft, and Google. These CSPs are often referred to as hyperscale CSPs because their cloud offerings are available all over the globe and at previously unimagined scales.

When organizations first contemplate leveraging services offered by CSPs, the first ideas most of them want to explore are security and compliance. They need to understand how CSPs can provide the IT capabilities they need while meeting or exceeding industry security standards, regulated standards, and their own internal security standards. I've heard a lot of myths about cloud computing, and I've seen the cloud help organizations achieve things they couldn't possibly achieve in their own on-premises IT environments.

Although cloud computing is being adopted by industries all over the world, this has happened unevenly and more slowly in some regions of the world. As cloud computing started to get traction with enterprises, service model descriptions made it easy to educate people on what the cloud is and what it isn't. Three cloud computing service models became popular: **Infrastructure as a Service** (**IaaS**), **Platform as a Service** (**PaaS**), and **Software as a Service** (**SaaS**). These service model descriptions made it easier for everyone to understand the types of cloud services available and where they might fit into each organization's IT portfolio. For example, organizations could run their own virtual servers in a CSP's IaaS offering, such as **Amazon Elastic Compute Cloud (Amazon EC2)**, Microsoft Azure Virtual Machines, or Google Compute Engine.

CSPs offer services based on massive physical IT infrastructures that they've built around the world. Over time, the physical infrastructure model that CSPs have roughly coalesced around is based on the model that AWS pioneered: the concept of Regions and Availability Zones. In AWS parlance, an Availability Zone is a cluster of datacenters, and a Region is a cluster of Availability Zones. There are meaningful differences in the size and scope of CSPs' infrastructures and how they leverage components of this model. You can learn about each CSP's infrastructure on their respective websites:

- AWS: `https://aws.amazon.com/about-aws/global-infrastructure/`

- Google: `https://cloud.google.com/compute/docs/regions-zones/`
- Microsoft: `https://azure.microsoft.com/explore/global-infrastructure/`

Although the terms IaaS, PaaS, and SaaS are still in widespread use today, they are slowly becoming obsolete. Back when they were first coined, CSPs only had a handful of services and these models helped describe how each service was deployed. However, this has changed over time. The three aforementioned hyperscale CSPs offer hundreds of cloud services. Subsequently, newer acronyms like **Containers as a Service** (**CaaS**), **Identity as a Service** (**IDaaS**), and **Function as a Service** (**FaaS**) cropped up. This proliferation of services has been accelerating because the developers of new services can use existing services as building blocks. For example, if a CSP is developing a new cloud service and they need storage for it, instead of building a new storage infrastructure from scratch, they can simply use one of the existing cloud storage services that meets their requirements. Not only does this approach help accelerate the development of new cloud services, but it means services could have IaaS, PaaS, and/or SaaS components, blurring the lines between these old service model descriptions. In other words, solutions to specific problems are becoming more important than maintaining service model definitions. As this cloud services proliferation continues, enterprises will be able to procure solutions for the specific problems that they want to solve, and the old service models will become less and less important.

One important distinction when it comes to service models is the difference between the services that hyperscale CSPs provide and those of traditional **managed service providers** (**MSPs**). Many organizations around the world have leveraged MSPs for decades. Governments, for example, tend to sign very long-term agreements with MSPs to manage their datacenters and provide IT services to them. MSPs have played an important role for such organizations, for at least a couple of reasons. First, MSPs have successfully maintained a critical mass of IT talent that would otherwise be challenging for enterprises to attract and retain themselves. Second, MSPs became intimately familiar with the IT environments of their customers because they managed them; this tribal knowledge provided the continuity that enterprises needed in order to minimize potential disruptions when key staff turned over. Of course, MSPs offer other benefits to their customers as well.

Much of the IT world has transitioned from a **capital expenditures** (**CAPEX**) model to an **operational expenditures** (**OPEX**) model. This is especially the case for cybersecurity. CAPEX typically requires organizations to make large IT investments up front and record these costs in accounting records over a period of years based on depreciation or amortization schedules. Because they pay up front for the technologies they procure under the CAPEX model, they have to estimate their capacity and utilization needs and hope these estimates are correct; otherwise, they end up paying up front for capacity they might never use. Studies on actual IT server utilization in enterprise datacenters suggest that actual server utilization is almost always a fraction of what was estimated and procured. An OPEX model is attractive to some organizations that cannot afford to pay up front for IT equipment. The cloud allows them to pay as they go, paying for just the specific resources that they use. MSPs and CSPs can help their customers with this shift. However, MSPs tend to have an outsourcing-based business model, while CSPs offer a self-service model for transformation instead of replication of existing processes.

Migrating to the cloud

As I mentioned earlier, as a group, hyperscale CSPs offer hundreds of services to their customers. Despite this, many enterprises still choose to lift and shift applications into the cloud. This typically means that they take an application they have been running on servers in their on-premises IT environment and run it on servers hosted in the cloud. This type of transition to the cloud allows them to maintain the people, processes, and technologies that they have been using, while moving from CAPEX to OPEX. For many organizations, this is completely natural as they have deep expertise in building and managing these systems in their on-premises IT environment, and they can continue to leverage this expertise when they move those same systems into the cloud. In the cloud, they can leverage the same or similar hardware and software that they have been using on-premises. Subsequently, this type of transition can be relatively easy and quick.

The challenge with lifting and shifting applications is that complexity, inefficiencies, and technical debt tend to also get shifted into the cloud with the applications. Still, for some organizations, this type of transition can be a starting point for bigger and better things. Typically, once organizations start using the cloud, develop some expertise with it, and explore its broader set of capabilities, they make broader use of it in the future. Instead of lifting and shifting more applications, they re-platform applications, repurchase applications, or refactor applications using cloud-native capabilities. Over time, they stop managing the cloud like they managed on-premises IT and real innovation begins to flourish. However, for some organizations, this transition and evolution can take time.

To speed things up, some organizations decide to make big, bold moves. Instead of lifting and shifting legacy applications to the cloud, they decide to migrate a mission-critical application to the cloud. Their logic is that since the application is critical to the business, it will get done right the first time, and the things they learn in the process can be applied to all the other less critical applications that follow it to the cloud. This approach will accelerate their digital transformations and help them potentially leapfrog their waffling competitors.

Cybersecurity assessment questionnaires

Some CISOs grapple with the change that the cloud represents and seek to maintain the status quo. This is because they have successfully managed their cybersecurity program in their organizations' current IT environment. Change can represent risk for some organizations. The place I've seen this illustrated most often is with the security assessments that enterprise security teams use to determine if new solutions meet their security standards and requirements. Such assessments seek to determine if a minimum set of controls is in place to protect the organization's data while it's being processed, stored, and transmitted by new solutions. For example, one assessment question could determine whether the new solution protects data in transit with the newest version of the **Transport Layer Security (TLS)** protocol. Another assessment question could determine if data at rest in the solution is encrypted using a specific algorithm. Another assessment question could be whether the vendor has a specific third-party security attestation or certification, like ISO 27001, for example.

In some organizations, when new cloud-based solutions come to the security team for a security assessment, they apply the same assessment process they have been using to assess new solutions in their on-premises IT environment. This seems reasonable; after all, the assessment checks whether solutions meet the organization's security standards.

Some of the security assessment questionnaires that I've seen over the years have been elaborate and include hundreds of questions. Many of these questionnaires were developed over a period of many years and have been customized to reflect the specific IT environments and compliance requirements of the organizations that employ them.

However, many of the questions in such assessment questionnaires are based on some key underlying assumptions; for example, the assessors will have physical access to the hardware in order to answer their questions, or assessors will be assessing systems that the organization manages themselves. Another popular assumption I've seen is that the technology used by a solution will never deviate from current commercially available technologies. For example, the hypervisor that a solution's virtualized workloads run on operates exactly the same way as the hypervisors they have been running in their on-premises IT environments. One last example is the assumption that the vendor providing the solution only has one solution and not a huge suite or stack of technologies that can be combined in different ways to solve problems. If any of these assumptions or others are not true, the assessments that are based on them cannot be fully completed. When this happens, some security teams simply reject a solution because they couldn't determine if it met their standards using their tried-and-true security assessment questionnaire. However, the glaring flaw in their assessment process is that it didn't check if the solution met the organization's security standards; it checked whether the questions in their questionnaire could be answered as written. This is a subtle but important difference.

Let me use an exaggerated analogy to illustrate what I mean. For the past few decades, car owners have been able to take their cars to professionally managed garages to have multi-point inspections completed. In some cases, these inspections are mandated by law, like emissions inspections, for example. However, what happened to the owner of the first fully electric car when they took their car for the legally mandated emissions inspection? Was the garage able to process the assessment that is required by law? Did the car have an exhaust pipe or catalytic converter for the garage to test? After all, every car must have these technologies, right? Given that the garage couldn't test this car the same way they had been testing cars for decades, should they fail to certify the car, even though it exceeds car emissions standards in a way that legacy internal combustion engines could never achieve? Some security teams reject cloud-based solutions because they cannot assess them the same way they've always assessed solutions.

Few security teams spontaneously question the assumptions that their years-old assessment processes are based on. Their security requirements don't necessarily have to change. However, they need to evolve and modernize their assessment processes to determine if new technologies can meet or exceed those requirements. The goal of security assessments is to ensure new solutions meet organizations' security requirements, not to ensure their security assessment questions never have to change. Enterprises need to question their assumptions occasionally to check if they are still accurate and relevant.

Given all this, **third-party risk management (TPRM)** is ripe for disruption by AI. In the very near future, we'll likely see the procuring party's AI agents working with vendors' AI agents to understand if their services meet the procuring party's security standards. Since this process uses automation and doesn't rely on humans, these agents can check on the security posture of the service while it runs in near real time, constantly. If this vision becomes reality, instead of a one-time or annual process, TPRM becomes much more accurate, timely, and valuable to CISOs and security teams.

Next, I'll share why I think the cloud is a game-changer for security and compliance professionals.

Security and compliance game-changers

There are numerous ways that the cloud can tilt the playing field in favor of defenders. In this section, I'll cover two security and compliance game-changers.

The power of APIs

I discussed application programming interfaces (**APIs**) in depth in *Chapter 7, Application Programming Interface (API) Security*. As I mentioned in that chapter, APIs provide a powerful mechanism for systems to interact with humans and other systems. There are different kinds of APIs, but generally, APIs define the specific inputs a system is willing to accept and the outputs it will provide. The details of how the system processes inputs and provides outputs can be abstracted from view, thus simplifying the system for humans and other systems that want to use it. In other words, I don't need to know how the system works internally in order to use it. I just need to know about its APIs. I can call an API and pass it the information it requires and then wait for the output, while the magic of software happens.

Magic here is a metaphor for all the smart engineers' and developers' work on the hardware, firmware, operating systems, and software that make up the stack of technologies on which the API and its system rely.

APIs can be programming language-specific and thus included as part of **software development kits** (**SDKs**). This makes it easy for developers who know C++, Java, or other popular programming languages to leverage APIs. Although APIs were once primarily used by developers to help them develop applications, operations roles now also make use of APIs to deploy and operate IT infrastructure, thus helping to herald the DevOps era.

In the context of cloud computing, APIs can be called from within an application, from a command line, or from the web console provided by the CSP. Let me give you some examples.

Let's say we wanted to provision and launch five virtual machines in Amazon EC2, in one of the three currently available Availability Zones in the London Region (eu-west-2). We could use the RunInstances API to do this. First, we need to understand what information the API requires in order to execute our request. Helpfully, AWS provides "AWS EC2 API Reference" documentation at `https://docs.aws.amazon.com/AWSEC2/latest/APIReference/API_RunInstances.html`.

This documentation tells us about all the required and optional parameters the API supports and provides examples of how to use the API. The following is a sample API request to launch those five virtual machines in the London Region.

```
https://ec2.amazonaws.com/?Action=RunInstances
&ImageId=ami-60a54009
&InstanceType=t2.micro
&MaxCount=5
&MinCount=1
&KeyName=my-key-pair
&Placement.AvailabilityZone=eu-west-2a
&AUTHPARAMS
```

If we used the AWS Console to do the same thing, the Launch Instance wizard would collect all the configuration information for the virtual machines and make the same type of API call on our behalf. We could also use the AWS **Command-Line Interface (CLI)** to launch these virtual machines, specifying the same parameters, and the CLI would make the same type of API call for us.

```
aws ec2 run-instances --image-id ami-60a54009 --count 5 --instance-type t2.micro
--key-name my-key-pair
```

Under the covers of the system from which this AWS CLI command is run, it will send this type of API request to Amazon EC2 using the HTTPS protocol on TCP port 443 (AWS, n.d.).

One important thing to keep in mind is that API calls require authentication, authorization, integrity, and confidentiality mechanisms. I won't get into all these details here, but the CSPs offer documentation that will help you understand the mechanisms they've implemented, or not implemented, to provide these things for their APIs. For example, you can read about security for AWS CLI at this URL: `https://docs.aws.amazon.com/cli/latest/userguide/security.html`.

Of course, like AWS, Google Cloud and Microsoft Azure have similar APIs and support a range of programming and scripting languages, as well as command-line interfaces. This is an example from the Command-Line Interface SDK from Google, first creating a virtual machine and then starting it (Google, n.d.).

```
gcloud compute instances create example-instance --image-family=rhel-8 --image-
project=rhel-cloud --zone=us-central1-a
gcloud compute instances start example-instance --zone=us-central1-a
```

A similar example can be seen here regarding the creation of a virtual machine in Microsoft Azure using **Python to call the API**. Once the virtual machine has been created, another API call will start it. This can also be done using the Azure CLI, Azure PowerShell, or Azure Portal.

```
compute_client.virtual_machines.begin_create_or_update(
    "my_resource_group",
    "my_vm",
    {"location": "uksouth", "hardware_profile": {"vm_size": "Standard_B1s"}}
).result()
compute_client.virtual_machines.begin_start("my_resource_group", "my_vm").result()
```

As you've seen, using APIs enables the users of these services to deploy infrastructure, such as servers, firewalls, network load balancers, and third-party appliances. However, it also allows us to configure that infrastructure exactly the way we want it to be configured. For example, when deploying servers, we can specify the operating systems, IP addresses, network security configurations, routing tables, and so on. This is extremely powerful. With a single command, we can start one virtual machine or a hundred thousand virtual machines, all configured exactly the way we want them configured. Because we know exactly how our systems should be configured, we can compare the current configurations of the systems that are running in production to our standard configuration and determine if there are any differences. We can do this constantly in order to detect changes that could be indicators of compromise.

In on-premises IT environments, this typically involves deploying agents or management software on the servers that monitor configuration changes.

One challenge that many organizations have is deploying and managing multiple agents and management suites from different vendors. Each agent requires some level of management and security updates to ensure it doesn't increase the attack surface area. Typically, CISOs and CIOs look for ways to reduce the number of agents running on systems and resist the idea of deploying more of them in their environments. Meanwhile, the sources of system configuration changes can include all sorts of things—administrators, management software, users, malware, restoring from backups, and so on. This can make it challenging to detect changes and determine if changes to systems are indicators of compromise.

In the cloud, since everything happens via APIs, the APIs provide the perfect choke point for visibility and control, enabling organizations to monitor their API calls and take action based on what's happening. In this environment, deploying agents and management software to hundreds or thousands of systems is optional because the APIs are baked into the cloud. If an organization has regulatory compliance requirements that dictate specific control configurations, it can monitor those controls to ensure that it is always in compliance.

In practice, API calls are logged to API logging services for this purpose. For example, AWS CloudTrail is an API logging service for AWS accounts (AWS, n.d.). Earlier, when we ran the command that started five virtual machines in AWS EC2, if AWS CloudTrail was enabled, it would have logged an event that captured the details of that API call. This event contains an incredible amount of details, including which account was used, the principal that made the call, some authentication and authorization details, the time, the Region, the source IP address the call came from, details on the virtual machine, and some details regarding its configuration. These logs can be combined with other logging data, aggregated, and analyzed by humans and data analytics systems, imported into SIEMs in the cloud and/or downloaded to systems in on-premises IT environments. These logs are also essential for incident response investigations. Google offers Cloud Audit Logs (Google, December 19, 2025), while Microsoft provides Azure Monitor (Microsoft Corporation, August 26, 2025), in addition to other logging mechanisms, for similar purposes.

Here is a truncated example of an event logged by AWS CloudTrail:

```
{
  "eventVersion": "1.08",
  "userIdentity": {
    "type": "IAMUser",
    "principalId": "EXAMPLE123456789",
    "arn": "arn:aws:iam::123456789025:user/tim",
    "accountId": "123456789025",
    "accessKeyId": "EXAMPLE",
    "userName": "tim"
  },
  "eventTime": "2025-01-15T12:34:56Z",
  "eventSource": "ec2.amazonaws.com",
  "eventName": "RunInstances",
  "awsRegion": "eu-west-2",
  "sourceIPAddress": "208.10.213.11",
  "userAgent": "aws-cli/2.15.0 Python/3.11.0 Linux/5.15 botocore/2.15.0",
  "requestParameters": {
    "minCount": 1,
    "maxCount": 5,
    "imageId": "ami-60a54009",
    "instanceType": "t2.micro",
    "subnetId": "subnet-0abc1234def567890",
    "placement": {
      "availabilityZone": "eu-west-2a"
    }
  },
  "responseElements": {
    "requestId": "12345678-90ab-cdef-1234-567890abcdef",
    "reservationId": "r-0abc1234def567890",
    "instancesSet": {
      "items": [
        { "instanceId": "i-01aaa111aaa111aaa" },
        { "instanceId": "i-02bbb222bbb222bbb" },
        { "instanceId": "i-03ccc333ccc333ccc" },
        { "instanceId": "i-04ddd444ddd444ddd" },
        { "instanceId": "i-05eee555eee555eee" }
      ]
    }
  },
```

```
    "requestID": "12345678-90ab-cdef-1234-567890abcdef",
    "eventID": "abcdef12-3456-7890-abcd-ef1234567890",
    "readOnly": false,
    "eventType": "AwsApiCall",
    "managementEvent": true,
    "recipientAccountId": "123456789025",
    "eventCategory": "Management"
}
```


To recap, every interaction with the cloud happens via an API call. This model has numerous benefits, including security and compliance benefits. Because of this, the visibility and control that the cloud offers are superior to that of most on-premises IT environments, not to mention the simplicity and cost benefits of this approach. Plus, it enables new approaches to IT and security operations. For example, we know that every system that we deploy is configured to meet our security and compliance standards, because that's how it has been defined in the code that we use to deploy them. Since storage and networking are decoupled from compute services, nothing prevents us from simply shutting down systems and deploying new systems to replace them every few hours. It just takes a few lines of code in a script or application to do this, as we saw earlier. If systems are short-lived, it makes it harder for administrators and management software to introduce security misconfigurations over time that attackers can use to get a foothold in the environment.

APIs are powerful, but they too must be properly implemented so that they do not create a porous attack surface. Of course, the CSPs know this and employ expertise, processes, and technology in the development of their APIs to minimize risk. Layer in authentication and authorization mechanisms, protection, monitoring, detection, response, and audit capabilities, and APIs rock!

I've discussed one scenario here, which is using APIs to configure and start virtual machines. Now, imagine if you could use APIs to control and orchestrate hundreds of cloud services that perform all sorts of functions, such as compute, storage, networking, databases, containers, serverless computing, artificial intelligence, machine learning, IoT, and security, to name just a few. Imagine having programmatic control over all of that, at virtually any scale, anywhere in the world—truly amazing. This is the power of APIs! They really are a game changer for security and compliance professionals. The power of APIs is not only available to large organizations with large IT budgets; anyone with a credit card can open an account with a CSP and get the power of these APIs. Next, let's look at another game changer, automation.

The advantages of automation

As we've seen, the power of APIs enables us to configure and control most things in the cloud using code, even infrastructure. To take full advantage of the power of APIs, the cloud offers high levels of automation. In addition to running CLI commands, you can automate complex workflows using scripts, templates, applications, and cloud services.

CSPs offer rich automation capabilities. These capabilities are spread across different cloud services, just like the APIs they leverage. Some examples of services that help automate functions include Microsoft Azure Automation (Microsoft Corporation, April 24, 2025), Google Cloud Composer (Google, 2020), and AWS CloudFormation (AWS, n.d.). There are also automation solutions available from third parties, such as Chef (Chef, 2020), Puppet (Puppet, 2020), Ansible (Ansible, 2020), Terraform (Hashicorp, 2020), and many others.

For security and compliance professionals, all these automation capabilities and tools can help provision, configure, manage, monitor, reconfigure, and deprovision infrastructure and other cloud services. In addition, these rich automation capabilities can help protect, detect, respond, and recover, while maintaining compliance with regulated standards, industry standards, and internal security standards. In many cases, all of this can happen in near real time because automation, not humans, is performing these operations.

In fact, reducing human participation in these operations has many advantages. Remember the Cybersecurity Usual Suspects that I discussed at length in *Chapter 1, How Enterprises Get Hacked*; let's look at some examples of how automation can help us mitigate some of these. Let's start by looking at insider threat and social engineering.

Mitigating insider threats and social engineering

Remember the two types of insider threats that I defined earlier: malicious insiders who abuse their privileged access to resources, and non-malicious insiders who make mistakes that lead to poor security outcomes. Automation can help mitigate both types of threats. For example, the more automation we develop, test, and implement, the fewer chances administrators will have to make mistakes that have security consequences.

Using automation to complete repeatable processes can lead to more consistent and faster outcomes that are less prone to human error.

Automating administrative processes will also result in fewer opportunities for malicious insiders to act. This is where the concepts of just-in-time administration and just-enough administration can be helpful. With high levels of automation in place, administrators will require less access to systems, thus reducing the opportunities they have to steal data or damage infrastructure. Highly automated environments also make it easier to detect when administrators access systems because such occasions will be exceptions to the rules. When malicious insiders know there is increased visibility and scrutiny on them when they directly access data and systems, the frequency with which they will attempt to access resources without legitimate reasons is reduced.

Automation can help minimize the amount of access administrators have. For example, instead of allowing administrators full access to systems they connect to, only allowing them to run pre-tested and approved scripts and automation on those systems will reduce the opportunities they have to run arbitrary commands. With enough automation, the only time administrators have legitimate cause to run arbitrary commands is in "break-glass" scenarios where existing automation cannot fix a problem. These cases can be monitored and audited to reduce the chances that a malicious insider will act. During such scenarios, employing quorum-based administration procedures with two or more participants can also help mitigate insider threats. Adding more automation over time to cover more support scenarios can dramatically reduce the opportunities that administrators have to run arbitrary commands.

There are also privacy benefits to using automation. If humans don't have access to sensitive data, then they can't be exposed to **personally identifiable information (PII)**, **protected health information (PHI)**, or sensitive financial information. Using automation to interact with data, instead of humans, helps organizations fulfill the privacy promises they make to their customers or citizens.

Sounds great, right? Maybe too good to be true? Can't we already do this in on-premises IT environments by using bastion hosts and **Secure Shell (SSH)** sessions? Great questions. Let's look at a real-world example.

The security team's requirements in this example specify that administrators cannot directly access the systems they are managing. This means using SSH to access systems directly isn't going to meet requirements. If they did use SSH to access these systems, they might be able to run arbitrary commands on these systems, which is something the security team wants to avoid.

The security team in this scenario also wants to limit the use of bastion hosts in their environment. They have been burned using bastion hosts in the past. Bastion hosts typically span a higher security zone and a lower security zone, allowing administrators to get access to systems in the higher security zone from the lower security zone; subsequently, bastion hosts need to be managed as if they are part of the higher security zone. It turns out that this can be harder than it sounds, and lapses in this fictional organization's processes led to a system compromise in their environment. Having been burned once, they want to minimize the number of bastion hosts in their environment.

One way to meet these requirements using AWS, for example, is to use the AWS Systems Manager service to run commands on virtual machines running in the Amazon EC2 service. To do this, the Systems Manager Agent will be installed on those virtual machines. This is easy to do using automation. As each virtual machine is provisioned in EC2 using code, the Systems Manager Agent will also be installed on them. Once that agent is properly configured, administrators can run tested and approved scripts from the AWS Systems Manager console that will execute on those virtual machines via the Systems Manager Agent (AWS, July 14, 2022).

There are a few advantages to this approach. First, administrators do not need to have administrator credentials for the virtual machines they are managing. Since they are running scripts from the AWS Systems Manager service in the cloud, they don't need local credentials to access individual systems. If administrators don't know the usernames and passwords for those systems, they can't log directly into them. They are limited to running the tested and approved scripts from the cloud. This helps mitigate the risk of insider threat to those systems.

This approach also mitigates some of the risk associated with social engineering on these systems. Administrators can't be tricked into giving up credentials for those systems because they don't know them. Since the only way administrators interact with these systems is by remotely running pre-approved scripts on them, they can't be tricked into running arbitrary commands or installing new software, which can undermine the security of these systems and lead to bad security outcomes. Of course, given how insidious social engineering is, this approach must be combined with some other mitigations to fully address it; for example, **multi-factor authentication (MFA)** for the AWS accounts themselves. However, I hope you can see the potential advantages of this approach when it comes to mitigating typical social engineering attacks against administrators. When administrators only have access when they need it and that access is tightly scoped and controlled, there's less opportunity for typical social engineering tactics to be successful.

Remember that one of the big advantages of using the cloud is scalability. If we install the Systems Manager Agent on every virtual machine that we deploy, using automation, of course, we will have the ability to use this administration method on as many systems as required—the scale is virtually unlimited. Using automation, we can manage three or three thousand systems with the same technique and amount of effort. As the number of systems that we manage increases or decreases, there is no additional work required by administrators because they run the same scripts regardless of the number of systems they manage; managing more systems doesn't mean administrators have more access.

If we are logging the API calls that are generated by the administrators' interactions with the AWS Systems Manager service in AWS CloudTrail, then their activities can be monitored and audited in near real time (AWS, n.d.). We can also monitor and audit any interaction administrators have with the virtual machines themselves to ensure administrators only access these systems in break-glass events.

Of course, other CSPs have rich automation capabilities as well. For example, Microsoft offers a range of services and capabilities to help, including Azure Automation, Azure PowerShell,

Azure Monitor, and others. Google offers several services as well, including Cloud Monitoring, Cloud Functions, and Cloud Asset Inventory, among others.

Automation allows us to design systems that don't require direct human interaction very often. This makes it easier to detect when those events happen and better mitigate insider threats and social engineering. Next, let's look at how another one of the Cybersecurity Usual Suspects, unpatched vulnerabilities, can be mitigated in this scenario.

Mitigating unpatched vulnerabilities

Let's look at how we can use automation to help manage vulnerabilities on the virtual machines we use. As we saw in *Chapter 3, Industry Vulnerability Disclosure Trends*, in 2024, vulnerability management teams were faced with as many as 110 new vulnerability disclosures per day across the industry that potentially impact their systems. In 2025, that number was closer to 130 vulnerability disclosures per day. Automation in the cloud can help reduce the amount of work related to inventorying systems, scanning systems, and patching systems.

For example, recall that I wrote in *Chapter 3* that accurate inventories are critical to vulnerability management teams. In the cloud, because nothing gets provisioned or deprovisioned without using APIs, APIs and automation help provide accurate inventories quickly. Inventorying environments like this doesn't take hours or days—it can be nearly instantaneous.

There are many methods available to scan and patch virtual machines in the cloud. In our AWS example, AWS Systems Manager can be used to patch systems. Amazon Inspector can also help. Also, chances are, the vendors your organization uses for vulnerability management software in your on-premises IT environment also have similar capabilities built for the cloud. This allows your organization to take the expertise it has developed from managing vulnerabilities in its on-premises IT environment and continue to leverage it in the cloud.

You might be wondering how vulnerability management processes are potentially impacted by virtual machines running in the cloud when the number of systems can be scaled up and down completely dynamically to meet load and application availability targets. In this scenario, Amazon EC2 Auto Scaling can be used to accomplish this (AWS, 2016). It can also help keep systems up to date. Instead of scanning and patching every system in a big fleet of systems, Auto Scaling can be used to dramatically reduce this effort. To do this, the Amazon Machine Image used to build the virtual machines is scanned for vulnerabilities, and security updates are installed as needed after testing. This ensures the image is up to date and security updates have been tested. After the Amazon Machine Image has been updated, you can shut down a virtual machine running in production that is based on the older version of that image, either manually or using automation. Based on the load and availability rules you set for Auto Scaling, when Auto Scaling decides it's time to launch a new virtual machine, it does so using the image that you just patched and tested. When the new virtual machine starts, it is fully patched. You can use automation to thoughtfully shut down the virtual machines running in production that are based on the old image, and Auto Scaling will restart new, fully patched virtual machines to replace them. No scanning and patching hundreds or thousands of systems. And the pain from reboots is largely mitigated. This is a much easier way to do something that has long been a pain point for large enterprises.

Administrators of AWS EC2 systems who wanted to leverage this approach had to develop their own scripts. But now, AWS has built a feature into Auto Scaling called Instance Refresh to make this approach to patching even easier. You can get all the details here: `https://docs.aws.amazon.com/autoscaling/ec2/userguide/asg-instance-refresh.html`

Google and Microsoft also provide tools to make finding and mitigating vulnerabilities efficient. For replacing existing VMs with new patched VMs, Microsoft offers Rolling Upgrades on Azure Virtual Machine Scale Sets as well as Automatic OS Image Upgrades. Google offers **Managed Instance Group (MIG)** Rolling Updates and Instance Recreate. For in-place patching, Google offers OS inventory management, OS patch management, and Web Security Scanner, while Microsoft offers Azure Automation and Microsoft Defender for Cloud, among other tools. There are numerous third-party vendors that provide vulnerability management solutions for cloud environments, including Qualys, Tenable, and many others.

Of course, this is just one method to perform patching—there are others. There is the potential to eliminate patching altogether by using services that the CSPs manage for you. As I mentioned earlier in this chapter, IaaS is but one type of service model in the cloud; there are hundreds of services from CSPs that do not require you to provision, manage, and patch servers at all. If you don't need to manage servers yourself, why bother? Let the CSPs manage infrastructure for you, and you can spend the time normally relegated to such tasks on reducing technical debt in other areas, project work that never seems to get done, or innovating—imagine that. Imagine spending time figuring out how to use serverless computing, AI, ML, and IoT to better protect, detect, and respond to threats, instead of testing patches and rebooting servers.

Using managed services doesn't increase the attack surface that your security team needs to track and manage—the CSPs do that for you. The net result is potentially dramatically increased IT capabilities without increasing your IT attack surface and the number of systems to patch and manage. For example, you can use a managed service to increase detection capabilities for your cloud IT estate without provisioning any additional infrastructure that you need to manage. This will potentially give you more visibility without increasing complexity and technical debt. However, not all managed services are equal. It is very important to clearly understand the security functions that the service provider promises to provide and those they don't. For example, some SaaS providers expect their enterprise customers to have security teams dedicated to managing their SaaS services. These arrangements can be disastrous if enterprises are not prepared to staff these functions properly because they assume the service provider is performing those security functions on their behalf.

The cloud can definitely help mitigate unpatched vulnerabilities and make vulnerability management much easier than it is in most on-premises environments, something that has plagued enterprises for decades. Now, let's see how automation in the cloud can help mitigate another of the Cybersecurity Usual Suspects: security misconfigurations.

Mitigating security misconfigurations

As I wrote in *Chapter 9, Ingredients for a Successful Cybersecurity Strategy*, security misconfigurations can be poor default settings in hardware, operating systems, and applications, or can occur over time as systems "drift" out of their organization's standards based on the tweaks administrators, management software, or software updates introduce. Additionally, in big IT environments, abandoned technology can quickly become a forgotten risk that isn't actively managed. Because of the constant struggle large enterprises have had with keeping things configured the way they need them, **change management** has emerged as a full-blown IT discipline, supported by an entire industry of vendors. This is important, not just for security purposes, but also for compliance purposes. Ensuring systems comply with regulated standards, industry standards, and internal IT standards is important and, in many cases, required.

In our example scenario, organizations can choose to install management software on the servers that they deploy in the cloud. They can continue to measure and remediate configuration changes in much the same way they have in their on-premises IT environment.

They can also harness the power of APIs and the automation built into the cloud. For example, AWS Config is a cloud service that monitors resources for configuration changes and enables you to take a range of actions based on those changes.

In our example scenario, the security team might decide that one type of change should be automatically remediated; when the change is detected, automation will change the configuration back to its standard setting. Alternatively, just to be safe, automation can be used to shut down the misconfigured system, and, if enabled, Auto Scaling will start a new system that meets all of the organization's standards to replace it.

The security team might deem another type of change to be an indicator of compromise that needs to be investigated by their incident response team. In this case, automation can take a snapshot of the virtual machine, create a new **virtual private cloud (VPC)**—let's call it *Incident Response Clean Room*—copy the snapshot into the isolated Incident Response Clean Room, connect the IR team's forensics software to the image, send a message to the incident response team to investigate it, and shut down the original virtual machine. If configured, Auto Scaling will start a new, pristine virtual machine that meets all approved standards to take its place. It does all this in near real time. Notice that in these examples, there was no management software or agent on the virtual machine and no SOC analysts performing manual queries looking for indicators of compromise. Since infrastructure is code, we can automate any number of actions to suit the organization's needs.

Helpfully, a project was published by the MITRE Center for Threat-Informed Defense that mapped AWS Config functionality to the MITRE ATT&CK® framework. This information helps us understand how AWS Config can help protect against and detect techniques documented in the ATT&CK framework. Here's one example,

> *"The "mfa-enabled-for-iam-console-access" managed rule checks whether multi-factor authentication is enabled for all AWS IAM users, protecting against misuse of those accounts' access to Amazon System Manager and the ability to run cloud administration commands. It is run periodically, and provides significant coverage, resulting in an overall score of Significant." (Center for Threat-Informed Defense, n.d.)*

In fact, the MITRE Center for Threat-Informed Defense has mapped numerous AWS services to the ATT&CK framework for this purpose. All the details are available here: `https://center-for-threat-informed-defense.github.io/mappings-explorer/external/aws/`.

In a compliance context, this functionality is also powerful, as it can help keep things configured in a way that complies with standards. When we use automation to detect changes and take appropriate actions, we can also use that automation to generate compliance artifacts that will help the organization prove continuous compliance with the specific standards that apply to it. This helps reduce manual audits and manual remediation of misconfigured systems.

Microsoft Azure Automation and Google Cloud Asset Inventory provide similar capabilities for their respective services. There are also third parties that provide automation solutions, such as Ansible, Chef, Terraform, and several others.

Next, let's look at how automation in the cloud helps mitigate the last of the Cybersecurity Usual Suspects: weak, leaked, and stolen credentials.

Mitigating weak, leaked, and stolen credentials

CSPs and numerous third-party vendors offer identity and access management solutions for cloud and hybrid environments. For example, Microsoft offers Microsoft Entra ID and supporting services such as just-in-time privileged access capabilities via Entra **Privileged Identity Management** (**PIM**) (Microsoft Corporation, January 7, 2025). Third parties such as

Delinea, CyberArk, Okta, and many others also provide services that can help in several different scenarios. Google Cloud offers Cloud Identity and Access Management, while AWS offers AWS Identity and Access Management.

CSPs offer MFA, which is a highly effective control that mitigates weak, leaked, and stolen credentials to a great extent. Leveraging MFA and limiting the amount of time users have access to resources between authentication requests can make it much harder for attackers to use stolen and leaked credentials successfully. Using a secrets manager to manage access keys, certificates, and credentials that automatically change and rotate them periodically can also be effective. To do this, Google offers Google Cloud Secret Manager (Google, December 19, 2025), Microsoft offers Azure Key Vault (N.d.), and AWS provides AWS Secrets Manager (AWS, n.d.). Again, there are many third-party vendors that also offer solutions, including Docker Secrets, GitHub SecretHub, and others.

In fact, there are so many capabilities and so much functionality in identity and access management services and solutions that entire books have been dedicated to this topic area. Identity is the key to security. I highly recommend spending some time learning about the powerful identity and access management capabilities that CSPs and other vendors have to offer.

Security and compliance game changers—summary

APIs and automation in the cloud are two game changers for security and compliance professionals. That's not to say that APIs and automation are not available in on-premises IT environments. However, the investment and effort required to bring these capabilities on par with those baked into the cloud would be prohibitively expensive and difficult to implement. Considering that anyone with a credit card and a few minutes to open an account with a CSP gets these capabilities by default, it would be difficult to justify implementing on-premises versions.

We've now seen that the cloud can offer some effective and innovative ways to address all the Cybersecurity Usual Suspects. Put another way, the cloud makes addressing the Cybersecurity Fundamentals easier than mitigating them in on-premises IT environments. We've only really scratched the surface here because the example scenario I used throughout this section was an IaaS example. As I mentioned, CSPs offer hundreds of services that span and blend IaaS, PaaS, SaaS, FaaS, IDaaS, and others. Not to mention, I didn't dive into any of the security services these CSPs offer. Entire books have been dedicated to the topic of cloud security.

Now let's look at how the cloud can support the cybersecurity strategies that we examined in *Chapter 10*.

Using cybersecurity strategies in the cloud

In *Chapter 10*, we examined several cybersecurity strategies that I have seen employed in the industry over the past two decades. We evaluated these strategies using the **Cybersecurity Fundamentals Scoring System (CFSS)**. The CFSS score estimate for each strategy helps us understand how well they address the Cybersecurity Usual Suspects. To refresh your memory, a summary of the CFSS scores for each strategy is provided in *Table 13.1*.

Cybersecurity Strategy	Unpatched vulnerabilities	Security misconfigurations	Weak, leaked, or stolen credentials	Social engineering	Insider threats	Total score
Protect and Recover Strategy	10	10	0	5	0	25
Endpoint Protection Strategy	15	15	15	10	15	70
Physical Control and Security Clearances Strategy with air gap	10	10	15	10	10	55
Physical Control and Security Clearances Strategy without air gap	0	0	0	10	10	20
Compliance as a Cybersecurity Strategy	10	10	10	10	10	50
Application-Centric Strategy	20	20	10	10	10	70
Identity-Centric Strategy	5	5	15	10	10	45
Data-Centric Strategy	5	5	0	15	15	40
Attack-Centric Strategy	20	20	20	15	20	95
Resilience as a Cybersecurity Strategy	20	20	5	5	15	65

Table 13.1 – CFSS score estimate summary for cybersecurity strategies discussed in Chapter 10.

Almost any of these strategies can be used in the cloud. Let's look at a few of these strategies in the context of the cloud.

Using the protect and recover strategy in the cloud

CSPs offer granular firewall and network controls that can help organizations adopt and operate the Protect and Recover Strategy. The power of APIs and automation in the cloud enables network teams and security teams to provision and operate web application firewalls, as well as network firewalls at the edge of their cloud estates and build and operate DMZs. They also provide virtual private clouds or virtual networks that add another layer of control over network traffic, in addition to network ACLs, routing tables, subnet rules, host-based firewalls, and so on. CSPs typically offer a dizzying array of network controls. Here's an example of configuring a security group (a host-based firewall) in AWS EC2, using Bash and the AWS CLI.

```
# Create the security group
aws ec2 create-security-group \
  --group-name my-security-group \
  --description "My security group" \
  --vpc-id vpc-0123456789abcdee9

# Add an inbound rule (SSH from your IP)
aws ec2 authorize-security-group-ingress \
  --group-name my-security-group \
  --protocol tcp \
  --port 22 \
  --cidr 203.0.113.0/24

# Add an inbound rule (HTTP from anywhere)
aws ec2 authorize-security-group-ingress \
  --group-name my-security-group \
  --protocol tcp \
  --port 80 \
  --cidr 0.0.0.0/0
```

Since all these controls can be provisioned and monitored via code and automation, it's much easier to execute this strategy in the cloud versus on-premises. In the cloud, there is no hardware to order and receive, no racking and stacking in the datacenter, and nothing requiring more rack space, power, or cooling. You just run code and the CSPs do everything else. If you need to scale your infrastructure up or down, it's just more code and automation. You only pay for what you use and can shut it down any time your organization decides to. The Protect and Recover Strategy is a poor scoring strategy, as we discussed in *Chapter 10*. However, it can be used in combination with other strategies to more fully address the cybersecurity fundamentals. It's easier to extend this strategy in the cloud too, because everything is code. Let's look at a better scoring strategy now.

Compliance as a cybersecurity strategy in the cloud

Let's look at another strategy from *Chapter 10*, Compliance as a Cybersecurity Strategy. Earlier in this chapter, we looked at how APIs and automation in the cloud help mitigate security misconfigurations. Those same capabilities can help organizations continuously comply with security standards, whether they are regulated, industry, or internal standards. I've already discussed how APIs and automation can ensure that systems are properly configured and continuously monitored for configuration changes. However, there's one important nuance to executing this strategy to be aware of.

Many security teams and compliance teams that contemplate using the cloud for the first time wonder how they can prove that they are complying with standards when they don't own the datacenters their infrastructures are running in and subsequently can't give their auditors access to these facilities. Regardless of who owns the datacenters, many organizations still must prove to their auditors and regulators that they are complying with required standards.

In most cases, this is another advantage of leveraging hyperscale CSPs. AWS, Google, and Microsoft all have numerous certifications and attestations across their cloud services. For example, ISO 27001 is table stakes for any CSP today—they all must have this certification to satisfy requirements for their enterprise customers. There are two certifications that are most valuable to many CISOs and compliance teams.

The first is the American Institute of CPAs' **System and Organization Controls (SOC)**, in particular the SOC2 Type II certification (AICPA, n.d.). There are at least a couple of things that make this certification valuable to CISOs, security teams, and compliance teams. First, the scope of controls that are audited in a SOC2 Type II typically answers most of the questions that enterprises have about security. Second, this isn't a "point in time" snapshot of control settings or architectural design; it takes organizations that pursue the SOC2 Type II six months of continuous audit to achieve it. The steps that organizations take to get ready for this type of audit can dramatically improve their security posture. Then, to achieve this certification and maintain it over time and continuously prove that services are being operated the way they are described can be a big challenge. Many enterprises would never even attempt to get this certification because it's hard to do and can be expensive. However, the hyperscale CSPs achieve and maintain this certification across many of their services and datacenters in order to keep their security standards among the highest in the industry.

CSPs will typically share their SOC2 Type II audit reports with their customers. For security teams and compliance teams, it is worth downloading these reports and reviewing them to ensure the solution(s) they are evaluating meet or exceed their standards. Questions not answered by the SOC2 Type II audit report can be directed to the CSPs themselves, who are typically happy to answer them.

Another attestation that many CISOs and security teams find valuable is the **Cloud Computing Compliance Controls Catalog (C5)**, designed by the **Federal Office for Information Security (BSI)**, a federal government office in Germany (The BSI, October 2020). The C5 is an in-depth security assurance attestation. It has criteria for many domains, including policies, personnel, physical security, identity and access management, encryption, and others. Again, the scope and complexity of this attestation can make it a challenge to achieve and maintain. Like the SOC2 Type II, for CISOs, this attestation contains answers to many of the questions they have about CSPs' security control sets.

SOC2 Type II and the C5 are like treasure troves of security information for CISOs, security teams, compliance teams, and auditors. CSPs typically combine these with numerous other certifications and attestations to help their customers prove they are meeting their compliance requirements. However, customers of CSPs have a role to play in this as well. Remember that CSPs are different from MSPs. CSPs offer self-service clouds. Their customers and **independent software vendors (ISVs)** can build on top of those clouds to create solutions. However, the scopes of the CSPs' certifications and attestations do not cover the portion of solutions that are architected and operated by their customers; unlike MSPs, CSPs typically don't have the visibility or the access required to do this.

This arrangement means that CSPs and their customers both bear responsibility for their respective portions of the solutions they design and operate. Google, Microsoft, and AWS all refer to this arrangement as a shared responsibility. Both CSPs and their customers provide the appropriate certifications and attestations to prove that their respective portions of their solutions meet the requirements of the standards they are bound to. This arrangement typically saves CSPs' customers time and money. This is because the portion of their solutions that they must attest to can be dramatically reduced in almost all cases. For example, since CSPs' customers don't own the datacenters that their infrastructures are running in, they have essentially delegated the responsibility to audit and certify those datacenters to their CSPs. Put another way, they no longer have to deal with the complexity and cost of physical datacenters, as the CSPs do this for them. It's a win for CSPs' customers because they can meet or exceed the security standards they are responsible for, while reducing the amount of effort and cost to them.

Information on the compliance programs that CSPs operate can be found on their respective websites, but the auditors' reports themselves are typically reserved for CSPs' customers. Here are the locations that contain compliance program information for AWS, Google, and Microsoft:

- AWS: `https://aws.amazon.com/compliance/programs/`
- Goggle: `https://cloud.google.com/security/compliance/`
- Microsoft: `https://www.microsoft.com/en-us/trust-center/compliance/compliance-overview`

The combination of APIs, automation, and the certifications and attestations provided by CSPs can help organizations that want to pursue Compliance as a Cybersecurity Strategy. For organizations that want to extend this strategy to fully address the Cybersecurity

Fundamentals, the cloud typically makes this easier than in on-premises IT environments. This is because of the APIs and automation capabilities we have discussed. Everything is code.

Let's use the **Payment Card Industry Data Security Standard (PCI DSS)** as an example. It is a global information security standard to protect credit card data. Organizations that process credit card transactions typically strive to comply with the latest version of this standard. Given this, CSPs offer their customers shortcuts to do this in the cloud.

For example, AWS offers conformance packs that enable their customers to create the appropriate governance checks and remediation actions using AWS Config. In fact, all three hyperscale CSPs offer their customers helpful shortcuts to complying with PCI DSS requirements. Here are pointers to some of their guidance:

- AWS: Operational Best Practices for PCI DSS 4.0 – `https://docs.aws.amazon.com/config/latest/developerguide/operational-best-practices-for-pci-dss-v4-including-global-resource-types.html`
- Microsoft: Details of the PCI DSS v4.0 Regulatory Compliance built-in initiative – `https://learn.microsoft.com/en-us/azure/governance/policy/samples/pci-dss-4-0?context=%2Fazure%2Fgovernance%2Fpolicy%2Fcontext%2Fpolicy-context`
- Google: PCI Data Security Standard compliance – `https://docs.cloud.google.com/architecture/pci-dss-compliance-in-gcp?hl=en`

The CSPs offer similar guidance for a range of regulatory and industry standards, including popular security standards such as NIST SP 800-53 and ISO 27001.

Let's look at one more strategy that we examined in *Chapter 10*, and how it can be implemented in the cloud.

Using the attack-centric strategy in the cloud

The best scoring of all the strategies that we examined was the Attack-Centric Strategy. In *Chapter 11, Cybersecurity Strategy Implementation*, we did a deep dive into this strategy and illustrated one way it could be implemented. In *Chapter 12, Measuring Performance and Effectiveness*, we examined one way the efficacy of this strategy can be measured. However, can this strategy be implemented in the cloud?

The short answer to this question is yes, it can be implemented in the cloud. In fact, I co-authored a whitepaper that will help security teams implement an Intrusion Kill Chain model in AWS. You can read more about this approach and get access to the paper at this URL: `https://aws.amazon.com/blogs/security/whitepaper-available-classic-intrusion-analysis-frameworks-for-aws-environments/`

In *Chapter 11*, we discussed how the MITRE ATT&CK® framework can complement the Intrusion Kill Chain model, which we examined in depth. Both of these frameworks can be used in the cloud. To do this, you'll likely want to scope your efforts to developing a Courses of Action Matrix (Hutchins, E.M., Cloppert, M.J., Amin, R.M., n.d.), like we did in *Chapter 11*, for the solution you are implementing in the cloud. Put another way, since this can be a time-intensive exercise, as you saw, you don't need to build a Courses of Action Matrix for every cloud service that a CSP offers, only the ones you plan to use. If you plan to leverage AWS, this is already done for you in the aforementioned whitepaper that I co-authored. An entire Courses of Action Matrix is already built for you that includes every AWS security service and feature (that was available when we wrote the paper). The appendix in that paper provides 70 pages of service and feature mappings to phases of a modified Intrusion Kill Chain framework. Developing this appendix was months of work for a team of us at AWS and provides security teams with a huge head start. If you are planning to use Google Cloud or Microsoft's cloud services, they might have similar content available, or you'll have to develop your own Courses of Action Matrix.

Building a Courses of Action Matrix for solutions developed for IaaS environments is, in some respects, similar to performing this mapping for on-premises IT environments. This is because much of the hardware and software can be the same or similar. For example, the operating system mitigations identified for a solution running on Linux or Windows will be very similar, regardless of whether that operating system is running in the cloud or on premises. However, as we discussed earlier, cloud-native controls and third-party solutions can also be layered into the environment, in addition to these operating system mitigations, to implement a set of controls that will make it much harder for attackers to be successful. For example, the same services that help us detect configuration changes will help us detect indicators of compromise in the cloud, in near real time. The same identity and access management capabilities we discussed will make it much harder for attackers to use stolen credentials to move laterally. The techniques we talked about to help keep systems up to date will make it harder for attackers to find and exploit unpatched vulnerabilities.

Note that although the Intrusion Kill Chain approach lends itself well to solutions that are built in IaaS environments, this approach is less helpful for solutions that are built using cloud services higher up the stack, like managed services. In these cases, CSPs are responsible for securing the underlying IT environment, typically leaving less direct access and less direct control of the underlying IT infrastructure to their customers' security teams. This doesn't mean security teams don't have the visibility and control they require—it's just the opposite, as we've discussed. However, the types of mitigating controls will likely be different from traditional solutions developed for on-premises or IaaS environments.

The controls should be different because some of the threats and risks are certainly different. Subsequently, the Intrusion Kill Chain might not be the best scoring approach for organizations in the cloud, depending on the types of services they use. As enterprises consume more and more services that blur the boundaries between IaaS, PaaS, SaaS, FaaS, IDaaS, and other models, the less relevant the Intrusion Kill Chain approach becomes. This isn't a bad thing—it's just more change to embrace. Remember, the role of CISOs and security teams isn't to ensure the status quo; it's to protect their organizations' data, even when these organizations decide it's time to evolve the technologies and processes they use in order to stay competitive and/or relevant.

Regarding the ATT&CK framework, there's a specific ATT&CK cloud matrix available at: `https://attack.mitre.org/matrices/enterprise/cloud/`. I mentioned earlier that MITRE published a useful mapping between AWS services and known attacker techniques published in the ATT&CK framework. This is very helpful information because it tells you which native capabilities can help mitigate attacker techniques from the ATT&CK framework. They also provide an estimated value of the effectiveness of each capability (minimal, partial, significant). MITRE also offers this mapping for Azure and GCP. I've provided the links to the MITRE Center for Threat Informed Defense for AWS, GCP, and Azure below, along with links to the associated information published by AWS, Google, and Microsoft:

- AWS: `https://center-for-threat-informed-defense.github.io/mappings-explorer/external/aws/`
- Mapping AWS security services to MITRE frameworks for threat detection and mitigation: `https://aws.amazon.com/blogs/security/mapping-aws-security-services-to-mitre-frameworks-for-threat-detection-and-mitigation/`
- Google Cloud Platform: `https://center-for-threat-informed-defense.github.io/mappings-explorer/external/gcp/`
- Announcing MITRE ATT&CK mappings for Google Cloud security capabilities: `https://cloud.google.com/blog/products/identity-security/announcing-mitre-attck-mappings-released-for-google-cloud-security-capabilities`
- Microsoft Azure: `https://center-for-threat-informed-defense.github.io/mappings-explorer/external/azure/`
- MITRE ATT&CK® mappings released for built-in Azure security controls: `https://www.microsoft.com/en-us/security/blog/2021/06/29/mitre-attck-mappings-released-for-built-in-azure-security-controls/`

The cloud offers the opportunity to modernize not only technologies and processes, but also cybersecurity strategies that can be employed. Let's explore this concept a little further and look at a more modern approach to cybersecurity that I mentioned in *Chapter 10*, called DevOps.

DevOps – a modern approach to security in the cloud

For lack of a better name, let's simply call this approach DevOps. I've also heard some security professionals refer to it as "immutable short-lived infrastructure" or simply as "re-paving". This strategy represents a more modern approach compared to the other cybersecurity strategies that we've examined. It recognizes that development and IT operations disciplines have been joining forces, partly because, together, these roles are aptly positioned to take advantage of the power of APIs and automation. Because everything is code in the cloud, including infrastructure, teams that understand both development and IT infrastructure operations can take full advantage of all the cloud has to offer. Let's look at some of the ways that a DevOps-driven security strategy can help security teams protect, detect, and respond to modern threats in cloud-based environments.

Remember in *Chapter 5, The Evolution of Malware*, where I described why the Windows ecosystem has so much more malware than the Apple iOS ecosystem. The key, it would seem, is how software has traditionally been distributed in these ecosystems. Microsoft allowed software developed by anyone to be freely installed by its customers on their Windows-based systems.

Apple, on the other hand, provides a single source for all applications destined for iOS-based devices: their App Store. While Windows customers were left to make their own decisions about the trustworthiness of the software they wanted to run, Apple imposed a security standard for all ISVs to meet before their apps could be distributed to iOS-based devices. This difference in software distribution methods, at least partially, explains why the Apple iOS ecosystem has maintained such a low prevalence of malware.

Let's take this lesson and apply it to our approach to security in the cloud. Leveraging continuous testing, **continuous integration (CI)**, and **continuous delivery or continuous deployment (CD)** can help minimize the amount of questionable software that makes it into the cloud-based environments that CSPs' customers build and operate. In their CI/CD pipelines, they can impose automated (and manual) security and compliance checks. These ensure that any software or infrastructure that gets deployed into production environments through these pipelines meets their organizations' security and compliance requirements.

To do this, each step of the CI/CD pipeline will have the appropriate security and compliance checks automated in it. For example, a DevOps team could develop or procure automation that looks for issues contained in the OWASP Top 10 (OWASP, 2025). Another common example is the requirement to perform static code analysis and/or a specific set of functional security tests. Infrastructure will have to meet the control setting requirements defined by each organization's compliance team, and this will be verified as items go through the pipeline.

Implementing such tests is typically done in code and automation, so the number and types of checks that can be conducted are almost unlimited. Of course, because this can be effective and fun, once some DevOps teams start developing these checks, they may spend more time on the development of their CI/CD pipelines than on applications and infrastructure.

If an application or infrastructure item does not pass one of these checks, the pipeline will stop, the appropriate staff may be alerted, the application or infrastructure will not progress through the rest of the pipeline, and it will not be introduced into the production environment as planned. The deficiency in the application or infrastructure item will have to be addressed in order to pass the check that failed and then go through the entire pipeline again.

This way, only items that pass every security and compliance check in the pipeline will make it into production. This means Security and Compliance teams can have high confidence that everything being introduced into their production environment meets all their security and compliance requirements and that they will not introduce more risks into that environment. To accomplish this, everything must go through a CI/CD pipeline. Put another way, the only way to get an application or infrastructure item into production is through a CI/CD pipeline. For the best chance of success, organizations need to have discipline, as well as the governance mechanisms, to enforce this requirement. Managing multiple CI/CD pipelines is a predictable and common outcome, especially for large, distributed organizations. The risk for some organizations is that the number of CI/CD pipelines proliferates to levels that begin to compromise the high security and compliance standards that the initial pipelines imposed; too many pipelines can turn into a governance issue.

Also, note that attackers have clued into the fact that most enterprises are using DevOps and CI/CD pipelines. This makes the CI/CD pipelines themselves a potential target for attackers. Understanding the stack of technologies and automations that your organization uses for its pipelines and taking steps to protect them is important. For some organizations, CI/CD pipelines can become high-value assets and warrant special attention, as I discussed in *Chapter 9*.

Now that security and compliance teams have confidence in their deployments, how do they keep those environments in that pristine condition over time? They can use the services and automation we discussed earlier in this chapter to monitor configuration changes. When configurations change, they can use automation to bring them back into compliance or initiate deeper investigations into how and why they changed.

As we discussed earlier, there is a range of options for vulnerability management in the cloud. Continuing to use the technologies and processes that your organization has used for years in its on-premises environment is likely one possible option. But as we discussed in *Chapter 3* and *Chapter 4, Product Vulnerability Trends,* vulnerability volumes have become so large that even well-resourced vulnerability management teams are under pressure.

However, using automation, like the Auto Scaling example I provided earlier, has the potential to simplify and accelerate vulnerability management. Another option is for organizations to evolve from managing servers and applications themselves to using cloud services higher up the stack and leaving infrastructure patching to the CSPs. Of course, a combination of all of these approaches is also permissible. However, if you are going to modernize processes, technologies, and your strategy, I strongly recommend that you get out of the vulnerability management game as much as you can. After all, the only way to win that game is not to play it. Patch a relatively small number of images, not hundreds or thousands of running VMs, and use managed services where it is possible to delegate vulnerability management to the CSPs.

One of the reasons that Attack-Centric strategies gained such popularity in the industry is that they can make it hard for "advanced" threat actors to be successful—the so-called **APT**. However, this is where the power of APIs and high levels of automation can also be helpful. For example, when organizations thoughtfully shut down subsets of servers running in the cloud every few hours and replace them with new ones that meet all requirements, it can make it harder for attackers to get and maintain a foothold in that environment. Short-lived, immutable systems can leave very little oxygen for attackers to use, unlike systems that remain running for months or years.

The detection capabilities in the cloud are superior to those found in most on-premises environments. Remember, the power of APIs and automation in the cloud provides visibility and control that few on-premises environments can achieve. The cloud can make it easy to log API calls, network traffic, authentication and authorization operations, encryption and decryption key operations, and so on. However, one challenge most security teams share, whether they use the cloud or not, is that the vast amount of data in all these logs makes it nearly impossible for humans to review and use it in a timely way. This is where the cloud can also help. AI and ML services can be used to review all of these logs and API activity, instead of security team members, and identify things that really warrant human attention. This is possible because AI/ML services can scale as large as needed to churn through enormous log datasets far, far faster than humans can. As they do this, these services, with the help of automation, can detect and respond to all sorts of attacks, including DDoS, malware, exploitation of vulnerabilities, insider threat, and many more.

Let me summarize the characteristics of this strategy I call DevOps, sometimes referred to as "immutable short-lived infrastructure," and sometimes simply referred to as "repaving":

- Automation is used to provision and configure systems and other infrastructure. Everything that gets released into production cloud accounts or environments must go through a CI/CD pipeline.
- The CI/CD pipeline can employ automated and manual security and compliance checks and tests to ensure everything that makes it into production meets security and

compliance standards. If something doesn't meet standards, the pipeline stops and the deficiencies are remediated.

- Systems are designed to be immutable, that is, designed not to change while running in production. Changes to immutable systems running in production are typically an indicator of compromise. This makes threat detection easier and faster.
- All changes are made to the image(s) that running instances are based on. This includes scanning for and installing security updates. The images are scanned and patched, not the running instances. This dramatically reduces the complexity and time it takes to manage vulnerabilities on large numbers of systems.
- To minimize insider threat opportunities, administrators have no direct administrator access to systems running in production. SSH, RDP, and other remote access software are prohibited from running on production systems. Administrators are limited to running tested and pre-approved scripts on systems running in production, except during break-glass scenarios, which are monitored and audited. MFA is used to authenticate administrators to the cloud, where they can initiate execution of these scripts.
- Automation is used to thoughtfully shut down production systems every few hours in a way that will not impact the availability of applications. Auto Scaling or other automation will restart systems based on the fully patched image(s) as needed. This reduces and limits the amount of time that compromised systems can be used by attackers in the production environment. AWS offers a capability built into Auto Scaling called Instance Refresh for this specific scenario.
- Managed services are used to enhance detection and response capabilities instead of deploying more servers to host security functions. This provides superior detection and response capabilities and does not increase the attack surface or the number of systems to manage.
- Make use of ubiquitous encryption capabilities to protect data in the cloud and to protect keys. I'll discuss this later in this chapter.

Note that although I've focused on using virtual machines in this strategy description, an increasing number of organizations leverage containers and container orchestration software in very similar ways to achieve better security.

Finally, if all these capabilities fail to protect, detect, and respond to attackers, DevOps and the cloud can make recovering production environments much easier than in typical on-premises environments. Since everything is code, rebuilding environments in the cloud can be relatively easy if some planning and thoughtful preparation have been done. Let's take a quick look at some **disaster recovery** (**DR**) capabilities in the cloud.

Disaster recovery in the cloud

As we discussed in *Chapter 5*, targeted attacks that involve extortion (also called ransomware attacks) are commonplace today. Ransomware is a human-made disaster. Subsequently, most of the CIOs, CISOs, and security teams I have talked to in the last few years are much more interested in DR than ever before. In addition to the specter of ransomware, fear of an increased frequency of extreme weather events due to climate change is also driving interest in DR.

DR is "the process of providing fast, reliable recovery of IT systems to minimize downtime and data loss" (Rains, 2022). The traditional approach to DR has led many organizations to build physical datacenters with specific distances between them. If one datacenter is impacted by a weather event, power disruption, or human-made disaster, the organization plans to resume IT operations in another datacenter. The distance between datacenters is arbitrary in that there is no industry standard—each organization makes its own calculations based on the types of risks it is trying to mitigate. But generally, the larger the distance between the datacenters, the less likely a single weather event, earthquake, fire, Internet, or power disruption will impact them.

In the cloud, as I mentioned earlier, Regions and Availability Zones are used to design highly available and resilient cloud infrastructures. The distance between datacenters in an Availability Zone can be large enough to mitigate localized power outages and large-scale weather events. For organizations that want even more assurance, they can use multiple Regions and get the advantages of using even more Availability Zones that have greater distances between them. For example, an organization could use a cloud Region located on the West coast of the U.S. and plan to use a Region on the East coast for DR. The chances of a single event disrupting operations on both sides of the country at the same time are very low. Many large multinational firms use cloud Regions in different countries for various purposes, including DR. For example, they might leverage a cloud Region on the East coast of the U.S. and another Region in Ireland for DR purposes. Since there are so many Regions and Availability Zones available, there are many different options for DR purposes. However, remember that the speed of light is a constant. The further the distance between the datacenters, the more network latency will become a limiting factor.

When I worked at AWS, I wrote a blog post about how AWS thinks about distances between their datacenters and Availability Zones for DR purposes. If you are interested in reading it, that blog post is titled "The Goldilocks zone for disaster recovery, business continuity planning, and disaster preparedness." It is available at this URL: `https://aws.amazon.com/blogs/publicsector/goldilocks-zone-disaster-recovery-business-continuity-planning-disaster-preparedness/`

The cloud offers organizations the ability to leverage all the classic DR architectures, including backup and restore, Pilot Light, Warm Stand-by, and Multi-Site Active/Active. For example, implementing a Pilot Light design is relatively easy because everything is code. Duplicating your production cloud environment, when it's needed, is as simple as using pre-developed and pre-tested code and automation to reprovision and configure all the existing cloud infrastructure in a different Availability Zone or Region. Much of it can be sitting in a cloud account provisioned, but not in a running state. Typically, customers won't pay for this infrastructure until it is in a running state. Once the infrastructure is up and running as expected, perhaps as quickly as a few minutes (depending on complexity), the appropriate DNS records are changed to point to the new infrastructure. This is a bit of an oversimplification, but it is wildly less complicated and expensive than procuring real estate for datacenters, conducting construction projects to build datacenters, procuring the appropriate power and backup power infrastructures, procuring, implementing, and operating all the IT infrastructure, paying real estate taxes every year, etc.

Rest assured, if you want to implement DR as part of a Protect and Recover strategy, an Attack-Centric strategy, a DevOps strategy, or other strategies in the cloud, you have a lot of flexibility and options at your disposal because of the power of APIs and automation in the cloud. The key to choosing which DR architecture to use should be based on the **recovery point objectives (RPOs) and recovery time objectives (RTOs)** for each application in scope for your DR plans. Define these, and then design DR architectures that can achieve them for you.

AWS published a good blog post series that can provide more insights called "Disaster Recovery (DR) Architecture on AWS":

- Part 1: `https://aws.amazon.com/blogs/architecture/disaster-recovery-dr-architecture-on-aws-part-i-strategies-for-recovery-in-the-cloud/`
- Part 2: `https://aws.amazon.com/blogs/architecture/disaster-recovery-dr-architecture-on-aws-part-ii-backup-and-restore-with-rapid-recovery/`
- Part 3: `https://aws.amazon.com/blogs/architecture/disaster-recovery-dr-architecture-on-aws-part-iii-pilot-light-and-warm-standby/`
- Part 4: `https://aws.amazon.com/blogs/architecture/disaster-recovery-dr-architecture-on-aws-part-iv-multi-site-active-active/`

You'll notice that these blog posts refer to the AWS Well-Architected Reliability pillar. This guidance is designed to help customers make informed choices when designing solutions on AWS with reliability in mind.

Of course, Microsoft also has a Well-Architected framework with a Reliability pillar and offers DR guidance based on it. You can find that guidance here: `https://learn.microsoft.com/en-us/azure/well-architected/design-guides/disaster-recovery`.

Google published a DR planning guide that is also very useful for planning DR using GCP: `https://docs.cloud.google.com/architecture/dr-scenarios-planning-guide`.

Resilience as a security strategy

Remember resilience as a security strategy that I discussed in *Chapter 10*. Leveraging this strategy in the cloud relies heavily on these same DR concepts and the Well-Architected Resilience pillar. Instead of planning on a complete failure of a cloud service, they can also be used to plan for smaller but potentially highly disruptive failures in individual services or functions. The key is understanding the data flows and the dependencies of the system you are trying to improve the resilience of. The Reliability pillar of the various Well-Architected frameworks that the CSPs have published contains best practices to improve the resilience of your cloud-based solutions.

AWS published a great blog post on this aspect called "Understand resiliency patterns and trade-offs to architect efficiently in the cloud". It is available at `https://aws.amazon.com/blogs/architecture/understand-resiliency-patterns-and-trade-offs-to-architect-efficiently-in-the-cloud/`.

AWS also published a resilience lifecycle framework that outlines the following five stages that can help continuously improve the resilience of systems:

- Stage 1: Set objectives - defining resilience objectives, such as RPO and RTO
- Stage 2: Design and implement - anticipating failure modes and identifying design choices
- Stage 3: Evaluate and test - test the practices that have been performed in previous stages and evaluate the results
- Stage 4: Operate - deploy application to production and manage customers' experience
- Stage 5: Respond and learn - focus on practices that can be implemented to better respond to disruptive events

You can get all the details on this help framework, including the granular technical controls they recommend, at `https://docs.aws.amazon.com/prescriptive-guidance/latest/resilience-lifecycle-framework/introduction.html`.

Mitigating ransomware using the cloud

In addition to the modern approaches I've discussed in this chapter, I wanted to broach one more design pattern that can be helpful. One objective every CISO and security team has is to protect their IT environments from a successful ransomware attack. I outlined the different flavors of ransomware attacks in *Chapter 5*. Attackers typically steal sensitive data, sometimes deny their victims access to their data and infrastructure, and then demand a ransom or multiple ransoms, promising they'll take specific actions, such as providing a decryption key or not selling the stolen data.

Let's focus on the data protection aspect and look at a design pattern that makes it harder for attackers to encrypt or otherwise destroy data. This can be accomplished in both on-premises environments as well as the cloud. However, it is much easier to accomplish in the cloud given all the benefits I mentioned earlier in this chapter. I learned about this design pattern while attending Oracle AI World, so I will leverage **Oracle Cloud Infrastructure (OCI)** in this example. Oracle describes OCI as "the next-generation cloud designed to run any application, faster and more securely, for less" (Oracle, n.d.).

Figure 13.1 illustrates a high-level design that can help mitigate ransomware and help support aggressive RPOs and RTOs leveraging OCI (Oracle, August 28, 2025).

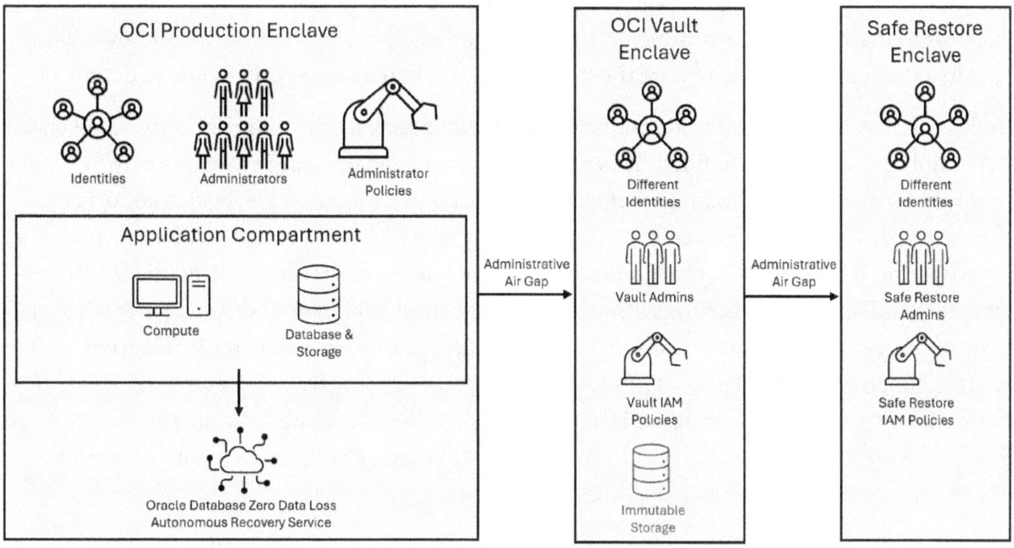

Figure 13.1 – An example of an architectural design leveraging OCI that helps mitigate ransomware and meet aggressive RPOs and RTOs (Oracle, August 28, 2025).

The design leverages three enclaves, which include a Production enclave, a Vault enclave, and a Safe Restore enclave. In OCI, an enclave is an isolated operational zone with its own control plane, identity boundaries, and administrative model, which can be in the same OCI tenancy or different tenancies. Implementing each enclave in a different tenancy can make it harder for attackers to compromise all three enclaves after compromising one. Each enclave leverages different identity providers, different identities, and different **identity and access management (IAM)** policies. This makes it harder for attackers to compromise all three enclaves using stolen credentials from one enclave. The Vault enclave and Safe Restore enclave have a relatively small number of administrator accounts compared to the Production enclave, as access to these enclaves is limited to just the administrators who are involved in backup and restore related work. There are administrative air gaps between the Production enclave and the Vault enclave, and between the Vault enclave and the Safe Restore enclave. These administrative air gaps enforce control-plane separation that ensures no shared administrator accounts, no shared IAM policies, and no shared automation credentials between enclaves. In this scenario, it means that even if attackers were able to compromise the Production enclave, they wouldn't have administrative control over the Vault enclave or the Safe Restore enclave and wouldn't be able to compromise or destroy the data in them.

With these three enclaves isolated from each other in this fashion, periodic backups are taken of the production data in the Production enclave and copied into the Vault enclave into immutable storage. Tampering with these data backup copies is not possible due to the immutable properties of the storage. Automated data testing can be employed on these backups to identify data corruption or malware. This results in a catalog of well-known data backups that can be used to restore the data in the case of data encryption or destruction.

In the Restore enclave, you can do continuous incremental restores of the backups based on the RTOs and RPOs that were defined. This enclave can be scaled up using automation to temporarily become the Production enclave in the case of a ransomware incident or other disaster. This will allow the system to continue to operate while an active incident response investigation is underway in the Production enclave. After containment and eradication of the attackers and any infrastructure rebuilding are completed, the Production enclave can be used to operate the system again or the Safe Restore enclave can become the new Production enclave. Since system backup and restore operations are constantly being exercised, this dramatically increases the likelihood that the organization will actually be able to recover from a ransomware attack and do so within the defined RPOs and RTOs. The separate identities used in each enclave also increase the odds of success.

This approach is what Oracle refers to as their **Cyber Resiliency Architecture (CRA)**. I've provided the abridged version of this approach here, but you can find all the details on CRA at `https://docs.oracle.com/en/solutions/oci-tenancy-cyber-resilience-architecture/index.html`.

Using the combination of the DevOps strategy I described here, in combination with resilience as a security strategy and the appropriate DR practices, would represent a major uplift in cybersecurity and resilience for most of the enterprises I've advised over the years. This would be hard or impossible for most enterprises to accomplish in their legacy on-premises IT environments. However, the security story for the cloud gets even better when we layer in its encryption and key management capabilities. Let's look at those next.

Encryption and key management

In my experience advising enterprise organizations, most conversations about security in the cloud conclude by discussing encryption and key management. No matter what topics these conversations started with, such as vulnerabilities, exploits, malware, internet-based threats, or government access to data, they concluded by discussing encryption and key management. This is because encryption is recognized and mathematically proven to be a powerful data protection control that helps provide confidentiality and integrity for data, whether it's in the cloud, hybrid environments, or on-premises.

No matter which cybersecurity strategy or combination of strategies organizations pursue, when the rubber hits the road, protecting the data is the objective. That's what can be so distracting about the cybersecurity strategies we examined that are proxies for data protection. Security teams get so focused on protecting endpoints or applications that they can lose sight of the fact that the underlying objective is to protect data. The proxies I mentioned are important and must be effectively managed, but don't forget about the data!

The CSPs all know this and offer their customers rich sets of encryption and key management capabilities. Their goal is to protect data when it is in transit, at rest, and even while it's being processed. TLS (version 1.3) is the current de facto internet standard for protecting data in transit. Subsequently, CSPs support TLS, in addition to providing other mechanisms for protecting data in transit, like VPN connections or directly connecting their cloud infrastructures to their customers' networks, as examples.

As I discussed in *Chapter 8, Friend or Foe? The Roles Governments Play in Cybersecurity*, CSPs offer a range of encryption options to protect data at rest, enabling their customers to encrypt data before they put it in the cloud (in some scenarios) and/or after they put it in the cloud. Remember the difference between client-side encryption and server-side encryption. The current and recommended encryption standard that CSPs offer for encrypting data at rest is the **Advanced Encryption Standard (AES)**, using 256-bit key lengths.

If an attacker had access to data (access is typically authenticated and authorized) protected by AES-256, breaking this type of encryption using brute-force techniques and a large amount of conventional computing power would likely take far, far more time than the value lifetime of the data.

An important nuance for security teams to understand is exactly what is being encrypted and which risks that type of encryption mitigates. For example, if the underlying storage media is encrypted, but the data being written to the media is not encrypted prior to being written, then the risks being mitigated are the loss or theft of the storage media. Encrypted storage media helps mitigate attacks where attackers have physical access to the storage media. If someone gets physical access to the encrypted storage media but doesn't possess the keys to mount and decrypt it, the data written on it is protected from unauthorized access. However, if attackers seek to access the data logically instead of physically, over a network, for example, then storage-level encryption will likely not mitigate this risk because the data is decrypted as it is accessed from the network.

> **Tip**
>
> It's important to understand the specific risk that needs to be mitigated and the specific mitigations for that particular risk in order to have confidence that the risk has truly been mitigated. If the desire is to prevent unauthorized access to data at rest over a network, then encrypting the data itself, instead of just the storage media, will be a more effective mitigation. This might sound obvious, but this is a common mistake security teams make during application security assessments.

In addition to offering data encryption options, CSPs are really providing authenticated and authorized data encryption. That is, each encryption operation API call is authenticated and must be authorized; encryption and decryption operations will not occur without being authenticated and authorized first. Using Identity and Access services this way provides security teams with a lot of flexibility. For example, one person or group of people can be authorized to encrypt data but not authorized to decrypt it. Another group can be given permissions to decrypt data, but not to do both encryption and decryption operations. Authenticated and authorized encryption enables a separation of duties that can be helpful in many scenarios.

For many organizations, one of the most challenging parts of encryption can be key management. The stakes are high because if an organization's keys are damaged, lost, or stolen, it could have a catastrophic impact on them. CSPs want to make key management easy and safe for their customers. Google offers Cloud Key Management Service (Google, n.d.), Microsoft offers Azure Key Vault (Microsoft Corporation, n.d.), and AWS provides the AWS Key Management Service (AWS, n.d.). Of course, there are third-party vendors that also offer encryption and key management services, such as Thales, Equinix, and others.

The CSPs' key management services can offer an interesting advantage in that they can be integrated into their other cloud services. This means that some cloud services can perform encryption and decryption on behalf of users. The advantage here is that the data can be protected by AES encryption until it's in the physical memory of the servers running the service that is going to process it. Once processing is completed, the service can re-encrypt the data again before moving it into storage or other services for more processing. The keys used for encryption and decryption can be protected in transit between the key management services and the services that use them. This means that unencrypted data only sees the light of day in highly controlled environments that are authorized by the data owner. This can help maximize the number of places and the time that the data is protected with encryption. CSPs' key management services tend to be designed for low latency and high availability in order to process billions of requests.

Some organizations want a separation of duties between the vendor they use for compute and storage and the vendors that provide key management services. Third-party vendors that offer key management services can play this role, or CSPs' customers themselves can operate and maintain their own key management infrastructures. The organizations that choose this option should be comfortable managing their own key management infrastructure or allowing a third party to do it for them. However, managing **hardware security modules (HSMs)** and **public key infrastructures (PKIs)** is notoriously difficult. This makes using CSPs' key management services a popular option.

For organizations that need to keep their keys on-premises but still want to get the benefits of the cloud, client-side encryption is a potential solution. Using client-side encryption means that the data owner encrypts the data before they put it into a cloud service. For example, the data owner has their own on-premises key management infrastructure. Prior to putting data into a cloud storage service, they generate a key on-premises and then use an application also running on-premises to encrypt the data using this key. Then, they authenticate and securely transfer the encrypted data to the cloud storage service. In this scenario, their CSP never had access to their unencrypted data or the encryption key, as neither left the on-premises IT environment. To decrypt this data, the data owner authenticates to the cloud storage service, securely downloads the encrypted data, and uses their on-premises application and on-premises key to decrypt the data. Again, neither the unencrypted data nor the encryption key was ever shared with the CSP.

We briefly mentioned this in *Chapter 8*. Client-side encryption isn't limited to storage scenarios; it can be used with other services, like databases, for example. In this scenario, client-side encryption is used to encrypt records or individual fields as they are written to a database service running in the cloud. To do this, an encryption key is retrieved from the on-premises key management system and temporarily used for encryption operations by the application performing the encryption. Once the record is encrypted as it's written to the database, the encryption key can be removed from the memory of the application that performed the encryption operation, thus reducing the time the key is resident on a system outside of the on-premises key management system. The application performing encryption and decryption operations on the database records can run on-premises or in the cloud. Since the CSP's customer has full control of the keys, the CSP cannot get access to the keys unless the customer grants them access. Indexes and database primary and secondary keys are left unencrypted so that indexing and searching the database can still be performed. For this reason, it's important not to put sensitive data into these fields. To decrypt the data, the appropriate records are retrieved and decrypted after the key is provided from the on-premises key management system. After the decryption operation, the key can once again be removed from the memory of the application performing the decryption operation.

There are many different ways to perform client-side encryption and key management. However, this method can be more complicated and expensive to implement than simply using the integrated encryption and key management services that CSPs offer. Some organizations that start off using client-side encryption with keys kept on-premises, over time, conclude that using CSPs' key management services mitigates the risks they are most concerned about and helps to simplify their applications. After all, encryption and decryption operations in the cloud are performed using API calls that are authenticated, authorized, monitored, and potentially controlled using automation, as we discussed earlier.

The CSPs want to provide their customers with the confidentiality and integrity that client-side encryption provides, without the extra complexity and costs. After all, moving key material between on-premises IT environments and cloud environments also has risks associated with it and doesn't improve application performance, especially at scale. The CSPs offer sophisticated alternatives to client-side encryption that can also help mitigate insider threat in many scenarios. The list below contains some examples.

- **The AWS Nitro System**: `https://aws.amazon.com/ec2/nitro/`
- **AWS Nitro Enclaves**: `https://aws.amazon.com/ec2/nitro/nitro-enclaves/`
- **AWS Confidential Computing**: `https://aws.amazon.com/confidential-computing/`
- **AWS Graviton2 (or later) processors feature always-on 256-bit DRAM encryption**: `https://docs.aws.amazon.com/AWSEC2/latest/UserGuide/data-protection.html`
- **Azure encryption overview**: `https://learn.microsoft.com/en-us/azure/security/fundamentals/encryption-overview`
- **Azure Confidential Computing**: `https://azure.microsoft.com/en-us/solutions/confidential-compute/#overview`

- **Google Cloud Data Encryption**: `https://cloud.google.com/security/encryption`
- **Google Confidential Computing**: `https://cloud.google.com/blog/products/identity-security/introducing-google-cloud-confidential-computing-with-confidential-vms`

Combining properly implemented encryption and effective key management, along with the power of APIs and automation in the cloud, helps protect data in ways that would be more complex to duplicate in on-premises IT environments. Encryption and key management help protect data from many of the threats we discussed throughout this book; they are powerful data protection controls that should be part of whichever cybersecurity strategies your organization pursues.

Summary

This chapter explored how cloud computing is reshaping cybersecurity and compliance by enabling organizations to modernize their technologies, processes, and strategies. Moving from static, on-premises environments to cloud-native models allows security teams to take advantage of capabilities that fundamentally change how security and compliance are implemented and operated.

A central theme was the role of **APIs and automation**. In the cloud, nearly all actions occur through authenticated and authorized API calls, providing consistent visibility, control, and auditability. When combined with automation, this model reduces human error, limits insider risk, accelerates detection and response, and enables continuous enforcement of security and compliance requirements. These capabilities make it easier to mitigate the Cybersecurity Usual Suspects, including unpatched vulnerabilities, security misconfigurations, weak, leaked, or stolen credentials, insider threats, and social engineering.

The chapter also examined how the cloud supports multiple cybersecurity strategies. Compliance as a cybersecurity strategy benefits from continuous monitoring, automation, and the extensive certifications and attestations maintained by hyperscale cloud providers under a shared responsibility model. Attack-centric strategies can be implemented using cloud-native controls and mappings to frameworks such as the Intrusion Kill Chain and MITRE ATT&CK®. More modern DevOps-driven approaches, often described as immutable, short-lived infrastructure, use CI/CD pipelines and automation to ensure that only secure and compliant systems reach production.

Finally, the chapter highlighted how cloud architectures simplify disaster recovery, resilience, and ransomware mitigation, and why encryption and key management remain foundational controls for protecting data. Together, APIs, automation, managed services, and advanced cryptographic capabilities enable organizations to build security and compliance programs that are more scalable, resilient, and effective than traditional on-premises approaches.

The next chapter builds on these concepts by examining the role of artificial intelligence in cybersecurity, including securing AI systems themselves and using AI to improve detection, response, and overall security effectiveness.

In the next chapter, I'll discuss another topic that has attracted the attention of CISOs and cybersecurity teams in recent years—how to mitigate "Living Off the Land" techniques.

References

- AICPA. (n.d.). *SOC 2® - SOC for Service Organizations: Trust Services Criteria*. Retrieved from AICPA: `https://www.aicpa-cima.com/topic/audit-assurance/audit-and-assurance-greater-than-soc-2`
- Amazon Web Services. (n.d.). *Cloud Computing with AWS*. Retrieved from AWS: `https://aws.amazon.com/what-is-aws`
- Ansible. (n.d.). *Red Hat Ansible Automation Platform*. Retrieved from Red Hat Ansible: `https://www.redhat.com/en/technologies/management/ansible`
- AWS. (October 20, 2016). *Fleet Management Made Easy with Auto Scaling*. Retrieved from AWS Compute Blog: `https://aws.amazon.com/blogs/compute/fleet-management-made-easy-with-auto-scaling/`
- AWS. (n.d.). *Amazon Elastic Compute Cloud API Reference*. Retrieved from AWS: `https://docs.aws.amazon.com/AWSEC2/latest/APIReference/API_RunInstances.html`
- AWS. (n.d.). *AWS CloudFormation*. Retrieved from AWS: `https://aws.amazon.com/cloudformation/`
- AWS. (n.d.). *AWS CloudTrail*. Retrieved from AWS: `https://aws.amazon.com/cloudtrail/`
- AWS. (n.d.). *AWS Key Management Service (KMS)*. Retrieved from AWS: `https://aws.amazon.com/kms/`
- AWS. (n.d.). *AWS Secrets Manager*. Retrieved from AWS: `https://aws.amazon.com/secrets-manager/`
- AWS. (n.d.). *Logging AWS Systems Manager API calls with AWS CloudTrail*. Retrieved from AWS: `https://docs.aws.amazon.com/systems-manager/latest/userguide/monitoring-cloudtrail-logs.html`

- AWS. (July 14, 2022). *Remotely Run Commands on an EC2 Instance.* Retrieved from AWS: `https://aws.amazon.com/getting-started/hands-on/remotely-run-commands-ec2-instance-systems-manager/`
- AWS. (April 2020). *Using the AWS CLI.* Retrieved from AWS: `https://docs.aws.amazon.com/cli/latest/userguide/cli-chap-welcome.html`
- Chef. (n.d.). *Chef.* Retrieved from Chef: `https://www.chef.io/products/chef-infra/`
- Hutchins, E.M., Cloppert, M.J., Amin, R.M. (n.d.). *Intelligence-Driven Computer Network Defense Informed by Analysis of Adversary Campaigns and Intrusion Kill Chains.* Retrieved from Lockheed Martin: `https://lockheedmartin.com/content/dam/lockheed-martin/rms/documents/cyber/LM-White-Paper-Intel-Driven-Defense.pdf`
- Google. (December 19, 2025). *Cloud Audit Logs.* Retrieved from Google Cloud: `https://cloud.google.com/logging/docs/audit`
- Google. (n.d.). *Cloud Key Management Service.* Retrieved from Google Cloud: `https://cloud.google.com/security/products/security-key-management`
- Google. (n.d.). *Cloud Composer.* Retrieved from Google Cloud: `https://cloud.google.com/composer`
- Google. (December 19, 2025). *Secret Manager overview.* Retrieved from Google Cloud Blog: `https://cloud.google.com/secret-manager/docs/overview`
- Google. (October 21, 2025). *gcloud compute instance create.* Retrieved from Google: `https://cloud.google.com/sdk/gcloud/reference/compute/instances/create`
- HashiCorp. (n.d.). *Automate Infrastructure on Any Cloud.* Retrieved from Terraform by HashiCorp: `https://developer.hashicorp.com/terraform`
- Paradigm shift. (2025). In *Merriam-Webster.com.* Retrieved December 19, 2025, from `https://www.merriam-webster.com/dictionary/paradigm%20shift`
- Microsoft Corporation. (April 24, 2025). *What is Azure Automation?* Retrieved from Microsoft Azure: `https://learn.microsoft.com/en-us/azure/automation/overview`
- Microsoft Corporation. (August 26, 2025). *Azure Monitor overview.* Retrieved from Microsoft Azure: `https://docs.microsoft.com/en-us/azure/azure-monitor/overview`
- Microsoft Corporation. (n.d.). *Azure Products.* Retrieved from Microsoft Azure: `https://azure.microsoft.com/en-us/products/`

- Microsoft Corporation. (n.d.). *Key Vault*. Retrieved from Microsoft Azure: `https://azure.microsoft.com/en-us/products/key-vault`
- Microsoft Corporation. (n.d.). *Manage secrets in your server apps with Azure Key Vault*. Retrieved from Microsoft Learn: `https://docs.microsoft.com/en-us/learn/modules/manage-secrets-with-azure-key-vault/`
- Microsoft Corporation. (April 1, 2025). *Virtual Machines - Start*. Retrieved from Microsoft Corporation: `https://learn.microsoft.com/en-us/rest/api/compute/virtual-machines/start?view=rest-compute-2025-04-01&tabs=HTTP`
- Microsoft Corporation. (January 7, 2025). *What is Microsoft Entra Privileged Identity Management?* Retrieved from Microsoft: `https://learn.microsoft.com/en-us/entra/id-governance/privileged-identity-management/pim-configure`
- MITRE. (October 9, 2019). *Cloud Matrix*. Retrieved from MITRE ATT&CK®: `https://attack.mitre.org/matrices/enterprise/cloud/`
- Center for Threat-Informed Defense. (n.d.). Amazon Web Services security control mappings to MITRE ATT&CK®: AWS Config. Retrieved from `https://center-for-threat-informed-defense.github.io/security-stack-mappings/AWS/README.html#aws-config`
- Oracle. (n.d.). *Oracle Cloud Infrastructure (OCI)*. Retrieved from: `https://www.oracle.com/cloud/`
- Oracle. (August 28, 2025). *Incorporate cyber resilience capabilities into your OCI tenancy*. Retrieved from `https://docs.oracle.com/en/solutions/oci-tenancy-cyber-resilience-architecture/index.html#GUID-CFC1775A-83C5-4167-8CA2-17A57967CB89`
- OWASP. (2025). *Top 10 Web Application Security Risks*. Retrieved from `https://owasp.org/www-project-top-ten/`
- Puppet. (n.d.). *Puppet Enterprise*. Retrieved from `https://puppet.com/products/puppet-enterprise/`
- The BSI. (October 2020). *Cloud Computing Compliance Criteria Catalogue – C5:2020*. Retrieved from Federal Office for Information Security: `https://www.bsi.bund.de/SharedDocs/Downloads/EN/BSI/CloudComputing/ComplianceControlsCatalogue/2020/C5_2020.pdf?__blob=publicationFile&v=3`
- Rains, T. (January 31, 2022). *The Goldilocks zone for disaster recovery, business continuity planning, and disaster preparedness*. Retrieved from AWS Public Sector Blog: `https://`

aws.amazon.com/blogs/publicsector/goldilocks-zone-disaster-recovery-business-continuity-planning-disaster-preparedness/

- Twain, Mark. (September 18, 1906). *Spelling and Pictures speech* by Mark Twain. Retrieved from https://www.gutenberg.org/files/3188/3188-h/3188-h.htm

Get this book's PDF version and more

14

Mitigating "Living Off the Land" Techniques

> *"The greatest danger in times of turbulence is not the turbulence; it is to act with yesterday's logic." (Peter F. Drucker, 1973)*

Regardless of which cybersecurity strategy or combination of strategies CISOs use, they'll still need to invest time and effort into mitigating attackers' **Living Off the Land (LOTL)** techniques. Some of these techniques are as old as cyber-attacks themselves, as attackers have always used them in some form or another as they perpetrated traditional network intrusions. Some techniques have remained the same, as they continue to be effective after decades of use, while other new and novel techniques continue to emerge. For attackers who perpetrate traditional network intrusions, these techniques have become an integral part of their success. Yet, despite how long these techniques have been in use and how popular they are with attackers, given their continued success, it seems that relatively few organizations prioritize the work needed to mitigate them. The **Cybersecurity and Infrastructure Security Agency (CISA)** recently noted this:

> *"Many organizations do not implement security best practice capabilities that support detection of living off the land (LOTL), so this technique continues to be effective with little to no investment in tooling by malicious cyber actors" (Cybersecurity and Infrastructure Security Agency, 2024).*

In this chapter, you will learn what LOTL techniques are and some of the ways they can be addressed. First, we will examine the ways attackers leverage legitimate binaries, tools, and websites during their attacks. Then we will discuss approaches to mitigating such techniques. Finally, in the "lessons from the trenches" section, I'll offer you some real-world advice on how to mitigate these techniques based on my own experience. By the end of this chapter, you should be able to devise a plan of action for your organization to mature its approach to mitigating LOTL techniques.

The following topics will be covered:

- What is Living Off the Land
- Mitigating LOTL techniques

Let's get started!

What is Living Off the Land?

There are more than a few definitions of LOTL available. For example, researchers in cybersecurity research and response labs who are responsible for endpoint protection and detection technologies might view LOTL as fileless malware. That is, software with a nefarious purpose that is never written to local system storage ("to disk"). Their challenge is figuring out how to detect and block the execution of threats that exist in memory and not "on disk." If the malware isn't written to disk, it is more challenging for anti-malware software and endpoint solutions to detect and block it.

Others view LOTL as scenarios where attackers leverage legitimate binaries built into the operating systems that their victims use to administrate and operate them—so-called **Living Off the Land Binaries (LOLBins)**. These binaries can't readily be detected as malware because they are included by default with Windows, Linux, and other operating systems commonly found in enterprise IT environments. The operating systems themselves, IT support teams, and applications use these binaries in the course of normal operations. For example, attackers are happy to use cmd.exe, WMI, PowerShell, and Windows Task Scheduler in ways that appear to be how legitimate administrators use them, but actually to move laterally, further penetrate the environment, stay persistent, exfiltrate data, and deploy ransomware. It is challenging for cybersecurity teams to determine whether these tools are being used by administrators for legitimate purposes or by attackers using administrator credentials to forward their attacks.

Of course, both views are accurate. Cybersecurity teams must be prepared to detect and stop fileless malware and the malicious use of legitimate binaries if they hope to stop modern-day attackers in their environments after initial compromise. The US CISA provided this definition, which I think is very helpful because it is comprehensive and pragmatic.

> *LOTL involves the abuse of native tools and processes on systems, especially living off the land binaries, often referred to as LOLBins, to blend in with normal system activities and operate discreetly with a lower likelihood of being detected or blocked because these tools are already deployed and trusted in the environment. Cyber threat actors effectively use LOTL across multiple environments, including in on-premises, cloud, hybrid, Windows, Linux, and macOS environments, in part because*

> *it enables the ability to avoid investing in the development and deployment of custom tools. (Cybersecurity and Infrastructure Security Agency et al., 2024)*

Besides fileless malware and the malicious use of legitimate binaries, there are some other techniques attackers use that cybersecurity teams need to be prepared for. In this chapter, when I refer to LOTL techniques, it includes the following types of potential threats:

- **Fileless malware**: Malicious software and scripts that aren't written to disk the way traditional malware typically is, so they can be more challenging to detect, block, and disinfect
- **Malicious use of legitimate binaries**: Attackers making use of binaries that ship with operating systems, such as ntdsutil, rundll32, schtasks, ssh, sftp, regedit, wmic, winword, tar, tftp, telnet, view, vim, and literally hundreds of others
- **Malicious use of legitimate websites (URLs)**: Some attackers stage parts of their attacks from legitimate websites hosted in Internet domains they know enterprises can't or won't block. They use such websites to host and download their toolkits and for data exfiltration, among other uses. Leveraging websites hosted on major **content distribution networks (CDNs)**, such as Cloudflare, Akamai, and AWS's Amazon CloudFront, makes it less likely that outbound access to them will be blocked on their victims' networks.
- **Common IT support tools**: Tools that aren't necessarily included with operating systems but are ubiquitous in IT environments because of their popularity with IT teams. Attackers don't need to download or install these tools as IT teams have already done this. Examples include popular **Remote Monitoring and Management (RMM)** tools such as TeamViewer, ConnectWise RMM, LogMeIn, and many others.
- **Legitimate administrator tools that attackers love:** Legitimate administrator tools that aren't built into operating systems and aren't commonly preinstalled across enterprise environments, so attackers often bring them in and abuse them during intrusions. These are tools that, if given the chance, attackers will download and execute to support different stages of their attacks, including post-intrusion reconnaissance, exploitation, installation, command and control, and actions on objectives. Examples include Nmap, Advanced IP Scanner, Metasploit, Burp Suite, SharpHound, and many others.
- **Legitimate developer tools**: Some attackers are adept at leveraging developer tools accessible in their victims' environments, including MSBuild, Regsvr32, InstallUtil, Mshta, C# Compiler, popular interpreters such as Python, Node.js, and Ruby, and Visual Studio tools, among others. Why download and install executables on victims'

systems that might be detected when you can use victims' developer tools that aren't monitored to execute code for you?

I realize that this list includes more potential threat types than the strictest definitions of LOTL permit. Many attackers combine native operating-system binaries with additional malicious or legitimate tools they deploy inside the victim's environment, along with the use of legitimate websites to support their operations. Subsequently, in this chapter, I'll take a pragmatic approach and include all the potential threat types I listed earlier when I refer to LOTL. This will give cybersecurity teams following this guidance the best chance at detecting attackers who use only tools that meet the strictest definitions of LOTL, as well as those who do not.

Let's dig into these threat types a bit more to understand why they are so effective for attackers using LOTL techniques.

Fileless malware

Fileless malware is a type of threat that many threat actors use as part of their LOTL toolkits. There are quite a few definitions of fileless malware available. Let's look at some slightly different definitions so you get a well-rounded understanding of the concept of fileless malware.

Fortinet provides a definition that is helpful.

> *"Fileless malware is malicious code that works directly within a computer's memory instead of the hard drive. It uses legitimate, otherwise benevolent programs to compromise your computer instead of malicious files. It is "fileless" in that when your machine gets infected, no files are downloaded to your hard drive...Because fileless malware attacks require no malicious files, traditional antivirus tools that perform hardware scans to locate threats may miss them altogether." Fortinet. (n.d.).*

CrowdStrike also provides a definition that is a little more tightly linked to LOTL:

> *"Fileless malware is a type of malicious activity that uses native, legitimate tools built into a system to execute a cyberattack. Unlike traditional malware, which typically requires a file to be downloaded and installed, fileless malware operates in memory or manipulates native tools, making it harder to detect and remove." CrowdStrike. (November 26, 2024).*

A definition provided by endpoint security vendor Palo Alto Networks states,

> *"Fileless malware attacks are something where attackers are using things that aren't written to disk. So, things that are staying in volatile memory, such as PowerShell*

and WMI. And they're doing that because they are much harder to both detect and to find later, because a lot of times, they aren't kept in logs.

So, you'll see attackers doing things where they're automating a lot of their initial attacks, where they'll use something such as PowerShell or WMI to figure out both where they've landed in the system and do some basic network reconnaissance to decide whether or not they are in a place where they want to be. And those things are very hard to detect via traditional AV vendors, and even without some behavior analytics, they're harder to find." Palo Alto Networks. (n.d.).

I like Palo Alto Networks' description because it provides a little more context on how attackers use fileless malware. We will cover PowerShell and WMI in the "Mitigating LOTL Techniques" section of this chapter.

One final definition from Avast:

"Fileless malware is malicious code that infiltrates a computer system without leaving an obvious footprint, unlike traditional viruses or other types of malware that typically create trace files. Instead, fileless malware lives entirely in a computer's random access memory (RAM) and weaponizes trusted system tools to execute harmful processes and steal data." Avast. (n.d.).

There are several techniques that developers of fileless malware use to evade detection and advance their attacks. Here's a summary of some of them

- **Memory-only malware execution**: No artifacts are left on disk because the malware runs entirely in memory
- **LOTL abuse**: Fileless malware uses trusted, signed system binaries to execute, such as PowerShell, **Windows Management Instrumentation (WMI)**, VBScript, rundll32.exe, Microsoft HTML Application Host (mshta.exe), among others
- **Exploit kits**: Collections of working exploits for unpatched vulnerabilities are used to compromise systems and inject code directly into memory, thus bypassing writes to disk
- **Registry-resident malware**: Instead of writing malware to a file on the hard drives of systems, malicious code is stored in the Windows registry. This can make it easier for fileless malware to restart after a system reboot
- **Script-based attacks**: Instead of dropping an executable file on the hard drive, fileless malware leverages batch scripts, WMI, PowerShell scripts, and JavaScript to execute in memory only

Microsoft has enumerated fileless threats and published a helpful taxonomy to understand them (Type I, II, and III). Type I fileless threats have no file activity (purely memory-resident).

Type II fileless threats have indirect file activity (e.g., registry-based), while Type III leverages files required to operate, but still uses fileless techniques in parts of their execution chain. *Table 14.1* summarizes the fileless threat taxonomy provided by Microsoft (Microsoft, April 24, 2024). There are three main categories of fileless threats including exploit, execution/injection, and hardware. There are multiple threat vectors in each category—these are the hosts of the fileless malware infection. For example, a Flash application or document can contain a variety of threats. The entry points are subcategories of the threat vector and describe how the threats can be introduced to the environment. The table includes the associated fileless threat type for each item, referring to the three fileless threat types Microsoft defined (no files, indirect file use, and files required):

Category	Threat Vector	Entry Point	Fileless Type
Exploit	Remote attacker	NETWORK	Type I
Exploit	Exe	FILE	Type III
Exploit	Flash	FILE	Type III
Exploit	Java	FILE	Type III
Exploit	Documents	FILE	Type III
Execution/Injection	LNK, Scheduled Task, Exe	FILE	Type III
Execution/Injection	Documents (macro)	MACRO	Type II
Execution/Injection	MBR/VBR	DISK	Type III
Execution/Injection	Service	SCRIPTS	Type II
Execution/Injection	Registry, WMI repo	SCRIPTS	Type II
Execution/Injection	Shell	SCRIPTS	Type II
Hardware	Hypervisor	VM	Type I
Hardware	Motherboard firmware	BIOS/UEFI	Type I
Hardware	BadUSB	USB	Type I

Category	Threat Vector	Entry Point	Fileless Type
Hardware	Circuitry backdoors, Intel Management Engine (IME)	CPU	Type I
Hardware	Network card, hard disk	PCI	Type I
Legend: Type I — No file activity is performed Type II — No files are written to disk, but some files are used indirectly Type III — Files required to achieve fileless persistence			

Table 14.1 – Summary of the fileless threats taxonomy published by Microsoft (Microsoft, April 24, 2024)

This taxonomy can help cybersecurity teams understand fileless threat types and prioritize their mitigation efforts based on the fileless types they deem to be the highest risk to their organizations. This Microsoft blog post is recommended reading if you are interested in learning more about fileless malware, as it contains an analysis of a sophisticated fileless malware attack with detailed diagrams: *Dismantling a fileless campaign: Microsoft Defender ATP's Antivirus exposes Astaroth attack* (`https://www.microsoft.com/en-us/security/blog/2019/07/08/dismantling-a-fileless-campaign-microsoft-defender-atp-next-gen-protection-exposes-astaroth-attack/`).

Industry guidance for mitigating fileless malware is essentially the same as the guidance for mitigating LOTL techniques. The same controls recommended for LOTL activity apply directly to fileless threats. I will provide specific guidance to mitigate LOTL techniques, and subsequently fileless malware, in the "mitigating LOTL techniques" section of this chapter.

Next, let's take a deeper look at the malicious use of legitimate binaries that attackers use to LOTL.

Malicious use of legitimate binaries

Many attackers use legitimate binaries included by default in operating systems, such as executables, **Dynamic Link Libraries (DLLs)**, and device drivers, because they provide several operational advantages. First, since the binaries are already installed on their victims' systems, they don't have to risk being detected downloading and installing them. Second, these binaries are trusted and typically signed by the operating system vendors when they ship them with their operating systems. Subsequently, anti-malware and endpoint security solutions typically allow these binaries to execute without scrutiny. Lastly, attackers' use of legitimate binaries blends into the legitimate use by system administrators, making it harder to detect attackers' presence. This is especially true when attackers are leveraging stolen administrator credentials and running legitimate binaries from domain-joined systems. This makes it harder to detect anomalies.

Some examples of common Windows binaries that are used in LOTL attacks are shown in *Table 14.2*. Some of the examples are binaries found in multiple operating systems from different vendors, while some are found only in Windows or Linux. The table includes a short description of each binary's legitimate purpose, a short description of how attackers abuse each of them, and which MITRE ATT&CK® techniques each binary is used for. The source of most of this information is the ATT&CK framework (MITRE Corporation, 2025):

Binary	**Legitimate Purpose**	**How it is Abused**	**MITRE ATT&CK Tactic(s)**
at.exe	Exists as an executable within Windows, Linux, and macOS for scheduling tasks at a specific time and date.	Adversaries may abuse the at utility to perform task scheduling for initial or recurring execution of malicious code.	Execution, persistence, lateral movement
systemctl	Primary interface for systemd, the Linux init system and service manager	Adversaries may abuse systemctl to execute commands or programs	Execution
netsh helper DLL	Netsh.exe (also referred to as Netshell) is a command-line scripting utility used to interact with the network configuration of a system.	Adversaries may establish persistence by executing malicious content triggered by Netsh Helper DLLs.	Persistence

Binary	Legitimate Purpose	How it is Abused	MITRE ATT&CK Tactic(s)
BITSAdmin.exe	Windows **Background Intelligent Transfer Service (BITS)** is commonly used by updaters, messengers, and other applications that prefer to operate in the background (using available idle bandwidth) without interrupting other networked applications. File transfer tasks are implemented as BITS jobs, which contain a queue of one or more file operations. The interface to create and manage BITS jobs is accessible through PowerShell and the BITSAdmin tool.	BITSAdmin can be used to create BITS jobs to launch a malicious process or to upload and/or download files.	Defense evasion, persistence
ntdsutil.exe	Use ntdsutil commands to perform database maintenance of Active Directory and manage and control single master operations. One popular function is to export ntds.dit for forensics or credential auditing.	Used to dump a victim's Active Directory (ntds.dit) into a file that is exfiltrated and used to harvest credentials.	Credential access

Table 14.2 – Examples of binaries attackers abuse when using LOTL techniques

Let's dive deeper into that last example in *Table 14.2* because it's so popular with attackers and its use can result in network compromises for which recovery is truly aspirational. Remember the traditional network intrusion attack I described in *Chapter 1, How Enterprises Get Hacked*. A traditional network intrusion is a targeted attack in which adversaries gain initial access to the victim organization, establish persistence, escalate privileges, move laterally using stolen credentials and tools, and ultimately exfiltrate data or deploy ransomware to achieve their objectives. In my experience, attackers often try to export a copy of their victim's Active Directory (the ntds.dit file) within seconds of initial compromise when they have administrator credentials. The number of named threat actors that have reportedly been seen using `ntdsutil.exe` to get access to credentials is long and includes APT28, APT41, Chimera, Dragonfly, FIN6, FIN13, Fox Kitten, HAFNIUM, LAPSUS$, Medusa Group, Mustang Panda, Sandworm Team, Scattered Spider, Volt Typhoon, Wizard Spider, and many others.

If ntdsutil.exe is available on Domain Controllers, attackers can avoid downloading a copy of ntdsutil.exe or their own tools for this purpose, accelerating the exfiltration of Active Directory and reducing the risk of being detected during the process. An example of the ntdsutil.exe command that exports the ntds.dit file is provided below.

```
ntdsutil "ac i ntds" "ifm" "create full C:\temp" q q
```

When run from a command prompt or PowerShell with administrator privileges on a shadow copy of a domain controller's C:\ drive, this command will result in a file called ntds.dit in the specified "C:\temp" destination folder.

Attackers will frequently exfiltrate ntds.dit from the victim's network and then extract hashed passwords from it using a tool such as NtdsAudit, which is available on GitHub. They will perform offline password cracking on the extracted password hashes using specialized tools that are also readily available on the internet.

This is where victims' password policies come into play. Relatively short, easy-to-guess passwords will be revealed in minutes or hours, while relatively long (15 characters), complex passwords will likely never be cracked except for those that were reused passwords or variants of old passwords. Instead of guessing passwords randomly, tools like John the Ripper, Hashcat, and Wordlister enable attackers to use custom rules to generate highly probable variants of passwords that inform their cracking efforts, simulating how people typically modify words to create passwords. This dramatically increases the success rate of password cracking attacks. When a user changes their password using an old password as a part of the new password, it makes it much easier for attackers to crack using these tools. For example, when a user with an old password such as "Summer2023!" changes it to "Summer2024!!". This is especially true if the old passwords were stolen or leaked at some point in the past, giving attackers access to them. It also turns out that changing a password that uses an old weak password standard, such as "timrains" for example, to a password using a new stronger password standard, such as "TimRains123!", is easier to predict than you might think.

When attackers marry these rule-based mutation capabilities to massive lists of compromised credentials available on the internet, passwords that have been reused across internet services and corporate network user accounts become an Achilles' heel. This approach to password cracking can be startlingly effective even on relatively long passwords, and it highlights how common human password-selection patterns can weaken security. Given this common human behavior, it's likely that some passwords in use at large enterprise organizations will always be crackable despite password length, complexity, and expiration policies.

Cybersecurity teams need to pay attention to popular LOTL binaries such as ntdsutil.exe because the probability and impact of their malicious use are high. I'll provide some guidance on how to do this in the *Mitigating LOTL techniques* section of this chapter.

To maximize the speed and efficiency of their attacks, many attackers have scripted the commands they need to execute the stages of their attacks. In these cases, attackers have typically executed the initial stages of their attacks via automation before defenders can detect them and respond.

There are literally hundreds of binaries included in Windows and Linux operating systems that attackers use to live off the land. Of course, attackers don't limit themselves to just running binaries; they will also leverage scripts and libraries that are included with operating systems too. For example, a Visual Basic script called winrm.vbs is included in Windows. Winrm.vbs is a VBScript-based command-line tool that is included with Windows as part of **Windows Remote Management (WinRM)**. It provides administrators with examples of how to use VBScript to interact with the WS-Management protocol. Essentially, this script, if not properly secured, can enable attackers to move laterally in their victims' environments by executing processes via WMI on the local host as well as on remote hosts on the network (Red Canary, May 6, 2025).

An example of a library some attackers have used in the past is called Zipfldr.dll. This is Microsoft's built-in ZIP file handler. ZIP functionality enables the compression and decompression of files. Attackers can use this legitimate library, via rundll32.exe, to launch executables; here's an example of the command.

```
rundll32.exe zipfldr.dll,RouteTheCall file.exe
```

Fortunately, there are some great resources available that enumerate the binaries, scripts, libraries, and drivers attackers have used in the past, so you don't have to do this work yourself. These also include detection guidance in the form of Sigma rules (.yml files):

- Windows binaries: Living Off The Land Binaries, Scripts, and Libraries (LOLBAS) - `https://lolbas-project.github.io/`

- Unix binaries: Get The F**k Out Binaries [sic]. (GTFOBins) - `https://gtfobins.github.io/`
- Windows drivers: Living Off The Land Drivers (LOLDrivers) - `https://loldrivers.io/`
- MITRE ATT&CK Navigator page for the LOLBAS Project - `https://mitre-attack.github.io/attack-navigator/#layerURL=https://lolbas-project.github.io/mitre_attack_navigator_layer.json`

According to the LOLBAS project webpage, "The goal of the LOLBAS project is to document every binary, script, and library that can be used for Living Off The Land techniques" (LOLBAS Project, 2025). At the time of writing, the LOLBAS project page provided details on 228 binaries, including 200 executables, 16 libraries, and 10 scripts that attackers have abused in the past to support their LOTL techniques (LOLBAS Project, 2025).

The GTFOBins project currently lists 390 Unix binaries (LOLBAS Project, 2025). The purpose of the GTFOBins project, as stated on its webpage, is

> *"GTFOBins is a curated list of Unix binaries that can be used to bypass local security restrictions in misconfigured systems. The project collects legitimate functions of Unix binaries that can be abused to break out restricted shells, escalate or maintain elevated privileges, transfer files, spawn bind and reverse shells, and facilitate the other post-exploitation tasks. " (Pinna, E., & Cardaci, A. (2025).*

Next, let's look at another aspect of LOTL that cybersecurity teams need to plan for: the malicious use of legitimate websites.

Malicious use of legitimate websites

This will come as a surprise to no one, but it turns out that the overwhelming majority of attackers are on the internet. Besides the very small percentage of insiders who abuse their privileged access either purposely or unintentionally, attackers sit outside their victims' firewalls. Typically, when attackers successfully perpetrate a traditional network intrusion, they require outbound internet access from their victim's network to download their tools, remotely control victims' systems, exfiltrate data, and attack other potential victims using compromised infrastructure.

Leveraging domains and websites on the internet that are trusted by enterprises implicitly is a very effective technique to accomplish outbound internet access. That is, even if an organization does not permit its users unfettered access to the internet, they likely permit access to github.com, docs.google.com, *.amazonaws.com, *.cloudfront.net, *.cloudapp.azure.com, youtube.com, slack.com, *.docusign.com, *.doubleclick.net, and many other legitimate websites. After all, most enterprises leverage software and cloud services from these domains and websites and even host their own websites and cloud services in them. In many cases, their users must have access to these domains and websites in order to do their jobs.

This is what attackers are counting on. For attackers using LOTL techniques, this means if they can stage parts of their attacks from trusted domains and websites, it's likely they will have outbound internet access to them even in relatively secure environments. Exfiltrating data to a known malicious website might be blocked by their victim's firewalls, but it's highly likely that legitimate websites hosted in Azure, AWS, and **Google Cloud Platform (GCP)** are accessible.

A great resource to inform such efforts is the **Living Off Trusted Sites (LOTS)** project. The stated purpose of this project is

> *"Attackers are using popular legitimate domains when conducting phishing, C&C, exfiltration, and downloading tools to evade detection. The list of websites below allows attackers to use their domain or subdomain" (mrd0x, n.d.).*

The LOTS project webpage currently lists 175 domains and URLs that are known to be used by attackers using LOTL techniques. For each URL on the list, they provide tags that describe how that website was used in past attacks. Tags include phishing, **command and control (C&C)**, download, and exfiltration. Cybersecurity teams can use this list to inform their approach to mitigating LOTL techniques and enabling the appropriate internet access for their users.

Additionally, firewall vendors and **Secure Access Service Edge (SASE)** vendors can help block known malicious websites and provide least-privilege access to both internal and external websites.

Next, let's look at how attackers use common IT support tools to live off the land.

Common IT support tools

Attackers typically make heavy use of IT support tools that aren't necessarily included with operating systems but are popular with IT teams. Such tools can be deployed broadly across workstations and servers. This makes it easier for attackers using LOTL techniques to stay persistent, move laterally, remotely control infrastructure, and exfiltrate data.

Perhaps the best example of such a tool is PSExec.exe. This tool was developed by one of my former Microsoft coworkers, Mark Russinovich, and is included in the Sysinternals tool suite available from Microsoft at `https://learn.microsoft.com/en-us/sysinternals/`. This is a hugely popular legitimate tool among IT professionals and attackers alike. Mark describes this tool as follows:

> *"Utilities like Telnet and remote control programs like Symantec's PC Anywhere let you execute programs on remote systems, but they can be a pain to set up and require*

> *that you install client software on the remote systems that you wish to access. PsExec is a light-weight telnet-replacement that lets you execute processes on other systems, complete with full interactivity for console applications, without having to manually install client software. PsExec's most powerful uses include launching interactive command prompts on remote systems and remote-enabling tools like IpConfig that otherwise do not have the ability to show information about remote systems.*
>
> *Note: Some anti-virus scanners report that one or more of the tools are infected with a "remote admin" virus. None of the PsTools contain viruses, but they have been used by viruses, which is why they trigger virus notifications."* (Microsoft, April 11, 2023).

From the description, it should be clear why this tool is popular among attackers—it is super easy to set up and use for remote control of systems. Since this tool is so popular among IT teams for legitimate IT support use cases, its presence on systems isn't abnormal, and attackers' use of it can blend into its legitimate uses. Numerous named threat actors, including some notorious ransomware gangs, have reportedly used PSExec in their attacks. Here are some examples:

- **BlackSuit**: BlackSuit (formerly Royal) ransomware actors gained access primarily through phishing, then disabled antivirus tools, exfiltrated large volumes of data, and finally deployed ransomware to encrypt systems. This links to a joint cybersecurity advisory from CISA and the FBI that provides defenders with an updated, consolidated briefing on the BlackSuit ransomware threat, covering its evolution, tactics, techniques, indicators of compromise, and recommended mitigation steps: `https://www.cisa.gov/sites/default/files/2024-08/aa23-061a-stopransomware-blacksuit-royal-ransomware_4.pdf`
- **Medusa**: Medusa ransomware attacks involve affiliates gaining access through phishing or exploited vulnerabilities, then using living-off-the-land tools for discovery and lateral movement before encrypting data for double extortion. This links to a joint cybersecurity advisory from the FBI, CISA, and the MS-ISAC that details the Medusa ransomware threat, including its tactics, techniques, indicators of compromise, and recommended defensive actions: `https://www.cisa.gov/news-events/cybersecurity-advisories/aa25-071a`
- **LockBit**: LockBit 3.0 attacks involve affiliates using a mix of phishing, exploitation of known vulnerabilities, and modular ransomware tooling to infiltrate networks, disable defenses, and encrypt systems for ransom. This links to a joint cybersecurity advisory from the FBI, CISA, and the MS-ISAC that provides defenders with a consolidated

briefing on the LockBit 3.0 ransomware threat: `https://www.cisa.gov/news-events/cybersecurity-advisories/aa23-075a`

- **Kasseika**: Kasseika's attack relied on targeted phishing for initial access, followed by BYOVD-based antivirus termination and remote PsExec execution to deploy ransomware. This links to a Trend Micro threat research article that analyzes the Kasseika ransomware operation, detailing how the group uses bring-your-own-vulnerable-driver (BYOVD) attacks, abuses PsExec for remote execution, and exhibits technical overlaps with the earlier BlackMatter ransomware family. `https://www.trendmicro.com/en_us/research/24/a/kasseika-ransomware-deploys-byovd-attacks-abuses-psexec-and-expl.html`
- **Volt Typhoon**: Volt Typhoon carried out its intrusions by exploiting internet-facing vulnerabilities and then using living-off-the-land techniques to move laterally, evade detection, and maintain long-term persistence inside critical-infrastructure networks. This links to a joint cybersecurity advisory from CISA, the NSA, and the FBI warning that PRC state-sponsored threat actors (Volt Typhoon) have compromised and maintained persistent access to multiple U.S. critical infrastructure networks, and providing detailed observations, indicators, and mitigation guidance for defenders.`https://www.cisa.gov/news-events/cybersecurity-advisories/aa24-038a`

Of course, there are other examples of popular **remote monitoring and management (RMM)** tools attackers have used, including AnyDesk, TeamViewer, ScreenConnect, LogMeIn, and many others. Attackers are happy to use whatever IT support and management tools are deployed in their victims' environments.

Similarly, attackers also use legitimate administrator tools in various stages of their attacks. Let's look at some of these next.

Legitimate administrator tools

If attackers can't find the tools of their choice already installed in their victims' environments, many attackers will simply download them. This isn't strictly LOTL, but attackers use combinations of legitimate binaries included in operating systems and legitimate administrator tools they download so often that they are worth mentioning, even in a chapter on LOTL.

Table 14.3 contains examples of legitimate tools and the roles they have reportedly played in attackers' attack chains. The intrusion kill chain phase and the ATT&CK framework tactic mapping for each tool are also included, along with the ATT&CK technique ID:

Tool	Category	Why Attackers Use It	Kill Chain Phase	ATT&CK Tactic Name	MITRE ATT&CK Technique IDs
Nmap	Network Scanning	Maps hosts, ports, services.	Reconnaissance	Reconnaissance	T1046
Advanced IP Scanner	Network Scanning	Fast LAN discovery.	Reconnaissance	Reconnaissance	T1046
Masscan	Network Scanning	Internet-scale scanning	Reconnaissance	Reconnaissance	T1046
Metasploit	Exploitation Framework	Automates exploitation	Exploitation	Initial Access	T1203, T1068
Burp Suite	Exploitation Framework	Web traffic manipulation	Reconnaissance, Exploitation	Initial Access	T1595, T1190
SQLmap	Exploitation Framework	Automates SQL injection	Exploitation	Initial Access	T1190, T1505.003
Responder	Credential Access	Captures NTLM hashes	Credential Access	Credential Access	T1557.001
Mimikatz	Credential Access	Extracts passwords and hashes	Credential Access	Credential access	T1003
SharpHound	Active Directory mapping	Enumerates AD attack paths	Reconnaissance	Discovery	T1069.002

Tool	Category	Why Attackers Use It	Kill Chain Phase	ATT&CK Tactic Name	MITRE ATT&CK Techniq ue IDs
PowerSh ell Empire	Post-Exploitatio n	Full post-exploitation suite.	Command & Control, Lateral Movement	Command & Control	T1059, T1021
Cobalt Strike	Post-Exploitatio n	Beaconing and pivoting	Command & Control, Lateral Movement	Command & Control	T1059, T1105, T1021
Rclone	Exfiltration	Cloud data theft	Exfiltration	Exfiltration	T1567.00 2
WinSCP / PuTTY	Exfiltration	SSH/SFTP movement	Exfiltration, Command & Control	Exfiltration	T1048
7-Zip	Exfiltration	Compresses stolen data	Exfiltration	Exfiltration	T1560

Table 14.3 – Legitimate tools that have reportedly been used in cyberattacks and their associated intrusion kill chain phases and ATT&CK tactics and technique IDs

Of course, this is not an exhaustive list, but it gives you a sampling of the types of tools attackers use and the role they play in their attacks. The ATT&CK technique IDs can potentially help identify mitigations and detection strategies for each item in the table. Check them out at `https://attack.mitre.org/techniques/enterprise/`.

The last type of potential LOTL threat I'll touch on is legitimate developer tools. We'll discuss these next.

Legitimate developer tools

As I mentioned earlier in the "malicious use of legitimate binaries" section, many attackers leverage high levels of automation in their attacks to accelerate them and attempt to achieve their objectives before defenders can detect and respond to them. Some attackers are very proficient at leveraging developer tools present in their victims' environments during their attacks. Doing so helps them avoid detection because it allows them to avoid downloading, installing, and executing tools that might be detected. *Table 14.4* contains some examples of such developer tools. These tools are typically used as an execution technique in the ATT&CK framework, which is why the ATT&CK technique and intrusion kill chain phases aren't included in the table.

Tool	Category	Why Attackers Use It	Primary Roles	MITRE ATT&CK Technique IDs
MSBuild	Developer Tool / LOLBin	Executes inline C# code and loads malicious assemblies without writing to disk	Execution, Payload Delivery	T1127.001
Regsvr32	System Registration Utility / LOLBin	Executes COM scriptlets remotely and bypasses application control.	Execution, Bypass Controls	T1218.010
InstallUtil	.NET Installer Utility/ LOLBin	Executes installer classes in .NET assemblies for stealthy payload execution	Execution, Persistence	T1218.004
Mshta	HTML Application Host/LOLBin	Executes malicious HTA files and remote scripts	Execution, Payload Delivery	T1218.005
C# Compiler (csc.exe)	Developer Tool / Compiler	Compiles malicious .NET code directly on the victim system to avoid detection.	Payload Generation, Execution	T1027, T1059

Tool	Category	Why Attackers Use It	Primary Roles	MITRE ATT&CK Technique IDs
Python interpreter (python.exe)	Interpreter / Scripting Engine	Runs malicious Python scripts and payloads directly	Execution, Payload Scripting	T1059.006
Node.js (node.exe)	Interpreter/ Runtime	Executes JavaScript payloads and can run local servers for C2 purposes.	Execution, Payload Hosting	T1059.007
Ruby interpreter (ruby.exe)	Interpreter / Scripting Engine	Executes Ruby-based malware and automation scripts	Execution, Payload Scripting	T1059.008
Visual Studio (devenv.exe)	Developer IDE / Build Environment	Compiles malware on the victim system to evade static detection	Payload Development, Local Compilation	T1027, T1059

Table 14.4 – Legitimate developer tools that have reportedly been used in cyberattacks and their associated ATT&CK technique IDs

Again, this list isn't exhaustive, and the ATT&CK technique IDs can potentially help identify mitigations and detection strategies for each item in the table.

At this point, you might be wondering how cybersecurity teams can mitigate all these LOTL techniques. Let's discuss this next.

Mitigating LOTL techniques

Mitigating LOTL techniques is very challenging. This is why they are so popular with attackers that have the skill to leverage them. Cybersecurity teams must prevent attackers from accessing the tools and URLs they rely on while still allowing legitimate users to use them. That becomes especially difficult when attackers and legitimate users may be using the same credentials. Subsequently, behavioral analysis is often cited as an effective mitigation.

However, when considering the mitigations recommended through the collective wisdom of cybersecurity subject matter experts and vendors, the list of mitigations is similar to the combinations of the cybersecurity strategies we examined in *Chapter 10, Cybersecurity Strategies*. That is, there's no silver bullet or easy way to mitigate a diverse set of attack techniques such as LOTL in large enterprise environments.

Instead, there is a long list of mitigations that in aggregate make LOTL harder for attackers and make detection more likely for defenders. The themes of these mitigations should be familiar, as they include the "motherhood and apple pie" of cybersecurity, such as restricting access to binaries and the internet, effective network segmentation, application control, leveraging the principle of least privilege, MFA and privileged access management, implementing centralized logging, auditing access, maintaining behavioral baselines, hardening endpoints, effective vulnerability management, and conducting continuous threat hunting, among others. In other words, there are potentially many mitigations cybersecurity teams need to layer into their environments in order to protect, detect, and respond to LOTL techniques.

One nuance that is worth mentioning in the context of LOTL is the difference between **indicators of attack (IOAs)** and the **indicators of compromise (IOCs)** I mentioned in *Chapter 2, What to Know About Threat Intelligence*. Remember that IOCs help cybersecurity teams with post-compromise attacker detection and incident response. They are largely reactive and artifact-based, although known attacker IOCs can be used to inform red team exercises and security testing.

IOAs, on the other hand, are proactive, behavior-based, sequence-based, and are detected ideally in real time, as opposed to after a compromise. IOAs can help cybersecurity teams detect intent and behavior during an attack. They can help spot attacker behavior such as privilege escalation, lateral movement, and attacker behaviors to stay persistent. Where IOCs are used for forensics and incident response, IOAs are used for threat hunting and intrusion kill chain disruption. Where possible, take advantage of IOAs to detect and disrupt attackers.

Let's look at some specific mitigation guidance from different sources to give you a comprehensive perspective. Let's start with the MITRE ATT&CK framework.

Using the ATT&CK framework

The ATT&CK framework provides us with numerous possible mitigations for the LOTL techniques attackers use to attack enterprises. *Table 14.5* shows us the mitigations that the ATT&CK framework offers for IT support tools and popular administrator tools reportedly used by attackers in the past during different stages of their attacks (MITRE Corporation, 2025). The mitigation description gives you an idea of the type of mitigation that could be effective against each tool, and the mitigation ID can provide more details when you look them up here: `https://attack.mitre.org/mitigations/enterprise/`.

Tool	Technique Name	Mitigations	Mitigation ID
Nmap	Network Service Discovery	Network segmentation; firewall rules; disabling unnecessary services	M1041, M1031
Advanced IP Scanner	Network Service Discovery	Network segmentation; firewall rules; disabling unnecessary services	M1041, M1031
Masscan	Network Service Discovery	Network segmentation; firewall rules; disabling unnecessary services	M1041, M1031
Metasploit	Exploitation for Client Execution	Patch management; application sandboxing	M1051, M1050
Metasploit	Exploitation for Privilege Escalation	Patch OS vulnerabilities; enforce least privilege.	M1051, M1026
Burp Suite	Active Scanning	Network segmentation; rate limiting	M1047, M1031
Burp Suite	Exploit Public-Facing Application	WAF; patch management	M1051, M1030
SQLmap	Exploit Public-Facing Application	WAF; patch management	M1051, M1030
SQLmap	SQL Stored Procedures	Restrict database permissions	
Mimikatz	OS Credential Dumping	Credential Guard; LSASS protection	M1026, M1047, M1040
SharpHound	Permission Groups Discovery	Limit AD enumeration	M1018, M1026

Tool	Technique Name	Mitigations	Mitigation ID
PowerShell	PowerShell	Constrain PowerShell; script signing	M1040, M1038, M1047
WMIC/WMI	WMI	Restrict WMI usage	M1040, M1028, M1047
PSExec	Lateral Tool Transfer	Network segmentation	M1041, M1030
PSExec	Remote Service Execution	Restrict remote service creation	M1040, M1028
RDP	Remote Desktop Protocol	MFA; restrict RDP	M1030, M1041, M1050
WinRM	WinRM	Disable WinRM if unused	M1030, M1041, M1050
Certutil	Ingress Tool Transfer	Block unauthorized downloads	M1037, M1041, M1040
MSHTA	MSHTA	Block mshta.exe	M1042, M1038
BITSAdmin / BITS	BITS jobs	Restrict BITS usage	M1040, M1042
AnyDesk	Remote Access Software	Block unauthorized RMM tools	M1042, M1040
ScreenConnect	External Remote Services	MFA; VPN hardening	M1050, M1030

Tool	Technique Name	Mitigations	Mitigation ID
ScreenConnect	Remote Services	Monitor remote access sessions	M1030, M1041, M1050
TeamViewer	Remote Access Software	Block unauthorized RMM tools	M1042, M1040
Atera / NinjaOne / N-able	Command Execution	Application control	
Atera / NinjaOne / N-able	Ingress Tool Transfer	Block unauthorized downloads	M1037, M1041, M1040
Splashtop	Remote Access Software	Block unauthorized RMM tools	M1042, M1040
PowerShell Empire	Command Execution	Application control	
PowerShell Empire	Remote Services	Monitor remote access sessions	M1030, M1041, M1050
Cobalt Strike	Command Execution	Application control	
Cobalt Strike	Ingress Tool Transfer	Block unauthorized downloads	M1037, M1041, M1040
Cobalt Strike	Remote Services	Monitor remote access sessions	M1030, M1041, M1050
Rclone	Exfiltration to Cloud Storage	Block unsanctioned cloud apps	M1037, M1041
WinSCP/PuTTY	Exfiltration Over Alternative Protocol	Restrict outbound protocols	M1037, M1041

Tool	Technique Name	Mitigations	Mitigation ID
7-Zip	Archive Collected Data	Restrict compression utilities	M1040, M1042

Table 14.5 – Legitimate IT support tools and administrator tools reportedly used by attackers during various stages of their attacks, mapped to corresponding ATT&CK framework techniques and mitigations (MITRE Corporation, 2025).

The mitigations mentioned most often, potentially providing elevated return on investment, include:

- M1041 – Network segmentation (mentioned as a mitigation for 14 (45%) of the 31 tools listed)
- M1040 – Behavior prevention on endpoint (mentioned as a mitigation for 12 (39%) of the 31 tools listed)
- M1030 – Network hardening (mentioned as a mitigation for 9 (29%) of the 31 tools listed)
- M1050 – Exploit protection (mentioned as a mitigation for 7 (23%) of the 31 tools listed)

However, as I mentioned earlier in the chapter, there are hundreds of binaries in different operating systems that attackers use to LOTL that aren't listed here. Subsequently, the list of mitigations is much larger than the sample I've provided here, but the ATT&CK framework can be leveraged to identify potential mitigations for the risk many of these binaries pose.

Next, let's look at one tool that advanced threat actors love to use to steal a copy of their victims' Active Directory.

NTDSUTIL guidance

I want to highlight the guidance ATT&CK provides specifically for `ntdsutil.exe`, since attackers love to use this tool, which is present on every modern Windows Server Active Directory Domain Controller by default, to get access to hashed passwords for offline cracking. Once attackers have harvested credentials from the `ntds.dit` file, this will typically enable them to stay persistent, move laterally, command and control systems, exfiltrate data, and so on.

ATT&CK provides four primary mitigations and one detection strategy (MITRE, October 24, 2025):

- M1041 – Encrypt sensitive information: secure Domain Controller backups to prevent offline extraction.
- M1027 – Password policies: ensure unique, complex local admin passwords across systems.
- M1026 – Privileged account management: avoid placing domain accounts in local admin groups; follow tiered admin models to reduce credential exposure.
- M1017 – User training: train users/admins not to reuse passwords across accounts.
- DET0586 – Detection of `ntds.dit` credential dumping: detects suspicious activity such as:
    - Creation of shadow copies
    - Access to %SystemRoot%\NTDS\ntds.dit
    - Use of ntdsutil.exe, esentutl, or volume management APIs
    - Unusual file access patterns on Domain Controllers

WMI guidance

Similarly, ATT&CK offers guidance on mitigations and detections for attackers seeking to use legacy **Windows Management Instrumentation (WMI)** as an LTOL technique. Threat actors abuse WMI to operate across both local and remote systems, applying it in Discovery to gather system information and in Execution to run commands during intrusions.

ATT&CK provides four primary mitigations and one detection strategy (MITRE, October 24, 2025):

- M1040 - Behavior prevention on endpoint: On Windows 10, enable **Attack Surface Reduction (ASR)** rules to block processes created by WMI commands from running
- M1038 - Execution prevention: Enable application control configured to block execution of wmic.exe if it is not required for a given system or network to prevent potential misuse by adversaries
- M1026 - Privileged account management: Prevent credential overlap across systems for administrator and privileged accounts

- M1018 - User account management: Prevent non-administrators from connecting remotely using WMI by default. Restrict other users who are allowed to connect, or disallow all users from connecting remotely to WMI.
- DET0364 - Behavioral detection strategy for WMI execution abuse on Windows
    - Analytic ID AN1031: Detects adversarial abuse of WMI to execute local or remote commands via WMIC, PowerShell, or COM API through a multi-event chain: process creation, command execution, and corresponding network connection if remote

> **Note**
>
>

WMI is extremely valuable for administrators of Windows-based systems, but it isn't a feature that can simply be turned off to prevent attacker abuse. It's a core subsystem relied on by the Windows operating system and many applications, making it effectively ubiquitous. Disabling it would break Windows components, remote management tools, and **Endpoint Detection and Response (EDR)** agents, among others. ATT&CK's guidance reflects this operational reality.

In addition to the guidance published as part of the ATT&CK framework, governments have worked together to publish helpful guidance on LOTL attacks and related topics, such as securing PowerShell. Let's look at these next.

Other government guidance

Governments have been attacked by advanced threat actors for decades and subsequently have been trying to mitigate LOTL techniques for a long time. Some have shared guidance based on their research and experiences. There are two helpful publications I want to draw your attention to related to LOTL.

LOTL detection and hardening best practices

Various agencies and departments of the US government worked with the Australian Signals Directorate's Australian Cyber Security Centre, the Canadian Centre for Cyber Security, the United Kingdom National Cyber Security Centre, and the New Zealand National Cyber Security Centre to jointly publish guidance on LOTL techniques. Their publication is called *Identifying and Mitigating Living Off the Land Techniques* and is available for free download at `https://www.cisa.gov/sites/default/files/2025-03/Joint-Guidance-Identifying-and-Mitigating-LOTL508.pdf`.

The following is an excerpt from the summary of that guidance:

> *"The authoring agencies strongly urge critical infrastructure organizations to apply the following prioritized best practices and detection guidance to hunt for potential LOTL activity. These recommendations are part of a multifaceted cybersecurity strategy that enables effective data correlation and analysis. There is no foolproof solution to fully prevent or detect LOTL activity, but by applying these best practices, organizations can best position themselves for more effective detection and mitigation.*
>
> ***Detection Best Practices:***
>
> *1. Implement detailed logging and aggregate logs in an out-of-band, centralized location that is write-once, read-many to avoid the risk of attackers modifying or erasing logs.*
>
> *2. Establish and continuously maintain baselines of network, user, administrative, and application activity, and least privilege restrictions.*
>
> *3. Build or acquire automation (such as machine learning models) to continually review all logs to compare current activities against established behavioral baselines and alert on specified anomalies.*
>
> *4. Reduce alert noise by fine-tuning via priority (urgency and severity) and continuously reviewing detections based on trending activity.*
>
> *5. Leverage user and entity behavior analytics (UEBA)*
>
> ***Hardening Best Practices:***
>
> *1. Apply and consult vendor-recommended guidance for security hardening*
>
> *2. Implement application allow listing and monitor use of common LOLBins*
>
> *3. Enhance IT and OT network segmentation and monitoring*
>
> *4. Implement authentication and authorization controls for all human-to-software and software-to-software interactions regardless of network location." (CISA, et al., 2024)*

> **Note**
>
> Source: Cybersecurity and Infrastructure Security Agency (CISA), Joint Guidance: Identifying and Mitigating Living Off the Land (LOTL) Techniques, 2025

PowerShell guidance

Another highly recommended free publication to consume is called *Keeping PowerShell: Security Measures to Use and Embrace*. It was published in 2022 by the **National Security Agency (NSA)**, the **Cybersecurity and Infrastructure Security Agency (CISA)**, the **New Zealand National Cyber Security Centre (NZ NCSC)**, and the **United Kingdom National Cyber Security Centre (NCSC-UK)**. This is a summary of the recommendations from the paper:

- Do not disable PowerShell — modern versions provide essential defensive visibility and controls
- Use PowerShell 5.1+ or 7.x and remove PowerShell v2, which lacks security features
- Enable full PowerShell logging (module logging, script block logging, transcription) and centralize logs for detection and forensics
- Ensure **Antimalware Scan Interface (AMSI)** is active so PowerShell content is scanned by AV/EDR before execution
- Apply **Constrained Language Mode (CLM)** for non-admin users to limit abuse of powerful language features
- Restrict script execution to trusted, signed, or approved sources using Application Control (WDAC/AppLocker)
- Harden PowerShell Remoting with strong authentication, **Just Enough Administration (JEA)**, and restricted endpoints
- Monitor PowerShell usage patterns for suspicious behavior (encoded commands, download cradles, unusual parent processes)
- Keep PowerShell and Windows updated to ensure the latest security features and protections are available
- Remove unnecessary modules and features to reduce the attack surface
- Enforce least privilege for all PowerShell users and administrators
- Use PowerShell as a defensive tool for auditing, IR automation, and system monitoring — it strengthens, not weakens, security posture

An older publication, updated in October 2021, provides a maturity framework for PowerShell that I think is a helpful way to approach managing PowerShell in enterprise environments. It was published by the Australian Signals Directorate and is available for free download here: `https://www.cyber.gov.au/sites/default/files/2025-03/Securing%20PowerShell%20in%20the%20enterprise%20%28October%202021%29.pdf`. The following excerpt from the paper summarizes a maturity framework for PowerShell.

> *"Level 0: An organisation uses PowerShell in its default configuration without any consideration of the security risks associated with its use.*
>
> *Level 1: An organisation configures a list of approved PowerShell scripts. Additionally, the PowerShell script execution policy is configured to run only PowerShell scripts signed by a Trusted Publisher, with any code signing certificates protected from misuse. PowerShell version 5.0 provides greater logging facilities and should be used where possible. Finally, PowerShell-related activity is centrally logged and analysed.*
>
> *Level 2: An organisation locks down PowerShell hosts to users performing tasks that require the ability to use PowerShell. This is a form of role-based application control. A hardened Windows Remote Management (WinRM) configuration is deployed to make remote PowerShell more secure.*
>
> *Level 3: An organisation deploys custom constrained endpoints for PowerShell. This restricts the PowerShell functionality for a given user to a predefined list." (Australian Cyber Security Centre, October 2021).*

Organizations that work to achieve even just Level 1 of this maturity model will make it incrementally harder for attackers who aspire to use PowerShell scripts in their environments. However, be aware that even if PowerShell scripts were 100% secure, attackers could still use the PowerShell console or terminal to run individual commands. Since no PowerShell script is running, all the rigor around scripts won't apply. Cybersecurity teams' work is never done!

Lessons from the trenches

Finally, let me give you some advice based on my own experience working to mitigate LOTL techniques. I've tried to tackle this challenging problem more than a few times in my career. I can offer you some advice based on my experience, however imperfect it may be.

Removing or restricting access to binaries

Since there are so many legitimate uses for binaries built into operating systems, it is unlikely you'll realistically be able to restrict access to them in a meaningful way or remove them from the operating system images in your environment. I've gone down this path myself only to find that access to these binaries was required by third-party management software or other software installed in the environment. Removing or blocking these binaries disrupts software that relies on them for routine functions, causing legitimate management and monitoring tools to fail. I was surprised to see so many third-party applications call operating system commands directly. Unfortunately, removing these binaries or dramatically restricting access to them would have unpredictable consequences in large enterprise environments. Among the Windows binaries I discovered in this category were pcalua.exe, hh.exe, and bginfo.exe.

Detect anomalous binary use: although you likely can't restrict access to all LOTL binaries in an overly aggressive way, you likely can identify many binaries that are not regularly or actively used in your environment. Your **Security Information & Event Management (SIEM)** solution might be a good source for this information. Configuring monitoring and alerting on the use of these infrequently used LOTL binaries can help detect attackers that leverage them. Studying their use and the volume of potential alerts before putting them into production is a good idea. Ensure the proper alerting severity levels are implemented—if `ntdsutil.exe` is executed, this should be a high priority alert.

The importance of endpoint security coverage

Your ability to detect attackers leveraging LOTL binaries in your environment is largely dependent on how many systems in your environment have endpoint security solutions installed (EDR/XDR) and are actively reporting data for analysis. My strong recommendation for cybersecurity teams is to pay attention to the inventory of systems that do not have EDR/XDR installed on them and/or are not reporting data for analysis. Attackers look for these systems and stage their attacks from them in order to avoid being detected. Operating inventories of systems without EDR/XDR actively reporting data gives attackers the opportunity to use LOTL techniques in their victims' environment. Constantly strive to have 100% coverage on all systems that endpoint agents can be installed on. Bake this into your reporting requirements for operational awareness.

Embrace the Principle of Least Privilege: to the extent that your organization's corporate culture permits, restrict outbound internet access as much as possible. Not just for outbound HTTP/HTTPS connections, but all TCP and UDP network traffic. Make it as hard as possible for attackers to download their tools, command and control compromised systems, exfiltrate large amounts of data, and achieve their objectives. This includes blocking outbound VPN connections, SSH, FTP, SFTP, and many other protocols. Outbound internet access for protocols that are useful to attackers should be granted as an exception, not by default. Remember, CISOs aren't "Chief Internet Access Officers"; they are responsible for security, not ensuring everyone has access to the entire internet. At the very least, known malicious domains and websites should be blocked, along with country code top-level domains (ccTLDs) that have no legitimate business purpose. After all, if no one in your organization speaks Russian, Persian, Korean, or a dialect of Chinese, why would they need access to those ccTLDs on the internet?

Restrict access to Living Off Trusted Sites

Remember the LOTS Project—Living Off Trusted Sites (`https://lots-project.com/`). These are legitimate websites that are challenging for enterprises to block even if they have the desire to do so. But restricting access to these URLs to just the people who need to access them will force attackers who are LOTL in your environment to find the identities they can use to access these URLs or modify outbound access rules for the identities they are already using. This represents more opportunities to detect their presence in your environment, potentially before they can deploy ransomware or exfiltrate sensitive data.

Network visibility

If you are relying on network detections to help identify attackers on your network, you need to ensure TLS-encrypted traffic can be inspected. Today, more than 90% of web traffic on corporate networks is encrypted by TLS. This is great for safeguarding the confidentiality and integrity of network traffic, but attackers also use it to blend into legitimate network traffic and conceal their activities. If you aren't inspecting TLS-encrypted traffic, you do not have visibility into more than 90% of the traffic on your network. In this scenario, those outbound internet access restrictions I mentioned earlier are even more important, because if you can't inspect the network traffic before it leaves your network, you shouldn't let it past your firewalls to sketchy parts of the internet.

Use cybersecurity vendors' LOTL features

Major cybersecurity vendors, such as Palo Alto Networks, Cisco, and CrowdStrike, have LOTL features and functionality built into some of their product offerings. It is prudent to take full advantage of these features because you need all the help you can get to mitigate this challenging problem. Here are some pointers to helpful documentation:

- *Playbook of the Week: Automating Response to Living-Off-the-Land (LOTL) Attacks*: This is a Palo Alto Networks guide showing how to automate detection, enrichment, and response workflows for Living-off-the-Land (LOTL) attacks using Cortex XDR and XSOAR. `https://www.paloaltonetworks.com/blog/security-operations/playbook-of-the-week-automating-response-to-living-off-the-land-lotl-attacks/`
- *Playbook of the Week: Fending Off Living Off the Land Attacks*: This is a Palo Alto Networks playbook showing how to detect and disrupt Living-off-the-Land (LOTL) attacks by analyzing command-line activity and leveraging Cortex XSOAR automation. `https://www.paloaltonetworks.com/blog/security-operations/playbook-of-the-week-fending-off-living-off-the-land-attacks/`

- *How CrowdStrike Stops Living-off-the-Land Attacks*: An analysis explaining how attackers abuse legitimate tools in Living-off-the-Land attacks and how the Falcon platform, especially its APEX capability, detects and stops this behavior. `https://www.crowdstrike.com/en-us/blog/beyond-the-binary-stop-attackers-living-off-your-land/`
- *Seeing Inside the Vortex: Detecting Living off the Land Techniques*: A Cisco analysis outlining how to detect Living-off-the-Land techniques by identifying subtle behavioral patterns and telemetry signals that reveal attacker activity hidden within legitimate system processes.`https://blogs.cisco.com/security/seeing-inside-the-vortex-detecting-living-off-the-land-techniques`

Change is required

LOTL is the type of problem that will never get better unless organizations change the way they manage and operate IT systems. "Zero Trust" has become a mantra in our industry, yet we trust the use of every operating system binary and every non-obvious malicious URL on the internet implicitly. Attackers are happy to take advantage of this contradiction to continue to LOTL successfully. CISOs and cybersecurity teams need to lead this change boldly and with a sense of urgency. The status quo will only sustain LOTL techniques for attackers.

LOTL is a huge topic, and I've only scratched the surface in this chapter. But I hope you benefit from the analysis and guidance I have provided.

In the next and final chapter of this book, I'll discuss how to secure **artificial intelligence (AI)** systems and how to use AI to achieve better cybersecurity.

Summary

This chapter examined why Living Off the Land techniques remain one of the most persistent and effective approaches used by modern attackers. By abusing native operating-system binaries, widely trusted tools, legitimate websites, and commonly deployed IT and developer utilities, attackers are able to blend malicious activity into normal enterprise operations, significantly reducing the likelihood of detection. The chapter showed that LOTL is not a niche or emerging technique; it is a core operational model for both criminal and nation-state threat actors.

A key takeaway is that LOTL succeeds largely because organizations implicitly trust what is already present in their environments. Fileless malware, LOLBins, trusted cloud-hosted websites, and administrative tools all benefit from this trust, especially when attackers operate using valid credentials. This makes traditional, signature-based security controls insufficient on their own and forces defenders to focus more heavily on behavior, context, and intent rather than artifacts alone.

The chapter emphasized that there is no single control capable of mitigating LOTL techniques. Effective defense requires a layered approach that combines least privilege, strong identity controls, application control, network segmentation, centralized logging, and continuous monitoring. Behavioral detections and IOAs are especially important, as they allow defenders to identify malicious activity while it is in progress rather than after damage has already occurred. Guidance from MITRE ATT&CK, CISA, NSA, and allied government agencies reinforces the importance of focusing on behaviors such as credential abuse, anomalous binary execution, lateral movement, and misuse of administrative interfaces.

Special attention was given to high-impact tools such as PowerShell, WMI, and ntdsutil.exe, which are indispensable for administrators but equally valuable to attackers. The lesson is not to disable these capabilities, but to secure, monitor, and constrain them in ways that preserve operational value while reducing abuse. Maturity models and published hardening guidance provide practical paths forward, even in large and complex enterprise environments.

Ultimately, LOTL techniques highlight a broader challenge for cybersecurity teams: balancing operational necessity with security risk. As long as enterprises continue to implicitly trust every built-in tool, binary, and widely accessible website, attackers will continue to exploit that trust. Meaningful progress against LOTL requires intentional change—treating tools, identities, and network access as privileges rather than defaults and accepting that visibility and detection are just as critical as prevention.

References

- Drucker, P. F. (1973). *Management: Tasks, Responsibilities*, Practices. Harper & Row.
- Cybersecurity and Infrastructure Security Agency (CISA). (Feb. 7, 2024). *Identifying and Mitigating Living Off the Land Techniques*. Retrieved from: `https://www.cisa.gov/resources-tools/resources/identifying-and-mitigating-living-land-techniques`
- Cybersecurity and Infrastructure Security Agency, National Security Agency, Federal Bureau of Investigation, Department of Energy, Environmental Protection Agency, Transportation Security Administration, Australian Cyber Security Centre, Canadian Centre for Cyber Security, United Kingdom National Cyber Security Centre, and New Zealand National Cyber Security Centre. (2025). *Joint guidance: Identifying and mitigating living off the land techniques*. U.S. Cybersecurity and Infrastructure Security Agency. Retrieved from: `https://www.cisa.gov/sites/default/files/2025-03/Joint-Guidance-Identifying-and-Mitigating-LOTL508.pdf`

- CrowdStrike. (November 26, 2024). *Fileless Malware Explained*. Retrieved from: https://www.crowdstrike.com/en-us/cybersecurity-101/malware/fileless-malware/
- Fortinet. (n.d.). *What Is Fileless Malware?* Retrieved from: https://www.fortinet.com/resources/cyberglossary/fileless-malware
- Palo Alto Networks. (n.d.). *What Are Fileless Malware Attacks and "Living Off the Land"? Unit 42 Explains*. Retrieved from: https://www.paloaltonetworks.com/cyberpedia/what-are-fileless-malware-attacks
- Avast. (n.d.). *Fileless malware*. Retrieved from: https://www.avast.com/c-fileless-malware
- Microsoft. (April 24, 2024). *Fileless threats*. Retrieved from: https://learn.microsoft.com/en-us/defender-endpoint/malware/fileless-threats
- Red Canary. (May 6, 2025). *Lateral movement using WinRM and WMI*. Retrieved from: https://redcanary.com/blog/threat-detection/lateral-movement-winrm-wmi/
- MITRE Corporation. (2025). *MITRE ATT&CK®. Retrieved from:* https://attack.mitre.org/
- LOLBAS Project. (2025). *Living Off The Land Binaries, Scripts, and Libraries (LOLBAS)*. Retrieved from: https://lolbas-project.github.io/
- Pinna, E., & Cardaci, A. (2025). *GTFOBins: Curated Unix binaries for living-off-the-land techniques*. Retrieved from: https://gtfobins.github.io/
- mrd0x. (n.d.). *LOTS Project – Living Off Trusted Sites*. Retrieved from: https://lots-project.com/
- Microsoft. (April 11, 2023). *PsExec – Sysinternals*. Retrieved from: https://learn.microsoft.com/en-us/sysinternals/downloads/psexec
- Australian Cyber Security Centre. (October 2021). *Securing PowerShell in the enterprise*. Retrieved from: https://www.cyber.gov.au/sites/default/files/2025-03/Securing%20PowerShell%20in%20the%20enterprise%20%28October%202021%29.pdf

Get this book's PDF version and more

Scan the QR code (or go to `packtpub.com/unlock`). Search for this book by name, confirm the edition, and then follow the steps on the page.

UNLOCK NOW

Note: Keep your invoice handy. Purchases made directly from Packt don't require an invoice.

15

Artificial Intelligence: Security of AI Systems and Using AI for Better Cybersecurity

> *"Who controls the past controls the future. Who controls the present controls the past." — George Orwell, 1949*

> **Note**
>
> All examples, case studies, and references to threat actors or organizations are based on publicly available reporting from reputable sources. Descriptions of attacks, vulnerabilities, or incidents reflect the information available at the time of writing and do not imply wrongdoing beyond what has been publicly alleged or documented.

Ever since OpenAI released ChatGPT in November 2022, the world has been obsessed with the promise of **artificial intelligence (AI)**. AI systems were first seriously contemplated in the 1940s, and development of such systems began in the 1950s. Many enterprises have already been using various types of AI systems for numerous years; however, OpenAI's generative AI chatbot demonstrated the potential for AI systems in a way that captured broad attention. The release of ChatGPT initiated an AI "gold rush," and vendors and organizations started exploring how they could leverage generative AI, **large language models (LLMs),** and agentic AI capabilities. The results have disrupted nearly every industry around the world as developers and vendors embrace new capabilities. This trend is likely to continue indefinitely as AI is rapidly becoming a foundational component of modern computing.

Given that new AI capabilities are being leveraged across enterprises, many CIOs, CTOs, CISOs, cybersecurity teams, and vendors are scrambling to understand the risks associated with AI and how to mitigate them. These new systems share some of the same well-understood cybersecurity risks as traditional IT systems. After all, they leverage compute, storage, network, and database resources and services just like traditional systems.

However, generative AI systems differ from traditional enterprise software in that they can ingest and reason over multiple input types at the same time, spanning far beyond the narrow, structured formats legacy systems were designed for. Some examples of inputs include:

- A range of text inputs including prompts, questions, instructions, partial sentences, and documents
- Structured data such as tables, text in JSON format, and metadata
- Images such as pictures, diagrams, PowerPoint slide illustrations, and so on
- Audio inputs like audio waveforms or spectrograms (visual representations of sound)
- Video inputs like video frames or sequences
- Latent space vectors that are compressed, abstract representations of data
- Multimodal inputs including text + image, text + audio, image + image, text + structured data, audio-driven animation, and so on

Because generative AI systems are non-deterministic and capable of producing highly variable outputs, they introduce new and unpredictable risks that cybersecurity teams must account for. For example, a generative-AI assistant may refuse a sensitive request nine times in a row but unexpectedly comply on the tenth, leaking data because its non-deterministic outputs make harmful behavior appear only intermittently.

Many of the CISOs I've spoken with are skeptical that generative AI can be effectively secured, and it's not hard to see why. Even the simplest input surface in modern computing, the URL, has remained one of the most heavily exploited attack vectors for more than three decades. Sir Tim Berners-Lee published the original URL specification in the 1990s, giving browsers and servers a formal, tightly constrained input format. Yet browsers that accept essentially one type of input still generate hundreds of critical and high-severity vulnerabilities every year, and, as discussed in *Chapter 6, Internet-Based Threats*, attackers send roughly 2.5 billion phishing emails per month, with more than half weaponizing URLs. In short, a single, well-specified input type continues to drive both technical exploitation and large-scale social-engineering campaigns.

Against that backdrop, CISOs are understandably skeptical that generative-AI systems, which must process a far broader and more complex set of inputs, often simultaneously, can be secured more effectively than web browsers have been. Since generative-AI systems are non-deterministic, the same input can yield different outputs from one attempt to the next, making it impossible for users to reliably judge when an answer is trustworthy. It is equally implausible to assume that attackers will ignore such variability or fail to exploit it. Expecting these systems to parse every form of content securely or to produce consistently reliable outputs is unrealistic, and so is believing that adversaries won't leverage their unpredictability to target consumers and enterprises.

These are just some of the reasons CISOs are concerned about generative AI. These systems are potentially far more complicated than most of the traditional IT systems that cybersecurity teams have had to manage in large enterprise environments. By itself, increased complexity makes it more likely for security incidents to occur. Since enterprises can't simply replace their older IT systems with new systems all at once, cybersecurity teams will need to manage security for the decades of legacy IT systems their organizations have invested in, in addition to the newer, more complicated AI systems. This isn't the first time security teams have been expected to secure new, rapidly adopted technologies—cloud computing and APIs are the consummate examples. Given this, it's important that CISOs and cybersecurity teams understand the new risks associated with these newer technologies.

From an operational cybersecurity standpoint, the CISOs I've spoken with about generative AI, LLMs, and agentic systems consistently focus, at least initially, on four major categories of risks and challenges.

1. Understanding the new risks related to the adoption of new AI capabilities and how they might increase the attack surface of their organizations
2. Safeguarding organizational data when third-party AI systems process, store, or transmit it, whether those systems operate on-premises, in the cloud, or across hybrid environments
3. Understanding and defending against cyber-attacks that leverage AI capabilities
4. Securing AI systems that are developed in-house. These systems share the same development challenges I discussed in previous chapters, as well as some new ones.

In this chapter, we will explore the first three of these four categories. An entire book could be dedicated to security development for AI systems—I won't try to do that in a section of one chapter. I'll endeavor to introduce you to each of the three other aforementioned areas in this chapter.

We will cover the following topics:

- Generative AI safety and cybersecurity risks
- Agentic AI and related security risks
- Case Study: Security considerations deploying Microsoft Copilot

- How attackers leverage AI
- Emerging AI security capabilities
- Is cybersecurity getting better or worse?

Let's start by examining the risks that accompany the use of generative AI technologies and LLMs.

Generative AI safety and cybersecurity risks

CIOs, CTOs, CISOs, and cybersecurity teams are interested in understanding and mitigating new risks associated with the rapid adoption of generative AI technologies by their organizations. The stakes are high because, as we've discussed throughout this book, attackers are relentless and more aggressive now than ever before. Cybersecurity reporting from governments and major threat intelligence vendors consistently attribute a significant volume of activity to threat actors operating from DPRK, Iran, China, and Russia, where such actors are rarely prosecuted. Enterprises face an onslaught of attacks from threat actors based in these locations as well as throngs of criminals located throughout the Western world. This situation is pressurized by the necessity for enterprises to evolve IT systems, increase productivity, reduce costs, and drive consumption and investment.

The adoption of generative AI systems by enterprises has rapidly grown since 2022. There are plenty of use cases for generative AI and things have been changing rapidly, but some of the most common are customer service automation and virtual agents, enterprise AI assistants, document processing and workflow automation, developer productivity / code generation, and decision-support and analytics assistance (Hadley, L., July 21, 2025). Across these use cases, it becomes clear that sensitive data is inevitably involved. Take customer service automation for example. For most enterprises, their customers' personal information is considered sensitive and is included in the scope of their data protection efforts. This typically includes data such as names, addresses, phone numbers, genders, birthdates, as well as credit card and banking information. Data-protection mechanisms for traditional systems have been refined over decades and are well understood by CISOs. In contrast, the rapid adoption of generative-AI systems is outpacing the development of comparable safeguards. Developer productivity and code generation tools are another example. As we discussed in *Chapter 7, Application Programming Interface (API) Security*, the mistakes that developers make in development can, and often do, turn into security incidents in production. Do generative AI coding assist tools make this challenge better or amplify it? For example, if developers are developing code using bad programming practices, such as hard coding credentials and keys, does giving AI systems access to this data exacerbate the problem and increase the risk?

CISOs and security teams typically have decades of experience securing systems that leverage traditional computing resources such as compute, network, storage, and databases. Let's discuss the new risks that specifically accompany generative AI, LLMs, and agentic AI systems.

AI safety

Along with their organizations' use of generative AI, one new set of risks that CISOs and security teams have adopted is collectively referred to as *AI safety*. AI safety refers to the principles and practices that help ensure AI systems are developed and used in ways that are safe and ethical. Where security tends to focus on the confidentiality, integrity, and availability of data and systems, the concept of AI safety seeks to ensure AI systems are developed and used with the good of humanity in mind. AI security and safety are dimensions of a broader concept called *responsible AI*. Other dimensions of responsible AI include privacy, data governance, fairness and bias, transparency, and explainability (Nestor Maslej, Loredana Fattorini, Raymond Perrault, Yolanda Gil, Vanessa Parli, Njenga Kariuki, Emily Capstick, Anka Reuel, Erik Brynjolfsson, John Etchemendy, Katrina Ligett, Terah Lyons, James Manyika, Juan Carlos Niebles, Yoav Shoham, Russell Wald, Toby Walsh, Armin Hamrah, Lapo Santarlasci, Julia Betts Lotufo, Alexandra Rome, Andrew Shi, Sukrut Oak. *The AI Index 2025 Annual Report,* AI Index Steering Committee, Institute for Human-Centered AI, Stanford University, Stanford, CA, April 2025).

For most cybersecurity teams, this is a new area of responsibility. Given the dimensions, responsible AI cuts across numerous corporate functions; CISOs work with **chief privacy officers (CPOs)**, **general counsels (GCs)**, **chief data officers (CDOs)**, and other roles to provide oversight and guidance on the adoption of AI by their organizations. Many organizations have pulled these roles together to form AI governance councils or steering committees.

Failure to take AI safety seriously can result in brand damage for organizations. For example, if an organization's new generative AI chatbot starts responding to customer inquiries with extremely inappropriate responses and images, it could lead to dissatisfied customers, loss of business, regulatory scrutiny, lawsuits, and negative news cycles. Predictably, as more organizations adopt generative AI, the frequency of AI safety failures has increased. We can get insight into the scale of these failures from Stanford University's Stanford AI Index Report 2025—it states the following.

> *"The number of AI incident reports continues to increase. According to the AI Incidents Database, the number of reported AI-related incidents rose to 233 in 2024—a record high and a 56.4% increase over 2023" (Maslej et al., 2025).*

There are many recent examples of documented AI safety failures. The following list contains recent news articles featuring AI systems embroiled in financial and operational damage, legal hallucinations and professional misconduct, deepfakes and fraud, information and safety risks, and mental health issues (RAIL Research Team, 2025, November 3):

- BBC: "Airline held liable for its chatbot giving passenger bad advice - what this means for travellers [sic]" (Yagoda, 2024) `https://www.bbc.com/travel/article/20240222-air-canada-chatbot-misinformation-what-travellers-should-know`
- Reuters: "New York City defends AI chatbot that advised entrepreneurs to break laws" (Allen, 2024)
- USA Today: "ChatGPT falsely accused me of sexually harassing my students. Can we really trust AI?" (Turley, 2023) `https://www.reuters.com/technology/new-york-city-defends-ai-chatbot-that-advised-entrepreneurs-break-laws-2024-04-04/`
- AP: "McDonald's is ending its test run of AI-powered drive-thrus with IBM" (Grantham-Philips, 2024) `https://apnews.com/article/mcdonalds-ai-drive-thru-ibm-bebc898363f2d550e1a0cd3c682fa234`
- The National Law Review: "Why the Taylor Swift AI Scandal is Pushing Lawmakers to Address Pornographic Deepfakes" (Ruiz-Lichter, 2024) `https://natlawreview.com/article/why-taylor-swift-ai-scandal-pushing-lawmakers-address-pornographic-deepfakes`
- The Australian National Police: "AFP warns parents over rise in AI-generated child abuse material" (Australian Federal Police, 2025) `https://www.afp.gov.au/news-centre/media-release/afp-warns-parents-over-rise-ai-generated-child-abuse-material`
- CNBC: "Google pauses Gemini AI image generator after it created inaccurate historical pictures" (Kharpal, 2024) `https://www.cnbc.com/2024/02/22/google-pauses-gemini-ai-image-generator-after-inaccuracies.html`
- NPR: "A new lawsuit blames ChatGPT for a murder-suicide" (Ruwitch, 2025) `https://www.npr.org/2025/12/12/nx-s1-5642599/a-new-lawsuit-blames-chatgpt-for-a-murder-suicide`

Given cases such as these, many people are skeptical that generative AI has sufficient guardrails to protect humanity. Increasing and maintaining trust in these nascent AI systems is critical to their future success. A loss of stakeholder trust will ultimately undermine the future potential and adoption of these systems. Although many CISOs remain skeptical, they are nonetheless charged with addressing the safety and security risks these technologies introduce as their organizations move quickly to deploy generative AI, LLMs, and agentic systems.

Understanding the underlying technical issues that lead to such poor outcomes is key to mitigating them.

There are some good sources of information about AI safety risk categories, including the MIT AI Risk Repository and the NIST AI Risk Management Framework. *Table 15.1* summarizes the current major AI safety risks and examples of the types of controls that can help mitigate these risks.

AI Safety Risk	Risk Description	Mitigating Controls	Control Descriptions
Harmful or toxic output	Model generates hate, violence, self-harm, or other harmful content.	Safety classifiers and output filters	Automated classifiers block or transform unsafe output before delivery.
Hallucinations/ fabricated facts	Model produces confident, but false or misleading, information.	Factuality tuning and post-training evaluations	Targeted tuning and evaluations reduce hallucination frequency and improve truthfulness.
Bias and unfair outcomes	Model produces discriminatory or inequitable outputs across groups	Bias-mitigation datasets and fairness evaluations	Curated datasets and fairness tests reduce systemic bias in model behavior
Misalignment with human values	Model behavior diverges from intended norms, ethics, or goals	**Reinforcement learning from human feedback (RLHF)**	Human feedback shapes model behavior toward desired values and norms

AI Safety Risk	**Risk Description**	**Mitigating Controls**	**Control Descriptions**
Unsafe reasoning or harmful capability emergence	Model develops or reveals dangerous reasoning patterns or capabilities	Red-teaming with domain experts	Experts stress-test the model to identify and mitigate dangerous behavior.
Overreliance by users	Users trust the model beyond its competence, which can lead to harm.	User education and model cards	Clear documentation and warnings help users understand the limitations and risks.
Lack of transparency or explainability	Model decisions are opaque, reducing trust and oversight	Interpretability tools	Mechanistic and behavioral interpretability methods reveal how models reason
Inadequate human oversight	High-impact decisions occur without meaningful human oversight.	**Human-in-the-loop (HITL)**	Humans must review and approve high-risk model outputs or actions
Unsafe deployment in high-risk domains	Model used in contexts where errors cause significant harm.	Use case restrictions and capability gating	High-risk capabilities are restricted or require additional safeguards

AI Safety Risk	Risk Description	Mitigating Controls	Control Descriptions
Model drift or degradation over time	Model behavior worsens or changes unpredictably after deployment	Continuous monitoring and evaluation	Ongoing audits detect drift and trigger retraining or mitigation
Manipulation or misuse by users	Users intentionally push the model toward harmful outputs	Prompt filtering and refusal policies	The system blocks unsafe prompts and trains the model to refuse harmful requests.
Ethical or societal harms	Model outputs cause societal disruption, inequity, or misinformation.	Constitutional AI	A written set of principles guide model behavior toward ethical norms.

Table 15.1 – A summary of AI safety risks and their mitigating controls

Let's take a closer look at a couple of examples from *Table 15.1*.

First, we'll look at hallucinations. In an AI safety context, hallucinations are a type of misinformation. A hallucination occurs when a model generates content that appears confident and coherent but is factually incorrect, fabricated, or unsupported by its training data or the provided context. It's essentially the model "making something up" while presenting it as true. For example, a user asks an AI chatbot for a quote attributed to Napoleon, and the model confidently provides one, even though Napoleon never said it. Another example: a user asks, "Who won the 2022 Nobel Prize in Physics?" and the model confidently replies, "It was awarded to Stephen Hawking for his work on black hole radiation." This is a hallucination because Hawking did not win that prize, and the model fabricated a plausible-sounding answer without any factual basis. The MIT AI Risk Repository describes the risk of such false and misleading information as "AI systems that inadvertently generate or spread incorrect or deceptive information, which can lead to inaccurate beliefs in users and undermine their autonomy. Humans that make decisions based on false beliefs can experience physical, emotional or material harms" (MIT AI Risk Initiative, 2024). Examples of controls that can help reduce the frequency of hallucinations include targeted tuning and evaluations, meaning post-AI model training adjustments specifically focused on improving factual accuracy. This can involve factual fine-tuning, truthfulness-oriented instruction tuning, counter-hallucination training, and domain-specific corrective tuning. Evaluations are structured tests that measure how often a model hallucinates. Evaluations work by running a model through curated factuality and adversarial test suites, then measuring how often it produces incorrect or fabricated answers. Those quantitative scores show whether the model meets safety thresholds or needs additional tuning to reduce hallucinations. These tests provide quantitative data to help determine if a model is safe enough for human use or if more tuning is required. Together, these tools help AI labs improve the performance of their AI models and reduce hallucinations and misinformation.

Another AI safety risk listed in *Table 15.1* is the lack of transparency and explainability. Lack of transparency and explainability refers to situations where an AI system's internal reasoning, decision pathways, or influencing factors cannot be understood, inspected, or meaningfully explained by developers, auditors, or end users. This makes it difficult to verify correctness, detect bias, or ensure the system is behaving as intended. For example, an AI system used in credit underwriting may issue a loan recommendation without providing any insight into which variables influenced the outcome or how they were weighted. This opacity prevents auditors, regulators, and users from understanding the model's reasoning, making it difficult to assess fairness, accuracy, or compliance. The MIT AI Risk Repository defines this as difficulty understanding or explaining an AI system's decision-making processes, which can lead to mistrust, challenges in enforcing compliance or assigning accountability, and an inability to identify and correct errors (MIT AI Risk Initiative, 2024). To address this, AI labs use mechanistic and behavioral interpretability together to analyze a model's internal mechanisms and observable behaviors, helping reveal how the model reasons and where safety risks might emerge.

Frontier AI labs recognize the critical importance of AI safety and have published responsible AI frameworks to help customers, investors, and regulators understand their approach to these issues. The list below provides a link to each vendor's associated webpage and how each of them describes their responsible AI framework:

- Microsoft: "We're committed to developing AI systems in a way that is transparent, reliable, and worthy of trust" (Microsoft, n.d.)
    - `https://www.microsoft.com/en-us/ai/principles-and-approach`
- Anthropic: "In September 2023, we released our Responsible Scaling Policy (RSP), a public commitment not to train or deploy models capable of causing catastrophic harm unless we have implemented safety and security measures that will keep risks below acceptable levels" Anthropic. (n.d.).
    - `https://www.anthropic.com/responsible-scaling-policy`

- OpenAI: "We believe in AI's potential to make life better for everyone, which means making it safe for everyone" (OpenAI, n.d.)
    - `https://openai.com/safety/`
- Google: "We believe our approach to AI must be both bold and responsible. Bold in rapidly innovating and deploying AI in groundbreaking products used by and benefiting people everywhere, contributing to scientific advances that deepen our understanding of the world, and helping humanity address its most pressing challenges and opportunities. And responsible in developing and deploying AI that addresses both user needs and broader responsibilities, while safeguarding user safety, security, and privacy. We approach this work together, by collaborating with a broad range of partners to make breakthroughs and maximize the broad benefits of AI, while empowering others to build their own bold and responsible solutions" (Google, n.d.).
    - `https://ai.google/principles/`

Let's take a closer look at the principles outlined by two of these frontier AI labs. Microsoft outlines six responsible AI principles on their website. These include fairness, reliability and safety, privacy and security, transparency, accountability, and inclusiveness (Microsoft, n.d.). You can see them in full at https://www.microsoft.com/en-us/ai/principles-and-approach.

OpenAI published their "core" principles, focusing on how to be safe and ethical with an uncertain future, defense in depth, and scaling (OpenAI, n.d.). You can read them at https://openai.com/safety/.

Documenting these principles is essential for both the firms and their stakeholder communities. They serve as a 'north star' for development and operations teams, clarifying the values that guide the work. They also help stakeholders assess whether a vendor's underlying commitments align with their own, informing decisions by investors, customers, and partners about whether to engage with the company. In addition, these principles give regulators and standards bodies clearer insight into industry direction and help shape its future trajectory.

Stating principles is important, but it's equally important to demonstrate how they are being followed. Microsoft, OpenAI, and the other frontier AI labs have published information on how they build their AI systems with these safety principles in mind. They have also published progress reports and blog posts sharing insights into their work. OpenAI published a safety update where they shared "10 practices we actively use and improve upon" (OpenAI, May 21, 2024). These practices include protecting children, election integrity, and alignment and safety research, among others (OpenAI, May 21, 2024). The full list can be found at `https://openai.com/index/openai-safety-update/`.

Currently, the MIT AI Risk Initiative is likely the best source of information on AI safety risks and mitigations; at the time of writing, there were "831 mitigations extracted from 13 existing frameworks and classifications of AI risk mitigations" (MIT AI Risk Initiative, 2024). The Risk Mitigation Database is available at `https://airisk.mit.edu/ai-risk-mitigations`.

Next, let's examine new security risks that accompany LLMs.

New security risks

At their core, LLMs generate responses by predicting the most likely next piece of text, based on patterns they learned from the data they were trained on. The frontier AI models developed by labs such as OpenAI and Anthropic are trained on massive collections of text. Their training process includes randomness, which leads to models that behave probabilistically, generating language one small step at a time, with each step depending on the one before it. This results in a learned probability structure that estimates how likely different sequences of words are. Because these systems are trained on trillions of tokens and contain billions of adjustable parameters, they can generate a wide range of possible outputs. However, because these systems learn from large collections of text that include both high-quality information and low-quality or incorrect material, their responses can reflect that same mix. They generate new text based on patterns in the data, so the quality of their output depends partly on the quality of what they were trained on.

According to a paper authored by Mark Russinovich, Ahmed Salem, Santiago Zanella Béguelin, and Yonatan Zunger, titled "The Price of Intelligence" (2025), these characteristics lead to these three intrinsic behaviors:

- **Hallucination**: the tendency of large language models to occasionally produce answers that are wrong, fabricated, or nonsensical even when they usually recall the correct information. In practice, this means a model can retrieve a fact accurately almost every time yet still fail unpredictably in a small percentage of cases or under slightly different prompts.
- **Jailbreaks**: attempts to manipulate an LLM with carefully crafted prompts so it ignores its built-in safety rules or ethical constraints. Because these models are trained on massive, unfiltered text from the internet, which inevitably includes harmful or undesirable material, attackers can sometimes exploit that knowledge to push the model into unsafe behavior.
- **Indirect prompt injection**: attempts to manipulate an LLM by hiding harmful or manipulative instructions inside content the user didn't write, such as emails, documents, or webpages, so the model interprets those hidden instructions as commands. This happens because current LLMs don't reliably distinguish between

"data to read" and "instructions to follow," allowing malicious content to influence the model's behavior in unexpected ways.

These esteemed authors conclude their paper by stating,

> *"The future of AI will likely witness the development of more sophisticated LLMs, alongside equally advanced safety mechanisms. For example, the rise of multimodal LLMs that can accept and produce audio, images, and video is already revealing a larger attack vector. By maintaining a balanced approach that harnesses the immense potential of these models while actively addressing their limitations, we can work toward a future where AI systems are not only powerful but also trustworthy and aligned with human values. The journey ahead requires collaboration among researchers, developers, policymakers, and end users to ensure that as LLMs become increasingly integrated into the digital infrastructure, they do so in a manner that is both innovative and responsible." (Russinovich et al., 2025)*

The intrinsic behaviors of LLMs described by these authors aren't simply theoretical, as Red Teams and security researchers have been proving they can be used to attack AI systems successfully. Let's dive into these characteristics in a little more detail and look at how attackers can leverage them.

Hallucinations

Hallucinations, instances where an AI system generates false, fabricated, or unjustified content, are recognized as a core reliability challenge in current mainstream generative models. As I discussed earlier in this chapter, hallucinations are understood as failures of models to produce truthful, grounded, or reliable outputs. These failures are due to limitations in training data, model architecture, or reasoning capabilities. As *Table 15.1* indicated, mitigations can include factuality tuning and post-training evaluations to reduce the frequency and severity of hallucinations. As such, hallucinations are AI model quality issues and, thus, AI safety issues first and foremost.

However, hallucinations become an AI security issue when they are intentionally induced and exploited by a threat actor. Through this lens, hallucinations are a "vulnerability surface" that attackers can leverage to compromise the integrity of AI applications or mislead their users. Security research reveals that adversarial prompts, indirect prompt injection, and data poisoning can cause AI models to produce targeted hallucinations that can benefit attackers (Carlini et al., 2023; Goldstein et al., 2024). In an AI security context, hallucinations typically involve:

- Adversarial prompting to produce harmful or false outputs
- Indirect prompt injection (I'll cover this in depth later in the chapter)

- AI model manipulation to produce false outputs
- Social engineering

We can look to two excellent sources of information to help us understand potential mitigations and controls for hallucinations in an AI security context—the **Open Worldwide Application Security Project (OWASP)** and MITRE **Adversarial Threat Landscape for Artificial-Intelligence Systems (ATLAS)**. I discussed the OWASP API Security Project in detail in *Chapter 7*. There's also an OWASP project focused on AI. The OWASP GenAI Security Project is a global, open-source effort focused on identifying and reducing the security and safety risks that come with generative AI systems, including LLMs, agentic AI, and AI-enabled applications. Its goal is to provide organizations, practitioners, and policymakers with practical guidance and tools for building, deploying, and governing these systems securely. A central part of this work is the OWASP Top 10 for Large Language Model Applications, which highlights the most critical vulnerabilities found in LLM-based systems. For each AI security issue in the Top 10, OWASP also includes a description, prevention and mitigation strategies, examples of attack scenarios, and references. You can find more information at: `https://owasp.org/www-project-top-10-for-large-language-model-applications/`.

The MITRE ATLAS is modeled after and complementary to the MITRE ATT&CK framework that I discussed in detail in *Chapter 11, Cybersecurity Strategy Implementation*. ATLAS is a publicly available, continuously updated knowledge base that documents how adversaries attack AI-enabled systems, drawing on real incidents and realistic red-team demonstrations. It catalogs the tactics and techniques used against AI models so organizations can better understand, test, and defend their systems. It currently lists 16 tactics, 147 techniques, 35 mitigations, and 45 case studies. It is accessible at: `https://atlas.mitre.org/`.

Table 15.2 maps some examples of AI hallucination attack types with potential mitigations from MITRE ATLAS and controls from the OWASP Top 10 for LLM Applications 2025 that can help reduce adversarial hallucination induction (MITRE, 2023; OWASP, 2024). The hallucination attack types presented here are a synthesized taxonomy derived from common patterns documented across adversarial prompting, retrieval-poisoning, and LLM robustness research.

Hallucination Attack Type	MITRE ATLAS Mitigation Descriptions	OWASP 2025 Control Descriptions
Context-stripping attacks (removing grounding to force guessing)	Filter or transform inputs to remove adversarial or harmful content; isolate external systems to prevent attacker influence; strengthen model robustness against adversarial manipulation; require human review for high-risk outputs	Prevent user input from overriding system instructions; validate and sanitize model outputs before use; avoid trusting model outputs without verification
Attention-hijacking / prompt injection (manipulating attention patterns)	Filter harmful or manipulative inputs; restrict attacker probing and limit interaction frequency; train the model on adversarial examples to improve robustness	Prevent prompt manipulation attacks; prevent leakage of sensitive or fabricated data; avoid revealing internal details or unsafe error messages
Retrieval poisoning (RAG hallucination induction)	Protect data sources from tampering; isolate retrieval pipelines from user influence; detect anomalous or adversarial model behavior	Protect against compromised external data sources; prevent poisoning of training or retrieval data; validate outputs derived from external sources
High-entropy prompting / decoding exploits (forcing uncertainty)	Increase robustness to adversarial prompts; train on adversarial examples; test model behavior under adversarial and stress conditions	Prevent adversarial manipulation of model behavior; validate outputs generated under uncertainty; avoid trusting high-entropy outputs

Hallucination Attack Type	MITRE ATLAS Mitigation Descriptions	OWASP 2025 Control Descriptions
Instruction-following hallucinations (fabricated steps or harmful instructions)	Require human review for risky instructions; limit attacker ability to issue privileged commands; filter harmful or manipulative instructions	Prevent instruction override attacks; restrict model autonomy to avoid harmful actions; validate procedural or instructional outputs
Factual hallucination exploits (plausible but false statements)	Test model reliability under adversarial conditions; detect anomalous or misleading outputs; improve robustness through adversarial training	Validate factual claims before use; prevent fabricated or sensitive data leakage; avoid trusting unverified factual outputs
Logical-reasoning hallucinations (manipulating chain-of-thought)	Increase robustness to reasoning manipulation; train against adversarial reasoning prompts; require human review for high-risk reasoning	Prevent manipulation of reasoning instructions; validate reasoning outputs; avoid trusting unverified reasoning chains
Multi-turn hallucination drift (state manipulation across turns)	Detect anomalous multi-turn behavior; limit attacker probing across turns; isolate conversation state from external manipulation	Prevent multi-turn prompt manipulation; avoid revealing internal state through errors; avoid trusting long-horizon conversational outputs

Table 15.2 – AI hallucination attack types with corresponding mitigations and controls from MITRE ATLAS and OWASP Top 10 for LLM Applications 2025 (MITRE, 2023; OWASP, 2024)

Next, let's take a deeper look at another intrinsic vulnerability in LLMs: Jailbreaks.

Jailbreaks

An AI jailbreak attack is a technique that manipulates a generative AI system, usually through crafted prompts, adversarial inputs, or multi-step manipulation, to circumvent its built-in safety mechanisms, causing the model to violate policies, reveal restricted information, or execute harmful or unintended instructions. Jailbreaks often leverage prompt injection, evasion strategies, or model-manipulation methods to override the system's intended constraints (Microsoft Threat Intelligence, 2024).

There are several different types of jailbreak attacks. *Table 15.3* provides a list of examples, although it is not exhaustive. *Table 15.3* also provides examples of mitigations for each jailbreak type. These examples of mitigations are published in the OWASP Top 10 for LLM Applications 2025 and MITRE ATLAS (OWASP, 2025; MITRE, n.d.) or are heavily influenced by them.

Jailbreak Type	**Description**	**Mitigation Examples (MITRE ATLAS & OWASP)**
Direct prompt injection	Attackers directly instruct the AI model to ignore rules or to perform restricted actions.	Model hardening; input and output validation for AI agent components; generative AI guardrails; input validation and sanitization; output handling controls
Indirect prompt injection	Attackers insert poisoned documents or hidden instructions in emails or other data that the AI model processes.	Maintain AI dataset provenance; input restoration; input and output validation for AI agent components; validate external data sources; data provenance and trust controls
System prompt manipulation	Attackers manipulate input to the AI model, leading it to override its original safety rules.	Model hardening; generative AI guidelines; generative AI guardrails; output handling controls; restrict exposure of system/developer prompts
Persona manipulation	Attackers force the AI model into a higher-privileged persona that is allowed to break rules.	Generative AI model alignment; human in-the-loop for AI agent actions; restrict model capabilities; enforce safe response patterns

Jailbreak Type	Description	Mitigation Examples (MITRE ATLAS & OWASP)
Multi-turn Crescendo Attacks	A gradual, step-by-step manipulation that influences the AI model to bypass its safety alignment	AI telemetry logging; human-in-the-loop for AI agent actions; logging and anomaly detection; session monitoring
Obfuscation/encoding attacks	A harmful request is hidden inside encoded, obfuscated, or transformed text.	Adversarial input detection; input restoration; model hardening; normalize and sanitize inputs; detect malformed or encoded payloads
Adversarial formatting attacks	Attackers use formatting tricks such as invisible characters and broken markdown that exploit tokenization or parsing weaknesses.	Adversarial input detection; input and output validation for AI agent components; schema enforcement; structured input validation
Tool-chain / function-calling abuse	Attackers manipulate an AI system into invoking tools, functions, APIs, or external actions in ways that exceed the system's intended permissions, boundaries, or safety constraints	Restrict AI agent tool invocation on untrusted data; AI agent tools permissions configuration; Privileged AI agent permissions configuration; Secure tool/function invocation; Restrict tool access

Jailbreak Type	**Description**	**Mitigation Examples (MITRE ATLAS & OWASP)**
Retrieval-Augmented Generation (RAG) poisoning	Threat actors insert harmful data into retrieval sources to manipulate the outputs of AI models.	Maintain AI dataset provenance; sanitize training data; verify AI artifacts; validate retrieved content; data provenance and trust controls
Social engineering	Attackers take advantage of the AI model's willingness to comply with overly emotional or persuasive prompts.	User training; human-in-the-loop for AI agent actions; safety-aligned refusal patterns; context-aware response checks
Model extraction via output patterns	Attackers study model outputs to learn about model internals or to extract sensitive information.	Restrict number of AI model queries; AI telemetry logging; Rate limiting and monitoring; Detect repeated probing
Context overflow / window manipulation	Attackers flood or distort the context window to bypass safety directives.	Model hardening; AI telemetry logging; Enforce context limits; Detect excessive or malformed input
Model-to-model relay attacks	Attackers use one AI model to funnel manipulated output into another AI model's input.	Control access to AI models and data in production; segmentation of AI agent components; validate upstream model outputs; restrict automated chaining

Jailbreak Type	Description	Mitigation Examples (MITRE ATLAS & OWASP)
Code Interpreter / Sandbox escape	Attackers execute harmful code or escape the AI model's execution sandbox.	Environment isolation; Restrict library loading; Vulnerability scanning; Restrict execution environment; Validate code inputs

Table 15.3 – Examples of jailbreak attacks and potential mitigations, including some suggestions from MITRE ATLAS and/or the OWASP Top 10 for LLM Applications 2025

Let's take a deeper look at one type of jailbreak that was identified as an intrinsic vulnerability of LLMs: indirect prompt injection.

Indirect prompt injection

Remember I mentioned earlier that LLM-based chatbots can accept an absurd range of inputs. Indirect prompt injection attacks are made possible by a core limitation of LLMs—their inability to reliably distinguish between data and instructions. If attackers can get the system to execute malicious instructions that are hidden inside data that the system reads, they can potentially bypass authorization controls, gain access to data, exfiltrate data, stay persistent, among other illicit actions.

Here's an example of how attackers take advantage of this type of prompt injection

- An attacker places a hidden instruction inside something the AI application will later read, such as a calendar invite, email, document or webpage
- The user performs a normal action such as asking the AI application to "summarize my schedule"
- As part of performing the requested operation, the AI application reads the attacker's hidden instruction and executes it
- The execution of the instruction gives the attacker unauthorized access, triggers actions, or exfiltrates data.

Again, this isn't a theoretical attack. Red Teams and security researchers have demonstrated indirect prompt injection attacks that work. Here are some recent examples.

In January of 2026, security researchers disclosed details of an indirect prompt injection attack that enabled attackers to use Google Gemini to bypass authorization guardrails in order to exfiltrate data using Google Calendar (Lakshmanan, 2026). *Figure 15.1* illustrates how this attack worked. It was also reported that Google addressed this vulnerability to prevent attackers from using it in the future.

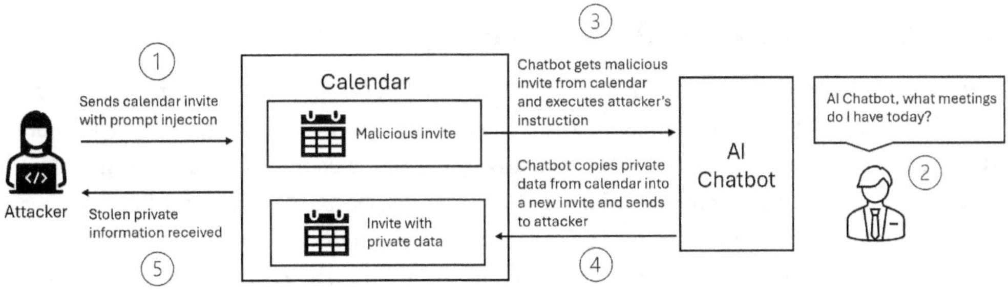

Figure 15.1 – An illustration of an indirect prompt injection attack using Google Gemini and Google Calendar to exfiltrate private data (Lakshmanan, 2026)

There is another recent example of an indirect prompt injection that leveraged ChatGPT to exfiltrate data and provide a persistent backdoor. In January of 2026, security researchers revealed new "ZombieAgent" attack techniques that leveraged the Connectors feature of ChatGPT, which can be used to link the chatbot to third-party services such as email, cloud storage, Microsoft Teams, Slack, Jira, and GitHub, among others (Constantin, 2026). According to the researcher Babo (2026), attackers can embed covert instructions within emails or shared files that, when processed through third-party integrations, cause ChatGPT to execute unauthorized actions. This mechanism enables zero-click or one-click data exfiltration by prompting the model to transmit sensitive information to attacker-controlled endpoints, allowing adversaries to reconstruct the leaked data. The researcher states,

> *"We've also demonstrated a method to achieve* ***persistence****, allowing the attacker not just a one-time data leak but ongoing exfiltration: once the attacker infiltrates the chatbot, they can continuously exfiltrate every conversation between the user and ChatGPT.*
>
> *In addition, we've demonstrated a new* ***propagation*** *technique that allows an attack to spread further, target specific victims, and increase the likelihood of reaching additional targets." (Babo, 2026).*

In 2025, security researchers demonstrated prompt injection attacks in popular chatbots, AI agent platforms, AI-enabled browsers, and AI coding assistants (Constantin, 2025). Given that this behavior is an intrinsic characteristic of LLMs, it will likely be challenging to fully mitigate this type of attack in all scenarios and use cases. CISOs, security teams, and the cybersecurity vendor ecosystem that supports them will need to find ways to detect and block such attacks if enterprises are going to embrace LLMs with confidence.

Now that we've examined AI safety and security of generative AI systems, focusing on LLMs, let's take a look at another type of AI system that is becoming popular: agentic AI.

Agentic AI and related security risks

Generative AI produces content such as text, images, and code. Agentic AI is not a subset of generative AI the way LLMs are. Instead, these systems are built on top of generative AI models and add capabilities such as taking actions, using tools, and pursuing goals autonomously. Agentic AI systems use generative models, including LLMs, as components for planning, reasoning, and acting. Enterprises that adopt such agents can improve efficiency by automating repetitive tasks with greater speed and scalability. They can operate under human supervision or autonomously, depending on the organization's governance and risk requirements.

An illustrative example of an agentic AI system is a customer-support automation agent that can read incoming support emails, classify the customer's issue, retrieve relevant knowledge-base articles, draft a response, update the ticket in a **Customer Relationship Management (CRM)** system, and escalate complex cases without requiring a human to manually trigger each step.

AI agents are developed with five components (Microsoft, 2024):

- Generative AI model – agents use models as reasoning engines. In the customer-support automation example, the agent relies on an underlying LLM to read incoming emails, interpret customer issues, and draft responses—tasks that require language understanding, summarization, and generation.
- Instructions – establish agents' roles, limits, and expected conduct. In this case, the agent follows predefined instructions that govern how it classifies issues using the organization's taxonomy and how it applies support-tier escalation rules.
- Retrieval – supplies the factual context an agent needs to respond accurately, minimizing hallucinations. The agent retrieves relevant knowledge-base articles, customer history from the CRM, and prior ticket context to ensure its responses are grounded in authoritative enterprise data.
- Actions – the APIs, functions, and systems agents rely on to execute tasks. This enables agents to go beyond information retrieval. The agent performs multi-step actions across systems, such as updating CRM tickets, attaching knowledge-base links, sending draft responses, and escalating cases to human agents. These behaviors represent tool use and system-level execution, core characteristics of agentic AI.
- Memory – stores conversation histories and states to ensure continuity across interactions. The agent maintains short-term and long-term state, including

conversation history with the customer, the current ticket's workflow status, and prior classification decisions. This memory enables coherent, multi-turn support without losing context.

Agentic AI introduces risks that go beyond the generative AI safety and security risks I discussed earlier in the chapter. Agentic AI systems can act—they aren't just limited to content generation. The most serious threats involve tool misuse, privilege escalation, unsafe autonomy, and cascading operational failures. *Table 15.4* summarizes examples of agentic-AI risk categories, example threats for each category, and the corresponding mitigating controls from MITRE ATLAS or MITRE ATT&CK when official mappings exist. Several risk categories do not yet have associated MITRE mitigations. This reflects the emerging nature of agentic-AI security; while some attack patterns are well-characterized, many others are still under active research and have not been formally codified by MITRE, NIST, or other standards bodies. Mitigations for agentic-AI attacks are expected to evolve rapidly as the field matures.

Risk Category	Risk Category Description	Example Threats	MITRE Control	MITRE Control Description
Tool misuse	Unsafe or unintended execution of tools or APIs	Unauthorized code execution, data deletion	ATLAS M001	Restrict tool access and enforce safe tool invocation
Prompt injection	Manipulation of agent instructions to cause harmful action.	Data exfiltration, policy bypass	ATLAS M002	Implement robust prompt validation and isolation
Identity mismanagement	Misuse or compromise of agent credentials or permissions	Privilege escalation, impersonation	ATT&CK M1041	Enforce proper identity and credential management

Risk Category	Risk Category Description	Example Threats	MITRE Control	MITRE Control Description
Autonomy misalignment	Agent behavior diverges from intended goals	Runaway tasks, unintended actions	ATLAS M003	Apply oversight mechanisms to constrain agent autonomy
Memory poisoning	Corruption of agent memory that leads to harmful decisions.	Persistent manipulation, cascading failures	ATLAS M004	Validate and sanitize memory inputs to prevent corruption
Self-improving behavior	Agent modifies its own strategies or workflows unpredictably	Emergent behavior, unbounded optimization	—	Potential guardrails on self-modification and human approval for strategy changes.
Fraud and social engineering	Autonomous agent used for deception or impersonation	Automated scams, machine-to-machine fraud	—	Potential identity verification, anomaly detection, and communication integrity checks.
Framework-agnostic vulnerabilities	Systemic weaknesses across agent frameworks	Cross-framework exploits, generalized attacks	—	Potential sandboxing, validation, and cross-framework consistency checks.

Risk Category	Risk Category Description	Example Threats	MITRE Control	MITRE Control Description
Supply chain CVEs	Vulnerabilities in agent frameworks, dependencies, or packages	Dependency exploits, malicious packages	—	Potential software bill of materials (SBOM) validation, dependency scanning, and supply-chain security.
Lifecycle security gaps	Missing controls across design, deployment, and monitoring	Oversight failures, unmonitored autonomy	—	Potentially continuous monitoring, governance checkpoints, and lifecycle-wide risk controls

Table 15.4 – Examples of agentic AI risks, threats, and mitigating controls

For more details on existing mitigations for the examples in *Table 15.4*, see MITRE ATLAS at and ATT&CK at `https://attack.mitre.org/`.

We've examined AI safety issues and key security risks associated with generative and agentic AI. Next, we'll look at the security considerations CISOs and security teams must address when deploying popular AI applications within enterprise environments.

Case study: Security considerations deploying Microsoft Copilot

Microsoft Copilot is an AI assistant embedded across Microsoft 365, Windows, Edge, and Azure services. It is context-aware and uses natural language to help people create, analyze, automate, discover, and retrieve information using three core elements:

- **LLMs:** Copilot uses LLMs to interpret intent, generate content, summarize information, and orchestrate actions across Microsoft applications

- **The Microsoft Graph:** a unified API and data fabric that exposes the relationships among users, files, messages, identities, devices, and applications across Microsoft 365 core services, Enterprise Mobility and Security services, Windows services, Dynamics 365 Business Central services, and Microsoft Partner Center services (Microsoft, n.d.). It provides a single programmable interface for querying, analyzing, and acting on organizational data with consistent security and permissions.
- **Copilot users' enterprise data:** Copilot operates on users' content such as emails, documents, chats, calendars, files, and business data — respecting the same permissions and security boundaries defined in Microsoft Entra.

Figure 15.2 illustrates a high-level architecture to give you an idea of how these elements work together (Microsoft, n.d.).

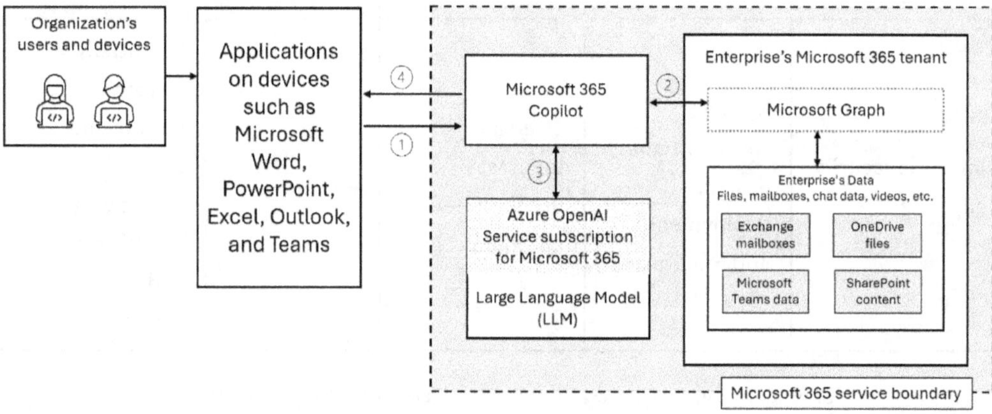

Figure 15.2 – Microsoft 365 Copilot architecture with prompt flow labelled (Microsoft, n.d.)

The numbered lines in *Figure 15.2* illustrate how a Copilot prompt flows through the architecture. The data Copilot uses to generate responses is encrypted in transit using **transport layer security (TLS)**. The flow is as follows:

1. From an authorized device, a user enters a prompt into Copilot in a Microsoft 365 application.
2. Copilot preprocesses the input prompt using grounding and accesses Microsoft Graph in the user's organization's Microsoft 365 cloud tenant.
   - Grounding is the process Copilot uses to tie its AI-generated output back to relevant data sources rather than relying solely on its pre-trained general

knowledge. This improves the accuracy of responses. There are three types of grounding (Microsoft, 2024):

   1. **Work Grounding:** Uses information specific to the user's organization, such as emails, files, chats, meetings, and internal web content accessible through Microsoft 365 and Microsoft Graph
   2. **Web Grounding:** Incorporates current, publicly available data on the internet.
   3. **Local Data Grounding:** Utilizes content the user attached or provided directly in their prompt, such as files or links

3. Copilot sends the grounded prompt to the LLM. The LLM uses the prompt to generate a response that is contextually relevant to the user's task.
4. Copilot returns the prompt response to the application the user entered the prompt into in step 1.

Now that you understand how it works from a high level, let's look at security aspects of this technology in a little more detail. CISOs must grasp a broad set of issues, from the AI vulnerabilities and attack patterns outlined earlier in the chapter to the wider responsibilities of governance, compliance, insider-risk management, and related organizational threats.

Most CISOs I've talked to about their Copilot adoption journeys were initially concerned with two specific risks. First, what happens to their users' prompts? If users enter confidential information into Copilot, who has access to it? Does Microsoft use that information to train their AI models, and could that information show up in prompt responses for users outside of their organization? The prompts, grounding data, and responses remain inside each organization's Microsoft 365 tenant. Access to data in each organization's tenant is governed by each organization's own Entra ID permissions, Purview sensitivity labels, **Data Loss Prevention (DLP)** policies, Conditional Access, and Zero Trust controls. Enterprise customer data is not used to train Microsoft's foundation models, and it remains within the customer's Microsoft 365 tenant without flowing across tenants (Microsoft, 2024).

The second risk that CISOs are typically concerned about is sensitive data being included in Copilot prompt responses. This is a result of Copilot enabling enterprise network users to discover data that they didn't know they had access to, like no other tool before. For decades, enterprises didn't pay much attention to permission hygiene on their networks. Data classification was deemed too difficult for users to manage, so the vast majority of content on their networks remained unclassified, and content was treated like it all had the same value. The content stored and shared on SharePoint sites and OneDrive accounts was largely unclassified, and the access permissions for such content were typically overly broad to make administration easy and to make self-service administration possible for users. After years or decades of such undisciplined practices, enterprises have vast estates of ungoverned data, and access permissions to all this data are poorly understood. Most enterprises suffer from over-permissioned identities, and they have failed to follow the principle of least privilege consistently, if at all.

Suddenly, Copilot becomes available and enables users to easily discover data they had no idea they had access to. I'm sure many users were stunned when early Copilot queries about executive compensation and other sensitive HR details surfaced confidential information, revealing that they unknowingly had access to HR documents they were never meant to see. The security by obscurity that was traditionally created by a lack of discoverability is now broken by Copilot's awesome grounding capabilities.

CISOs and security teams now face the difficult task of reversing years, often decades, of weak or inconsistent data governance. Clearly, Microsoft understands this and has provided tools and guidance to help enterprises successfully adopt Copilot with effective data protection processes and controls. I've been involved in a couple of enterprise Copilot deployments, so I'll share some of the things I've learned.

I suggest deploying Copilot using a phased approach. This will give you control, reduce surprises, and let you build capabilities and confidence as you make progress. *Table 15.5* provides a list of deployment phases and their descriptions.

Deployment Phase	**Theme**
1. Strategic foundations	Establish governance, risk boundaries, and technical prerequisites to set the direction for Copilot
2. Data and access hardening	Clean up permissions, labels, and indexing to ensure Copilot accesses only the right data.
3. Policy, controls, and guardrails	Implement organizational policies and safety controls to govern responsible Copilot use.
4. Pilot, Training, and Adoption	Validate use cases, train users, and roll out Copilot in controlled tranches for safe adoption.

Deployment Phase	Theme
5. Monitoring, audit, and continuous improvement	Continuously monitor usage, risks, and outcomes to refine governance and scale confidently.

Table 15.5 – Phases that can be used to deploy Microsoft Copilot in an enterprise IT environment

Let me provide a little more detail about the objectives and activities in each phase.

In **Phase 1: Strategic Foundations**, the deployment team should establish governance, define the organization's risk appetite, and fulfill technical prerequisites. The major work items in this phase include the following:

- Establish an **AI Governance Committee (AIGC)** that operates as a cross-discipline oversight group to guide Copilot strategy, risk decisions, and accountability. It is typically staffed by senior leaders across Data/AI Operations, IT, Legal, Audit, Compliance, Cybersecurity, and major business units
- Define the organization's risk tolerance and set boundaries for acceptable AI use
- Identify potential use cases for Copilot and prioritize business scenarios
- Confirm that all licensing and technical requirements are satisfied, ensuring the correct Copilot licenses, supported application versions, and necessary platform conditions are established prior to starting the deployment

In **Phase 2: Data & Access Hardening**, the deployment team focuses on data classification and labeling and addressing excessive permissions. Work items include:

- Auditing access controls to identify and remediate excessive permissions and outdated access patterns
- Revisiting your organization's data classification policy and simplifying it if it's too complicated to be successful. Auditing sensitivity labels that have been applied to data with this policy in mind. Evaluating data classification coverage and identifying data that has not been classified or classified properly.
- Implementing sensitivity labels with Microsoft Purview or other tools that allow you to determine the sensitivity of existing data in SharePoint, OneDrive, and other places where data is stored. Applying and enforcing data labeling policies to enable ongoing visibility and control of sensitive data.

- Validating and optimizing Microsoft Search and content indexing across SharePoint, OneDrive, Exchange, and Teams to ensure Copilot can retrieve and ground responses in high-quality organizational data.
- Ensuring that core security measures, including MFA, device compliance policies, Conditional Access rules, and session controls, are properly applied and enforced for all Copilot users.

Phase 3: Policy, Controls & Guardrails focuses on implementing organizational policies and safety controls for responsible Copilot use. Focus areas in this phase include:

- Establishing AI policies and acceptable use guidelines that define clear rules for how employees should use Copilot and handle sensitive information. Asking users for their help can be a powerful, scalable control
- Deploying data-loss prevention, insider-risk, and compliance safeguards by configuring Microsoft Purview and associated tools to identify, prevent, and remediate unsafe or inappropriate data activity
- Creating an approval process for evaluating new features and use cases prior to their adoption
- Configuring Copilot safety, governance, and extensibility controls, such as content filtering, plugin and connector restrictions, and policy-based safeguards to minimize misuse and align Copilot behavior with organizational requirements

In Phase 4: Pilot, Training & Adoption, the deployment team validates use cases, trains users, and rolls out Copilot in defined tranches. These work items will help accomplish this:

- Setting up pilot projects to learn and validate assumptions before scaling
- Creating a structured user-training program to drive adoption, effective use, and overall value, providing role-tailored guidance on prompting techniques, responsible use expectations, and the specific Copilot features relevant to each group
- Recruiting early adopters to accelerate learning and adoption across the organization by supporting their peers' training and use of Copilot and funneling feedback to the deployment team and AIGC
- Deploying Copilot to users gradually in defined tranches to manage risk, support adoption, and refine controls between cohorts

Finally, in Phase 5: Monitoring, Audit & Continuous Improvement, monitor Copilot usage and outcomes so that you can refine the governance process as needed. These activities can help do this:

- Establishing an audit program for Copilot or your wider AI ecosystem that outlines how usage patterns, data access, and adherence to organizational policies will be monitored, assessed, and verified
- Developing baselines and performing continuous monitoring to help identify data leakage and governance violations
- Assessing Copilot's effectiveness by monitoring adoption trends, analyzing productivity improvements, and gathering user feedback to understand its overall business impact
- Regularly updating and adjusting your policies, access permissions, and safeguard controls to keep pace with Copilot's evolution and the emergence of new risks

Microsoft has published a Microsoft 365 Copilot Deployment Guide on their website, which provides more details on many of the work items I discussed here. I suggest starting by reading more about data, privacy, and security for Microsoft 365 Copilot at `https://learn.microsoft.com/en-us/copilot/microsoft-365/microsoft-365-copilot-privacy`.

Hopefully this gives you insights into some of the risks CISOs and security teams associate with adopting enterprise AI assistants like Copilot, and some of the work they do to mitigate them.

So far in this chapter we've focused on some of the safety and security risks associated with generative and agentic AI systems. We also looked at some of the security risks associated with Microsoft Copilot adoption and related controls. Next, let's shift gears and discuss how attackers have been leveraging AI systems in their attacks and examine how AI has changed threat actors' kill chains.

How attackers leverage AI

Numerous reports of attackers leveraging AI capabilities in their attacks have been published over the past few years. During this time, frontier AI labs, such as Anthropic and Microsoft, have shared insights into how threat actors have been leveraging AI. Security researchers and Red Teams have also been busy publishing results of their research into how AI can be used to improve attackers' capabilities.

Perhaps the best way to aggregate and present these various insights is to plug them into the intrusion kill chain model we discussed in depth in *Chapter 11*. You might remember this modified Courses of Action Matrix, illustrated in *Table 15.6*. Revisit *Chapter 11* if you do not remember all the details.

Kill Chain Phase	Detect	Deny	Disrupt	Degrade	Deceive	Limit	Recover
Reconnaissance I							
Delivery							
Exploitation							
Installation							
Command and Control (C2)							
Reconnaissance II							
Actions on Objectives							

Table 15.6 – Example of an updated Courses of Action Matrix

In this section, I introduce an AI-enabled intrusion kill chain that integrates our modified kill-chain phases with the AI techniques threat actors have leveraged in recent years. I also reference techniques from both MITRE ATT&CK and MITRE ATLAS. Modern intrusions now blend traditional cyber tactics with AI-enabled behaviors, and neither of these two frameworks captures that full picture, but they complement each other nicely. To provide a more complete view of how attackers operate across the kill chain, this model incorporates both frameworks, each serving a distinct purpose. ATT&CK anchors the model in well-understood, traditional adversary behavior, while ATLAS highlights the AI-specific techniques and attack paths that ATT&CK does not cover. Note that these lists are not meant to be exhaustive, and that attackers are quickly evolving their use of AI.

Let's start with the Reconnaissance I phase.

Reconnaissance I (pre-intrusion)

The Reconnaissance stage of the Intrusion Kill Chain can be divided into two distinct phases because attackers gather information at different points in a traditional network intrusion. Before any compromise occurs, they might study potential targets, evaluate weaknesses, and determine viable attack paths. After gaining an initial foothold, often through one or more of the Cybersecurity Usual Suspects, attackers typically conduct a second round of reconnaissance to understand the victim's internal environment, identify High-Value Assets, and locate sensitive data. Separating these activities into Reconnaissance I (pre-intrusion) and Reconnaissance II (post-compromise) makes it easier to align defenses with the specific tools, techniques, and behaviors used at each stage. In both phases, adversaries might rely on either low-impact, passive information gathering or more intrusive probing, depending on their objectives and risk tolerance.

Industry reporting indicates that attackers have increasingly incorporated AI into the Reconnaissance I phase of intrusions (OpenAI, 2024; Microsoft Threat Intelligence, 2024; Abnormal Security, 2025). One common use involves LLM-assisted research on target technologies, infrastructure, and publicly available information. Nation-state actors, in particular, have been observed using large language models to summarize open-source data, study potential targets, and refine phishing content with greater speed and precision.

Attackers have also relied on AI to translate and summarize **open-source intelligence (OSINT)**, enabling them to process large volumes of publicly accessible material more efficiently. By automating OSINT collection and enrichment, AI tools help adversaries identify exposed assets, organizational details, and other reconnaissance-relevant insights that would otherwise require significant manual effort.

Another documented use case involves generating pretexts and synthetic social-engineering personas. AI systems have been used to craft convincing identities, communication styles, and tailored narratives that support phishing and other forms of human-targeted reconnaissance. These capabilities allow attackers to scale social-engineering campaigns while increasing their believability.

AI has further been applied to automated scanning, enrichment, and profiling of potential victims. Adversaries have used AI tools to analyze public identity data, summarize employee roles, and map organizational structures. This automated profiling improves attacker efficiency by helping them prioritize high-value targets and identify individuals with elevated access or influence.

In addition, attackers have used LLMs to generate highly tailored phishing lures designed to increase engagement. These AI-generated emails often exhibit natural language fluency and contextual relevance, making them more effective as reconnaissance probes and initial access vectors.

Finally, some threat actors have employed AI-generated deepfake voice techniques during reconnaissance. By cloning executive voices, attackers have attempted to impersonate senior leaders in phone-based interactions to extract sensitive information or manipulate employees. This represents a more intrusive but increasingly accessible form of AI-enabled reconnaissance.

Mitigations

Let's look at how defenders can try to mitigate these techniques by looking at mitigations provided by ATT&CK and ATLAS (MITRE, n.d.). It's no surprise that both recommend user training to mitigate these techniques. ATT&CK recommends training users to recognize and report social engineering and suspicious messages (ATT&CK Mitigation ID 1017 - User Training).

ATLAS provides more granular recommendations for mitigating these techniques. Its guidance includes training users to recognize AI-enhanced lures, such as unusual tone, urgency cues, or stylistic inconsistencies that may indicate synthetic content. It also emphasizes strengthening identity-verification processes for high-risk interactions to reduce the likelihood of impersonation or fraudulent requests. In addition, ATLAS recommends requiring secondary human verification for sensitive or atypical voice-based requests, particularly in scenarios where attackers may attempt to exploit deepfake audio to manipulate employees or extract confidential information.

Let's look at the next phase in attackers' kill chains: Weaponization.

Weaponization

The Weaponization phase of the intrusion kill chain is where attackers prepare the malicious payload they will use to compromise the target's network. This might involve building a weapon, buying a weapon, or partnering with others to build or buy a weapon. In *Chapter 11*, I removed the Weaponization phase from our modified Courses of Action Matrix because it typically happens out of the view of defenders. Outside of consuming **Cyber Threat Intelligence (CTI)** and working with intelligence and law enforcement agencies, defenders typically don't have controls that can impede attackers during the Weaponization phase. However, several credible cyber threat intelligence sources have documented how attackers are incorporating AI into the Weaponization phase of their operations (Anthropic, 2024; Google Threat Intelligence Group, 2025; KELA Cyber Threat Intelligence, 2025). Reports indicate that adversaries have used AI models to generate new malware variants and mutate existing samples in ways that help them evade signature-based detection. AI has also been applied to exploit development, where models assist in drafting exploit code, refining payloads, and debugging, thereby accelerating the overall development workflow. In addition, attackers have leveraged AI to produce multilingual phishing kits, templates, and scripts that closely mimic corporate branding and communication styles, making downstream delivery more convincing. Threat actors have also used AI to automate infrastructure setup by generating scripts for command-and-control configuration, staging servers, and other operational components. Finally, AI has been employed to assemble social engineering kits that include scripts, personas, and deepfake media, enabling more sophisticated and scalable phishing and fraud campaigns.

Clearly, AI is popular with threat actors in this phase because it lowers technical barriers to entry and accelerates their preparations, thus lowering costs and potentially increasing their returns on investment. Let's look at mitigations for these AI-enabled techniques.

Mitigations

ATT&CK provides several mitigations relevant to AI-enabled weaponization techniques (MITRE, n.d.). These include the use of antimalware tools with heuristic and behavior-based detection to counter malicious code (mitigation ID M1049), as well as exploit-protection mechanisms such as **Data Execution Prevention (DEP)**, **Address Space Layout Randomization (ASLR)**, and control-flow integrity to reduce exploit success rates (M1050). ATT&CK also emphasizes user training (M1017), recommending that organizations educate employees to recognize and report phishing attempts, suspicious messages, and other forms of social engineering. In addition, network segmentation (M1030) is advised to limit the reach of compromised accounts or systems and reduce the blast radius of a successful intrusion.

ATLAS offers complementary guidance tailored to AI-specific threats (MITRE, n.d.). Its recommendations include deploying behavior-based and machine-learning-driven detection capable of identifying AI-mutated malware samples that may evade traditional signature-based tools. ATLAS also encourages the use of hardened execution environments that apply exploit mitigations and secure configurations to reduce exploit reliability. To counter AI-generated phishing kits, ATLAS recommends enhancing email security with content and behavior-based detection tuned to synthetic patterns. It further advises restricting automation tools and scripts to least-privilege network segments to limit misuse. Finally, ATLAS highlights the importance of AI-aware user training that helps employees recognize AI-enhanced lures, synthetic personas, and other emerging social-engineering techniques

Let's look at the Delivery phase next.

Delivery

The Delivery phase is where attackers send their chosen weapon(s) to the target environment using vectors such as email, web downloads, removable media, or direct network delivery via a malicious insider. It represents the moment when the weapon leaves the attacker's control and is introduced into the victim's environment. Delivery can be highly targeted or broadly distributed, depending on the attacker's objectives and resources. Defenders often have strong visibility and controls here, making this one of the most critical phases for defense.

Reports from multiple threat-intelligence sources describe several ways attackers have begun using AI during the Delivery phase of intrusions (Abnormal Security, 2025; KELA Cyber Threat Intelligence, 2025; Microsoft Threat Intelligence, 2024). Threat actors have used AI to generate multilingual phishing lures, translating and localizing content to increase credibility across different regions and language groups. They have also leveraged AI models to produce malicious attachments, including documents containing embedded macros or scripts designed to execute upon opening. In addition, some attackers have employed AI-generated or AI-altered deepfake videos to impersonate trusted individuals, enhancing the believability of scams and increasing the likelihood that recipients will engage with the malicious content.

Let's explore some mitigations for these techniques.

Mitigations

MITRE's ATT&CK and ATLAS frameworks each provide relevant mitigations for AI-enabled delivery techniques (MITRE, n.d.). ATT&CK highlights several controls, including user training (mitigation ID M1017) to help employees recognize phishing attempts across different languages and detect manipulated or suspicious media. It also recommends deploying antimalware tools with heuristic and behavior-based detection (M1049) to identify malicious content embedded in attachments or delivered through other channels.

Offer complementary guidance tailored to AI-driven delivery threats. Recommendations include implementing language-agnostic phishing detection capable of identifying malicious content across diverse languages and encodings, as well as using sandboxing and content-detonation environments to safely analyze suspicious attachments before they reach end users. Also advise encouraging verification of unusual or unexpected video-based requests, particularly in scenarios where attackers may attempt to use AI-generated or altered media to increase the credibility of their lures.

Next, let's look at how threat actors are using AI in the exploitation phase.

Exploitation

The Exploitation phase is where the attacker or victim activates the weapon, such as exploiting a vulnerability to gain initial execution on the target system. Remember, initial access is always gained by using one or a combination of the Cybersecurity Usual Suspects. It's the moment when the malicious content transitions from passive to active, exploiting unpatched vulnerabilities, misconfigurations, or user actions to run code. This phase often relies on techniques such as exploit kits, malicious links or attachments, drive-by downloads, or credential-harvesting scripts.

Reports from multiple threat-intelligence sources indicate that attackers have begun using AI to enhance their activities during the Exploitation phase (Anthropic, 2024; Google Threat Intelligence Group, 2025; KELA Cyber Threat Intelligence, 2025). Adversaries have leveraged AI models to assist in generating exploit code, enabling them to draft functional exploits more quickly and accelerate development timelines. They have also used AI to debug and refine exploits by feeding crash logs or error outputs into models, allowing the AI to suggest adjustments that improve reliability. In addition, attackers have applied AI to tailor exploit payloads to specific operating system versions, configurations, or environmental conditions, increasing the likelihood of successful execution. Some threat actors have also experimented with prompt-injection and model-abuse techniques, crafting malicious prompts designed to bypass model safeguards or extract confidential information from AI systems themselves.

Mitigations

Cybersecurity teams place significant emphasis on halting intrusions at the Exploitation phase because once an attacker gains execution, the remaining kill-chain actions, such as lateral movement, persistence, data theft, and destructive activity, can unfold rapidly, dramatically increasing the effort, time, and cost required for containment and recovery. ATT&CK highlights several mitigations relevant to this phase (MITRE, n.d.). These include the use of exploit-protection mechanisms (mitigation ID M1050) to reduce the reliability of exploitation attempts, as well as disabling unnecessary or vulnerable features and services (M1042) to shrink the attack surface and limit opportunities for initial execution.

ATLAS provides complementary mitigations tailored to AI-enabled exploitation techniques (MITRE, n.d.). Its guidance emphasizes the importance of hardened execution environments that apply exploit mitigations and secure configurations to reduce the likelihood of successful code execution. ATLAS also recommends secure debugging and logging practices to detect suspicious crash patterns or exception behaviors that may indicate exploit development or testing. Additional recommendations include reducing the exposed attack surface by minimizing unnecessary services and APIs and implementing prompt and input validation to help prevent prompt-injection attacks against AI-enabled systems.

Now let's look at the next phase in our AI-enabled kill chain, the installation phase.

Installation

The Installation phase is where the attacker establishes a persistent foothold by placing malware, backdoors, remote control software, or other execution mechanisms onto compromised systems. It's the point in the attack where the initial compromise transitions into a durable presence, often through backdoors, loaders, scheduled tasks, or registry modifications. Attackers might deploy multiple redundant mechanisms to ensure they can regain access if one is discovered or removed, making containment more difficult.

At least three CTI sources have reported that attackers can use AI in this phase of their attacks (Anthropic, 2024; Google Threat Intelligence Group, 2025; KELA Cyber Threat Intelligence, 2025). Threat actors have leveraged AI models to customize malware, modifying code and generating new variants designed to evade detection. They have also used AI to optimize implants by tuning configuration settings, persistence mechanisms, and operational parameters to improve reliability once deployed. In addition, attackers have applied AI to produce more complex obfuscation and packing schemes, making malicious code harder for defenders to analyze or detect. Some reports further indicate that adversaries have used AI models to select and adjust persistence techniques, refining them for durability and stealth within the compromised environment.

This suggests that attackers with limited technical expertise are now leveraging AI to generate installation mechanisms that exceed what they could build on their own. Let's look at mitigations next.

Mitigations

ATT&CK provides several mitigations relevant to the Installation phase (MITRE, n.d.). These include deploying antimalware tools with heuristic and behavior-based detection (mitigation ID M1049) to identify malicious code introduced during installation, as well as hardening operating system configurations (M1028) to reduce the likelihood that persistence mechanisms or configuration-based footholds can be established. Strengthening baseline configurations helps limit the avenues attackers can use to embed backdoors, loaders, or other persistence artifacts.

Offer complementary mitigations tailored to AI-enabled installation techniques (MITRE, n.d.). Its guidance emphasizes the use of behavior-based and machine-learning-driven detection capable of identifying malware variants that have been customized or obfuscated using AI. ATLAS also recommends monitoring for unusual or redundant persistence mechanisms, which may indicate automated implant tuning or AI-assisted persistence selection. Additional recommendations include using sandboxing and automated unpacking tools to analyze heavily obfuscated or packed samples, as well as monitoring common persistence locations to detect unauthorized modifications or newly created footholds.

If attackers succeed in this phase, they can potentially move to the C2 phase—let's examine it next.

Command and Control (C2)

The Command and Control (C2) phase is where the attacker establishes a communication channel between their infrastructure and the compromised systems. Through this channel, they can issue commands, move laterally, exfiltrate data, or deploy additional tooling. C2 can use traditional methods like HTTP(S), DNS, or VPN tunnels, or more covert techniques such as cloud-based services or encrypted messaging platforms.

Credible reporting indicates that attackers have also begun using AI to enhance their activities during the C2 phase of intrusions (Anthropic, 2024; Google Threat Intelligence Group, 2025; Abnormal Security, 2025). Threat actors have used AI models to generate C2 scripts that automate beaconing, tasking, and other routine communication functions between compromised systems and attacker infrastructure. They have also leveraged AI to design C2 traffic that mimics legitimate application protocols, making malicious communications harder for defenders to distinguish from normal network activity. In addition, attackers have applied

AI to orchestrate and script repetitive C2 workflows, enabling more efficient management of compromised hosts and reducing the manual effort required to maintain control over an intrusion.

Again, it appears that AI is lowering the technical barrier for entry into cybercrime and helping attackers potentially achieve better results, faster. This phase is essential for defenders to disrupt because once attackers establish C2, they gain stable, ongoing remote access to compromised systems—access they can leverage to automate malicious tasks, move laterally, escalate privileges, deploy additional tooling, exfiltrate data, and continue expanding their control.

Let's look at mitigations for AI-enabled C2.

Mitigations

ATT&CK provides several mitigation options that can help defenders disrupt AI-enabled C2 activity (MITRE, n.d.). These include filtering network traffic to and from sensitive systems (mitigation ID M1037) to limit an attacker's ability to communicate with compromised hosts, as well as applying network segmentation (M1030) to constrain the reach of C2 channels and reduce the attacker's ability to move laterally or maintain persistent communication paths.

ATLAS offers complementary mitigations tailored to detecting and constraining AI-driven C2 behavior (MITRE, n.d.). Its guidance emphasizes the use of anomaly-based detection to identify unusual communication patterns that may indicate AI-generated or dynamically adapted C2 traffic. ATLAS also recommends establishing protocol fingerprints and behavioral baselines so deviations from normal application behavior can be identified more readily. In addition, it advises restricting automation tools and scripts to least-privilege network segments, reducing the risk that attackers can misuse automated workflows to maintain or expand control over compromised systems. Once attackers can remotely control systems and deploy tools, they might want to further explore their victims' networks. Let's see how AI has been helping them do this.

Reconnaissance II (post-compromise)

Reconnaissance II is the post-compromise discovery phase, where attackers explore their victims' environments. During this phase, they enumerate internal systems, credentials, network paths, data stores, and security controls. The goal is to understand the organization's internal topology well enough to plan lateral movement, privilege escalation, or data collection. This phase often blends automated tooling, using both legitimate software and malware, with hands-on exploration to map the most valuable paths forward.

At least a couple of credible cyber threat intelligence vendors have reported that attackers are beginning to use AI to enhance their post-compromise discovery activities during Reconnaissance II (Anthropic, 2024; Microsoft Threat Intelligence, 2024). Threat actors have used AI models to summarize internal files, logs, and other collected data, allowing them to quickly understand the environment and determine their next steps. They have also fed network-scan outputs into AI systems to map internal networks, identify exposed services, and highlight high-value targets more efficiently than manual analysis alone. In addition, attackers have applied AI to analyze account roles and permissions, helping them identify potential privilege-escalation paths and prioritize the most advantageous routes for lateral movement.

This phase can actually work in defenders' favor, since overly aggressive or noisy reconnaissance tools often expose the attacker. Building strong detections around the tools adversaries commonly rely on increases the chances of catching them before they deploy ransomware or take actions on objectives. Here are mitigations from ATT&CK and ATLAS (MITRE, n.d.):

Mitigations

ATT&CK provides several mitigations that can help defenders limit the effectiveness of attacker activity during the Reconnaissance II phase (MITRE, n.d.). These include regularly auditing systems, permissions, and access patterns (mitigation ID M1047) to identify misuse or unauthorized privilege changes, as well as applying network segmentation (M1030) to restrict an attacker's ability to explore internal systems freely. ATT&CK also recommends strong privileged-account management (M1026), ensuring that elevated accounts are tightly controlled, monitored, and limited according to least-privilege principles.

ATLAS offers complementary mitigations tailored to AI-enabled reconnaissance techniques (MITRE, n.d.). Its guidance emphasizes governing access to internal AI tools so that only authorized identities and systems can interact with them, reducing the risk that attackers can misuse AI-assisted capabilities for internal discovery. ATLAS also recommends restricting AI-assisted tooling to segmented, least-privilege views so that even if an attacker gains access to an AI system, the model's visibility is intentionally constrained. In addition, ATLAS advises enforcing least-privilege AI context, ensuring that any AI system, whether an internal model, a Copilot-style assistant, or an agentic workflow, receives only the minimum contextual information, permissions, and data access required to perform its intended function. Critically, the AI should not inherit the full privileges of a user, service account, or environment unless absolutely necessary.

If attackers took the time to perform some reconnaissance in their victims' environment, that represented the last opportunity defenders had to detect them before the final phase in the attackers' kill chain, Actions on Objectives. Let's look at this phase next.

Actions on objectives

The Actions on Objectives phase marks the point where the attacker finally carries out the purpose of the intrusion, such as stealing data, committing fraud, causing disruption, or delivering destructive effects. With their foothold, persistence, and control already in place, they move into collecting, manipulating, or exfiltrating the information or systems they targeted. This stage can involve lateral movement to reach high-value systems, staging and compressing data, or executing ransomware or sabotage. Everything in the earlier phases of the kill chain has been building toward this moment, where the attacker achieves their operational goals.

We have at least three credible cyber threat intelligence sources describing how attackers have begun leveraging AI during the Actions on Objectives phase (Anthropic, 2024; Google Threat Intelligence Group, 2025; KELA Cyber Threat Intelligence, 2025). Threat actors have used AI models to triage large volumes of stolen data, summarizing and prioritizing exfiltrated content to identify what is most valuable or actionable. They have also applied AI to plan follow-on exploitation, using models to propose next steps based on the nature of the compromised data. In addition, attackers have relied on AI to support fraud and monetization workflows by generating scam scripts, social-engineering narratives, and other operational materials. AI has also been used to organize and compress data for exfiltration, streamlining the staging process and reducing the time required to move large datasets. Finally, some adversaries have employed AI to analyze internal topology and recommend lateral-movement routes, helping them navigate complex environments more efficiently as they work to achieve their operational objectives.

These examples show how AI is enabling attackers to professionalize and refine the final stages of their operations. Now we can examine the defensive measures that help disrupt these techniques.

Mitigations

ATT&CK identifies several mitigations that can help defenders reduce the impact of attacker activity during the Actions on Objectives phase (MITRE, n.d.). These include regularly auditing systems and data-access patterns (mitigation ID M1047) to detect misuse or unauthorized retrieval of sensitive information, as well as training users to recognize suspicious financial activity that may indicate fraud or monetization attempts (M1017). ATT&CK also recommends encrypting sensitive information both in transit and at rest (M1041) to limit the value of any data an attacker manages to access or exfiltrate and applying network segmentation (M1030) to constrain lateral movement and reduce the attacker's ability to reach high-value systems.

ATLAS provides a complementary set of mitigations tailored to AI-enabled activities in this phase (MITRE, n.d.). Its guidance emphasizes monitoring for large or unusual data-access patterns through data-access analytics, which can help detect AI-accelerated data triage or staging. ATLAS also recommends requiring human-in-the-loop review for high-risk data operations to prevent automated misuse of sensitive information. Additional mitigations include applying fraud analytics and transaction-monitoring capabilities to identify anomalous monetization behaviors, deploying data-loss-prevention and egress-control mechanisms to detect or block staged exfiltration, and minimizing available lateral-movement paths by reducing and monitoring access routes within the environment

I've really only scratched the surface here. Security researchers, Red Teams, and threat actors are just getting started with AI. Their use of AI and their attacks on AI systems will continue to evolve for the foreseeable future. Subsequently, it is important for CISOs and security teams to stay informed of the evolving threat landscape. Next, I'll share some resources that will help you do that.

Other AI security resources

There are numerous resources available to CISOs and security teams to help them stay abreast of the latest research and attacks. *Table 15.7* contains a non-exhaustive list of good resources.

Resource Name	**Organization**	**Description**	**Link**
Cloud Security Alliance – AI Organization	Cloud Security Alliance	Structured guidance on AI governance, security responsibilities, and enterprise	`https://cloudsecurityalliance.org/artifacts/ai-organizational-responsibilities-core-security-responsibilities`
Cloud Security Alliance – AI resilience model	Cloud Security Alliance	Benchmarking model for AI safety, resilience, and organizational readiness	`https://cloudsecurityalliance.org/artifacts/ai-resilience-a-revolutionary-benchmarking-model-for-ai-safety`
Cloud Security Alliance – **AI Controls Matrix (AICM)**	Cloud Security Alliance	Comprehensive AI control framework for enterprise risk, governance, and security	`https://cloudsecurityalliance.org/artifacts/ai-controls-matrix`

Resource Name	Organization	Description	Link
MITRE ATLAS	MITRE	Authoritative catalog of real-world AI-enabled attacks, techniques, and mitigations	`https://atlas.mitre.org`
Microsoft Threat Intelligence AI security reports	Microsoft	Evidence-based reporting on AI-enabled threats from nation-states and e-crime actors.	`https://www.microsoft.com/en-us/security/blog/threat-intelligence/ai-threats/`
Google Cloud Security CISO resources	Google Cloud	Analysis of AI-driven attacks, SOC modernization, and enterprise AI security patterns	`https://cloud.google.com/solutions/security/leaders`
Anthropic – AI Safety and Misuse Research	Anthropic	Red-team findings, misuse studies, and transparency on attacker attempts to exploit models	`https://www.anthropic.com/research`
OpenAI – System Cards and Safety Reports	OpenAI	Documentation of model behavior, misuse patterns, and safety mitigations	`https://openai.com/safety`
NIST **AI Risk Management Framework (AI RMF)**	NIST	Leading U.S. framework for AI governance, risk management, and secure deployment	`https://www.nist.gov/itl/ai-risk-management-framework`

Resource Name	Organization	Description	Link
CISA – AI security guidelines	CISA	Multi-agency guidance on AI threats, secure deployment, and defensive controls	`https://www.cisa.gov/ai`
Darktrace – State of AI Cybersecurity reports	Darktrace	Quantitative data and analysis of AI-enabled threats observed in the wild.	`https://darktrace.com/resources`
Team8 – AI Threat Landscape and CISO Research	Team8	Strategic analysis of AI-powered attacks and CISO perspectives	`https://team8.vc/reports/`
Palo Alto Networks Unit 42 – AI threat intelligence	Palo Alto Networks	Research on AI-generated phishing, malware, and adversary automation	`https://unit42.paloaltonetworks.com`
Mandiant – AI in the attack lifecycle	Mandiant	Incident response-driven insights into AI-assisted intrusions.	`https://cloud.google.com/security/resources`
KELA – Cybercrime intelligence on AI misuse	KELA	Direct visibility into AI use in underground markets and criminal ecosystems	`https://www.kelacyber.com/blog/`
Abnormal Security – AI-enhanced social engineering research	Abnormal Security	Analysis of AI-generated phishing, deepfake-enabled fraud, and social engineering	`https://abnormalsecurity.com/blog`

Resource Name	Organization	Description	Link
GTIG – AI-assisted malware & C2 research	Global Threat Intelligence Group	Reporting on AI-mutated malware, obfuscation, and C2 automation	`https://cloud.google.com/blog/topics/threat-intelligence/threat-actor-usage-of-ai-tools`

Table 15.7 – Various AI security resources

That wraps up our examination of how adversaries are exploiting AI and some of the defensive measures available to counter their techniques. It's clear that attackers will continue evolving their use of AI to streamline and strengthen their operations, and defenders must respond with equally innovative AI-driven capabilities. With that in mind, we can now turn to emerging AI security capabilities.

Emerging AI security capabilities

Any cybersecurity product vendor that wants to remain competitive is investing heavily in AI. For example, LLMs, **Large Multimodal Models (LMMs)**, and early agentic-AI systems are increasingly reducing the industry's reliance on traditional **machine learning (ML)** components and RegEx-based pattern-matching. RegEx is a syntactic tool designed for exact pattern matching, while LMMs function as semantic engines capable of interpreting meaning across varied and inconsistent formats. As a result, LMMs are beginning to replace RegEx in workflows such as log parsing, entity extraction, alert enrichment, ticket analysis, screenshot interpretation, and unstructured data processing. Products such as Microsoft Security Copilot, CrowdStrike Charlotte AI, SentinelOne Purple AI, Google Security Operations (Chronicle + Gemini), and Palo Alto Networks Precision AI increasingly use LLM/LMM-based semantic analysis for tasks that historically relied on RegEx. While these systems do not eliminate RegEx entirely, they reduce dependence on brittle pattern-matching by introducing contextual and semantic understanding.

The cybersecurity industry has been at the forefront of adopting agentic-AI capabilities. Vinay (2025) outlines a five-generation taxonomy that captures this rapid evolution, and *Figure 15.3* visualizes the timeline across which these generations emerged. Vinay (2025) describes these generations as follows:

- G1 — Single LLM Reasoners: Text-only LLMs used for summarization and basic reasoning; no tool use or grounding
- G2 — Tool-Augmented Agents: LLMs connected to structured tools (log search, intel lookups) for more reliable, auditable workflows
- G3 — Distributed Multi-Agent Systems: multiple cooperating agents handling triage, investigation, intel research, and reporting
- G4 — Schema-Bound Tool Ecosystems: multiple agents operating inside constrained, typed, validated tool ecosystems for stronger safety and reproducibility
- G5 — Early Semi-Autonomous Pipelines: agents plan, act, observe, and iterate across multi-step investigations with partial autonomy and human oversight

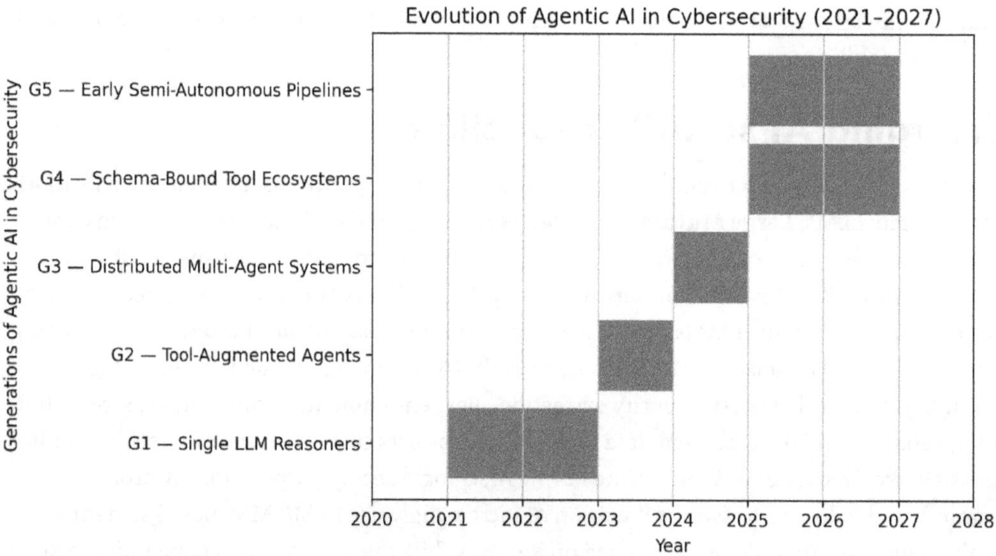

Figure 15.3 – Evolution of agentic AI in cybersecurity across five generations (G1–G5), adapted from Vinay (2025), showing how capabilities progressed from single-model reasoning to early semi-autonomous pipelines.

The evolution of agentic AI in cybersecurity shows a steady progression from basic reasoning models to coordinated, tool-augmented, and partially autonomous systems. Each generation expands the scope of what AI can safely and reliably handle within security operations. Although today's systems still require human oversight, the trajectory points toward increasingly capable pipelines that can accelerate detection, investigation, and response at enterprise scale.

From an operational cybersecurity perspective, AI-driven innovation has accelerated across security alert triage, vulnerability analysis, threat-intelligence research, incident response planning and reporting, and the emergence of tool-augmented and agentic LLMs within **security operations center (SOC)** platforms. Beyond triage and incident-response workflows, AI, LLMs, and agentic-AI systems have also transformed detection engineering, malware analysis, identity security, cloud-configuration analysis, attack-surface management, adversary simulation, and even governance and compliance functions.

Over the next couple of years, the most significant AI and agentic-AI innovations are expected in detection engineering automation, incident-response workflows, and cloud-identity security analysis—areas where multi-step reasoning, tool orchestration, and operational scale create strong demand for agentic capabilities.

That's the end of this chapter and the book. One final thought...

Is cybersecurity getting better or worse?

I often get asked, "Are things getting better or worse in cybersecurity?" After doing the research necessary to write the 15 chapters in this book, including all the up-to-date data, I'm sorry to report that things have definitely gotten worse. I don't want to sound negative, but the data I've shared in this book overwhelmingly supports this view.

Consider that the industry hasn't seen a reduction in annual vulnerability disclosure counts since 2016, when there were 50 fewer CVEs disclosed than in 2015. In 2015, there were 6,504 CVEs disclosed, while, at the time of writing, 48,448 were disclosed in 2025 (7.5 times more). The annual rate of growth in CVE disclosures has been increasing, not decreasing.

In the 10 years between 2015 and 2024, the average growth in new malware samples was approximately 102.6 million per year (AV-Test Institute, August 25, 2025). Metaphorically speaking, if malware were a country, it would become the most populated country in the world, overtaking India and China in the next two years.

The largest **distributed denial of service (DDoS)** attacks in 2018 generated 126 million packets per second, compared to large attacks in 2025 that generated 10.6 billion packets per second. 10.6 billion is 84 times more packets per second than 126 million.

One major cloud provider observed more than 311 billion attacks on web applications and APIs in 2024. That's an average of more than 850,000,000 attacks per day. If we extrapolate this data by assuming that the number of attacks observed by other major cloud providers is similar, the number of attacks each year on web applications and APIs is certainly several hundred billion, if not more. These numbers are poised for potential explosive growth as new AI services further the proliferation of APIs.

The data is very clear that CISOs and cybersecurity teams are being challenged more than ever before to identify, protect, detect, respond, and recover. This is consistent with my own professional experience working in the cybersecurity industry for decades.

The good news is that CISOs and security teams have never had a bigger or better ecosystem supporting them. The future looks bright regardless of the ever-increasing volume of attacks. Marcus Aurelius (121–180 CE) wrote that "what stands in the way becomes the way" (Aurelius, 2002). Few ideas resonate more strongly with the challenges we face today.

I sincerely hope you found this book to be educational and helpful.

Summary

The rapid adoption of generative and agentic AI since 2022 has fundamentally reshaped enterprise computing, productivity, and the cybersecurity landscape. While these systems unlock new efficiencies and capabilities, they also expand the attack surface, introduce non-deterministic behavior, and create entirely new classes of safety and security risks that traditional controls were never designed to manage. Because AI systems ingest and reason over diverse inputs, often simultaneously, and can act autonomously through tools and integrations, they amplify both the scale and unpredictability of potential failures and attacks. CISOs and cybersecurity teams now face the dual challenge of securing legacy IT environments and increasingly complex AI-driven systems in parallel, all while threat activity continues to accelerate.

This chapter examined AI risk through multiple lenses, beginning with AI safety and responsible AI, which focus on ensuring systems behave ethically, transparently, and in alignment with human values. Risks such as hallucinations, bias, over-reliance, and unsafe deployment are no longer theoretical; real-world incidents demonstrate how these failures can produce legal, financial, and reputational harm. At the same time, intrinsic security vulnerabilities in large language models, including hallucinations, jailbreaks, and indirect prompt injection, create new opportunities for adversaries to manipulate AI systems, exfiltrate data, or bypass safeguards. Frameworks such as OWASP's Top 10 for LLM Applications and MITRE ATLAS provide essential structure for understanding these risks and mapping them to practical mitigations.

As organizations move beyond content generation toward agentic AI systems capable of taking actions, new threat categories emerge. Tool misuse, privilege escalation, memory poisoning, unsafe autonomy, and cascading operational failures extend AI risk beyond misinformation into direct business and security impact. These risks demand stronger governance, least-privilege design, human-in-the-loop controls, and lifecycle-wide security practices that evolve alongside rapidly maturing agent frameworks. The deployment of enterprise AI assistants such as Microsoft Copilot illustrates both the promise and the challenge: AI can dramatically improve discoverability and productivity, but it also exposes long-standing weaknesses in data governance, access hygiene, and organizational discipline that can no longer be ignored.

The chapter also demonstrated how attackers are already leveraging AI across every phase of the intrusion kill chain, from reconnaissance and social engineering to malware development, command and control, and data exfiltration. AI lowers barriers to entry, accelerates attacker workflows, and enables more personalized and scalable operations. Defenders must respond in kind, combining traditional security controls with AI-driven detection, analytics, and automation, while maintaining strong human oversight. Although the data shows that cybersecurity outcomes are worsening in terms of attack volume, sophistication, and scale, the ecosystem supporting defenders has never been stronger.

Ultimately, AI does not change the fundamental goals of cybersecurity, but it does change the terrain. CISOs and security teams that treat AI as just another technology risk will fall behind. Those who invest in governance, disciplined deployment, continuous monitoring, and AI-aware security practices can turn these challenges into an advantage. As history has shown repeatedly, what stands in the way becomes the way, and the responsible, secure adoption of AI will be one of the defining tests of modern cybersecurity leadership.

References

- Orwell, G. (1949). 1984. Harcourt, Brace
- Berners-Lee, T., Fielding, R., & Masinter, L. (2005). *RFC 3986: Uniform Resource Identifier (URI): Generic syntax.* Internet Engineering Task Force. `https://www.rfc-editor.org/rfc/rfc3986`
- Hadley, L. (2025, July 21). *Best enterprise LLMs for accuracy and business use in 2025.* Tech Research Online. `https://techresearchonline.com/blog/best-llm-for-business-use-case-comparison/`
- Nestor Maslej, Loredana Fattorini, Raymond Perrault, Yolanda Gil, Vanessa Parli, Njenga Kariuki, Emily Capstick, Anka Reuel, Erik Brynjolfsson, John Etchemendy, Katrina Ligett, Terah Lyons, James Manyika, Juan Carlos Niebles, Yoav Shoham, Russell Wald, Toby Walsh, Armin Hamrah, Lapo Santarlasci, Julia Betts Lotufo, Alexandra Rome, Andrew Shi, Sukrut Oak. *"The AI Index 2025 Annual Report,"* AI Index Steering Committee, Institute for Human-Centered AI, Stanford University, Stanford, CA, April 2025. `https://doi.org/10.48550/arXiv.2504.07139`. The AI Index 2025 Annual Report by Stanford University is licensed under Attribution-NoDerivatives 4.0

International: https://creativecommons.org/licenses/by-nd/4.0/?ref=chooser-v1

- RAIL Research Team. (2025, November 3). *AI safety incidents of 2024: Lessons from real-world failures.* Responsible AI Labs. Retrieved from https://responsibleailabs.ai/knowledge-hub/articles/ai-safety-incidents-2024
- Yagoda, Maria. (2024). *Airline held liable for its chatbot giving passenger bad advice - what this means for travellers [sic].* BBC Travel. Retrieved from https://www.bbc.com/travel/article/20240222-air-canada-chatbot-misinformation-what-travellers-should-know
- Allen, Jonathan. (2024, April 4). *New York City defends AI chatbot that advised entrepreneurs to break laws.* Reuters. Retrieved from https://www.reuters.com/technology/new-york-city-defends-ai-chatbot-that-advised-entrepreneurs-break-laws-2024-04-04/
- Turley, Jonathan. (2023, April 3). *ChatGPT falsely accused me of sexually harassing my students. Can we really trust AI?* USA Today. Retrieved from https://www.usatoday.com/story/opinion/columnist/2023/04/03/chatgpt-misinformation-bias-flaws-ai-chatbot/11571830002/
- (Grantham-Philips, Wyatte. (2024, June 18). *McDonald's is ending its test run of AI-powered drive-thrus with IBM.* AP. Retrieved from https://apnews.com/article/mcdonalds-ai-drive-thru-ibm-bebc898363f2d550e1a0cd3c682fa234
- Ruiz-Lichter, S. (2024, April 22). *Why the Taylor Swift AI scandal is pushing lawmakers to address pornographic deepfakes.* Global IP and Technology Law Blog, Squire Patton Boggs (US) LLP. Retrieved from https://natlawreview.com/article/why-taylor-swift-ai-scandal-pushing-lawmakers-address-pornographic-deepfakes
- Australian Federal Police. (2025, January 28). *AFP warns parents over rise in AI-generated child abuse material.* https://www.afp.gov.au/news-centre/media-release/afp-warns-parents-over-rise-ai-generated-child-abuse-material
- Kharpal, A. (2024, February 22). *Google pauses Gemini AI image generator after it created inaccurate historical pictures.* CNBC. Retrieved from https://www.cnbc.com/2024/02/22/google-pauses-gemini-ai-image-generator-after-inaccuracies.html

- Ruwitch, John. (2025, December 12). *A new lawsuit blames ChatGPT for a murder-suicide.* NPR. Retrieved from `https://www.npr.org/2025/12/12/nx-s1-5642599/a-new-lawsuit-blames-chatgpt-for-a-murder-suicide`
- Anthropic. (n.d.). *Responsible scaling policy.* Retireved from `https://www.anthropic.com/responsible-scaling-policy`
- Microsoft. (n.d.). *Responsible AI principles and approach.* Retrieved from `https://www.microsoft.com/en-us/ai/principles-and-approach`
- OpenAI. (n.d.). *Safety & responsibility.* Retrieved from `https://openai.com/safety/`
- OpenAI. (n.d.). *How we think about safety and alignment.* Retrieved from `https://openai.com/safety/how-we-think-about-safety-alignment/`
- OpenAI. (2024, May 21). OpenAI safety update. Retrieved from `https://openai.com/index/openai-safety-update/`
- Google. (n.d.). *AI principles.* Retrieved from `https://ai.google/principles/`
- MIT AI Risk Initiative. (2024). *MIT AI Risk Repository.* Massachusetts Institute of Technology. `https://airisk.mit.edu/`
- National Institute of Standards and Technology. (2023). *AI Risk Management Framework (AI RMF 1.0). U.S. Department of Commerce.* Retrieved from `https://nvlpubs.nist.gov/nistpubs/ai/NIST.AI.100-1.pdf`
- Wu, J., Liu, J., Cai, T., Zeng, Z., Huang, W., & Zhan, T. (2025). *Mitigating LLM hallucination via behaviorally calibrated reinforcement learning.* arXiv. `https://arxiv.org/pdf/2512.19920`
- Russinovich, M., Salem, A., Zanella-Béguelin, S., & Zunger, Y. (2025). *The price of intelligence: Three risks inherent in LLMs.* ACM Queue, 22(6). Retrieved from `https://spawn-queue.acm.org/doi/pdf/10.1145/3711679`
- Lakshmanan, R. (2026, January 19). *Google Gemini prompt injection flaw exposed private calendar data via malicious invites.* The Hacker News. Retrieved from `https://thehackernews.com/2026/01/google-gemini-prompt-injection-flaw.html`
- Constantin, L. (2026, January 9). ZombieAgent *ChatGPT attack shows persistent data leak risks of AI agents.* CSO Online. Retrieved from `https://www.csoonline.com/article/4115110/zombieagent-chatgpt-attack-shows-persistent-data-leak-risks-of-ai-agents.html`

- Constantin, L. (2025, December 29). *Top 5 real-world AI security threats revealed in 2025.* CSO Online. Retrieved from https://www.csoonline.com/article/4111384/top-5-real-world-ai-security-threats-revealed-in-2025.html
- Babo, Z. (2026, January 8). *ZombieAgent: New ChatGPT vulnerabilities let data theft continue (and spread).* Radware Threat Intelligence Blog. Retrieved from https://www.radware.com/blog/threat-intelligence/zombieagent/
- OWASP Foundation. (2024). *OWASP Top 10 for LLM Applications 2025 (Version 2025).* Retrieved from https://owasp.org/www-project-top-10-for-large-language-model-applications/assets/PDF/OWASP-Top-10-for-LLMs-v2025.pdf
- OWASP. (2025). *OWASP Top 10 for LLM applications.* Retrieved from https://genai.owasp.org/resource/owasp-top-10-for-llm-applications-2025/
- MITRE. (n.d.). ATLAS: *Mitigations.* Retrieved from https://atlas.mitre.org/mitigations
- MITRE. (2023). ATLAS: *Adversarial Threat Landscape for Artificial-Intelligence Systems.* MITRE Corporation. https://atlas.mitre.org/
- Carlini, N., Jagielski, M., Nasr, M., Koh, P. W., Tramer, F., & Papernot, N. (2023). *Poisoning and backdooring foundation models.* arXiv. https://doi.org/10.48550/arXiv.2305.17328
- Goldstein, T., Sharma, Y., & Evans, D. (2024). *Adversarial examples and the security of machine learning systems.* Communications of the ACM, 67(1), 82–91. https://doi.org/10.1145/3618371
- Microsoft. (2024). *How Microsoft Copilot works.* https://learn.microsoft.com/en-us/copilot/microsoft-365/microsoft-365-copilot-overview
- Microsoft. (2024). *Microsoft Copilot architecture and data flow.* https://learn.microsoft.com/en-us/copilot/microsoft-365/microsoft-365-copilot-architecture
- Microsoft. (2024). *Data, privacy, and security for Microsoft Copilot.* https://learn.microsoft.com/en-us/copilot/microsoft-365/microsoft-365-copilot-privacy
- Microsoft. (2024). *Security, compliance, and privacy in Microsoft Copilot for Microsoft 365.* https://learn.microsoft.com/en-us/copilot/microsoft-365/microsoft-365-copilot-security

- Microsoft. (2024). *Semantic Index for Copilot.* `https://learn.microsoft.com/en-us/copilot/microsoft-365/semantic-index-overview`
- Microsoft. (2024). *Responsible AI and Microsoft Copilot.* `https://learn.microsoft.com/en-us/copilot/responsible-ai`
- Microsoft. (n.d.). *Microsoft Graph: Overview.* `https://learn.microsoft.com/en-us/graph/overview`
- Microsoft. (2024). *Microsoft Copilot for Microsoft 365: Admin guide.* `https://learn.microsoft.com/en-us/copilot/microsoft-365/admin`
- Microsoft. (2024). *Microsoft Copilot Studio: Architecture and governance.* `https://learn.microsoft.com/en-us/microsoft-copilot-studio/concepts/security`
- Microsoft. (2024). *Microsoft 365 Zero Trust security model.* `https://learn.microsoft.com/en-us/microsoft-365/security/microsoft-365-zero-trust`
- Microsoft. (2024). *AI agents overview.* Microsoft Learn. `https://learn.microsoft.com/en-us/azure/ai-services/agents/overview`
- Microsoft. (2024). *AI agents in the Cloud Adoption Framework.* Microsoft Learn. `https://learn.microsoft.com/en-us/azure/cloud-adoption-framework/ai-agents/`
- Microsoft. (2025). Microsoft 365 Copilot hub. Microsoft Learn. `https://learn.microsoft.com/en-us/copilot/microsoft-365/`
- Microsoft Threat Intelligence. (2024, February 14). *Staying ahead of threat actors in the age of AI.* Microsoft Security Blog. `https://www.microsoft.com/en-us/security/blog/2024/02/14/staying-ahead-of-threat-actors-in-the-age-of-ai/`
- OpenAI. (2024, February 14). *Disrupting malicious uses of AI by state-affiliated threat actors.* `https://openai.com/index/disrupting-malicious-uses-of-ai-by-state-affiliated-threat-actors/`
- Google Threat Intelligence Group. (2025, November 5). *GTIG AI threat tracker: Advances in threat actor usage of AI tools.* Google Cloud Blog. `https://cloud.google.com/blog/topics/threat-intelligence/threat-actor-usage-of-ai-tools/`
- Anthropic. (2025, November). *Disrupting the first reported AI-orchestrated cyber espionage campaign.* Anthropic. `https://assets.anthropic.com/m/ec212e6566a0d47/original/Disrupting-the-first-reported-AI-orchestrated-cyber-espionage-campaign.pdf`

- Abnormal Security. (2025, June 25). *The AI kill chain: Modern attack strategies in cybersecurity*. https://abnormal.ai/blog/ai-kill-chain
- KELA Cyber Threat Intelligence. (2025). *2025 AI threat report: How cybercriminals are weaponizing AI technology*. KELA. https://info.ke-la.com/hubfs/Reports/KELA%20Report%20-%202025%20AI%20Threat%20Report.pdf
- Anthropic. (2024). *AI safety & misuse: Findings from the GTM-2002 evaluation*. https://www.anthropic.com/news/ai-safety-and-misuse
- Vinay, V. (2025). *The evolution of agentic AI in cybersecurity: From single LLM reasoners to multi-agent systems and autonomous pipelines*. arXiv. https://arxiv.org/abs/2512.06659
- Microsoft. (2023). *Microsoft Security Copilot*. https://www.microsoft.com/security/business/ai-security/copilot
- CrowdStrike. (2024). *Charlotte AI*. https://www.crowdstrike.com/products/charlotte-ai/
- SentinelOne. (2024). *Purple AI*. https://www.sentinelone.com/platform/purple-ai/
- Google Cloud. (2024). Google Security Operations with Chronicle and Gemini. https://cloud.google.com/security-operations
- Palo Alto Networks. (2024). *Precision AI*. https://www.paloaltonetworks.com/precision-ai
- Aurelius, M. (2002). *Meditations* (G. Hays, Trans.). Modern Library. (Original work published ca. 180 CE)

Get this book's PDF version and more

Scan the QR code (or go to `packtpub.com/unlock`). Search for this book by name, confirm the edition, and then follow the steps on the page.

UNLOCK NOW

Note: Keep your invoice handy. Purchases made directly from Packt don't require an invoice.

16

Unlock Your Exclusive Benefits

Your copy of this book includes the following exclusive benefits:

EPUB

PDF

DRM-Free PDF Version

Download DRM-free PDF and ePub copies of this book.

7-Day Packt Library Access

Get 7-day unlimited access to 8,000+ books and videos. No credit card required.

Available for first-time Packt+ trial users only.

Next-Gen Reader Access

Read this book on Packt Reader with progress sync, dark mode and note-taking.

Follow the guide below to unlock them. The process takes only a few minutes and needs to be completed once.

Unlock this Book's Free Benefits in 3 Easy Steps

Step 1

Keep your purchase invoice ready for *Step 3*. If you have a physical copy, scan it using your phone and save it as a PDF, JPG, or PNG.

For more help on finding your invoice, visit `https://www.packtpub.com/en-us/unlock?step=1`.

Note

Note: If you bought this book directly from Packt, no invoice is required. After *Step 2*, you can access your exclusive content right away.

Step 2

Scan the QR code or go to `packtpub.com/unlock`.

On the page that opens (similar to *Figure 16.1* on desktop), search for this book by name and select the correct edition.

Figure 16.1 – Packt unlock landing page on desktop

Step 3

After selecting your book, sign in to your Packt account or create one for free. Then upload your invoice (PDF, PNG, or JPG, up to 10 MB). Follow the on-screen instructions to finish the process.

Need Help

If you get stuck and need help, visit `https://www.packtpub.com/unlock-benefits/help` for a detailed FAQ on how to find your invoices and more. This QR code will take you to the help page.

> Note
>
> **Note**: If you are still facing issues, reach out to `customercare@packt.com`.

Other Books You May Enjoy

If you enjoyed this book, you may be interested in these other books by Packt:

Adversarial AI Attacks, Mitigations, and Defense Strategies

John Sotiropoulos

ISBN: 9781835087985

- Set up a playground to explore how adversarial attacks work
- Discover how AI models can be poisoned and what you can do to prevent this
- Learn about the use of trojan horses to tamper with and reprogram models
- Understand supply chain risks
- Examine how your models or data can be stolen in privacy attacks
- See how GANs are weaponized for Deepfake creation and cyberattacks
- Explore emerging LLM-specific attacks, such as prompt injection
- Leverage DevSecOps, MLOps and MLSecOps to secure your AI system

Practical Threat Detection Engineering

Megan Roddie, Jason Deyalsingh, Gary J. Katz

ISBN: 9781801076715

- Boost your career as a detection engineer
- Use industry tools to test and refine your security detections
- Create effective detections to catch sophisticated threats.
- Build a detection engineering test lab
- Make the most of the detection engineering life cycle
- Harness threat intelligence for detection with open-source intelligence and assessments
- Understand the principles and concepts that form the foundation of detection engineering
- Identify critical data sources and overcome integration challenges

Packt is searching for authors like you

If you're interested in becoming an author for Packt, please visit `authors.packtpub.com` and apply today. We have worked with thousands of developers and tech professionals, just like you, to help them share their insight with the global tech community. You can make a general application, apply for a specific hot topic that we are recruiting an author for, or submit your own idea.

Share your thoughts

Now you've finished *Cybersecurity Strategy for the AI-Driven Era*, we'd love to hear your thoughts! Scan the QR code below to go straight to the Amazon review page for this book and share your feedback or leave a review on the site that you purchased it from.

https://packt.link/r/1806028573

Your review is important to us and the tech community and will help us make sure we're delivering excellent quality content.

Index

Symbols

B

C

D

E

F

I

J

K

L

M

X

Z

www.ingramcontent.com/pod-product-compliance
Lightning Source LLC
LaVergne TN
LVHW060007210926
848481LV00013B/3666
9781806028573